**Essentials
of Managerial
Finance**

New York   Chicago   San Francisco   Atlanta   Dallas   Montreal   Toronto   London

Essentials of Managerial Finance

J. Fred Weston
Eugene F. Brigham
University of California, Los Angeles

HOLT, RINEHART and WINSTON, INC.

Preface

STRUCTURE OF ESSENTIALS

Essentials of Managerial Finance is designed to present the fundamental materials of a business finance course with a minimum amount of technical, nonessential detail. *Essentials* is, in a sense, a reformulation of our larger book, *Managerial Finance*. The order of chapters and the presentation of material differs somewhat from that of *Managerial Finance*. *Essentials* is divided into eight major sections. Part I presents some introductory material on the nature of financial management and the business environment. Part II, "Financial Analysis, Planning, and Control," presents some basic tools that are used in the remaining parts of the book. Part III, "Long-Term Investment Decisions," examines the capital budgeting decisions; Part IV, "Valuation and Financial Structure," considers the implications of financing these investments by use of debt versus equity capital. Part V, "Working Capital Management," discusses current asset management and short- and intermediate-term financing. Following this, Part VI, "Long-Term Financing," analyzes the alternative types and forms of long-term securities, emphasizing ways in which the financial manager can use these different securities to lower his cost of capital. Part VII deals with the two tangential —but highly important—topics: (1) mergers and (2) corporate failure. The final section, Part VIII, presents an integrated view of financial management, considering the timing of financial policy over the business cycle and over the stages of a firm's life cycle.

Other differences between the two books reflect the evolution in our thinking about how materials in a finance course should be taught. They also reflect the thinking of a large number of people who have used *Managerial Finance*, as well as of people who reviewed an earlier draft of

v

Essentials. We recognize, of course, that there is probably no single optimal order of presentation for the material, nor is it possible to obtain a consensus on a single organization.

Although we feel the organization of *Essentials* can be effectively justified in comparison with alternatives, we do recognize that individual instructors may wish to alter our order of presentation. Thus, we have endeavored to make each chapter self-contained and have provided a Glossary, which permits the assigning of chapters out of the order presented in the text. By referring to the Glossary the student will be able to obtain a working definition for any expressions in a chapter reserved for a later assignment.

We have presented difficult concepts and principles early in the text. Thus, the concepts presented may be used in making financial management decisions throughout the book, and, through repetition, reinforce an effective understanding of the basic ideas.

BASIC ORIENTATION OF ESSENTIALS

As indicated, *Essentials of Managerial Finance* is designed to present the fundamental material in a business finance course with a minimum amount of technical, nonessential detail. *Managerial Finance,* on the other hand, explores in depth the controversial, difficult, conceptual problems. A contrast between two types of mathematics books will provide a useful analogy. One math book might develop theorems and proofs of the theorems, while another might present the theorems and illustrate their use without formal development of their proofs. *Managerial Finance* is comparable to the mathematics book that presents all proofs; *Essentials* is comparable to the book that utilizes theorems in practical applications and in making decisions.

This contrast may be illustrated with specific comparisons between the two texts. In the Capital Budgeting chapter in *Managerial Finance,* for example, we analyze the theoretical differences between the internal rate of return and the net present value methods of evaluating alternatives. In the same chapter in *Essentials,* on the other hand, we explain and illustrate each of the alternative methods, then state our conclusion that on theoretical grounds the net present value method is generally preferable. We refer interested readers to *Managerial Finance* for the proof of our proposition. Another difference between the two books is illustrated in certain aspects of cost of capital—specifically, the cost of retained earnings versus the cost of new external equity funds. *Managerial Finance* explores some of the nagging theoretical issues at great length. In *Essentials,* we present our conclusions on how the costs of retained earnings and the cost of new equity should be calculated for practical cost of capital calculations. Still another example of the difference in the treatment of materials between the two books can be observed in the discussion of mergers and financial rehabilitation. On both topics, *Managerial Finance* analyzes a wide range of legal and accounting aspects as well as economic and financial principles. *Essentials* presents a shorter treatment, emphasizing only the fundamental materials required for a general background and understanding of these topics as they relate to effective financial management.

INTEGRATION OF MATERIALS

The reorganization of *Essentials of Managerial Finance* described in the opening paragraphs, with the elimination of certain details described above, enables the reader to follow easily the central theme of the text—maximizing the value of the business firm. Stripping away excess detail also helped us to see the theme better and enabled us to pull together some material that was not previously integrated as well as it might have been. The best examples of this would be (1) the material on working capital analysis and (2) the interrelationship between the cost of capital, capital budgeting, and dividend policy.

END-OF-CHAPTER PROBLEMS AND THE STUDY GUIDE

Many man-hours have been spent on the questions, problems, and solutions for *Essentials of Managerial Finance*. On the basis of extended classroom use in mimeographed form, the problems have all been carefully checked for clarity and accuracy, new ones added, and the less successful ones eliminated.

We are also aware that some problems are relatively complex and that students sometimes have difficulty setting them up. To overcome this problem, we have provided a *Study Guide*, which presents an illustrative prototype problem similar to each of the more difficult problems contained in the text. The *Study Guide* will not be necessary for all readers, but its availability should make it possible for any reader to prepare adequate answers to any problems contained in the text.

SUMMARY

In summary, *Essentials of Managerial Finance* draws on *Managerial Finance*, but is a separate and distinct book. From the standpoint of the reader interested in obtaining a statement of principles and illustrations of their application, without being delayed by a consideration of the foundation and proofs of principles, *Essentials* provides continuity and readability. End-of-chapter questions and problems have been extensively reworked to remove ambiguities, to improve clarity, and to provide dependable solutions in the *Instructor's Manual*. The *Study Guide* will also provide readers with aids to effective comprehension of the materials of managerial finance.

Los Angeles, California
February 1968

J. Fred Weston
Eugene F. Brigham

Contents

PART IV   Valuation and Financial Structure

PART V   Working Capital Management

PART I
Introduction

Chapter 1

The Finance Function

Like so many things in the contemporary world, the subject matter of finance has undergone some significant changes in recent years. Prior to 1950, the primary function of finance was the *obtaining* of funds. Later on, more attention was given to the *use* of funds, and one of the important developments of the early 1950s was a systematic analysis of the internal management of the firm with a focus on flows of funds within the corporate structure.[1]

As procedures for using financial control in the internal management process have developed, the finance function has become an increasingly important part of the firm's general management. In the past, the financial officer was simply told how much money the firm needed and then given the responsibility for obtaining these funds. Under the new system, the financial manager is confronted with fundamental questions about the operations of the business enterprise. These questions—the new domain of finance—have been stated as follows:

1. How large should an enterprise be, and how fast should it grow?
2. In what form should it hold its assets?
3. What should be the composition of its liabilities? [2]

---

[1] Bion Miller Howard and Upton, *Introduction to Business Finance* (New York: McGraw Hill, 1953).

[2] Ezra Solomon, *The Theory of Financial Management* (New York: Columbia University Press, 1963), pp. 8–9.

3

As it stands today, the focus of finance is on decisions and actions which affect the value of the firm. Reflecting this focus, the central theme of *Essentials of Managerial Finance* is the valuation of the business enterprise. The firm's value today depends upon the expected stream of earnings that it will generate in the future and on the riskiness of these projected future earnings. To illustrate, two firms may each be expected to earn $100,000 a year in the indefinite future. If the earnings of one firm are relatively certain—for example, its business may consist of ownership of United States Treasury bonds and its income may consist of the interest received on these bonds—while the earnings of the other firm are somewhat uncertain because it is engaged in a risky enterprise—for example, drilling offshore oil wells—then the first firm, because of its lower risk, will probably have a higher capital value. The low-risk company, for example, might have a total market value of $1.5 million, while the high-risk company might have a market value of $1 million.

Financial decisions affect both the size of the earnings stream, or profitability, and the riskiness of the firm. These relationships are diagramed in Figure 1-1. Policy decisions affect risk and profitability, and these two factors jointly determine the value of the firm.

Figure 1-1   Valuation as the Central Focus of the Finance Function

The primary policy decision is that of choosing the business or the industry in which to operate. Once this choice has been made, both profitability and risk are determined by decisions relating to the size of the firm, the types of equipment that are used, the extent to which debt is employed, and the firm's liquidity position.

Decisions about these factors generally affect both risk and profitability. For example, an increase in the cash position reduces risk; since cash is not an earning asset, however, it also reduces profitability. Similarly, use of additional debt will generally raise the rate of return, or the profitability, of the stockholders' net worth; at the same time, however, more debt means more risk. Financial analysis seeks to strike the particular balance between risk and profitability that will maximize the value of the firm.

The nature and content of a field of study are likely to be responsive to the pressing problems of the day. For an understanding of the evolution in finance, it is necessary to review some of the important new developments that have taken place both in the economies of the Free World and in the internal operations of business firms. Among the developments that have had an impact on the finance function are the following:

1. Rise of large-scale business units, which makes the tasks formerly handled by the company president too large for any one person to handle
2. Increased product and market diversification by firms
3. Growth of spending on research and development, which has accelerated the tempo of change in the economy
4. Increased emphasis on growth in the economy and its major segments
5. Accelerated progress in transportation and communication, which has brought the countries of the world closer together
6. Narrowing profit margins, which reflect heightened competition

These changes have resulted in new ways of managing, and these new methods, in turn, have had important impacts on the financial manager. First, large-scale operations require decentralization and divisional responsibility for profit. Methods must be developed for segregating the contributions of smaller groups of activities and evaluating these contributions. Second, the emphasis on growth and diversification requires both ability to finance expansion and considerable adaptability on the part of the firm. Third, increased competition and narrowing profit margins heighten the need for techniques to make operations more efficient.

These developments and their impact have produced what has been referred to as a management revolution.[3] Whether these changes deserve the term "revolution" or whether they simply reflect continuing changes that might be referred to as an "evolution," they have significantly broadened the responsibilities of financial management. The basic changes that have taken place in the environment have been associated with the development of powerful new techniques and new ways of managing. One such change is the revolution of information-processing techniques using the computer to acquire, store, retrieve, and analyze all kinds of business information. Computers are used to monitor the behavior of cash, receivables, inventories, and physical facilities. Another example is the accelerated development of management science techniques—linear programing, game theory, simulation, and so on. All are essentially mathematical techniques dealing with complex relations among business data.

Related to the development of management science techniques is the significant progress which has been made in management planning and

---

[3] T. F. Bradshaw, "The Place and Status of the Financial Executive Today," in *Financial Executive's Job*, Financial Management Series, No. 99 (New York: American Management Association, 1952), pp. 16–17.

control techniques. These involve (1) establishing over-all profit goals, (2) establishing departmental and divisional goals which, taken together, achieve the over-all profit goal, (3) measuring progress and results against standards, and (4) taking action through adjustments to keep the company moving toward its goals.

The increased need for planning and control to carry out the enterprise profit goal has made the financial manager a key executive and has broadened his responsibilities. Thus, the new role of the financial manager suggests that the basic pattern of this book be divided into the following broad areas:

1. Financial analysis and control
2. Financial planning
3. Valuation and financial structure decisions
4. Working capital management
5. Long-term financing decisions
6. Valuation in mergers and corporate readjustments

Emphasis is given to planning, analysis, and control, and to the tasks of raising funds for the firm. Consideration is also given to the interactions with the broader environment in which the firm operates.

The remainder of this chapter covers the orientation of managerial finance, shows how financial management fits into the broader management framework, shows the relation of managerial finance to related disciplines, and gives illustrations of the crucial impact of finance during the life histories of individual firms. The following chapter describes the tax environment and the impact of taxes on business decisions. Both chapters provide the background necessary for the presentation of principles and procedures of financial analysis and control set forth in Part II.

ORIENTATION OF MANAGERIAL FINANCE

Scope of Financial Management

Traditionally, the literature of business finance has emphasized either management of working capital or acquisition of funds. The acquisition of funds, or episodic financing, typically commits the firm for long periods and involves sizeable amounts of money. Errors here can be exceedingly costly. However, as the interval between episodes is long, the acquisition of funds takes only a small fraction of the financial manager's time.

Much of the financial officer's time is devoted to management of working capital. For this reason some persons have suggested that finance books concentrate on this aspect of his duties. But a new and at least equally important emphasis is required: the place of the financial manager in the general management framework and the increased role of the financial manager in the vital activities of planning and control. However, the increased importance of new areas does not decrease the importance of traditional decision-making areas.[4] This book, therefore, attempts to give full emphasis to the three major approaches to the financial manager's functions: (1) financial planning and control, (2) management of working capital, and (3) individual financing episodes.

The Insider versus the Outsider View

Should the study of finance take the insider's or the outsider's point of view? Phrased in another way, should a finance book emphasize the administrative, or the managerial, point of view, or should it be aimed at the person who is interested in business finance as a customer, a stockholder, or a voter? These two points of view are not incompatible. Although this book emphasizes the professional manager's job, neither point of view can be effectively developed without consideration of the other.

The financial manager, whose preoccupation is with internal administration of the firm, must still take into account the reaction of outsiders to his operations. The claims and pressures of outsiders must be adjusted to the responsibilities and problems of internal financial administration. Hence it seems essential to base financial decisions on a consideration of both points of view. Nevertheless, the internal point of view deserves primary emphasis because the financial manager is responsible for the financial affairs of the enterprise.

Small-Firm versus Large-Firm Financing

Similarly, the issue of the large firm versus the small firm as the appropriate focus of attention in finance courses is a false one. Principles of business finance are just as applicable to the small firm as to the large. The basic ideas are fundamentally the same, even though there will be different factual environments in their application.

The distinction between corporate finance and other forms of business financing is also an artificial division. As the materials in Chapter 2 on the tax environment indicate, the boundaries between corporate and noncorporate forms are becoming increasingly blurred, particularly for small firms. Further, important large-scale businesses are carried on in the form of business trusts.[5]

---

[4] This point is summarized well by Marshall D. Ketchum, "Looking Around: Financial Management," *Harvard Business Review,* 34, (January–February 1956), pp. 131–132.

[5] An example is the American Optical Company, one of the leaders in its industry. It is organized as a Massachusetts trust, a form of organization described in Weston and Brigham, *Managerial Finance,* Second Edition, Ch. 2.

This book seeks to focus on generalizations that are applicable across a broad range of financing activities. It emphasizes effective use of principles, adaptation to the firm's external environment, and the role of the financial manager as a part of the general management process. A further foundation for this latter aspect is now developed.

MANAGEMENT FRAMEWORK

The last 10–15 years have witnessed a blossoming of the literature on management theory and policy, which are the core of business school doctrine. These developments are too important to be ignored in any individual area of business studies. The contributions are particularly important for financial management. As a consequence of these developments, the financial manager's status has been elevated into a vital part of management. It is necessary to provide at least a summary statement of the nature of management activities in which the financial manager potentially performs a key role.

The process of managing is decision making—that is, choosing among alternatives. The job of the financial *manager* is to accomplish his tasks, both episodic and day-to-day financing, through people. Thus there are two aspects of management: (1) the general management activity—working with people and (2) the specific functions or activities—what gets done. The general and the specific functions of management as they relate to finance are outlined below.

Functions of Management

Although the functions of general management differ among different authorities, the following enumeration has gained wide acceptance: [6]

Organizing
Staffing
Directing
Planning
Controlling

Organizing is the identification and determination of activities which need to be undertaken in order to achieve enterprise objectives. Organization represents the grouping of activities into departments for the specialization of managerial activities and functions. Specialization in turn requires

---

[6] This section has benefited from Harold Koontz and Cyril O'Donnell, *Principles of Management* (New York: McGraw-Hill, 1964, pp. 1–67).

the definition of managerial authority and of responsibility relations for carrying out the activities to achieve the objectives.

Staffing involves the selection among candidates for positions, the training of subordinates, and the appraisal of activities. Job requirements must be defined, and inducements must be offered to elicit effective performance.

Directing requires the guidance and supervision of subordinates and their lines of communication.

Planning is the formulation of enterprise goals or objectives, the selection among alternative courses of action, and the initiation of policies and programs to achieve objectives.

Controlling is seeing that things get done and improving performance. It requires setting standards, measuring performance against enterprise objectives and standards, evaluating performance, and acting promptly to take corrective actions. Policies, programs, and procedures are modified in order to improve performance.

These general functions of management may now be contrasted with specific areas of management decisions. Four activities usually appear on most statements of the basic operations of a business: production, personnel, finance, and marketing. Finance is always included in such a list because financial activities are crucial for the well-being of a firm and play a strategic role in the performance of all general functions of management.

With this background on the nature of both general and specific activities of management, the role of financial management may now be set out.

Finance and General Functions of Management

The financial manager performs important activities in connection with each of the general functions of management. With respect to *organizing,* an important guideline is to group activities in such a way that areas of responsibility and accountability are defined. In the large-scale organization this procedure usually implies some degree of decentralization. The profit center (for example, a division) is a method of decentralizing activities for developing strategic control points. Financial data are developed and analyzed for use in evaluating the performance of a related group of operations.

The determination of the nature and extent of *staffing,* or manpower requirements, is aided by the financial budget program. The ability of an enterprise to attract and to retain high-quality talent is greatly affected by its financial capabilities.

Direction is based to a considerable degree on instruments of financial reporting, such as budgets, balance sheets, and income statements. The information contained in such financial reports enables the manager to guide his subordinates.

Planning involves heavy reliance on financial tools and analysis. Forecasts and budgets are key instruments for financial planning.

Control requires use of the techniques of financial analysis and the development of financial ratios and standards. Financial reports must be supplemented, of course, by direct observation and a broad understanding of enterprise processes.

In summary, informed and enlightened use of financial information is necessary for coordinating the enterprise activities and for achieving harmony between individual motives and enterprise goals.

This completes a brief description of the nature of general management and the key role of finance in it. Description of financial management as an area of decision making is the subject matter of the remainder of this book. Now it will be possible to see the relation of financial decisions to the broader aspects of managing a business enterprise.

Place of Finance in the Organization

The financial manager in the firm often carries the title of treasurer. Sometimes he is called vice-president in charge of finance, controller, treasurer-controller, or secretary-treasurer. Whatever his title, the financial manager is usually close to the top of the organizational structure of the firm. Typically, he is a member of the first level of the corporate staff in a large organization.

Characteristically, financial planning is conducted by top-level management. Consequently, the chief financial manager is often a vice-president; or sometimes the president himself will carry the responsibilities of the financial manager. In large firms, major financial decisions are often made by a finance committee. For example, finance committees are used in General Motors, United States Steel, and American Telephone and Telegraph. In smaller firms the owner-manager himself typically conducts the financial operations, although he may delegate many other management functions.

One reason for the high place occupied by the financial manager in the organizational structure is the importance of planning, analysis, and control operations for which he is responsible. Often a "financial control" staff reports directly to the president or operates as an analytical staff for vice-presidents in charge of production, marketing, engineering, and other operations.

Another reason why financial authority is rarely decentralized or delegated to subordinates is that many financial decisions are crucial for the survival of the firm. Decisions which have major financial implications, such as taking on a new product or discarding an old one, adding a plant or changing locations, floating a bond or a stock issue or entering into sale and leaseback arrangements are all major episodes in the life of a corporation.

Moreover, significant economies can be achieved through centralizing financial operations. A large corporation requiring $50 million can float a bond issue at a much lower interest cost per dollar than the rate at which a small firm can borrow $1,000. A small firm borrowing $1,000 will probably pay from 6 to 8 percent up to 14 to 18 percent. The large corporation is likely to be able to borrow at a rate ranging from 4½ to 6½ percent. It would be misleading, however, to imply that the advantages of centralization lie only in interest savings. The terms of the financial contract are also likely to be improved—a matter that may be of greater importance to the borrower than the interest rate. Contract terms refer to the extent to which borrowers can buy additional fixed assets, declare dividends, incur debt, and so forth.

Although the responsibility for carrying out major financial decisions is likely to be centered in the hands of a high-level official, a large number of day-to-day operations are conducted by the treasurer's office. These tasks are likely to be carried out by subordinates in lower level jobs. They include handling cash receipts and disbursements, borrowing from commercial banks on a regular and continuing basis, and formulating cash budgets.

MANAGERIAL FINANCE AND RELATED DISCIPLINES

Paradoxically, although some aspects of the finance function are conducted at the highest levels of the organization, a person aspiring to become a financial manager in a large company is likely to start as a trainee in a job with heavy accounting duties. Therefore, questions about the relation of finance to other studies naturally arise.

Accounting and Finance

Some persons find it difficult to distinguish between accounting and finance. They observe that in both subjects the same terminology and financial records are often used. Hence it appears to them that accounting and finance are the same thing. But accounting is primarily data gathering; finance is data analysis for use in decision making. Though accounting has become increasingly useful in recent years in providing the information necessary for good management decisions, financial executives are responsible for analysis, planning, and control.

Quantitative Methods and the Behavioral Sciences

Financial management deals with data and with people. The responsibilities for data analysis provide opportunities for application of the new and powerful tools of linear programing, game theory, and simulation referred to previously. Many of the concepts set out in this book may be utilized most effectively in business operations in conjunction with these new techniques. As the financial area can make much use of these skills, the student of finance is well advised to acquire them.

Operation of a business involves the interaction of physical assets, data, and people. The behavioral sciences are therefore also an essential part of the financial manager's training. Business involves authority relations between individuals and groups—political science. It also draws on sociology, which is the study of the behavior of people in groups. Of great importance, of course, is psychology, which deals with the mind, personality, and emotional make-up of both managers and managed.

Familiarity with these diverse areas of knowledge is required for the making of sound financial decisions. But perhaps of most direct significance for financial policies is the *economic* environment, whose nature and impact need to be sketched at least briefly at this point.

Economics and Finance

Economics may be defined as a study of the efficient use of scarce resources or of the best means to fulfill socially defined ends or goals. The kinds of decisions made by firms in marketing, production, finance, and personnel are properly the subject matter of economics, and business finance is therefore an aspect of the economic theory of the firm. The characteristics of the economic environment are of vital significance for financial policies in ways now briefly indicated.

Separation of Savings and Investment. The United States is a money economy. Savings and investment are performed by different persons. People save through institutions such as savings banks, commercial banks, savings and loan associations, life insurance companies, and pension funds. These institutions are called "financial intermediaries." Businesses obtain funds from the intermediaries to make investments in land, buildings, equipment, and inventories. Financial intermediaries today own approximately two thirds (by value) of the securities of all firms, contrasted with less than one quarter (by value) of the securities at the turn of the century.[7]

Financing today is much more impersonal than it was earlier. Previously, wealth and income were not so equally distributed as they are today. People invested their funds directly in their own businesses or in local enterprises about which they had direct knowledge. Either they knew the persons running the firms or they were familiar with the operations. But

---

[7] Raymond Goldsmith, *The Share of Financial Intermediaries in National Wealth and National Assets, 1900–1949.* Occasional Paper No. 42 (New York: National Bureau of Economic Research, 1954), p. 4, Table A.

today many people save through financial intermediaries, which in turn buy the securities of the firms. Finance, therefore, is fundamentally a process for allocating economic resources among different users. The ability to obtain funds is the ability to obtain command over the real resources of the economy. This suggests another basic characteristic of the economic environment.

Price and Profit System. Prices and profits allocate resources in the United States. Allocation is made, not by administrative boards, but by relative prices and by income shares. Profit maximization, subject to risk-limiting strategies, is the framework for studying the operations of the firm. Most economics texts treat profit maximization, its variations, and its substitute goals in a formal way, with demand and supply curves to describe how the price system performs its functions. This book illustrates the concepts of profit maximization and other business strategies in terms of specific kinds of financial decisions.

A money economy, in which savings and investment are performed by different groups of persons guided by prices and profits, has other characteristics which carry implications for financial managers.

Fluctuations and Economic Instability. Fluctuations in the general level of business are a major cause of changes in the level of an individual firm's sales. Such changes result in changes in the firm's financing requirements. Differences in the degree of fluctuations influence the extent to which a financial manager may take on the risk of fixed-interest or fixed-rental obligations. Economic fluctuations result in many diverse forms of financing contracts.

Growth. The economy of the United States has grown and will probably continue to grow at the rate of about 3 to 5 percent a year. To maintain its place in the economy, an industry must grow at least at this same rate. To hold its share of its industry market, a firm must also grow. Sales growth implies a continued growth in the firm's plant and equipment, inventories, receivables, and other assets. The financial manager's job is to obtain the funds to finance the expansion of the firm's ownership of these means of production and sale.

Price Movements. In addition to the fluctuations in business and in the growth of the economy as a whole, there are fluctuations in price levels. Financial planning is necessary if a firm is to benefit from price level changes. The financial structure of the firm should reflect expectations about future price level changes.

Interest Rates and Stock Market Prices. Fluctuations in interest rates and stock prices represent fluctuations in the cost of funds and the relative attractiveness of different forms and sources of financing. Interest rate levels are also an index of availability of loanable funds. These factors are used by the financial manager in analyzing the alternative forms of financing and in timing entry into the money markets.

   Competition and Technological Change.   Competition among firms, existing products, and newly created products pervades the economy. Technological changes present opportunities and threats to a firm. Adequate finances are required for the firm to make the adjustments necessary for survival and growth in the ever-changing economy, and it is the financial manager who must bear the responsibility for the availability of necessary funds.

   Understanding the nature of the external environment, noting its impact on the firm, and recognizing the role of the firm in the operation of the economy—all are crucial and vital aspects of the decision process. The aim of the present book is to provide a meaningful body of concepts to guide the use of a broad variety of tools for financial decisions that advance the progress of the firm and the society of which it is a part.[8]

CRUCIAL ROLE OF FINANCING DECISIONS

The role of finance in the conduct of the firm has been expressed most aptly in the following statement: "A firm's success and even survival, its ability and willingness to maintain production and to invest in fixed or working capital are to a very considerable extent determined by its financial policies, both past and present." [9] This statement can be amply documented by examples of the lives of many firms. Let us consider a few.

   General Motors was established in 1908 by W. C. Durant as a consolidation of a few companies in the automobile industry. When the working capital crisis of 1920–1921 developed, General Motors received financing aid from the Morgans and the du Ponts, and Durant lost his control of the company.

   In contrast is the experience of Henry Ford. The Ford Motor Company needed some $75 million to meet its working capital needs. A group of Wall Street bankers formed a committee and offered to help Ford out of his diffi-

---

   [8] Cf. "It is important to recognize the fact that business also operates in a world of ideas. What business can or cannot do, as well as the way in which it must operate, is determined in part by the predominating concepts or theories in the society within which it exists. These may be religious, social, economic, or political and may be expressed in such forms as ethical standards, social values, and the objectives and methods of government."—Larson, *Guide to Business History* (Cambridge, Mass.: Harvard University Press, 1948), p. 5.

   [9] Irwin Friend, "What Business Can Do to Prevent Recessions," in *Problems in Antirecession Policy* (New York: Committee for Economic Development, 1954), p. 6.

culty in return for a portion of the control of the Ford Motor Company. Ford declined the proposal.

But Ford had to raise $75 million. How did he do it? First, he shipped his auto inventories to his dealers, with a telegram requesting cash. This forced them to borrow individually. He raised $25 million in this manner. Second, he allowed accounts and bills payable for raw materials to accumulate. Third, he reduced overhead in the factory and in the office. Fourth, by vigorous collection methods he collected some outstanding accounts receivable, foreign accounts, and by-product accounts. Fifth, he sold some $8 million of liberty bonds on hand. By all these methods he was able to meet his working capital needs and maintain complete control over his company.

A more recent illustration involves a consumer finance company. In 1946 the company sold promissory notes of $400,000 to an insurance company. Later the firm needed additional funds, but was unable to arrange with the holders of the original notes for an additional loan. The loan agreement had been so drawn that it was virtually necessary to call the entire issue and place a new one of $1 million with another institutional investor. Because calling the original issue involved a substantial penalty, the company made it a point to see that the new loan agreement provided that additional funds could be secured from either the same lender or other lenders without the consent of the present holders and without paying penalties if any of the existing notes were to be retired. This illustration points up some of the pitfalls of absence of planning in setting up loan agreements.

These examples illustrate a more general principle. It has been said with great truth that financing is the critical management function in that it provides the means of remedying weak management in other areas. If production or marketing efforts, for example, have deteriorated, adequate financial means may be used to rehabilitate and restore the weak departments to renewed effectiveness. On the other hand, money alone is no substitute for strength in the other operating areas of the firm. Finance is thus an interdependent part of the total fabric of the firm.

SUMMARY

The financial manager plays a key role in the firm. He has a central responsibility in analysis, planning, and control, factors that guide the firm's resources into the most profitable lines and hold a tight rein on costs.

The importance of the financial manager is evidenced by his occupying a top-level position in the organization structure of the firm. Financial decisions are crucial for the well-being of a firm, because they determine the ability of the company to obtain plant and equipment when needed, to carry the required amount of inventories and receivables, to avoid burdensome fixed charges when sales and profits fall, and to avoid losing control of the company.

These new dimensions in the nature and scope of the responsibilities of the financial manager have determined the central theme of this book, which is indicated by the following set of relations:

$$\text{DECISIONS} \rightleftarrows \begin{array}{c} \text{PROFITABILITY} \\ \text{RISK} \end{array} \longrightarrow \text{VALUE}$$

QUESTIONS

1-1 What are some similarities between business management and the management of the U. S. Department of Defense? some differences?

1-2 What has been the impact of the development of financial intermediaries on business finance?

1-3 Suppose you are called upon to take over as chief executive officer (usually the president) of a large firm struggling to avoid bankruptcy. Your first task is to reorganize the business. Prepare an organization chart showing the place of the financial manager in the managerial hierarchy.

1-4 Give illustrations of the financial implications of production, marketing, and personnel decisions. In terms of the organization chart prepared in question 3, do these illustrations suggest cross communications between the financial officer and the production, sales, and personnel officers?

1-5 Are financial decisions likely to be more crucial for a failing business or for a successful, growing business? Would you as chief executive officer be more concerned about your financial manager in the failing firm or in the thriving firm?

1-6 What are the most important activities of the financial manager in terms of their importance to the firm's future and the amount of the financial manager's time they take up? Are these relationships likely to be the same for (a) large versus small firms, (b) stable versus growing firms, and (c) strong versus weak firms?

PROBLEMS

1-1 An appliance manufacturer has been selling directly to distributors on a net 15-day credit basis. His sales have been $1,080,000 a year and his average collection period is twenty days. He has 7 percent of sales in inventory. His balance sheet is shown below.

BALANCE SHEET

Cash	$ 15,000	Accounts payable	$ 75,000
Receivables, net	60,000	Other current liabilities	25,000
Inventories	75,000	Total current liabilities	$100,000
Total current assets	$150,000	Common stock	100,000
Net property	100,000	Earned surplus	50,000
Total assets	$250,000	Total claims on assets	$250,000

Because of excess production capacity and an attempt to increase the profit margin, the manufacturer begins to sell directly to retailers, in addition to selling to distributors. Standard terms on these sales are net 30.

a) How much additional financing will be required by the new sales if the additional sales amount to $540,000 and the average collection period is 40 days?

b) If this is the only change, how will the new balance sheet appear?

c) What aspect of finance does this problem illustrate?

(Use the convention of 360 days in a year.)

1–2   An office equipment retailer plans to add a new type of desk to his existing line. He expects annual sales of $540,000 from the new line. Net profit after salaries and taxes each year is 2.2 percent of sales. The owner takes no salary. The average payables for the new line will be 7 percent of sales.[10] However, the store will need 7 percent of sales in its inventory at all times, and the average collection period will be 30 days.

BALANCE SHEET

Accounts receivable	_____	Accounts payable	_____
Inventory	_____	Retained earnings	_____
		Subtotal	_____
		Additional financing (needed to balance)	_____
Total assets	_____	Total claims on assets	_____

Fill in the skeleton balance sheet above as of the end of the first year. Discuss the critical factors in the problem and the lesson to be learned from it.

---

[10] Payables would, of course, equal the payment period on purchases multiplied by average purchases per day. But if the ratio of materials costs to sales is constant, accounts payable can also be expressed as some multiple or percentage (in this problem, 7 percent) times sales.

Chapter 2

The Tax Environment[1]

The federal government is often called the most important stockholder in the American economy. This is not literally true, as the government does not "own" corporate shares in the strict sense of the word, but it is by far the largest recipient of business profits. Income of unincorporated businesses is subject to tax rates ranging up to 70 percent, and income of corporations is taxed at a 48 percent rate. State and sometimes city or county taxes must be added to these federal taxes, and dividends received by stockholders are subject to personal income taxes at the stockholders' individual tax rates.

With such a large percentage of business income going to the government, it is not surprising that taxes play an important role in financial decisions. Whether to lease or to buy, to use common stock or debt, to make or not to make a particular investment, to merge or not to merge—all these decisions are influenced by tax factors. This chapter summarizes some basic elements of the tax structure relating to financial decisions.

OVERVIEW OF TAX AND EXPENDITURE PATTERNS

The overriding importance of governments—federal, state, and local—and the trend toward their increasing importance are shown by the figures in

---

[1] This chapter has benefited from the assistance of Mr. R. Wendell Buttrey, tax attorney and lecturer on taxation at the University of California, Los Angeles.

Table 2–1. In 1950 total tax revenues amounted to $68.7 billion, or 24.1 per-
cent of that year's gross national product (GNP). By 1966 taxes had
climbed to $212.2 billion, or 28.7 percent of GNP. State and local govern-
ments' share of the total revenues rose somewhat more rapidly than that of
total governmental receipts—from 27.4 percent in 1950 to 32.9 percent
in 1966.

Table 2–1   LEVEL OF GOVERNMENT RECEIPTS IN RELATION TO
GROSS NATIONAL PRODUCT, 1950 AND 1966
(dollars in billions)

	1950		1966	
	Amount	Percent	Amount	Percent
Federal government receipts*	$ 49.9	72.6	$142.4	67.1
State and local government receipts*	18.8†	27.4	69.8†	32.9
Total government receipts	$ 68.7	100.0	$212.2	100.0
Gross national product	$284.8		$739.5	
Government receipts as a percent of GNP	24.1		28.7	

* Based on the national income and product accounts.
† Federal grants-in-aid to state and local governments have been eliminated to avoid
double counting.
SOURCE: *Economic Report of the President, 1967* (Washington, D. C.: U. S. Government
Printing Office, 1967), pp. 213, 286.

Table 2-2 shows the principal sources of federal income for the years
1950 and 1966. Individual and corporate income taxes provided the bulk
of the revenues in each year, with the percentage contributed by personal

Table 2–2   FEDERAL REVENUES BY SOURCES, FISCAL YEARS 1950 AND
1966 (dollars in billions)

	1950		1966	
	Amount	Percent	Amount	Percent
Individual income taxes	$15.7	43.1	$ 48.8	46.6
Corporate income taxes	10.4	28.6	25.6	24.5
Excise taxes	7.5	20.6	10.9	10.4
Estate and gift taxes	0.7	1.9	2.7	2.6
Customs	0.4	1.1	1.4	1.3
Miscellaneous receipts	1.7	4.7	15.3	14.6
	$36.4	100.0	$104.7	100.0

SOURCE: *Economic Report of the President, 1967* (Washington, D. C.: U. S. Government
Printing Office, 1967), p. 282.

income taxes rising over the period, as personal incomes rose more rapidly than corporate profits. The relative importance of excise taxes has declined greatly.

The main sources of state and local government revenue, shown in Table 2-3, are licenses and other fees, property taxes, and sales taxes.[2] Income taxes, both personal and corporate, are of minor importance, but transfers from the federal government amounted to over 14 percent of state and local revenues in 1965. The most important change in the relative positions of the various sources of taxes is the decreased importance of the property tax and the increased importance of licenses, fees, and other revenues.

Table 2–3   STATE AND LOCAL GOVERNMENT REVENUES BY
             SOURCES, FISCAL YEARS 1950 AND 1965 (dollars in billions)

	1950		1965	
	Amount	Percent	Amount	Percent
Property taxes	$ 7.3	38.6	$22.9	30.9
Sales and gross receipts taxes	5.2	27.5	17.1	23.0
Individual income taxes	0.8	4.2	4.0	5.4
Corporation net income taxes	0.6	3.2	1.9	2.6
Revenues from the federal government	2.5	13.2	11.0	14.8
Licenses, fees, and other revenues	2.5	13.2	17.3	23.3
Totals	$18.9	100.0	$74.2	100.0

SOURCE: *Economic Report of the President* (Washington, D. C.: U. S. Government Printing Office, 1967), p. 289.

CORPORATE INCOME TAXES

Rate Structure. The first $25,000 of corporate taxable income is taxed at a 22 percent rate; all income over $25,000 is taxed at a 48 percent rate.[3] If a firm's taxable income was $100,000, for example, the tax would be computed as follows:

$$22\% \times 25,000 \quad \$\ 5,500$$
$$48\% \times 75,000 \quad \underline{36,000}$$
$$\$41,500$$

[2] It is important to note that these are *aggregate* statistics for all states and municipalities. There are considerable variations among governmental units, particularly with regard to the use of income taxes.

[3] Technically, there is a "normal" corporate tax of 22 percent plus a surtax of 26 percent on all income over $25,000.

The 22 percent rate would apply to the first $25,000 and the 48 percent rate would apply to the remaining $75,000, the total tax amounting to $41,500. Table 2–4 shows that the average corporate income tax is moderately progressive up to $1 million, when it becomes virtually 48 percent.

Table 2–4   MARGINAL AND AVERAGE TAX RATES OF THE CORPORATION INCOME TAX, 1968 (in percentages)

Corporate Income (in dollars)	Marginal Tax Rate*	Average Tax Rate†
0–25,000	22%	22.00%
25,001–26,000	48	23.00
26,001–32,000	48	27.69
32,001–38,000	48	30.89
38,001–44,000	48	33.23
44,001–50,000	48	35.00
50,001–60,000	48	37.17
60,001–70,000	48	38.71
70,001–80,000	48	39.88
80,001–90,000	48	40.78
90,001–100,000	48	41.50
100,001–150,000	48	43.67
150,001–200,000	48	44.75
200,001–500,000	48	46.70
500,001–1,000,000	48	47.35
1,000,001–5,000,000	48	47.87
5,000,001–10,000,000	48	47.94
10,000,001–100,000,000	48	47.99
100,000,001–500,000,000	48	48.00

* The *marginal tax rate* is the tax on each additional dollar of taxable income received. The tax on each of the first $25,000 is 22 cents; on each dollar over $25,000, the marginal tax rate jumps to 48 cents. The total taxes paid, when divided by the taxable income, gives the average tax rate.
† Applied to the upper limit of each class interval.

This relatively simple tax structure has wide implications for business planning. Because the tax rate more than doubles when corporate income rises above $25,000, it clearly pays to break moderately sized companies into two or more separate corporations in order to hold the income of each unit under $25,000 and thus keep the tax rate at 22 percent.[4] We shall see

---

[4] This is less true today than it was prior to 1964. The Revenue Act of 1964 imposed an additional 6 percent tax on the first $25,000 of income of multiple corporations (1) when they are controlled by an individual or a group and (2) when they do not elect to file consolidated tax returns. In spite of this additional tax, in many cases there is still a tax advantage to forming multiple corporations.

later, however, that the income tax is not the only factor bearing on this discussion.

Corporate Capital Gains and Losses[5]

Corporate taxable income consists of two components: (1) profits from the sale of capital assets and (2) all other income, defined as *ordinary income.*

Capital assets are defined as assets used by a firm but not bought and sold in the ordinary course of its business. For example, a machine tool would be a capital asset to a manufacturing company that used the tool, but it would not be a capital asset to a dealer in machine tools or to the tool manufacturer. Gains and losses on the sale of capital assets are defined as *capital gains,* and under certain circumstances they receive special tax treatment.

The sale of a capital asset held for six months or less gives rise to a *short-term* capital gain or loss, while its disposal, when held for more than six months, produces a *long-term* gain or loss. Net short-term gains (gains minus losses) are added to the firm's ordinary income and taxed at regular corporate income tax rates. For long-term capital gains, the tax is limited to 25 percent. For example, if a corporation holds the common stock of another corporation as an investment for more than six months and then sells it at a profit, the gain is subject to a tax of 25 percent.

Depreciable Assets

If an asset is subject to depreciation, for example, a machine tool, its cost is defined as the original purchase price less accumulated depreciation. To illustrate, suppose a machine cost $10,000, and $5,000 of depreciation has been taken on it. Its book value, by definition, is $5,000 ($10,000 — $5,000). If the company sells the machine, it may incur a capital gain or loss. For example, if it sells the machine for $3,000, it incurs a $2,000 loss ($5,000 book value — $3,000 received).

If the company sells the machine for more than its book value, it may incur *either* a capital gain *or* ordinary income for tax purposes. If the gain is a recapture of depreciation, indicating that the firm had been depreciating the asset too rapidly (and charging off this depreciation as an expense to reduce ordinary income), the gain is ordinary income and is taxed accordingly. For example, if it sells the machine for $7,000, it incurs a $2,000 gain ($7,000—$5,000). *This gain is not classified as a capital*

---

[5] Corporate capital gains and losses (as well as most other tax matters) are subject to many technical provisions. This section and the others dealing with tax matters include only the most general provisions. For special cases the student is referred to *Federal Tax Course* (Englewood Cliffs, N. J.: Prentice-Hall, 1968), *passim.*

gain, however; it constitutes the recapture of depreciation and is taxed as ordinary income.

The sale of a depreciable asset is subject to capital gains when the gain exceeds the amount of depreciation taken. To continue with the preceding example, if our machine had been sold for $12,000, then a total profit of $7,000 ($12,000 — $5,000) would have been incurred. Of this amount, $5,000 would represent the recapture of depreciation (since this amount of depreciation had been charged off) and would be taxed as ordinary income; the remaining $2,000 would be classified as a capital gain for tax purposes and would be taxed at a rate of 25 percent.

Deductibility of Capital Losses

A net capital loss is not deductible from ordinary income. For example, if in 1967 a corporation has an ordinary income of $100,000 and a net capital loss of $25,000, it still pays a tax on the ordinary income at the normal rate of 22 percent on the $25,000 and 48 percent on the $75,000, a total tax of $41,500. The net capital loss may, however, be carried over for five years and used to offset capital gains during that period. For example, if this corporation has a net capital gain of $75,000 in 1968, its *taxable net capital gain* in that year is $75,000 less the carry-over of $25,000, or $50,-000. The tax on the net gain is 25 percent, or $12,500, which is added to the tax on its ordinary income. The maximum period a capital loss may be carried forward in this manner is five years.

Dividend Income

Another important rule is that 85 percent of dividends received by one corporation from another is exempt from taxation.[6] For example, if corporation H owns stock in corporation S and receives $100,000 in dividends from corporation S, it has to pay taxes on only $15,000 of the $100,000. Assuming H is in the 48 percent tax bracket, the tax is $7,200, or 7.2 percent of the dividends received. The reason for this reduced tax is that to subject intercorporate dividends to the full corporate tax rate would, eventually, lead to triple taxation. First, firm S would pay its regular taxes, then firm H would pay a second tax. Finally, H's own stockholders would be subject to taxes when they receive dividends. The 85 percent dividend exclusion thus reduces the multiple taxation of corporate income.

---

[6] If the corporation receiving the dividends owns 80 percent or more of the stock of the dividend-paying firm, it may file a consolidated tax return. In this case, there have been no dividends as far as the Internal Revenue Service is concerned, so there is obviously no tax on dividends received. On the internal books of the related corporations there may be an accounting entry entitled "dividends" used to transfer funds from the subsidiary to the parent, but this is no concern to the IRS.

Payment of Tax in Installments

Before 1952, corporations paid their tax obligations in quarterly installments in the year *following* the year in which the income was earned. For example, if a corporation earned $100,000 in 1949 and the tax payable on this income was $50,000, the corporation paid $12,500 in each of four quarterly installments on March 15, June 15, September 15, and December 15, 1950. Under the so-called Mills plan beginning in 1952, corporations were moved toward a pay-as-you-go basis. By 1960 the larger corporations were paying 25 percent of their tax liability on each September 15 and December 15 of the year in which the income was earned (on an estimated basis), and 25 percent of the tax liability on each March 15 and June 15 of the year following that in which the liability was incurred. New provisions of the Internal Revenue Act of 1964 speed up collection even more, and by 1970 large corporations will be paying 25 percent of their estimated tax bill on the 15th of April, June, September, and December of the *current* year.

It will be seen in a subsequent chapter that the amount of taxes owed to the government constitutes an interest-free source of funds. As the movement toward pay-as-you-go corporate taxes progresses, new sources of financing must be found; thus planning for the speed-up in tax collections is important to American business.

Net Operating Carry-Back and Carry-Forward

For any year ending after December 31, 1958, any ordinary corporate operating loss can be carried back three years and forward five years. The law states that the loss must first be carried back to the earliest year, the remainder applied to the second earliest year, and so on. For example, an operating loss in 1969 may be used to reduce taxable income in 1966, 1967, 1968, 1970, 1971, 1972, 1973, and 1974, and it *must* follow that sequence. The purpose of permitting this loss averaging is to avoid penalizing corporations whose incomes fluctuate widely.

To illustrate, suppose the Ritz Hotel made $100,000 before taxes in all years except 1969, when it suffered a $600,000 operating loss. The Ritz would use the *carry-back* feature to recompute its taxes for 1966, use $100,-000 of the operating losses to reduce the 1966 profit to zero, and recover the amount of taxes paid in that year. Since $500,000 of unrecovered losses would still be available, Ritz would do the same thing for 1967 and 1968. Then, in 1970, 1971, and 1972, it would apply the *carry-forward* loss to reduce its profits to zero in each of these years.

The right to carry losses forward and backward has made some corporations attractive buys. For example, Atlas Corporation and Howard

Hughes bought RKO Pictures because of a $30 million tax-loss credit. A corporation may acquire another firm that has had a tax loss, operate it as a subsidiary, and then present consolidated returns for tax purposes. Newspapers frequently contain advertisements such as "Tax-Loss Corporation for Sale," "Attractive Tax Loss Available." The corporation may be a doubly attractive buy if the purchaser is able to operate the business effectively and turn it into a profitable corporation at the same time that he benefits from the tax-loss carry-forward.

The tax law of 1954 placed certain restrictions on this privilege. (1) If more than 50 percent of the stock changes hands within two years after the purchase and (2) if the old business is essentially abandoned, no loss carry over is provided. The objective of the limitation is to prevent a firm from merging for the sole purpose of taking advantage of the tax law. If it merges for this purpose and files consolidated returns, the loss privilege may be disallowed. Moreover, deductions are denied where an acquisition appears to have been motivated largely by the prospects of such deductions.[7]

Improper Accumulation

A special surtax on improperly accumulated income is provided for by Section 531 of the Internal Revenue Code, which states that earnings accumulated by a corporation are subject to penalty rates *if the purpose of the accumulation is to enable the stock owners to avoid the personal income tax.* Of income not paid out in dividends, $100,000 is prima facie retainable for the reasonable needs of the business. This is a benefit for small corporations. But there is a penalty rate on all amounts over $100,000 shown to be unnecessary to meet the reasonable needs of the business. The penalty rate is 27.5 percent on the first $100,000 of improperly accumulated taxable income and 38.5 percent on all amounts over $100,000.

The 1954 law provides that the burden of proof of improper accumulation falls on the United States Treasury if the taxpayer files a statement supporting his accumulation. In other words, if the taxpayer presents a statement explaining why he is retaining the earnings, it is up to the Treasury to prove that his statement is not justified. Before 1954, the burden of proof was on the taxpayer to convince the Treasury and the courts that retention was justified.

Retained earnings are used to pay off debt, to finance growth, and to provide the corporation with a cushion against possible cash drains caused by losses. How much a firm should properly accumulate for uncertain con-

---

[7] Sylvan Tobolowsky, "Tax Consequences of Corporate Organization and Distributions," *Journal of Taxation,* 12 (January 1960), pp. 8–15.

tingencies is a matter of judgment. Fear of the penalty taxes that may be imposed under Section 531 may cause a firm to pay out a higher rate of dividends than it otherwise would.[8]

Sometimes Section 531 may stimulate mergers. A clear illustration is provided by the purchase of the Toni Company (home permanents) by the Gillette Safety Razor Company.[9] The sale was made early in 1948, when Toni's sales volume had begun to level off. Since earnings retention might be difficult to justify, the owners of Toni, the Harris brothers, were faced with the alternatives of paying penalty rates for improper accumulation of earnings or of paying out the income as dividends. Toni's income after corporate taxes was $4 million a year, and, with the Harris brothers' average personal income tax of 75 percent, only $1 million a year would have been left after they paid personal taxes on dividends. By selling Toni for $13 million, they realized a $12 million capital gain (their book value was $1 million). After paying the 25 percent capital gains tax on the $12 million, or $3 million, the Harrises realized $10 million after taxes ($13 million sale price less $3 million tax). Thus, Gillette paid the equivalent of 3¼ years' after-corporate-tax earnings for Toni, while the Harris brothers received 10 years' after-personal-income-tax net income for it. The tax factor made the transaction advantageous to both parties.

Election of Legal Form for Tax Purposes

The broad aspects of the federal corporate income tax have now been covered. For many business decisions, the federal income tax on individuals is equally important, so the main outlines of this part of the tax system must be discussed. First, however, it is necessary to note that under certain circumstances proprietorships and partnerships can elect to be taxed as corporations. Similarly, certain incorporated businesses may elect to be taxed as proprietorships or partnerships.

This possibility of operating a business in one form but being taxed as another type of concern is highly important; it allows qualified firms to have the best of both worlds. In the next section the individual tax structure is examined and compared with the corporate tax structure, thus providing a basis for making an intelligent choice as to which form of organization a firm should elect for tax purposes.

---

[8] See materials in James K. Hall, *The Taxation of Corporate Surplus Accumulations* (Washington, D. C.: U. S. Government Printing Office, 1952), especially Appendix 3.

[9] See J. K. Butters, K. Lintner, and W. L. Cary, *Effects of Taxation, Corporate Mergers* (Boston: Harvard Business School, 1951), pp. 96–111. The lucid presentation by these authors has been drawn on for the general background, but the data have been approximated to make the illustration simple. The principle involved is not affected by the modifications of the facts.

PERSONAL INCOME TAX

Of some five million firms in the United States, over four million are organized as individual proprietorships or as partnerships. The income of businesses organized as individual proprietorships or partnerships is taxed as personal income to the owners or the partners unless they have elected to have the firm taxed as a corporation. The net income of a proprietorship or a partnership is reported to provide a basis for determining the individual's income tax liability. Thus, as a business tax, the individual income tax may be as important as the corporate income tax.

Individual Income Tax Structure

The tax rates applicable to the single individual are set forth in Table 2-5, and rates applicable to married couples filing joint returns are shown in

Table 2-5   MARGINAL AND AVERAGE 1967 TAX RATES OF THE INDIVIDUAL INCOME TAX (Single taxpayers or separate returns)

Taxable Income	Tax Calculation			Average Tax Rate	
	Base Amount +	Marginal Tax Rate =	Tax*	Individual	Corporate
$0–$500	$0	14%	$70	14.0%	22.0%
500–1,000	70	15	145	14.5	22.0
1,000–1,500	145	16	225	15.0	22.0
1,500–2,000	225	17	310	15.5	22.0
2,000–4,000	310	19	690	17.3	22.0
4,000–6,000	690	22	1,130	18.8	22.0
6,000–8,000	1,130	25	1,630	20.4	22.0
8,000–10,000	1,630	28	2,190	21.8	22.0
10,000–12,000	2,190	32	2,830	23.5	22.0
12,000–14,000	2,830	36	3,550	25.3	22.0
14,000–16,000	3,550	39	4,330	27.0	22.0
16,000–18,000	4,330	42	5,170	28.7	22.0
18,000–20,000	5,170	45	6,070	30.3	22.0
20,000–22,000	6,070	48	7,030	31.9	22.0
22,000–26,000	7,030	50	9,030	34.7	23.0
26,000–32,000	9,030	53	12,210	38.1	27.7
32,000–38,000	12,210	55	15,510	40.8	30.9
38,000–44,000	15,510	58	18,990	43.1	33.2
44,000–50,000	18,990	60	22,590	45.2	35.0
50,000–60,000	22,590	62	28,790	48.0	37.2
60,000–70,000	28,790	64	35,190	50.3	38.7
70,000–80,000	35,190	66	41,790	52.2	39.9
80,000–90,000	41,790	68	48,590	54.0	40.8
90,000–100,000	48,590	69	55,490	55.5	41.5
100,000–150,000	55,490	70	90,490	60.3	43.7
150,000–200,000	90,490	70	125,490	62.7	44.8
200,000–500,000	125,490	70	335,490	67.1	46.7
500,000–1,000,000	335,490	70	685,490	68.5	47.4
1,000,000–5,000,000	685,490	70	3,485,490	69.7	47.9
5,000,000–100,000,000	3,485,490	70	69,985,490	70.0	48.0

* Based on upper limit of each class interval.

Table 2-6. Since joint returns are permitted whether or not one spouse earns the entire income, this privilege has the effect of lowering applicable tax rates.

Table 2-6   MARGINAL AND AVERAGE 1967 TAX RATES OF THE PERSONAL INCOME TAX (joint returns)

	Tax Calculation			Average Tax Rate	
Taxable Income	Base Amount	+ Marginal Tax Rate =	Tax*	Individual	Corporate
$0–$1,000	$0	14%	$140	14.0%	22.0%
1,000–2,000	140	15	290	14.5	22.0
2,000–3,000	290	16	450	15.0	22.0
3,000–4,000	450	17	620	15.5	22.0
4,000–8,000	620	19	1,380	17.4	22.0
8,000–12,000	1,380	22	2,260	18.8	22.0
12,000–16,000	2,260	25	3,260	20.4	22.0
16,000–20,000	3,260	28	4,380	21.9	22.0
20,000–24,000	4,380	32	5,660	23.6	22.0
24,000–28,000	5,660	36	7,100	25.4	24.8
28,000–32,000	7,100	39	8,660	27.1	27.7
32,000–36,000	8,660	42	10,340	28.7	29.9
36,000–40,000	10,340	45	12,140	30.4	31.8
40,000–44,000	12,140	48	14,060	32.0	33.2
44,000–52,000	14,060	50	18,060	34.7	35.5
52,000–64,000	18,060	53	24,420	38.2	37.8
64,000–76,000	24,420	55	31,020	40.8	39.4
76,000–88,000	31,020	58	37,980	43.2	40.6
88,000–100,000	37,980	60	45,180	45.2	41.5
100,000–120,000	45,180	62	57,580	48.0	42.6
120,000–140,000	57,580	64	70,380	50.3	43.4
140,000–160,000	70,380	66	83,580	52.2	43.9
160,000–180,000	83,580	68	97,180	54.0	44.4
180,000–200,000	97,180	69	110,980	55.5	44.8
200,000–300,000	110,980	70	189,980	60.3	45.8
300,000–400,000	180,980	70	250,980	62.7	46.4
400,000–1,000,000	250,980	70	670,980	67.1	47.4
1,000,000–10,000,000	670,980	70	6,970,980	69.7	47.9
10,000,000–100,000,000	6,970,980	70	69,920,980	70.0	48.0

* Based on upper limit of each class interval.

For some decisions, the taxpayer will compare the marginal tax rates. If a taxpayer has income from other sources and is deciding on whether to set up a new venture as a proprietorship or a corporation, he will be concerned with the tax rate applicable to the additional income. In comparing the relative advantages of the corporate versus noncorporate form of business organization, he is likely to compare the personal individual income tax rates to which his income will be subject with the marginal corporate income tax rates.

When the taxpayer's income will be derived mainly from the enterprise he contemplates forming, he is more likely to compare the average rates of taxation. The relation between the average tax rates of the corporate income tax and the individual income tax is shown in Figure 2-1. For single returns, the individual rate rises above the corporate rate at about $10,000. For joint returns, the individual tax rises above the corporate at $54,000, at which point the amount of taxes on individual income is $19,-320 and that on corporate income is $19,420. From this point on, the individual tax rate rises to 70 percent, while the corporate rate rises more slowly toward 48 percent.

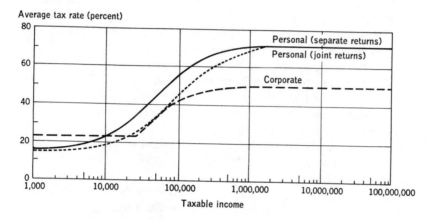

Average tax rate (percent)

Taxable income

Figure 2-1 Comparison between Average Rates of Personal Income Tax and Corporation Income Tax (1967 Tax Rates)

Thus, for a firm with net income of $1 million, there is no question but that the corporate form of business should be used. The tax advantage helps to explain why our largest businesses utilize the corporate form of organization. At incomes in the region of the $54,000 dividing line, whether the corporate or the noncorporate form will be most advantageous depends upon the facts of the case. If a firm finds it necessary to pay out a substantial part of its earnings, the noncorporate form is likely to be advantageous, because the "double taxation" is avoided. On the other hand, the corporate form is satisfactory if the nature of the business operation makes it possible to set up a number of corporations for the purpose of keeping the tax rate at 22 percent.

Capital Gains and Losses

As with corporations, the distinction between short-term and long-term gains and losses is the six-month holding period. Net short-term gains are taxed at regular rates; the tax on long-term gains may be computed in either of two ways. First, the taxpayer may pay a flat rate of 25 percent on net long-term gains. Alternatively, he may elect to pay the ordinary tax rate on *one half* the amount of the net long-term gains. The taxpayer should compute his tax under each of these methods and then select the one that results in the lower tax bill. For example, a married couple with an income of $32,000 from noncapital sources and a $10,000 long-term capital gain would compute their tax in two ways: (1) apply the normal tax rates on $32,000 plus ½ ($10,000) = $37,000 or (2) apply the normal tax on $32,000 plus 25 percent of $10,000. The first method would produce a tax of $10,790; the second, a tax of $11,160. The taxpayer would naturally elect the first method in this case. In general, for joint returns the 25 percent option is beneficial only if the taxable income exceeds $44,000, the point at which the marginal tax rate goes to 50 percent.

In contrast to the treatment permitted corporations, if an individual's capital losses exceed his capital gains, the net loss may be deducted from ordinary income up to a maximum of $1,000. In other words, an individual may deduct against ordinary income up to $1,000 of his net capital losses in any one year. If the net capital loss is in excess of $1,000, any amount above $1,000 may be carried forward until it is exhausted. Capital losses may not be carried back.

Moreover, the Revenue Act of 1958 provides that individuals who invest in the stock of small corporations and suffer a loss on that stock may, for tax purposes, treat such a loss up to $25,000 a year ($50,000 on a joint return) as an ordinary loss rather than as a capital loss. A corporation is considered a small corporation, and the loss on its stock can be treated as an ordinary loss, if its common stock does not exceed $500,000 and if its total net worth—common stock plus retained earnings—does not exceed $1 million. This provision also encourages the formation of, and investment in, small corporations.

Although the foregoing tax factors make it difficult to generalize on whether the corporate or the noncorporate form is more advantageous from a tax standpoint, the essential variables for making an analysis are provided. In general, the advantage now seems to be on the side of the corporation, particularly since a firm may obtain the many benefits of its corporate status and yet elect to be taxed as a proprietorship or a partnership.

Dividend Income

The first $100 of dividend income received by an individual stockholder is excluded from taxable income. If stock is owned jointly by a husband and a wife, the exclusion is $200. However, if only one spouse owns stock, the total exclusion is generally only $100.

To illustrate, if a family's gross income consists of $12,000 of salary plus $500 of dividends on stock owned by the husband, the gross taxable income (before deductions) is $12,400. However, if the stock is jointly owned, the taxable gross income would be $12,300, because $200 of the dividend income would be excluded.

Personal Deductions

A $600 deduction is allowed for the taxpayer and each of his dependents; the deduction is doubled on any taxpayer or dependent who is over sixty-five years old or is blind. A family of four—husband, wife, and two dependent children, none blind or over sixty-five—would thus have personal deductions of 4 times $600, or $2,400.

Other Deductions

Certain other items are also deductible from income before computing taxes—medical expenses (subject to limitations), interest payments, state and local taxes, contributions, among others. A taxpayer has the choice of either itemizing these deductions or taking the standard deduction, which is computed as the lower of $1,000 or 10 percent of gross taxable income.

Illustration. A family of four filing a joint return has an income consisting of $11,000 salary and $500 dividends on stock owned jointly by the husband and the wife. They take the standard deduction. Their gross income is $11,500, but $200 dividends are excluded, leaving a gross taxable income of $11,300. Personal deductions are $2,400 and the standard deduction is $1,000, the lesser of $1,000 or 10 percent of $11,300; their taxable income is therefore $7,900. From Table 2-6 we find that the tax is $1,361, calculated as $620 plus 19 percent of $3,900.

SUMMARY

This chapter provides some basic background on the tax environment within which business firms operate.

Corporate Taxes

The *corporate tax rate* structure is simple: the tax rate is 22 percent on income up to $25,000, and 48 percent on all income over $25,000. Taxes are paid in quarterly installments during the year the income is earned. *Operating losses* may be carried back for three years and forward for five years. *Capital losses* may not be treated as a deduction from operating income, but they may be used to offset capital gains. Corporate capital losses may be carried forward for five years.

Eighty-five percent of the *dividends received* by a corporation owning stock in another firm is excluded from the receiving firm's taxable income; the receiving firm must pay full taxes on the remaining 15 percent of the dividends. *Dividends paid* are not treated as a tax-deductible expense. Regardless of the size of its earnings a corporation does not have to pay dividends if it needs funds for expansion. If, however, the funds are not used for a legitimate purpose and if earnings are retained merely to enable stockholders to avoid paying personal income taxes on dividends received, the firm will be subject to an *improper accumulations tax.*

Personal Income Tax

Unincorporated business income is taxed at the personal tax rates of the owners. Personal income tax rates for both individuals and married persons filing jointly are *progressive*—the higher one's income, the higher his tax rate. Personal income tax rates start at 14 percent of taxable income and rise to 70 percent of taxable income over $200,000. Corporate income tax rates range between 22 and 48 percent. Thus at lower incomes the personal income tax rate is lower if a business is organized as a proprietorship or a partnership; at higher incomes the corporate tax rate is lower. This fact has a significant bearing on whether a business chooses to be taxed as a corporation or as an individual. Note, however, that under certain circumstances *unincorporated businesses can elect to be taxed as corporations,* and vice versa.

Short-term *capital gains* are taxed at ordinary rates; long-term gains, at 25 percent or one half the normal tax rate, whichever is lower. Capital losses can be used to offset capital gains. Net capital losses in any year can be deducted from ordinary income up to a limit of $1,000 a year. Capital losses in excess of $1,000 can be carried forward indefinitely until used up.

The foregoing material on the United States tax system is not designed to make a tax expert of the reader. It provides a few essentials for recognizing tax aspects of business financial problems and for developing an awareness of the kinds of situations that should be taken to tax specialists for further guidance. These basics will, however, be referred to frequently in the remainder of the text, for income taxes are often an important factor in the making of business financial decisions.

QUESTIONS

2–1 Compare the marginal and the average tax rates of corporations with taxable incomes of $5,000, $50,000, $500,000, $5,000,000, and $50,000,000. Can you make such a comparison for sole proprietorships or for partnerships?

2–2 Which is the more relevant tax rate, the marginal or the average, in determining the form of organization for a new firm? Have recent changes in the tax laws made the form of organization more or less important than formerly?

2–3 For tax purposes, how does the treatment of interest expense compare with the treatment of common stock dividends from each of the following standpoints: a firm paying the interest or the dividends, an individual recipient, a corporate recipient?

2–4 Compare the treatment of capital gains and losses with ordinary gains and losses in income tax returns.

2–5 What is the present corporate carry-back and carry-forward tax provision for ordinary income? What is the purpose of this provision?

2–6 What is the purpose of the Internal Revenue Code provision dealing with improper accumulation of corporate surplus?

2–7 Does the corporate tax rate structure give small firms the incentive to operate as multiple corporations?

2–8 Why is personal income tax information important for a study of business finance?

2–9 How do the tax rates for capital gains and losses affect an individual's investment policies and opportunities for financing a small business?

PROBLEMS

2–1 A corporation has a net income of $43,350 before interest charges. Assuming interest charges amount to $3,350:

a) How much income tax must the corporation pay?
b) What is the marginal tax rate?

2–2 Warren T. Lasser is a married man with one child. His gross income for 1968 is $12,000, which includes $1,250 of corporate dividends received by his wife. He files a joint return and takes the standard deduction. What is his personal income tax liability for 1968?

2–3 The taxable income (losses are shown in parentheses) of the Austin Corporation, formed in 1961, is shown below.

1962	$(300,000)
1963	150,000
1964	200,000
1965	300,000
1966	(150,000)

Corporate tax rates for these years are as follows:

1962 and 1963—first $25,000, 30%; excess, 52%
1964—first $25,000, 22%; excess, 50%
1965 and 1966—first $25,000, 22%; excess, 48%

What is the corporate tax liability for each year?

2–4 The Western Corporation income statement for 1965 is shown here.

Gross taxable income	$150,000
Tax payable (prepaid)	65,500
Net income after taxes	$ 84,500

PSR Manufacturing Corporation had a $75,000 loss in 1965. Western feels that its managerial talent can turn PSR into a profitable operation. If the two companies merged prior to January 1, 1966, what would be the merged corporation's income for 1965 after any refund of prepaid taxes? What is the difference in tax liability for Western before and after the merger?

2–5   In 1965 Alvin Manufacturing earned $150,000 before taxes on sales of $3 million. In 1963 it acquired working control of Markson Products, Inc., for $125,000 and disposed of the stock in 1965 for $350,000. (Alvin controlled less than 80 percent of Markson.) In addition, dividends paid by Markson to Alvin during 1965 amounted to $15,000.

a) What is Alvin's tax for 1965?

b) What would Alvin's tax have been if Markson had declared a further dividend of $50,000 in 1965 and if Alvin had sold the stock, purchased in 1963, for 300,000?

2–6   A corporation has income of $100,000 after all expenses.

a) What is the corporation's income tax liability?

b) Suppose the operations of the company are such that it could justify setting up five separate corporations (for example, a real estate company operating in five separate sections of a city). What tax is paid by each of the five corporations? the total tax paid by all five? (Assume that each corporation had a net profit of $20,000.)

c) As its sole income, Company ABC receives the total after-tax income of the five corporations in the form of dividends. What is the total amount of tax paid by the six firms, assuming they file a consolidated tax return? unconsolidated tax returns?

PART II

Financial Analysis, Planning, and Control

Chapter 3

Financial Analysis

Planning is the key to the financial manager's success. Financial plans may take many forms; a good plan must be related to the firm's existing strengths and weaknesses. Its strengths must be understood if they are to be used to proper advantage; its weaknesses must be recognized if corrective action is to be taken. For example, are inventories adequate to support the projected level of sales? Does the firm have too heavy an investment in accounts receivable, and does this condition reflect a lax collection policy? The financial manager can plan his future financial requirements in accordance with the forecasting and budgeting procedures developed in succeeding chapters, but his plan must begin with the type of financial analysis developed below.

BASIC TYPES OF FINANCIAL RATIOS

Each particular type of analysis has a purpose or use that determines the different types of relationships emphasized in the analysis. The analyst may, for example, be a banker considering whether or not to grant a short-term loan to a firm. He is primarily interested in the firm's liquid position and stresses ratios that measure liquidity. In contrast, long-term creditors place far more emphasis on earning power and on operating efficiency than on liquidity. They know that unprofitable operations will erode asset values; a strong current position is no guarantee that funds will be available to repay

37

a 20-year bond issue. Equity investors are similarly interested in long-term profitability and efficiency. Management is, of course, concerned with all these aspects of financial analysis—it seeks to repay its debts to the banker and to earn profits for the stockholder.

It is useful to classify ratios into four fundamental types:

1. *Liquidity ratios,* which are designed to measure the firm's ability to meet its maturing short-term obligations
2. *Leverage ratios,* which measure the extent to which the firm has been financed by debt
3. *Activity ratios,* which measure how effectively the firm is using its resources
4. *Profitability ratios,* which measure management's over-all effectiveness as shown by the returns generated on sales and investment

Specific examples of each type of ratio are given in the following sections with an actual case history used to illustrate their calculation and use. The company's name and specific figures are disguised, of course, but the case is a good one to illustrate the process of financial analysis.

Walker-Wilson Manufacturing Company. The Walker-Wilson Manufacturing Company produces specialized machinery used in the automobile repair business. Formed in 1946, when Charles Walker and Ben Wilson set up a small plant to produce certain tools they had developed while in the Army, Walker-Wilson grew steadily and earned the reputation of being one of the best small firms in its line of business. In December 1966, both Walker and Wilson were killed in a crash of their private plane. For the next 2 years the firm was managed by Walker-Wilson's accountant, but in 1968 the widows, who are the principal stockholders in Walker-Wilson, acting on the advice of the firm's bankers and attorneys, engaged David Thompson as president and general manager.

Thompson is experienced in this line of business, especially in production and sales, but he does not have a detailed knowledge of his new company. He has therefore decided to conduct a detailed appraisal of the firm's position and, on the basis of this position, to draw up a plan for future operations. The most recent balance sheet and income statement—the starting points for any financial analysis—are presented in Tables 3-1 and 3-2.[1]

---

[1] There is no "standard form" for the balance sheet, income statement, or other financial statements. Moreover, certain words can be given more than one meaning, and a single concept can be called by several different titles. For example, "net income after taxes" is also called "net income," "net profit," "income," and "profit." Depreciation can refer to the accumulated reserve for depreciation or to the annual charge against operating income. The balance sheet is also called the "statement of condition"; and the income statement the "profit and loss statement." These and other ambiguities can cause confusion, but if one is careful to determine the context within which the word is used, this confusion can be minimized.

Table 3–1   *WALKER-WILSON COMPANY*
                        ILLUSTRATIVE BALANCE SHEET
                            December 31, 1968

Assets		*Claims on Assets*	
Cash	$ 50,000	Accounts payable	$ 60,000
Marketable securities	150,000	Notes payable, 8%	100,000
Receivables, net	200,000	Accruals	10,000
Inventories	300,000	Provision for federal in-	
Total current assets	$ 700,000	come taxes	130,000
Gross plant and		Total current liabilities	$ 300,000
equipment	$1,800,000	First mortgage bonds,	
Less reserve for		5% *	500,000
depreciation	500,000	Debentures, 6%	200,000
Net plant and		Common stock	600,000
equipment	$1,300,000	Retained earnings	400,000
		Total net worth	$1,000,000
Total assets	$2,000,000	Total claims on assets	$2,000,000

* The annual sinking fund requirement is $20,000.

Liquidity Ratios

Generally the first concern of the financial analyst is liquidity—is the firm able to meet its maturing obligations? Walker-Wilson has debts totaling $300,000 that must be paid within the coming year. Can these obligations be satisfied? Although a full liquidity analysis requires the use of cash budgets (described in Chapter 5), ratio analysis, by relating the amount of cash and other current assets to the current obligations, provides a quick and easy-to-use measure of liquidity.

1. Current Ratio. The current ratio is computed by dividing current liabilities into current assets. Current assets normally include cash, marketable securities, accounts receivable, and inventories; current liabilities consist of accounts payable, short-term notes payable, current maturities of long-term debt, accrued income taxes, and other accrued expenses (principally wages). The current ratio is the generally accepted measure of short-term solvency, since it indicates the extent to which the claims of short-term creditors are covered by assets that are expected to be converted to cash in a period roughly corresponding to the maturity of the claims.

Table 3–2   *WALKER-WILSON COMPANY*
ILLUSTRATIVE INCOME STATEMENT
For Year Ended December 31, 1968

Net sales		$3,000,000
Cost of goods sold		2,580,000
Gross profit		$ 420,000
Less: Operating expenses		
Selling	$22,000	
General and administrative	40,000	
Rent on office	28,000	90,000
Gross operating income		$ 330,000
Depreciation		100,000
Net operating income		$ 230,000
Add: Other income		
Royalties		15,000
Gross income		$ 245,000
Less: Other expenses		
Interest on notes payable	$ 8,000	
Interest on first mortgage	25,000	
Interest on debentures	12,000	45,000
Net before income tax		$ 200,000
Federal income tax (at 40 percent *)		80,000
Net income after income tax available to common stock-		$ 120,000
holders		
Less: Common stock dividends		100,000
Increase in retained earnings		$ 20,000

* For most of the illustrations in the text a 50 percent corporate tax rate is used.

The calculation of the current ratio for Walker-Wilson is shown below.

$$\text{current ratio} = \frac{\text{current assets}}{\text{current liabilities}} = \frac{\$700,000}{\$300,000} = 2.3 \text{ times}$$
$$\text{industry average} = 2.5 \text{ times}$$

The current ratio is slightly below the average for the industry, 2.5, but not low enough to cause concern. It appears that Walker-Wilson is about in line with most other firms in this particular line of business. Since current assets are near-maturing, it is highly probable that they could be liquidated at close to book value. With a current ratio of 2.3 Walker-Wilson could liquidate current assets at only 42.9 percent of book value and still pay off current creditors in full.

2. Quick Ratio, or Acid Test. The quick ratio is calculated by deducting inventories from current assets and dividing the remainder by current liabilities. Inventories are typically the least liquid of a firm's current assets and the asset on which losses are most likely to occur in the event of liquidation. Therefore, this measure of ability to pay off short-term obligations without relying on the sale of inventories is important.

$$\text{quick, or acid test ratio} = \frac{(\text{current assets} - \text{inventory})}{\text{current liabilities}} = \frac{\$400,000}{\$300,000}$$
$$= 1.3 \text{ times}$$
$$\text{industry average} = 1.0 \text{ time}$$

The industry average quick ratio is 1, so Walker-Wilson's 1.3 ratio compares favorably with other firms in the industry. Thompson knows that if the marketable securities can be sold at par and if he can collect the accounts receivable, he can pay off his current liabilities without selling any inventory.

Leverage Ratios

Leverage ratios, which measure the contributions of owners as compared with the financing provided by the firm's creditors, have a number of implications. First, creditors look to the equity, or owner-supplied funds, to provide a margin of safety. If owners have provided only a small proportion of total financing, the risks of the enterprise are borne mainly by the creditors. Second, by raising funds through debt, the owners gain the benefits of maintaining control of the firm with a limited investment. Third, if the firm earns more on the borrowed funds than it pays in interest, the return to the owners is magnified. For example, if assets earn 6 percent and debt costs but 4 percent, there is a 2 percent differential, which accrues to the stockholders. Leverage cuts both ways, however; if the return on assets falls to 3 percent, the differential between that figure and the cost of debt must be made up from equity's share of total profits. In the first instance, where assets earn more than the cost of debt, leverage is favorable; in the second it is unfavorable.

In practice, leverage is approached in two ways. One approach involves examining balance sheet ratios and determining the extent to which borrowed funds have been used to finance the firm. The other approach measures the risks of debt by income statement ratios designed to determine the number of times fixed charges are covered by operating profits. These sets of ratios are complementary, and most analysts examine both types of leverage ratios.

3. Debt to Total Assets. This ratio, generally called the debt ratio, measures the percentage of total funds that have been provided by creditors. Debt includes current liabilities and all bonds. Creditors prefer moderate debt ratios, since the lower the ratio, the greater the cushion against creditors' losses in the event of liquidation. In contrast to the creditors' preference for a low debt ratio, the owners may seek high leverage either (1) to magnify earnings or (2) because raising new equity means giving up some degree of control. But if the debt ratio is too high, there is a danger of encouraging irresponsibility on the part of the owners. The stake of the owners can become so small that speculative activity, if it is successful, will yield a substantial percentage return to the owners. On the other hand, if the venture is unsuccessful, only a moderate loss is incurred by the owners, because their investment is small.

$$\text{debt ratio} = \frac{\text{total debt}}{\text{total assets}} = \frac{\$1,000,000}{\$2,000,000} = 50\%$$
$$\text{industry average} = 33\%$$

Walker-Wilson's debt ratio is 50 percent; this means that creditors have supplied half the firm's total financing. Since the average debt ratio for this industry—and for manufacturing generally—is about 33 percent, Walker-Wilson would find it difficult to borrow additional funds without first raising more equity capital. Creditors would be reluctant to lend the firm more money, and Thompson would probably be subjecting the stockholders to undue dangers if he sought to increase the debt ratio still more by borrowing.

4. *Times Interest Earned.* The times-interest-earned ratio is determined by dividing earnings before interest and taxes (gross income in Table 3-2) by the interest charges. The times-interest-earned ratio measures the extent to which earnings can decline without resultant financial embarrassment to the firm because of inability to meet annual interest costs. Failure to meet this obligation can bring legal action by the creditors, possibly resulting in bankruptcy. Note that the before-tax profit figure is used in the numerator. Because income taxes are computed after deducting interest expense, the ability to pay current interest is not affected by income taxes.

$$\text{times interest earned} = \frac{\text{profit before taxes plus interest charges}}{\text{interest charges}}$$

$$\frac{\$245,000}{\$45,000} = 5.4 \text{ times}$$
$$\text{industry average} = 8.0 \text{ times}$$

Walker-Wilson's interest charges consist of three payments totaling $45,000 (see Table 3-2). The firm's gross income available to service these charges is $245,000, so the interest is covered only 5.4 times. Since the industry average is 8 times, the company is covering its interest charges by a minimum margin of safety and deserves only a fair rating. This ratio reinforces the conclusion based on the debt ratio that the company is likely to face some difficulties raising additional funds from debt sources.

5. *Fixed Charge Coverage.* The number of times fixed charges are covered is determined by dividing profit before fixed charges by the total fixed charges—interest, lease payments, sinking fund requirements, and the tax related to sinking fund payments.[2] This more inclusive ratio provides an important supplement to the times-interest-earned figure, as it recognizes that financial problems may arise from the nonpayment of lease obligations or sinking fund charges as well as from the failure to meet interest payments.

$$\text{fixed-charge coverage} = \frac{\text{income available for meeting fixed charges}}{\text{fixed charges}}$$

$$= \frac{\text{gross income} + \text{rent on office}}{\text{interest} + \text{rent} + \text{before-tax sinking fund}}$$

$$= \frac{\$245,000 + \$28,000}{\$45,000 + \$28,000 + \$33,333}$$

$$= \frac{\$273,000}{\$106,333} = 2.6 \text{ times}$$

$$\text{industry average} = 4.0 \text{ times}$$

---

[2] A sinking fund, discussed in detail in Chapter 17, is a required annual payment designed to amortize a bond issue. Sinking fund payments are not deductible for income tax purposes, so they must be paid with after-tax profits. This means, in effect, that the firm must earn sufficient profits before taxes to enable it to pay its tax bill and still have enough left to meet the sinking fund requirement. For this reason the tax requirement must be included in the denominator of the fixed-charge-coverage ratio.

Since it is in the 40 percent tax bracket, Walker-Wilson must have a before-tax income of $33,333 to enable it to pay the tax and still have $20,000 left after taxes. The general equation for finding the necessary before-tax income is:

$$\begin{array}{l}\text{before-tax income required for} \\ \text{sinking fund payment}\end{array} = \frac{\text{sinking fund payment}}{1.0 - \text{tax rate}}$$

$$= \frac{\$20,000}{1.0 - 0.4} = \frac{\$20,000}{0.6}$$

$$= \$33,333$$

Walker-Wilson's fixed charges are covered 2.6 times, as opposed to an industry average of 4 times. Again, this indicates that the firm is somewhat weaker than creditors would prefer it to be and further points up the difficulties Thompson would likely encounter if he should attempt additional borrowing.

Activity Ratios

Activity ratios measure how effectively the firm employs the resources at its command. These ratios all involve comparisons between the level of sales and the investment in various asset accounts. The activity ratios presume a proper balance between sales and the various asset accounts—inventories, accounts receivable, fixed assets, and others. As we shall see in the following chapter, this is indeed a good assumption.

6. *Inventory Turnover.* The inventory turnover we shall use is sales divided by inventories.

$$\text{inventory turnover} = \frac{\text{sales}}{\text{inventory}} = \frac{\$3,000,000}{\$300,000} = 10 \text{ times}$$
$$\text{industry average} = 9 \text{ times}$$

Walker-Wilson's turnover of 10 compares favorably with an industry average of 9 times. This suggests that the company does not hold excessive stocks of inventory; excess stocks are, of course, unproductive and represent an investment with a low or zero rate of return. This high inventory turnover also reinforces Thompson's faith in the current ratio. If the turnover had been low—perhaps 3 or 4 times—he would have wondered whether the firm was holding damaged or obsolete materials not actually worth their stated value.

Two problems arise in calculating and analyzing the inventory turnover ratio. First, sales are at market prices, and if inventories are carried at cost, as they generally are, it would be more appropriate to use cost of goods sold in place of sales in the numerator of the formula. Established compilers of financial ratio statistics such as Dun & Bradstreet, however, use the ratio of sales to inventories carried at cost. To develop a figure that can be compared with those developed by Dun & Bradstreet, it is therefore necessary to measure inventory turnover with sales in the numerator, as we do here.

The second problem lies in the fact that sales occur over the entire year, whereas the inventory figure is for one point in time. This makes it better to use an average inventory, computed by adding beginning and ending inventories and dividing by two. If it is determined that the firm's business is highly seasonal, or if there has been a strong upward or downward sales trend during the year, it becomes essential to make this relatively simple adjustment. Neither of these conditions holds for Walker-Wilson; to maintain comparability with industry averages, therefore, Thompson did not use the average inventory figure.

7. *Average Collection Period.* The average collection period, which is an alternative ratio for measuring the accounts receivable turnover, is computed as follows: First, the annual credit sales are divided by 360 to get the average daily sales.[3] Second, daily sales are divided into accounts receivable to find the number of days' sales tied up in receivables. This is defined as the average collection period, for it represents the average length of time that the firm must wait after making a sale before receiving cash.

$$\text{sales per day} = \frac{\$3,000,000}{360} = \$8,333$$

$$\text{average collection period} = \frac{\text{receivables}}{\text{sales per day}} = \frac{\$200,000}{\$8,333} = 24 \text{ days}$$

$$\text{industry average} = 20 \text{ days}$$

The calculations for Walker-Wilson show an average collection period of 24 days, slightly above the 20-day industry average. This ratio can also be evaluated by the terms on which the firm sells its goods. For example, Walker-Wilson's sales terms call for payment within 30 days, so the 24-day collection period is excellent. Even if the firm sold on a 20-day payment basis, the performance could be considered satisfactory, because some payment delays are customary. However, if the ratio's trend over the past few years has been rising while the credit policy has not changed, steps should be taken to expedite the collection of accounts receivable.

One nonratio financial tool should be mentioned in connection with accounts receivable analysis—the aging schedule, which breaks down accounts receivable according to how long they have been outstanding. This schedule for Walker-Wilson is given below.

Age of Account (days)	Percent of Total Value of Accounts Receivable
0–10	50
11–30	20
31–45	15
46–60	3
over 60	12
	100

[3] For convenience the financial community generally uses 360 rather than 365 as the number of days in the year for purposes such as the present one.

The 24-day collection period looked good by comparison with the 30-day terms, but the aging schedule shows that the firm is having serious collection problems with some of its accounts. Thirty percent are overdue, many for over a month. Others pay quite promptly, bringing the average down to only 24 days, but the aging schedule shows this average to be somewhat misleading.

8. Fixed Assets Turnover. The ratio of sales to fixed assets measures the turnover of capital assets.

$$\text{fixed asset turnover} = \frac{\text{sales}}{\text{fixed assets}} = \frac{\$3,000,000}{\$1,300,000} = 2.3 \text{ times}$$
$$\text{industry average} = 5.0 \text{ times}$$

Walker-Wilson's turnover of 2.3 times compares poorly with the industry average of 5 times, indicating that the firm is not using its fixed assets to as high a percentage of capacity as are the other firms in the industry. Thompson should bear this fact in mind when his production officers request funds for new capital investments.

9. Total Assets Turnover. The final activity ratio measures the turnover of all the firm's assets—it is calculated by dividing sales by total assets.

$$\text{total assets turnover} = \frac{\text{sales}}{\text{total assets}} = \frac{\$3,000,000}{\$2,000,000} = 1.5 \text{ times}$$
$$\text{industry average} = 2 \text{ times}$$

Walker-Wilson's turnover of total assets is well below the industry average. The company is simply not generating a sufficient volume of business for the size of the asset investment. Sales should be increased, or some assets should be disposed of, or both steps should be taken.

Profitability Ratios

Profitability is the net result of a large number of policies and decisions. The ratios examined thus far reveal some interesting things about the way the firm is operating, but the profitability ratios give final answers as to how effectively the firm is being managed.

10. Profit Margin on Sales. This ratio, computed by dividing net income after taxes by sales, gives the profit per dollar of sales.

$$\text{profit margin} = \frac{\text{net profit after taxes}}{\text{sales}} = \frac{\$120,000}{\$3,000,000} = 4\%$$
$$\text{industry average} = 5\%$$

Walker-Wilson's profit margin is somewhat below the industry average of 5 percent, indicating that the firm's sales prices are relatively low or that its costs are relatively high, or both. Unit sales prices can decline by 4 percent or costs rise by 4 percentage points before the firm suffers an overall loss. In general, profit margins indicate the magnitude of the margin of protection against losses resulting from falling prices or rising costs.

11. Return on Total Assets. The ratio of net profit to total assets measures the return on total investment in the firm.[4]

$$\text{return on total assets} = \frac{\text{net profit after taxes}}{\text{total assets}} = \frac{\$120,000}{\$2,000,000} = 6.0\%$$
$$\text{industry average} = 10\%$$

Walker-Wilson's 6 percent return is well below the 10 percent average for the industry. This low rate results from the low profit margin on sales and from the low turnover of total assets.

12. Return on Net Worth. The ratio of net profit after taxes to net worth measures the rate of return on the stockholders' investment.

$$\text{return on net worth} = \frac{\text{net profit after taxes}}{\text{net worth}} = \frac{\$120,000}{\$1,000,000} = 12.0\%$$
$$\text{industry average} = 15\%$$

Walker-Wilson's 12 percent return is below the 15 percent industry average.

Summary of the Ratios

The individual ratios, which are summarized in Table 3-3, can give Thompson a reasonably good idea of Walker-Wilson's main strengths and weaknesses. First, the company's liquidity position is reasonably good—its current and quick ratios appear to be satisfactory by comparison with the industry averages. Second, the leverage ratios suggest that the company is rather heavily indebted. With a debt ratio substantially higher than the industry average and with coverage ratios well below the industry averages, it is doubtful that Walker-Wilson could do much additional debt financing except on relatively unfavorable terms. Even if Thompson could borrow more, to do so would be subjecting the company to the danger of default and bankruptcy in the event of a business downturn.

Turning to the activity ratios, the inventory turnover and average col-

---

[4] Interest can also be included in the numerator of this ratio, but we have not done so for two reasons: (1) for manufacturing companies this addition is inconsequential and (2) the published averages exclude interest. Later in the book, however, when we deal with utilities, we do add back interest, as this has a material bearing on the ratio and is the general practice.

Table 3–3 SUMMARY OF FINANCIAL RATIO ANALYSIS

Ratio	Formula for Calculation	Calculation	Industry Average	Evaluation
Liquidity				
Current	$\dfrac{\text{current assets}}{\text{current liab.}}$	$\dfrac{\$\ 700{,}000}{\$\ 300{,}000} = 2.3$ times	2.5 times	Satisfactory
Quick, or acid test	$\dfrac{(\text{current assets} - \text{inventory})}{\text{current liabilities}}$	$\dfrac{\$\ 400{,}000}{\$\ 300{,}000} = 1.3$ times	1.0 times	Good
Leverage				
Debt to total assets	$\dfrac{\text{total debt}}{\text{total assets}}$	$\dfrac{\$1{,}000{,}000}{\$2{,}000{,}000} = 50\%$	33%	High
Times interest earned	$\dfrac{\text{profit before taxes plus interest charges}}{\text{interest charges}}$	$\dfrac{\$\ 245{,}000}{\$\ 45{,}000} = 5.4$ times	8.0 times	Fair
Fixed charge coverage	$\dfrac{\text{income available for meeting fixed charges}}{\text{fixed charges}}$	$\dfrac{\$\ 273{,}000}{\$\ 106{,}333} = 2.6$ times	4.0 times	Low
Activity				
Inventory turnover	$\dfrac{\text{sales}}{\text{inventory}}$	$\dfrac{\$3{,}000{,}000}{\$\ 300{,}000} = 10$ times	9 times	Satisfactory
Average collection period	$\dfrac{\text{receivables}}{\text{sales per day}}$	$\dfrac{\$\ 200{,}000}{\$\ 8{,}333} = 24$ days	20 days	Satisfactory
Fixed assets turnover	$\dfrac{\text{sales}}{\text{fixed assets}}$	$\dfrac{\$3{,}000{,}000}{\$1{,}300{,}000} = 2.3$ times	5.0 times	Poor
Total assets turnover	$\dfrac{\text{sales}}{\text{total assets}}$	$\dfrac{\$3{,}000{,}000}{\$2{,}000{,}000} = 1.5$ times	2 times	Low
Profitability				
Profit margin on sales	$\dfrac{\text{net profit after taxes}}{\text{sales}}$	$\dfrac{\$\ 120{,}000}{\$3{,}000{,}000} = 4\%$	5%	Low
Return on total assets	$\dfrac{\text{net profit after taxes}}{\text{total assets}}$	$\dfrac{\$\ 120{,}000}{\$2{,}000{,}000} = 6.0\%$	10%	Low
Return on net worth	$\dfrac{\text{net profit after taxes}}{\text{net worth}}$	$\dfrac{\$\ 120{,}000}{\$1{,}000{,}000} = 12.0\%$	15%	Somewhat Low

lection period both indicate that the company's current assets are pretty well in balance, but the low fixed asset turnover suggests that there has been too heavy an investment in fixed assets. The low fixed asset turnover means, in effect, that the company probably could have operated with a smaller investment in fixed assets. And had the excessive fixed asset investment not been made, the company could have avoided some of its debt financing and would now have lower interest payments. This, in turn, would have led to improved leverage and coverage ratios.

The profit margin on sales is low, indicating that costs are too high, or that prices are too low, or both. In this particular case, the sales prices are in line with other firms, and high costs are, in fact, the cause of the low margin. Further, the high costs can be traced (1) to high depreciation charges and (2) to high interest expenses. These costs are, in turn, both attributable to the excessive investment in fixed assets.

Returns on both the total investment and net worth are also below the industry average. These relatively poor results are directly attributable to the low profit margin on sales, which lowers the numerator of the ratios, and to the excessive investment, which raises the denominator.

Trend Analysis

The preceding ratio analysis gives a reasonably good picture of Walker-Wilson's operation, but it is incomplete in one important respect—it ignores the time dimension. The ratios are snapshots of the picture at one point in time, but there may be trends in motion that are in the process of rapidly eroding a relatively good present position. Conversely, an analysis of the ratios over the past few years may suggest that a relatively weak present position is being improved at a rapid rate.

The method of trend analysis is illustrated in Figure 3-1, which shows a graph of Walker-Wilson's sales, current ratio, debt ratio, fixed asset turnover, and return on net worth. These figures are compared with industry averages. Industry sales have been rising steadily over the entire period, and the industry average ratios have been relatively stable throughout. Thus, any trends in the individual company's ratios are due to its own internal conditions, not to environmental influences affecting all firms. Second, Walker-Wilson's deterioration since the death of the two principal officers is also apparent. Prior to 1966, Walker-Wilson was growing more rapidly than the average firm in the industry; during the next two years, however, sales actually declined.

Walker-Wilson's liquidity position as measured by its current ratio has also gone downhill in the past two years. Although the ratio is only slightly below the industry average at the present time, the trend suggests that a real

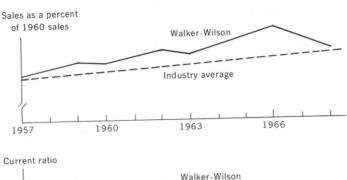

Sales as a percent of 1960 sales

Walker-Wilson

Industry average

1957   1960   1963   1966

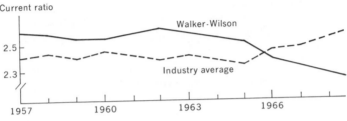

Current ratio

Walker-Wilson

2.5

2.3

Industry average

1957   1960   1963   1966

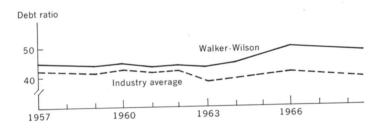

Debt ratio

50

Walker-Wilson

40

Industry average

1957   1960   1963   1966

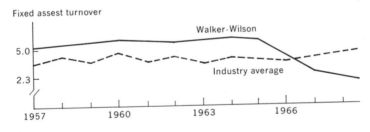

Fixed assest turnover

Walker-Wilson

5.0

2.3

Industry average

1957   1960   1963   1966

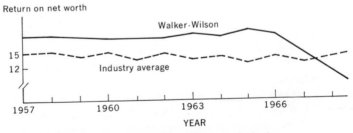

Return on net worth

Walker-Wilson

15

12

Industry average

1957   1960   1963   1966

YEAR

Figure 3-1   Illustration of Trend Analysis

liquidity crisis may develop during the next year or two unless corrective action is taken immediately.

The debt ratio trend line shows that Walker-Wilson followed industry practices closely until 1966, when the ratio jumped a full 10 percentage points above the industry average. Similarly, the fixed asset turnover declined during 1966, even though sales were still rising. The records reveal that the company borrowed heavily during 1966 to finance a major expansion of plant and equipment. Walker and Wilson had intended to use this additional capacity to generate a still higher volume of sales and to retire the debt out of expected high profits. Unfortunately, their untimely death led to a decrease in sales rather than an increase, and the expected high profits that were to be used to retire the debt did not materialize. The analysis suggests that the bankers were correct when they advised Mrs. Walker and Mrs. Wilson of the firm's need for a change in management.

SOURCES OF COMPARATIVE RATIOS

In the analysis of the Walker-Wilson Company, industry average ratios were frequently used. Where may one obtain such averages? Some important sources are listed below.

Dun & Bradstreet. Probably the most widely known and used of the industry average ratios are those compiled by Dun & Bradstreet, Inc. "Dun & Brad" provides fourteen ratios calculated for a large number of industries. Sample ratios and explanations are shown in Table 3-4. The complete data give the fourteen ratios, with the interquartile ranges [5] for 125 lines of business activity based on their financial statements. The 125 types of business activity consist of 71 manufacturing and construction categories, 30 types of wholesalers, and 24 types of retailers.

Robert Morris Associates. Another group of useful ratios can be found in the annual *Statement Studies* compiled and published by the Robert Morris Associates (RMA), which is the national association of bank loan officers. These are representative averages based on financial statements received by banks in connection with loans made. Eleven ratios are

---

[5] The median and quartile ratios can be illustrated by an example. The median ratio of current assets to current debt of manufacturers of airplane parts and accessories, as shown in Table 3–4, is 2.01. To obtain this figure the ratios of current assets to current debt for each of the 55 concerns were arranged in a graduated series, with the largest ratio at the top and the smallest at the bottom. The median ratio of 2.01 was the ratio halfway between the top and the bottom. The ratio of 3.08, representing the upper quartile, was one quarter of the way down the series from the top (or halfway between the top and the median). The ratio of 1.52, representing the lower quartile, was one quarter of the way up from the bottom (or halfway between the median and the bottom).

Table 3–4 DUN & BRADSTREET RATIOS FOR SELECTED INDUSTRIES, 1966

Line of Business (and number of concerns reporting)	Current assets to current debt (times)	Net profits on net sales (per cent)	Net profits on tangible net worth (per cent)	Net profits on net working capital (per cent)	Net sales to tangible net worth (times)	Net sales to net working capital (times)	Collection period (days)	Net sales to inventory (times)	Fixed assets to tangible net worth (per cent)	Current debt to tangible net worth (per cent)	Total debt to tangible net worth (per cent)	Inventory to net working capital (per cent)	Current debt to inventory (per cent)	Funded debts to net working capital (per cent)
3522* Agricul. Implements & Machinery (74)	3.78	7.15	21.44	36.82	8.13	5.27	25	6.1	21.5	22.5	47.5	71.3	44.6	17.8
	2.27	4.12	14.59	20.68	4.60	3.21	39	3.9	33.5	49.3	80.0	104.9	72.0	37.0
	1.52	3.23	8.30	14.95	2.98	2.34	52	3.1	63.6	115.3	149.6	161.4	98.4	50.9
3722-23-29 Airplane Parts & Accessories (59)	2.40	8.12	27.78	44.96	8.27	4.46	34	8.6	27.9	43.2	58.0	73.8	87.9	14.1
	1.81	5.25	18.11	32.21	5.29	3.43	46	5.9	48.4	61.5	103.5	103.4	100.0	47.5
	1.42	3.10	11.90	17.76	4.20	2.72	61	3.9	75.5	112.5	179.1	154.7	141.9	65.8
3714 Automobile Parts & Accessories (84)	3.77	6.75	18.89	32.11	6.54	3.89	35	8.0	25.7	23.5	47.3	60.5	56.5	14.6
	2.58	4.59	14.60	20.32	4.63	2.99	42	5.3	39.6	38.0	77.8	86.2	79.7	41.6
	2.03	3.22	8.65	14.09	3.23	2.19	51	4.2	55.5	63.4	116.9	100.5	113.7	59.9
2515 Bedsprings & Mattresses (49)	3.60	2.69	11.53	15.03	8.52	5.85	30	11.7	15.6	22.9	48.7	54.8	55.6	3.6
	2.33	2.06	6.46	10.95	5.79	3.48	42	8.2	28.1	45.9	72.8	76.8	93.6	26.6
	1.87	0.80	2.71	5.11	4.34	2.61	55	5.5	49.3	76.3	133.9	114.5	154.8	52.1
2082 Breweries (27)	3.34	6.48	15.15	63.72	11.34	3.23	8	21.6	53.7	13.1	20.4	33.3	108.2	9.6
	2.59	4.75	10.38	34.27	8.51	2.49	16	16.4	59.4	21.3	38.6	46.5	137.8	118.6
	1.88	1.28	2.55	8.23	5.13	1.72	24	11.4	81.9	34.1	97.5	87.7	194.9	176.2
287 Chemicals, Agricultural (33)	2.98	3.87	11.78	44.91	13.41	5.11	32	10.4	29.5	33.6	58.4	62.1	89.5	24.1
	1.73	2.02	7.58	17.73	6.72	3.46	55	6.6	53.6	73.1	111.0	106.6	122.9	47.9
	1.33	0.95	1.56	2.80	4.15	1.98	87	5.0	71.2	123.0	165.9	160.5	237.3	75.2
281 Chemicals, Industrial (60)	2.77	8.15	16.07	50.01	7.05	3.09	39	10.1	42.6	20.1	31.8	65.2	76.1	44.0
	2.28	5.53	12.45	30.32	5.03	1.95	50	6.9	68.8	30.0	58.9	84.7	98.5	94.2
	1.51	3.93	9.03	17.95	3.39	1.52	59	5.5	88.9	50.0	106.0	100.1	128.7	152.4
1511 Contractors, Building Construction (188)	2.06	3.14	19.04	33.04	20.41	12.51	†	†	9.5	61.7	119.4	†	†	11.9
	1.49	1.38	12.39	16.38	11.52	8.09	†	†	22.2	138.0	188.4	†	†	27.4
	1.27	0.74	6.20	9.14	5.79	4.32	†	†	42.1	239.8	318.0	†	†	83.4

* SIC categories.
† Building trades contractors have no inventories in the credit sense of the term. As a general rule, they have no customary selling terms, such contracts being a special job for which individual terms are arranged.
SOURCE: *Key Business Ratios in 125 lines,* 1966 (New York: Dun & Bradstreet, Inc.). Reprinted by permission of Dun & Bradstreet.

computed for 156 lines of business. The firms represented in the sample tend to be the larger and financially stronger firms; the averages contained in the RMA studies, therefore, provide a relatively high-quality basis for comparison.

Quarterly Financial Report for Manufacturing Corporations. The Federal Trade Commission and the Securities and Exchange Commission jointly publish quarterly data on manufacturing companies. Both balance sheet and income statement data are developed from a systematic sample of corporations. The reports are published within perhaps six months after the financial data have been made available by the companies. They include an analysis by industry groups and by asset size, as well as financial statements in ratio form (or common-size analysis). The FTC-SEC reports are a rich source of information and are frequently used for comparative purposes.

Individual Firms. Credit departments of individual firms compile financial ratios and averages (1) on their customers in order to judge their ability to meet obligations and (2) on their suppliers in order to evaluate their financial ability to fulfill contracts. The First National Bank of Chicago for instance, compiles semiannual reports on the financial data for finance companies. The National Cash Register Company gathers data for a large number of business lines.

Trade Associations and Public Accountants. Financial ratios for many industries are compiled by trade associations and constitute an important source to be checked by a financial manager seeking comparative data. In addition, accounting firms specializing in certain lines (for example, textiles or canning) will compile averages of financial ratios for the confidential use of their clients. These averages are usually the best obtainable. In addition to balance sheet data, they provide detailed information on operating expenses, which makes possible an informed analysis of the efficiency of the firms.

USE OF FINANCIAL RATIOS IN CREDIT ANALYSIS

Thus far in the chapter we have discussed a rather long list of ratios and have learned what each ratio is designed to measure. Sometimes it will be unnecessary to go beyond a few calculations to determine that a firm is in very good or very bad condition, but often the analysis is equivalent to a detective-story investigation—what one ratio will not indicate, another may. Also, a relation vaguely suggested by one ratio may be corroborated by another. For these reasons, it is often useful to calculate a number of different ratios.

In numerous situations, however, a few ratios will tell the story. For example, a credit manager who has a large number of invoices flowing across his desk each day may limit himself to three ratios as evidence of whether the prospective buyer of his goods will pay promptly. (1) He uses the current ratio to determine how burdened the prospective buyer is with current liabilities. (2) He uses the debt ratio to determine how much of the prospective buyer's own funds are invested in the business. If the funds of the prospective buyer are low, he is probably short of working capital and is likely to fall behind in his payments. (3) He uses one of the profitability ratios to see whether or not the firm has favorable prospects. If the profit margin is high enough, it may justify the risk of dealing with a slow-paying customer. Profitable companies are likely to grow and, thus, to become better customers in the future. However, if the profit margin is low relative to other firms in the industry, if the current ratio is low, and if the debt ratio is high, a credit manager probably will not approve a sale involving an extension of credit.

Of necessity, the credit manager is more than a calculator and a reader of financial ratios. Qualitative factors may override quantitative analysis. Oil companies, for instance, in selling to truckers often find that the financial ratios are adverse and that if they based their decisions solely on financial ratios, they would not make sales. Or, to take another example, profits may have been low for a period, but if the customer understands why profits have been low and can remove the cause of the difficulty, a credit man may be willing to approve a sale to him. The credit man's decision is also influenced by his own firm's profit margin. If the selling firm is making a large profit on sales, then it is in a better position to take credit risks than if its margin is low. Ultimately, the credit manager must judge a customer with regard to his character and management ability, and intelligent credit decisions must be based on careful consideration of conditions in the selling as well as the buying firm.

SUMMARY OF FINANCIAL RATIO ANALYSIS

Financial ratio analysis enables the financial manager to gauge the progress of his firm and to judge how it appears to others, especially stockholders and creditors. The number and the kinds of ratios he uses depend upon the nature of the industry and the size and age of the firm. The ratios discussed in this chapter are summarized with norms for large manufacturing firms, where such ratios are available, in Table 3-5. For most types of analyses the financial manager need not utilize all the ratios indicated above. Usually only a selected few are necessary, but the financial manager will also find it useful to make trend comparisons, comparisons with other firms, or both.

Table 3–5 SUMMARY OF FINANCIAL RATIOS AND REFERENCE GUIDES FOR LARGE MANUFACTURING FIRMS

I.	Liquidity	
	1. Current ratio	2/1
	2. Quick ratio	1/1
II.	Leverage	
	3. Debt to total assets	40 percent
	4. Times interest earned	8 times
	5. Fixed charge coverage	4 times
III.	Activity	
	6. Inventory turnover	9 times
	7. Average collection period	varies with credit terms
	8. Fixed assets turnover	varies
	9. Total asset turnover	varies
IV.	Profitability	
	10. Gross profit on sales	4–6 percent
	11. Return on total assets	10–12 percent
	12. Return on net worth	13–15 percent

It is also important to realize that for many types of decisions financial ratios are only a beginning. They give the financial manager just a fraction of the information he needs for making a decision. Ultimately, the financial manager's success rests on his judgment of men and on his foresight into future events.

SUMMARY

Ratio analysis, which relates balance sheet and income statement items to one another, permits the charting of the history of a firm and the evaluation of its present position. Thorough analysis also allows the financial manager to anticipate reactions of investors and creditors and, thus, gives him a good insight into how his request for funds is likely to be met.

Basic Types of Ratios

Ratios are classified into four basic types: (1) liquidity, (2) leverage, (3) activity, and (4) profitability. Data from the Walker-Wilson Manufacturing Company are used to compute each type of ratio and to show how financial analysis is made in practice. An almost unlimited number of ratios may be calculated, but in practice a limited number of each type are sufficient. What are probably the twelve most common and useful ratios are discussed in this chapter.

Use of Ratios

A ratio is not a meaningful number in and of itself—it must be compared with something before it becomes useful. The two basic kinds of comparative analysis are (1) trend analysis and (2) comparisons with other firms in the same industry. *Trend analysis* involves computing the ratios of a particular firm for several years and comparing the ratios over time to see if the firm is improving or deteriorating. *Comparative analysis,* as defined here, means comparing the key ratios of the firm under study with those of another firm in the same industry or, even better, with an industry average. These two types of comparisons are often combined in the kind of graphic analysis illustrated in Figure 3–1.

Some reference to ratios will be made in each remaining chapter in the text, so it is imperative that the student be thoroughly familiar with the nature of the key ratios. The following chapter will help in gaining this understanding, as it begins by showing how certain ratios are directly related to others.

QUESTIONS

3–1 "A uniform system of accounts, including identical forms for balance sheets and income statements, would be a most reasonable requirement for the SEC to impose on all publicly owned firms." Discuss.

3–2 There are four groups of financial ratios: liquidity, leverage, activity, and profitability. Financial analysis is conducted by four types of analysts: management, equity investors, long-term creditors, and short-term creditors.
   a) Explain the nature of type of ratio.
   b) Explain the emphasis of each type of analyst.
   c) Could the same basic approach to financial analysis be taken by each group of analysts?

3–3 How can a composite of industry averages be used as a norm for comparison with the financial ratios of an individual firm?

3–4 Why can norms with relatively well-defined limits be stated in advance for some financial ratios but not for others?

3–5 Why should financial ratio calculations be supplemented by trend analysis?

PROBLEMS

3–1 The following data were taken from the financial statements of the Medfone Corporation for the calendar year 1968. The norms given below are from Dun & Bradstreet financial ratios for the metal stamping industry.
   a) Fill in the ratios for Medfone.
   b) Indicate by comparison with the industry norms the errors in management policies reflected in these financial statements.

MEDFONE CORPORATION
BALANCE SHEET
December 31, 1968

Cash	$ 20,000	Accounts payable	$ 15,000
Receivables	25,000	Notes payable (5%)	20,000
Inventory	75,000	Other current liab.	10,000
Total current assets	120,000	Total current liab.	45,000
Net property	55,000	Long-term debt (6%)	20,000
		Net worth	110,000
Total assets	$175,000	Total claims on assets	$175,000

MEDFONE CORPORATION
INCOME STATEMENT
For Year Ended December 31, 1968

Sales		$250,000
Cost of goods sold		
Materials	$95,000	
Labor	60,000	
Heat, light, and power	9,000	
Indirect labor	15,000	
Depreciation (10%)	5,500	184,500
Gross profit		$ 65,500
Selling expenses	$25,000	
General and administrative expenses	20,500	45,500
Operating profit		20,000
Less: Interest expense		1,200
Net profit before taxes		18,800
Less: Federal income taxes		9,400
Net profit		$ 9,400

FINANCIAL RATIOS

Ratio	Medfone	Norm
$\dfrac{\text{current assets}}{\text{current liabilities}}$	_____	2.5 times
$\dfrac{\text{sales}}{\text{inventories}}$	_____	9.9 times
$\dfrac{\text{average collection period}}{\text{sales}}$	_____	33 days
$\dfrac{\text{sales}}{\text{total assets}}$	_____	1.3 times (assumed)
$\dfrac{\text{net profit}}{\text{sales}}$	_____	3.3%
$\dfrac{\text{net profit}}{\text{net worth}}$	_____	3.8%
$\dfrac{\text{net profit}}{\text{total assets}}$	_____	10.7%

3–2 For one set of the pairs of companies listed below, chart the following financial ratios over the past 7 years. (This problem requires library research. Data may be obtained from company reports or from an investment manual such as Moody's Industrials or Standard and Poor's Industrials).

Current ratio
Total debt to net worth
Sales to total assets
Average collection period
Sales to inventory (inventory turnover)
Profit after fixed charges and taxes to sales
Profit after fixed charges and taxes to net worth

General Motors and Chrysler
Boeing and Douglas Aircraft
Sperry Rand and International Business Machines
Standard Oil of New Jersey and Standard Oil of California
General Electric and Westinghouse

a) Compare the trends in the return on net worth for each of the two companies in the pair you are analyzing.

b) Indicate the reasons for any difference in trends in rate of return on net worth suggested by your time-trend analysis.

Chapter 4

Financial Control

The preceding chapter described certain ratios commonly used in financial analysis. This chapter extends the analysis to show how the ratios relate to one another, and then looks at two other tools of financial analysis—break-even charts and sources and uses of funds statements.

DU PONT SYSTEM OF FINANCIAL CONTROL[1]

The du Pont system of financial control has achieved wide recognition in American industry, and properly so. It brings together the activity ratios and profit margin on sales and shows how these ratios interact to determine the profitability of assets. The nature of the system, modified somewhat, is set forth in Figure 4-1.

The right side of the figure develops the turnover ratio. This section shows how current assets (which consist of inventories, accounts receivable, and cash), when added to fixed assets, gives total investment. Total investment, when divided into sales, gives the turnover of investment.

---

[1] The best current description of the du Pont system is contained in T. C. Davis, *How the du Pont Organization Appraises Its Performance.* Financial Management Series, No. 94 (New York: American Management Association Treasurer's Department, 1950), and *Executive Committee Control Charts,* prepared by E. I. du Pont de Nemours and Company (Wilmington, Delaware: E. I. du Pont de Nemours & Co., 1959).

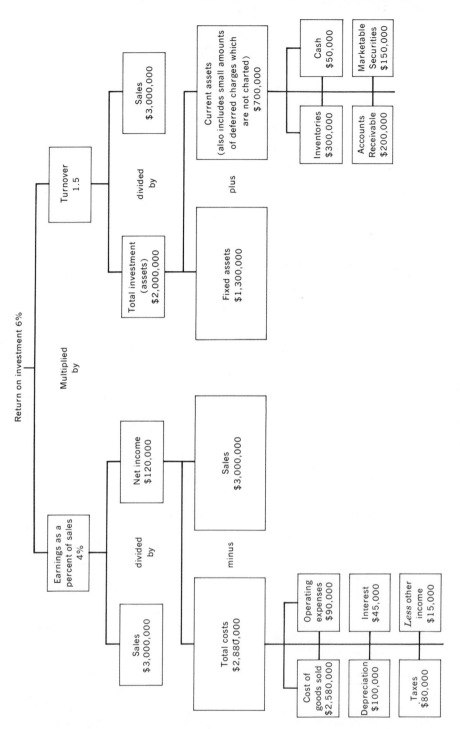

Figure 4-1   Modified du Pont System of Financial Control

The left side of the figure develops the profit margin on sales. The individual expense items, plus income taxes, are subtracted from sales to produce net profits after taxes. Net profits, when divided by sales, gives the profit margin on sales. When the asset turnover ratio is multiplied by the profit margin on sales, the product is the return on total investment in the firm. This can be seen from the following formula.

$$\frac{sales}{investment} \times \frac{profit}{sales} = \frac{profit}{investment}$$

These relationships can be illustrated by reference to the Walker-Wilson Company analyzed in Chapter 3. Walker-Wilson's turnover was seen to be 1.5 times, as compared to an industry average of 2 times, and its margin on sales was 4 percent, as compared to 5 percent for the industry. Multiplied together, turnover and profit margin produced a return on assets equal to 6 percent, a rate well below the 10 percent industry average. If Thompson is to bring Walker-Wilson back to the level of the rest of the industry, he should strive to boost both his profit margin and his total asset turnover. Tracing back through the du Pont system should help him in this task.

Extending the du Pont System to Include Leverage

Walker-Wilson's return on total investment was only 6 percent, well below the 10 percent industry average. However, the firm's 12 percent return on net worth is only slightly below the 15 percent industry average. How can the return on net worth end up so close to the industry average when the return on total assets is so far below the average? The answer is that Walker-Wilson uses so much debt.

Only one half of Walker-Wilson's assets are financed with net worth; the other half is financed with debt. This means that the entire 6 percent return on assets (which is computed after interest charges on debt) goes to the common and preferred stockholders, so their return is boosted substantially. The precise formula for measuring the effect of financial leverage on stockholder returns is shown below.

$$\text{percentage return on net worth} = \frac{\text{percentage return on assets}}{\text{percent of assets financed by net worth}}$$

$$= \frac{\text{percentage return on assets}}{1.0 - \text{debt ratio}}$$

Calculation for Walker-Wilson:

$$\text{return on net worth} = \frac{6\%}{1.0 - 0.50} = \frac{6\%}{0.5} = 12\%$$

Calculation for the industry average:

$$\text{return on net worth} = \frac{10\%}{1.0 - 0.33} = \frac{10\%}{0.67} = 15\%$$

This formula is useful for showing how financial leverage can be used to increase the rate of return on net worth.[2] But increasing returns on net worth by using more and more leverage causes the leverage ratios to rise higher and higher above the industry norms. Creditors resist this tendency, so there are limitations to the practice. Moreover, greater leverage increases the risk of bankruptcy and thus endangers the firm's stockholders. Since Mrs. Walker and Mrs. Wilson, the widows of the firm's founders, are entirely dependent on income from the firm for their support, they would be in a particularly bad position should the firm go into default. Consequently, Thompson would be ill-advised to attempt to use leverage to boost the return on net worth much further.

RATES OF RETURN IN DIFFERENT INDUSTRIES

Would it be better to have a 5 percent margin on sales and an assets turnover of 2 times, or a 2 percent sales margin and a turnover of 5 times? It makes no difference whatever—in either case the firm has a 10 percent return on investment. Actually, of course, most firms are not free to make the kind of choice posed in the above question. Depending on the nature of its industry, the firm *must* operate with more or fewer assets, and it will experience a turnover that depends on the characteristics of its particular line of business. In the case of a dealer in fresh fruits and vegetables, fish, or other perishable items, the turnover should be high—every day or two would be most desirable. In contrast, some lines of business require very heavy fixed investment or involve long production periods. A hydroelectric utility company, with its heavy investment in dams and transmission lines, for example, requires heavy fixed investment; a shipbuilder or an aircraft producer, for example, needs a long production period. Such companies

---

[2] There are limitations on this statement—specifically, the return on net worth increases with leverage only if the return on assets exceeds the rate of interest on debt after giving account to the tax deductibility of interest payments. This whole concept is explored in detail in Chapter 8, which is devoted entirely to financial leverage.

necessarily have a low asset turnover rate, but a correspondingly higher profit margin on sales.

If a grocery chain has a high turnover, and a chemical producer, with its heavy investment in fixed assets, a low turnover, would you expect to find differences in their profit margins on sales? In general, you would—the chemical producer should have a considerably higher profit margin to offset its low turnover. Otherwise, the grocery business would be much more profitable than the chemical, investment would flow into the grocery industry, and profits in this industry would be eroded to the point where the rate of return was about equal to that in the chemical industry.

We know, however, that leverage must be taken into account when considering the rate of return on net worth. If the firms in one industry have a somewhat lower return on total assets but use slightly more financial leverage than do those in another industry, both sets of firms may end up with approximately the same rate of return on net worth.[3]

These points, which are all necessary to a complete understanding of ratio analysis, are illustrated in Table 4-1. Here we see how turnover and

Table 4–1   TURNOVER, PROFIT MARGINS, AND RETURNS
ON NET WORTH, 1966

	Sales to Total Assets	Profit to Sales	Profit to Total Assets	Debt to Total Assets	Profit to Net Worth*
All manufacturing firms	1.60×	5.6%	8.9%	41%	15.2%
Hercules, Inc. (chemical producer)	1.15	8.5	9.8	32	14.4
Safeway Stores (food retailer)	5.23	1.8	9.4	40	15.6

* The figures in this column may be found as:

$$\text{profit to net worth} = \frac{\text{profit to total assets}}{1 - \text{debt to total assets}}$$

SOURCES: Moody's Investors Service, SEC-FTC Bulletins, Robert Morris Associates, and Annual Statement Studies.

profit margins interact with each other to produce varying returns on assets, and also how financial leverage affects the returns on net worth. Hercules, Inc., Safeway Stores, and the average of all manufacturing firms are compared. Hercules, with its very heavy fixed asset investment, is seen to have a relatively low turnover, while Safeway, a typical chain food store, has a very

---

[3] The factors that make it possible for firms to use more leverage are taken up in Chapters 8 and 9. It may be stated now, however, that the primary factor favoring leverage is sales stability.

high sales-to-assets ratio. However, Hercules ends up with about the same rate of return on assets because its high profit margin on sales compensates for its low turnover. Both Safeway and Hercules use financial leverage to increase their return on net worth.

BREAK-EVEN ANALYSIS

Break-even analysis, another important financial tool, is basically an analytical technique for studying the relations among fixed costs, variable costs, and profits. If a firm's costs were all variable, the problem of break-even volume would never arise. But by having some variable and some fixed costs, the firm must suffer losses up to a given volume.

Break-even analysis is a formal profit-planning approach based on established relations between costs and revenues. It is a device for determining the point at which sales will just cover total costs. If the firm is to avoid losses, its sales must cover all costs—those which vary directly with production and those which do not change as production levels change. Costs that fall into each of these categories are outlined below.

Fixed Costs*	*Direct or Variable Costs*
Depreciation on plant and equipment	Factory labor
Rentals	Materials
Interest charges on debt	Sales Commissions
Salaries of research staff	
Salaries of executive staff	
General office expenses	

    * Some of these costs—salaries and office expenses—could be varied to some degree, but firms are reluctant to reduce these expenditures in response to temporary fluctuations in sales.

The nature of break-even analysis is depicted in Figure 4-2, the basic break-even chart. The chart is on a unit basis, with volume produced shown on the horizontal axis and costs and income measured on the vertical axis. Fixed costs of $40,000 are represented by a horizontal line: that is, they are the same (fixed) regardless of the number of units produced. Variable costs are assumed to be $1.20 a unit. Total costs rise by $1.20, the amount of the variable costs, for each additional unit produced. Production is assumed to be sold at $2 a unit, so the total income is pictured as a straight line, which must also increase with production. The positive slope (or the rate of ascent) of the total-income line is steeper than that of the total-cost line. This must be true, because the firm is gaining $2 of revenue for every $1.20 paid out for labor and materials, the variable costs.

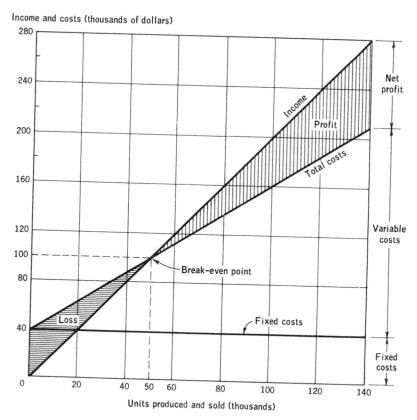

Figure 4-2 Break-Even Chart

Up to the break-even point, found at the intersection of the total-income and total-cost lines, the firm suffers losses. After that point the firm begins to make profits. Figure 4-2 indicates a break-even point at a sales and costs level of $100,000 and a production level of 50,000 units.

More exact calculations of the break-even point can be carried out by trial and error or algebraically. In section A of Table 4-2 profit-and-loss relations are shown for various levels of sales; in section B the algebraic calculations are carried out.

Break-Even Point Based on Totals

Calculating break-even points on the basis of dollar sales instead of on units of output is especially useful (Table 4-3). The main advantage of this method is that it enables one to determine a general break-even point for a firm that sells several related products at varying prices. Furthermore, the procedure requires a minimum of data. Only three values are needed: sales,

Table 4–2   RELATIONS AMONG UNITS PRODUCED, TOTAL VARIABLE
             COSTS, FIXED COSTS, TOTAL COSTS, AND TOTAL INCOME

A. Trial-and-Error Calculations

Units Sold	Total Variable Costs	Fixed Costs	Total Costs	Sales	Net Profit (Loss)
20,000	$ 24,000	$40,000	$ 64,000	$ 40,000	$(24,000)
40,000	48,000	40,000	88,000	80,000	(8,000)
50,000	60,000	40,000	100,000	100,000	—
60,000	72,000	40,000	112,000	120,000	8,000
80,000	96,000	40,000	136,000	160,000	24,000
100,000	120,000	40,000	160,000	200,000	40,000
120,000	144,000	40,000	184,000	240,000	56,000
140,000	168,000	40,000	208,000	280,000	72,000

B. Algebraic Solution to Break-Even Volume

1) The break-even quantity is defined as that volume of output at which revenue is just equal to total costs (fixed costs plus variable costs).

2) Let:
$$P = \text{sales price per unit}$$
$$Q = \text{quantity produced and sold}$$
$$F = \text{fixed costs}$$
$$V = \text{variable costs per unit}$$

3) Then:
$$P \cdot Q = F + V \cdot Q$$
$$P \cdot Q - V \cdot Q = F$$
$$Q(P - V) = F$$
$$Q = \frac{F}{P - V} \text{ at break-even } Q$$

4) Illustration:
$$Q = \frac{\$40,000}{\$2.00 - \$1.20}$$
$$= 50,000 \text{ units}$$

fixed costs, and variable costs. Sales and total-cost data are readily available from annual reports of corporations and from investment manuals. Total costs can be determined by deducting net profits from sales. Total costs must then be segregated into fixed and variable components. The major fixed charges (rent, interest, depreciation, and general and administrative expenses) may be taken from the income statement. Finally, variable costs are calculated by deducting fixed costs from total costs.

Table 4-3   CALCULATION OF BREAK-EVEN POINT
BASED ON TOTALS

$$\text{Break-even point (sales volume)} = \frac{\text{total fixed costs}}{1 - \dfrac{\text{total variable costs}}{\text{total sales volume}}}$$

Procedure: Take any quantity and use the related data to determine the break-even point. For example, assume that 20,000 units are produced and use the data in Table 4-2.

$$\text{Break-even point} = \frac{\$40,000}{1 - \dfrac{\$24,000}{\$40,000}} = \frac{\$40,000}{0.4} = \$100,000$$

Rationale:

1) At the break-even point, sales (S) are equal to fixed cost (FC) plus variable cost (VC):

$$S = FC + VC \tag{1}$$

2) Because both the sales price and the variable cost per unit are assumed to be constant in break-even analysis, the ratio VC/S is also constant and may be found from the annual income statement.

3) Since variable cost is a constant percentage of sales, equation (1) can be rewritten as:

$$S = FC + \frac{VC}{S}(S)$$

$$S\left(1 - \frac{VC}{S}\right) = FC$$

$$S = \frac{FC}{1 - \dfrac{VC}{S}} \text{ at break-even } S$$

Operating Leverage

Operating leverage is defined as the extent to which fixed costs are used in operations, and break-even analysis can be used to reflect the degree of operating leverage employed. The formal definition does not fully convey the meaning of leverage, but an example may help. If you were trying to lift the end of a large box in order to place a roller under it, you might insert an iron rod under the box with a sturdy object like a stone as the fulcrum to obtain leverage in lifting. With this lever system a relatively small amount of pressure can lift a very heavy box. To complete the analogy, the fixed-cost element is the lever that allows a small change in sales to induce a relatively large change in profits.

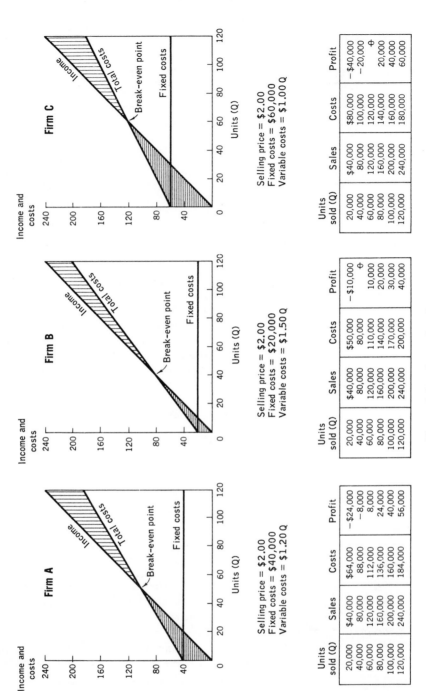

Firm A

Selling price = $2.00
Fixed costs = $40,000
Variable costs = $1.20 Q

Units sold (Q)	Sales	Costs	Profit
20,000	$40,000	$64,000	−$24,000
40,000	80,000	88,000	−8,000
60,000	120,000	112,000	8,000
80,000	160,000	136,000	24,000
100,000	200,000	160,000	40,000
120,000	240,000	184,000	56,000

Firm B

Selling price = $2.00
Fixed costs = $20,000
Variable costs = $1.50 Q

Units sold (Q)	Sales	Costs	Profit
20,000	$40,000	$50,000	−$10,000
40,000	80,000	80,000	¢
60,000	120,000	110,000	10,000
80,000	160,000	140,000	20,000
100,000	200,000	170,000	30,000
120,000	240,000	200,000	40,000

Firm C

Selling price = $2.00
Fixed costs = $60,000
Variable costs = $1.00 Q

Units sold (Q)	Sales	Costs	Profit
20,000	$40,000	$80,000	−$40,000
40,000	80,000	100,000	−20,000
60,000	120,000	120,000	¢
80,000	160,000	140,000	20,000
100,000	200,000	160,000	40,000
120,000	240,000	180,000	60,000

Figure 4-3 Operating Leverage

The significance of the degree of operating leverage is further brought out by Figure 4-3. Three firms, A, B, and C, with differing degrees of leverage are contrasted. Firm A is considered to have a normal amount of fixed costs in its operations. It uses automated equipment, with which one operator can turn out a few or many units at the same labor cost, to about the same extent as the average firm in the industry. Firm B has lower fixed costs, but note the steeper rate of increase in variable costs of firm B over firm A. Firm B, however, breaks even at a lower level of operations than firm A. At a production level of 40,000 units, firm A is losing $8,000, but firm B breaks even.

On the other hand, firm C has the highest fixed costs. It is highly automated, using expensive, high-speed machines that require very little labor per unit produced; with such an operation its variable costs rise slowly. Because of the high overhead resulting from charges associated with the expensive machinery, C's break-even point is higher than that for either A or B. Once firm C reaches its break-even point, however, its profits rise faster than those of the other firms.

High fixed costs and low variable costs provide the greatest percentage change in profits both upward and downward. The profit behavior follows from economic logic. High fixed costs arise from employing larger amounts of capital, which permit the firm to operate with reduced labor and, thereby, smaller variable costs.

The relative importance of fixed costs is likely to reflect both the technology of the industry and the stability of sales. The nature of the business influences how much equipment will be used in the production process. If sales are stable, the firm will acquire more specialized equipment. If sales fluctuate greatly, the firm will seek more flexibility by using less machinery relative to more purchased parts or labor.

Cash Break-Even Analysis

Another use of break-even analysis is the analysis of the firm's situation on a cash basis. Some of the firm's fixed costs are noncash outlays, and for a period some of its revenues may be in receivables. The cash break-even chart for firm D, constructed on the assumption that $30,000 of the fixed costs from the previous illustration are depreciation charges and, therefore, a noncash outlay, is shown in Figure 4-4. Because fixed cash outlays are only $10,000, the cash break-even point is at 12,500 units rather than 50,000 units, which is the profit break-even point.

Cash break-even analysis does not fully represent cash flows—for this a cash budget is required. But the cash break-even analysis is useful because it provides a picture of the flow of funds from operations. A firm could incur

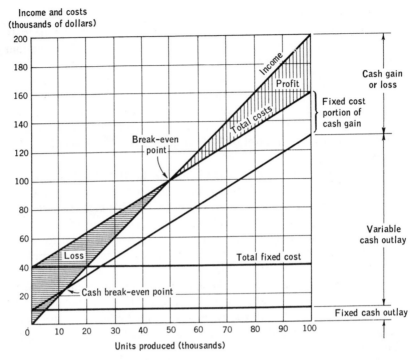

Figure 4-4   Cash Break-Even Analysis

a level of fixed costs that would result in losses during periods of poor business but in large profits during upswings. If cash outlays are small, even during periods of losses the firm might still be operating above the cash break-even point. Thus the risks of insolvency, in the sense of inability to meet cash obligations, would be small. This allows a firm to reach out for higher profits through automation and operating leverage.

Limitations of Break-Even Analysis

Break-even analysis is useful in studying the relations among volume, prices, and cost structure and is thus helpful in pricing, cost control, and other financial decisions. It has limitations, however, as a guide to managerial actions.

Break-even analysis is especially weak in what it implies about the sales possibilities for the firm. Any given break-even chart is based on a constant selling price, so in order to study profit possibilities under different prices a whole series of charts is necessary, one chart for each price.

With regard to costs, break-even analysis is also deficient—the relations indicated by the chart do not hold at all outputs. As sales increase, existing plant and equipment are worked to capacity, and both this situation and the use of additional workers and overtime pay cause variable costs to rise sharply. Additional equipment and plant are required, thus increasing fixed costs. Finally, over a period the products sold by the firm change in quality and quantity; such changes in product mix influence the level and slope of the cost function. In short, break-even analysis is useful as a first step in developing the basic data required for pricing and making financial decisions. More detailed analysis is required before final judgments can be made.

SOURCES AND USES OF FUNDS

The sources and uses of funds statement is one of the most useful tools in the financial manager's analytical kit. The basic purpose of the funds statement is to indicate, on a historical basis, where cash came from and where it was used.

When a firm requests a loan, one of the first questions occurring to a loan officer is, What has the firm done with the money it had? This question is answered by the sources and application statement. The information it provides may indicate that the firm is making progress or that problems are arising.

Rough-and-Ready Sources and Applications Analysis

To construct the sources and uses statement, one first tabulates the changes in balance sheet items from one year to the next. Each change in the balance sheet may be classified as either a source of funds or a use of funds, according to the following pattern:

Use of funds: (1) increase in asset item or (2) decrease in liability item

Source of funds: (1) decrease in asset item or (2) increase in liability item

An illustration of the financial manager's rough-and-ready analysis of sources and uses of funds is embodied in Tables 4-4 and 4-5.

Dallas obtained funds by drawing down cash balances, by selling marketable securities, by increasing other current liabilities, by incurring long-term debt, and by retaining earnings. Total funds from these sources were $39 million. An additional $10 million arose from the increase in the reserve for depreciation. Depreciation expense itself does not produce cash, but it is a noncash outlay. Since it was deducted from revenues to arrive at

Table 4–4   *DALLAS FERTILIZER AND CHEMICAL COMPANY*
COMPARATIVE BALANCE SHEETS AND SOURCES AND USES OF FUNDS
(in millions of dollars)

	12/31/67	12/31/68	Sources	Uses
Cash	$ 10	$ 5	$ 5	
Marketable securities	25	15	10	
Net receivables	15	20		$ 5
Inventories	25	30		5
Gross fixed assets	150	180		30
Less: Allowance for depreciation*	(40)	(50)	10	
Net fixed assets	110	130		
Total assets	$185	$200		
Accounts payable	$ 10	$ 6		4
Notes payable	15	10		5
Other current liabilities	10	14	4	
Long-term debt	60	70	10	
Preferred stock	10	10	—	—
Common stock	50	50	—	—
Retained earnings	30	40	10	
Total claims on assets	$185	$200	$49	$49

* The allowance for depreciation is actually a liability account, even though it appears on the left side of the balance sheet. Note that it is deducted, not added, when totaling the column.

Table 4–5   *DALLAS FERTILIZER AND CHEMICAL COMPANY*
STATEMENT OF SOURCES AND USES OF FUNDS, 1968
(in millions of dollars)

Uses	*Amount*	*Percent*
Gross fixed assets expansion	$30	61.2
Inventory investment	5	10.2
Increase in receivables	5	10.2
Reduction in notes payable	5	10.2
Reduction in accounts payable	4	8.2
Total use of funds	$49	100.0
Sources		
Increase in long-term debt	$10	20.4
Increase in retained earnings	10	20.4
Noncash depreciation outlay	10	20.4
Sale of marketable securities	10	20.4
Reduction in cash holdings	5	10.2
Increase in other liabilities	4	8.2
Total source of funds	$49	100.0

the retained earnings figure, it must be added back as a source of funds in cash flow analysis.[4]

The total sources of funds, then, is $49 million. This amount was used to finance an increase in accounts receivable, to purchase inventories and fixed assets, and to reduce notes payable. Dallas Chemical had a net income of $12 million in 1968 and paid out $2 million in dividends, so the retained earnings of $10 million completely reconciles the surplus account.

What does this rough-and-ready statement of sources and uses of funds tell the financial manager? It tells him that plant size was expanded and that fixed assets amounting to $30 million were acquired. Inventories and net receivables also increased as sales increased. The firm needed funds to meet working capital and fixed assets demands.

Previously, Dallas had been financing its growth through bank credit (notes payable). In the present period of growth, management decided to obtain some of its financing from permanent sources (long-term debt). It obtained enough long-term debt not only to finance some of the asset growth but also to pay back some of its bank credit and reduce accounts payable. In addition to the long-term debt, funds were acquired from retained earnings and from depreciation charges of $10 million. Moreover, the firm had been accumulating marketable securities in anticipation of this expansion program, and these were sold to pay for new buildings and equipment. Finally, cash had been accumulated in excess of the firm's needs and was also worked down.

This example illustrates how the financial manager's rough-and-ready approach to sources and uses can give him a fairly complete picture of recent operations. Such an approach is not bogged down in details. Because refined adjustments usually amount to less than 4 or 5 percent of the total amounts involved, the financial manager can omit them and still obtain a good perspective on the flow of funds in his company or departments.

---

[4] Treating depreciation as a source of funds is sufficiently worrisome to students to warrant elaboration. Consider Dallas's condensed 1968 income statement. Assume that sales are for cash and that all costs (except depreciation) and taxes are paid during the period.

Sales	$300,000,000
Costs excluding depreciation	270,000,000
Depreciation	10,000,000
Profit before taxes	20,000,000
Taxes	8,000,000
Profit after taxes	$ 12,000,000

Disregarding any possible changes in balance sheet accounts, how much cash was available from operations to finance new investment, to repay debt, and so on? The answer is $22 million, the sum of profits after taxes plus depreciation. In the actual case, of course, other events transpired and produced a different figure for total sources of funds. This example does show, however, the rationale behind the statement that depreciation is a source of funds.

SUMMARY

The preceding chapter described certain ratios commonly used in financial analysis. This chapter first extended the analysis to show how some of the ratios are related to one another and then presented two other tools of financial analysis —break-even charts and sources and uses of funds statements.

Du Pont System

The du Pont system shows how the return on investment is dependent upon turnover and the profit margin. The system is generally expressed in the form of the following equation:

$$\frac{\text{sales}}{\text{investment}} \times \frac{\text{profit}}{\text{sales}} = \frac{\text{profit}}{\text{investment}}$$

The first term, investment turnover, times the profit margin equals the rate of return on investment. The kinds of actions discussed in the preceding chapter can be used to effect needed changes in turnover and the profit margin and thus to improve the return on investment.

The du Pont system can be extended to encompass financial leverage and thus to examine the manner in which turnover, sales margins, and leverage all combine to determine the rate of return on net worth. The following equation is used to show this relationship:

$$\text{percent return on net worth} = \frac{\text{percent return on assets}}{1.0 - \text{debt ratio}}$$

The formula is useful for examining the way financial leverage can be used to increase the rate of return on net worth.

Rates of Return in Different Industries

The extended du Pont system shows why firms in different industries—even though they have widely different turnovers, profit margins, and debt ratios— may end up with very similar rates of return on net worth. In general, firms dealing with relatively perishable commodities would be expected to have high turnovers but low profit margins, and firms whose production processes require heavy investments in fixed assets would be expected to have low turnover ratios but high profit margins.

Break-Even Analysis

Break-even analysis is a method of relating fixed costs, variable costs, and total revenues to show the level of sales that must be attained if the firm is to operate at a profit. The analysis can be based on the number of units produced or total dollar sales; it can also be used for the entire company or for a particular product or division. Further, with minor modifications, break-even analysis can be put on a cash basis instead of on a profit basis.

Sources and Uses of Funds

The sources and uses of funds statement is used to indicate where cash came from and how it was used. When a firm wishes to borrow funds, one of the first questions occurring to a loan officer is, what has the firm done with the money it had? This question is answered by the sources and uses statement. The information it provides may indicate that the firm is making progress or that problems are arising.

The du Pont system, break-even analysis, and sources and uses statements are all fundamental tools in the financial manager's kit and will be encountered time and time again throughout the remainder of this book.

QUESTIONS

4–1   "The higher the rate of return on investment, the better the firm's manage-
       ment." Is this statement true for all firms? Explain. If you disagree with
       the statement, give examples of businesses in which it might not be true.

4–2   What factors would you attempt to change if you wanted to increase a
       firm's rate of return (a) on assets or (b) on net worth?

4–3   Profit margins and turnover rates vary from industry to industry. What
       industry characteristics account for these variations? Give some contrast-
       ing examples to illustrate your answer.

4–4   Why is it particularly important for a rapidly growing young firm to con-
       cern itself with systems of control?

4–5   Are lower total costs *always* beneficial to a company? Why?

4–6   Which relation would you, as a financial manager, prefer: a profit margin
       of 10 percent with a capital turnover of 2 or a profit margin of 25 percent
       and a capital turnover of 1? Can you think of any firm with a relation
       similar to the latter?

4–7   What benefits can be derived from break-even analysis?

4–8   What is operating leverage? Explain how profits or losses can be magnified
       in a firm with a great deal of operating leverage as opposed to a firm
       without this characteristic.

4–9   What portion of the selling price of a product goes toward covering fixed
       costs? Relate your answer to marginal cost analysis.

4–10   What data are necessary to construct a break-even chart?

4–11   What is the general effect of each of the following changes on a firm's
       break-even point?

       a) An increase in selling price with no change in units sold.
       b) A change from leasing of a machine for $5,000 to a purchase of the
          machine for $100,000. The useful life of this machine will be 20 years,
          with no salvage value. Assume straight line depreciation.
       c) A reduction in variable labor costs.

4–12   What are the most important determinants of fixed asset and inventory
       requirements for a manufacturing firm?

4–13   Why do turnover ratios differ for firms in the same industry?

PROBLEMS

4–1 Fill in the following outline of the du Pont pattern of analysis for one set
of the pairs of companies listed below. (This problem requires library research. Data may be obtained from company annual reports or from an
investment manual such as Moody's Industrials or Standard & Poor's Industrials.)

General Motors and Chrysler
Boeing and Douglas Aircraft
Sperry Rand and International Business Machines
Standard Oil of New Jersey and Standard Oil of California
General Electric and Westinghouse

Sales to operating investment	_____%	Cash to sales (percentage)	_____
		Average collection period (days)	_____
		Inventory turnover (times)	_____
Return on investment	_____%	Net fixed asset turnover (times)	_____
		Total operating assets	$_____
		Operating expenses to sales (percentage)	_____
Profit to sales	_____%	Net income before fixed charges and taxes to total assets (percentage)	_____
		Net income after fixed charges and taxes	$_____

a) Using data for the most recent year available, compare the return on
investment for the two companies.
b) Indicate reasons for the observed differences in rates of return suggested by the du Pont analysis.

4–2 For the Ajax Corporation the following relations exist: each unit of output
is sold for $20; for output up to 20,000 units the fixed costs are $60,000;
variable costs are $8 a unit.

a) What is the firm's gain or loss at sales of 4,000 units? of 6,000 units?
b) What is the break-even point? Illustrate by a chart.
c) What occurs to the break-even point if the selling price rises to $24?
What is the significance of the change to financial management? Illustrate by a chart.
d) What occurs to the break-even point if the selling price rises to $24
but variable costs rise to $12 a unit? Illustrate by a chart.

4–3 The consolidated balance sheets for the Moore Corporation at the beginning
and end of 1968 are shown below.

MOORE CORPORATION
BALANCE SHEET
Beginning and End 1968
(in millions of dollars)

	(Jan. 2)	(Dec. 31)	Sources	Use
Cash	$ 20	$ 10		
Marketable securities	15	0		
Net receivables	30	40		
Inventories	70	100		
Total current assets	$135	$150		
Gross fixed assets	100	200		
Less: Reserves for depreciation	(35)	(55)		
Net fixed assets	65	145		
Total assets	$200	$295		
Accounts payable	$ 20	$ 25		
Notes payable	20	5		
Other current liabilities	10	20		
Long-term debt	10	35		
Common stock	50	85		
Retained earnings	90	125		
Total claims on assets	$200	$295		

The company bought $100 million worth of assets. The charge for current depreciation was $20 million. Earnings after taxes were $55 million, and the company paid out $20 million in dividends.

a) Fill in the amount of source or use in the appropriate column.
b) Prepare a percentage statement of sources and uses of funds.
c) Briefly summarize your findings.

Chapter 5

Financial Planning and Budgeting

The planning process is an integral part of the financial manager's job. As will be seen in subsequent chapters, long-term debt and equity funds are raised infrequently and in large amounts. Further, the cost per dollar raised by selling such securities decreases as the size of the issue increases; this reduces the tendency to raise outside capital at frequent intervals. Because of these considerations, it is important that the firm have a working estimate of its total needs for funds for the next few years. It is therefore useful to examine methods of forecasting the firm's over-all needs for funds; this is the subject of the first section of this chapter.

In addition to his long-range forecasts, the financial manager is also concerned with short-term needs for funds. It is embarrassing to a corporate treasurer to "run out of money." Even though he may be able to negotiate a bank loan on short notice, his plight may cause the banker to question the soundness of the firm's management and, accordingly, to reduce the company's line of credit with the bank. We must, therefore, give attention to short-term budgeting with special emphasis on cash forecasting, or *cash budgeting,* as it is commonly called. This is the subject of the second part of the chapter.

LONG-RANGE FINANCIAL FORECASTING

The most important variable that influences a firm's financing requirements is its projected dollar volume of sales. Hence, a good sales forecast is an essential foundation for forecasting financial requirements. The two principal methods of forecasting financial requirements are described in the following sections. Both use sales as the starting point for the forecast—the first method uses a fixed ratio relation between sales and asset components; the second, a variable ratio relationship.

Percent-of-Sales Method

The simplest approach to forecasting financial requirements expresses the firm's needs in terms of the percentage of annual sales invested in each individual balance sheet item. As an example, consider the Moore Company, whose balance sheet as of December 31, 1968, is shown in Table 5-1. The company's sales are running at about $500,000 a year, which is its capacity limit, and the profit margin after tax on sales is 4 percent. During 1968 the company earned $20,000 after taxes and paid out $10,000 in dividends; it plans to continue paying out half of net profits as dividends. How much additional financing will be needed if sales expand to $800,000 during 1969? The calculating procedure, using the percent-of-sales method, is explained below.[1]

Table 5-1

THE MOORE COMPANY
BALANCE SHEET
December 31, 1968

Assets		Liabilities	
Cash	$ 10,000	Accounts payable	$ 50,000
Receivables	85,000	Accrued taxes and wages	25,000
Inventories	100,000	Mortgage bonds	70,000
Fixed assets (net)	150,000	Common stocks	100,000
		Retained earnings	100,000
Total assets	$345,000	Total liab. and net worth	$345,000

First, isolate those balance sheet items which can be expected to vary directly with sales. In the case of the Moore Company this step applies to *all* the assets—a higher level of sales would necessitate more cash for transactions, more receivables, higher inventory levels, and additional fixed plant capacity. On the liability side, accounts payable as well as accruals may be expected to increase with increases in sales. Retained earnings will

---

[1] We recognize, of course, that as a practical matter business firms plan their needs in terms of specific items of equipment, square feet of floor space, and other factors, not as a percentage of sales. However, the outside analyst does not have access to this information, and the manager, even though he has the information on specific items, needs to check his forecasts in aggregate terms. The percent-of-sales method serves both these needs surprisingly well.

go up so long as the company is profitable and does not pay out 100 percent of earnings, but the percentage increase is not constant. However, neither common stock nor mortgage bonds would increase spontaneously with an increase in sales.

Those items which can be expected to vary directly with sales are tabulated as a percentage of sales in Table 5–2. For every $100 increase in sales, assets must increase by $69, and this $69 must be financed in some manner. Accounts payable will increase spontaneously with sales, as will accruals, and these two items will supply $15 of new funds for each $100 increase in sales. Subtracting the 15 percent for spontaneously generated funds from the 69 percent funds requirement leaves 54 percent—thus, for each $100 increase in sales the Moore Company must obtain $54 of financing either from retained earnings or from external sources.

Table 5–2   *THE MOORE COMPANY*
BALANCE SHEET ITEMS EXPRESSED AS A PERCENT OF SALES
December 31, 1968

Cash	2.0%	Accounts payable	10.0%
Receivables	17.0	Accrued taxes and wages	5.0
Inventories	20.0	Mortgage bonds	n.a.
Fixed assets (net)	30.0	Common stock	n.a.
		Retained earnings	n.a.
Total assets	69.0%	Total liab. and net worth	15.0%

n. a. = not applicable

Assets as a percent of sales	69.0%
Less: Spontaneous increase in liabilities	15.0
Percent of each additional dollar of sales that must be financed	54.0%

In the case at hand, sales are scheduled to increase from $500,000 to $800,000, or by $300,000. Applying the 54 percent to the expected increase in sales leads to the conclusion that $162,000 will be needed.

Some of this need will be met by retained earnings. Total sales during 1969 will be $800,000, and if the company earns 4 percent after taxes on this volume, profits will amount to $32,000. Assuming that the 50 percent dividend payout ratio is maintained, dividends will be $16,000, and $16,000 will be retained. Subtracting the retained earnings from the $162,000 that was needed leaves a figure of $146,000—this is the amount of funds that must be obtained through borrowing or selling new common stock.

Notice what would have happened if the Moore Company's sales forecast for 1969 had been only $515,000—a not-too-bad 3 percent gain. Applying the 54 percent net need for funds to the $15,000 sales increase gives an $8,100 funds requirement. Retained earnings ($10,300) would more than cover these requirements, so the firm would have no need of outside capital. Thus, the example shows not only that higher levels of sales bring about a need for funds, but also that while small percentage increases can be financed through retained earnings, larger increases cause the firm to go into the market for outside capital. In other words, a certain level of growth can be financed from internal sources, but higher levels of growth require external financing.

The percent-of-sales method of forecasting financial requirements is neither simple nor mechanical, although an explanation of the ideas requires simple illustrations. Experience in applying the technique in practice suggests the importance of understanding (1) the basic technology of the firm and (2) the logic of the relation between sales and assets for the particular firm in question. A substantial amount of experience and judgment is required to apply the technique in actual practice.

The percent-of-sales method is most appropriately used for forecasting relatively short-term changes in financing needs. It is less useful for longer term forecasting for reasons that are best described in connection with the analysis of the regression method of financial forecasting given below.

Scatter Diagram, or Regression, Method

An alternative method used to forecast financial requirements is the scatter diagram, or regression, method. A scatter diagram is a graphic portrayal of joint relations. Proper use of the scatter diagram method requires practical but not necessarily statistical sophistication.

Table 5–3 RELATIONS BETWEEN INVENTORY AND SALES

Year		Sales	Inventory	Inventory as a Percent of Sales
1963		$ 50,000	$22,000	44
1964		100,000	24,000	24
1965		150,000	26,000	17
1966		200,000	28,000	14
1967		250,000	30,000	12
1968		300,000	32,000	11
.		.	.	.
.		.	.	.
.		.	.	.
1973	(estimated)	500,000	40,000	8

Table 5–3 and Figure 5–1 illustrate the use of the regression method and also demonstrate its superiority over the percent-of-sales method for long-range forecasting. As in all financial forecasting, the sales forecast is the starting point. The financial manager is given the sales forecast, or he may participate in formulating it. Suppose he has data through 1968 and is making a forecast of inventories for 1973, as indicated in Table 5–3. If he is using the regression method, he draws a line through the points for 1963 through 1968, as shown in Figure 5–1. The line that fits the scatter of points in this example is a straight line. It is called the line of best fit, or the regres-

Figure 5-1   Illustrative Relation between Sales and Inventory

sion line. Of course, all points seldom fall exactly on the regression line, and the line itself may be curved as well as linear.[2]

If the percent-of-sales method had been used, some difficulties would have arisen immediately. Table 5–3 gives percent of sales for 1963 through 1968. What relation could be used? the 44 percent for 1963? the 11 percent for 1968? some average of the relations? If the relation for 1968 had been used, a forecast of $55,000 for inventories in 1973 would have been made. This forecast represents a large error.

The regression method is thus seen to be superior for forecasting financial requirements, particularly for longer term forecasts. When a firm is likely to have a base stock of inventory or fixed assets, the ratio of the item to sales declines as sales increase. In such cases the ratio, or percent-of-sales method, results in large errors.[3]

In Table 5–4 the data for the Standard Oil Company of Texas are used to demonstrate the scatter diagram method for a complete financial forecast. In Figure 5–2, only selected variables are plotted. Chart (a) shows the relation between gross national product (hereafter called GNP) and the Standard Oil Company sales. A forecast of GNP, a good measure of the general level of business activity, is used to project company sales in chart (a) of Figure 5–2. Charts (b), (c), and (d) relate Standard Oil Company sales to net accounts receivable, inventories, and net fixed assets.

The procedure for carrying out a scatter diagram analysis is outlined below.

1. Forecast or project the sales of the firm by GNP, industry sales, or other logical business indicators.
2. Plot the scatter diagrams for major asset, liability, and net worth categories related to sales.
3. Fit the regression line by free hand (inspection) or by numerical calculations.

---

[2] In these illustrations inventories are used as the item to be forecast. Much theory suggests that inventories increase as a square root of sales. This characteristic would tend to turn the line of regression between inventories and sales slightly downward. Also, improvements in inventory-control techniques would curve the line of relation downward. However, the increased diversity of types, models, and styles tends to increase inventories. Applications by the authors' students of the regression method to hundreds of companies indicate that the linear straight line relations typically represent the line of best fit or, at worst, involve only small error. If the line were in fact curved over, a curved line could be fit to the data and used for forecasting purposes.

[3] The widespread use of the percentage method makes for lax control. It should be easy to improve on a $55,000 inventory level and still be inefficient because the correct target amount is closer to $40,000. A clear example of the use of correlation relations instead of ratios to set controls for travel expenses is set out in W. A. Wallis and H. V. Roberts, *Statistics* (New York: The Free Press, 1956), pp. 549–555.

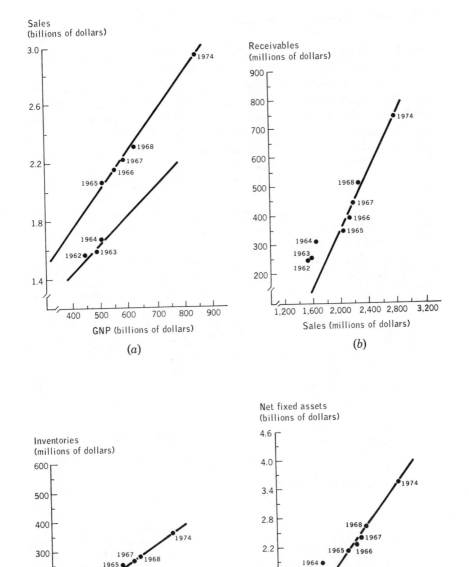

Figure 5-2   Scatter Diagrams: Standard Oil Company of Texas

Table 5–4 GROSS NATIONAL PRODUCT AND STANDARD OIL COMPANY OF TEXAS DATA
(in millions of dollars)

Year	GNP (billions of dollars)*	Sales	Cash, Marketable Securities	Inventories	Receivables	Total Current Assets	Net Fixed Assets	Misc. Assets	Accounts Payable	Provision for Income Tax
1962	440	$1,559	$193	$243	$250	$686	$1,629	$136	$164	$54
1963	480	1,565	189	238	253	675	1,759	143	165	48
1964	500	1,663	217	219	318	754	1,864	164	226	53
1965	520	2,046	219	252	347	820	2,105	191	286	56
1966	552	2,150	202	240	399	871	2,274	208	333	50
1967	586	2,203	204	267	446	917	2,397	230	344	50
1968	623	2,285	172	279	519	971	2,589	236	347	60

Year	Other Current Liab.	Long-term Debt	Common Stock and Capital Surplus	Retained Earnings and Surplus Reserves	Total Assets and Claims on Assets	Net Income to Common	Cash Dividends to Common	Payout Percentage Dividends ÷ Earnings	Retained Earnings
1962	$259	$179	$ 797	$1,215	$2,451	$258	$126	49%	$132
1963	259	175	797	1,347	2,578	254	126	50	128
1964	324	173	797	1,487	2,782	266	126	47	140
1965	394	172	962	1,569	3,117	286	126	44	160
1966	434	185	1,148	1,563	3,353	305	133	44	172
1967	451	183	1,148	1,741	3,545	314	139	44	175
1968	478	216	1,378	1,724	3,796	337	144	43	193

* In 1947 prices.

85

4. Project the regression lines and determine the level of each balance sheet category for the forecast value of sales. (Projections for the Standard Oil Company of Texas are summarized in Table 5–5).

5. The difference between asset requirements and financing sources directly related to sales indicates financial requirements.

As is true of the ratio methods of forecasting financial requirements, the regression method can be used to forecast only the items of the balance sheet that are directly influenced by sales. Some items are directly tied to sales; others are not.

Balance sheet items directly tied to increase in sales		Balance sheet items not directly tied to increase in sales	
Assets	*Liabilities*	*Assets*	*Liabilities*
Cash	Accounts payable	Investments	Notes payable
Receivables	Provision for income		Long-term debt
Inventories	tax		Preferred stock
Fixed assets	Accruals		Common stock
	Retained earnings		

As the above listing indicates, most of the asset items—the balance sheet items to be financed—vary with the increase in sales. When sales increase, these items are likely to increase in some predictable fashion. On the right-hand side of the balance sheet, some items similarly increase with incremental sales. Retained earnings, as indicated in the discussion of the ratio method, increase with total sales, not just incremental sales.

In the example provided in Table 5–5, the company's sales are projected to increase by some $495 million over the six-year period. Total assets are expected to rise from $3,796 million to $5,213 million, an increase of $1,417 million. The increases in retained earnings and other selected current liability items can provide part of the additional funds required, but additional financing of some $123 million will be needed.[4]

The difference between the financing required (increases in the asset items) and the financing provided (increases in certain liability and net worth items) is the additional financing required. This financing stems from four major sources: notes payable, long-term debt, preferred stock, and common stock.

These are the major alternative sources of financing. Forecasting financial requirements thus leads to an estimate of financing needed. How the needed financing is to be raised is the subject matter of subsequent chapters. First, however, it is necessary to examine the cash budget.

---

[4] The figures presented here for the Standard Oil Company of Texas are used only to illustrate the methodology.

Table 5–5 *STANDARD OIL COMPANY OF TEXAS*
PRO FORMA BALANCE SHEETS
1968 Estimates Compared with 1968 Actual
(in millions of dollars)

	1968 Actual	1968 Estimated	1974 Estimated
GNP (in billions of dollars)	$ 623	$ 623	$ 850*
Company sales	2,285	2,285	2,780
Assets			
Cash and marketable securities	173	210	223
Receivables	519	480	750
Inventories	279	275	355
Total current assets	971	965	1,328
Miscellaneous assets	236	236	345
Net fixed assets	2,589	2,590	3,540
Total assets	$3,796	$3,791	$5,213
Liabilities			
Accounts payable	$ 348	$ 348	$ 455
Income taxes payable	60	60	74†
Other current liabilities	70	57	63
Total current liabilities	478	465	592
Long-term debt	216	216	216
Total liabilities	694	681	808
Capital			
Common stock	1,378	1,378	1,378
Retained earnings	1,724	1,724	2,904
Total capital	3,102	3,102	4,282
Subtotal	3,796	3,783	5,090
Additional financing needed	0	8	123
Total liab. and net worth	$3,796	$3,791	$5,213

* 5.5 percent growth rate.
† Assumed 20 percent of net income.

BUDGETING

The methods of financial forecasting covered thus far in this chapter are more effective for long-term planning than for short-term planning. The reason for this is that a firm's needs for inventories and plant equipment must, for large volume changes, conform to its level of sales. Assets are therefore closely related to sales in the long run. In the short run, however, the firm may have excess capacity which enables it to expand sales without proportional additions to inventories, plant, and equipment. Or, in the short term, sales may contract; what happens to assets in this case depends upon the expected duration and severity of the sales decline and upon the ability of management to adjust to a changed sales volume.

Budgeting is a management tool used for shorter term planning and control. In short, budgeting is a method of planning and control that emphasizes monthly and one- or two-year plans for the future. Historically, budgeting was treated as a device to limit expenditures. The more modern approach is to view the budgeting process as a tool for obtaining the most productive and profitable use of the company's resources.

Nature of the Budgeting Process

Fundamentally, the budgeting process is a search to improve operations; it is a continuous effort to get the job done in the best possible way. The budget requires a set of performance standards, or targets. Budgets are reviewed to compare plans and results; this process has been called "controlling to plan." It is a continuous monitoring procedure, reviewing and evaluating performance with reference to the previously established standards.

Establishing standards requires a realistic understanding of the activities carried on by the firm. Arbitrary standards, set without a basic understanding of the minimum costs as determined by the nature of the firm's operations, can do more harm than good. Budgets imposed in an arbitrary fashion may represent impossible targets at the one extreme or standards that are too lax at the other. If standards are unrealistically high, frustrations and resentment will develop. If standards are unduly lax, costs will be out of control, profits will suffer, and morale will become flabby. However, a set of budgets based on a clear understanding and careful analysis of operations can play an important positive role for the firm.

Budgets, therefore, can provide valuable guides to both high-level executives and middle-management personnel. Well-formulated and effectively developed budgets make subordinates aware of the fact that top management has a realistic understanding of the nature of the operations in the business firm. Thus, the budget becomes an important communication link between top management and the divisional personnel whom they guide.

Budgets also represent planning and control devices which enable management to anticipate change and adapt to it. Business operations in today's economic environment are complex and subject to heavy competitive pressures. In such an environment many kinds of changes take place. The rate of growth of the economy as a whole fluctuates, and these fluctuations affect different industries in a number of different ways. If a firm plans ahead, the budget and control process can provide management with a better basis for understanding of the firm's operations in relation to the general environment. This increased understanding, in turn, leads to faster reactions to developing events, thus increasing the firm's ability to perform effectively.

The budgeting process, in summary, improves internal coordination. This element reflects the basic theme of this book: to show how financial decisions affect the profits and value of the firm and to show how these decisions may be improved. Decisions at every stage—for each product and at the research, engineering, production, marketing, personnel, and financial levels—all have an impact on the firm's profits. Planning and control is the essence of profit planning, and the budget system provides an integrated picture of the firm's operations as a whole. Therefore, the budget system enables each manager to see the relation of his part of the enterprise to the totality of the firm. For example, a production decision to alter the level of work-in-process inventories, or a marketing decision to change the terms under which a particular product is sold, can be traced through the entire budget system to show its effects on the firm's over-all profitability. The budgeting system is therefore a most important financial tool.

The Budget System

The over-all nature of the budget process is outlined in Figure 5–3. Budgeting is a part of the total planning activity in the firm, so we must begin with a statement of corporate goals or objectives. The statement of goals, shown in the box at the top of the figure, determines the second part of the figure, the corporate long-range plan, shown in the second box. A segment of the corporate long-range plan includes a long-range sales forecast. This forecast requires a determination of the number and types of products that will be manufactured both at the present and in the future years encompassed by the long-range plan. This is the product mix strategy.

Shorter term forecasts and budgets are formulated within the framework of the long-range plan. One might, for example, begin with a sales forecast covering six months or one year. The short-term sales forecast provides a basis for (and is, in turn, dependent on) the broad range of policies indicated in the center of Figure 5–3. First, there are manufacturing policies covering the choice of types of equipment, plant layout, and production-line arrangements. In addition, the kind of durability built into the products and their associated costs will be considered. Second, a broad set of marketing policies must be formulated. These relate to such items as (1) the development of the firm's own sales organization versus the use of outside sales organizations; (2) the number of salesmen and the method by which

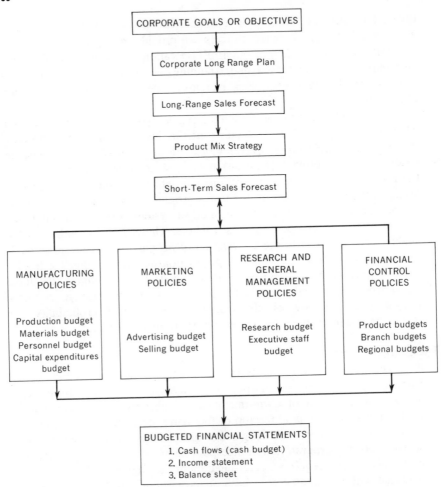

Figure 5-3   Over-All View of the Total Budgeting Process and Relations

they will be compensated; (3) the forms, types, and amounts spent on advertising; and other factors. Third are the research and general management policies. Research policies relate to relative emphasis on basic versus applied research and the product areas emphasized by both types of research. Fourth are financial policies, discussed in the following section.

Financial Control Policies

Financial control policies include the organization and content of various types of financial control budgets. These include a budget for individual products and for every significant activity of the firm. In addition, budgets will be formulated to control operations at individual branch offices. These budgets, in turn, are grouped and modified to control regional operations.

In a similar manner, policies established at the manufacturing, marketing, research, and general management levels give rise to a series of budgets. For example, the production budget will reflect the use of materials, parts, labor, and facilities, and each of the major elements in a production budget is likely to have its own individual budget program. Thus, there is likely to be a materials budget, a labor or personnel requirements budget, and a facilities or long-run capital expenditures budget; and, after the product is produced, the next step in the process will call for a marketing budget. Related to the over-all process are the general office and executive requirements, which will be reflected in the general and administrative budget system.

The results of projecting all these elements of cost are reflected in the budgeted, or projected, income statement. The anticipated sales give rise to the various types of investments needed to produce the products; these investments, plus the beginning balance sheet, provide the necessary data for developing the assets side of the balance sheet.

But these assets must be financed; hence, a cash flow analysis—the cash budget—is required. The cash budget indicates the combined effects of the budgeted operations on the firm's cash flow. A positive net cash flow will indicate that the firm has ample financing. On the other hand, if an increase in the volume of operations leads to a negative cash flow, additional financing will be required. This leads directly to choices of financing, which is the subject of a considerable portion of the remainder of the book.

Since the structure of the income statement and balance sheet have already been covered in preceding chapters, the rest of this section will deal with the two remaining aspects of the budgeting process—the cash budget and the concept of variable, or flexible, budgets.

CASH BUDGETING

The cash budget, as indicated, determines not only the total amount of financing that will be required but its timing as well. The cash budget indicates the amount of funds that will be needed month by month or even week by week and is one of the financial manager's most important tools. Because a clear understanding of the nature of cash budgeting is important, the process is described by means of an example which makes the elements of the cash budget explicit.

Marvel Toy is a medium-sized toy manufacturer. Sales are highly seasonal, with the peak falling in September, when retailers stock up for the Christmas season. All sales are made on terms that allow a cash discount on payments made within 30 days; if the discount is not taken, the full amount must be paid in 60 days. But Marvel, like most other companies, finds that some of its customers delay payment up to 90 days. Experience shows that on 20 percent of the sales, payment is made within 30 days; that on 70 percent of the sales, payment is made during the second month after the sale; and that on 10 percent of the sales, payment is made during the third month.

Production is geared to future sales. Purchased materials and parts amount to 70 percent of sales, and Marvel purchases materials and parts the month before the company expects to sell the finished product. Marvel's own purchase terms permit it to delay payment on its own purchases for one month. In other words, if August sales are forecast at $30,000 and if purchases during July amount to $21,000, this amount is actually paid in August.

Wages and salaries, rent, and other cash expenses are given in Table 5–6. The company also has a tax payment of $8,000 coming due in August, and its capital budgeting plans call for the purchase in July of a new machine tool costing $10,000, payment to be made in September. Assuming the company needs to keep a $5,000 cash balance at all times and it has $6,000 on July 1, what are Marvel's financial requirements for the period July through December?

The cash requirements are worked out in the cash budget shown as Table 5–6. The top half of the table provides a worksheet for calculating collections on sales and payments on purchases. The first line in the worksheet gives the sales forecast for the period May through December—May and June sales are necessary to determine collections for July and August. Next, cash collections are given. The first line of this section shows that 20 percent of the sales during any given month are collected that month. The second shows the collections on the prior month's sales—70 percent of sales in the preceding month. The third line gives collections from sales two months earlier—10 percent of sales in that month. The collections are summed to find the total cash receipts from sales during each month under consideration.

With the worksheet completed, the cash budget itself can be considered. Receipts from collections are given on the top line. Next, payments during each month are summarized. The difference between cash receipts and cash payments is the net cash gain or loss during the month; for July, there is a net cash loss of $4,200. The initial cash on hand at the beginning of the month is added to the net cash gain or loss during the month to yield the cumulative cash that will be on hand if no financing is done; at the end of July, Marvel Toy will have cumulative cash equal to $1,800. The de-

Table 5-6 MARVEL TOY COMPANY CASH BUDGET

					Work Sheet				
	May	June	July	Aug.	Sept.	Oct.	Nov.	Dec.	Jan.
Sales (net of cash discounts)	$10,000	$10,000	$20,000	$30,000	$40,000	$20,000	$20,000	$10,000	$10,000
Collections									
First month (20%)	$ 2,000	2,000	4,000	6,000	8,000	4,000	4,000	2,000	2,000
Second month (70%)		7,000	7,000	14,000	21,000	28,000	14,000	14,000	7,000
Third month (10%)			1,000	1,000	2,000	3,000	4,000	2,000	2,000
Total	$ 2,000	$ 9,000	$12,000	$21,000	$31,000	$35,000	$22,000	$18,000	$11,000
Purchases (70% next month's sales)	$ 7,000	$14,000	$21,000	$28,000	$14,000	$14,000	$ 7,000	$ 7,000	
Payments		7,000	14,000	21,000	28,000	14,000	14,000	7,000	7,000
Receipts									
Collections			$12,000	$21,000	$31,000	$35,000	$22,000	$18,000	$11,000
Cash Budget									
Payments									
Purchases			14,000	21,000	28,000	14,000	14,000	7,000	
Wages and salaries			1,500	2,000	2,500	1,500	1,500	1,000	
Rent			500	500	500	500	500	500	
Other expenses			200	300	400	200	200	100	
Taxes				8,000					
Payment on Machine					10,000				
Total payments			$16,200	$31,800	$41,400	$16,200	$16,200	$ 8,600	
Net cash gain (loss) *during month*			(4,200)	(10,800)	(10,400)	18,800	5,800	9,400	
Initial cash at start of month			6,000	1,800	(9,000)	(19,400)	(600)	5,200	
Cumulative cash (if no financing)			1,800	(9,000)	(19,400)	(600)	5,200	14,600	
Desired level of cash			5,000	5,000	5,000	5,000	5,000	5,000	
Cash above minimum needs(or financing needs)—Cumulative minus desired			(3,200)	(14,000)	(24,400)	(5,600)	200	9,600	

93

sired cash balance, $5,000, is subtracted from the cumulative cash balance to determine the amount of financing that the firm needs if it is to maintain the desired level of cash. At the end of July we see that Marvel will need $3,200.

This same procedure is used in the following months. Sales will expand seasonally in August, and with the increased sales will come increased payments for purchases, wages, and other items. Moreover, the $8,000 tax bill is due in August. Receipts from sales will go up too, but the firm will still be left with a $10,800 cash deficit during the month. The total financial requirements at the end of August will be $14,000—the $3,200 needed at the end of July plus the $10,800 cash deficit for August.

Sales peak in September and the cash deficit during this month will amount to another $10,400. The total need for funds through September will increase to $24,400. Sales, and, consequently, purchases and the payment for past purchases, will fall markedly in October, but the collections will be the highest of any month, because they mainly reflect the high September sales. As a result, Marvel Toy will enjoy a healthy $18,800 cash surplus during October. This surplus can be used to pay off borrowings, so the need for financing will decline by $18,800 to $5,600.

Marvel will have another cash surplus in November, and this extra cash will permit it to eliminate completely the need for financing. In fact, the company is expected to have $200 in extra cash by the month's end, and another cash surplus in December will swell the extra cash to $9,600. With such a large amount of unneeded funds, Marvel's treasurer will doubtlessly want to make investments in some type of interest-bearing securities or put the funds to use in some other way.

VARIABLE, OR FLEXIBLE, BUDGETS

Budgets are planned allocations of a firm's resources, based on forecasts for the future. Two important elements influence actual performance. One element is the impact of external influences—developments in the economy as a whole and competitive developments in the firm's own industry. The firm has essentially no control over these factors. The second element, which is controllable by the firm, is the level of efficiency at a given volume of sales. It is useful to separate the impact of these two elements, as this separation is necessary for evaluating individual performances.

The essence of the variable budget system is to introduce flexibility into budgets by recognizing that certain types of expenditures will vary at different levels of output. Thus, a firm might have an alternative level of outlay budgeted for different volumes of operation—high, low, medium. One of management's responsibilities is to determine which of these alternative budgets should be in effect for the planning period under consideration.

The scatter diagram method, described in the first part of this chapter in connection with financial forecasting, may also be utilized to establish the basis for flexible budgeting. The use of the concept can be illustrated by a specific example. Suppose that a retail store has had the experience indicated by the historical data set forth in Table 5–7. It is apparent from the

Table 5–7   *HUBLER DEPARTMENT STORE*
RELATIONSHIP BETWEEN SALES AND EMPLOYEES

Month	Sales (in millions of dollars)	Number of Employees
January	4	42
February	5	51
March	6	60
April	7	75
May	10	102
June	8	83
July	5	55
August	9	92

data that the number of employees the firm needs is dependent upon the dollar volume of sales that occurs during a month. This is seen more easily from a scatter diagram like that of Figure 5–4. The freehand regression line is sloped positively because the number of employees increases as the

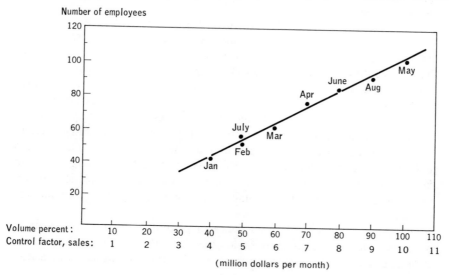

Figure 5-4   Hubler Department Store Scatter Diagram and Regression Line

volume of sales increases. The independent variable, dollar volume of sales, is called the *control variable*. Variations in the control variable cause changes in total expenses. The volume of sales can be forecast, and the number of employees can be read from the regression chart.

Table 5–8 **HUBLER DEPARTMENT STORE**
BUDGET ALLOWANCE

Volume (in percentages)	Employees	Weekly Payroll Estimate (average wage, $100)
60	62	$ 6,200
70	72	7,200
80	82	8,200
90	92	9,200
100	102	10,200
110	112	11,200

The relations can be expressed in tabular form (Table 5–8). Given the forecast of the volume of operations, standards are provided for the expected number of employees and the weekly payroll.[5]

Problems of Budgeting

Four major problems are encountered when using budget systems. First, budgetary programs can grow to be so complete and so detailed that they become cumbersome, meaningless, and unduly expensive. Overbudgeting is dangerous.

Second, budgetary goals may come to supersede enterprise goals. But budgets are a tool, not an end in themselves. Enterprise goals by definition supersede subsidiary plans of which budgets are a part. Also, budgets are based on future expectations which may not be realized. There is no acceptable reason for neglecting to alter budgets as circumstances change. This reasoning is the core of the argument in favor of more flexible budgets.

Third, budgets can tend to hide inefficiencies by continuing initial expenditures in succeeding periods without proper evaluation. Budgets growing from precedent usually contain undesirable expenditures. They should not be used as umbrellas under which slovenly, inefficient management can hide. Consequently, the budgetary process must contain provision for reexamination of standards and other bases of planning by which policies are translated into numerical terms.

Finally, some case study evidence suggests that the use of budgets as a pressure device defeats their basic objectives. Budgets, if used as an instrument of tyranny, cause resentment and frustrations, which in turn lead

---

[5] Note that the regression analysis provides even more flexibility in budgeting than do the high, medium, and low levels mentioned earlier.

to inefficiency. In order to counteract this effect, it has been recommended that top management increase the participation of subordinates during the preparatory stages of the budgets.

USE OF FINANCIAL PLANS AND BUDGETS

Forecasts, or long-range plans, are necessary in all the firm's operations. The personnel department must have a good idea of the scale of future operations if it is to plan its hiring and training activities properly. The production department must be sure that the productive capacity is available to meet the projected product demand, while the finance department must be sure that funds are available to meet the firm's financial requirements.

The tools and techniques discussed in this chapter are actually used in several separate, but related, ways. First, the percent-of-sales method or, preferably, the scatter diagram method is used to make a long-range forecast of financial requirements over the next three to five years. This forecast is then used to make the strategic financing plans during the planning period. The company might, for example, plan to meet its financial requirements with retained earnings and short-term bank debt during 1969 and 1970, then float a bond issue in 1971, use retained earnings in 1972, and finally sell an issue of common stock in 1973. Fairly long lead times are necessary when companies sell bonds or stocks; otherwise, they might be forced to go into the market during unfavorable periods.

In addition to this long-run strategic financial planning, the financial manager must also make accurate short-run forecasts to be sure that the bank funds will be available to meet seasonal and other short-run requirements. He might, for example, have a meeting with his bank loan officer to discuss his company's need for funds during the coming year. Prior to the meeting, he would have his accountants prepare a detailed cash budget showing the need for money during each of the coming 12 months. The cash budget would show the maximum amount that would be needed. during the year, how much would be needed during each month, and how cash surpluses would be generated at some point to enable the firm to repay the bank loans.

The financial manager would also have his firm's most recent, as well as its projected, balance sheets and income statements, and he would have calculated the key financial ratios to show both its actual and its projected financial positions to the banker. If its financial position is sound and if its cash budget appears reasonable, the bank will commit itself to make the required funds available. Even if the bank decides that the company's request is unreasonable and denies the loan request, the financial manager will have time to seek other sources of funds. While it might not be pleasant to have to look elsewhere for money, it is much better to know ahead of time that the loan request will be refused.

With these forecasting techniques in mind, we consider in subsequent chapters the ways the firm can meet its financial requirements. Should it use debt or equity? long-term or short-term debt? And, given its decisions on these questions, how does the financial manager obtain the required capital?

SUMMARY

Financial forecasting is carried on at two levels—long-range forecasting and short-range forecasting, that is, forecasting requirements for several months. Naturally, the shorter the period covered by the forecast, the higher the level of accuracy.

Long-Range Financial Forecasting

The most important causal variable in determining financial requirements is a firm's projected dollar volume of sales. Hence, a good sales forecast is an essential foundation for forecasting financial requirements. The two principal methods used to make financial forecasts are (1) the percent-of-sales method and (2) the regression method. The first has the virtue of simplicity—the forecaster computes past relationships between asset and liability items and sales, assumes these same relationships will continue, and then applies the new sales forecast to get an estimate of the financial requirements.

Since the percent-of-sales method assumes that the balance sheet/sales relationships will remain constant, it is only useful for relatively short-run forecasting. When longer forecasts are being made, the regression method is preferable because it allows for changing balance sheet/sales relationships.

Short-Range Financial Forecasting

The principal tool for making short-run financial forecasts is the cash budget. Cash budgets, if used properly, are highly accurate and can pinpoint the funds that will be needed, when they will be needed, and when cash flows will be sufficient to retire any loans that might be necessary.

Use of Financial Forecasts

The tools and techniques discussed in this chapter are used in several separate but related ways. First, one of the long-range forecasting techniques is used to make a long-run forecast of the firm's financial requirements over the three to five years following the long-run planning period. This forecast is then used to make the strategic financing plans during the planning period. Long lead times are necessary when companies sell bonds or stocks; otherwise, financial managers might be forced to go into the market for funds during unfavorable periods.

In addition to this long-run, strategic forecasting, the financial manager must also make accurate short-run forecasts to be sure that bank funds will be available to meet seasonal and other short-run requirements. If the firm's financial position is sound and if its cash budget appears reasonable, the bank will commit itself to make the required funds available. If the bank decides that the company's request is unreasonable and denies it, the financial manager will have time to seek other sources of funds.

QUESTIONS

5–1   What is the first step in forecasting financial requirements? Why is this the first step?

5–2   For what reasons does a firm hold cash?

5–3   Compare the relative advantages of holding cash as opposed to investing in short-term marketable securities.

5–4   If a firm's average collection period is 25 days and its daily credit sales are $1,000, what is the theoretical amount for accounts receivable on the balance sheet?

5–5   Describe the regression method for forecasting financial needs. What are the strengths and the weaknesses of this method?

5–6   What should be the approximate point of intersection between the sales/ asset regression line and the vertical axis for the following: inventory, accounts receivable, fixed assets? State your answer in terms of positive, zero, or negative intercept. Can you think of any accounts that might have a negative intercept?

5–7   How does forecasting financial requirements in advance of needs assist the financial manager perform his responsibilities more effectively?

5–8   Do you suppose the management of working capital would occupy more of the financial manager's time in a retailing concern or in an electric utility company? Why?

5–9   Explain how a downturn in the business cycle could either cause a cash shortage for a firm or have the opposite effect and generate excess cash.

5–10   Why do many "young" firms find it difficult to obtain working capital loans from commercial banks? Do you suppose that a given young firm would have an easier time getting a working capital loan than a loan to finance fixed assets?

5–11   What alternatives are available to a company when it finds it has excessive working capital in the form of cash?

5–12   Explain this statement: "Current assets to a considerable extent represent permanent assets."

5–13   If the United States lacked a highly developed banking system, making it difficult if not impossible for business to borrow to meet seasonal needs, what would be the effects on the cash balances maintained by business firms? What would be the effect on the general level of business and economic activity?

PROBLEMS

5-1   The Grossman Supply Company is a wholesale steel distributor. It purchases steel in carload lots from more than twenty producing mills and sells to several thousand steel users. The items carried include shapes, plates, wire products, bolts, windows, pipe, and tubing.

The company owns two warehouses, each housing 10,000 square feet, and contemplates the erection of another warehouse of 15,000 square feet. The nature of the steel-supply business requires that the company maintain large inventories to take care of customer requirements in the event of mill strikes or other delays.

In examining patterns from 1960 through 1965, the company found a rather consistent relation between the following accounts as a percent of sales.

Current assets	50
Net fixed assets	20
Accounts payable	5
Other current liabilities, including accruals and provision for income taxes but not for bank loans	5
Net profit after taxes	2

The company's sales for 1966 were $4 million, and its balance sheet on December 31, 1966, was as follows:

GROSSMAN SUPPLY COMPANY
BALANCE SHEET
December 31, 1966

Current assets	$2,000,000	Accounts payable	$ 200,000
Fixed assets	800,000	Notes payable	600,000
		Other current liabilities	200,000
		Total current liabilities	1,000,000
		Mortgage loan	200,000
		Common stock	500,000
		Earned surplus	1,100,000
		Total liabilities and	
Total assets	$2,800,000	net worth	$2,800,000

The company expects its sales to grow by $300,000 each year. If this growth is achieved, what will its financial requirements be at the end of the 5-year period? Assume that accounts not tied directly to sales (for example, notes payable) remain constant. Assume also that the company pays no dividends.

a) Construct a *pro forma* balance sheet for the end of 1971, using "additional financing needed" as the balancing item.

b) What are the crucial assumptions made in your projection method?

5–2 The annual sales of the Townsend Company are $1 million. Common stock and notes payable are constant. The percent of sales in each balance sheet item that varies directly with sales are as follows:

Cash	4
Receivables	12
Inventories	12
Net fixed assets	18
Accounts payable	10
Provision for income tax	4
Other current liabilities	5
Profit rate (after taxes) on sales	6

a) On the assumption that any excess funds will be invested in government securities, complete the balance sheet below:

TOWNSEND COMPANY
BALANCE SHEET
December 31, 1966

Cash		Accounts payable	
Receivables		Notes payable	$ 80,000
Inventory		Provision for income tax	
Total current assets		Other current liabilities	
Fixed assets		Total current liabilities	
		Common stock	$100,000
		Retained earnings	
		Total liabilities and	
Total assets	_____	net worth	_____

b) Now suppose that in one year sales increase by $200,000, to $1.2 million. What will be the new balance sheet (no dividends paid)?

c) For any given increase in sales in one year, what will be the additional external financing requirements, expressed as a percentage of sales?

5–3 The current balance sheet of the Merton Corporation is shown here.

MERTON CORPORATION
BALANCE SHEET
December 31, 1966

Assets		Liabilities and Net Worth	
Cash	$ 50,000	Accounts payable	$ 45,000
Accounts receivable	240,000	Accruals	35,000
Inventories	180,000	Federal taxes payable*	40,000
Total current assets	$470,000	Total current liabilities	$120,000
Fixed assets, net	120,000	Net worth	470,000
Total assets	$590,000	Total claims on assets	$590,000

* Payable $20,000 on March 15 and $20,000 on June 15.

The level of business activity is expected to rise 20 percent by the end of the 6-month period January through June 1967. An expansion program requiring an additional investment of $60,000 in fixed assets is planned for this period. Assume that receivables, inventories, payables, and accruals increase by 20 percent. The estimated income statement for the 6-month period is shown below.

MERTON CORPORATION
INCOME STATEMENT
For Six Months Ended June 30, 1967

Net sales		$900,000
Cost of goods sold	$620,000	
Other operating expenses	210,000	
Depreciation expense	30,000	
Total cost of sales		860,000
Net income before federal income taxes		$ 40,000
Federal income taxes		19,200*
Net income after federal income taxes		$ 20,800

* Assume these taxes will not be paid until after the cash budgeting period.

a) Prepare a cash budget covering the six-month period as one unit of time.
b) Construct an estimated balance sheet for the end of the 6-month period.
c) Calculate the current ratio and total debt-to-net-worth ratio of the firm on June 30, 1967.
d) Assume that Merton raises $100,000 cash by selling long-term debt. What will be the effect on the two ratios obtained in c?
e) What is the financial significance of the problem of rapidly expanding sales?

5-4 Indicate the effects of the transactions listed below on each of the following: total current assets, working capital, current ratio, and net profit. Use + to indicate an increase, — to indicate a decrease, and 0 to indicate no effect. State necessary assumptions and assume an initial current ratio of more than 1 to 1.

	Total Current Assets	Working Capital	Current Ratio	Effect on Net Profit
1) Cash is acquired through issuance of additional common stock.	____	____	____	____
2) Merchandise is sold for cash.	____	____	____	____
3) Federal income tax due for the previous year is paid.	____	____	____	____
4) A fixed asset is sold for less than book value.	____	____	____	____
5) A fixed asset is sold for more than book value.	____	____	____	____

		Total Current Assets	Working Capital	Current Ratio	Effect on Net Profit
6)	Merchandise is sold on credit.	___	___	___	___
7)	Payment is made to trade creditors for previous purchases.	___	___	___	___
8)	A cash dividend is declared and paid.	___	___	___	___
9)	Cash is obtained through bank loans.	___	___	___	___
10)	Short-term notes receivable are sold at a discount.	___	___	___	___
11)	Previously issued stock rights are exercised by company stockholders.	___	___	___	___
12)	A profitable firm increases its fixed asset depreciation allowance account.	___	___	___	___
13)	Marketable securities are sold below cost.	___	___	___	___
14)	Uncollectible accounts are written off against the allowance account.	___	___	___	___
15)	Advances are made to employees.	___	___	___	___
16)	Current operating expenses are paid.	___	___	___	___
17)	Short-term promissory notes are issued to trade creditors for prior purchases.	___	___	___	___
18)	Ten-year notes are issued to pay off accounts payable.	___	___	___	___
19)	A wholly depreciated asset is retired.	___	___	___	___
20)	A *cash* sinking fund for the retirement of bonds is created; a reserve for bond sinking fund is also created.	___	___	___	___
21)	Bonds are retired by the use of the cash sinking fund.	___	___	___	___
22)	Accounts receivable are collected.	___	___	___	___
23)	A stock dividend is declared and paid.	___	___	___	___
24)	Equipment is purchased with short-term notes.	___	___	___	___

	Total Current Assets	Working Capital	Current Ratio	Effect on Net Profit
25) The allowance for doubtful accounts is increased.	____	____	____	____
26) Merchandise is purchased on credit.	____	____	____	____
27) Controlling interest in another firm is acquired by the issuance of additional common stock.	____	____	____	____
28) Earnings are added to the reserve for bond sinking fund.	____	____	____	____
29) An unconsolidated subsidiary paid the firm a cash dividend from current earnings.	____	____	____	____
30) The estimated taxes payable has been increased.	____	____	____	____

PART III

Long-Term Investment Decisions

Chapter 6

The Interest Factor in Financial Decisions

The investment in fixed assets should, logically, be taken up at this point. However, the long-term nature of fixed investments makes it necessary to consider first the theory of compound interest—the "math of finance." Compound interest is essential to an understanding of capital budgeting, the topic of the following chapter, but interest rate theory is also an integral part of several other topics taken up later in the text. Financial structure decisions, lease versus purchase decisions, bond refunding operations, security valuation techniques, and the whole question of the cost of capital are some other subjects that cannot be understood without a knowledge of compound interest.

Many people are afraid of the subject of compound interest; hence, they simply avoid it. It is certainly true that many successful businessmen —even some bankers—know essentially nothing of the subject. However, as technology advances, as more and more engineers become involved in general management, and as modern business administration programs turn out more and more highly qualified graduates, this "success in spite of himself" pattern will become more and more difficult to achieve. Furthermore, fear of compound interest relationships is quite unfounded—the subject matter is simply not that difficult. Practically all problems involving compound interest can be handled quite satisfactorily with only a few basic formulas.

COMPOUND VALUE

A person deposits $1,000 in a savings and loan association that pays 4 percent interest compounded annually. How much will he have at the end of one year? To treat the matter systematically, let us define the following terms:

P = principal, or beginning amount
i = interest rate
I = dollar amount of interest earned during a period
V = ending amount, or the sum of $P + I$

V may now be calculated as

$$V = P + I$$
$$= P + Pi$$
$$= P(1 + i) \tag{6-1}$$

This last equation shows that the ending amount is equal to the beginning amount times the factor $(1 + i)$. For the example, where $P = \$1,000$, V is found as:

$$V = \$1,000(1.0 + .04) = \$1,000(1.04) = \$1,040$$

If the person leaves the $1,000 on deposit for five years, to what amount will it have grown at the end of that period? Equation 6–1 can be used to construct Table 6–1, which indicates the answer.

Table 6–1 COMPOUND INTEREST CALCULATIONS

Year	Beginning Amount (P)	Times	(1 + i)=	Ending Amount (V)
1	$1,000		1.04 =	$1,040
2	1,040		1.04 =	1,082
3	1,082		1.04 =	1,125
4	1,125		1.04 =	1,170
5	1,170		1.04 =	1,217

Note that V_2, the balance at the end of the second year, is found as

$$V_2 = P_2(1 + i) = P_1(1 + i)(1 + i) = P_1(1 + i)^2$$

Similarly, V_3, the balance after three years, is found as

$$V_3 = P_3 (1 + i) = P_1 (1 + i)^3$$

In general, V_n, the compound amount at the end of any year n, is found as

$$V_n = P(1 + i)^n \tag{6-2}$$

This is the fundamental equation of compound interest, and it can readily be seen that equation 6–1 is simply a special case of equation 6–2 where $n = 1$.

While it is necessary to understand the derivation of equation 6–2 in order to understand much of the material in the remainder of this chapter (as well as material to be covered in subsequent chapters), the concept can be applied quite readily in a mechanical sense. Tables have been constructed for values of $(1 + i)^n$ for wide ranges of i and n; Table 6–2 is illustrative. Table A-1, in Appendix A, is a more complete table.

Table 6–2   COMPOUND VALUE OF $1

Year	1%	2%	3%	4%	5%	6%	7%	8%	9%	10%
1	1.010	1.020	1.030	1.040	1.050	1.060	1.070	1.080	1.090	1.100
2	1.020	1.040	1.061	1.082	1.102	1.124	1.145	1.166	1.188	1.210
3	1.030	1.061	1.093	1.125	1.158	1.191	1.225	1.260	1.295	1.331
4	1.041	1.082	1.126	1.170	1.216	1.262	1.311	1.360	1.412	1.464
5	1.051	1.104	1.159	1.217	1.276	1.338	1.403	1.469	1.539	1.611
6	1.062	1.126	1.194	1.265	1.340	1.419	1.501	1.587	1.677	1.772
7	1.072	1.149	1.230	1.316	1.407	1.504	1.606	1.714	1.828	1.949
8	1.083	1.172	1.267	1.369	1.477	1.594	1.718	1.851	1.993	2.144
9	1.094	1.195	1.305	1.423	1.551	1.689	1.838	1.999	2.172	2.358
10	1.105	1.219	1.344	1.480	1.629	1.791	1.967	2.159	2.367	2.594
11	1.116	1.243	1.384	1.539	1.710	1.898	2.105	2.332	2.580	2.853
12	1.127	1.268	1.426	1.601	1.796	2.012	2.252	2.518	2.813	3.138
13	1.138	1.294	1.469	1.665	1.886	2.133	2.410	2.720	3.066	3.452
14	1.149	1.319	1.513	1.732	1.980	2.261	2.579	2.937	3.342	3.797
15	1.161	1.346	1.558	1.801	2.079	2.397	2.759	3.172	3.642	4.177

Letting IF (interest factor) $= (1 + i)^n$, equation 6–2 may be written as $V = P (IF)$. It is necessary only to go to an appropriate interest table to find the proper interest factor. The correct interest factor for the above illustration is found in Table 6–2. Look down the Year column to 5 and across to the appropriate number in the 4% column to find the interest factor—1.217. Then, using this interest factor, we find the compound value of the $1,000 after five years as

$$V = P(IF) = \$1,000(1.217) = \$1,217.$$

Notice that this is precisely the same figure that was obtained by the long method in Table 6–1.

PRESENT VALUE

Suppose you were offered the alternative of either $1,217 at the end of five years or X dollars today. There is no question but that the $1,217 will be paid in full (perhaps the payer is the United States government) and, having no current need for the money, you would deposit it in a savings association paying a 4 percent dividend. (Four percent is defined to be your "opportunity cost.") How small must X be to induce you to accept the promise of $1,217 five years hence?

Referring to Table 6–2, it is seen that the initial amount of $1,000 growing at 4 percent a year yields $1,217 at the end of five years. Hence, you should be indifferent in your choice between $1,000 today and $1,217 at the end of five years.

Finding present values (or discounting, as it is commonly called) is simply the reverse of compounding, and equation 6–2 can quite readily be transformed into a present value formula. Dividing both sides by $(1 + i)^n$ and dropping the subscript n from V_n, we have:

$$P = \frac{V}{(1 + i)^n} = V\left[\frac{1}{(1 + i)^n}\right] \qquad (6\text{--}3)$$

Tables have been constructed for the term in brackets for various values of i and n; Table 6–3 is an example. A more complete table, Table A-2, is found in Appendix A. For the illustrative case being considered, look down the 4% column to the fifth row. The figure shown there, 0.822,

Table 6–3   PRESENT VALUE OF $1

Year	1%	2%	3%	4%	5%	6%	7%	8%	9%	10%	12%	14%	15%
1	.990	.980	.971	.962	.952	.943	.935	.926	.917	.909	.893	.877	.870
2	.980	.961	.943	.925	.907	.890	.873	.857	.842	.826	.797	.769	.756
3	.971	.942	.915	.889	.864	.840	.816	.794	.772	.751	.712	.675	.658
4	.961	.924	.889	.855	.823	.792	.763	.735	.708	.683	.636	.592	.572
5	.951	.906	.863	.822	.784	.747	.713	.681	.650	.621	.567	.519	.497
6	.942	.888	.838	.790	.746	.705	.666	.630	.596	.564	.507	.456	.432
7	.933	.871	.813	.760	.711	.665	.623	.583	.547	.513	.452	.400	.376
8	.923	.853	.789	.731	.677	.627	.582	.540	.502	.467	.404	.351	.327
9	.914	.837	.766	.703	.645	.592	.544	.500	.460	.424	.361	.308	.284
10	.905	.820	.744	.676	.614	.558	.508	.463	.422	.386	.322	.270	.247

is the interest factor used to determine the present value of $1,217 payable in five years, discounted at 4 percent.

$$P = V\ (IF)$$
$$= \$1,217(0.822)$$
$$= \$1,000$$

COMPOUND VALUE OF AN ANNUITY

An annuity is defined as a series of payments of a fixed amount for a specified number of years. Each payment occurs at the end of the year.[1] For example, a promise to pay $1,000 a year for three years is a three-year annuity. If one were to receive such an annuity and were to deposit each annual payment in a savings account paying 4 percent interest, how much would he have at the end of three years? The answer is shown graphically in Figure 6–1. The first payment is made at the end of year 1, the second at the end of year 2, and so on. The last payment is not compounded at all; the next to the last is compounded for one year; the second from the last for two years; and so on back to the first, which is compounded for $n-1$ years.

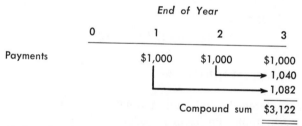

Figure 6–1. **Graphic Illustration of an Annuity: Compound Sum**

When the compound values of each of the payments are added, their total is the sum of the annuity. For the example, this total is $3,122.

Expressed algebraically, with S_n defined as the compound sum, R as the periodic receipts, and n as the length of the annuity, the formula for S_n is:

$$S_n = R_1(1+i)^{n-1} + R_2(1+i)^{n-2} + \ldots + R_{n-1}(1+i)^1 + R_n$$
$$= R\,[(1+i)^{n-1} + (1+i)^{n-2} + \ldots + (1+i)^1 + 1]$$
$$= R\,[IF]$$

[1] Had the payment been made at the beginning of the period, each receipt would simply have been shifted back one year. The annuity would have been called an *annuity due;* the one in the present discussion, where payments are made at the end of each period, is called a *regular annuity* or, sometimes, a *deferred annuity.*

The expression in brackets has been given values for various combinations of n and i. An illustrative set of these annuity interest factors is given in Table 6–4; a more complete set may be found in Table A-3 in Appendix A. To find the answer to the three-year $1,000 annuity problem, simply

Table 6–4   SUM OF AN ANNUITY OF $1 FOR *N* YEARS

Year	1%	2%	3%	4%	5%	6%	7%	8%
1	1.000	1.000	1.000	1.000	1.000	1.000	1.000	1.000
2	2.010	2.020	2.030	2.040	2.050	2.060	2.070	2.080
3	2.030	3.060	3.091	3.122	3.152	3.184	3.215	3.246
4	4.060	4.122	4.184	4.246	4.310	4.375	4.440	4.506
5	5.101	5.204	5.309	5.416	5.526	5.637	5.751	5.867
6	6.152	6.308	6.468	6.633	6.802	6.975	7.153	7.336
7	7.214	7.434	7.662	7.898	8.142	8.394	8.654	8.923
8	8.286	8.583	8.892	9.214	9.549	9.897	10.260	10.637
9	9.369	9.755	10.159	10.583	11.027	11.491	11.978	12.488
10	10.462	10.950	11.464	12.006	12.578	13.181	13.816	14.487

turn to Table 6–4, look down the 4% column to the row for the third year, and multiply the factor 3.122 by $1,000. The answer is the same as the one derived by the long method illustrated in Figure 6–1.

$$S_n = R \times IF$$
$$= \$1,000 \times 3.122 = \$3,122 \qquad (6\text{–}4)$$

PRESENT VALUE OF AN ANNUITY

Suppose you were offered the following alternatives: a three-year annuity of $1,000 a year or a lump-sum payment today. You have no need for the money during the next three years, so if you accept the annuity you would simply deposit the receipts in a savings account paying 4 percent interest. How large must the lump-sum payment be to make it equivalent to the annuity? Again, a graphic illustration will help explain the problem.

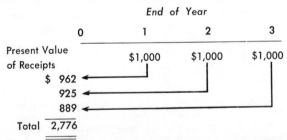

Figure 6–2.   Graphic Illustration of an Annuity: Present Value

The present value of the first receipt is $R\left[\dfrac{1}{1+i}\right]$; the second is $R\left[\dfrac{1}{1+i}\right]^2$; and so on. Defining the present value of an annuity of n years as A_n, we may write the following equation:

$$A_n = R\left[\frac{1}{1+i}\right]^1 + R\left[\frac{1}{1+i}\right]^2 + \ldots + R\left[\frac{1}{1+i}\right]^n$$

$$= R\left[\frac{1}{(1+i)} + \frac{1}{(1+i)^2} + \ldots + \frac{1}{(1+i)^n}\right]$$

$$= R\,[IF] \tag{6--5}$$

Again, tables have been worked out for the interest factor, the term in the brackets. Table 6–5 is illustrative; a more complete table is found in Table A-4 in Appendix A. From this table the IF for a three-year 4 percent annuity is found to be 2.775. Multiplying this factor by the $1,000 annual receipt gives $2,775, the present value of the annuity. This figure departs from the long-method answer shown in Figure 6–2 only by a rounding difference.

$$A_n = R \times IF$$
$$= \$1,000 \times 2.775$$
$$= \$2,775 \tag{6--6}$$

Table 6–5   PRESENT VALUES OF AN ANNUITY OF $1

Year	1%	2%	3%	4%	5%	6%	7%	8%	9%	10%
1	0.990	0.980	0.971	0.962	0.952	0.943	0.935	0.926	0.917	0.909
2	1.970	1.942	1.913	1.886	1.859	1.833	1.808	1.783	1.759	1.736
3	2.941	2.884	2.829	2.775	2.723	2.673	2.624	2.577	2.531	2.487
4	3.902	3.808	3.717	3.630	3.546	3.465	3.387	3.312	3.240	3.170
5	4.853	4.713	4.580	4.452	4.329	4.212	4.100	3.993	3.890	3.791
6	5.795	5.601	5.417	5.242	5.076	4.917	4.766	4.623	4.486	4.355
7	6.728	6.472	6.230	6.002	5.786	5.582	5.389	5.206	5.033	4.868
8	7.652	7.325	7.020	6.733	6.463	6.210	6.971	5.747	5.535	5.335
9	8.566	8.162	7.786	7.435	7.108	6.802	6.515	6.247	5.985	5.759
10	9.471	8.983	8.530	8.111	7.722	7.360	7.024	6.710	6.418	6.145

ANNUAL PAYMENTS FOR ACCUMULATION OF A FUTURE SUM

Suppose we want to know the amount that must be deposited at 5 percent for each of the next five years in order to have $10,000 available to pay off a debt at the end of the fifth year. Dividing both sides of equation 6–4 by IF, we get

$$R = \frac{S_n}{IF}$$

Looking up the interest factor for five years at 5 percent in Table 6–4 and dividing this figure into $10,000, we get

$$R = \frac{\$10,000}{5.526} = \$1,810$$

Thus, if $1,810 is deposited each year in an account paying 5 percent interest, at the end of five years the account will have accumulated $10,000.

ANNUAL RECEIPTS FROM AN ANNUITY

Suppose that on September 1, 1968, you receive an inheritance of $7,000. The money is to be used for your education and is to be spent during the academic years beginning September 1969, 1970, and 1971. If you place the money in a bank account paying 4 percent annual interest and make three equal withdrawals at each of the specified dates, how large can each withdrawal be to leave you with exactly a zero balance after the last one has been made?

The solution requires application of the present value of an annuity formula, equation 6–6. Here, however, we know that the present value of the annuity is $7,000, and the problem is to find the three equal annual payments when the interest rate is 4 percent. This calls for dividing both sides of equation 6–6 by IF to make equation 6–7.

$$A_n = R(IF) \tag{6–6}$$

$$R = \frac{A_n}{IF} \tag{6–7}$$

The interest factor (*IF*) is found in Table 6–5 to be 2.775, and substituting this value into equation 6–7 we find the three equal annual withdrawals to be $2,523 a year:

$$R = \frac{\$7,000}{2.775} = \$2,523$$

This particular type of calculation is used frequently in setting up insurance and pension plan benefit schedules, and it is also used to find the periodic payments necessary to retire a loan within a specified period. For example, if you wanted to retire a $7,000 bank loan drawing interest at 4 percent on the unpaid balance in three equal installments, each payment would be $2,523. In this case, you would be the borrower and the bank would be "buying" an annuity with a present value of $7,000.

PRESENT VALUE OF AN UNEVEN SERIES OF RECEIPTS

Recall that the definition of an annuity includes the words *fixed amount*—in other words, annuities deal with constant, or level, payments or receipts. Although many financial decisions do involve constant payments, many important decisions are concerned with uneven flows of cash. In particular, the kinds of fixed asset investments dealt with in the following chapter very frequently involve uneven flows. Consequently, it is necessary to expand the present analysis to deal with varying payment streams. Since most of the applications call for present values, not compound sums or other figures, this section is restricted to the present value.

To illustrate the calculating procedure, suppose someone offered to sell you a series of payments consisting of $300 after one year, $100 after two years, and $200 after three years. How much would you be willing to pay for the series, assuming the appropriate discount rate (interest rate) is 4 percent? To determine the purchase price, simply compute the present value of the series; the calculations are worked out in Table 6–6 below.

Table 6–6   CALCULATING THE PRESENT VALUE OF AN UNEVEN SERIES OF PAYMENTS

Year	Receipt	×	Interest Factor	=	Present Value
1	$300		.962		$288.60
2	100		.925		92.50
3	200		.889		177.80
			Present value of investment		$558.90

The receipts for each year are shown in the second column; the discount factors (from Table 6–3) are given in the third column; and the product of these two columns, the present value of each individual receipt, is given in the last column. When the individual present values in the last column are added, the sum is the present value of the investment, $558.90. Under the assumptions of the example, you should be willing to pay this amount for the investment.

Had the series of payments been somewhat different—say $300 at the end of the first year, then nine annual payments of $100 each—we would probably want to use a different procedure for finding the investment's present value. We could, of course, set up a calculating table, such as Table 6–6, but the fact that most of the payments are part of an annuity permits us to use a short cut. The calculating procedure is shown in Table 6–7, and the logic of the table is diagrammed in Figure 6–3.

Table 6–7   CALCULATING PROCEDURE FOR AN UNEVEN SERIES OF PAYMENTS THAT INCLUDES AN ANNUITY

1) P.V. of $300 due in 1 year: $300(0.962)	$ 288.60
2) P.V. of 9-year annuity with $100 receipts:	
a) P.V. at beginning of next year.	
$100(7.435) = $743.50	
b) P.V. of $743.50: $743.50(0.962)	715.25
3) P.V. of total series	$1,003.85

Section 1 of the table deals with the $300 received at the end of the first year; its present value is found to be $288.60. Section 2 deals with the nine $100 payments. In part (a) the value of a $100, nine year, 4 percent annuity is found to be $743.50. However, the annuity does not start until *next* year, so it is worth less than $743.50 today. Specifically, it is worth the present value of $743.50, discounted back one year at 4 percent, or $715.25; this calculation is shown in part (b) of section 2. When the present value of the initial payment is added to the present value of the annuity component, the sum is the present value of the entire investment, or $1,003.85. The logic of the calculations is diagrammed in Figure 6–3.

SEMIANNUAL AND OTHER COMPOUNDING PERIODS

In all the examples used thus far it has been assumed that returns were received once a year, or annually. For example, in the first section of the chapter, dealing with compound values, it was assumed that funds were placed on deposit in a savings and loan association and grew by 4 percent a year. However, suppose the advertised rate had been 4 percent compounded *semiannually*. What would this have meant? Consider the following example.

END OF YEAR

0	1	2	3	4	5	6	7	8	9	10
Present	300	100	100	100	100	100	100	100	100	100

Values
$288.60 ◄─┘
    $743.50 ◄───────┘
    715.25 ◄───┘
$1,003.85

Figure 6-3 Graphic Illustration of Present Value Calculations

A person deposits $1,000 in a bank savings account and receives a return of 4 percent compounded semiannually. How much will he have at the end of one year? Semiannual compounding means that interest is actually paid each six months, a fact taken into account in the tabular calculations in Table 6–8. Here the annual interest rate is divided by two, but

Table 6–8 COMPOUND INTEREST CALCULATIONS WITH SEMIANNUAL COMPOUNDING

Period	Beginning Amount (P)	times	(1 + i)	Ending Amount
1	$1,000.00	×	(1.02)	$1,020.00
2	1,020.00	×	(1.02)	1,040.40

twice as many compounding periods are used because interest is paid twice a year. Comparing the amount on hand at the end of the second six-month period, $1,040.40, with what would have been on hand under annual compounding, $1,040, shows that semiannual compounding is better from the standpoint of the saver. This result occurs, of course, because he earns interest on interest more frequently.

General formulas can be developed for use when compounding periods are more frequent than once a year. To demonstrate this, equation 6–2 is modified as follows:

$$V_n = P(1 + i)^n \tag{6-2}$$

$$V_n = P\left(1 + \frac{i}{m}\right)^{mn} \tag{6-8}$$

Here m is the number of times per year compounding occurs. When banks compute daily interest, the value of m is set at 365 and equation 6–8 is applied.

The tables can be used when compounding occurs more than once a year. Simply divide the nominal, or stated, interest rate by the number of times compounding occurs, and multiply the years by the number of compounding periods per year. For example, to find the amount to which $1,000 will grow after five years if semiannual compounding is applied to a stated 4 percent interest rate, divide 4 percent by 2 and multiply the five years by 2. Then look in Table 6–2 (or Appendix Table A-1) under the 2 percent column and the row for the 10th year. You find an interest factor of 1.219. Multiplying this by the initial $1,000 gives a value of $1,219, the amount to which $1,000 will grow in five years at 4 percent compounded semiannually. This compares with $1,217 for annual compounding.

The same procedure is applied in all the cases covered—compounding, discounting, single payments, and annuities. To illustrate semiannual compounding in finding the present value of an annuity, for example, consider the case described in the Present Value of an Annuity section above—$1,000 a year for three years, discounted at 4 percent. With annual compounding (or discounting) the interest factor is 2.775, and the present value of the annuity is $2,775. For semiannual compounding look under the 2% column and 6-year row of Table 6–5, to find an interest factor of 5.601. This is now multiplied by half of $1,000, or the $500 deposited each six months, to get the present value of the annuity—$2,800. The payments come a little more rapidly—the first $500 is paid after only six months (similarly with other payments) so the annuity is a little more valuable if payments are received semiannually rather than annually.

APPROPRIATE INTEREST RATE

Throughout the chapter an assumed interest rate has been used in the examples. Before closing, however, it is necessary to give some idea of what the appropriate interest rate for a particular investment might be.

The starting point is, of course, the general level of interest rates in the economy as a whole. This level is set by the interaction of supply-and-demand forces, with demand for funds coming largely from businesses, individual borrowers, and, when it is running a deficit, the federal government. Funds are supplied by individual and corporate savers and, under the control of the Federal Reserve System, by the creation of money by banks. Depending on the relative levels of supply and demand, the basic pattern of interest rates is determined.

There is no one rate of interest in the economy—rather, there is, at any given time, an array of different rates. The lowest rates are found on the safest investments, the highest rates on the most risky ones. Usually, there is less risk on investments that mature in the near future than on longer term investments, so generally higher rates are associated with long-term investments. There are other factors that affect interest rate differentials (also called "yield" differentials), but a discussion of these factors is best deferred until later in the book.

A person faced with the kinds of decisions considered in this chapter must accept the existing set of interest rates found in the economy. If he has money to invest, he can invest in short-term United States government securities and incur no risk whatever. However, he will generally have to accept a relatively low yield on his investment. If he is willing to accept a little more risk, he can invest in high-grade corporate bonds and get a higher fixed rate of return. If he is willing to accept still more risk, he can move into common stocks to obtain variable (and hopefully higher) returns (dividends plus capital gains) on his investment. Other alternatives include bank and savings and loan deposits, long-term governments, mortgages, apartment houses, and so on.

Risk Premiums

With only a limited amount of money to invest, one must pick and choose among investments, and the final selection will involve a choice between risk and returns. Suppose, for example, that you are indifferent between a five-year government bond yielding 4 percent a year, a five-year corporate bond yielding 5 percent, and a share of stock on which you can expect to receive a 6 percent return. Given this situation, you can take the government bond as a riskless security, and you attach a 1 percent risk premium to the corporate bond and a 2 percent risk premium to the share of stock. Risk premiums, then, are the added returns that risky investments must command over the less risky ones.

Opportunity Costs

Although there are very many potential investments available in the economy, at any given time a particular individual actively considers only a limited number of them. After making adjustments for risk differentials, he ranks the various alternatives from the most attractive to the least. Then, presumably, our investor puts his available funds in the most attractive investment. If he is offered a new investment, he must compare it with the best of the existing alternatives. If he takes the new investment, he must give up the opportunity of investing in the best of his old alternatives. *The yield on the best of the alternatives is defined as the opportunity cost of investing in the new alternative.* The interest rates used in the preceding examples were all determined as opportunity costs available to the person in the example. This concept is also used in the following chapter, where we consider business decisions to invest in fixed assets, or the *capital budgeting decision.*

SUMMARY

A knowledge of compound interest and present value techniques is essential to an understanding of many important aspects of finance—capital budgeting, financial structure, security valuation, and many other topics. The basic principles of compound interest, together with the most important formulas used in practice, were described in this chapter.

Compound Value

Compound value (V_n), or compound amount, is defined as the sum to which a beginning amount of principal (P) will grow over n years when interest is earned at the rate of i percent a year. The equation for finding compound values is given here.

$$V_n = P(1 + i)^n$$

Tables giving the present value of $1 for a large number of different years and interest rates have been prepared. The present value of $1 is called the interest factor (IF); illustrative values are given in Table 6–2, and a more complete set of interest factors is given in Appendix Table A–1.

Present Value

The present value of a future payment (P) is the amount which, if we had it now and invested it at the specified interest rate (i), would equal the future payment (S) on the date the future payment is due. For example, if one is to receive $1,217 after five years and decides that 4 percent is the appropriate interest rate (it is called "discount" rate when computing present values), then he could find the present value of the $1,217 to be $1,000 by applying the following equation:

$$P = S \left[\frac{1}{(1 + i)^n} \right] = \$1,217 \ [0.822] = \$1,000$$

The term in brackets is called the present value interest factor (IF), and values for it have been worked out in Tables 6–3 and A–2.

Compound Value of an Annuity

An annuity is defined as a series of payments of a fixed amount (R) for a specified number of years. The compound value of an annuity is the total amount one would have at the end of the annuity period if each payment was invested at a certain interest rate and held to the end of the annuity period. For example, suppose we have a three-year $1,000 annuity invested at 4 percent. There are formulas for annuities, but tables are available for the relevant interest factors. The IF for the compound value of a three-year annuity at 4 percent is 3.122, and it can be used to find the present value of the illustrative annuity:

$$\text{compound value} = IF \times \text{annual receipt} = 3.122 \times \$1,000 = \$3,122$$

Thus, $3,122 is the compound value of the annuity.

Present Value of an Annuity

The present value of an annuity is the lump sum one would need to have on hand today in order to be able to withdraw equal amounts (R) each year and end up with a balance exactly equal to zero at the end of the annuity period. For example, if one wanted to withdraw $1,000 a year for three years, he could deposit $2,775 today in a bank account paying 4 percent interest, withdraw the $1,000 in each of the next three years, and end up with a zero balance. Thus, $2,775 is the present value of an annuity of $1,000 per year for three years when the appropriate discount rate is 4 percent. Again, tables are available for finding the present value of annuities. To use them, one simply looks up the interest factor (IF) for the appropriate number of years and interest rate, then multiplies the IF by the annual receipt.

$$\text{present value of annuity} = IF \times \text{annual receipt} = 2.775 \times \$1,000 = \$2,775$$

Relation of Interest Factors to One Another

All interest factors (IF) given in the tables are for $1; for example, 2.775 is the IF for finding the present value of a three-year annuity. It must be multiplied by the annual receipt, $1,000 in the example, to find the actual value of the annuity. Students—and even financial managers—sometimes make careless mistakes when looking up interest factors, using the wrong table for the purpose. This can be avoided if one recognizes the following sets of relations.

Compound value, single payment. The IF for the compound value of a single payment, with the normal interest rates and holding periods generally found, is *always* greater than 1.0 but seldom larger than about 3.0.

Present value, single payment. The IF for the present value of a single payment is *always* smaller than 1.0; for example, 0.822 is the present value IF for 4 percent held for five years. The *compound* value IF is larger than 1.0; the *present* value IF is smaller than 1.0.

Compound value of an annuity. The IF for the compound value of an annuity is *always* larger than the number of years the annuity has to run. For example, the IF for a three-year annuity will be larger than 3.0, while the IF for a 10-year annuity will be larger than 10.0. Just how much larger depends on the interest rate—at low rates the interest factor is slightly larger than N; at high rates it is very much larger.

Present value of an annuity. The IF for the present value of an annuity is smaller than the number of years it has to run. For example, the IF for the present value of a three-year annuity is less than 3.0.

Other Uses of the Basic Equations

The four basic interest formulas can be used in combination to find such things as the present value of an uneven series of receipts. The formulas can also be transformed to find (1) the annual payments necessary to accumulate a future sum and (2) the annual receipts from a specified annuity.

Appropriate Interest Rate

The appropriate interest rate to use is critical when working with compound interest problems. The true nature of the interest rates to be used when working with business problems can be understood only after the chapters dealing with the cost of capital have been examined; this chapter concluded with a brief discussion of some of the factors that determine the appropriate rate of interest for a particular problem—the risk of the investment and the investor's opportunity cost of money.

QUESTIONS

6–1 What types of financial decisions require explicit consideration of the interest factor?

6–2 Compound interest relations are important for decisions other than financial ones. Why are they important to marketing managers?

6–3 Would you rather have an account in a savings and loan association that pays 5 percent interest compounded semiannually or 5 percent interest compounded daily? Why?

6–4 For a given interest rate and a given number of years, is the interest factor for the sum of an annuity larger or smaller than the interest factor for the present value of the annuity?

6–5 Suppose you are examining two investments, A and B. Both have the same maturity, but A pays a 6 percent return and B yields 5 percent. Which investment is probably riskier? How do you know it is riskier?

PROBLEMS

6–1 At a growth rate of 8 percent, how long does it take a sum to double?

6–2 Which amount is worth more at 5 percent: $1,000 today or $1,400 after 7 years?

6–3 On December 30, Philip P. Potter buys a building for $20,000, payable 10 percent down and the balance in twenty-five equal annual installments that are to include principal plus 6 percent compound interest on the declining balance. What are the equal installments?

6–4 a) What amount would be paid for a $1,000 10-year bond that pays $25 interest semiannually ($50 a year) and is sold to yield 6 percent, compounded semiannually?

b) What would be paid if the bond is sold to yield 4 percent?

c) What would be paid if semiannual interest payments are $30 and the bond is sold to yield 10 percent?

6–5 The Westwood Company is establishing a sinking fund to retire a $200,000 mortgage which matures on December 31, 1978. The company plans to put a fixed amount into the fund each year for 10 years. The first payment will be made on December 31, 1969, the last on December 31, 1978. The company anticipates that the fund will earn 5 percent a year. What annual contributions must be made to accumulate the $200,000 as of December 31, 1978?

6–6 You are considering two investment opportunities, A and B. A is expected to pay $100 a year for the first 10 years, $200 a year for the next 20 years, and nothing thereafter. B is expected to pay $400 a year for 11 years, and nothing thereafter. You find that alternative investments of similar risk yield 3 percent and 7 percent for A and B respectively.

a) Find the present value of each investment. Show calculations.

b) Which is the more risky investment? Why?

c) Assume that your rich uncle will give you your choice of investments without cost to you, and that (i) you must hold the investment for its entire life (cannot sell it) or (ii) you are free to sell it at its going market price. Which investment would you prefer under each of the two conditions?

Chapter 7

Capital Budgeting

Capital budgeting involves the entire process of planning expenditures whose returns are expected to extend beyond one year. The choice of one year is arbitrary, of course, but it is a convenient cutoff time for distinguishing between types of expenditures. Obvious examples of capital outlays are expenditures for land, buildings, and equipment. Also, an advertising or a promotion campaign or a program of research and development is likely to have an impact beyond one year, hence, come within the classification of a capital budgeting expenditure.[1]

It is not the purpose of this definition to set up artificial boundaries or criteria for particular kinds of outlays. The basis for the distinction is a practical one. When outlays are made and the results continue over an extended period, several implications of considerable importance for the firm follow.

---

[1] Though this discussion is focused on capital budgeting related to expenditures on fixed assets, the theory and techniques are equally applicable to all kinds of asset investments by business. Therefore, while the authors follow traditional practices of relating capital budgeting to investment in fixed assets, it should be remembered that the techniques discussed are applicable to all types of management decisions. In concept, investments in cash, receivables, or inventory must be justified by earning a satisfactory return on these asset items.

SIGNIFICANCE OF CAPITAL BUDGETING

A number of factors combine to make capital budgeting one of the most important areas of strategic decision making with which financial management is involved. First and foremost, the fact that the results continue over an extended period means that the decision maker loses some of his flexibility. He must make a commitment into the future. For example, the purchase of an asset with an economic life of 10 years requires a long period of waiting before the final results of the action can be known. The decision maker must commit funds for this period and, thus, become a hostage of future events.

Asset expansion is fundamentally related to expected future sales. A decision to buy or to construct a fixed asset that is going to last five years involves an implicit five-year sales forecast. Indeed, the economic life of an asset purchased represents an implicit forecast for the duration of the economic life of the asset. Hence, failure to forecast accurately will result in overinvestment or underinvestment in fixed assets.

An erroneous forecast of asset needs can result in serious consequences for a firm. If the firm has invested too much in assets, it will be incurring unnecessarily heavy expenses. If it has not spent enough on fixed assets, two serious consequences may arise. First, its equipment may not be sufficiently modern to enable it to produce competitively. Second, if it has inadequate capacity, it may lose a portion of its share of the market to rival firms. To regain lost customers characteristically requires heavy selling expenses or price reductions, or both.

Another problem is to properly phase the availability of capital assets. For example, the executive vice-president of a decorative-tile company recently gave the authors an illustration of the importance of capital budgeting. His firm tried to operate near capacity most of the time. For about four years there had been intermittent spurts in the demand for its product, and when these spurts occurred, the firm had to turn away orders. After a sharp increase in demand, the firm would add capacity by renting an additional building, then purchasing and installing the appropriate equipment; it would take six to eight months to have the additional capacity ready. At his point the company would find that there was no demand for its increased output—other firms had already expanded their operations and had taken an increased share of the market, with the result that demand for this firm had leveled off. If the firm had properly forecast demand and had planned its increase in capacity six months or one year in advance, it would have been able to maintain its market—indeed, to obtain a larger share of the market.

Good capital budgeting will also improve the timing of asset acquisitions and the quality of assets purchased. This situation follows from the nature of capital goods and of their producers. Capital goods are not ordered by firms until they see that sales are going to press on capacity. Such occasions occur simultaneously for many firms. When the heavy orders come in, the producers of capital goods go from a situation of idle capacity to one where they cannot meet all the orders that have been placed. Consequently, large backlogs of orders accumulate. Since the production of capital goods involves a relatively long work in process period, a year or more of waiting may be involved before the additional capital goods are available. This factor has obvious implications for purchasing agents and plant managers.

Another reason for the importance of capital budgeting is that asset expansion typically involves substantial expenditures. When a firm is going to spend a considerable amount of money, it must make the proper plans—large amounts of funds are not available automatically. A firm contemplating a major capital expenditure program may need to arrange its financing several years in advance to be sure of having the funds required for the expansion.

Finally, it has been said with a great deal of truth that many firms fail not because they have too much capital equipment but because they have too little. While the conservative approach of having a small amount of capital equipment may be appropriate at times, such an approach may also be fatal if a firm's competitors install modern, automated equipment that permits them to produce a better product and sell it at a lower price.

AN OVER-ALL VIEW OF CAPITAL BUDGETING

Capital budgeting is, in essence, an application of a classic proposition from the economic theory of the firm: namely, a firm should operate at the point where its marginal revenue is just equal to its marginal cost. When this rule is applied to the capital budgeting decision, marginal revenue is taken to be the percentage rate of return on investments, while marginal cost is the firm's cost of capital.

A simplified version of the concept is depicted in Figure 7–1. Here the horizontal axis measures the dollars of investment during a year, while the vertical axis shows both the percentage cost of capital and the rate of return on projects. The projects are denoted by the boxes—project A, for example, calls for an outlay of $3 million and promises a 17 percent rate of return; project B requires $1 million and yields about 16 percent; and

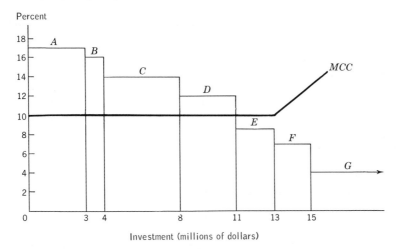

Figure 7-1   Illustrative Capital Budgeting Decision Process

so on. The last investment, project G, simply involves buying 4 percent government bonds, which may be purchased in unlimited quantities.

The curve *MCC* designates the marginal cost of capital, or the cost of each additional dollar acquired for purposes of making capital expenditures.[2] As it is drawn in this hypothetical illustration, the cost of capital is constant at 10 percent until the firm has raised $13 million, after which it turns up. To maximize profits, the firm should accept projects A through D, obtaining and investing $11 million, and should reject E, F, and G.

At the applied level, the process is considerably more complex than this simple example would suggest. Projects do not just appear; a continuing stream of good investment opportunities results from hard thinking, careful planning, and often, large outlays for research and development. In addition, some very difficult measurement problems are involved; the sales and costs associated with particular projects must be estimated, frequently for many years into the future. Last, some difficult conceptual problems arise over the methods of calculating rates of return and the cost of capital.

Businessmen are required to take action, however, even in the face of the kinds of problems described, and this requirement has led to the development of procedures that assist in making optimal investment decisions. One of these procedures, forecasting, has been discussed in Chapter 5, while the important subject of the cost of capital is deferred to

---

[2] The cost of capital concept is discussed at length in Chapter 10.

Chapter 10. The essentials of the other elements of capital budgeting are taken up in the remainder of this chapter.

Investment Proposals

Aside from the actual generation of ideas, the first step in the capital budgeting process is to assemble the proposed new investments, together with the data necessary to appraise them. Although practices vary from firm to firm, proposals dealing with asset acquisitions are frequently grouped according to the following categories:

1. Replacements
2. Expansion: additional capacity in existing product lines
3. Expansion: new product lines
4. Other

These groupings are somewhat arbitrary, and it is frequently difficult to decide the appropriate category for a particular investment. In spite of such problems, the scheme is used quite widely and, as shall be seen, with good reason.

Ordinarily, replacement decisions are the simplest to make. Assets wear out and become obsolete, and they must be replaced if production is to continue. The firm has a very good idea of the cost savings to be obtained by replacing an old asset, and it knows the consequences of nonreplacement. All in all, the outcomes of most replacement decisions can be predicted with a high degree of confidence.

An example of the second investment classification is a proposal for adding more machines of the type already in use or the opening of another branch in a city-wide chain of food stores. Expansion investments are frequently incorporated in replacement decisions. To illustrate, an old, inefficient machine may be replaced by a larger and more efficient one.

A degree of uncertainty—sometimes extremely high—is clearly involved in expansion, but the firm at least has the advantage of examining past production and sales experience with similar machines or stores. When it considers an investment of the third kind, expansion into new product lines, little if any experience data are available on which to base decisions. To illustrate, when General Motors decided to develop the diesel engine for commercial application, it had very little idea of either the development costs or the specific applications to which the engine could be put. Under such circumstances, any estimates must at best be treated as very crude approximations.

The "other" category is a catchall and includes intangibles; an example is a proposal to boost employee morale by installing a music system.

Major strategic decisions such as plans for overseas expansion or mergers might also be included here, but more frequently they are treated separately from the regular capital budget.

Administrative Details

The remaining aspects of capital budgeting involve administrative matters. Approvals are typically required at higher levels within the organization as we move away from replacement decisions and as the sums involved increase. One of the most important functions of the board of directors is to approve the major outlays in a capital budgeting program. Such decisions are crucial for the future well-being of the firm.

The planning horizon for capital budgeting programs varies with the nature of the industry. When sales can be forecast with a high degree of reliability for 10 to 20 years, the planning period is likely to be correspondingly long; electric utilities are an example of such an industry. Also, when the product-technology developments in the industry require an 8-to-10-year cycle to develop a new major product, as in certain segments of the aerospace or the electronics industries, a correspondingly long planning period is necessary.

After a capital budget has been adopted, payments must be scheduled. Characteristically, the finance department is responsible for scheduling payments and for acquiring funds to meet payment schedule requirements. In addition, the finance department will be primarily responsible for cooperating with other members of operating divisions to compile systematic records on the uses of funds and the uses of equipment purchased in capital budgeting programs. Effective capital budgeting programs require such information as the basis for periodic review and the evaluation of capital expenditures.

The foregoing represents a brief overview of the administrative aspects of capital budgeting; the analytical problems involved are considered next.

CHOOSING AMONG ALTERNATIVE PROPOSALS

In most firms there are more proposals for projects than the firm is able or willing to finance. Some proposals are good, others are poor, and methods must be developed for distinguishing between them. Essentially, the end product is a ranking of the proposals and a cutoff point for determining how far down the ranked list to go.

In part, proposals are eliminated because they are *mutually exclusive.*

Mutually exclusive proposals are alternative methods of doing the same job. If one piece of equipment is chosen to do the job, the others will not be required. Thus, if there is a need to improve the materials handling system in a chemical plant, the job may be done either by conveyer belts or by fork trucks. The selection of one method of doing the job makes it unnecessary to use the others. They are mutually exclusive items.

Independent items are pieces of capital equipment that are being considered for different kinds of projects or tasks that need to be accomplished. For example, in addition to the materials handling system, the chemical firm may need equipment to package and to measure the end items. The work would require a packaging machine, and the purchase of equipment for this purpose would be independent of the equipment purchased for materials handling.

To distinguish among the many items that compete for the allocation of the firm's capital funds, a ranking procedure must be developed. This procedure involves, first, calculating the estimated benefits from the use of equipment and, second, translating the estimated benefits into a measure of the advantage of the purchase of the equipment. Thus, an estimate of benefits is required, and a conversion of the benefits into a ranking measure must be developed.

IMPORTANCE OF GOOD DATA

Most discussions of measuring benefits are relatively brief, but it is important to emphasize *that in the entire capital budgeting procedure, probably nothing is of greater importance than a reliable estimate of the cost savings or revenue increases that will be achieved from the prospective outlay of capital funds.* But these estimates are likely to be more closely related to the facts of particular situations than they are subject to generalizations.

The nature of the task of calculating savings from a proposed investment is indicated by a brief consideration of the items that may affect benefits; examples are changes in quality and quantity of direct labor, in amount and cost of scrap and rework time, and in maintenance expenses, down time, safety, flexibility, and so on. So many variables are involved that it is obviously impossible to make neat generalizations. However, this should not minimize the crucial importance of the required analysis of the benefits derived from capital expenditures. Each capital equipment expenditure must be examined in detail for possible additional costs and additional savings.

All the subsequent procedures for ranking projects are no better than the data input. Above all, the data formulation requires good judgment in expressing the amount of the benefits. This is not a routine clerical task to be performed on a mechanical basis. It requires continuous monitoring and evaluation of estimates by individuals competent to make such evaluations: engineers, accountants, economists, cost analysts, and other qualified persons.

After the estimates of costs and benefits have been made, they are utilized for ranking alternative investment proposals. How this grading is accomplished is the next topic.

RANKING INVESTMENT PROPOSALS

Among the many methods for ranking investment proposals, three are discussed here. The first, payback, is included because it is so widely used; it is not, however, a conceptually sound method. The other two procedures are included because they are conceptually sound.[3] The name and a brief description of each are set forth below. *Future returns are, in all cases, defined as the net proceeds before depreciation but after taxes that result from a project. In other words, returns are synonymous with cash flows from investments.*

1. Payback method—number of years required to return the original investment.
2. Internal rate method—interest rate which equates the present value of future returns to the investment outlay.
3. Net present value method—present value of future returns discounted at the appropriate cost of capital minus the cost of the investment.

The nature and characteristics of the three methods are illustrated and explained. To make the explanations more meaningful, the same data are used to illustrate each method. Assume that two projects are being considered by a firm. Each requires an investment of $1,000. The firm's cost of capital is 10 percent.[4] The net returns from the equally risky investments A and B are as follows:

---

[3] There are also a number of "average rate of return" methods that are encountered in practice. We consider them all to be fundamentally unsound and have elected not to discuss them here.

[4] A discussion of how the cost of capital is calculated is presented in Chapter 10. At this point cost of capital should be considered as the firm's opportunity cost of making a particular investment.

Table 7–1   NET CASH FLOWS (profit after taxes plus depreciation)

Year	A	B
1	$500	$100
2	400	200
3	300	300
4	100	400
5		500
6		600

Payback Period

The *payback period* is the number of years it takes the firm to recover its original investment by net returns before depreciation but after
taxes. The payback period is two and one-third years for project A and
four years for project B. If the firm were employing a three-year payback
period, project A would be accepted but project B would be rejected.

Though the payback period is very easy to calculate, it can lead to
the wrong decisions. As the illustration demonstrates, it ignores income beyond the payback period. If the project is one maturing in later years, the
use of the payback period can lead to the selection of less desirable investments. Projects with longer payback periods are characteristically those
involved in long-range planning—developing a new product or tapping a
new market. These are just the strategic decisions which determine a firm's
fundamental position, but they also involve investments which do not yield
their highest returns for a number of years. This means that the payback
method may be biased against the very investments that are most important to a firm's long-run success.

In spite of its shortcomings, the payback method has been widely used
by American industry. A survey made by the Machinery and Allied Products Institute indicated that 60 percent of the surveyed firms use the payback period. On equipment with a service life of 10 years or more, 28
percent of those using the method set a three-year payback and 34 percent
set a five-year payback. Only 16 percent use a payoff period of more than
five years. Thus, the relatively belated initiation of effective long-range planning by American firms is probably related to the widespread use of the
payback period in analyzing alternative investments. Since its emphasis is
on the very short run, the payback method simply does not require inquiry
into the far-distant future.

Recognition of the longer period over which an investment is likely to
yield savings points up another weakness in the use of the payback method
for ranking investment proposals: its failure to take into account the interest factor. To illustrate, consider two assets each costing $300 and each
having the following cash flows:

Year	X	Y
1	200	100
2	100	200
3	100	100

Each project has a two-year payback; hence, each would appear equally desirable. However, we know that a dollar today is worth more than a dollar next year, so project X, with its faster cash flow, is certainly more desirable.

The use of the payback period is sometimes defended on the ground that returns beyond three or four years are fraught with such great uncertainty that it is best to disregard them altogether in a planning decision. However, this is clearly an unsound procedure. Some of the investments with highest returns are those which may not come to fruition for eight, nine, or ten years. The new product cycle in industries involving advanced technologies may not have a payoff for eight or nine years. Furthermore, even though returns that occur after three or four or five years are most uncertain, it is important to make a judgment about the likelihood of their occurring. To ignore them is to assign a zero probability to these distant receipts. This can hardly produce the best results.

A final defense of the payback method is that a firm which is short of cash must necessarily give great emphasis to a quick return of its funds so that they may be put to use in other places or in meeting other needs. It can only be said that this does not relieve the payback method of its many shortcomings, and that there are better methods for handling the cash shortage situation.[5]

Internal Rate of Return

As the flaws in the payback method were recognized, people began to search for methods of evaluating projects that would recognize that a dollar received immediately is preferable to a dollar received at some future date. The internal rate-of-return method is the first widely used procedure that takes this fact into account. The internal rate of return itself is defined as *the interest rate that equates the present value of the expected future receipts to the cost of the investment outlay.*

The internal rate of return must be found by trial and error. First, compute the present value of the cash flows from an investment, using an arbitrarily selected interest rate. Then compare the present value so ob-

---

[5] We interpret a cash shortage to mean that the firm has a high opportunity cost for its funds, and a high cost of capital. We would consider this high cost of capital in the following ranking procedures—the internal rate of return or the net present value method—and thus take account of the cash shortage.

tained with the investment's cost. If the present value is higher than the cost figure, try a higher interest rate and go through the procedure again. Conversely, if the present value is lower than the cost, lower the interest rate and repeat the process. Continue until the present value of the flows from the investment are approximately equal to its cost. *The interest rate that brings about this equality is defined as the internal rate of return.*[6]

This calculation process is illustrated in Table 7–2 for projects A and B. First, the 4 percent interest factors are obtained from Appendix Table A-1. These factors are then multiplied by the cash flows for the corresponding years, and the present values of the annual cash flows are placed in the appropriate columns. For example, the IF (interest factor) 0.96 is multiplied by $500, and the product, $480, is placed in the first row of column A.

The present values of the yearly cash flows are then summed to get the investment's total present value. Subtracting the cost of the project from this figure gives the net present value. As the net present values of both investments are positive at the 4 percent rate, increase the rate to 10 percent and try again. Once again the net present values are positive, so the rate is stepped up to 15 percent. *At this point the net present value of investment A is approximately zero, which indicates that its internal rate of return is approximately 15 percent. Continuing, B is found to have an internal rate of return of approximately 20 percent.*

Assuming that the firm uses a cost of capital of 10 percent, if the two projects are independent, both should be accepted. If they are mutually exclusive, B ranks higher and, thus, should be accepted, while A should be rejected.

What is so special about the particular interest rate that equates the cost of a project with the present value of its receipts? Suppose that a firm obtains all of its capital by borrowing from a bank, and that the interest cost of this debt is 6 percent. If the internal rate of return on a particular project is calculated to be 6 percent, the same as the cost of capital, then the firm would be able to invest in the project, use the cash flow generated by the investment to pay off the principal and interest on the bank loan, and come out exactly even on the transaction. If the internal rate of return exceeded 6 percent, the project would be profitable, while if the internal

---

[6] In order to reduce the number of trials required to find the internal rate of return, it is important to minimize the error at each iteration. One reasonable approach is to make as good a first approximation as possible, then to "straddle" the internal rate of return by making fairly large changes in the interest rate early in the iterative process. In practice, if many projects are to be evaluated or if long periods are involved, one would not work out the calculations by hand but would use a computer.

rate of return was less than 6 percent, taking on the project would result in losses. It is this characteristic that makes us interested in the internal rate of return.

Net Present Value Method

Another discounted cash flow technique for analyzing investment opportunities is called the net present value method, or sometimes simply the present value method. *To implement this approach, simply find the present value of the expected net cash flow of an investment, discounted at the cost of capital, and subtract from it the initial cost outlay of the project.*[7] If the net present value is positive, the project should be accepted; if negative, it should be rejected. If the two projects are mutually exclusive, the one with the higher net present value should be chosen.

If the assumption of a 10 percent cost of capital is continued, the net present values of our illustrative projects A and B have already been found. The second set of calculations in Table 7–2—that for a 10 percent interest factor—shows investment A to have a net present value of $80, B to have one of $400. On this basis, both should be accepted if they are independent, but B should be the one accepted if they are mutually exclusive, because its net present value is higher than A's.

Both discounted cash flow methods—the internal rate of return and net present value—meet the objections to the payback method. They consider all the revenues from a project, and they take account of the time value of money. Under ordinary circumstances, the two approaches give identical investment decisions.[8] Generally, we shall concentrate on the net present value method.

DETERMINING CASH FLOWS

Thus far the problem of measuring cash flows—the benefits used in the present value calculations above—has not been dealt with directly. This matter will now be discussed and a few simple examples given.

---

[7] If costs are spread over several years, this must be taken into account. Suppose, for example, that a firm bought land in 1965, erected a building in 1966, installed equipment in 1967, and started production in 1968. One could treat 1965 as the base year, comparing the present value of the costs as of 1965 to the present value of the benefit stream as of that same date.

[8] For a discussion of the differences between the net present value and internal rate-of-return methods, see J. Fred Weston and Eugene F. Brigham, *Managerial Finance, Second Edition* (New York: Holt, Rinehart and Winston, 1966), Chapter 7 and Appendix A.

Table 7-2 PRESENT VALUE CALCULATIONS

Investment = $1,000

Year	Cash Flow	
	A	B
1	$500	$100
2	400	200
3	300	300
4	100	400
5		500
6		600

4 Percent

Year	IF*	Present Value	
		A	B
1	0.96	480	96
2	0.92	368	184
3	0.89	267	267
4	0.86	86	344
5	0.82		410
6	0.79		474
Present value		1,201	1,775
Net P.V.		201	775

10 Percent

Year	IF*	Present Value	
		A	B
1	0.91	455	91
2	0.83	332	166
3	0.75	225	225
4	0.68	68	272
5	0.62		310
6	0.56		336
Present value		1,080	1,400
Net P.V.		80	400

15 Percent

Year	IF*	Present Value	
		A	B
1	0.87	435	87
2	0.76	304	152
3	0.66	198	198
4	0.57	57	228
5	0.50		250
6	0.43		258
Present value		994	1,173
Net P.V.		(6)	173

20 Percent

Year	IF*	Present Value	
		A	B
1	0.83	415	83
2	0.69	276	138
3	0.58	174	174
4	0.48	48	192
5	0.40		200
6	0.33		198
Present value		913	985
Net P.V.		(87)	(15)

24 Percent

Year	IF*	Present Value	
		A	B
1	0.81	405	81
2	0.65	260	130
3	0.52	156	156
4	0.42	42	168
5	0.34		170
6	0.28		168
Present value		863	873
Net P.V.		(137)	(127)

32 Percent

Year	IF*	Present Value	
		A	B
1	0.76	380	76
2	0.57	228	114
3	0.43	129	129
4	0.33	33	132
5	0.25		125
6	0.19		114
Present value		770	690
Net P.V.		(230)	(310)

Simplified Model for Determining Cash Flows

One way of considering the cash flows attributable to a particular investment is to think of them in terms of comparative income statements. This is illustrated in the following example.

The Widget Division of the Culver Company, a profitable, diversified manufacturing firm, purchased a machine five years ago at a cost of $7,500. The machine had an expected life of 15 years at time of purchase and a zero estimated salvage value at the end of the 15 years. It is being depreciated on a straight line basis and has a book value of $5,000 at present. The division manager reports that he can buy a new machine for $10,000 (including installation) which, over its 10-year life, will expand sales from $10,000 to $11,000. Further, it will reduce labor and raw materials usage sufficiently to cut operating costs from $7,000 to $5,000. The old machine's current market value is $1,000. Taxes are at a 50 percent rate and are paid quarterly, and the firm's cost of capital is 10 percent. Should Culver buy the new machine?

The decision calls for three steps: (1) estimate the actual cash outlay attributable to the new investment, (2) determine the present value of the incremental cash flows, and (3) see if the internal rate of return exceeds the cost of capital or if the net present value is positive. These steps are set forth below.

1. Estimated Cash Outlay. Culver must make a $10,000 payment to the manufacturer of the machine, but its next quarterly income tax bill will be reduced by $2,000. The tax reduction occurs because the old machine, which is carried at $5,000, will be written down by $4,000 ($5,000 less $1,000 salvage value) immediately if the new one is purchased. To illustrate, suppose the Culver Company's taxable income in the quarter in which the new machine is purchased would be $100,000 without the purchase of the new machine and the consequent write-off of the old machine. With a 50 percent tax rate, Culver would have to write a check for $50,000 to pay its tax bill. However, if it buys the new machine and sells the old one, it takes an operating loss of $4,000—the $5,000 book value on the old machine less the salvage value. (The loss is an operating loss, not a capital loss, because it is in reality simply recognizing that depreciation charges, an operating cost, were too low during the old machine's five-year life.) With this $4,000 additional operating cost, taxable income is reduced from $100,000 to $96,000, and the tax bill from $50,000 to $48,000. This means, of course that the firm's cash outflow for taxes is $2,000 less because it purchased the new machine. In addition, there is a cash inflow of $1,000 from the sale of the old machine. The result is that the purchase of the new machine involves a net cash outlay of $7,000; this is its cost for capital budgeting purposes.[9]

Invoice price of new machine	$10,000
Less: Tax savings	−2,000
Salvage of old machine	−1,000
Net cash outflow	$ 7,000

2. Present Value of Benefits. The first column in Table 7-3 shows the Widget Division's estimated income statement as it would be without the new machine; the second column shows the statement as it will look if the new investment is made. (It is assumed that these figures are applicable for each of the next 10 years; if this is not the case, then cash flow estimates

Table 7–3   COMPARATIVE INCOME STATEMENT FRAMEWORK FOR CONSIDERING CASH FLOWS

	Without New Investment	*With New Investment*
Sales	$10,000	$11,000
Operating costs	−7,000	−5,000
Depreciation	−500	−1,000
Taxable income	$ 2,500	$ 5,000
Income taxes	−1,250	−2,500
Profit after taxes	$ 1,250	$ 2,500
Cash flow $(P + D)$	$ 1,750	$ 3,500
Change in cash flow: $3,500 − $1,750 = $1,750		

Note: The effects of the sale of the old machine on the income statement are not considered here. These effects are accounted for in the estimate of the cash outlay for the new machine.

must be made for each year.) The difference between the new and the old cash flows, $1,750, is the incremental cash flow produced by the new machine; this is the benefit stream to be discounted at the cost of capital.

---

[9] It is also useful to point out at this time that when the investment tax credit is allowed, the outlay cost of new investments in machinery and equipment is reduced by the amount of the investment tax credit. In other words, if the asset has a cost of $1,000 and a depreciable life of at least eight years, the outlay cost will be reduced by a 7 percent tax credit, or by $70. This obviously raises the net present value over what it would otherwise be and thus stimulates investment. It is for this reason, of course, that Congress created the investment tax credit. When Congress feels the economy needs to be stimulated, the tax credit is put into force. When Congress feels that the economy is "overheated" and should be restrained, the credit is suspended. The tax credit has therefore been used as an instrument of fiscal policy.

The interest factor for a 10-year 10 percent annuity is found to be 6.145 from Appendix Table A-4. This factor, multiplied by the $1,750 incremental cash flow, shows the investment to have a present value of $10,754.

3. Net Present Value. Subtracting the $7,000 cost figure from the $10,754 gives the investment a net present value of $3,754. Since the net present value is positive, the new machine should be purchased.[10]

Worksheet for Replacement Decisions

Table 7-4 shows a worksheet for making replacement decision calculations. The top section of the table sets forth the cash outflows at the time the investment is made. All these flows occur immediately, so no discounting is required, and the present value factor is 1.0. No tax adjustment is necessary on the invoice price of the new machine, but, as we saw above, the $4,000 loss on the old machine gives rise to a $2,000 tax reduction, which is deducted from the price of the new machine. Also, the $1,000 salvage value on the old machine is treated as a reduction in cash outflows necessary to acquire the new machine. Notice that since the $1,000 is a recovery of capital investment it is not considered to be taxable income; hence, no tax adjustment is made for the salvage value.

In the lower section of the table we see that revenues increase by $3,000 a year—a sales increase of $1,000 plus a cost reduction of $2,000. However, this amount is taxable, so with a 50 percent tax the after-tax benefits are reduced to $1,500. This $1,500 is received each year for 10 years, so it is an annuity. The present value of the annuity, discounted at the 10 percent cost of capital, is $9,217.

Cash inflows also come from the depreciation on the new machine— $1,000 before, or $500 after, taxes. Again, this is a 10-year annuity, and its present value is $3,073. Observe that the depreciation on the old machine is *subtracted* from the inflows section. The logic here is that, had the replacement *not* been made, the company would have had the benefit of the $500 depreciation each year for the next 10 years. With the replacement, however, all this depreciation is taken as an operating loss immediately and is shown as the tax loss on sale in the upper section of the table.

Table 7-4 gives the same net present value, $3,754, as was derived under the comparative income statement approach. In general, the tabular approach is somewhat more convenient for use in the management decisions illustrated in the end-of-chapter problems.

---

[10] Alternatively, the internal rate of return on the project could have been computed and found to be 21 percent. Since this is substantially in excess of the 10 percent cost of capital, the internal rate-of-return method also indicates that the investment should be undertaken.

Table 7–4   CALCULATIONS FOR REPLACEMENT DECISIONS

	Amount before Tax	Amount after Tax	Year Event Occurs	Present Value Factor at 10%	Present Value
Outflows at time investment is made:					
Investment in					
new equipment	10,000	10,000	0	1.00	$10,000
Salvage value					
of old	(1,000)	(1,000)	0	1.00	(1,000)
Tax loss on sale	(4,000)	(2,000)	0	1.00	(2,000)
Total outflows (present value of costs)					$ 7,000
Inflows, or annual returns:					
Benefits*	3,000	1,500	1–10	6.145	9,217
Depreciation on					
new (annual)	1,000	500	1–10	6.145	3,073
Depreciation on					
old (annual)†	(500)	(250)	1–10	6.145	(1,536)
Salvage value on new‡	—	—	—	—	—
Total inflows (present value of benefits)					$10,754
Present value of inflows less present value of outflows			= $3,754		

* $1,000 sales increase + $2,000 cost saving = $3,000 benefit.
† Had the replacement not been made, Culver would have had $500 depreciation a year on the old machine—$5,000 book value divided by 10 years. But since they made the replacement, this depreciation is no longer available. The $5,000 has been recovered as $1,000 salvage plus $4,000 deductible loss. The depreciation of $500 a year must, therefore, be subtracted from inflows. It would be possible, of course, for Culver not to sell the old machine, not to take the immediate loss, and to continue getting the $500 yearly depreciation. If Culver chose to do this, however, the present value would be only $1,536 as against $3,000 ($2,000 + $1,000) for the sale and tax loss.
‡ The new machine has a zero estimated salvage value at the time it is purchased. However, the table is structured to show how salvage value would be handled in cases where it is applicable.

PROJECT ACCEPTABILITY

A general fallacy is to consider that what is true of the individual parts will be true of the whole. This problem also arises in connection with capital budgeting. Though individual projects appear to promise a relatively attractive yield, when they are taken together difficulties might be involved in achieving all the favorable projects simultaneously. One problem is that other firms in the same industry may be engaging in similar capital expenditure programs in an attempt to increase their capacity or, by cost reductions, to obtain a larger share of the product market. For a given growth rate in the industry, it is obviously impossible for every firm to obtain increases in sales that would fully utilize all the capital expenditure projects being undertaken.

Another problem is that while individual projects promise favorable yields, to undertake a large number of projects simultaneously might involve a very high rate of expansion by the individual firm. Such substantial additional personnel requirements and organizational problems may be involved that over-all rates of return will be diminished. Top management, at some point in the capital budgeting process, must therefore make a decision regarding the total volume of favorable projects that may be successfully undertaken without causing a significant reduction in the prospective returns from individual projects.

A firm might, for example, have the investment opportunities shown in Table 7–5 and only $6 million available for investment. In this situation,

Table 7–5   THE PROSPECTIVE-PROJECTS SCHEDULE

Nature of Proposal	Amounts of Funds Required	Cumulative Total	Internal Rate of Return
1. Purchase of leased space	$2,000,000	$ 2,000,000	23%
2. Mechanization of accounting system	1,200,000	3,200,000	19
3. Modernization of office building	1,500,000	4,700,000	17
4. Addition of power facilities	900,000	5,600,000	16
5. Purchase of affiliate	3,600,000	9,200,000	13
6. Purchase of loading docks	300,000	9,500,000	12
7. Purchase of tank trucks	500,000	10,000,000	11
			10% cutoff
8. Installation of conveyor system	200,000	10,200,000	9
9. Construction of new plant	2,300,000	12,500,000	8
10. Purchase of executive aircraft	200,000	12,700,000	7

the firm would probably accept projects 1 through 4 and project 6, for a total investment of $5.9 million. Under no circumstances should it accept projects 8, 9, or 10, as they all earn less than the cost of capital.

SUMMARY

Capital budgeting is of the greatest significance to a firm because it involves commitments for large outlays whose benefits (or drawbacks) extend well into the future. Decisions in these areas will, therefore, have a major impact on the future well-being of the firm. This chapter focused on how such decisions might be made more effective and might contribute to the health and growth of a firm. The discussion stressed the development of systematic procedures and rules for preparing a list of investment proposals, for evaluating them, and for selecting a cutoff point.

The chapter emphasized that one of the most crucial phases of the process of evaluating capital budget proposals is obtaining a dependable estimate of the savings or increases in revenues that will be obtained from undertaking the project. It cannot be overemphasized that the firm must allocate to competent and experienced personnel the making of these judgments.

Ranking Investment Proposals

Three commonly used procedures for ranking investment proposals were discussed in the chapter:

1. *Payback,* defined as the number of years required to return the original investment. Although the payback method is used frequently, it has serious conceptual weaknesses because it ignores the facts (1) that some receipts come in beyond the payback period and (2) that a dollar received today is more valuable than a dollar received in the future.

2. *Internal rate of return,* defined as the interest rate that equates the present value of future returns to the investment outlay. Although it is more difficult to calculate the internal rate of return than the payback, the rate-of-return method overcomes the conceptual flaws noted in the use of the payback method.

3. *Net present value,* defined as the present value of future returns discounted at the cost of capital minus the cost of the investment. This method, like the internal rate of return, meets the objections raised against the payback method. Ordinarily, the net present value and internal rate of return methods produce identical results.

Determining Cash Flows

The cash inflows from an investment consist of the incremental profit after taxes plus the incremental depreciation; the cash outflow is the cost of the investment less the sum of any salvage value received on an old machine plus any tax loss when an old machine is sold.

The Composition Problem

Although individual projects appear to promise a relatively attractive yield, when they are taken together difficulties might arise in achieving all the favorable projects simultaneously. Several factors must be considered in this connection: expansion plans of other firms in the industry, capital limitations, personnel problems if expansion rates are too high, and so on. Top management, at some point in the capital budgeting process, must make a decision regarding the total volume of favorable projects that can be successfully undertaken without causing a significant reduction in the prospective returns from individual projects.

QUESTIONS

7–1 Why will a firm often continue to use obsolete equipment instead of installing new replacements? How does the use of this obsolete equipment affect the company and the economy?

7–2 Are there conditions under which a firm might be better off if it chooses a machine with a rapid payback rather than one with the largest rate of return?

7–3 Company X uses the payback method in evaluating investment proposals and is considering new equipment whose additional earnings will be $150 a year. The equipment costs $500 and its expected life is 10 years (straight line depreciation). The company uses a 3-year payback as its criterion. Should the equipment be purchased under the above assumptions?

7–4 What are the most critical problems that arise in calculating a rate of return for a prospective investment?

7–5 What other factors in addition to rate-of-return analysis should be considered in determining capital expenditures?

7–6 Would it be beneficial for a firm to review its past capital expenditures and capital budgeting procedures? Why?

7–7 Fiscal and monetary policies are tools used by the government to stimulate the economy. Explain, using the analytical devices developed in this chapter, how each of the following might be expected to stimulate the economy by stimulating investment.

a) The investment tax credit
b) A speed-up of tax-allowable depreciation (for example, the accelerated methods permitted in 1954 or the guideline revisions of 1962)
c) An easing of interest rates
d) Passage of the War on Poverty Program

PROBLEMS

7–1 The Jordan Company is using a machine whose original cost was $15,000. The machine is 5 years old and has a current market (salvage) value of $2,000. The asset is being depreciated over a 15-year original life toward a zero estimated salvage value. Depreciation is on a straight line basis and the tax rate is 50 percent.

Management is contemplating the purchase of a replacement whose cost is $10,000 and whose estimated salvage value is $2,000; the expected savings with the new machine are $3,000 a year. Depreciation is on a straight line basis over a 10-year life, and the cost of capital is 10 percent.

a) Should the firm replace the asset?
b) What factors in addition to the quantitative factors listed above are likely to require consideration in a practical situation?

Set up your solution in the manner described in Table 7–4. Assume a 50 percent tax rate.

7–2   The Denver Company is considering the purchase of a new machine tool to replace an obsolete one. The machine being used for the operation has both a tax book value and a salvage value of zero; it is in good working order and will last, physically, for at least an additional 10 years. The proposed machine will perform the operation so much more efficiently that Denver Company engineers estimate that labor, material, and other direct costs of the operation will be reduced $3,000 a year if it is installed. The proposed machine costs $12,000 delivered and installed, and its economic life is estimated to be 10 years, with zero salvage value. The company expects to earn 14 percent on its investment after taxes (14 percent is the firm's cost of capital). The tax rate is 50 percent, and the firm uses straight line depreciation.

a) Should Denver buy the new machine?
b) Assume that the tax book value of the old machine had been $4,000, that the annual depreciation charge would have been $400, and that it had no sale value. How do these assumptions affect your answer?
c) Change part *b* to give effect also to the sale of the old machine for $2,000.
d) Change part *b* to assume that the annual savings would be $4,000. (The change in part *c* is not made; the machine is *not* sold for $2,000.)
e) Rework part *a* assuming the relevant cost of capital is now 5 percent. What is the significance of this? What can be said about parts *b*, *c*, and *d* under this assumption?
f) What other factors are likely to affect investment decisions of this type?

7–3   Each of two mutually exclusive projects involves an investment of $1,000. Cash flows (after-tax profits plus depreciation) total $660 a year for 2 years for project S and $265 a year for 6 years for project L.

a) Compute the present value of each project if the firm's cost of capital is 6 percent, 10 percent, 20 percent.
b) Compute the internal rate of return for each project.
c) Which project is better?
d) Graph the present values of the two projects, putting PV on the Y axis and the cost of capital on the X axis.
e) What is the significance of your results?

PART IV

Valuation and Financial Structure

Chapter 8

Financial Structure and the Use of Leverage

Once the financial manager has determined his firm's financial requirements, his next task is to see to it that these funds are on hand. Assuming that the company has a history of sound management and is not trying to expand too rapidly, there should be no problem in raising the necessary capital. However, capital comes in many forms—long and short-term debt, secured and unsecured debt, preferred stock, common stock, retained earnings, and such hybrid instruments as convertibles and long-term leases. What are the characteristics of these different securities? Which particular form is the best one to use in a given situation? Or should a package consisting of some of each kind be tried? These are the questions to which we now turn. Our first task, and the one considered in this chapter, is to examine the firm's financial structure and the effects of using financial leverage.

BASIC DEFINITIONS

To avoid ambiguity in the use of key concepts, the meanings of frequently used expressions are given here. *Financial structure* refers to the right-hand side of the balance sheet—the financing of the resources acquired by the firm. *Capital structure* is the permanent financing of the firm, represented by long-term debt, preferred stock, and net worth. *Net worth* is the *common* stockholders' equity and includes common stock, capital surplus, earned surplus (retained earnings), and net worth reserves.[1]

Finally, our key concept for this chapter is *financial leverage,* or the *leverage factor,* defined as the ratio of total debt to total assets. For example, a firm having assets of $100 million and total debt of $50 million would have a leverage factor of 50 percent. Some writers use only long-term debt in the numerator of the ratio, but this is not a generally accurate measure of financial leverage. While long-term debt might be more or less appropriate in an industry such as electric utilities, where little short-term debt is employed, it would be clearly inappropriate in other industries, such as aerospace, where firms rely on current debt as an important source of financing. Further, the smaller firms in most industries tend to make extensive use of short-term liabilities, particularly trade accounts payable. Therefore, to ignore current debt in measuring the risk incurred by using financial leverage would be to ignore the major (sometimes the only) form of debt employed.

THEORY OF FINANCIAL LEVERAGE

Perhaps the best way to understand the proper use of financial leverage is to analyze its impact on profitability under varying conditions. Suppose there are three firms in a particular industry, and these firms are identical except for their financial policies. Firm A has used no debt and consequently has a leverage factor of zero; firm B, financed half by debt and half by equity, has a leverage factor of 50 percent; firm C has a leverage factor of 75 percent. Their balance sheets are shown below.

FIRM A

		Total debt	$ 0
		Net worth	200
Total assets	$200	Total claims	$200

---

[1] Note that preferred stock is excluded from net worth here. Preferred stock is a hybrid security with some of the characteristics of common stock and some of the characteristics of bonds. When viewed from the point of view of the firm's creditors, preferred is very much like common. From the viewpoint of common stockholders, preferred shares are similar to debt. Consequently, preferred stock can be classified either as a part of net worth or as debt, depending on the purpose of the analysis. If we look at leverage from the creditors' point of view, preferred is included with equity. If we look at leverage from the position of the common stockholder, it is excluded from net worth. This seemingly ambiguous point is discussed in more detail in Chapter 16.

FIRM B

		Total debt (6%)	$100
		Net worth	100
Total assets	$200	Total claims	$200

FIRM C

		Total debt (6%)	$150
		Net worth	50
Total assets	$200	Total claims	$200

How do these different financial patterns affect stockholder returns? As can be seen from Table 8-1, the answer depends upon the state of the industry's economy. When the economy is depressed, sales and profit margins are low and the firms earn only 2 percent on assets. When conditions become somewhat better, the return on assets is 5 percent. Under normal conditions the returns rise to 8 percent, while in a moderate boom the figure goes to 11 percent. Finally, under extremely favorable circumstances the companies have a 14 percent return on assets. These percentages, multiplied by the $200 of assets, give the earnings before interest and taxes for the three companies under the various states of the economy.

Table 8–1 demonstrates how the use of financial leverage magnifies the impact on the stockholders of changes in the rate of return on assets. When economic conditions go from normal to good, for example, returns on assets go up 37.5 percent. Firm A uses no leverage, gets no magnification, and consequently experiences the same 37.5 percent jump in the rate of return to stockholders. Firm B, on the other hand, enjoys a 60 percent increase in stockholder returns as a result of the 37.5 percent rise in returns on assets. Firm C, which uses still more leverage, has an 86 percent increase. Just the reverse holds in economic downturns, of course: the 37.5 percent drop in returns on assets when the economy goes from normal to bad results in return-on-net-worth declines of 37.5 percent, 60 percent, and 86 percent for firms A, B, and C, respectively.

Using the same illustrative numbers, Figure 8–1 gives a graphic presentation of the interaction between the rates of return on assets and net worth, given the three different leverage factors. The interesting point to note here is the intersection of the three lines at the point where assets are returning 6 percent, the interest cost of debt. At this point the return on net worth is 3 percent. The assumed 50 percent tax rate reduces the 6 percent return on total assets to a return of 3 percent on net worth, regardless of the degree

Table 8–1 STOCKHOLDER RETURNS UNDER VARIOUS LEVERAGE
AND ECONOMIC CONDITIONS

| | Economic Conditions | | | | | |
	Very Poor	Poor	Break-even	Normal	Good	Very Good
Rate of return on total assets before interest	2%	5%	6%	8%	11%	14%
Dollar returns on total assets before interest	$4	$10	$12	$16	$22	$28
Firm A. Leverage Factor 0%						
Earnings in dollars	$4	$10	$12	$16	$22	$28
Less: Interest expense	0	0	0	0	0	0
Gross income	4	10	12	16	22	28
Taxes (50%)*	2	5	6	8	11	14
Available to common stock	2	5	6	8	11	14
Percent return on common stock	1%	2.5%	3%	4%	5.5%	7%
Firm B. Leverage Factor 50%						
Earnings in dollars	$4	$10	$12	$16	$22	$28
Less: Interest expense	6	6	6	6	6	6
Gross income	(2)	4	6	10	16	22
Taxes (50%)*	(1)	2	3	5	8	11
Available to common stock	(1)	2	3	5	8	11
Percent return on common stock	—1%	2%	3%	5%	8%	11%
Firm C. Leverage Factor 75%						
Earnings in dollars	$4	$10	$12	$16	$22	$28
Less: Interest expense	9	9	9	9	9	9
Gross income	(5)	1	3	7	13	19
Taxes (50%)*	(2.5)	.5	1.5	3.5	6.5	9.5
Available to common stock	(2.5)	.5	1.5	3.5	6.5	9.5
Percent return on common stock	—5%	1%	3%	7%	13%	19%

* The tax calculation assumes that losses are carried back and result in tax credits.

of leverage. When returns on assets are higher, leverage improves stockholder returns and is said to be *favorable;* when assets earn less than 6 percent, returns to stockholders are reduced and the leverage is defined as
*unfavorable. In general, whenever the return on assets exceeds the cost of
debt, leverage is favorable, and the higher the leverage factor the higher
the rate of return on common equity.*

Rate of return on net worth

Figure 8-1   Relation between Rates of Return on Assets and Rates of Return on Net Worth under Different Leverage Conditions

EFFECTS OF FINANCIAL LEVERAGE

To show that the results of alternative financial decisions are useful in judging the relative merits and demerits of various plans, a specific example is given. This example illustrates how future earnings prospects affect financing decisions.

The Universal Machine Company, whose latest balance sheet is shown in Table 8-2, manufactures equipment used by steel producers. As is typically the case for the producers of durable capital assets, the company's sales fluctuate widely, far more than does the over-all economy. For example, during nine of the last 25 years, sales have been below the break-even point, so losses have been relatively frequent. In the past few years, however, machinery demand has been heavy and has actually been rising, and if Universal is to continue sharing in this expansion it will have to increase capacity. For this increase, $3 million is required. James Walter, the financial vice-president, learns that he can net $3 million by selling bonds with a 5 percent coupon. Alternatively, he can raise the money by selling 75,000 shares of common stock.

Table 8–2   *UNIVERSAL MACHINE COMPANY*
                              BALANCE SHEET*
                              December 31, 1968

Cash	$ 200,000	Accounts payable	$1,200,000
Receivables (net)	1,100,000	Other current liabilities	800,000
Inventories	1,600,000	Total liabilities	$2,000,000
Plant (net)	2,500,000	Common stock ($10 par)	2,500,000
Equipment (net)	2,800,000	Surplus	3,700,000
Total assets	$8,200,000	Total claims on assets	$8,200,000

* Figures are rounded for convenience.

During the past five years, Universal's sales have fluctuated between $500,000 and $4,000,000; at the latter volume the firm is operating at full capacity and has to turn down orders. With the additional plant expansion, sales capacity will increase to $6 million. Fixed costs, after the planned expansion, will be $500,000 a year, and variable costs (excluding interest on the debt) will be 40 percent of sales.

Although Walter's recommendation will be given much weight, the final decision for the method of financing rests with the company's board of directors. Procedurally, the financial vice-president will analyze the situation, evaluate all reasonable alternatives, come to a conclusion, and then present the alternatives with his recommendations to the board. For his own analysis, as well as for presentation to the board, Walter prepares the material shown in Table 8-3.

In the top third of the table, earnings before interest and taxes are calculated for different levels of sales ranging from $0 to $6 million. The firm suffers an operating loss up to $1 million of sales, but beyond that point it shows a rapid rise in gross profit.

The middle third of the table shows the financial results that will occur with bond financing at the various sales levels. First, the $150,000 annual interest charges are deducted from the earnings before interest and taxes calculated above. Next, taxes are taken out. Notice that if the sales level is so low that losses are incurred, the firm receives a tax credit. Finally, net profits after taxes are divided by the 250,000 shares outstanding to obtain earnings per share of common stock.[2]

In the bottom third of the table the financial results that will occur with stock financing are calculated. No interest payments are involved, so the earnings-before-tax figure is the same as the one computed at the top of

---

[2] The shares outstanding can be calculated by dividing the $2,500,000 common stock figure given on the balance sheet by the $10 par value.

Table 8–3

UNIVERSAL MACHINE COMPANY
PROFIT CALCULATIONS AT VARIOUS SALES LEVELS

Sales	$0	$500,000	$1,000,000	$2,000,000	$4,000,000	$6,000,000
Fixed costs	$500,000	$500,000	$500,000	$500,000	$500,000	$500,000
Variable costs (40% of sales)	–0–	200,000	400,000	800,000	1,600,000	2,400,000
Total costs (except interest)	$500,000	$700,000	$900,000	$1,300,000	$2,100,000	$2,900,000
Earnings before interest and taxes	$(500,000)	$(200,000)	$100,000	$700,000	$1,900,000	$3,100,000
Financing with Bonds						
Less: Interest (5% × $3,000,000)	$150,000	$150,000	$150,000	$150,000	$150,000	$150,000
Earnings before taxes	$(650,000)	$(350,000)	$(50,000)	$550,000	$1,750,000	$2,950,000
Less: Income taxes (50%)*	(325,000)	(175,000)	(25,000)	275,000	875,000	1,475,000
Net profit after taxes	$(325,000)	$(175,000)	$(25,000)	$275,000	$875,000	$1,475,000
Earnings per share on 250,000 shares of common	$–1.30	$–0.70	$–0.10	$1.10	$3.50	$5.90
Financing with Stock						
Earnings before taxes†	$(500,000)	$(200,000)	$100,000	$700,000	$1,900,000	$3,100,000
Less: Income taxes (50%)*	(250,000)	(100,000)	50,000	350,000	950,000	1,550,000
Net profit after taxes	$(250,000)	$(100,000)	$50,000	$350,000	$950,000	$1,550,000
Earnings per share on 325,000 shares of common	$–0.78	$–0.31	$+0.15	$1.08	$2.92	$4.77

* Assumes tax credit on losses.
† Earnings before tax is the same as earnings before interest and tax because interest is zero with stock financing.

151

the table. Net profit after taxes is divided by 325,000 shares—the original 250,000 plus the new 75,000—to find earnings per share.

Walter next plots the earnings per share under the two methods of financing, as shown in Figure 8-2. If sales were depressed toward zero, the debt financing line cuts the Y axis at −$1.30, below the −$0.78 intercept of the common stock financing line. The debt line has a steeper slope and rises faster, however, showing that earnings per share will go up faster with increases in sales if debt is used. The two lines cross at sales of about $2 million. Below that volume of sales the firm would be better off issuing common stock, but above that level debt financing would produce higher earnings per share.

If Walter and his board of directors *knew for sure* that sales would

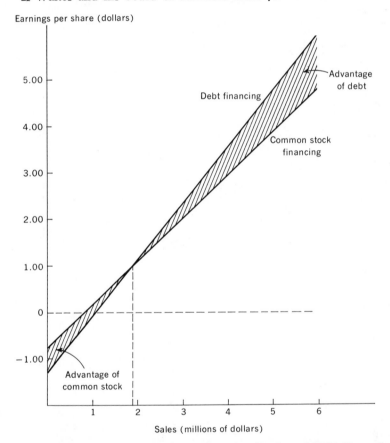

Figure 8-2   Earnings per Share for Stock and Debt Financing

never again fall below $2 million, bonds would be the preferred method of financing the asset increase. But they cannot know this for certain and, in fact, they probably have good reason to expect future business cycles to drive sales down to, and even below, this critical level. They know that during the past five years sales have been as low as $500,000. If sales fall to this level again, the company would not be earning enough to cover its interest charges. Such a situation, if it continues for several years, could jeopardize the very existence of the firm. On the other hand, if sales continue to expand, there would be higher earnings per share from using bonds, and no officer or director would want to forgo these substantial advantages.

When industry standards for leverage are applied, we see that the firm's debt ratio, after financing, will be 45 percent as compared to a norm for manufacturing firms of only 36 percent. (See Table 8–4.) Since Universal Machine is a capital goods producer and is thus subject to wider fluctuations than the average manufacturer, it might be argued that a 45 percent debt ratio is too high for Universal Machine.

Walter's recommendations and the decision of each director will depend (1) upon each person's appraisal of the future and (2) upon his psychological attitude toward risk. The pessimists, or risk averters, will prefer to employ common stock, while the optimists, or those less sensitive to risk, will favor bonds. This example, which is typical of many real-world situations, suggests that the major disagreements over the choice of forms of financing are likely to reflect uncertainty about the future levels of the firm's sales. Such uncertainty, in turn, reflects the characteristics of the firm's environment—general business conditions, industry trends, and quality and aggressiveness of management.

VARIATIONS IN FINANCIAL STRUCTURE

As might be expected, wide variations in the use of financial leverage may be observed among industries and among the individual firms in each industry. Illustrative of these differences is the range of ratios of total debt to total assets shown in Table 8-4 for certain broad groups of industries. Service industries use the most leverage, reflecting the facts (1) that services include certain financial institutions that typically have high liabilities and (2) that there are many smaller firms in the service industries, and small firms as a group are heavy users of debt. Public utility use of debt stems from a heavy fixed asset investment, coupled with extremely stable sales. Mining and manufacturing firms use relatively little debt because of their exposure to fluctuating sales.

Table 8–4   VARIATION IN FINANCIAL LEVERAGE IN INDUSTRY
            GROUPS, 1961-1962

Name of Industry	Debt to Total Assets (in percentages)
Service	63
Public utilities	58
Wholesale trade	53
Agriculture	49
Retail trade	48
Mining	38
Manufacturing	36

SOURCE: United States Treasury Department, Internal Revenue Service, *Statistics of Income, U.S. Business Tax Returns, 1962* (Washington, D.C.: U.S. Government Printing Office, 1964).

Within the broad category "manufacturing," wide variations are observed for individual industries. Table 8-5 presents an array of total-debt-to-

Table 8–5   TOTAL-DEBT-TO-ASSETS RATIOS FOR SELECTED MANU-
            FACTURING INDUSTRIES

Manufacturing Industries	Percent
Fabrics: Cotton, silk, wool, synthetic	27
Household furniture except upholstered	32
Automotive parts and accessories	35
Flour and other grain mill products	35
Iron and steel forgings	35
Iron and steel foundries	39
Drugs and medicines	40
Machine tools and metalworking equipment	40
Canned and dried fruits and vegetables	41
Industrial chemicals	42
Electronic components and accessories	42
Precision instruments	44
Books	45
Bread and other bakery products	46
Ready mixed concrete	47
Sporting and athletic goods	48
Meat packing	49
Dairy products	53
Veneer and plywood	55
Distilled liquor, wines, and liqueurs	59

SOURCE: *Annual Statement Studies,* 1966 Edition (Philadelphia: Robert Morris Associates, 1966).

total-assets ratios for selected manufacturing industries. The lowest ratios are found among textile companies, in which competitive pressures continue to be great. Low debt ratios are also found among the durable goods industries. The highest debt ratios are found in consumer nondurable goods, where demand is relatively insensitive to fluctuations and general business activity.

Even within a given industry there are wide variations in the use of financial leverage, as illustrated for the electric utility industry in Table 8-6. These variations reflect a number of different considerations, including the volatility of business in the companies' operating areas, the extent to which they use preferred stock, and their managements' willingness to assume risk. Montana Power, for example, sells a large proportion of its electricity to copper producers, whose volume of business, hence demand for power,

Table 8–6   DEBT-TO-TOTAL-ASSETS RATIO (Selected Electric Utility Companies, 1962)

Montana Power	37
Detroit Edison	41
Central Illinois Light & Power	54
Consolidated Edison	56
Tampa Electric	57
Missouri Public Service	63

SOURCE: *Moody's Public Utility Manual, 1963.*

is quite cyclical. This largely explains its low debt ratio. Missouri Public Service, by contrast, has a stable demand pattern, which permits its relatively high leverage factor.

FACTORS INFLUENCING FINANCIAL STRUCTURE

Thus far the discussion has touched on the factors that are generally considered when a firm formulates basic policies relating to its financial structure. The more important of these capital structure determinants are now listed and briefly discussed.

1. Growth rate of future sales
2. Stability of future sales
3. Competitive structure of the industry
4. Asset structure of the industry
5. Control position and attitudes toward risk of owners and management
6. Lender attitudes toward firm and industry

Growth Rate of Sales

The future growth rate of sales is a measure of the extent to which the earnings per share of a firm are likely to be magnified by leverage. If sales and earnings grow at an 8-to-10 percent rate a year, for example, financing by debt with limited fixed charges should magnify the returns to owners of the stock.[3] This can be seen from Figure 8–2 above.

On the other hand, the common stock of a firm whose sales and earnings are growing at a favorable rate commands a high price; thus, it sometimes appears that equity financing is desirable. The firm must weigh the benefits of using leverage against the opportunity of broadening its equity base when it chooses between future financing alternatives. Such firms may be expected to have a moderate-to-high rate of debt financing. For example, at the end of 1960 International Business Machines had a debt ratio of 37 percent. Litton Industries, another growth company, had a debt ratio of 60 percent.[4]

Sales Stability

Sales stability and debt ratios are directly related. With greater stability in sales and earnings, a firm can incur the fixed charges of debt with less risk than it can when its sales and earnings are subject to periodic declines; in the latter instance it will have difficulty in meeting its obligations. The stability of the utility industry, combined with relatively favorable growth prospects, has resulted in high leverage ratios in that industry.

Entry Conditions

Debt-servicing ability is dependent upon the profitability as well as the volume of sales. Hence, the stability of profit margins is as important as the stability of sales. The ease with which new firms may enter the industry and the ability of competing firms to expand capacity will influence profit margins. A growth industry promises higher profit margins, but such margins are likely to narrow if the industry is one in which the number of firms can be easily increased through additional entry. For example, pleasure-boat manufacturing and neighborhood bowling alleys were highly profitable industries in the later 1950's, and it was relatively easy for new firms

---

[3] Such a growth rate is also often associated with a high profit rate.

[4] There is, however, another consideration at work in the case of profitable, growing firms. The fact that they are profitable means that relatively large amounts of funds are being generated, and these are equity funds that can be used to finance further expansion. But rapidly growing companies have needs for asset expansion that typically exceed the retained earnings available from high profit rates. Others have emphasized the same point; for example, Gordon Donaldson, *Corporate Debt Capacity* (Boston: Harvard University, 1961). In general, it appears that growing firms are the ones that employ debt to the greatest extent.

to enter these industries and go into competition with the older firms. As these industries matured during the early 1960's, the capacity of the old and the new firms grew at an increased rate. As a consequence, profit margins declined.

Other firms in other industries are better able to resist competitive pressures. For example, to duplicate the unique technical, service, and distribution facilities of the International Business Machines Corporation would be very difficult, a fact suggesting that profit margins for this firm are less subject to erosion.

Asset Structure

Asset structure influences the sources of financing in several ways. Firms with long-lived fixed assets, especially when demand for their output is relatively assured—for example, utilities—use long-term mortgage debt extensively. Firms whose assets are mostly receivables and inventory whose value is dependent on the continued profitability of the individual firm—for example, those in wholesale and retail trade—rely less on long-term debt financing and more on short term.

Management Attitudes

The management attitudes that most directly influence the choice of financing are those concerning (1) control of the enterprise and (2) risk. Large corporations whose stock is widely owned may choose additional sales of common stock because they will have little influence on the control of the company. Also, because management represents a stewardship for the owners, it is often less willing to take the risk of heavy fixed charges.[5]

In contrast, the owners of small firms may prefer to avoid issuing common stock in order to be assured of continued control. Because they generally have confidence in the prospects of their companies, and because they can see the large potential gains to themselves resulting from leverage, managers of such firms are often willing to incur high debt ratios.

---

[5] It would be inappropriate to delve too far into motivational theory in an introductory finance textbook, but it is interesting to note that the managers of many larger, publicly owned corporations have a relatively small ownership position and derive most of their income from salaries. Some writers assert that in such cases managements do not strive for profits, especially if this effort involves using leverage with its inherent risk. Presumably, these managers feel that the risks of leverage for them, the ones who actually decide to use debt or equity, outweigh the potential gains from successful leverage. If sales are low, there is a chance of failure and the loss of their jobs, whereas if sales and profits are high, it is the stockholders, not management, who receive the benefits. While there is undoubtedly some merit to this argument, it should be pointed out that companies are increasingly using profit-based compensation schemes—bonus systems and stock-option plans—to motivate management to seek profitability as well as stability.

The converse can, of course, also hold—the owner-manager of a small firm may be *more* conservative than the manager of a large company. If the net worth of the small firm is, say, $1 million, and if it all belongs to the owner-manager, he may well decide that he is already pretty well off and elect not to risk using leverage in an effort to become still more wealthy. In the terms of the economists, he may have a diminishing marginal utility of money.

Lender Attitudes

Regardless of managements' analysis of the proper leverage factor for their firms, there is no question but that lenders' attitudes are frequently an important—sometimes the most important—determinant of financial structures. In the majority of cases, the corporation discusses its capital structure with lenders and gives much weight to their advice. But when management is so confident of the future that it seeks to use leverage beyond norms for the industry, lenders may be unwilling to accept such debt increases. They will emphasize that excessive debt reduces the credit standing of the borrower and the credit rating of the securities previously issued. The lender point of view has been expressed by a borrower, a financial vice-president, who stated that his policy is "to determine how much debt we can carry and still maintain an AA bond rating, then use that amount less a small margin for safety." [6]

GUIDELINES FOR FINANCIAL STRUCTURES

On the basis of the foregoing considerations, broad guidelines or reference levels for the financial structures of wide industrial segments are presented in Table 8-7. In examining these figures, keep in mind all that has been said about the importance of carefully appraising the individual situation and the dangers of relying on industry norms. The guidelines do, however, have a rational basis, and it would be wise to valuate critically the reasons behind any given company's decision to step outside the reference boundaries.

Manufacturing Industries

Detailed studies of financial ratios among manufacturing firms reveal wide variations among industries and, to a lesser degree, among firms in the same industry. Within a given industry, firms tend to cluster about a certain

---

[6] Bond ratings, which are discussed in detail in Chapter 17, are basically indices of the risk that lenders incur when buying particular bonds. A rating of AAA is the best, denoting the lowest risk, and AA is just below it.

Table 8–7   REFERENCE LEVELS FOR FINANCIAL STRUCTURES

	Percentage of Total Assets					
	Current Liabilities	Long-term Debt	Preferred Stock	Common Equity or Net Worth	Current Ratio	Times Interest Earned
Large, established firms						
Manufacturing	20–25%	15–20%	0–4%	55–65%	2×	8×
Utilities	5–10	45–50	10–15	30–35	1	4
Trade	30–35	16–18	0–2	50–55	2.5	7
Small, rapidly growing, profitable firms						
Manufacturing	40–45%	0–5%	0–10%	40–60%	1×	9×
Trade	50–60	0–5	0–5	30–40	1.5	10

financial structure, as the major factors influencing financial structure tend to operate in the same direction.

Table 8-7 suggests that the percentage of the financial structure in current liabilities should be smallest for utilities, next for manufacturing, and highest for firms engaged in wholesale and retail trade. As a group, manufacturing firms tend to operate with relatively small percentages of long-term debt in their financial structures. They incur long-term debt during periods of rapid expansion and follow the policy of paying off debt as rapidly as permitted by earnings retention or flotation of new shares of common stock. Preferred stock is used mainly as a substitute for debt where firms seek to gain the benefits of trading on the equity but are unwilling to bear the risks of fixed charges. The reference ranges suggested for manufacturing indicate that total-debt-to-total-assets ratios should approximate 40 percent.

Utility Industries

Current debt is a much smaller ratio of total assets for utilities than it is for any other industry. Cash is a small portion of total assets because of the synchronization of inflows and outflows of cash. The average collection period is short and receivables are low, because terms of sales are on presentation of invoice and service may be cut off if bills are not paid. By the nature of the business, inventories are small. Because of heavy fixed plant and stability of earnings, long-term debt is large. Preferred stock is used to a greater extent by utilities than by any other category of firms. The tax disadvantage of preferred stock is somewhat mitigated, because taxes are considered to be a cost of service, and utility rates (charges made for service) are adjusted upward to offset additional taxes incurred if preferred stock is substituted for debt.

For utilities, the ratio of preferred stock and debt to total assets runs about 60 to 65 percent. Greater clustering occurs in debt ratios of utility companies than of other industrial categories, though even here, as was seen from Table 8-6, variations can occur. It is interesting to speculate what the impact of the rapid substitution of nuclear energy plants for plants operated on fossil fuel, such as coal, will be over the next 10 to 15 or 20 years. The long life of the use of the specific durable assets which led to high debt ratios for utilities in past years may no longer be justified. With the rapid increase in the pace of technological change, particularly in the telephone and communications business, appropriate debt ratios may move downward.

Wholesale and Retail Trade

Firms engaged in wholesale and retail trade utilize current debt to the highest degree, but their use of long-term debt and preferred stock is smallest. Net worth percentages are moderately smaller for wholesale and retail trade than for manufacturing firms, with the ratio of debt to total assets rising to between 46 and 53 percent.

Current Ratio

The levels of current ratios reflect the characteristic asset structures in the three categories of industrial activity. The traditional 2-to-1 rule-of-thumb ratio fits most categories in the industrial field, but because of relatively small amounts of current assets, the 1-to-1 ratio for utilities is appropriate. Since trade firms have heavier inventories and receivables, a ratio of 2.5 or 3 to 1 is desirable here.

Times Interest Earned

Times interest earned is one of the tests widely applied by investors. The coverage suggested here reflects characteristic recommendations found in works on investments and security analysis.[7] Because these are the coverages expected by investors, the determination of the appropriate levels must reflect investor preferences as well as financial structure considerations. The logic involved here is to protect creditors by having expected earnings adequately cover interest requirements. The earnings level to be used should reflect the best judgment of future earnings levels, taking into

---

[7] See, for example, B. Graham, D. L. Dodd, and S. Cottle, *Security Analysis* (New York: McGraw-Hill, 1961), pp. 343–352.

account past experience and prospective changes in the economic environment that may affect earnings both in the industry and in the company under study, with allowance for possible declines.

Modification of Standards for Small Firms

In formulating broad reference guides for evaluating the financial structures of business firms, a number of factors in addition to the industry of the firm are important. Among these are the age, size, growth rate, and profitability of the firm. To reflect these factors and yet avoid unduly proliferating the categories, the second section of Table 8-7 indicates suitable modifications in the basic reference ranges for small, rapidly growing, profitable firms. A new, small firm starts from such a limited base that success, measured by profitability, is likely to be accompanied by rapid growth. Since they are likely to occur together, the influence of age, size, growth rate, and profitability may be conveniently grouped.

The small, successful firm is likely to employ leverage to a much greater degree than its older, larger counterpart. Current ratios will be lower, and the firm may actually be slow in meeting its bills. Because of this, the required coverage of fixed charges should be somewhat greater for protection to creditors. Debt-to-total-assets ratios may run as high as 60 percent for manufacturing firms and 70 to 75 percent for trade firms. As the firm grows and begins to present a record of success, its access to the equity markets is likely to improve. It will then probably have a common stock flotation that will help bring its financial structure into better balance.

The guidelines presented to this point have been very broad. They have been developed for the purpose of providing a framework for critical evaluation of the financial structures of firms. Finer distinctions must be made, however, and the following section describes how financial structures can be developed to reflect the characteristics of individual industries.

USE OF FINANCIAL RATIO COMPOSITES IN DETERMINING THE FINANCIAL PLAN

Chapter 3 has described how financial data summarized by industry averages can be used to evaluate the financial ratios for individual firms in these industries. Such industry composites can also be used to provide a basis for formulating the financial plan of an individual firm. Financial structures so developed conform to general industry practice. While simply conforming to the structure of other firms in a particular line of business is not necessarily desirable, such a standard can be a useful starting point. This is especially true if the capital structure of a new enterprise is being planned; here the use of such guidelines can be helpful in suggesting what the financial requirements are likely to be.[8]

Developing a *pro forma* balance sheet,[9] based on the average of financial ratios of firms in a given line of business, is the first step. To use the method of financial ratio composites to construct the *pro forma* financial plan, it is necessary to know only two things: (1) the industry of the firm and (2) its size, measured by estimated annual sales. An illustration of the technique is given for an industrial machinery firm with estimated annual sales of $120,000.

The Dun & Bradstreet median financial ratio composites for the industry for the most recent year are:

Sales to net worth	3 times
Current debt to net worth	40 percent
Total debt to net worth	60 percent
Current ratio	3 times
Net sales to inventory	4 times
Average collection period	42 days
Fixed assets to net worth	40 percent

On the basis of this information, the following *pro forma* balance sheet can be constructed:

PRO FORMA BALANCE SHEET

Cash	$ 4,000		Current debt	$16,000
Accounts receivable	14,000		Long-term debt	8,000
Inventory	30,000		Net worth	40,000
Current assets		$48,000		
Fixed assets		16,000		
Total assets		$64,000	Total liab. and net worth	$64,000

Calculations:

1. Net worth = sales ÷ net worth turnover
$$\frac{\$120,000}{3} = \$40,000$$

2. Total debt = 60% of net worth
$$\$40,000 \times 60\% = \$24,000$$

---

[8] Provisions must also be made for organization expenses and various start-up costs, such as losses incurred. The losses incurred may result from relatively heavy fixed costs that will cause losses until the sales volume grows to the point where initial fixed capacity is effectively utilized.

[9] A *pro forma* financial statement is one that is *projected*. It is an estimate of how a future statement will appear.

3. Current debt = 40% of net worth
$$\$40,000 \times 40\% = \$16,000$$
4. Long-term debt = total debt − current debt
$$\$24,000 - \$16,000 = \$8,000$$
5. Total claims on assets = net worth + total debt
$$\$40,000 + \$24,000 = \$64,000$$
6. Current assets = current debt × current ratio
$$\$16,000 \times 3 = \$48,000$$
7. Inventory = sales ÷ inventory turnover
$$\frac{\$120,000}{4} = \$30,000$$
8. Accounts receivable = average collection period × sales per day
$$\frac{\$120,000}{360} \times \frac{42}{1} = \$14,000$$
9. Cash = current assets − (receivables + inventory)
$$\$48,000 - (\$14,000 + \$30,000) = \$4,000$$
10. Fixed assets = net worth × 40%
$$\$40,000 \times 40\% = \$16,000$$
11. Total assets = current asets + fixed assets
$$\$48,000 + \$16,000 = \$64,000$$

Profitability and income statement relations can also be developed by reference to industry data, with the data being based on any of the wide variety of sources of financial ratio compilations described in Chapter 3. Alternatively, a financial manager may develop his own guidelines by constructing averages based on a selected number of firms most similar (in his judgment) to his own business—for example, firms of comparable age and size operating in his same geographic market area.

The use of financial ratio composites as a guideline to financial structures may be questioned on theoretical grounds. Because these composites are computed averages, some firms must be above the average and some below. But it is of interest to know on which side of the average an individual firm stands. Further, a strong practical consideration reinforces the value of such comparisons—bank lending officers and other credit and financial analysts place heavy reliance on such comparisons between individual firms and industry norms. Thus the financial structure of the firm will, in practice, be checked against industry data.

Of course, neither financial managers nor lenders need be held in a strait jacket by an industry average. The average is primarily a standard for reference, and many factors may cause an individual firm to depart from the industry pattern. For example, it has already been noted that age, size, growth rate, control position of owners, and management attitudes toward risk may all strongly influence the financial policies of a firm.

Financial structures suggested by industry practices actually represent only a starting point. Sound reasons may exist to cause an individual firm's financial structure to depart from the reference levels provided by industry data. But it is important that the financial manager understand the reasons for these differences and be able to explain them effectively to potential creditors. Sometimes the differences may represent elements of strength or the almost unavoidable growing pains of a rapidly developing company. However, departures from industry norms may also signal weaknesses requiring correction.

SUMMARY

Financial leverage, which means using debt to boost rates of return on net worth over the returns available on assets, is the primary topic covered in this chapter. Whenever the return on assets exceeds the cost of debt, leverage is favorable and the return on equity is raised by using it. However, leverage is a two-edged sword, and if the returns on assets are less than the cost of debt, then leverage reduces the returns on equity. This reduction is greater the more leverage a firm employs. As a net result, leverage may be used to boost stockholder returns, but using it is done at the risk of increasing losses if the firm's economic fortunes decline.

Financial structure, defined as the method of financing a firm's assets, represents another way of looking at the leverage question. In part, financial structures are determined by management. But firms are constrained by the amount of debt lenders are willing to advance, and this willingness is partially conditioned by the characteristics of the industry and by the financial structures of other firms in the industry. For this reason, the authors have analyzed the factors causing capital structures to differ among industries.

Thus far, the analysis has been more intuitive than rigorous. In the following two chapters the concepts developed up to this point will be extended to the formal theory of the cost of capital and the theory of security valuation. The way investors appraise the relative desirability of increased returns versus higher risks is seen to be a most important consideration, and one that, in general, invalidates the theory that firms should strive for maximum earnings per share regardless of the risks involved.

QUESTIONS

8–1   How will each of the following be changed by the occurrences listed below: financial structure, capital structure, and net worth?

a) The firm has retained earnings of $100 for the year.

b) A preferred stock issue is refinanced with bonds.

c) Bonds are sold for cash.

d) The firm repurchases 10 percent of its outstanding common stock with excess cash.

e) An issue of convertible bonds is converted.

8-2 From an economic and social standpoint, is the use of financial leverage justifiable? Explain by listing some advantages and disadvantages.

8-3 Financial leverage and operating leverage are similar in one very important respect. What is this similarity and why is it important?

8-4 What are some reasons for variations of debt ratios among the firms in a given industry?

8-5 Why is the following statement true? "Other things being the same, firms with relatively stable sales are able to incur relatively high debt ratios."

8-6 Why do public utility companies usually pursue a different financial policy from that of trade firms?

8-7 The use of financial ratios and industry averages in the financial planning and analysis of a firm should be approached with caution. Why?

8-9 Some economists believe that the swings in the business cycles have not been as wide in recent years as they were in the past. Assuming that they are correct in their analysis, what effect can this added stability have on the types of financing used by firms in the United States? Would your answer be true for all firms?

PROBLEMS

8-1 One useful test or guide for evaluating a firm's financial structure in relation to its industry is by comparison with financial ratio composites for its industry. A new firm or one contemplating entering a new industry may use such industry composites as a guide to what its financial position is likely to approximate after the initial settling-down period.

The following data represent the ratios for the furniture manufacturing industry for 1968:

Estimated annual sales	$400,000
Sales to net worth	4 times
Current debt to net worth	50%
Total debt to net worth	80%
Current ratio	2.2 times
Net sales to inventory	8 times
Average collection period	40 days
Fixed assets to net worth	70%

EXCELSIOR FURNITURE DESIGNS
PRO FORMA BALANCE SHEET
1968

Cash	$_____	Current debt	$_____
Accounts receivable	_____	Long-term debt	_____
Inventory	_____	Total debt	_____
Current assets	_____	Net worth	_____
Fixed assets	_____		
Total assets	$_____	Total liab. and net worth	$_____

a) Complete the above *pro forma* balance sheet. (Round to nearest thousands.)

b) What does the use of the financial ratio composites accomplish?

c) What other factors will influence the financial structure of the firm?

8–2 In early 1967 the Gusher Company was thinking of raising $300 million additional funds to finance growth. About the same time the Streamer Company was thinking of raising $100 million to finance growth in sales.

From data given below, which firm should sell 4.5 percent debentures and which should sell common stock?

GUSHER AND STREAMER OIL COMPANIES
BALANCE SHEETS
(in millions of dollars)

	Gusher	Streamer
Current assets	$3,000	$ 650
Investments	400	100
Net fixed assets	4,600	1,750
Total assets	$8,000	$2,500
Current liabilities	$1,400	$ 300
Long-term debt	1,600	200
Total debt	$3,000	$ 500
Common stock outstanding:		
Gusher (200 million shares), $10 par	$2,000	
Streamer (40 million shares), $25 par		$1,000
Surplus (earned and paid in)	3,000	1,000
Net worth	$5,000	$2,000
Total claims	$8,000	$2,500
Sales (in billions of dollars):		
1962	5.4	1.7
1963	5.6	1.7
1964	5.8	1.8
1965	6.4	1.9
1966	7.1	2.0

Net income (in millions of dollars):	Gusher	Streamer
1962	540	136
1963	560	136
1964	580	144
1965	640	152
1966	700	152

GUSHER AND STREAMER OIL COMPANIES
INCOME STATEMENTS
For Period Ended June 30, 1966
(in millions of dollars)

	Gusher	Streamer
Sales	$7,100	$2,000
Total costs	6,128	1,820
Net income before taxes	$ 972	$ 180
Interest on debt (4.5% for Gusher, 4% for Streamer)	72	8
	$ 900	$ 172
Federal income taxes	200	20
Net income after taxes	$ 700	$ 152

	Gusher	Streamer
Sales to total assets	0.89	0.80
Earnings per share	$3.50	$3.80
Dividends per share	1.85	1.25
Price/earnings ratio*	20×	15×
Market price	$ 70	$ 57

* The price/earnings ratio is the market price per share divided by earnings per share. It represents the amount of money an investor is willing to pay for $1 of current earnings. All other things being the same, the price earnings ratio is higher for less risky stocks.

8–3   The Beaumont Company plans to expand assets by 50 percent and to finance the expansion is choosing between a straight 6 percent debt issue and common stock. Its current balance sheet and income statement are shown below.

BEAUMONT COMPANY
BALANCE SHEET
December 31, 1967

		Debt, 5%	$ 40,000
		Common stock, $10 par	100,000
		Earned surplus	60,000
Total assets	$200,000	Total claims	$200,000

BEAUMONT COMPANY
INCOME STATEMENT
For Year Ended December 31, 1967

Sales	$600,000	
Total costs (excluding interest)	538,000	
Net income before taxes	$ 62,000	Earnings per share: $\dfrac{30,000}{10,000} = \$3$
Debt interest	2,000	
Income before taxes	$ 60,000	Market price: $12 \times 3 = \$36$
Taxes at 50%	30,000	
Net income	$ 30,000	

If the Beaumont Company finances the $100,000 expansion with debt, the rate on the incremental debt will be 6 percent and the price/earnings ratio of the common stock will be 10 times. If the expansion is financed by equity, the new stock can be sold at $33⅓, the rate on debt will be 5 percent, and the price/earnings ratio of all the outstanding common stock will remain at 12 times earnings.

a) Assuming that net income before interest on debt and before taxes is 10 percent of sales, calculate earnings per share at sales assumptions of $0, $50,000, $200,000, $280,000, $400,000, $600,000, $800,000 and $1,-000,000, when financing is with common stock in contrast to debt. Assume no fixed costs.

b) Make a break-even chart for the earnings under a.

c) Using the price earnings ratio indicated, calculate the market value per share of common stock for each sales level for both the debt and the equity methods of financing.

d) Make a break-even chart of market value per share for the company with data found in c.

e) If the firm follows the policy of seeking to maximize the market price of its stock, which form of financing should be employed?

f) What other factors should be taken into account in choosing between the two forms of financing?

g) Would it matter if the presently outstanding stock was all owned by Mr. Beaumont and that this represented his entire net worth? Would it matter if the final decision maker, the president, was compensated entirely by a fixed salary? That he had a substantial number of stock options?

Chapter 9

Valuation and Rates of Return

In the discussion of the capital budgeting process in Chapter 7, it was seen that the discount rate used in the calculations is of vital importance. Relatively small changes in the discount rate produce significant changes in computed net present values and sometimes cause a reversal in the decision to accept or to reject a particular project. In the discussion of capital budgeting, it was *assumed* that the cost of capital—the discount rate used in the present value process—was known, and this rate was used in the calculations. Now, however, it is necessary to devote attention to the problem of deriving the cost of capital for individual firms.

Since the cost of capital to the firm is integrally connected with investors' returns on capital, the basic principles underlying valuation theory are discussed in the present chapter. The following chapter, building on valuation theory, considers the costs of various types of capital and shows how they may be combined to produce the firm's over-all cost of capital. In capital budgeting, the *cost of capital* is the fundamental quantity used as the discount rate when calculating net present values of investments.

DEFINITIONS OF VALUE

While it is impossible to ascribe any monetary returns to certain types of assets—works of art, for instance—the fundamental characteristic of business assets is that they give rise to income flows. Sometimes this flow is

169

easy to determine and measure—the interest return on a bond is an example. At other times the cash flows attributable to the asset must be estimated, as was done in Chapter 7 in the evaluation of projects. Regardless of the difficulties of measuring income flows, it is the prospective revenues from assets that gives them value.

Liquidating versus Going Concern Value

Several different definitions of "value" exist in the literature and are used in practice, with different ones being appropriate at different times. The first distinction that must be made is that between *liquidating value* and *going concern value*. Liquidating value is defined as the amount that could be realized if an asset or a group of assets (the assets of an entire firm, for example) are sold separate from the organization that has been using them. If the owner of a machine shop decides to retire, he might auction off his inventory and equipment, collect his accounts receivable, then sell his land and buildings to a grocery wholesaler for use as a warehouse. The sum of the proceeds from each category of assets that he receives would be the liquidating value of the assets. If his debts are subtracted from this amount, the difference would represent the liquidating value of his ownership in the business.

On the other hand, if the firm is sold as an operating business to a corporation or another individual, the purchaser would pay an amount equal to the going concern value of the company. If the going concern value exceeds the liquidating value, the difference represents the value of the organization as distinct from the assets.

Book Value versus Market Value

Another distinction must be made between *book value,* or the accounting value at which an asset is carried, and *market value,* the price at which an asset can be sold. If the asset in question is a firm, it actually has two market values—a liquidating value and a going concern value. Only the higher of the two is generally referred to as *the* market value.

Market Value versus Intrinsic Value

The distinction between *intrinsic value* and *market value* has been stated clearly yet succinctly by Graham, Dodd, and Cottle.

A general definition of intrinsic value would be "that value which is justified by the facts, e.g., assets, earnings, dividends, definite prospects, including the factor of management." The primary objective in using the adjective "intrinsic" is to emphasize the distinction between value and *current market price,* but not to invest this "value" with an aura of permanence. In truth, the computed intrinsic value is likely to change at least from year to year, as the various factors governing that value are modified. But in most cases intrinsic value changes less rapidly and drastically than market price, and the investor usually has an opportunity to profit from any wide discrepancy between the current price and the intrinsic value as determined at the same time.[1]

Although these authors develop this concept for security (that is, stocks and bonds) valuation, the idea is applicable to all business assets. What it involves, basically, is estimating the future net cash flows attributable to an asset, determining an appropriate capitalization, or discount rate, and then finding the present value of the cash flows. This, of course, is exactly what was done in Chapters 6 and 7 when the present values of investment opportunities were found.

CAPITALIZATION OF INCOME

The procedure for determining an asset's intrinsic value is known as the *capitalization-of-income method of valuation*. This is simply a fancy name for an old friend, the present value of a stream of earnings, discussed at length in Chapter 6. The following example illustrates the technique for valuing a bond. Following this, the technique is illustrated with preferred and common stocks. From this point on, whenever the word "value" is used, we mean the intrinsic value found by capitalizing future cash flows. Further, for purposes of exposition we shall assume that the current market prices of stocks or bonds are equal to their intrinsic values. This assumption is relaxed in future chapters, where we see that *differences* between management estimates of intrinsic values and market prices have a significant bearing on the type of security—stock or bond—used to raise funds at a given time.

Bond Valuation

Bond values are relatively easy to determine. So long as the bond is not expected to go into default, the expected cash flows are the annual interest payments plus the principal amount to be paid when the bond matures. Capitalization rates applied to bonds differ among bonds depending primarily upon differences in risk of default on interest or principal. A U. S. Treasury security, for example, would have less risk than one issued by the Westbrig Corporation; consequently, a lower discount (or capitalization) rate would be applied to its interest payments.

The actual calculating procedures employed in bond valuation are illustrated by the following examples.

---

[1] B. Graham, D. L. Dodd, and S. Cottle, *Security Analysis* (New York, McGraw-Hill, 1961), p. 28.

Example 1. After the Napoleonic Wars (1814) England sold a huge bond issue that was used to pay off many smaller issues of prior years which had been floated to pay for the war. Since the purpose of the new issue was to consolidate past debts, the individual bonds were called "Consols." Suppose the bonds had a par value of $1,000 (actually, they were stated in pounds) and paid $50 interest annually into perpetuity. What would the bonds be worth under current market conditions?

First, note that the value of any perpetuity [2] is computed as follows:

$$\text{value} = \frac{\text{constant annual receipts}}{\text{capitalization rate}} = \frac{R}{i}$$

We know that the Consol's annual in'erest payment is $50; therefore the only other thing we need in order to find its value is the appropriate capitalization rate. This is commonly taken as the going interest rate, or yield, on bonds of similar risk. Suppose we find such bonds to be paying 4 percent under current market conditions; then the Consol's value is determined as

$$\text{value} = \frac{R}{i} = \frac{\$50}{0.04} = \$1,250$$

If the going rate of interest rises to 5 percent, the value of the bond falls to $1,000 ($50/0.05 = $1,000). If interest rates continue rising, when the rate goes as high as 6 percent the value of the Consol will be only $833.33. Values of this perpetual bond at a range of interest rates are given in the following tabulation.

Current Market Interest Rate	Current Market Value
0.02	$2,500.00
0.03	1,666.67
0.04	1,250.00
0.05	1,000.00
0.06	833.33
0.07	714.29

Example 2. Now suppose the British government issues bonds with the same risk of default as the Consols, but with a three-year maturity. The new bonds also pay $50 interest and have a $1,000 par value. What will be

---

[2] A perpetuity is a bond that never matures; it pays interest indefinitely. The equation for finding the intrinsic value of a perpetuity is proved in J. Fred Weston and Eugene F. Brigham, *Managerial Finance, Second Edition,* p. 277.

the value of these new bonds at the time of issue if the going rate of interest is 4 percent? The solution requires the long form of the present value equation.[3]

Year	Receipt	4 Percent Discount Factors	Present Value
1	$50	0.962	$ 48.10
2	$50	0.925	46.25
3	$50 + $1,000	0.889	933.45
		bond value	$1,027.80

At the various rates of interest used in the preceding example, this three-year bond would have the following values.

Interest Rate	Capital Value
0.02 ·	$1,086.15
0.03	1,056.45
0.04	1,027.80
0.05	1,000.00
0.06	973.65
0.07	947.20

Note how much less the bond value changes with given changes in interest rates when the term to maturity is only three years. At a going rate of interest equal to 5 percent, both the perpetuity and the short-term bonds are valued at $1,000. When rates fall to 2 percent, the long-term bond rises to $2,500, while the short-term security goes to only $1,086. A similar situation occurs when rates rise above 5 percent. *This differential responsiveness to changes in interest rates always holds true—the longer the maturity of a security, the greater its reaction to a given change in capitalization rates.* Thus, even if the risk of default on two bonds is exactly the same, the value of the one with the longer maturity is exposed to more risk from a rise in interest rates. This greater risk explains why short-term bonds usually have lower yields, or rates of return, than long-term bonds. It also explains why corporate treasurers are reluctant to hold their near-cash reserves in the form of long-term debt instruments—these near-cash reserves are held for precautionary purposes, and a treasurer would be unwilling to sacrifice safety for a little higher yield on a long-term bond.

---

[3] If the bond had a longer maturity, 20 years for example, we would certainly want to calculate its present value by finding the present value of a 20-year annuity and then adding to that the present value of the $1,000 principal amount received at maturity. Special bond tables have been devised to simplify the calculation procedure.

Preferred Stock Valuation

Most preferred stocks entitle their owners to regular, fixed dividend payments similar to bond interest. Although some preferred issues are retired, this is unusual, and for the most part they are perpetuities, whose value is found as follows:

$$\text{value} = \frac{\text{preferred dividend}}{\text{capitalization rate}}$$

For example, General Motors has a preferred stock outstanding that pays a $3.75 annual dividend. The appropriate capitalization rate at the time the stock was issued (1925) was 7.5 percent, so it sold at $50 at the time of issue. Today, however, GM is a much stronger company and its preferred stock is much less risky. Also, interest rates are lower today than in the late 1920s. The combined result is that the yield on GM's preferred issue has fallen to 5¼ percent and the value of the stock has climbed to $71 a share.

$$\text{value} = \frac{\$3.75}{0.0525} = \$71$$

Common Stock Valuation

While the same principles apply to the valuation of common stocks as to bonds, preferred stocks, or other assets, two features make their analysis much more difficult. First is the degree of certainty with which receipts can be forecast. For bonds and preferred stocks, this forecast presents very little difficulty, as the interest payments or preferred dividends are known with relative certainty. But in the case of common stocks, the forecasting of future earnings, dividends, and stock prices is exceedingly difficult, to say the least. The second complicating feature is that, unlike interest and preferred dividends, common stock earnings and dividends are generally expected to grow, not remain constant. Hence, standard annuity formulas cannot be applied, and more difficult conceptual schemes must be used.

The investment value of a share of common stock depends upon the dollar returns an investor will receive if he buys the stock. Now what are the returns? They are, of course, the dividends the investor receives while he holds the stock plus the price he receives when he sells it; the ending price is equal to the beginning price plus capital gains or minus capital losses.

To illustrate, suppose you are thinking of buying a share of American Rubber common stock. If you buy the stock, you will hold it for one year. The current market price is $40 a share. You note that American Rubber is earning $3.60 a share and paying $2 a year in dividends, and that dividends, earnings, and the price of the company's stock have been rising at about 4 percent a year over the past 10 to 15 years. This 4 percent growth rate, incidentally, is about the same as the rate of growth in GNP and in stock prices generally.

Using this information and the investment evaluation techniques described in Chapters 6 and 7, you could calculate the expected rate of return on American Rubber's stock as follows:

$$\text{present price} = \frac{\text{dividend}}{(1+r)} + \frac{\text{price in 1 year}}{(1+r)}$$

$$\text{present price} = \frac{\text{dividend}}{(1+r)} + \frac{\text{present price} \times (1+\text{growth rate})}{(1+r)}$$

$$\$40 = \frac{\$2.00}{(1+r)} + \frac{\$40(1.04)}{(1+r)}$$

$$\$40 = \frac{\$2.00}{(1+r)} + \frac{\$41.60}{(1+r)} = \frac{\$43.60}{(1+r)}$$

$$1+r = \frac{\$43.60}{\$40.00} = 1.090$$

$$r = 1.090 - 1.00 = 0.090, \text{ or } 9\%$$

Let us examine the steps here, and the assumptions involved. First, note that the first equation sets up the purchase of the share of stock as an investment (1) with a cost equal to the present price and (2) with returns equal to the dividend plus the ending price one year from now. The second equation shows that the ending price is equal to the present price plus the 4 percent expected price increase. The remainder of the equations simply substitute in the appropriate values and solve the basic equation for r, the rate of return on the stock, which turns out to be 9 percent.

The expected rate of return, r, can be split into two components, one from capital gains and one from dividends. This is done below:

$$\text{dividend yield} = \frac{\text{expected dividends}}{\text{current price}} = \frac{\$2}{\$40} = 0.05, \text{ or } 5\%$$

$$\text{capital gains yield} = \frac{\text{expected price increase}}{\text{current price}} = \frac{\$1.60}{\$40.00} = 0.04, \text{ or } 4\%$$

In this instance, the expected dividend yield turns out to be 5 percent, and the capital gains yield 4 percent.

The total return, or yield, is equal to the dividend yield plus the capital gains yield.

$$\text{total return} = \text{dividend yield} + \text{capital gains yield}$$

$$= \frac{\text{expected dividend}}{\text{current price}} + \frac{\text{expected increase in price}}{\text{current price}}$$

Dividends are abbreviated to D, the current price to P, and the second term in the equation—the increase in price divided by the current price, or the growth rate—to G. The following fundamental equation is thus produced.

$$\text{rate of return} = \frac{D}{P} + G$$

To repeat, the rate of return on a share of common stock is equal to its dividend yield plus the expected growth in the price of the stock, or the capital gains.[4]

Two critical assumptions are involved in the calculations: (1) that the dividend will be paid and (2) that the stock price will continue to grow at a 4 percent rate.[5] For a stable, solid company like American Rubber the dividend assumption is probably a good one, but the growth assumption will almost surely not hold exactly. Depending on a great many factors—but most importantly the performance of the entire stock market—the ending price will turn out to be more or less than $41.60. And, depending on whether the final price is higher or lower than the one forecast, the rate of return will turn out to be more or less than anticipated. If, for example, the stock market soars and American Rubber goes up to $50 a share, the $10 capital gain plus the $2 dividend will provide a 30 percent rate of return. On the other hand, if the market slumps badly and American Rubber falls to $30, the return will be *minus* 20 percent.

One other point should be observed in connection with these calculations for American Rubber. Notice that the company is expected to earn $3.60 a share and to pay out $2 in dividends. This means that $1.60 will be retained. Suppose the company reinvests these retained earnings in projects that yield 9 percent. Future earnings will increase by $0.14 ($1.60 × 0.09). Capitalized at 9 percent, the additional earnings add $1.60 to the value of the stock ($0.14/0.09). This $1.60 is exactly equal to the expected capital gain found above. The company *has* been retaining about 45

---

[4] Strictly speaking, this equation holds only if the growth rate is expected to remain constant in the future. A number of articles have been written on the problem of varying growth rates, but it need not concern us here.

[5] We are only using a one-year holding period. In the general case, where the holding period is of any length, the equation is still used, but another assumption must be added. Namely, the dividend must grow at the same rate as the stock price. Again, for a stable company such as American Rubber this is a good assumption— dividends and stock prices *do* move more or less together.

percent of its earnings, and it *has* been earning about 9 percent on new equity. The fact that earnings have been retained and reinvested in profitable projects explains why American Rubber has enjoyed a record of rising stock prices.

This exposition has been based on only a one-year holding period, but it can be expanded to any holding period with exactly the same results. The procedures are much more complicated, however, as one can see by examining some of the technical materials cited in the readings book references.[6] We next look at the factors that cause differentials in the expected rates of returns among securities, and then examine historical patterns of returns on stocks and bonds.

FACTORS LEADING TO VARIATIONS IN RETURNS AMONG SECURITIES

Risk and Rates of Return

The most important factor leading to differential expected rates of return among different securities is differences in risk. Here *risk* is defined as uncertainty about the return that will actually be realized. For example, if the asset in question is a 60-day Treasury bill, the expected returns can be estimated quite accurately—there is little risk of not realizing the expected yield. If the security is a corporate bond, there is always some danger that the firm will default; thus, there is some uncertainty about the final return.

Uncertainty is greater yet when we move to common stocks. Dividends are not always predictable, and the capital gains component is quite uncertain. Within common stocks, different companies' stocks are more uncertain than others. Such well-established firms as AT&T, General Motors, and du Pont have long histories of earnings and dividends, and we can predict their long-term future performance reasonably well. On the other hand, there is more uncertainty in the case of new companies and those developing new and essentially untried products—in these cases, risk is high relative to the AT&Ts, GMs, and other blue chips.

Would you expect returns to be higher or lower on risky investments?

---

[6] While most authorities would agree with our beliefs that stock prices are determined by such fundamentals as earnings, dividends, and rates of return on retained earnings, some argue that securities, especially common stocks, are valued by an essentially irrational process which involves psychology, stockbroker recommendations, and several other factors. Such essentially random phenomena do have a profound influence on short-run price movements; nevertheless, we argue that the long-run value of a stock is determined by investors capitalizing expected future returns. As the more sophisticated institutional investors assume a more important role in the stock market, this is becoming increasingly true.

Although some individuals are gamblers by nature and seem to prefer more to less risk, investors as a group dislike risk, or are "risk averters." Given risk aversion, securities with higher risk must sell on the basis of higher expected yields. For example, 9 percent expected return might be acceptable for American Rubber's stock, but a more stable and predictable electric utility common stock might sell on a 7 percent return basis. On the other hand, investors might be unwilling to buy stock in a wildcat oil drilling concern unless they can expect to make 20 percent.[7]

For a given firm, its bonds are less risky to investors than its common stocks, so expected yields are higher on stocks than on bonds. Risks on preferred stocks lie between bonds and common stocks, so returns on these securities should also fall in the middle.

One might also observe that different degrees of risk are incurred by individual firms within particular industries. If, for example, one firm has a strong research and development (R&D) program, excellent recruitment and management training programs, and broad geographic and product diversification, while another has none of these features, the first will be regarded as less risky than the second and will sell on a lower yield basis. If small firms, because of less product or geographic diversification, lower R&D expenditures, greater management succession problems, or any other reasons are considered to be more risky than large firms, investors will require a higher rate of return on small firms' securities.

Marketability and Rates of Return

Investors also value flexibility, or maneuverability. If one becomes disenchanted with a particular investment or if he needs funds for consumption or other investments, it is highly desirable for him to be able to liquidate his holdings. Other things the same, the higher the liquidity, or marketability, the lower an investment's required rate of return. Accordingly, one would expect to find listed stocks selling on a lower yield basis than over-the-counter stocks, and publicly owned stocks selling at lower yields than stocks with no established market. Since investments in small firms are generally less liquid than those in large companies, we have another reason for expecting to find higher required yields among smaller companies.

Changes in Stock Price Levels

Equity yields differ among firms because of differences in inherent risks and marketability, but they also differ for an individual stock over time. If the demand for funds is particularly heavy, and if at the same time

---

[7] Investors in the drilling company recognize, of course, that they may well end up taking a 100 percent *loss* on the venture, but this is balanced by the chance that the company will strike it rich and pay a handsome return.

the supply is restricted, the law of supply and demand requires that the price of funds—the interest rate on debt or the required rate of return on equity—be higher than when supply and demand conditions are reversed. In the late 1940s, for example, many corporations were expanding and seeking equity funds to finance this expansion, while many investors were expecting a serious postwar depression and were not interested in purchasing stocks. The result was a very high required rate of return on equity issues and low common stock prices.

As it became clear that the booming economy was not headed for a depression, investors began putting more money into the equity markets. Simultaneously, productive capacity began to catch up with demand, lowering corporate demands for funds. The net result was a pronounced decline in required rates of return and a much higher level of stock prices. These changes are illustrated in Figure 9-1.

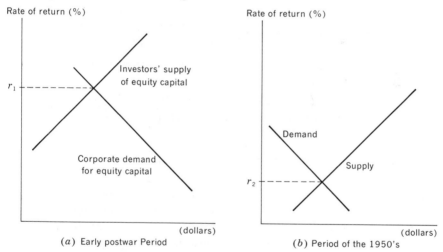

Figure 9-1   Hypothetical Supply and Demand for Equity Securities

Stock prices change for either of two reasons—changes in required rates of return or changes in growth expectations. For example, the 1949–1968 increase in stock prices may have been caused by either declining required equity yields, higher growth expectations, or a combination of the two.

This idea can be illustrated by reference to American Rubber. Recall that when the stock is selling for $40, is paying a $2 dividend, and is expected to grow at about 4 percent during the next year, the expected rate of return is calculated to be 9 percent.

Now suppose supply and demand conditions in the capital markets change so that the equilibrium rate of return—the point where supply equals demand—on American Rubber's stock declines to 8 percent. Assuming that dividend and growth expectations remain constant, this decline in the capitalization rate causes the current price to jump from $40 to $50. The reasons are explained below. First, note that the current price is determined as:

$$\text{current price or value} = \frac{\text{dividend}}{1 + \text{capitalization rate}} + \frac{\text{current price} \times (1 + \text{growth rate})}{1 + \text{capitalization rate}}$$

Substituting in the known quantities—the $2 dividend, the 8 percent capitalization rate, and the 4 percent growth rate—we find the current price of the stock.

$$\text{current price} = \frac{\$2.00}{1.08} + \frac{\text{current price}(1.04)}{1.08}$$

$$= \frac{\$2.00 + 1.04 \text{ current price}}{1.08}$$

$$1.08 \text{ current price} = \$2.00 + 1.04 \text{ current price}$$
$$1.08 \text{ current price} - 1.04 \text{ current price} = \$2$$
$$0.04 \text{ current price} = \$2.00$$

$$\text{current price} = \frac{\$2.00}{0.04} = \$50 \text{ a share}$$

Therefore, if the average investor expects American Rubber to pay a $2 dividend and to experience a 4 percent stock price appreciation from the reinvestment of retained earnings, and if he is to receive an 8 percent return on his investment, then the initial investment—the current price—must be $50.[8]

A change in growth expectations could produce a similar change. With the capitalization rate 9 percent and the growth rate 4 percent, the current price is $40. Now suppose the company announces a development that

---

[8] For those interested in generalized formulas, one applicable to a perpetual growth situation is:

$$P = \frac{D}{r - g}$$

where P = current price, D = current dividend, r = required rate of return, and g = the growth rate.

$$P = \frac{\$2.00}{0.08 - 0.04} = \frac{\$2.00}{0.04} = \$50 \text{ in the example}$$

leads investors to expect a higher rate of growth—say 5 percent per year. Substituting this new growth rate into the price equation and solving for the current price, we find a new price of $50 per share.

$$\text{current price} = \frac{\$2.00}{1.09} + \frac{\text{current price } (1.05)}{1.09} = \$50$$

For American Rubber, then, we see that a sharp stock price increase (or decrease) can arise from changes in market capitalization rates or growth expectations, or from a combination of the two. These ideas can be generalized for the stock market as a whole, and they can be used to explain changes in the level of stock prices.

Historical Rates of Return

Equity Yields. Various financial researchers investigating returns on publicly-owned stock over long periods have found them to average about 9 percent. When measured from stock market lows, returns are relatively high; conversely, when the market is high in the base period, stockholder yields are relatively low. For example, had one bought a portfolio of stocks at the average price prevailing in the depressed year 1949 and held them until 1965, his return would have been about 15 percent. The same group of stocks, bought during the high market in 1961, would have yielded a little over 6 percent by 1965.

Some rough averages of estimated stock yields under different market conditions are shown in Table 9-1. To the extent (1) that the future approximates the past and (2) that investors base expected future returns on those realized in the past, the figures in the table should give some idea of stockholders' required rates of return under different market, risk, and liquidity conditions.

Table 9–1   ESTIMATED RATES OF RETURN ON COMMON STOCKS

	Stock Market Condition		
Company Characteristics	*High*	*Normal*	*Low*
Low risk, high marketability	6½	7	9½
Average risk and marketability	7–8	8–10	12–15
High risk, low marketability	9	12	20

Debt Yields. Debt yields, or rates of return, also vary over time and with the characteristics of the individual loan. Many different statistics could be presented to support this assertion, but Table 9-2 illustrates it sufficiently. The year 1958 was a period of monetary ease; 1962 might be characterized as "normal" for recent years; and 1966 was a period of extremely tight money. A glance down any of the columns will show how bank interest rates varied between periods.

Table 9-2   BANK RATES ON BUSINESS LOANS IN 19 LARGE CITIES

	Size of Loan (in thousands of dollars)			
	1–10	10–100	100–200	200 and over
1958	5.5%	5.0%	4.6%	4.1%
1962	5.9	5.5	5.2	4.8
1966 (December)	6.8	6.7	6.5	6.2

SOURCE: *Federal Reserve Bulletin,* January 1967, p. 112.

Variations across the rows of the table are somewhat more difficult to explain. In part, interest rates on loans decline as the size of the loan increases because of the fixed costs of making and servicing loans. In addition, part of the decline occurs because small firms make small loans, and small firms are inherently more risky than large ones. But, at any rate, it is clear that returns on debt, like those on stock, vary over time and with the characteristics of the borrower.

The concepts of valuation and rates of return on debt and equity securities developed in this chapter are fundamentally related to the cost of capital concept. This is the subject of the following chapter.

SUMMARY

In the discussion of the capital budgeting process in Chapter 7, the discount rate used in the calculations was seen to be of vital importance. At that time, we simply assumed that the cost of capital—the discount rate used in the present value process—was known, and we used this assumed rate in the calculations. In this chapter, however, we turned our attention to the theory of the cost of capital.

Since the cost of capital is integrally related to investors' returns on capital, the basic principles underlying valuation theory were discussed and a number of definitions of value were presented: (1) liquidating versus going-concern value, (2) book versus market value, and (3) market versus "intrinsic" value. This last concept, intrinsic value, is fundamentally dependent upon discounted cash flow concepts and procedures, and it involves estimating future cash flows and discounting them back to the present at an appropriate rate of interest. This rate of interest, defined as the "required rate of return," is a function of the investment's risk and the investor's opportunity costs.

Rates of return on bonds and preferred stocks are simple to understand and to calculate, but common stock returns are more difficult. First, common stock returns consist of (1) dividends and (2) capital gains, not a single type of payment as occurs with bonds and preferred stocks. This fact necessitates the development of a rate of return formula that considers both dividends and capital gains; the rate of return formula for common stocks is, therefore, a two-part equation:

rate of return = dividend yield + capital gains yield

The second complicating feature of common stock is the degree of uncertainty involved. Bond and preferred stock payments are relatively predictable, but forecasting common stock dividends and, even more, capital gains, is a highly uncertain business.

Note also that risk is of two types: (1) a basic business risk having to do with the nature of the industry and the firm and (2) a financial risk dependent upon the extent to which financial leverage is employed. A firm that manufactures producers' durables—for example, railroad locomotives—is inherently more risky than an electric utility or chain of grocery stores. However, firms can and do alter their basic risks by using more or less financial (and also operating) leverage. As a result, a firm in a relatively stable industry may, because of excessive financial leverage, end up in a more risky position than one in an unstable industry.

As investors generally dislike risk, the required rate of return is higher on more risky securities. Bonds, as a class, are less risky than preferred stocks, and preferred stocks, in turn, are less risky than common stocks. As a result, the required rate of return is lowest for bonds, next for preferred stocks, and highest for common stocks. Within each of these security classes, there are variations among the issuing firms' risks; hence, required rates of return vary among firms. Also, supply and demand conditions in the capital markets change over time, so a given firm's securities will have different required rates of return at different points in time. Tables were presented to give some idea of the levels of the required rates of return on different types of securities and during different periods.

QUESTIONS

9–1 Most inheritance tax laws state that for estate tax purposes property shall be valued on the basis of "fair market value." Describe how an inheritance tax appraiser might use the valuation principles discussed in this chapter to establish the value (1) of shares of a stock listed on the New York Stock Exchange and (2) of shares representing 20 percent of a stock that is not publicly traded.

9–2 How does the level of interest rates influence stock and bond prices?

9–3 Using the theoretical concepts developed in this chapter and certain preceding ones, develop an argument to support the frequently encountered statement that a rising level of interest rates depresses the stock market. (It is true that higher interest rates tend to deflate the economy, hence corporate profits and stock prices, but this is not the desired answer to this question.)

9–4 Explain why bonds with longer maturities experience wider price movements from a given change in interest rates than do shorter maturity bonds. Preferably, give your answer (1) in words (intuitively) and (2) mathematically.

9–5 Describe the factors that determine the market rate of return on a particular stock at a given point in time.

9–6 Table 9–1 gives some estimates of rates of return on common stocks. Using this or similar tables, would you expect ten "experts" to reach the same conclusion about expected market yields on a given firm's common stock? Why or why not?

PROBLEMS

9–1 a) The Bay State Company is earning $4 million a year after taxes. Its common stock has a $10 par value; 3 million shares are authorized and 1 million shares are outstanding. What are the company's earnings per share?

b) Common stocks of electronic companies in the same risk class as Bay State sell to yield 5 percent on earnings. What would be the expected price of Bay State's stock? Why? (Note: earnings yield is earnings/price.)

c) At what price/earnings ratio does Bay State common sell?

d) If Bay State common sold on an 8 percent earnings yield basis, what would be its price? its price/earnings ratio?

e) Bay State pays a yearly dividend of $2 a share. If Bay State sells to yield 5 percent on earnings, what is the dividend yield basis on which it sells? (Note: dividend yield is dividend/price.)

9–2 a) The bonds of the Carolina Corporation are perpetuities bearing a 5 percent coupon and rated Aaa. Bonds of this type yield 4 percent. What is the price of Carolina's bonds? Their par value is $1,000.

b) Interest rate levels rise to the point where such bonds now yield 6 percent. What will be the price of the Carolina bonds now?

c) Interest rate levels drop to 5 percent. At what price will the Carolina bonds sell?

d) How would your answer to parts *a, b,* and *c* change if the bonds had a definite maturity date of 20 years?

9–3 Mike Dunn contemplates the purchase of a small electronics firm. Expected sales of the company are $2 million a year. For this line of business, firms earn 5.5 percent on sales after taxes.

Dunn feels that his money should earn a 20 percent return on investment in an area as risky as electronics. What is the largest amount he would pay for the electronics firm?

9–4 Because of ill health and old age Robert McKenzie contemplates the sale of his hardware store. His corporation has the following balance sheet:

Assets		Liabilities and Net Worth	
Cash	$ 8,000	Notes payable—bank	$ 3,500
Receivables, net	3,000	Accounts payable	5,000
Inventories	19,000	Accruals	1,500
Fixtures and equipment less $10,000 reserve for depreciation	20,000	Common stock plus surplus	40,000
		Total liabilities and	
Total assets	$50,000	net worth	$50,000

Annual before-tax earnings (after rent, interest, and salaries) for the preceding 3 years have averaged $12,000.

McKenzie has set a price of $60,000, which includes all the assets of the business except cash; the buyer assumes all debts. The assets include a 5-year lease and the goodwill associated with the name of McKenzie Hardware. Assume both McKenzie and the potential purchaser are in the 50 percent tax bracket.

a) Is the price of $60,000 a reasonable one? Explain.

b) What other factors should be taken into account in arriving at a selling price?

c) What is the significance, if any, of the rental option?

9–5 The Doyle Company is a small machine-tool manufacturer. It has been successful and has grown. Doyle is planning to sell an issue of common stock to the public for the first time. It faces the problem of setting an appropriate price on its common stock. The company feels that the proper procedure is to select firms similar to Doyle with publicly traded common stock and to make relevant comparisons.

The company finds several machine-tool manufacturers similar to it with respect to product mix, size, asset composition, and debt/equity proportions. Of these, Western and Olympic are most similar.

Relation	Western	Olympic	Doyle Totals
Earnings per share, 1966	$ 3.00	$ 5.00	$ 800,000
Average, 1960–1966	2.00	4.00	600,000
Price per share, 1966	24.00	50.00	—
Dividends per share, 1966	1.50	2.50	400,000
Average, 1960–1966	1.20	2.50	300,000
Book value per share	20.00	50.00	6,000,000
Market-book ratio	120%	100%	—

a) How would these relations be used in guiding Doyle in arriving at a market value for its stock?

b) What price would you recommend if Doyle sells 200,000 shares?

Chapter 10

The Cost of Capital

In the preceding chapter, the nature of the valuation process and the concept of expected rates of return were considered in some detail. In the discussion of the cost of capital, the subject of this chapter, extensive use will be made of these valuation concepts. First, the costs of the individual components of the capital structure—debt, preferred stock, and equity—are considered. Next, these individual component costs are brought together to form a weighted cost of capital. Finally, the conceptual ideas developed in the first two sections are illustrated with an example of the cost of capital calculation for an actual company.

DEBT CAPITAL

If a firm borrows $100,000 for one year at 6 percent interest, its before-tax dollar cost is $6,000 and its before-tax percentage cost is 6 percent. *As a first approximation, the cost of debt is defined as the rate of return that must be earned on debt-financed investments in order to keep unchanged the earnings available to common shareholders.*[1] Hence, the cost of debt

---

[1] Note that this definition is a *first approximation;* it will be modified to take account of the deductibility of interest payments for income tax purposes. Note also that the cost of debt is considered in isolation. The impact of the debt on the cost of equity, as well as on future increments of debt (in a sense, the true marginal cost of debt), will be treated when the weighted cost of capital is derived.

turns out to be the interest rate on debt, for if the firm borrows and invests the borrowed funds to earn a before-tax return just equal to the interest rate, then the earnings available to common stock remain unchanged. This is demonstrated below.

Example. The ABC Company has sales of $1 million, operating costs of $900,000, and no debt, and is taxed at the rate of 50 percent. Its income statement is shown in the Before column below. Then it borrows $100,000 at 6 percent and invests the funds in assets whose use causes sales to rise by $7,000 and operating costs to rise by $1,000. Hence, profits before interest rise by $6,000. The new situation is shown in the After column. Earnings after taxes are unchanged, as the investment just earns its cost of capital.

	Income Statements	
	Before	*After*
Sales	$1,000,000	$1,007,000
Operating costs	900,000	901,000
Earnings before interest and taxes (EBIT)	$ 100,000	$ 106,000
Interest	—	6,000
Earnings before taxes (EBT)	$ 100,000	$ 100,000
Taxes	50,000	50,000
Earnings after taxes (EAT)	$ 50,000	$ 50,000

Note that the cost of debt is applicable to *new* debt, not to the interest on old, previously outstanding debt. The primary concern with the cost of capital is to use it in a decision-making process—the decision whether to obtain capital to make new investments; the fact that the firm borrowed at high or low rates in the past is irrelevant.

PREFERRED STOCK

Preferred stock, described in detail in Chapter 16, is a hybrid between debt and common stock. Like debt, preferred stock carries a fixed commitment on the part of the corporation to make periodic payments, and in liquidation the claims of the preferred stockholders take precedence over those of the common stockholders. Unlike debt, however, failure to make the preferred dividend payments does not result in bankruptcy. Preferred stock is thus somewhat more risky to the firm than common stock, but it is less risky than bonds. Just the reverse holds for investors. To the investor, preferred is less risky than common, but more risky than debt.

The definition of the cost of preferred stock is similar to that of the cost of debt—it is that rate of return which must be earned on preferred stock-financed investments in order to keep unchanged the earnings available to common shareholders. This required rate of return turns out to be the preferred dividend per share (D_p) divided by the net price that the firm could realize from the sale of one share of a new issue of preferred stock (P_n).

$$\text{cost of preferred stock} = \frac{D_p}{P_n}$$

For example, if a firm sells an issue of $100 par value preferred stock with a $6 dividend and nets $95 a share after underwriting commissions, then its cost of preferred stock is 6.3 percent ($6/$95).

TAX ADJUSTMENT

As they stand, the definitions of the cost of debt and preferred stock capital are incompatible because, for tax purposes, interest payments are deductible and preferred dividends are not. The following example is an illustration.

Example. The ABC Company can borrow $100,000 at 6 percent, or it can sell 1,000 shares of $6 preferred stock to net $100 a share. Its before-investment situation is given in the Before column below. At what rate of return must it invest the proceeds from the new financing to keep the earnings available to common shareholders from changing?

		Invest in Assets Yielding		
		6%		*12%*
	Before	*Debt*	*Preferred*	*Preferred*
EBIT	$100,000	$106,000	$106,000	$112,000
I	—	6,000	—	—
EBT	100,000	100,000	106,000	112,000
T (50%)	50,000	50,000	53,000	56,000
Preferred dividends	—	—	6,000	6,000
Available for common dividends	$ 50,000	$ 50,000	$ 47,000	$ 50,000

As can be seen from the tabulations, if the funds are invested to yield 6 percent before taxes, earnings available to common stockholders are constant if debt is used, but they fall if the financing is with preferred stock. To maintain the $50,000 net earnings requires that funds generated from the sale of preferred stock be invested to yield 12 percent before taxes or 6 percent after taxes.

Cost-of-capital calculations may be made either on a before-tax or an after-tax basis. Ultimately, however, business decision makers must consider after-tax effects. Therefore, just as in Chapter 9 in the discussion of the rates of return on investments, only the cost of capital *after* corporate taxes will be dealt with. The cost of preferred stock is already on an after-tax basis as defined, but a simple adjustment is needed to arrive at the after-tax cost of debt. It is recognized that interest payments are tax deductible, and the cost of debt capital is reduced as follows:

$$\text{after-tax cost of debt} = (\text{before-tax cost}) \times (1.0 - \text{tax rate})$$

Example: before-tax cost of debt = 6 percent, tax rate = 48 percent
$$\text{after-tax cost} = (0.06)\ (1 - 0.48) = (0.06)\ (0.52) = 3.12 \text{ percent}$$

Had the tax rate been 50 percent, as is usually assumed for ease of calculations, the after-tax cost of debt would have been one half the interest rate.

COST OF EQUITY

The cost of equity capital is defined as the minimum rate of return that must be earned on equity-financed investments to keep unchanged the value of the existing common equity. In other words, if 10 percent is a corporation's cost of equity capital, then the value of the equity used to finance an investment will exceed its cost if—and only if—the internal rate of return on the investment exceeds 10 percent.

In general, there is a different cost of capital applicable to equity capital raised by retaining earnings than to that raised by selling new common stock. These points are covered below.

Retained Earnings[2]

The cost of retained earnings, or the return that must be earned on investments financed by retained earnings, is equal to the rate of return that investors expect to receive on the stock. To illustrate, consider Aubey

---

[2] Our treatment of the cost of retained earnings abstracts from certain complications caused by personal income taxes on dividend income and by brokerage costs incurred in reinvesting dividend income. We consider these points as being refinements not essential to an understanding of managerial finance, and, hence, have elected not to discuss them here. The problems are discussed at length in J. Fred Weston and Eugene F. Brigham, *Managerial Finance, Second Edition,* Chapter 12 and Appendix 12–B. We have also elected to disregard depreciation-generated funds when calculating the cost of capital. These funds have essentially the same cost as retained earnings.

Rents, a firm currently earning $2 a share, paying a $1 dividend, and selling at $20 a share. The company's earnings, dividends, and stock price have all been growing at about 5 percent a year, and this growth rate is expected to continue indefinitely. Using this information and the procedures developed in Chapter 9, we compute the expected rate of return on the stock as follows:

$$\text{expected, or required, rate of return} = \frac{\text{dividend}}{\text{price}} + \text{expected growth}$$

$$= \frac{\$1}{\$20} + 5\% = 10\%$$

The expected growth rate in the price of the shares is 5 percent; on the $20 initial price, this leads to a $1 increase in the value of the stock. This price increase will be attained (barring changes in the general level of stock prices) if the company retains $1 and invests this amount to yield 10 percent. However, if the $1 of retained earnings is invested to yield only 5 percent, then earnings will grow by only $0.05 during the year, not by the expected $0.10 a share. The new earnings will be $2.05, not the expected $2.10. This represents a growth of only 2½ percent, not 5 percent. If investors believe that the firm will earn only 5 percent on retained earnings in the future and thus attain only a 2½ percent growth rate, they will reappraise the value of the stock downward as follows:

$$\text{current price} = \frac{\text{dividend}}{(1+r)} + \frac{\text{current price} \times (1 + \text{expected growth})}{(1+r)}$$

$$P = \frac{\$1.00}{1.10} + \frac{P \times (1.025)}{1.10}$$

$$= \frac{\$1.00 + 1.025P}{1.10}$$

$$1.10P = \$1.00 + 1.025P$$

$$1.100P - 1.025P = \$1.00$$

$$0.075P = \$1.00$$

$$P = \$13.33$$

Note, however, that Aubey Rents suffered this price decline because it invested equity funds—retained earnings—at less than its cost of capital. Had it refrained from making this investment and paid all its earnings out in dividends, it would have cut its growth rate to zero. However, the price of the stock would not have fallen, because investors would still have been getting the required 10 percent rate of return on their investments.

$$R = \frac{D}{P} + G = \frac{\$2}{\$20} + 0 = 10 \text{ percent}$$

All the return would have been coming in the form of dividends, but the rate of return would have been the required 10 percent.

New Common Stock

The cost of new common stock is higher than the cost of retained earnings, because of the flotation costs involved in selling new common stock. To demonstrate, let us continue with the example of Aubey Rents. The company has 10,000 shares of stock outstanding, no debt, and is expected to earn $20,000, or $2 a share during the coming year. Investors anticipate that the company will continue its policy of paying out 50 percent of earnings as dividends, so $1 is the dividend expectation for the coming year. The firm has also been growing at 5 percent a year, and this growth rate is expected to be maintained. Investors require a 10 percent rate of return on the stock, so it is selling for $20 a share.

Now suppose Aubey Rents sells 5,000 shares of stock to the public at $20 a share, incurs a selling cost of $2 a share, and thus nets $18 a share, or a total of $90,000. If this $90,000 is invested to yield 10 percent, will the earnings, dividend, and price expectations be met? First, we calculate the new earnings per share, giving effect to the stock sale and to the new investment.

$$\text{incremental profits} = \$90,000 \times 0.10 = \$9,000$$
$$\text{total profits} = \$20,000 + \$9,000 = \$29,000$$
$$\text{incremental shares} = 5,000$$
$$\text{total shares} = 10,000 + 5,000 = 15,000$$
$$\text{new earnings per share} = \frac{\$29,000}{15,000} = \$1.93$$

The $1.93 is below the expected $2 a share. The sale of the new shares has diluted earnings, and the price of the stock will fall below $20 a share. Thus, the investment has not met the definition of cost of capital—the return on the investment financed by new stock did not earn the cost of capital because the incremental profits were not sufficient to keep the price of the stock from falling.

What rate of return must be earned on funds raised by selling stock to make this action worthwhile or, to put it another way, what is the cost of new common stock? The answer is found by applying the following formula.

$$\text{cost of new common stock} = \frac{\text{required rate of return on common stock}}{1 - \text{percentage cost of floating new common stock}}$$

In our example, the flotation cost on new equity issues is 10 percent ($2/$20), so applying the formula we find the cost of new common stock to be 11.1 percent.

$$\text{cost of new common stock} = \frac{10\%}{1.0 - 0.10} = \frac{10\%}{0.9} = 11.1\%$$

If Aubey earns 11.1 percent on investments financed by new common stock issues, earnings per share will not fall below previous expectations, the price of the stock will not fall, and the investments will have covered their cost of capital.

Finding the Basic Required Rate of Return on Common Stock

It is obvious by now that the basic rate of return required by investors on a firm's common stock is a most important quantity. This required rate of return is the cost of retained earnings and, used with the cost of floating common stock, it forms the basis for the cost of capital from new stock issues. How is this all-important quantity estimated?

Although one *can* use very involved, highly complicated procedures for making this estimation, satisfactory estimates may, in general, be obtained in either of two ways.

1. Simply look at the average rate of return that investors have obtained in the past, assume that in the future stocks will continue to have about the same rates of return as in the past, and use these historical averages as estimates of the current cost of equity capital.

For this, we recommend the figures given in Table 9–1. To use the table for this purpose, one must first make judgment decisions (1) about the risk/liquidity position of the stock in question and (2) about the state of the stock market. Suppose, for example, we decide that our particular company is of about average risk and liquidity and that the stock market is about normal— the market is not, in our judgment, either abnormally high or abnormally low. In this case we would simply assign 9 percent as the basic cost of equity capital. Later on, if the market dropped sharply, we would re-evaluate the cost of equity upward, to 10 or, perhaps, even to 12 percent.

Notice that some very fine judgments are required in this process. It would be nice to pretend that these judgments are unnecessary and to specify a precise way of determining the exact cost of equity capital. Unfortunately, this is not possible. Finance is in large part a matter of judgment, and one simply must face this fact.

    2. An alternative procedure, the use of which is recommended in conjunction with the one described above, is to estimate the basic required rate of return as

$$\text{rate of return} = \frac{\text{dividends}}{\text{price}} + \text{average growth rate}$$

The rationale for this equation, which has been developed in detail in Chapter 9, is that stockholder returns are derived from dividends and capital gains. The total of the dividend yield plus the average growth rate over the past 5-to-10 years gives an estimate of the total returns that stockholders probably expect in the future from a particular share of stock.

    For normal companies—those which are growing at a rate approximately equal to that of the entire economy—the two procedures generally give similar results. If recent growth has been extremely high, so high that it is doubtful the rate can be maintained, then the first procedure is the better one.

WEIGHTED COST OF CAPITAL

Suppose a particular firm's cost of debt is estimated to be 2½ percent (the interest rate on new debt issues is 5 percent), its cost of equity is estimated to be 8 percent, and the decision has been made to finance next year's projects by selling debt. The argument is frequently advanced that the cost of these projects is 2½ percent because debt will be used to finance them.

    This position contains a basic fallacy. To finance a particular set of projects with debt implies that the firm is also using up some of its potential for obtaining new low-cost debt. As expansion takes place in subsequent years, at some point the firm will find it necessary to use additional equity financing, or else the debt ratio will become too large. Because of this, the firm should be viewed as an on-going concern and its cost of capital should be calculated as a weighted average of the various types of funds it uses: debt, preferred stock, and equity.

The Calculating Procedure

    Before discussing the proper set of weights to be employed in computing the weighted average, it is useful to look briefly at the calculating procedure. The method is demonstrated in the following example.

    Example. The right-hand side of the Simple Company's balance sheet is shown in column 2 of the table below, and the dollars are converted to percentages of the total in column 3. Column 4 gives the after-tax costs of the different types of capital: debt, preferred stock, and equity; column 5 shows the product of column 3 and column 4. Summing column 5 gives the weighted average cost of the firm's capital—0.0775, or 7.75 percent.

SIMPLE COMPANY

(1) *Capital Components*	(2) *Balance Sheet Figures*	(3) *Percent of Total*	(4) *Component Cost (after taxes)*	(5) *Column 3 times Column 4*	(6) *Column 2 times Column 4*
Debt	$ 30,000,000	30%	3%	0.0090	$ 900,000
Preferred stock	5,000,000	5	7	0.0035	350,000
Net worth	65,000,000	65	10	0.0650	6,500,000
Total	$100,000,000	100%		0.0775	$7,750,000

An alternative method that gives identical results is to multiply the dollar figures in column 2 by the component costs in column 4 to get the figures in column 6; then add column 6 and divide the sum by the total amount of capital. Thus, the total dollar cost of $7.750 million divided by the $100 million of capital is 7.75 percent. We use whichever method provides the easiest calculations for the specific application.

The Weighting System

Although both financial theorists and corporate financial managers disagree over particular aspects of debt policy, there is general agreement that firms do seek optimum capital structures. "Optimum" is defined as the capital structure that minimizes the average cost of capital, and the concept is illustrated below. To minimize confusion, it is assumed that firms have no preferred stock.

Figure 10-1 shows a scatter diagram between the cost of debt and the cost of equity capital plotted against the debt ratio for a hypothetical industry. Each dot represents one of the firms in the industry. For example, the dots labeled "1" represent firm 1, a company with only 10 percent debt. Firm 1's after-tax cost of debt is 3 percent, while its cost of equity is 12 percent. Firm 2 uses 20 percent debt and also has a 3 percent cost of debt and a 12 percent cost of equity. Firm 3, on the other hand, has a 14 percent cost of equity and a 4 percent cost of debt. It uses 35 percent debt, and investors consider this to be a sufficiently high debt level to require higher yields on the firm's securities. In this particular industry, the threshold level of debt that begins to worry investors is 20 percent. Below 20 percent debt, investors are totally unconcerned about any risk induced by debt; above 20 percent, they are aware of the higher risk and require compensation in the form of higher rates of return.

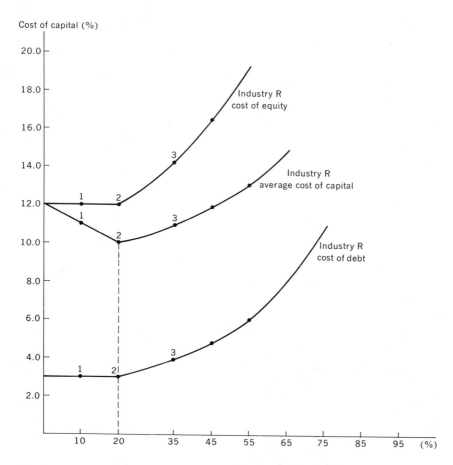

Figure 10-1   Hypothetical Cost of Capital Schedules for An Industry

The debt and the equity costs may be averaged on the basis of their respective weights of debt and equity capital. Firm 1 has a weighted average cost equal to 11.1 percent; firm 2 has a weighted average cost of 10.2 percent; and firm 3 has a weighted cost of 10.5 percent. These average costs, together with those of the other firms in the industry, are also plotted in Figure 10-1. We can see that firm 2 has the lowest average cost of capital— *20 percent debt is the debt ratio that minimizes the average cost of capital, so the optimal capital structure requires that firms use 20 percent debt.* According to the theory, the other firms in the industry should move toward a 20 percent debt ratio.

Shown in Figure 10-2 are the cost-of-capital schedules for firms in a risky industry (R) and a stable industry (S). Industry R, the one on which Figure 10-1 was based, might consist of diesel locomotive manufacturers

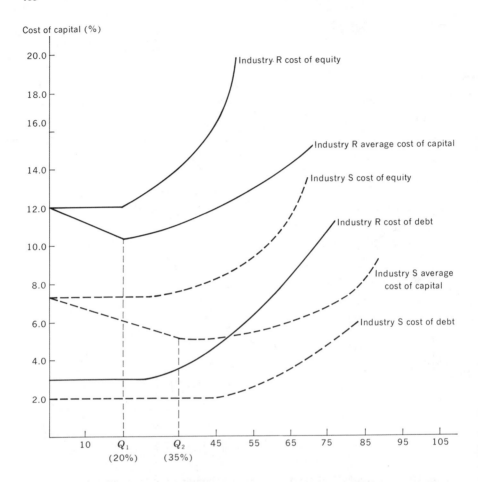

Figure 10-2   Hypothetical Cost of Capital Schedules for High-Risk and Low-Risk Industries

and industry S of electric utilities. The highest line on the graph shows the relationship between the cost of equity and the debt ratio for firms in industry R. With no debt, their cost of equity is 12 percent. It remains at this level until debt reaches 20 percent, but beyond this point costs rise because of the increasing risk of greater amounts of debt. The second curve from the bottom shows the relationship between the cost of debt and the debt ratio for the R firms. This curve starts at 3 percent after taxes, is constant for a while, and then rises as a larger percentage of assets is financed with debt. The average cost of capital for R firms, the second line from the top, is 12 percent where all financing is with relatively expensive equity capital. After declining for a while as additional low-cost debt is averaged in with equity, the average cost of capital for R industry begins to rise when debt has reached 20 percent of total capital. Beyond this point, the fact that both debt and equity are becoming more expensive offsets the fact that debt costs less than common equity.

While the same principles apply to firms in the less risky industry S, its cost functions are quite different from those of industry R. In the first place, S's over-all risk is lower, giving rise to lower debt and equity costs at all debt levels. Further, its relative stability means that less risk is attached to any given percentage of debt; therefore, its cost of both debt and equity —and, consequently, its average cost of capital—turn up farther to the right than do those for R firms. Its optimum debt ratio (Q_2) is at 35 percent as compared to only 20 percent for industry R firms.

Determining the actual optimum capital structure for a specific firm requires both analysis and judgment, and it is up to a firm's financial management to decide on the best capital structure for its company. Once this decision has been reached, the weighting system for the average cost of capital calculation is also determined. Unless otherwise noted, we will assume that management deems its present capital structure to be optimal, and we shall use this set of weights in our calculations.[3]

CALCULATING COST OF CAPITAL FOR AN ACTUAL COMPANY

The procedures discussed above are now applied to an actual company, the Continental Can Company, to illustrate the cost-of-capital calculation. Continental Can is a large firm, with assets of over $950 million and sales

---

[3] If the book value of a firm's capital differs from its market value, it is possible to define two alternative sets of capital weights. In strict accordance with theoretical concepts, it is preferable to use market value weights. If a firm's equity sells for more than its book value—the typical situation for most healthy firms—then using book value weights produces a weighted *average* cost of capital that is too low. However, the weighted *marginal* cost of capital is not generally influenced to any significant degree by the choice of weights used to calculate it. The reason for this is that the market value of *marginal* debt and equity is approximately equal to their book value.

Two additional points are also worth mentioning here. First, when book and market values differ, it is impossible to maintain capital structures constant in terms of both book and market values. That is, if debt constitutes 50 percent of capital when book values are used but only 30 percent when market values are used, then raising additional capital *necessarily* causes one or the other of these ratios to change. This is demonstrated on pp. 288–289 of *Managerial Finance, Second Edition.* The second point is that in practice most firms seem to consider their book value capital structures when making decisions about new financing. These two reasons, combined with the fact that weights do not particularly matter when considering the *marginal* cost of capital, lead us to use book weights in spite of the theoretical superiority of market value weights.

of over $1 billion. Sales and earnings are relatively stable, as food and beverage companies make up the bulk of the firm's customers. Dividends have been paid since 1923, even during the depression of the 1930s. Based on an indicated dividend rate of $2 and a current price of $50 per share, the dividend yield is 4 percent. Over the past 10 years, earnings, dividends, and the price of the stock have grown at a rate of about 6 percent, and all indications suggest that this same rate of growth will be maintained in the foreseeable future. Since internally generated funds provide sufficient equity, only the costs of internal equity, taken in accordance with the preceding discussion of retained earnings to be 10 percent, need be considered.

The average interest rate on Continental Can's outstanding long-term debt is 4.5 percent, but much of this debt was issued in earlier years when interest rates were generally lower than they are now. Current market yields are about 5.8 percent, and approximately this cost will be associated with new debt issues. After a 48 percent income tax, the cost of debt is estimated to be 3 percent. The preferred stock is stated to be 3.75 percent preferred, but it was also issued when rates were low. Based on current market yields, the estimated cost of preferred stock is 6 percent.

Table 10-1   *CONTINENTAL CAN COMPANY*
RIGHT-HAND SIDE OF BALANCE SHEET
December 31, 1965
(millions of dollars)

			Long-Term Funds Only	
Payables and accruals	$120	12.5%		
Tax accruals	33	3.5		
Total current liabilities	$153	16.0%		
Reserve for deferred taxes	$ 66	6.9%		
Other reserves (primarily pension fund)	11	1.1		
Total reserves	$ 77	8.0%		
Long-term debt	$160	16.7%	$160	22%
Preferred stock	7	0.8	7	1
Common equity	560	58.5	560	77
Long-term funds	727	76.0%	$727	100%
Total Financing	$957	100.0%		

The right-hand side of Continental Can's balance sheet is given in Table 10-1. A considerable portion of the firm's funds are "free" in the sense that no interest is charged for them—accounts payable, accruals, and reserves are in this class. Some would argue that in the calculation of the over-all cost of capital, this "free" capital, plus short-term debt, should be included. Under certain circumstances this procedure is valid; usually, however, only permanent, long-term capital need be considered. The principal reason for ignoring short-term capital and "free" capital is a practical one: the cost of capital is used primarily in capital budgeting for long-term assets, which are generally financed with long-term, permanent funds.[4] Of the target, or chosen long-term capital structure, 22 percent is debt, 1 percent is preferred stock, and 77 percent is common equity.

If management believed that some other capital structure was optimal, then other weights would be used, but for purposes of illustration it is assumed that the existing structure has been determined to be the optimum. On the basis of these weights and the previously determined costs of debt, equity, and preferred stock, the calculations shown in Table 10-2 indicate that Continental Can's weighted cost of capital is 8.4 percent.[5] So long as

Table 10–2   *CONTINENTAL CAN*
ILLUSTRATIVE CALCULATION OF COST OF CAPITAL
(dollars in millions)

	Using Dollar Amounts of Capital for Weights		
	Amount of Capital	*Component Cost*	*Amount of Cost (Column 1 times Column 2)*
	(1)	(2)	(3)
Long-term debt	$160	3%	$ 4.80
Preferred stock	7	6	0.42
Common equity	560	10	56.00
	$727		$61.22

$$\frac{\$61.22}{\$727} = 8.42\%$$

	Using Capital Proportions for Weights		
Long-term debt	22.0%	3%	0.0066
Preferred stock	1.0	6	0.0006
Common equity	77.0	10	0.0770
	100.0%		0.0842 = 8.42%

4 Another justification for ignoring "free" capital is that, in the capital budgeting process, these spontaneously generated funds are netted out against the required investment outlay, then ignored in the cost-of-capital calculation. To illustrate, consider a retail firm thinking of opening a new store. According to customary practices, the firm should (1) estimate the required outlay, (2) estimate the net receipts (additions to profits) from the new store, (3) discount the estimated receipts at the cost of capital, and (4). accept the decision to open the new store only if the net present value of the expected revenue stream exceeds the investment outlay. The estimated accruals, trade payables, and other costless forms of credit are deducted from the investment before making the calculation.

5 Using market instead of book value weights, the weighted cost of capital is 8.8 percent.

Continental Can finances in the indicated manner, its new funds should cost this amount.[6]

MARGINAL COST OF CAPITAL

In the preceding example of Continental Can, we assumed that the company would finance only with debt and internally generated equity, and on this basis we found the over-all weighted cost of capital to be 8.4 percent. What would have occurred had the firm's need for funds been so great that it was forced to sell new common stock? The answer is that its marginal cost of capital would have increased significantly. To show why this is so, we shall extend the Continental Can example.

First, suppose that during 1965 Continental Can had total earnings of $59 million available for common stockholders, paid $27 million in dividends, and retained $32 million. We know that to keep the capital structure in balance and the average cost of capital at 8.4 percent, the retained earnings should equal 77 percent of the net addition to capital. Therefore, the total new capital that can be obtained on the basis of the retained earnings is:

$$\text{retained earnings} = 0.77 \times \text{new capital}$$
$$\text{new capital} = \frac{\text{retained earnings}}{0.77}$$
$$= \frac{\$32 \text{ million}}{0.77} = \$41.6 \text{ million}$$

Next, we note that 1 percent of the new capital, or about $400,000, should be preferred stock and that 22 percent, or $9.2 million, should be debt. In other words, Continental Can can raise a total of $41.6 million—$32 million from retained earnings, $9.2 million in the form of debt, and $400,000 in the form of preferred stock—and still maintain its target capital structure in exact balance.

If all financing up to $41.6 million is in the prescribed proportions, the cost of each dollar of new capital up to that point is still 8.4 percent, the previously computed weighted cost of capital. As soon as the total required funds exceed $41.6 million, however, Continental Can must begin relying on more expensive new common stock. Therefore, beyond $41.6 million we must compute a new weighted cost of capital. Assuming Continental Can

---

[6] In this situation, the average and marginal costs of capital are constant and equal to one another.

would incur a flotation cost on new equity issues equal to 10 percent, we could compute the cost of capital for funds over $41.6 million as follows:

1. Find the cost of new equity:

$$\text{cost of new common stock} = \frac{\text{required rate of return}}{1 - \text{flotation costs}}$$

$$= \frac{10 \text{ percent}}{0.9} = 11.1\%$$

2. Get a new weighted cost of capital (marginal cost of capital), using new common stock:

	Proportion ×	Component Cost	= Product
Debt	22%	3.00	0.0066
Preferred stock	1	6.00	0.0006
Equity (new)	77	11.10	0.0855
	100.0%		0.0927 or 9.3%

Figure 10-3 gives another view of this concept. The relationships obtained are shown in graph (*a*). Here we see that up to $41.6 million—the total of retained earnings, incremental debt, and incremental preferred stock—the cost of capital is constant at 8.4 percent. Immediately beyond $41.6 million, however, the cost of capital jumps to 9.3 percent.

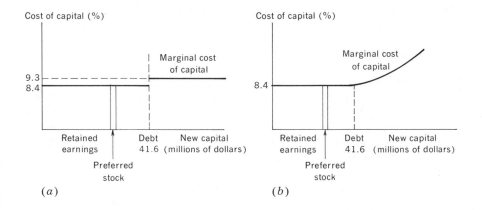

(a)   (b)

Figure 10-3   Relation between the Marginal Cost of Capital and the Amount of Funds Raised

Graph (*a*) is, of course, highly idealized; in fact, the actual cost of capital curve looks much more like that shown in graph (*b*) of Figure 10-3. Here we see that the curve is flat until it reaches the vicinity of 41.6 million; then it turns up gradually and continues rising. It will go up gradually rather than suddenly because the firm will probably make small adjustments in its target debt ratio, in the actual types of securities it uses, and so on. And the curve will continue to rise because, as more and more of its securities are put on the market during a fairly short period, it will experience more and more difficulty in getting the market to absorb the new securities. These two topics—the wide assortment of securities available to the financial manager and the ability of the securities markets to absorb the firm's debt and equity instruments—are considered in the following sections of the book. Note also that we cannot specify the exact cost of capital until we know how much capital will be raised. But the amount of capital that we raise depends on investment opportunities as determined in the capital budgeting decision. Capital budgeting and cost of capital operate jointly on each other, and both must be simultaneously determined. We shall return to this topic in Chapter 18, in which dividend policy and internal financing decisions are considered.

SUMMARY

In the preceding chapter, the nature of the valuation process and the concept of expected rates of return were considered in some detail. The present chapter used these valuation concepts to develop a weighted cost of capital for the firm. First, the cost of the individual components of the capital structure—debt, preferred stock, and equity—were analyzed. Next, these individual component costs were brought together to form a weighted cost of capital. Finally, the conceptual ideas developed in the first two sections were illustrated with an example of the cost of capital for an actual company—Continental Can.

Cost of Individual Capital Components

The cost of debt is defined to be the interest rate that must be paid on new increments of debt capital. Preferred stock cost to the company is the effective yield and is found as the annual preferred dividend divided by the net price the company receives when it sells new preferred stock. In equation form, the cost of preferred stock is

$$\text{cost of preferred stock} = \frac{\text{preferred dividend}}{\text{net price of preferred}}$$

Since interest payments on debt are deductible for tax purposes but preferred dividends are not, it is necessary to make an adjustment to reconcile the cost of debt and that of preferred stock. Our procedure is to put both costs on an after-tax basis. The cost of preferred as calculated above is already on an after-tax basis; debt cost can be adjusted for taxes by multiplying the effective interest rate by a tax factor.

after-tax cost of debt = interest rate $\times$ (1.0 − tax rate)

The cost of equity is defined as the minimum rate of return that must be earned on equity-financed investments to keep unchanged the value of the existing common equity. This required rate of return is the rate of return that investors expect to receive on the company's common stock—the dividend yield plus the capital gains yield. Generally, we assume that investors expect to receive about the same rates of return in the future that they have received in the past; therefore, we estimate the required rate of return on the basis of actual historical returns.

Equity capital comes from two sources, retained earnings and sale of new issues of common stock. The basic required rate of return is used for the cost of retained earnings, but new stock has a higher cost, because of the presence of flotation costs associated with the sale of stock. The cost of new common stock issues is computed as follows.

$$\text{cost of new stock} = \frac{\text{required rate of return on common stock}}{1.0 - \text{percentage cost of floating new common stock}}$$

New common stock is, therefore, more expensive than retained earnings.

Weighted Cost of Capital

The first step in calculating the weighted cost of capital is to determine the cost of the individual capital components as described above. The next step is to establish the proper set of weights to be used in the averaging process. Unless we have reason to think otherwise, we generally assume that the present capital structure of the firm is at an optimum, where optimum is defined as the capital structure that will produce the minimum average cost of capital for raising a given amount of funds. The optimum capital structure varies from industry to industry, with more stable industries having optimum capital structures that call for the use of more debt than in the case of unstable industries.

Relation between Cost of Capital and Amount of Funds Raised

Generally, the marginal cost of capital of a firm is constant until it has raised an amount of new capital equal to its retained earnings plus the amount of incremental debt and preferred stock that can be supported by retained earnings. Beyond this point, the firm must sell new common stock. Since new common stock has a higher cost than retained earnings, the marginal cost of capital rises when new common stock must be sold. Actually, the cost of capital rises gradually, not abruptly; firms make small adjustments in their target debt ratios, begin to use an assortment of securities, retain more of their earnings, and so on, as they reach the limit of internally generated equity funds. These important topics—the wide assortment of securities available to the financial manager, changing debt ratios, and the decision to retain earnings or pay them out in dividends—are covered in the following sections of the book.

QUESTIONS

10–1   Suppose the basic business risks to all firms in a given industry are similar.
   a) Would you expect all firms in each industry to have approximately the same cost of capital?
   b) How would the industry averages differ?

10–2   Why are internally generated retained earnings less expensive than equity raised by selling stock?

10–3   Prior to the 1930s the corporate income tax was not very important, as rates were fairly low. Also prior to the 1930s preferred stock was much more important than it has been since that period. Is there a relation between the rise of corporate income taxes and the decline in importance of preferred stock?

10–4   Describe how each of the following would affect the cost of capital to corporations in general.
   a) The federal government solves the problem of business cycles (that is, cyclical stability is increased).
   b) The Federal Reserve Board takes action to lower interest rates.
   c) The cost of floating new stock issues rises.

10–5   The formula $R = \dfrac{D}{P} + g$, where D = current dividend, P = the current price of a stock, and g = the past rate of growth in dividends, is sometimes used to estimate R, the cost of equity capital. Explain the reasoning behind the formula and this use of it.

PROBLEMS

10–1   On January 1, 1968, the total assets of XYZ Company were $100 million. By the end of the year total assets are expected to be $150 million. The firm's capital structure, shown below, is considered to be optimal. Assume there is no short-term debt.

Debt (3% coupon bonds)	$ 35,000,000
Preferred stock (4%)	15,000,000
Net worth	50,000,000
	$100,000,000

New bonds will have a 4 percent coupon rate and will be sold at par. Preferred will have a 5 percent rate and will also be sold at par. Common stock, currently selling at $50 a share, can be sold to net the company $45 a share. Stockholders' required rate of return is estimated to be 8 percent. Retained earnings are estimated to be $5 million (ignore depreciation). The marginal corporate tax rate is 50 percent.

    a) Assuming all asset expansion (gross expenditures for fixed assets plus related working capital) is included in the capital budget, what is the dollar amount of the capital budget? (Ignore depreciation.)

    b) To maintain the present capital structure, how much of the capital budget must be financed by equity?

    c) How much of the new equity funds needed must be generated internally? externally?

    d) Calculate the cost of each of the equity components.

    e) Compute the weighted average cost of equity.

    f) Compute an over-all average cost of capital for XYZ.

    g) According to the information given, would the over-all average cost of capital have been higher or lower if the firm's rate of expansion had been lower? Why?

10–2   The ABC Manufacturing Company has the following capital structure as of April 15, 1968; the board of directors has decided that these same proportions of *debt, preferred, and equity* capital are to be maintained.

Short-term debt	Trivial
Long-term debt (4½%)	$60,000,000
Preferred stock (5½%)	30,000,000
Net worth	90,000,000

Earnings per share have grown steadily from $1.25 in 1961 to $2.50 estimated for 1968, and the investment community, expecting this growth to continue, capitalizes current earnings per share at about 3½ percent, giving a current market price of $71.43. ABC is paying a current annual dividend of 80 cents, and expects the dividend to grow at the same rate as earnings.

New securities can be sold as follows: bonds to yield investors 4½ percent; preferred to yield 5½ percent; and common stock at the current market price less $2 a share selling commission. These figures all assume that the capital relations set out above are maintained, and that $20 million or less is raised during the year. If more than $20 million is obtained, the figures must be revised as follows: bonds, 5 percent; preferred, 6 percent; common stock selling cost, $4 a share. These latter figures apply to the entire amount of funds raised, if an excess of $20 million is acquired.

Compute the cost of capital (a) for less than $20 million and (b) for more than $20 million.

PART V

Working Capital Management

Chapter 11

Current Asset Management

Working capital refers to a firm's investment in short-term assets—cash, short-term securities, accounts receivable, and inventories. *Gross working capital* is defined as the firm's total current assets. *Net working capital* is defined as current assets minus current liabilities. If the term "working capital" is used without further qualification, it generally refers to gross working capital.

There are advantages and disadvantages to using the concept "working capital management." In the modern systems approach to business management everything is recognized to be related to everything else, and the operations of the firm are viewed as a total, integrated system. In this sense it is artificial to study one segment of the firm, such as its current assets or its current liabilities. On the other hand, if one is really to understand the integrated whole, he must first understand the individual parts of the business firm. Therefore, it seems useful to break the total problem down and to analyze the component parts before taking an integrated view, as we do in Part VII.

IMPORTANCE OF WORKING CAPITAL MANAGEMENT

There are a number of aspects of working capital management that make it an important topic for study. Among them are the following.

Time devoted to working capital management. Surveys indicate

209

that the largest portion of a financial manager's time is devoted to the day-by-day internal operations of the firm; this may be appropriately subsumed under the heading "working capital management." Indeed, a survey of financial literature will disclose that in the early 1950s more attention was probably given to working capital management and the day-by-day operations of the financial manager than was devoted to any other aspect of finance.

Investment in current assets. Characteristically, current assets represent more than one-half the total assets of a business firm. Because they represent a large investment and because this investment tends to be relatively volatile, current assets are worthy of the financial manager's careful attention.

Relation between sales growth and current assets. The relation between sales growth and the need to finance current assets is close and direct. For example, if the firm's average collection period is 40 days and if its credit sales are $1,000 a day, it will have an investment of $40,000 in accounts receivable. If sales rise to $2,000 a day, the investment in accounts receivable will rise to $80,000. Sales increases produce similar immediate needs for additional inventories and perhaps for working cash balances. All these needs must be financed, and since they arise so quickly, it is imperative that the financial manager keep himself aware of developments in the working capital segment of the firm. Of course, continued sales increases will require additional long-term assets, and these fixed asset additions must also be financed. However, fixed asset investments, while critically important to the firm in a strategic long-run sense, do not generally have the same urgency as do current asset investments.

Importance for small firms. Working capital management is particularly important for small firms. A small new firm may minimize its investments in fixed assets by renting or leasing plant and equipment. However, there is no way of avoiding an investment in receivables and inventories. Therefore, current assets are particularly significant for the financial manager of a small firm. Similarly, a small firm has relatively limited access to the long-term capital markets; therefore, it must necessarily rely heavily on trade credit and short-term bank loans, current liabilities.

THE CASH CYCLE

Working capital management emphasizes the cash flow problems of a firm. Growing firms require new investment—immediate investment in current assets and as full capacity is reached, investment in fixed assets as well. New investments must be financed. New financing carries with it commitments and obligations to service the financing.[1] A growing, profitable firm is likely to require more cash for investments in receivables, inventories, and fixed assets. Therefore, a growing, profitable firm can have a cash flow problem. The nature of this problem, and the cause and effect relation between working capital and sales, is illustrated below, where the consequences of a series of transactions are traced.

1. Two partners invest a total of $50,000 to create the Glamour Galore Dress Company. The plant is rented, but equipment and other fixed assets cost $30,000. The resulting financial situation is shown by balance sheet 1.

BALANCE SHEET 1

Assets		*Liabilities*	
Current Assets			
Cash	$20,000		
Fixed Assets		Capital stock	$50,000
Plant and equipment	30,000	Total liabilities and	
Total assets	$50,000	net worth	$50,000

2. Glamour Galore receives an order to manufacture 10,000 dresses. The receipt of an order in itself has no effect on the balance sheet. However, in preparation for the manufacturing activity, the firm buys $20,000 worth of cotton cloth on terms of net 30 days. Without additional investment by the owners, total assets increase by $20,000, financed by the trade accounts payable to the supplier of the cotton cloth.

After the purchase, the firm spends $20,000 on labor for cutting the cloth to the required pattern. Of the $20,000 total cost, $10,000 is paid in cash and $10,000 is owed in the form of accrued wages. These two transactions are reflected in balance sheet 2.

Total assets increase to $80,000. Gross working capital is increased, but net working capital, total current assets minus total current liabilities, remains constant. The current ratio declines to 1.67, and the debt ratio rises to 37 percent. The financial position of the firm is weakening. If it should seek to borrow at this point, Glamour Galore could not use the work in process inventories as collateral because a lender could find little use for partially manufactured dresses.

3. In order to complete the dresses, additional labor costs of $20,000 are incurred and paid in cash. It is assumed that the firm desires to main-

---

[1] By "servicing" financing we refer to interest and repayment of principal on debt as well as dividends and retained earnings (the cost of equity capital) on common stock.

BALANCE SHEET 2

Assets		Liabilities	
Current Assets		Accounts payable	$20,000
Cash	$10,000	Accrued wages payable	10,000
Inventories: Work in process:			
Materials	20,000	Total current liabilities	$30,000
Labor	20,000		
Total current assets	$50,000	Capital stock	50,000
Fixed Assets			
Plant and equipment	30,000	Total liabilities and	
Total assets	$80,000	net worth	$80,000

tain a minimum cash balance of $5,000. Since the initial cash balance is $10,000, Glamour Galore must borrow an additional $15,000 from its bank to meet the wage bill. The borrowing is reflected in notes payable in balance sheet 3. Total assets rise to $95,000, with a finished goods inventory of $60,000. The current ratio drops to 1.4, and the debt ratio rises to 48 percent. These ratios represent a further weakening of the financial position.

BALANCE SHEET 3

Assets		Liabilities	
Current Assets		Accounts payable	$20,000
Cash	$ 5,000	Notes payable	15,000
Inventory: Finished goods	60,000	Accrued wages payable	10,000
Total	$65,000	Total	$45,000
Fixed Assets		Capital stock	50,000
Plant and equipment	30,000		
Total assets	$95,000	Total liabilities and net worth	$95,000

4. Glamour Galore ships the dresses on the basis of the original order, invoicing the purchaser for $100,000 within 30 days. Accrued wages and accounts payable have to be paid now, so Glamour Galore must borrow an additional $30,000 in order to maintain the $5,000 minimum cash balance.

Note that in balance sheet 4 finished goods inventory is replaced by receivables, with the markup reflected as retained earnings. This causes the debt ratio to drop to 33 percent. Since the receivables are carried at selling price, the current assets increase to $105,000 and the current ratio rises to 2.3. Compared with the conditions reflected in balance sheet 3, most of the financial ratios show improvement. However, the absolute amount of debt is large.

BALANCE SHEET 4

Assets		*Liabilities*	
Current Assets		Notes payable	$ 45,000
Cash	$ 5,000	Total current liab.	$ 45,000
Accounts receivable	100,000	Capital stock	$ 50,000
Total	$105,000	Retained earnings	40,000
Fixed Assets		Total net worth	$ 90,000
Plant and equipment	30,000		
Total assets	$135,000	Total liab. and net worth	$135,000

Whether the firm's financial position is really improved depends upon the credit worthiness of the purchaser of the dresses. If the purchaser is a good credit risk, Glamour Galore may be able to borrow further on the basis of the accounts receivable.

5. The firm receives payment for the accounts receivable, pays off the bank loan, and is now in the highly liquid position shown by balance sheet 5. If a new order for 10,000 dresses is received, it will have no effect on the balance sheet, but a cycle similar to the one described above will begin.

BALANCE SHEET 5

Assets		*Liabilities*	
Current Assets		Capital	$50,000
Cash	$60,000	Earned surplus	40,000
Fixed Assets			
Plant and equipment	$30,000		
Total assets	$90,000	Total liab. and net worth	$90,000

This analysis of the cash cycle shows how the investments in inventories and in accounts receivable are tied directly to sales. The other major component of current assets, cash, is also related to sales volume. The relations are not one to one, however; that is, factors other than sales influence the investment in working capital. With this in mind, we now turn to a detailed examination of the factors controlling the specific amounts of funds that must be invested in current assets.

CONTROLLING INVESTMENT IN CASH
AND MARKETABLE SECURITIES

The starting point in controlling the investment in assets is effective control of cash and cash equivalent. Cash equivalent includes marketable securities—for example, short-term government securities—characteristically held for liquidity purposes. These interest-bearing liquid assets can be converted to cash rapidly if the firm should need additional cash. "Cash" is primarily held as balances with commercial banks, largely in the form of demand deposits. Approximately 85 to 90 percent of all transactions in the United States are accomplished through the use of "cash" in the form of demand deposits.

Businesses or individuals have three primary motives for holding cash: (1) the transactions motive, (2) the precautionary motive, and (3) the speculative motive.

The transactions motive for holding cash is to enable the firm to conduct its ordinary business—making purchases and sales. The types of flows described above for Glamour Galore indicate the kinds of needs involved in the transactions use of cash. In some lines of business, such as the utilities, where billings can be cycled throughout the month, cash inflows can be scheduled and synchronized closely with the need for the outflow of cash. Hence, we expect the cash-to-revenues ratio or cash-to-total-assets ratio for utility firms to be relatively low. In retail trade, by contrast, a large number of transactions may actually be conducted by physical currency. As a consequence, retail trade requires a higher ratio of cash to sales and of cash to total assets.

The seasonality of a business may give rise to a need for cash for the purchase of inventories. For example, raw materials may be available only during a harvest season and may be perishable, as in the food-canning business. Or sales may be seasonal, as are department store sales around the Christmas and the Easter holidays, giving rise to an increase in needs for cash.

The two other traditional motives for holding "cash" are actually satisfied in large part by holdings of near-money assets—short-term government securities and the like. The precautionary motive relates primarily to the predictability of cash inflows and outflows. If the predictability is high, less cash or cash equivalent will need to be held against an emergency or other contingency. Another factor that strongly influences the precautionary motive for holding cash is the ability to obtain additional cash on short notice when circumstances necessitate. Borrowing flexibility is primarily a matter of the strength of the firm's relations with banking institutions and other sources of potential augmentation of its cash holdings.

The speculative motive for holding cash is to be ready for profit-making opportunities that may arise. By and large, accumulations of cash for speculative purposes are not widely found. Holding cash is more a function of the behavior of individual investors. However, the cash and marketable securities account may rise to rather sizable levels as a temporary basis for accumulating the means of financing. A dramatic example of this was the rise in cash and marketable securities of Montgomery Ward in 1958 to $149 million, representing 22 percent of total assets.

ADVANTAGES OF ADEQUATE CASH

In addition to these general motives, sound working capital management requires maintenance of an ample amount of cash for several specific reasons. First, it is essential that the firm have sufficient cash to take trade discounts. The payment schedule for purchases is referred to as "the term of the sale." A commonly encountered billing procedure, or term of trade, allows a 2 percent discount if the bill is paid within 10 days, with full payment required in 30 days in any event. Since the net amount is due in 30 days, failure to take the discount means paying this extra 2 percent for using the money an additional 20 days. If you were to pay 2 percent for every 20-day period over the year, there would be eighteen such periods:

$18 = \dfrac{360 \text{ days}}{20 \text{ days}}$. This represents an annual interest rate of 36 percent.[2]

Most firms are able to borrow at a rate substantially lower than 36 percent a year.

Second, since the current and acid test ratios are key items in credit analysis, it is essential that the firm, in order to maintain its credit standing, meet the standards of the line of business in which it is engaged. A strong credit standing enables the firm to purchase goods from trade suppliers on favorable terms and to maintain its line of credit with banks and other sources of credit.

Third, ample cash is useful for taking advantage of favorable business opportunities that may come along from time to time. Finally, the firm should have sufficient liquidity to meet emergencies, such as strikes, fires, or marketing campaigns of competitors.

Using the knowledge about the general nature of cash flows presented above, the financial manager may be able to improve the inflow—outflow

---

[2] The method of calculating the effective interest rate on accounts payable is described in Chapter 12.

pattern of cash. He can do so by better synchronization of flows and by reduction of float.

Synchronization of Cash Flows

As an example of synchronization, cash flows may be improved by more frequent requisitioning of funds by divisional offices from the firm's main or central office. A concrete illustration makes the point clearly.

Some Gulf Oil Corporation divisional field offices, for instance, used to requisition funds once or twice a week; now the treasurer's office insists on daily requisitions, thus keeping some cash on tap as much as four days longer. John Shaw, assistant treasurer, told an American Management Association seminar last year that, on the basis of ten offices, each requiring $500,000 a week, these staggered requisitions free the equivalent of $10 million for one day each week. At 3 percent interest, this earns better than $42,000 a year.[3]

In addition, effective forecasting can reduce the investment in cash. The cash flow forecasting at Universal Commercial Investment Trust Credit Corporation illustrates this idea.[4] An assistant treasurer forecasts planned purchases of automobiles by the dealers. He estimates daily the number of cars shipped to the 10,000 dealers who finance their purchases through Universal CIT. He then estimates how much money should be deposited in Detroit banks that day to pay automobile manufacturers. On one day he estimated a required deposit of $6.4 million; the actual bill for the day was $6.397 million, a difference of one tenth of 1 percent. Though such close forecasting cannot be achieved by every type of firm, the system enables Universal CIT to economize on the amount of money it must borrow, and thereby to keep interest expense to a minimum.

Reduction of Float

Another important method of economizing on the volume of cash required is by reduction of "float." Float refers to funds in transit between cities. Checks received from customers in distant cities are subject to two types of delays: the time required for the check to travel in the mail and the time required for clearing through the banking system.

To reduce these two types of float, a "lock-box plan" can be used. If our firm makes sales in large amounts at far distances, we can establish a lock box in a post office located in the customer's area. We can arrange to have customers send payments to the postal box in their city, then to have a bank pick up the checks and deposit them in a special checking account. The bank then has the checks cleared in the local area and remits by wire

---

[3] *Business Week,* July 12, 1958.
[4] *Finance,* May 15, 1954, pp. 56–58.

to our bank of deposit. If our distant customers are scattered, we can establish the lock box in our local city and have the checks picked up by our bank. The bank begins the clearing process, notifying us that a check has been received. In this way the clearing process starts before our firm processes the check. By these methods float may be reduced by one to five days. Examples of freeing funds in the amount of $1.5 million or more by these methods have been cited by firms.

Investment of Funds

A firm may have cash to invest for a number of reasons. One is seasonal or cyclical fluctuations in business. As sales expand, inventories and receivables mount. As sales fall off, inventories and receivables decrease and become cash. Thus, during a seasonal or cyclical expansion, the firm will need to finance an increase in inventories and receivables. Some firms may borrow as their seasonal or cyclical needs for financing expand. Others, particularly firms in capital goods industries where fluctuations are violent, attempt to accumulate cash or near-cash during a downturn to be ready to finance an upturn in business volume.

Firms may also accumulate resources as a protection against a number of contingencies. When they make uninsurable product warranties, firms must be ready to meet claims that may arise. Firms in highly competitive industries must have resources to carry them through substantial shifts in the market structure. A firm in an industry in which new markets are emerging—for example, foreign markets—needs to have resources to meet developments; these funds may be on hand for fairly long periods.

Thus, because of uncertain contingencies, a firm may have cash funds to invest for a few weeks, a few months, a few years, or even indefinitely. Investment alternatives are available to meet the needs of the firm. Taking both yield and risk considerations into account, the alternatives are listed in Table 11–1.

Depending on how long he anticipates holding the funds, the financial manager decides upon a suitable maturity pattern for his holdings. The numerous alternatives can be selected and balanced in such a way that he obtains the maturities and risks appropriate to the financial situation of his firm. Commercial bankers, investment bankers, and brokers provide the financial manager with detailed information on each of the forms of investments in the list. Since their characteristics change with shifts in financial market conditions, it would be misleading to attempt to give detailed descriptions of these investment outlets here. The financial manager must keep up to date on these characteristics. He should follow the principle of making investment selections that offer maturities, yields, and risks appropriate to his firm.

Table 11-1   ALTERNATIVE MARKETABLE SECURITIES FOR
             INVESTMENTS

	Approximate Maturities*
U. S. Treasury bills	91 to 182 days
U. S. Treasury certificates	9 to 12 months
U. S. Treasury notes	1 to 5 years
Prime commercial paper	Varies, up to 270 days
Negotiable certificates of deposit†	Varies, up to 3 years
Savings certificates at commercial banks	6 months
Savings accounts at commercial banks	
Savings accounts at savings and loan associations	
Bonds and stocks of other corporations	
Bonds and stocks of the firm in question‡	

* The maturities are those at issue date. For outstanding securities, maturities varying almost by day or week are available.
† See Roy L. Reierson, "A New Money Market Instrument" (New York: Bankers Trust Company, March 24, 1961).
‡ See L. A. Guthart, "More Companies Are Buying Back Their Stock," *Harvard Business Review,* March 1965.

Because some funds are to be held for extended periods, they may be invested with the objective of a higher return than that available from government securities. Such investments may be made in the shares of other companies. "Mostly, however, these are investments pure and simple, not for the sake of control. They were purchased to put the buyer's surplus cash to work hard, producing a larger return than it could earn, say, in the government bond market." [5]

Investments in other companies follow several patterns. The percentage of ownership is characteristically small; thus it cannot be said that the dominant motive is control. Often the investments are made in firms in related industries. This practice is followed partly because the nature and outlook for such industries are better understood and partly because such investments may yield additional information useful for purchasing or sales activities. For example, suppliers to larger firms may often hold shares in the larger firms for the contacts that will be provided by shareholders' information and meetings. Clearly, control cannot be exercised by the smaller firm. However, the smaller firm may in this manner obtain market information that might otherwise be more difficult to obtain.

[5] "Part-Time Portfolios," *Forbes,* May 15, 1961, pp. 16–17.

MANAGEMENT OF INVESTMENT IN RECEIVABLES

In the present chapter, the term "trade credit" refers to accounts *receivable,* and it involves both the credit used to support and expand sales and the resulting investment required of the firm. In Chapter 12, where its potentials and limitations as a source of funds are discussed, trade credit refers to accounts *payable.*

The ratio of receivables to sales generally is in the range from 8 to 12 percent for manufacturing firms, representing an average collection period of approximately one month. The ratio of receivables to total assets centers on about 16 to 20 percent. However, wide variations are experienced among firms, particularly when nonmanufacturing industries are included.

The major determinants of the level of receivables are (1) volume of credit sales, (2) seasonality of sales, (3) rules for credit limits, (4) terms of sales and credit policies of individual firms, and (5) collection policies. Variations in the ratios of receivables to sales (or the average collection periods) among firms reflect the differential impact of the factors listed above.

Variations in terms of sale reflect the customs of the line of business. A very important influence, however, is the perishability of the product. For example, very short payment periods are found in the bakery products, milk products, and meat products industries. On the other hand, relatively high ratios of receivables to sales are observed in the construction, industrial machinery, agricultural machinery, office equipment, and printing and publishing industries. In addition, higher ratios of receivables to sales are found among larger firms, which obtain funds at lower cost and tend to be wholesalers of credit obtained from financial institutions and reloaned to smaller firms.

Credit Policy

The basis of a firm's credit policy is its industry's characteristic credit terms; generally, a firm must meet the terms provided by other firms in the industry. However, when a customer is a poor credit risk, the company giving the trade credit must be less lenient for its own protection. A central task in formulating credit policy is an evaluation of the credit-worthiness of the potential customer.

To evaluate the credit risk, the credit manager considers the five C's of credit: *character, capacity, capital, collateral, conditions.* "Character" refers to the probability that the customer will *try* to honor his obligations. This factor is of considerable importance, because every credit transaction implies a *promise* to pay. Will the creditor make an honest effort to pay his debts, or is he likely to try to get away with something? Experienced credit men frequently insist that the moral factor is the most important in a credit evaluation.

"Capacity" is a subjective judgment of the *ability* of the customer. This is gauged by his past record, supplemented by physical observation of the customer's plant or store and business methods. "Capital" is measured by the general financial position of the firm as indicated by a financial-ratio analysis, with special emphasis on the tangible net worth of the enterprise. "Collateral" is represented by assets which the customer may offer as a pledge for security of the credit extended to him. Finally, "conditions" refers to the impact of general economic trends on the firm or special developments in certain areas of the economy that may affect the customer's ability to meet his obligations.

The five C's of credit represent the factors by which the credit risk is judged. Information on these items is obtained from the firm's previous experience with the customer, supplemented by a well-developed system of information-gathering groups. Two major sources of external information are available. The first is the work of the credit associations. By periodic meetings of local groups and by direct communication, information on experience with creditors is exchanged. More formally, credit interchange, a system developed by the National Association of Credit Management for assembling and distributing information on debtors' past performance, is provided. The interchange reports show the paying record of the debtor, industries from which he is buying, and the trading areas in which his purchases are being made.[6]

The second is the work of the credit-reporting agencies, the best known of which is Dun & Bradstreet. Agencies that specialize in coverage of a limited number of industries also provide information. Representative of these are the National Credit Office and the Lyon Furniture Mercantile Agency. Some of the services of Dun & Bradstreet are briefly described to indicate the nature of the information obtainable.

The Dun & Bradstreet Reference Book is published six times a year and covers the entire United States and Canada. Regional and state editions are also published. The Reference Book contains listings of firms and their credit ratings by town location. The credit ratings shown in Table 11–2 indicate both estimated financial strength and a composite credit appraisal. A credit appraisal of "high" indicates that financial affairs ap-

---

[6] For additional information, see *Credit Managerial Handbook, Second Edition,* a publication of the National Association of Credit Management, (Homewood, Ill.: Irwin, 1965).

pear healthy and meet a number of important tests with reference to the five C's of credit.

When the rating of a firm is less than high, the financial manager may wish to obtain more specific information from credit reports sold by Dun & Bradstreet. The credit reports follow the forms indicated in Table 11-3. They provide a summary of the main information about the customer: his credit rating and history, a discussion of the business operations and their location, financial information, and payment experience. The payment experience indicates whether the customer takes discounts, whether he pays promptly, and by how many days he delays payment if he does not pay promptly.

The above information can be translated into risk classes, grouped according to the probability of risk associated with sales to a customer. The combination of rating and supplementary information might lead to the following groupings of loss experience.

Group Number	Loss Ratio (in percentages)
1	None
2	0–½
3	½–1
4	1–2
5	2–5
6	5–10
7	10–20
8	over 20

If the selling firm has a 20 percent margin over the sum of direct operating costs and all delivery and selling costs and if it is producing at less than full capacity, it may adopt the following credit policies. It may sell on customary credit terms to groups 1 to 5, sell to groups 6 and 7 under more stringent credit terms, such as cash on delivery, and require advance payments from group 8. So long as the bad debt loss ratios are less than 20 percent, the additional sales are contributing something to overhead.

Credit limits, which may be related to risk classes, set a maximum on the total amount of credit which may be extended to a firm without a review of the customer's general credit position. They may be based on experience with the customer and related to a calculation of his appropriate needs for credit. Credit limits may be set at some fraction of net worth.[7]

---

[7] A credit limit of one fifth of net worth is based on the following logic. Credit should not exceed the owner's stake. Assuming that the customer has four other major suppliers, the seller should not extend credit of more than one fifth of the total credit.

Table 11–2   KEY TO RATINGS

Estimated Financial Strength			Composite Credit Appraisal			
			HIGH	GOOD	FAIR	LIMITED
AA	Over	$1,000,000	A1	1	1¹/₂	2
A+	Over	750,000	A1	1	1¹/₂	2
A	$500,000 to	750,000	A1	1	1¹/₂	2
B+	300,000 to	500,000	1	1¹/₂	2	2¹/₂
B	200,000 to	300,000	1	1¹/₂	2	2¹/₂
C+	125,000 to	200,000	1	1¹/₂	2	2¹/₂
C	75,000 to	125,000	1¹/₂	2	2¹/₂	3
D+	50,000 to	75,000	1¹/₂	2	2¹/₂	3
D	35,000 to	50,000	1¹/₂	2	2¹/₂	3
E	20,000 to	35,000	2	2¹/₂	3	3¹/₂
F	10,000 to	20,000	2¹/₂	3	3¹/₂	4
G	5,000 to	10,000	3	3¹/₂	4	4¹/₂
H	3,000 to	5,000	3	3¹/₂	4	4¹/₂
J			J 3	3¹/₂	4	4¹/₂
K	Up to	3,000	K 3	3¹/₂	4	4¹/₂
L			L 3¹/₂	4	4¹/₂	5

K & L are being phased out

Classification for both Estimated Financial Strength and Credit Appraisal

Financial Strength Bracket — Explanation

1 $125,000 and Over

2   20,000 to 125,000

3
4   Up to 20,000

4 is being phased out

When only the numeral (1, 2, 3, or 4) appears, it is an indication that the estimated financial strength, while not definitely classified, is presumed to be within the range of the ($) figures in the corresponding bracket and that a condition is believed to exist which warrants credit in keeping with that assumption.

Suppose, for example, a customer has a $60,000 net worth. If the supplying firm judges that it supplies one fifth of its customer's credit and applies the rule of one fifth of net worth, the buyer's credit limit is $12,000.

In reviewing credit extensions, the financial manager should not be guided by bad debt loss ratios alone. These must also be related to the potential contribution that additional sales have made to overhead costs. Accounts receivable represent an investment. The return on this investment can be calculated by taking the contribution to additional net earnings and determining the return from the investment in receivables, as in any capital budgeting problem.

Table 11–2 KEY TO RATINGS (continued)

"INV." shown in place of a rating indicates that the report was under investigation at the time of going to press. It has no other significance.

Not Classified or Absence of Rating

The absence of a rating, expressed by two hyphens (--), is not to be construed as unfavorable but signifies circumstances difficult to classify within condensed rating symbols. It suggests the advisability of obtaining a report for additional information.

Absence of a Listing

The absence of a listing is not to be construed as meaning a concern is non-existent, has discontinued business, nor does it have any other meaning. The letters "NQ" on any written report mean "not listed in the Reference Book."

Year Business Started

The numeral shown is the last digit of the year date when the business was established or came under present control or management. Thus, 8 means 1958; 9 means 1959. No dates go past ten years. Thus the absence of a numeral indicates ten years or more. This feature is not used in connection with branch listings.

Courtesy of Dun & Bradstreet, Inc.

INVENTORY CONTROL

Manufacturing firms generally have three kinds of inventories: raw materials, work in process, and finished goods. The levels of raw material inventories are influenced by anticipated production, seasonality of production, reliability of sources of supply, and efficiency of scheduling purchases and production operations.

Work in process inventory is strongly influenced by the length of the production period, which is the time between placing raw material in production and completing the finished product. Inventory turnover can be increased by decreasing the production period. One means of accomplishing this is perfecting engineering techniques to speed up the manufacturing process. Another means of reducing work in process is to buy items rather than make them.

The level of finished goods inventories is a matter of coordinating production and sales. The financial manager can stimulate sales by changing credit terms or by allowing credit to marginal risks. Whether the goods remain on the books as inventories or as receivables, the financial manager has to finance them. Many times firms find it desirable to make the sale and thus take one step nearer to realizing cash. The potential profits can outweigh the additional collection risk.

Table 11-3

Dun & Bradstreet REPORT

SIC	D-U-N-S	DATE OF REPORT	STARTED	RATING
34 61	803-4520 ARNOLD METAL PRODUCTS CO	CD 13 APR 21 19-- N METAL STAMPINGS	1957	D 1½

53 S MAIN ST
DAWSON MICH   66666
TEL 215 999-0000

SUMMARY

SAMUEL B. ARNOLD   )
GEORGE T. ARNOLD   ) PARTNERS

PAYMENTS	DISC PPT
SALES	$177,250
WORTH	$42,961
EMPLOYS	8
RECORD	CLEAR
CONDITION	SOUND
TREND	UP

PAYMENTS

HC	OWE	P DUE	TERMS	APR 1 19--	SOLD
3000	1500	1 10	30	Disc	Over 3 yrs
2500	1000	1 10	30	Disc	Over 3 yrs
2000	500	2 20	30	Disc	Old account
1000			30	Ppt	Over 3 yrs
500			30	Ppt	Over 3 yrs

FINANCE

On Apr 21 19-- S. B. Arnold, Partner, submitted statement Dec 31 19--

Cash	$ 4,870	Accts Pay	$ 6,121
Accts Rec	15,472	Notes Pay (Curr)	2,400
Mdse	14,619	Accruals	3,583
	----------		----------
Current	34,961	Current	12,104
Fixed Assets	22,840	Notes Pay (Def)	5,000
Other Assets	2,264	NET WORTH	42,961
	----------		----------
Total Assets	60,065	Total	60,065

19-- sales $177,250; gross profit $47,821; net profit $4,204. Fire
insurance mdse $15,000; fixed assets $20,000. Annual rent $3,000.
Signed Apr 21 19-- ARNOLD METAL PRODUCTS CO by Samuel B. Arnold, Partner
Johnson Singer, CPA, Dawson

-----0-----

Sales and profits increased last year due to increased sub-contract
work and this trend is reported continuing. New equipment was purchased
last Sept for $8,000 financed by a bank loan secured by a lien on the
equipment payable $200 per month. With increased capacity, the business
has been able to handle a larger volume. Arnold stated that for the first
two months of this year volume was $32,075 and operations continue profitable.

BANKING

Medium to high four figure balances are maintained locally. An equipment loan is outstanding and being retired as agreed.

HISTORY

Style registered Feb 1 1965 by partners. SAMUEL, born 1918, married.
1939 graduate of Lehigh University with B.S. degree in Mechanical Engineering. 1939-50 employed by Industrial Machine Corporation, Detroit, and
1950-56 production manager with Aerial Motors Inc., Detroit. Started this
business in 1957. GEORGE, born 1940, single, son of Samuel. Graduated in
1963 from Dawson Institute of Technology. Served U.S. Air Force 1963-64.
Admitted to partnership interest Feb 1965.

OPERATION

Manufactures light metal stampings for industrial concerns and also
does some work on a sub-contract basis for aircraft manufacturers. Terms
net 30. 12 accounts. Five production, two office employees, and one salesman. LOCATION: Rents one-story cinder block building with 5,000 square feet
located in industrial section in normal condition. Housekeeping is good.
4-21   (803 77) PRA

Courtesy of Dun & Bradstreet, Inc.

Determinants of Size of Inventories

Although wide variations occur, inventory-to-sales ratios are generally concentrated in the 12-to-20 percent range, and inventory-to-total-assets ratios are concentrated in the 16-to-30 percent range.

The major determinants of investment in inventory are the following: (1) length and technical nature of the production processes, (2) durability versus perishability or style factor in the end product. Inventories in the tobacco industry are high because of the long curing process. Likewise, in the machinery-manufacturing industries, inventories are large because of the long work in process period. On the other hand, inventory ratios are low in coal mining and in oil and gas production; no raw materials are used and the goods in process are small in relation to sales. Because of the seasonality of the raw materials, inventories are large in the canning industry.

With respect to the durability and style factors, large inventories are found in the hardware and the precious-metals industries because durability is great and the style factor is small. Inventory ratios are low in baking because of the perishability of the final product. Inventories are low in printing because the items are manufactured to order and require negligible finished inventories.

A potential for improvement in inventory control is offered by the use of computers and operations analysis. Though the techniques are far too diverse and complicated for treatment in this text, the financial manager should be prepared to make use of the contributions of specialists who have developed effective procedures for minimizing the investment in inventory.[8]

Inventory Decision Models

As an illustration of the systematic approach to inventory control, the use of a basic EOQ (economical ordering quantity) procedure may be illustrated.[9] The level of inventories is determined by reliability of sources

---

[8] Illustrative of the techniques at the practical level is the following:

Raytheon's new system works like this: Tabulator cards are inserted in each package of five electronic tubes leaving Raytheon's warehouse. As the merchandise is sold, the distributor collects the cards and files his replacement order without doing paper work. He simply sends in the cards, which are identified by account number, type of merchandise, and price of the units he orders.

Western Union Telegraph Co. equipment accepts the punched cards and transmits information on them to the warehouse, where it is duplicated on other punched cards. A typical order of 5,000 tubes of varying types can be received in about 17 minutes, Raytheon says. It can be assembled in about 90 minutes and delivered to Boston's Logan. Airport in an additional 45 minutes. "Orders from 3,000 miles away can be delivered within 24 hours, a saving of 13 days in some cases.—Roger B. Rowand, "Tactics Vary as Firms Try to Cut Warehouse Costs, Speed Service," *Wall Street Journal,* May 26, 1961, pp. 1, 11.

[9] For elaborations of the technique, see R. B. Fetter and W. C. Dalleck, *Decision Models for Inventory Management* (Homewood, Ill.: Irwin, 1961).

of supply, degree of integration of the firm, perishability of the item, and other factors which depend upon the nature of the product. Within these limits, however, the manager can reduce inventory commitments. Analytical work in recent years has shown that the optimum size of investment in inventory can be controlled by determining the EOQ. Ordering quantity serves as an indicator of the investment in inventory in the following manner. If it is assumed (1) that the ordering quantity is 100 units, (2) that the firm's inventory is virtually zero by the time the new order arrives, and (3) that inventory is withdrawn at a regular rate, the amount of inventory on the average (A) will be

$$A = \frac{100 + 0}{2} = 50$$

Thus, the average size of inventory may be approximated by the order quantity divided by 2. A widely used formula for the determination of EOQ is

$$EOQ = \sqrt{\frac{2 \times R \times O}{P \times I}} = \sqrt{\frac{2 \times 100 \times 10}{1 \times 0.2}} = 100$$

where

EOQ = economical ordering quantity
R = sales for the period in units = 100
P = price paid per unit = \$1
O = processing cost per order = \$10
I = inventory carrying charge as a percentage of the
inventory value = 20% = 0.2

Intuitively, we would suppose that the higher the ordering or processing costs, the less frequently orders should be placed. On the other hand, the higher the carrying costs of inventory, the more frequently stocks should be ordered. These two features are incorporated in the formula. Notice also that if sales had been estimated at 200 units, the EOQ would have been 144 and the average inventory 72. Thus, a doubling of sales leads to less than a doubling of inventories.

The formula may be utilized to determine the EOQ and the average inventory under a series of assumptions with regard to values of the variables, as is shown in Table 11–4. The results of the calculations are charted in Figure 11–1. The graph shows sales and the corresponding average level of inventories as a series of lines somewhat curved over. The height and the slope of each line are different; they depend upon the values of such

Figure 11-1   Relation between Inventory and Sales Based on the Formula for the Economical Order Point

critical factors as order processing costs and inventory carrying costs. But the significant fact from the standpoint of the financial manager is that a stable and dependable relation exists between sales and inventories when the strategic variables influencing inventory policy are known. The financial manager can work with the production department in determining the EOQ. From the EOQ he can develop financial standards for inventory levels.

Use of economical ordering quantity models not only contributes to sound inventory management but also provides a basis for projecting requirements for investment in inventories.[10] In other words, sound asset

---

[10] The newer operations research techniques for inventory control that have been investigated by the authors also result in stable relations between the level of sales and the size of inventories.

Table 11–4   RELATION BETWEEN SALES AND INVENTORY LEVELS
RESULTING FROM USE OF ECONOMICAL ORDERING
QUANTITY

				Situation Number					
I		II		III		IV		V	
$P = \$1$		$P = \$1$		$P = \$1$		$P = \$1$		$P = \$1$	
$I = 20\%$		$I = 20\%$		$I = 10\%$		$I = 5\%$		$I = 30\%$	
$O = \$10$		$O = \$5$		$O = \$10$		$O = \$10$		$O = \$20$	
S	*A*	*S*	*A*	*S*	*A*	*S*	*A*	*S*	*A*
1,000	158	1,000	112	1,000	224	1,000	316	1,000	183
2,000·	224	2,000	158	2,000	316	2,000	447	2,000	258
3,000	274	3,000	194	3,000	387	3,000	548	3,000	316
4,000	316	4,000	224	4,000	447	4,000	632	4,000	365
5,000	354	5,000	250	5,000	500	5,000	707	5,000	408
6,000	387	6,000	274	6,000	548	6,000	774	6,000	447

$S =$ level of sales in units.
$A =$ level of inventories in units.

management results in stable relations, which facilitate forecasts of financing requirements.

Generality of Inventory Analysis

Managing assets of all kinds is basically an inventory-type problem —the same method of analysis applies to cash, receivables, and fixed assets, as well as to inventories themselves. First, a basic stock must be on hand to balance the inflows and outflows of the items, with the size of the stock depending upon the patterns of flows, whether regular or irregular. Second, because the unexpected may always occur, it is necessary to have safety stocks on hand. They represent the little extra to avoid the costs of not having enough to meet current needs. Third, additional amounts may be required to meet future growth needs. These are anticipation stocks. Related to anticipation stocks is the recognition that there are optimum purchase sizes, economical ordering quantities. In borrowing money or in buying raw materials for production or plants and equipment, it is cheaper to buy more than one at a time or just enough to meet immediate needs.

With the foregoing as a basic foundation, the theoretical basis for determining the optimal investment in inventory can be developed and illustrated in Figure 11–2. Some costs rise with larger inventories—included here would be warehousing costs, interest on funds tied up in inventories, insurance, obsolescence, and so forth. Other costs decline with larger inventories—included here would be the loss of profits resulting from sales lost because of running out of stock, costs of production interruptions caused by inadequate inventories, possible purchase discounts, and so on.

Those costs which decline with higher inventories are designated by curve D in Figure 11–2, while those which rise with larger inventories are designated by line R in the figure. Line T is the total of lines R and D, and it represents the total inventory carrying cost. To the left of the intersection of the R and D lines, the T line is falling. To the right of the intersection, the T line is rising. Thus, at the intersection of the R and D lines, the T line is at its lowest. This represents the optimum size of inventory investment.

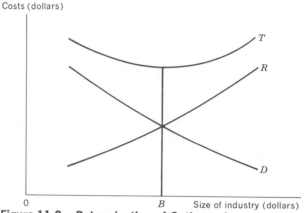

Figure 11-2   **Determination of Optimum Investment in Inventory**

This type of inventory investment analysis has wide applicability. It can be applied to investment in cash, receivables, and fixed assets, as well as to inventories. For example, consider the investment in plant and equipment. If a large investment is made in specialized equipment, variable production costs per unit will be reduced. On the other hand, such additional investment in plant and equipment produces higher depreciation and capital costs. So, again, some costs decline and some costs rise with size of investment in plant and equipment. Therefore an optimum investment point can be found.[11]

---

[11] Since the investment in plant and equipment is of more than one-year duration, extending in some cases to 20 years or more, not only must the type of analysis indicated by Figure 11–2 be taken into account, but the time value of money and the interest factor must be considered. This type of analysis was covered in Chapters 6 and 7.

SUMMARY

The du Pont system described in Chapter 4 makes it clear that a high rate of return on investment is dependent upon controlling the size of the firm's investment. The purpose of this chapter was to examine methods of controlling the investment in current assets. Investment in current assets is important because current assets constitute more than one half the total assets of the firm. Moreover, the relationship between sales growth and the need for funds to finance current assets is close and direct. For small, undercapitalized firms, working capital management is particularly important, because, while investment in fixed assets may be minimized by renting or leasing equipment and plant, investment in receivables and inventories cannot be reduced to the same degree.

The Cash Cycle

The chapter began by making clear the cause-and-effect relationship between current assets, frequently called working capital, and sales. Inventories must be on hand before sales are made, so a higher anticipated level of sales requires an investment in inventories. Next, most sales are made on credit, so even after the sale has been completed the firm's investment is not returned *until accounts receivable have been collected.* A thorough understanding of the cash cycle will go a long way toward enabling us to understand the flows of funds within the firm and, consequently, when it will require funds and when they can be repaid.

Control of Investment in Current Assets

Current assets consist primarily of cash and marketable securities, accounts receivable, and inventories. Ways of determining just how much of each should be kept on hand were analyzed in some detail in the chapter.

Cash and marketable securities are kept on hand for transaction purposes. There are clear advantages to having adequate cash on hand, but cash is a nonearning asset, so holdings should be kept to the minimum necessary level.

Accounts receivable are an important element of current assets. The major determinants of the level of receivables are the volume of credit sales, terms of sales, credit policies, and collection policies. The financial manager should understand how these factors interact to determine receivables and how he can alter the factors to control the level of receivables.

Inventories—raw materials, work in process, and finished goods—are necessary in most businesses. Rather elaborate systems for controlling the level of inventories have been designed. These systems frequently use computers for keeping records of all the items in stock, and an inventory control model that considers anticipated sales, ordering costs, and carrying costs can be used to determine reorder points for each item.

QUESTIONS

11–1 How can better methods of communications make it less necessary for firms to hold large cash balances?

11–2 The highly developed financial system of the United States, with its myriad of different near-cash assets, has greatly reduced cash balance requirements by reducing the need for transactions balances. Discuss.

11–3 Assuming a firm's volume of business remained constant, would you expect it to have higher cash balances (demand deposits) during a tight-money or an easy-money period? Does this situation have any ramifications for federal monetary policy?

11–4 If a firm sells on terms of net 30 and its accounts are on the average 30 days overdue, what will its investment in receivables be if its credit sales approximate $720,000?

11–5 "It is difficult to judge the performance of many of our employees, but not that of the credit manager. If he's performing perfectly, credit losses are zero, and the higher our losses (as a percent of sales), the worse his performance." Evaluate the statement.

11–6 Explain how a firm may reduce its investment in inventory by having suppliers hold raw materials inventories and customers hold finished goods inventories. What are the limitations of such a policy?

11–7 What factors are likely to reduce the holdings of inventory in relation to sales in the future? What factors will tend to increase the ratio? What, in your judgment, is the net effect?

11–8 What are the probable effects of the following on inventory holdings?

a) Manufacture of a part formerly purchased from an outside supplier.

b) Greater use of air freight.

c) Increase, from 7 to 17, in the number of styles produced.

d) Your firm receives large price reductions from a manufacturer of bathing suits if they are purchased in December and January.

PROBLEMS

11–1 The Pettit Production Company sells 150,000 oil-pipe connector units at $25 a unit. The costs of production are shown on the following page.

Selling price		$25
Cost of goods sold per unit:		
Direct material	$8	
Direct labor	7	
Factory overhead	5	20
Gross margin		$ 5
General and administrative expenses	$1	
Selling expenses	1	2
Net profit per unit		$ 3

The firm is operating with one shift. By going to a second shift it can sell an additional 150,000 units at the $25 price. The additional sales will have a probable credit loss of 10 percent and will involve collection costs of $50,000. Total factory overhead will rise by $250,000. General and administrative expenses are fixed ($150,000); selling expenses are constant at $1 a unit; and labor costs are fixed at $7 a unit.

a) Based on the data given, should the additional credit sales be made? (Work this problem using total rather than per unit figures.)

b) What other factors should be taken into account for such a decision?

11-2 The Pappas Machinery Company has sales of $40 million a year in good years and $25 million in poor years. Its fixed assets are $12 million; receivables and inventories are 40 percent of sales; total assets are constant at $30 million.

　　　The firm must have liquidity because of substantial risks under product warranties. In addition, the firm must be ready to meet extended terms provided by foreign competitors.

a) How much cash does the firm have available for investment in good years? in poor years?

b) Suggest three kinds of investments to be used by this firm.

11-3 The following relations for inventory purchase and storage costs have been established by analysis for the Irwin Manufacturing Corporation.

1. Orders must be placed in multiples of 100 units.
2. Requirements for the year are 50,000 units. (Use 50 weeks in a year for calculations.)
3. Price per unit is $3.
4. Inventory carrying charge is 10 percent of average inventory.
5. Purchasing cost per order is $18.75.
6. Desired safety stock is 3,000 units (on hand initially).
7. Two weeks are required for delivery.

a) What is the economical order size?

b) What is the optimal number of orders to be placed?

c) At what inventory level should a reorder be made?

Chapter 12

Major Sources of
Short-Term Financing

In the preceding chapter we traced the flow of cash through an illustrative business firm and discussed certain broad principles for managing investments in current assets. In the present chapter we take up the main forms of short-term credit, considering both the characteristics and the source of this credit.

Short-term credit is defined as debt originally scheduled for repayment within one year; in other words, short-term credit is equal to liabilities minus the current maturities of long-term debt. The three major sources of funds with short maturities are discussed in this chapter. Ranked in descending order by volume of credit supplied to business, the main sources of short-term financing are (1) trade credit between firms, (2) loans from commercial banks, and (3) commercial paper. To a lesser degree these sources also supply funds for longer terms, but their primary importance in short-term financing justifies treatment at this point.

TRADE CREDIT[1]

In the ordinary course of events, a firm buys its supplies and materials on credit from other firms, recording the debt as an *account payable*. Accounts payable, or trade credit, as it is commonly called, is the largest single

---

[1] In the previous chapter, we discussed trade credit from the point of view of minimizing investment in current assets. In the present chapter we look at "the
(Footnote continued on the following page.)

category of short-term credit and represents about 40 percent of the current liabilities of nonfinancial corporations. This percentage is somewhat larger for smaller firms; since small companies may not qualify for financing from other sources, they rely rather heavily on trade credit.

Trade credit is a "spontaneous" source of financing in that it arises from ordinary business transactions. For example, suppose a firm makes average purchases of $2,000 a day on terms of net 30. On the average it will owe 30 times $2,000, or $60,000 to its suppliers. If its sales, and consequently its purchases, double, accounts payable will also double to $120,000. The firm will have spontaneously generated an additional $60,000 of financing. Similarly, if the terms of credit are extended from 30 to 40 days, accounts payable will expand from $60,000 to $80,000. Thus, lengthening the credit period, as well as expanding sales and purchases, generates additional financing.

Credit Terms

The terms of sales, or credit terms, describe the payment obligation of the buyer. The four main factors that influence the length of credit terms are outlined below.

1. *Economic nature of product.*   Commodities with high sales turnover are sold on relatively short credit terms; the buyer resells the product rapidly, generating cash that enables him to pay the supplier. Groceries have a high turnover, but perishability also plays a role. The credit extended for fresh fruits and vegetables might run from five to ten days, whereas the credit extended on canned fruits and vegetables would more likely be 15 to 30 days. Terms for items that have a slow retail turnover, such as jewelry, may run six months or longer.

2. *Seller circumstances.*   Financially weak sellers must require cash or exceptionally short credit terms. For example, farmers sell livestock to meat-packing companies on a cash basis. In some industries, variations in credit terms can be used as a sales promotion device. Although the use of credit as a selling device endangers sound credit management, the practice does occur, especially when the seller's industry has excess capacity. Also, a large seller could use his position to impose relatively short credit terms. However, the reverse appears more often in practice; that is, financially strong sellers are suppliers of funds to smaller firms.

3. *Buyer circumstances.*   In general, financially sound retailers who sell on credit may, in turn, receive slightly longer terms. Some classes of

---

other side of the coin," viewing trade credit as a *source* of financing rather than a *use* of financing. In the previous chapter, the use of trade credit by our customers resulted in an asset investment called "accounts receivable." In the present chapter, the use of trade credit gives rise to a short-term obligation generally called "accounts payable."

retailers regarded as selling in particularly risky areas (such as clothing) receive extended credit terms, but they are offered large discounts to encourage early payment.

4. *Cash discounts.* A cash discount is a reduction in price based on payment within a specified period. Cash discounts often exceed the rate of interest at which the buyer can borrow, so it is important that a firm be cautious in its use of trade credit.[2] If it borrows and takes the cash discount, the period during which accounts payable remain on the books is reduced. The effective length of credit is thus influenced by the size of discounts offered.

Illustrative Credit Terms. Credit terms typically express the amount of the cash discount and the date of its expiration, as well as the final due date. Probably the most frequently encountered terms are 2/10, net 30. In other words, if payment is made within 10 days of the invoice date, a 2 percent cash discount is allowed. If the cash discount is not taken, payment is due 30 days after the date of invoice. The cost of not taking cash discounts can be substantial, as shown here.

Credit Terms	Cost of Credit If Cash Discount Not Taken
1/10, net 20	36.36%
1/10, net 30	18.18%
2/10, net 20	73.47%
2/10, net 30	36.72%

Employment of Trade Credit

Trade credit has double-edged significance for the firm. It is a source of credit for financing purchases and a use of funds by which a firm finances credit sales to customers. For example, if a firm sells on the average $3,000 of goods a day with an average collection period of 40 days, it will have accounts receivable at any balance sheet date of approximately $120,000.

If the firm buys $2,000 worth of materials a day and the balance is outstanding for 20 days, accounts payable will average $40,000. The firm

---

[2] The following equation may be used for calculating the cost of not taking discounts:

$$\text{cost} = \frac{\text{discount percent}}{(100 - \text{discount percent})} \times \frac{360}{(\text{final due date} - \text{discount period})}$$

To illustrate, the cost of not taking a discount when the terms are 2/10, net 30 is computed.

$$\text{cost} = \frac{2}{98} \times \frac{360}{20} = 0.0204 \times 18 = 36.72\%$$

is extending net credit of $80,000, the difference between accounts receivable and accounts payable.

It is important, therefore, that the firm make the maximum use of trade credit as a source of funds, but at the same time it should minimize the extent to which its own funds are tied up in accounts receivable.

Advantages of Trade Credit as Source of Financing

Trade credit, a customary part of doing business in most lines of activity, is convenient and informal. A firm that does not qualify for credit from a financial institution may receive trade credit because previous experience has familiarized the seller with the credit-worthiness of his customer. As the seller knows the merchandizing practices of the line of business, he is usually in a good position to judge the capacity of his customer and the risk of selling to him on credit. The amount of trade credit fluctuates with the buyers' purchases, subject to any credit limits that may be operative.

Whether trade credit costs more or less than other forms of financing is a moot question. Sometimes trade credit can be surprisingly expensive to the buyer. The user often does not have other alternative forms of financing available, and the costs to the buyer may be commensurate with the risks to the seller. But in some instances trade credit is used simply because the user may not realize how expensive it is. In such circumstances careful financial analysis may lead to the substitution of alternative forms of financing for trade credit.

At the other extreme, trade credit may represent a virtual subsidy or sales promotion device offered by the seller. The authors know, for example, of cases where manufacturers quite literally supplied *all* the financing for new firms by selling on credit terms substantially longer than those of the new company. In one instance a manufacturer, anxious to obtain a dealership in a particular area, made a loan to the new company to cover operating expenses during the initial phases and geared the payment of accounts payable to cash receipts. Even in such instances, however, the buying firm must be careful that it is not really paying a hidden financing cost in the form of higher product prices than could be obtained elsewhere.[3]

SHORT-TERM FINANCING BY COMMERCIAL BANKS

Commercial bank lending appears on the balance sheet as *notes payable* and is second in importance to trade credit as a source of short-term financing. Banks occupy a pivotal position in the short-term and intermediate-term money markets. Their influence is greater than appears from the dollar amounts they lend, because the banks provide marginal funds. As a

---

[3] For numerous examples, see Robert P. Hungate, "Inter-business Financing" (Unpublished Ph.D. dissertation, University of California, Los Angeles, January 1961).

firm's financing needs grow, the banks are called upon to provide the additional funds. If the request is denied, often the alternative is to slow down the rate of growth or to cut back operations.

Characteristics of Loans from Commercial Banks

The main characteristics of lending patterns of commercial banks are briefly described.

Forms of Loans. A single loan obtained from a bank by a business firm is not different in principle from a loan obtained by an individual. In fact, it is often difficult to distinguish a bank loan to a small business from a personal loan. A single loan is obtained by signing a conventional promissory note. Repayment is made in a lump sum at maturity (when the note is due) or in installments throughout the life of the loan.

A *line of credit* is a formal or an informal understanding between the bank and the borrower concerning the maximum loan balance the bank will allow the borrower. For example, a bank loan officer may indicate to a financial manager that the bank regards his firm as "good" for up to $80,000 for the forthcoming year. Subsequently, the manager signs a promissory note for $15,000 for 90 days—he is said to be "taking down" $15,000 of his total line of credit. This amount is credited to the firm's checking account at the bank. At maturity, the checking account will be charged for the amount of the loan. Interest may be deducted in advance or paid at maturity of the loan. Before repayment of the $15,000, the firm may borrow additional amounts up to $65,000.

A more formal procedure may be followed if the firm is quite large. To illustrate, Chrysler Corporation arranged a line of credit for over $100 million with a group of banks. The banks were formally committed to lend Chrysler the funds if they were needed. Chrysler, in turn, paid a commitment fee of approximately ¼ percent on the unused balance of the commitment to compensate the banks for tying up their funds.

Size of Loans. Banks make loans of all sizes. The bulk of loans from commercial banks by dollar amount is obtained by firms with total assets of $5 million and more. But, by number of loans, firms with total assets of $50,000 and less obtain about 40 percent of bank loans.

Maturity. Commercial banks concentrate on the short-term lending market. Short-term loans make up about two thirds of bank loans by dollar amount, whereas "term loans" (loans with maturities longer than one year) make up only one third.

Security. If a potential borrower is a questionable credit risk or if his financing needs exceed the amount which the loan officer of the bank considers to be prudent on an unsecured basis, some form of security is required. More than one half the dollar value of bank loans is secured; the forms of security are described in Chapter 13. In terms of the number of bank loans, two thirds are secured or endorsed by a third party who guarantees payment of the loan in the event the borrower defaults.

Minimum Balance. Banks typically require that a regular borrower maintain a minimum checking account balance equal to 15 or 20 percent of the outstanding loan. These balances, which are commonly called *compensating balances,* are a method of raising the effective interest rate. For example, if a firm needs $80,000 to pay off outstanding obligations, but must maintain a 20 percent compensating balance, it must borrow $100,000 to be able to obtain the required $80,000. If the stated interest rate is 5 percent, the effective cost is actually 6¼ percent—$5,000 divided by $80,000 equals 6.25 percent.[4]

Repayment of Bank Loans. Because the bulk of bank deposits is subject to withdrawal on demand, commercial banks seek to prevent firms from using bank credit for permanent financing. A bank may therefore require its borrowers to "clean up" their short-term bank loans for at least one month each year. If a firm is unable to become free of bank debt at least part of each year, it is using bank financing for permanent needs and should develop additional sources of long-term or permanent financing.

Cost of Commercial Bank Loans. Loans from commercial banks generally run about 4 to 7 percent, with the effective rate depending upon the characteristics of the firm and the level of interest rates in the economy. If the firm can qualify as a "prime risk" because of its size and financial strength, the rate of interest will be one half to three quarters of 1 percent above the rediscount rate charged by federal reserve banks to commercial banks. On the other hand, a small firm with below average financial ratios may be required to provide collateral security and to pay an effective rate of interest of 10 percent or more.

Determination of the effective or true rate of interest on a loan depends upon the stated rate of interest and the method of charging interest by the lender. If the interest is paid at the maturity of the loan, the stated rate of interest is the effective rate of interest. If the bank deducts the interest in advance (discounts the loan), the effective rate of interest is increased. On a $10,000 loan for one year at 5 percent, the discount is $500 and the borrower obtains the use of only $9,500. The effective rate of interest is

$$\frac{\$500}{\$9,500} = 5.3\%$$

If the loan is repaid in twelve monthly installments, the effective rate of interest is even higher. In this event the borrower pays $500 for the use

---

[4] Note, however, that if the compensating balance is set as a minimum monthly *average,* and if the firm would maintain this average anyway, the compensating balance requirement does not entail higher rates.

of about one half the amount he receives. The amount received is $10,000 or $9,500, depending upon the methods of charging interest. If interest is paid at maturity, the effective rate would be approximately

$$\frac{\$500}{\$5,000} = 10\%$$

Under the discounting method, the effective cost of the installment loan would be approximately

$$\frac{\$500}{\$4,750} = 10.53\%$$

Choice of Bank or Banks

Banks have close relations with their borrowers. Since there is considerable personal contact over the years, the business problems of the borrower are frequently discussed; thus the bank often provides informal management counseling services. A potential borrower seeking bank relations should recognize the important differences among banks as potential sources of funds. These differences can be summarized into the following seven points.

1. Banks have different basic policies toward risk. Some banks are inclined to follow relatively conservative lending practices, others engage in what are properly termed creative banking practices. The policies reflect partly the personalities of officers of the bank and partly the characteristics of the bank's deposit liabilities. Thus a bank with fluctuating deposit liabilities in a static community will tend to be a conservative lender. A bank whose deposits are growing with little interruption may follow "liberal" credit policies. A large bank with broad diversification over geographical regions or among industries served can obtain the benefit of combining and averaging risks. Thus, marginal credit risks that might be unacceptable to a small bank or to a specialized unit bank can be pooled by a branch banking system to reduce the over-all risks of a group of marginal accounts.

2. Some bank loan officers are active in providing counsel and in stimulating development loans with firms in their early and formative years. Certain banks have distinct departments to make loans to firms expected to become growth firms. The personnel of these departments can provide considerable counseling to customers.

3. Banks differ in the extent to which they will support the activities of the borrower in bad times. This characteristic is referred to as the degree of *loyalty* of the banks. Some banks may put considerable pressure on a business to liquidate its loans when the firm's outlook becomes clouded, whereas others will stand by the firm and work diligently to help it attain a more favorable condition.

4. The fourth characteristic by which banks differ is the degree of deposit stability. Instability arises not only from fluctuations in the level of deposits but also from the composition of deposits. Deposits can take the form of demand deposits (checking accounts) or time deposits (savings accounts, certificates of deposit, Christmas clubs). Total deposits tend to be more stable when time deposits are substantial. Differences in deposit stability go a long way toward explaining differences in the extent to which the banks are willing or able to help the borrower work himself out of difficulties or even crises.

5. Banks differ greatly in the degree of loan specialization. Larger banks have separate departments specializing in different kinds of loans, such as real estate, installment loans, and commercial loans, among others. Within these broad categories there may be a specialization by line of business, such as steel, machinery, or textiles. The strengths of smaller banks are likely to reflect the nature of the business and the economic environment in which the banks operate. They tend to become specialists in specific lines, such as oil, construction, and agriculture, to name a few. The borrower can obtain more creative cooperation and more active support if he goes to the bank that has the greatest experience and familiarity with his particular type of business. The financial manager should therefore choose his bank with care. A bank that is excellent for one firm may be unsatisfactory for another.

6. Size of bank may be an important characteristic. Since the maximum loan a bank can make to any one customer is generally limited to 10 percent of capital accounts (capital stock plus surplus accounts), it will generally not be appropriate for large firms to develop borrowing relationships with small banks.

7. With the heightened competition between commercial banks and other financial institutions, the aggressiveness of banks has increased. Modern commercial banks now offer a wide range of financial and business services. Most large banks have business development departments which provide counseling to firms and serve as an intermediary on a wide variety of their requirements.

COMMERCIAL PAPER

Nature

Commercial paper consists of promissory notes of *large* firms and is sold primarily to other business firms, insurance companies, pension funds, and banks. Though the amounts of commercial paper outstanding are less than 5 percent of bank loans outstanding, this form of financing is important to particular lines of business.

Maturity and Cost

Maturities of commercial paper vary from two to six months, with an average of about five months. The rates on prime commercial paper vary, but are generally about ½ percent below those on prime business loans.

Use

The use of the open market for commercial paper is restricted to a comparatively small number of concerns that are exceptionally good credit risks. Dealers prefer to handle the paper of concerns whose net worth is $5 million or more and whose annual borrowing exceeds $500,000.

Appraisal of Use

A number of advantages are claimed for the commercial paper market. (1) It affects the broadest and most advantageous distribution of paper. (2) It provides more funds at lower rates than do other methods. (3) The borrower avoids the inconvenience and expense of financing arrangements with a number of institutions, each of which requires a compensating balance. (4) Publicity and prestige accrue to the borrower as his product and his paper become more widely known. (5) Finally, the commercial paper dealer frequently offers valuable advice to his clients.

A basic limitation of the commercial paper market is that the size of the funds available is limited to the excess liquidity that corporations, the main suppliers of funds, may have at any particular time. Another disadvantage is that a debtor who is in temporary financial difficulty receives little consideration, because commercial paper dealings are impersonal. Bank relations, on the other hand, are much more personal, and a bank is much more likely to help a good customer weather a temporary storm than is a commercial paper dealer.

USE OF SECURITY IN SHORT-TERM FINANCING

It is ordinarily better to borrow on an unsecured basis, but frequently a potential borrower's credit rating is not sufficiently strong to justify the loan. If the loan can be secured by the borrower's putting up some form of collateral to be claimed by the lender in the event of default, then the lender may extend credit to an otherwise unacceptable firm.

Several different types of collateral can be employed—marketable stocks or bonds, land or buildings, equipment, inventory, and accounts receivable. Marketable securities make excellent collateral, but few firms hold portfolios of stocks and bonds. Similarly, real property (land and buildings) and equipment are good forms of collateral, but they are generally used as security for long-term loans. The bulk of secured short-term business borrowing involves the pledge of short-term assets—accounts receivable or inventories. These two types of loans are described in the following two sections.

FINANCING ACCOUNTS RECEIVABLE

Accounts receivable financing involves either the *pledge* or the *sale* of receivables. The pledging of accounts receivable is called *accounts receivable discounting*. The process is characterized by the fact that the lender takes the receivables but has recourse to the borrower (seller); if the person or the firm that bought the goods does not pay, the selling firm must take the loss. In other words, the risk of default on the accounts receivable pledged remains with the borrower. Also, the buyer of the goods is not ordinarily notified about the discounting of the receivables.

Factoring, the second basic type of receivables financing, is the purchase of accounts receivable by the lender without recourse to the borrower (seller). The buyer of the goods is notified of the transfer and makes payment directly to the lender. Since the factoring firm assumes the risk of default on bad accounts, it must do the credit checking; so it may be fairly said that factors provide not only money but also a credit department for the borrower.

Procedure for Discounting Accounts Receivable

The financing of accounts receivable is initiated by a legally binding agreement between the seller of the goods and the financing institution. The agreement sets forth in detail procedures to be followed and legal obligations of both parties. Once the working relation has been established, the seller will periodically take a batch of invoices to the financing institution. The lender reviews the invoices and makes an appraisal of the buyers. Invoices of companies that do not meet the lender's credit standards will not be accepted for discounting. The financial institution seeks to protect itself at every phase of the operation. Selection of sound invoices is the essential first step in safeguarding the financial institution. If the buyer of the goods does not pay the invoice, the bank still has recourse against the seller of the goods. However, if many buyers default, the seller will doubtlessly be unable to meet his obligation to the bank.

Accounts receivable financing is, to a considerable extent, a mass financing operation in which large numbers of invoices or accounts receivable are handled. The smaller the average size of the invoice, the greater the administrative work for the financing institution. Before World War II, the average loan balance outstanding for approximately half the borrowers using accounts receivable financing was less than $100,000, indicating that firms using accounts receivable financing were typically small firms. The development of accounts receivable financing has therefore contributed to the financing of small business.

Procedure for Factoring Accounts Receivable

The procedure for factoring is somewhat different from that for discounting. Again, an agreement between the seller and the factor is made to specify legal obligations and procedural arrangements. When the seller receives an order from a buyer, a credit approval slip is written and immediately sent to the factoring company for a credit check. If the factor does not approve the sale, the seller will generally refuse to fill the order. This procedure informs the seller prior to the sale about the buyer's credit-worthiness and acceptability to the factor. If the sale is approved, shipment is made and the invoice is stamped to notify the buyer to make payment directly to the factoring company.

The factor performs three functions in carrying out the normal procedure as outlined above: (1) credit checking, (2) lending, and (3) risk bearing. The seller can select various combinations of these functions by changing provisions in the factoring agreement. For example, a small or a medium-sized firm can avoid establishing a credit department. The factor's service might well be less costly than a department which may have excess capacity for the firm's credit volume. At the same time, if the firm uses part of the time of a noncredit specialist to perform credit checking, lack of education, training, and experience may result in excessive losses.

The seller may utilize the factor to perform the credit-checking and risk-taking functions, but not the lending function. The following procedure will be carried out on receipt of a $10,000 order. The factor checks and approves the invoices. The goods are shipped on terms n/30. Payment is made to the factor, who remits to the seller. But assume that the factor has received only $5,000 by the end of the credit period. He must still remit $10,000 to the seller (less his fee, of course). If the remaining $5,000 is never paid, the factor sustains a $5,000 loss.

Now consider the more typical situation in which the factor performs a lending function by making payment in advance of collection. The goods are shipped and, even though payment is not due for 30 days, the factor immediately makes funds available to the seller. Suppose $10,000 of goods is shipped; the factoring commission for credit checking is 2½ percent of the invoice price, or $250; and the interest expense is computed at a 9 percent annual rate on the invoice balance, or $75. The seller's accounting entry will read as follows.

Cash	$9,175
Interest Expense [5]	75
Factoring Commission	250
Reserve: Due from factor on collection of account	500
Accounts Receivable	$10,000

The $500 "due from factor on collection of account" in the entry is a reserve established by the factor to cover disputes between sellers and buyers on damaged goods, goods returned by the buyers to the seller, and failure to make outright sale of goods. The amount is paid to the seller firm when the factor collects on the account.

Factoring is normally a continuous process instead of the single cycle described above. The seller of the goods receives orders; he transmits the purchase orders to the factor for approval; on approval, the goods are shipped; the factor advances the money to the seller; the buyers pay the factor when payment is due; and the factor periodically remits any excess reserve to the seller of the goods. Once a routine is established, a continuous circular flow of goods and funds takes place between the seller, the buyers of the goods, and the factor.

Cost of Receivables Financing

Accounts receivable discounting and factoring services are convenient and advantageous, but they can be costly. The credit-checking commission is 1 to 3 percent of the amount of invoices accepted by the factor. The cost of money is reflected in the interest rate of 6 to 10 percent charged on the unpaid balance of the funds advanced by the factor. Where the risk to the factor is excessive, he purchases the invoices (either with or without recourse) at discounts from face value.

Evaluation of Receivables Financing

It cannot be said categorically that accounts receivable financing is always a good or a poor method of raising funds for an individual business. Among the advantages is, first, the flexibility of this source of financing. As the sales of a firm expand and it needs more financing, a larger volume of

---

5 Since the interest is only for one month, we take $\frac{1}{12}$ of the stated rate, 9 percent, and multiply this by the $10,000 invoice price.

$$\frac{1}{12} \times 0.09 \times \$10,000 = \$75$$

Note that the effective rate of interest is really above 9 percent, because the borrower does not get the full $10,000. In many instances, however, the factoring contract would call for interest to be computed on the invoice price *less* the factoring commission and the reserve account.

invoices is generated automatically. Because the dollar amounts of discounted invoices vary directly with sales, the amount of readily available financing increases. Second, receivables or invoices provide security for a loan which a firm might otherwise be unable to obtain. Third, factoring provides the services of a credit department that might otherwise be available to the firm only under much more expensive conditions.

Accounts receivable financing also has disadvantages. First, when invoices are numerous and relatively small in amount, the administrative costs involved may render this method of financing inconvenient and expensive. Second, the firm is using a highly liquid asset as security. For a long time accounts receivable financing was frowned upon by most trade creditors. In fact, such financing was regarded as confession of a firm's unsound financial position. It is no longer regarded in this light; many sound firms engage in receivables discounting or factoring. However, the traditional attitude causes some trade creditors to refuse to sell on credit to a firm which is discounting its receivables on grounds that to do so removes from the trade creditor a possible source of repayment.

Economically, the increased use of receivables financing has represented a substantial contribution to the financing of small businesses. It makes possible the financing of smaller firms and marginal credit risks for which other financing might not be available.

Future Use of Receivables Financing

We might make a prediction at this point—in the future, accounts receivable financing will increase in relative importance. Computer technology is rapidly advancing toward the point where credit records of individuals and firms can be kept in computer memory units. Systems have been devised so a store can have a unit on hand which, when an individual's magnetic credit card is inserted into a box, gives a signal that his credit is "good" and that a bank is willing to "buy" the receivable created when the store completes the sale. The cost of handling invoices will be greatly reduced over present-day costs, because the new systems will be so highly automated. This will make it possible to use accounts receivable financing for very small sales, and it will reduce the cost of all receivables financing. The net result will be a marked expansion of accounts receivable financing.

INVENTORY FINANCING

A relatively large volume of credit is secured by business inventories. If a firm is a relatively good credit risk, the mere existence of the inventory may be a sufficient basis for receiving an unsecured loan. If the firm is a relatively poor risk, the lending institution may insist upon security, which often takes the form of a chattel mortgage on the inventory.

Chattel Mortgage Security[6]

The chattel mortgage gives the lending institution a lien against property of the borrower. The chattel mortgage is sometimes inconvenient if the lending institution is really worried about the credit position of the borrowing firm, because, in order to establish a valid chattel mortgage, a meticulous description of the items and recordation with the county recorder may be required. Inventory description and legal control are difficult if the inventory is fluid. For example, a fruit and vegetable canner has inventory on hand from which he makes sales and into which additional inventories flow as the canning process takes place. In order to maintain the continuous legal validity of the chattel mortgage, a change in the inventory's items might require a change in the description of the inventory. Furthermore, in some jurisdictions a chattel mortgage on stock in trade is invalid.

Trust Receipts

Because of the weaknesses of the chattel mortgage, another type of security is used—the trust receipt. A trust receipt is an instrument acknowledging that the borrower holds the goods in trust for the lender. When trust receipts are used, the borrowing firm, on receiving funds from the lender, conveys a trust receipt for the goods. The goods can be stored in a public warehouse or held on the premises of the borrower. The trust receipt provides that the goods are held in trust for the lender, or are segregated in the borrower's premises on behalf of the lender and transmitted to the lender at the end of each day.

One defect of trust receipt financing is the requirement that a trust receipt must be issued for specific goods. For example, if the security is bags of coffee beans, the trust receipts would have to indicate the bags by number. In order to validate its trust receipts, the lending institution will have to send a man to the premises of the borrower to see that the bag numbers are correctly listed. Furthermore, complex legal requirements of trust receipts require the attention of a bank officer. Problems are compounded if borowers are widely separated geographically from the lender. To offset these inconveniences, field warehousing is coming into wide use as a method of securing loans with inventory.

---

6 A Uniform Commercial Code has been devised to make inventory financing, among other things, a much simpler process. Under the code, which has already been adopted by many states, inventories can be pledged without the necessity of identifying individual items.

Field Warehouse Financing

Like trust receipt and chattel mortgage financing, warehouse financing uses inventory as security. A public warehouse represents an independent third party engaged in the business of storing goods. Sometimes a public warehouse is not practical because of the bulkiness of goods and the expense of transporting them to and from the borrower's premises. Field warehouse financing represents an economical method of inventory financing in which the warehouse is established at the place of the borrower. To provide inventory supervision, the lending institution employs a third party in the arrangement, the field warehousing company. This company acts as the control (or supervisory) agent for the lending institution.

A field warehouse can be illustrated very simply. Suppose that a potential borrower has stacked iron in an open yard on his premises. A field warehouse can be established if a field warehousing concern places a temporary fence around the iron and erects a sign which says "This is a field warehouse supervised and conducted by the Smith Field Warehousing Corporation." These are minimal conditions, of course.

The example illustrates the two elements in the establishment of a warehouse: (1) public notification of the field warehouse arrangement and (2) supervision of the field warehouse by a custodian of the field warehouse concern. When the field warehousing operation is relatively small, the second condition is sometimes violated by hiring an employee of the borrower to supervise the inventory. This practice is viewed as undesirable by the lending institution because there is no control over the collateral by a person independent of the borrowing concern.[7]

The field warehouse financing operation is described best by a specific illustration. Assume that a tomato canner is interested in financing his operations by bank borrowing. The canner has sufficient funds to finance 15 to 20 percent of his operations during the canning season. These funds are adequate to purchase and process an initial batch of tomatoes. As the cans are put into boxes and rolled into the storerooms, the canner needs additional funds for both raw materials and labor.

Because of the credit rating of the canner, the bank decides that a

---

[7] This lack of independent control was the main cause of the breakdown that resulted in the huge losses connected with the loans to the Allied Crude Vegetable Oil Company headed by Anthony (Tino) DeAngelis. American Express Field Warehousing Company hired men from Allied's staff as custodians. Their dishonesty was not discovered because of another breakdown—the fact that the American Express touring inspector did not actually take a physical inventory of the warehouses. As a consequence, the swindle was not discovered until losses running into the hundreds of millions of dollars had been suffered. Cf. Norman C. Miller, *The Great Salad Oil Swindle,* (Baltimore, Md.: Penguin Books, 1965), pp. 72–77.

field warehousing operation is necessary to secure its lending. The field warehouse is established, and the custodian notifies the lending institution of the description by number of the boxes of canned tomatoes in storage and under his control. Thereupon the lending institution establishes for the canner a deposit on which he can draw. From this point on, the bank finances the operations. The canner needs only enough cash to initiate the cycle. The farmers bring more tomatoes; the canner processes them; the cans are boxed, and the boxes are put into the field warehouse; field warehouse receipts are drawn up and sent to the bank; the bank establishes further deposits for the canner based on the receipts; the canner can draw on the deposits to continue the cycle.

Of course, the canner's ultimate objective is to sell the canned tomatoes. As the canner receives purchase orders, he transmits them to the bank and the bank directs the custodian to release the inventories. It is agreed that, as remittances are received by the canner, they will be turned over to the bank. These remittances by the canner pay off the loans made by the bank.

Typically, a seasonal pattern exists. At the beginning of the tomato harvesting and canning season, the canner's cash needs and loan requirements begin to rise and reach a maximum by the end of the canning season. It is hoped that, just before the new canning season begins, the canner has sold a sufficient volume to have paid off the loan completely. If for some reason the canner has had a bad year, the bank may carry him over another year to enable him to work off his inventory.

Acceptable Products

In addition to canned foods, which account for about 17 percent of all field warehouse loans, many other product inventories provide a basis for field warehouse financing. Some of these are miscellaneous groceries, which represent about 13 percent; lumber products, about 10 percent; and coal and coke, about 6 percent.

These products are relatively nonperishable and are sold in well-developed, organized markets. Nonperishability protects the lender, if he should have to take over the security. For this reason a bank would not make a field warehousing loan on such perishables as fresh fish. However, frozen fish, which can be stored for a long time, can be field warehoused. An organized market aids the lender in disposing of an inventory which it takes over. Banks are not desirous of going into the canning or the fish business. They want to be able to dispose of an inventory within a matter of hours and with the expenditure of a minimum amount of time.

Cost of Financing

The fixed costs of a field warehousing arrangement are relatively high; this type of financing is therefore not suitable for an extremely small firm. If a field warehouse company sets up the field warehouse itself, it will typically set a minimum charge of about $350 to $600 a year, plus about 1 or 2 percent of the amount of credit extended to the borrower. In addition, the financing institution will charge from 6 to 10 percent interest. The minimum size of a field warehousing operation requires an inventory of about $100,000.

Appraisal

There are several advantages in the use of field warehouse financing as a source of funds for business firms. First, the amount of funds available is flexible, because the financing is tied to the growth of inventories, which in turn is related directly to financing needs. Second, the field warehousing arrangement increases the acceptability of inventories as loan collateral. Some inventories would not be accepted by a bank as security without a field warehousing arrangement. Third, the necessity for inventory control, safekeeping, and the use of specialists in warehousing has resulted in improved warehouse practices. The services of the field warehouse companies have often saved money for the firm in spite of the costs of financing mentioned above. The field warehouse company may suggest inventory practices which reduce the labor that the firm has to employ, and reduce inventory damage and loss as well.

The major disadvantage of a field warehousing operation is the fixed cost element, which reduces the feasibility of this form of financing for small firms.

SUMMARY

Short-term credit is defined as debt originally scheduled for repayment within one year. This chapter has discussed the three major sources of short-term credit —trade credit between firms, loans from commercial banks, and commercial paper.

Trade Credit

Trade credit, represented by accounts payable, is the largest single category of short-term credit and is especially important for smaller firms. Trade credit is a *spontaneous source of financing* in that it arises from ordinary business transactions; as sales increase, so does the supply of financing from accounts payable.

Although trade credit is a most useful method of financing, it is important that the financial manager be aware of its implicit cost. If discounts are offered for prompt payment, as they very often are, then the cost of not taking the discount amounts to an interest payment. Under certain common discount procedures the implicit interest cost of not taking discounts is quite high. For example, under terms of 2/10, net 30, where a 2 percent discount is allowed if payment is made within 10 days and the account is payable within 30 days, if the discount is not taken, the implicit interest cost is over 36 percent.

Bank Credit

Bank credit occupies a pivotal position in the short-term money market. Banks provide the marginal credit that allows firms to expand more rapidly than is possible through retained earnings and trade credit; to be denied bank credit often means that a firm must slow its rate of growth.

Bank loans are generally represented by *notes payable*. The loan itself is frequently arranged prior to the time it is needed—this is called *establishing a line of credit*. To insure that loan customers are also deposit customers, and also to raise the effective rate of interest on loans, banks frequently require minimum deposit balances known as *compensating balances*. When used, compensating balances are generally set at about 15 to 20 percent of the outstanding amount of the loan.

Bank interest rates are quoted in three ways—regular compound interest, discount interest, and installment interest where the interest charges are computed on the original amount of the loan rather than on the outstanding balance. Regular interest needs no adjustment—it is "correct" as stated. Discount interest requires a small upward adjustment to make it comparable to regular compound interest rates. Installment interest rates require a large adjustment; frequently the true interest rate is double the quoted rate for an installment loan.

Commercial Paper

Bank loans are personal in the sense that the financial manager meets with the banker, discusses the terms of the loan with him, and reaches an agreement that involves direct and personal negotiation. Commercial paper, on the other hand, although it is physically quite similar to a bank loan, is sold in a broad, impersonal market. A California firm might, for example, sell commercial paper notes to a bank in the Midwest.

Only the very strongest firms are able to use the commercial paper markets—the nature of these markets is such that the firm selling the paper must have a reputation so good that buyers of the paper are willing to buy the paper without any sort of credit check. *Interest rates* in the commercial paper market are the lowest available to business borrowers.

A disadvantage of commercial paper *vis-à-vis* bank credit, however, is that if a firm gets into any kind of temporary trouble, it will be completely excluded from the commercial paper market. Commercial banks, on the other hand, are frequently willing to lend support to a long-time customer even when it is having problems. This can be a big advantage to bank credit.

Use of Security in Short-Term Financing

It is ordinarily better to borrow on an unsecured basis, but frequently a potential borrower's credit rating is not sufficiently strong to justify the loan. If the loan can be secured by the borrower's putting up some forms of collateral to be claimed by the lender in the event of default, the lender may extend credit to an otherwise unacceptable firm. The most common type of collateral used for short-term credit are inventories and accounts receivable.

Accounts receivable financing can be done either by *pledging the receivables* (discounting) or by selling them outright, frequently called *factoring*. When the receivables are pledged, the borrower retains the risk that the person or firm who owes the receivable will not pay; this risk is typically passed on to the lender when factoring is involved. Because the factor takes the risk of default, he will typically investigate the purchaser's credit; therefore, the factor can perform three services—a lending function, a risk-bearing function, and a credit-checking function. When receivables are pledged, the lender typically performs only the first of these three functions. Consequently, factoring is generally quite a bit more expensive than pledging accounts receivable.

Inventory loans are rather difficult to administer under most circumstances. For certain types of inventory, however, the technique known as *field warehousing* is used to provide adequate security to the lender. Under a field warehousing arrangement, the inventory is under the physical control of a warehouse company, which releases the inventory only on order from the lending institution. Canned goods, lumber, steel, coal, and other standardized products are the type of goods usually covered in field warehouse arrangements.

QUESTIONS

12–1   It is inevitable that firms will obtain a certain amount of their financing in the form of trade credit, which is, to some extent, a free source of funds. What are some other factors that lead firms to use trade credit?

12–2   "Commercial paper interest rates are always lower than bank loan rates to a given borrower. Nevertheless, many firms perfectly capable of selling commercial paper employ higher cost bank credit." Discuss the statement, indicating (a) why commercial paper rates are lower than bank rates and (b) why firms might use bank credit in spite of its higher cost.

12–3   "Trade credit has an explicit interest rate cost if discounts are available but not taken. There are also some intangible costs associated with the failure to take discounts." Discuss.

12–4   What are some of the reasons that lead firms to offer high cash discounts?

12–5   A large manufacturing firm that had been selling its products on a 3/10, n/30 basis changed its credit terms to 1/20, n/90. What changes might be anticipated on the balance sheets of the manufacturer and its customers?

12–6   The availability of bank credit is more important to small firms than to large ones. Why is this so?

12–7   What factors should a firm consider in selecting its primary bank? Would it be feasible for a firm to have a primary deposit bank (the bank where most of its funds are deposited) and a different primary loan bank (the bank where it does most of its borrowing)?

12–8   Indicate whether each of the following changes would raise or lower the cost of accounts receivable financing, and why:

   a) The firm eases up on its credit standards in order to increase sales.
   b) The firm institutes a policy of refusing to make credit sales if the amount of the purchase (invoice) is below $100. Previously, about 40 percent of all invoices were below $100.
   c) The firm agrees to give recourse to the finance company for all defaults.
   d) The firm, which already has a recourse arrangement, is merged into a larger, stronger company.
   e) A firm without a recourse arrangement changes its terms of trade from net 30 to net 90.

12–9   Would a firm that manufactures specialized machinery for a few large customers be more likely to use some form of inventory financing or some form of accounts receivable financing? Why?

12–10   "A firm that factors its accounts receivable will look better in a ratio analysis than one that discounts its receivables." Discuss.

12–11   Why would it not be practical for a typical retailer to use field warehousing?

12–12   For each of the following, list one industry, together with your reasons for including it, that might be expected to use each type of credit:

   a) Field warehousing   d) Trust receipts
   b) Factoring   e) None of these
   c) Accounts receivable discounting

PROBLEMS

12–1   What is the equivalent annual interest rate that would be lost if a firm failed to take the cash discount under each of the following terms?

   a) 1/15, n/30   d) 2/10, n/40
   b) 2/10, n/60   e) 1/10, n/40
   c) 3/10, n/60

12–2   Given below is the balance sheet of the Consolidated Credit Corporation as of December 31, 1968.

CONSOLIDATED CREDIT CORPORATION
BALANCE SHEET
December 31, 1968
(in millions of dollars)

Cash	$ 60	Bank loans	$ 220
Net receivables	2,280	Commercial paper	775
Marketable securities	120	Others	335
Repossessions	3	Total due within a year	$1,330
Total current assets	$2,463	Long-term debt	940
Other assets	137	Total shareholders' equity	330
Total assets	$2,600	Total claims	$2,600

a) Calculate commercial paper as a percent of short-term financing, as a percent of total-debt financing, as a percent of all financing.

b) Why do finance companies such as Consolidated Credit use commercial paper to such a great extent?

c) Why do they use both bank loans and commercial paper?

12–3 The Kaplan Corporation had sales of $1.5 million during 1968 and earned a 2 percent return after taxes on total assets.

Although its terms of purchase are 30 days, its accounts payable represent 60 days' purchases. The president of the company is seeking to increase the company's bank borrowings in order to become current in meeting trade obligations.

The company's balance sheet is shown here.

KAPLAN CORPORATION
BALANCE SHEET
December 31, 1968

Cash	$ 20,000	Accounts payable	$ 200,000
Accounts receivable	100,000	Bank loans	200,000
Inventory	480,000	Accruals	100,000
Current assets	600,000	Current debt	500,000
Land and buildings	200,000	Mortgage on real estate	200,000
Equipment	200,000	Common stock, par 10 cents	100,000
		Retained earnings	200,000
		Total liabilities and	
Total assets	$1,000,000	net worth	$1,000,000

a) How much bank financing is needed to become immediately current on trade credit?

b) Would you as a bank loan officer make the loan? Why?

12–4 The Mattson Plastics Company has been growing rapidly. It is suffering
from insufficient working capital, however, and has therefore become slow
in paying bills. Of its total accounts payable, $100,000 is overdue. This
threatens the relation with its main supplier of powders used in the manufacture of various kinds of insulation materials for aircraft and missiles.
Over 80 percent of its sales are to six large defense contractors. Its balance
sheet, sales, and net profit for the year ended December 31, 1969, are
shown here.

MATTSON PLASTICS
BALANCE SHEET
December 31, 1969

Cash	$ 30,000	Trade credit	$ 250,000
Receivables	450,000	Bank loans	200,000
Inventories:		Accruals	50,000
Raw material	40,000		
Work in process	200,000	Total current debt	500,000
Finished goods	60,000	Chattel mortgages	300,000
		Capital stock	100,000
Total current assets	780,000	Surplus	100,000
Equipment	220,000		
Total assets	$1,000,000	Total liab. and net worth	$1,000,000
Sales	$2,050,000		
Profit after taxes	100,000		

a) If the same ratio of sales to total assets continues and if sales increase
to $2.550 million, how much nonspontaneous financing will be re-
quired?

b) The bank is reluctant to loan Mattson Plastics more than $150,000 to
$200,000 on an unsecured basis. Why?

c) Could Mattson obtain more funds by use of inventory financing?
Explain.

d) Would receivables financing be a possibility for Mattson? Explain.

e) *Assuming the facts listed below,* on the average what is the total amount
of receivables outstanding at any time? How much cash does the firm
actually receive by factoring the average amount of receivables? What
is the average duration of advances, on the basis of 360 days a year?
What is the total cost of the financing? What is the effective annual
financing charge (percentage) paid on the money received?

1) Receivables turn over five times a year.

2) Cash sales amount to $50,000.

3) The factor requires an 8 percent reserve for returns and disputed
items.

4) The factor also requires a 2 percent commission to cover the costs
of credit checking.

5) There is a 6 percent annual interest charge based on receivables less any reserve requirements and commissions. This payment is made at the beginning of the period and is deducted from the advance.

12–5 The Warren Company manufactures plastic toys. It buys raw materials, manufactures the toys in the spring and summer, and ships them to department stores and toy stores by the late summer or early fall. Warren factors its receivables. If it did not, the following would be its situation. For example, in October 1968, the balance sheet of Warren would have looked like this.

WARREN COMPANY
PRO FORMA BALANCE SHEET
October 31, 1968

Cash	$ 100,000	Accounts payable	$3,000,000
Receivables	3,000,000	Notes payable	2,000,000
Inventory	2,000,000	Accruals	200,000
		Total current debt	5,200,000
Total current assets	5,100,000	Common stock	500,000
		Mortgages	1,000,000
Fixed assets	2,000,000	Retained earnings	400,000
Total assets	$7,100,000	Total claims	$7,100,000

Warren provides advanced dating on its sales; thus its receivables are not due for payment until January 31, 1969. However, Warren would have been overdue on some $2 million of its accounts payable if the above situation actually existed.

Warren has an agreement with a finance company to factor the receivables. The factoring company charges a flat commission of 2 percent, plus 6 percent per year interest on the outstanding balance, and it deducts a reserve of 8 percent for returned and damaged materials. Interest and commission are paid in advance. No interest is charged on the reserved funds or on the commission.

a) Show the balance sheet of Warren on October 31, 1968, giving effect to the purchase of all the receivables by the factoring company and the use of the funds to pay accounts payable.

b) If the $3 million is the average level of outstanding receivables, and if they turn over 4 times a year (hence the commission is paid 4 times a year), what are the total dollar cost of financing and the effective annual interest rate?

12–6 The Karalus Company is a producer of building materials. The demand for its products is highly seasonal, concentrated in the spring and summer months. Its own production is therefore highly uneven.

Karalus would profitably allow a 10 percent trade discount to distributors if they were willing to accept deliveries during the slack season. The 10 percent concession would be advantageous to the distributors. However, as the distributors are generally underfinanced, they cannot accept deliveries without outside financing.

Outline a program of field warehousing to provide financing for the distributors.

Chapter 13

Intermediate-Term Financing

Intermediate-term financing is defined as debt originally scheduled for repayment in more than one year but less than five years. Anything shorter is a current liability and falls in the class of short-term credit, while obligations due in five or more years are thought of as long-term debt. This distinction is arbitrary, of course—we might just as well define long-term credit as credit starting with a maturity of 10 or more years. However, the one-to-five year distinction is commonly used, so we shall follow it here.

The major forms of intermediate-term financing include (1) *term loans,* (2) *conditional sales contracts,* and (3) *lease financing.* These types of credit are described in the present chapter.

TERM LOANS

A *term loan* is a business loan with a maturity of more than one year. There are exceptions to the rule, but ordinarily term loans are retired by systematic repayments (often called *amortization payments*) over the life of the loan. Security, generally in the form of a chattel mortgage on equipment, is often employed, but the larger, stronger companies are able to borrow on an unsecured basis.

The primary lenders on term credit are commercial banks, life insurance companies, and, to a lesser extent, pension funds. Bank loans are generally restricted to maturities of between one and five years, while insurance companies and pension funds make the bulk of their term loans for between five and fifteen years. Therefore, insurance company term loans are generally long-term, not intermediate-term, financing. Sometimes, when relatively large loans ($10 million and up) are involved, banks and insurance companies combine to make a loan, with the bank taking the short maturities and the insurance company the long maturities. Some specific features of term loans are discussed in the following sections.

Repayment Schedule

The repayment, or amortization, schedule is a particularly important feature of practically all term loans, so it is useful to describe how it is determined. The purpose of amortization, of course, is to have the loan repaid gradually over its life rather than falling due all at once. Amortization forces the borrower to retire the loan slowly, thus protecting both the lender and the borrower against the possibility that the borrower will not make adequate provisions for retirement during the life of the loan.

To illustrate how the amortization schedule is determined, let us assume that a firm borrows $1,000 on a 10-year term loan, that interest is computed at 5 percent on the declining balance, and that the principal and interest are to be paid in ten equal installments. What is the amount of each of the ten annual payments? To find this value we must use the present value concepts developed in Chapter 6.

First, notice that the lender advances $1,000 and receives in turn a 10-year annuity or R dollars each year. In the section headed Annual Receipts from an Annuity in Chapter 6 we saw that these receipts could be calculated as

$$R = \frac{A_n}{IF}$$

where R is the annual receipts, A_n is the present value of the annuity, and IF is the appropriate interest factor found either in Table 6-5 or in Appendix Table A-4. Substituting the $1,000 for A_n and the interest factor for a 10-year, 5 percent annuity, or 7.722, for IF, we get

$$R = \frac{\$1,000}{7.722} = \$130$$

Therefore, if our firm makes ten annual installments of $130 each, it will have retired the $1,000 loan and provided the lender a 5 percent return on his investment.

Table 13-1 breaks down the annual payments into interest and re-payment components, and in the process proves that level payments of $130 will, in fact, retire the $1,000 loan and give the lender his 5 percent return. This breakdown is important for tax purposes, as the interest payments are deductible.

Table 13-1   TERM LOAN REPAYMENT SCHEDULE

Year	Total Payment	Interest*	Amortization Repayment	Remaining Balance
1	$ 130	$ 50	$ 80	$920
2	130	46	84	836
3	130	42	88	748
4	130	38	92	656
5	130	34	96	560
6	130	28	102	458
7	130	23	107	351
8	130	18	112	239
9	130	13	117	122
10	130	8	122	—
Totals	$1,300	$300	$1,000	—

* Interest for the first year is $0.05 \times \$1,000 = \$50$; for the second year it is $0.05 \times \$920 = \$46$; and so on. The numbers are not exact because of rounding errors.

Characteristics of Direct Loans

Size of Loan. The typical term loan is small in terms of its dollar amount. Most commercial bank term loans are from $100,000 to $250,000. About 50 percent of life insurance loans run from about $1 million to $5 million. Commercial banks typically make smaller and shorter term loans; life insurance companies make larger and longer term loans on the average, although they also make a few short-term loans.

Size of Borrowers. It has been estimated that 90 percent of the term loans made by commercial banks are to small firms with assets of less than $5 million. Most of the term and direct loans made by insurance companies are to larger firms.

Industry of the Borrower. Earlier surveys have indicated that nearly 40 percent of term loans were confined to two major industry groups: (1) transportation, communication, and other public utilities and (2) petroleum, coal, chemicals, and rubber. These two groups also showed the highest ratio of term-to-total bank borrowing. This reflects the large proportion of their assets having relatively long service lives. By contrast, the smaller users of term credit were commodity dealers and sales finance companies, which have small fixed investment. A 1957 survey showed that the greatest relative increase in term loans was in trade, construction, and real estate— small firms growing rapidly.

Maturity. For commercial banks, the term loan runs five years or less, typically three years. For insurance companies, the most typical maturities have been 10 to 15 years. This difference reflects the fact that commercial banks are stronger in the short-term field, and insurance companies in the medium- and long-term field. As we pointed out above, banks and insurance companies occasionally cooperate in their term lending. For example, if a firm (usually a large one) seeks a 15-year term loan, a bank may take the loan for the first five years and an insurance company for the last 10 years.

Collateral. Commercial banks have required security on about 60 percent of the volume and 90 percent of the number of term loans made. They have taken as security mainly stocks, bonds, machinery, and equipment. Insurance companies also have required security on nearly a third of their loans, frequently using real estate as collateral on the longer loans.

In recent years institutional investors have increasingly taken compensation in addition to fixed interest payments on directly negotiated loans. The most popular form of additional compensation is an option to buy common stock, "the option being in the form of detachable warrants permitting the purchase of the shares at stated prices over a designated period.[1]

Use of Funds by Borrowers. During an earlier period, more than 50 percent of direct loans were used to refund outstanding bonds sold originally at higher interest rates. More recently, direct loans have provided primarily working capital, and secondarily, plant and equipment financing.

Repayment provisions. Most term loans are repayable in equal installments. Only a small percentage of the loans have any balloon segment of repayment at the end. Term loans are geared specifically to the ability of the firm to meet a certain repayment, or amortization, schedule.

Terms of Loan Agreements

The term loan assures funds to the borrower; he will not be faced with an inability to renew his loan if his needs for funds continue. Offsetting the advantages of having the assured use of funds for a period of from three to 20 years is a set of disadvantages that grow out of the inherent nature of the term loan. On a 90-day loan, since the commercial bank has the option to renew or not renew, the bank can take the occasion to reexamine the situation of the borrower. If it has deteriorated unduly, the loan officer simply does not renew the loan. On a term or direct loan, however, the bank or insurance company has committed itself for a period of

---

[1] C. M. Williams and H. A. Williams, "Incentive Financing," *Harvard Business Review,* 38, March–April 1960, p. 124.

years. Thus, there are certain restrictive provisions in the loan agreement designed to protect the lender for the duration of the loan. The most important of the typical restrictive provisions are listed below.

Current ratio. The current ratio must be maintained at some specified level—2½ to 1, 3 to 1, 3½ to 1, depending upon the borrower's line of business. Net working capital must be maintained at some minimum.

Additional fixed assets. There are restrictions on the amount of additional fixed assets that may be purchased by the borrower in the future. The lender seeks to protect himself against the borrower's sinking his funds excessively in fixed investments.

Additional long-term debt. Typically, there are prohibitions against incurring additional long-term indebtedness except with the permission of the lender. Furthermore, the lender does not permit the pledge of assets without the permission of the lender. Moreover, the loan agreement prohibits the borrower from assuming any contingent liabilities, such as guaranteeing the indebtedness of a subsidiary. Finally, the loan agreement probably restricts the borrower from signing long-term leases beyond specified amounts.

Management. The loan agreement may require that any major changes in management personnel, or in its composition, must be approved by the lender. The loan agreement requires life insurance on the principals of the business, especially if they are key personnel. In addition, the loan agreement may provide for the creation of a voting trust or a granting of proxies for a specified period to ensure that the management of the company will be under the control of the group on which the lender has relied in making the loan.

Financial statements. The lender will require the borrower to submit periodic financial statements for his review.

This list does not exhaust all the kinds of terms found in loan agreements, but it is illustrative. It serves to indicate the kind of protective provisions the bank or insurance company seeks to embody in the loan agreement.

Cost of Term Loans

Another major aspect of term lending is its cost. As with other forms of lending, the interest rate on term loans varies with the size of the loan and the quality of the borrower. Surveys show that on term loans of less than $500 the interest rate may run up to 10 percent. On loans of $1 million and above, term loan rates have been close to the prime rate. The size of the loan often reflects the quality of the borrower as well as the fixed cost involved in making small loans.

The interest rate may be related to the Federal Reserve rediscount rate. Often the loan agreement specifies that the interest rate will be based on the average of the rediscount rate in the borrower's Federal Reserve district during the previous three months, generally ½ percent to 1 or 2 percent above the rediscount rate. In other words, the loan rate can fluctuate during the life of the loan and is often tied to the rediscount rate. It may also be geared to the published prime rate charged by New York City banks.

Economic Aspects of Long-Term Loans

Finally, it is useful to comment on several aspects of the broader economic significance of long-term loans.

1. The long-term loan may make the economy less vulnerable to forced liquidation. Since the loan is not subject to renewal every 90 days, there is less danger of forced liquidation of loans accumulating during a depression when lenders become pessimistic and the financial position of the borrower deteriorates.

2. It brings insurance companies into direct lending to business. Before the 1930s, insurance companies invested in business primarily by buying bonds. In such a situation the insurance company was simply one among other bondholders. But now the relation is direct. The insurance company has considerable stability in its own liabilities. The flow of cash into an insurance company is highly predictable, and the danger of a wave of cash surrenders of life insurance policies during a recession has proved historically to be very small.[2] The insurance company, therefore, is in a position to allow an extension to a borrower if he gets into difficulties. This arrangement makes the economy less vulnerable to forced liquidation or to a continuous chain of liquidations in one area that forces liquidation in another, causing a downward spiral in the economy.

3. The term loan increases the availability of longer term debt for smaller businesses. However, it does not completely solve the small-business financing problem, because it does not represent equity funds (the funds are not left in the business permanently). Since amortization of the loan on a systematic basis is required, the small firm has the money only for a limited period and must have substantial cash throw-off ability in order to handle the term loan. The term loan does, however, extend the period over which the small business firm can grow by plowing back earnings.

---

[2] This statement must be qualified somewhat. In a period of extremely tight money such as 1966, insurance company policy loans (loans secured by the cash surrender value of policies) rise dramatically. The interest rate on policy loans is fixed, hence it does not rise with interest rates in general. This fixed rate is set high enough so that not too much policy loan borrowing occurs during "normal" times. However, policy loans become relatively attractive as the general level of interest rates rises, and in periods of extremely tight-money policy loans can constitute a serious cash drain for insurance companies.

CONDITIONAL SALES CONTRACTS

Conditional sales contracts are used to finance a substantial portion of the new equipment purchased by American business firms. Under the sales contract, the buyer agrees to buy a particular piece of equipment and to pay for it in installments over a one-to-five-year period. Until payment is completed, the seller of the equipment continues to hold title to the equipment. This fact gives rise to the name *conditional* sales contract—the sale is conditional upon satisfactory completion of the payments. While the contract is being paid off, the purchaser has possession of the equipment and uses it in his business. Also, it is typical for the firm that sold the equipment, a manufacturer or dealer, to sell the entire conditional sales contract to a finance company. What we have, in effect, is a long-term accounts receivable financing arrangement.

Procedure

Assume that a dentist needs a high-speed drill and that he has 30 percent of the purchase price. He makes the arrangements for the purchase from the manufacturer, and he agrees to finance the remaining 70 percent of the purchase price through a finance company or a bank. The dentist signs a conditional sales contract, which schedules payments based on the income he expects to earn. The payments are established exactly like those examined under the term-loan arrangement.

The conditional sales contract may be signed with the manufacturer, who sells it to a finance company or a bank. The financing institution usually requires a recourse agreement from the manufacturer for several reasons. The vendor (manufacturer) wants his money when the equipment leaves his factory. If the equipment is returned or repossessed, however, the manufacturer is in a better position than the financing institution to recondition and sell it. A financing institution cannot be expected to recondition a wide variety of specialized equipment. However, in a conditional sales contract it is usual to require that the financing institution repossess and return the equipment to the manufacturer within 60 days after the first default.

Products, Terms, and Appraisal

Products. Many kinds of equipment purchases are financed under conditional sales contracts. In descending order of frequency they are factory equipment, hotel and restaurant fixtures, equipment for beauty and barber shops, equipment for buses and trailers, medical equipment, diners and dining equipment, and bowling alley equipment. Studies of the credit positions of firms using installment equipment financing reveal that a high proportion of them are small firms with low credit ratings.

Terms. The terms of installment equipment financing are influenced mainly by the length of life of the equipment purchased. The down payment runs around one third of the equipment purchase price, and the maturity generally runs from two to three years. The cost of equipment financing is relatively high—usually 6 percent discounted on the face amount of the contract, an effective rate of interest of 14 or 15 percent. On heavy machinery purchased by prime credit risks the effective rate may run as low as 8 or 9 percent.

Appraisal. The main advantage of conditional sales financing is that it increases the ability of small firms to purchase equipment. Since the equipment generally produces income, the cash flow thus generated provides for repayment of the loan. In this sense the loan is self-liquidating. While the interest costs are high in an absolute sense, they may be low when related to the profitability of the equipment thereby acquired. The major limitation of conditional sales contract equipment financing is that it is by necessity limited to only the fixed asset portion of the assets of the firm.

LEASE FINANCING

Firms are generally interested in *using* buildings and equipment, not in owning them per se. One way of obtaining the use of facilities and equipment is to buy them, but an alternative is to lease rather than own. Prior to the 1950s, leasing was generally associated with real estate—land and buildings—but today it is possible to lease virtually any kind of fixed asset.

Leasing takes several different forms, the most important of which are sale and leaseback, service leases, and straight financial leases. These three major types of leasing are described below.

Sale and Leaseback

Under a sale and leaseback arrangement, a firm owning land, buildings, or equipment sells the property to a financial institution and simultaneously executes an agreement to lease the property back for a specified period under specific terms. If real estate—land or buildings—is involved, the financial institution is generally a life insurance company; if the property consists of equipment and machinery, the *lessor* could be an insurance company, a commercial bank, or a specialized leasing company.

Note that the seller, or lessee, immediately obtains the purchase price put up by the buyer, or lessor. At the same time, the seller-lessee retains the use of the property. This parallel is carried over to the lease payment schedule. Under a mortgage loan arrangement, the financial institution would receive a series of equal payments just sufficient to amortize the loan and provide the lender with a specified rate of return on his investment. The nature of the calculations was described above under the term loan arrangement. Under a sale and leaseback arrangement, the lease payments are set up in exactly the same manner—the payments are sufficient to return the full purchase price to the financial institution, in addition to providing it with a stated return on its investment.

Service Leases

Service, or operating, leases include both financing and maintenance services. International Business Machines Corporation is one of the pioneers of the service lease contract, and computers, together with automobiles and trucks, are the primary types of equipment involved in service leases.

Another important characteristic of the service lease is the fact that it is frequently not fully amortizing. In other words, the payments required under the lease contract are *not* sufficient to recover the full cost of the equipment. Obviously, however, the lease contract is written for considerably less than the expected life of the leased equipment, and the lessor expects to recover his cost in subsequent renewal payments.

A final feature of the service lease is the fact that such leases frequently contain a cancellation clause giving the lessee the right to cancel the lease and return the equipment before the expiration of the basic lease agreement. This is an important consideration for the lessee, for it means that he can return the equipment if technological developments render it obsolete.

Financial Leases

A strict financial lease is one that does *not* provide for maintenance services and that is *not* cancelable. The lessor is generally an insurance company if real estate is involved, and a commercial bank or specialized leasing company if the leased property is equipment. The typical arrangement involves the following steps:

1. The firm that will use the equipment selects the specific items it wants and negotiates the price and delivery terms with the manufacturer or the distributor.
2. Next, the user firm arranges with a bank or a leasing company to buy the equipment from the manufacturer or the distributor, and the user firm simultaneously executes an agreement to lease the equipment from the financial institution. The terms call for full amortization of the

financial institution's cost, plus a return of from 6 to 10 percent a year on the unamortized balance. The lessee is generally given an option to renew the lease at a reduced rental on expiration of the basic lease, but he does not have the right to cancel the basic lease without completely paying off the financial institution.

These leases are almost exactly the same as sale and leaseback arrangements, the only difference being that the leased equipment is new and the lessor buys it from a manufacturer or a distributor rather than from the user-lessee. A sale and leaseback may, then, be thought of as a special type of financial lease.

Internal Revenue Service Requirements for a Lease

The full amount of the annual lease payments are deductible for income tax purposes *provided the Internal Revenue Service agrees that a particular contract is a genuine lease and not simply an installment loan called a lease.* This makes it important that a lease contract be written in a form acceptable to the Internal Revenue Service. The following are the major requirements of bona fide lease transactions from the standpoint of the IRS:

1. The term must be less than 30 years, otherwise the lease is regarded as a form of sale.
2. The rent must represent a reasonable return to the lessor, "reasonable" being in the range of 6 to 10 percent on the investment.
3. The renewal option must be bona fide, and this requirement can best be met by giving the lessee the first option to meet an equal bona fide outside offer.
4. There shall be no repurchase option, or, if there is, the lessee should merely be given parity with an equal outside offer.

Cost Comparison

For an understanding of the possible advantages and disadvantages of lease financing, the cost of leasing must be compared with the cost of owning the equipment. In the typical case a firm that contemplates the acquisition of new equipment must also think about how to finance the equipment. When financing is necessary, the three major alternatives are (1) a term loan secured by a chattel mortgage on the equipment, (2) a conditional sales contract, and (3) a lease arrangement. To judge the cost of leasing, we must make a comparison of leasing versus the two borrow-to-purchase alternatives.

This comparison is best carried out in the manner presented in Table 13-2. Here it is assumed that the firm is acquiring a piece of equipment costing $1,000 and that it has the choice of borrowing the $1,000 at 5 percent, to be repaid in ten annual installments of $130 each, or of leasing the

Table 13–2 COMPARISON OF COST OF LEASING VERSUS BUYING

(1)	(2)	(3)	(4)	(5)	(6)	(7)	(8)	(9)	(10)	(11)	(12)	(13)
		Computing Net Cost of Owning										
		Applicable to Loan										
			Amortization									
Year	Total Payment	Interest	Payment	Remaining Balance	Depreciation	(3)+(6) Tax Deductible Expense	½(7) Tax Saving	(2)−(8) Net Cost of Owning	Lease Cost after Tax	(10)−(9) Advantage to Owning	5% Present Value Factor	(11)×(12) Present Value of Advantage to Owning
1	$130	$50	$80	$920	$100	$150	$75	$55	$65	10	0.952	9.52
2	130	46	84	836	100	146	73	57	65	8	0.907	7.26
3	130	42	88	748	100	142	71	59	65	6	0.864	5.18
4	130	38	92	656	100	138	69	61	65	4	0.823	3.29
5	130	34	96	560	100	134	67	63	65	2	0.784	1.57
6	130	28	102	458	100	128	64	66	65	(1)	0.746	(.75)
7	130	23	107	351	100	123	62	68	65	(3)	0.711	(2.13)
8	130	18	112	239	100	118	59	71	65	(6)	0.677	(4.06)
9	130	13	117	122	100	113	56	74	65	(9)	0.645	(5.80)
10	130	8	122	—	100	108	54	76	65	(11)	0.614	(6.75)
Totals	$1300	$300	$1,000	—	$1,000	$1300	$650	$650	$650			7.33

Assumptions:

1) The firm can borrow $1,000 at 5% to be repaid in ten equal annual installments. The annual payments are computed as:
   a) Interest factor for 10 years, 5% annuity = 7.722
   b) Required annual payment = $1,000 ÷ 7.722 = $130

2) The firm can arrange to finance its $1,000 equipment purchase under a 10-year lease plan calling for an annual rental of $130.

3) The equipment is worthless at the end of 10 years.

4) The firm uses straight line depreciation.

Note: If the equipment was expected to have a salvage value at the end of 10 years, this amount would constitute a *negative* payment (a receipt) and would reduce the net cost of owning. The salvage value would be deducted from the "net cost of owning" figure in column (9) for the tenth year.

machine for $130 a year. (Under the lease arrangement the firm is paying a 5 percent implicit interest rate; this is the rate the lessor is earning.)

Columns (2) through (5) show the payment schedule for the loan—note that this section is identical with the schedule shown in Table 13-1 for a term loan and that it would apply equally well to a 10-year conditional sales contract payment schedule. Column (6) gives the annual depreciation charges, assuming the firm owns the equipment and depreciates it on a straight line basis. Column (7) gives the total tax deductible expense, interest plus depreciation charges. These tax deductions reduce the tax bill by one half the amount of the deductions, assuming a 50 percent tax rate; this gives rise to the tax savings recorded in column (8). Now the total cash outlay associated with the borrow–purchase arrangement is the annual loan payment recorded in column (2); this is the gross cash outflow. Deducting the tax savings shown in column (8) from the payments in column (2) gives the net cash cost of owning recorded in column (9).

Assuming that the leasing company—which might well be the same bank that is willing to make the term loan—is willing to accept a 5 percent return on its investment, the annual lease payments must be $130, the same as those under the loan arrangement. This entire payment is deductible for income tax purposes, so the after-tax cost of the lease is $65 a year for 10 years. This figure is shown in column (10).

Column (9) shows the firm's net cash outlay each year if it elects to borrow the money and purchase the machine, while column (10) shows the net cash outflow if it elects the lease alternative. Subtracting column (9) from column (10) gives the cash flow advantage—plus or minus—to owning versus leasing. This figure is recorded in Column (11), which shows that owning involves smaller annual cash outlays in each of the first five years but that leasing requires smaller cash flows during the last five years.

We can no more add dollars payable in one year to those payable in another than we can add apples to oranges. We must, therefore, put the annual cash flow differentials between leasing and borrowing on a common basis; this requires converting them to present values. Column (12) gives the interest factors for 5 percent, the firm's cost of debt.[3] These interest factors, when multiplied by the cash flow differentials shown in Column

---

[3] As a technical point, we should state that the discount factor that should be applied is *not* the weighted cost of capital. Rather, it is the cost of debt. The logic behind this statement is explained in the excellent article "The Refunding Decision," by Oswald D. Bowlin in the March 1966 issue of *The Journal of Finance*. In brief, Bowlin points out that in comparing two financial alternatives there is essentially no risk to the firm in obtaining the savings attributable to one alternative over the other. This being the case, a discount rate that reflects the low risk is preferable to one that reflects the firm's average risk. For this reason, we have chosen to use the debt rate rather than the weighted cost of capital.

(11), give the present value of the differentials; these figures are given in Column (13).

When Column (13) is summed, we have the net present value of the advantage to owning. This figure can be either plus or minus. A positive result, as in the example, indicates that it is cheaper for the firm to borrow and purchase than it is to lease. A negative result would suggest that leasing has the advantage over buying.

What would happen to the relative cost of leasing versus owning if the example was modified to allow for accelerated depreciation? Accelerated depreciation would produce a higher tax shield, hence lower taxes, in the early years. This would reduce the net cost of owning (column 9) in the early years and raise it later on. Since the lease cost after tax (column 10) is unaffected, the result would be to increase the advantage to owning (column 11) in the early years and lower it in the later years. When the analysis is carried through to the Present Value column, the final result of accelerated depreciation would be to make owning relatively more attractive than it already is.

Raising the cost of capital factor (column 12) would have the same effect as switching to accelerated depreciation. The advantage of leasing comes in the later years, which are the ones that would be penalized most heavily by a higher cost of capital factor. The net result would be to increase the advantage of owning.

However, a table similar to Table 13-2, constructed from the lessor's point of view, would show that leases provide higher returns than loans, other things the same, because under a lease the lessor can take advantage of the accelerated depreciation. In such a situation the lessor is permitted some profit flexibility in setting lease terms, and competition among leasing companies could reduce the costs of leasing.

Table 13–3 VARIATIONS IN ASSUMED CONDITIONS AND THEIR IMPLICATIONS FOR COSTS OF OWNING VERSUS LEASING

Assumed Conditions	Consequences
Use of accelerated depreciation	Costs of owning lower
Implicit interest rates higher in leasing	Costs of leasing higher
Large residual values	Costs of owning lower
Rapid obsolescence	Costs of leasing lower

It may be useful to summarize some of the variations and their implications for the evaluation of owning versus leasing; this is done in Table 13-3. The material in the table summarizes frequently encountered arguments about advantages and disadvantages of leasing. Each assumed condition is subject to substantial qualification or error. Each will be considered in turn.

Use of accelerated depreciation. It is often argued that because of the ability to use accelerated depreciation methods, owning must be less expensive than leasing. Such an argument does not take into account the competitive aspects of the money and capital markets. Competition will force tax advantages, such as accelerated depreciation, to be shared between lessor and lessee. This relates to the point made just above. The payments pattern under leasing can be quite flexible. Thus, any opportunities available to equipment owners will have to be reflected in the competitive system of rates charged by leasing companies.

Implicit interest rates higher in leasing. The statement is frequently made that leasing always involves higher interest rates. This argument is of doubtful validity. First, when the nature of the lessee as a credit risk is considered, there may be no difference. Second, it is difficult to separate the money costs of leasing from the other services that may be embodied in a leasing contract. If, because of its specialist operations, the leasing company can perform the nonfinancial services, such as maintenance of the equipment, at lower cost than the lessee or some other institution could perform them, the effective cost of leasing may be lower than for funds obtained from borrowing or other sources. The efficiencies of performing specialized services may thus enable the leasing company to operate by charging a lower total cost than the lessor would have to pay for the package of money plus services on any other basis.

Large residual values. One important point that must be mentioned in connection with leasing is that the lessor owns the property at the expiration of the lease. The value of the property at the end of the lease is called the *residual value*. Superficially, it would appear that where residual values are large, owning will be less expensive than leasing. However, even this obvious advantage of owning is subject to substantial qualification. On leased equipment, the obsolescence factor is likely to be so large that it is doubtful whether residual values will be of a great order of magnitude. If residual values appear favorable, competition between leasing companies and other financial sources, and competition among leasing companies themselves, will force leasing rates down to the point where the potentials of residual values are fully recognized in the leasing contract rates. Thus, the existence of residual values on equipment is not likely to result in materially lower costs of owning. On the other hand, in connection with decisions whether to lease or to own land, the obsolescence factor is not involved except to the extent of deterioration in areas with changing population or use patterns. In a period of optimistic expectations about land values, there may be a tendency to overestimate rates of increase in land values. As a consequence, the current purchase of land may involve a price so high that the probable rate of return on owned land may be relatively small. Under this condition, leasing may well represent a more economical way of obtaining the use of land than owning. Conversely, if the probable increase in land values is not fully reflected in current prices, it will be advantageous to own the land.

Thus it is difficult to generalize whether current residual values or increases in the value of the land are likely to make the present cost of leasing higher or lower than the cost of owning. Generalization is impossible—the results depend on whether the individual firm has opportunities to take advantage of overoptimistic or overpessimistic evaluations of future value changes by the market as a whole.

Rapid obsolescence. Another fallacy is that leasing costs will be lower because of the rapid obsolescence of some kinds of equipment. If the obsolescence rate on equipment is high, leasing costs must reflect such a rate. Thus, in general terms, it might be argued that neither residual values nor obsolescence rates can basically affect·the cost of owning versus leasing.

In connection with leasing, however, it is possible that certain types of leasing companies may be better equipped to handle the obsolescence problem. For example, the Clark Equipment Company is a manufacturer, reconditioner, and specialist in materials handling equipment and has its own sales organization and system of distributors. This may enable Clark to write favorable leases for equipment. If the equipment becomes obsolete to one user, it may still be satisfactory for other users with different materials handling requirements, and Clark is ably situated to locate these other users.

Similarly, Management Assistance, Inc., provides an integrated operation in connection with the leasing of data processing equipment; it reconditions and maintains the equipment, in addition to providing a lease finance service. Data processing equipment that is obsolete for one firm may represent the most efficient (least cost) method of performing accounting functions in another firm. The active organization of Management Assistance, Inc., can thus shift the equipment to the user to whom it represents the most efficient method of performing the tasks required.

These illustrations indicate how the leasing company, by combining lending with other specialized services, may reduce the social costs of obsolescence and increase effective residual values. By such operations the total cost of obtaining the use of such equipment is reduced. Possibly other institutions that do not combine financing and other specialist functions, such as manufacture, reconditioning, servicing, and sales, may, in conjunction with financing institutions, perform the over-all functions as efficiently and at as low cost as do integrated leasing companies. However, this is a factual matter depending upon the relative efficiency of the competing firms in different lines of business and different kinds of equipment. To determine which combination of methods results in the lower costs, an analysis along the lines of the pattern outlined in Table 13-2 is required. Aside from the strictly quantitative considerations that would be reflected in such a table, it is useful to consider some of the possible qualitative advantages of leasing.

Possible Advantages of Leasing

Tax Deductions. One factor that shows up clearly in the cost calculation is tax deduction differentials between leasing and buying. If the lease is written for a relatively short period, it will have very large, *deductible* payments in the early years and smaller renewal payments in later years. In a sense, this amounts to a very rapid write-off, which is advantageous. However, the Internal Revenue Service rightly disallows as deductions lease payments under leases (1) that call for a rapid amortization of the lessor's costs and (2) that have a relatively low renewal or purchase option.

Investment Tax Credit. The investment tax credit is computed as a percentage of the initial cost of long-term assets, but is limited by the firm's computed taxes. For example, if the tax credit is 7 percent of new investment and if new investment is $10 million, the tax credit is $700,000. But if operating income is so low that taxes are running only $100,000 annually, the tax credit cannot be fully utilized.

Many companies are finding that their rapid rate of asset expansion, their low profits, or a combination of the two makes it impossible to use the entire amount of their tax credit. In these instances it may be possible to lease from a large bank or other supplier of lease funds, letting the lessor take the tax credit as purchaser of the asset. The lessee obtains a low implicit interest rate on the lease in return for giving up the investment tax credit. United Airlines undertook such an arrangement in 1964 when it leased some $25 million worth of jet engines from a group of six major banks. If this advantage is present and is of sufficient importance, it will be brought out in the cost calculations.

Increased Credit Availability. Two possible situations may exist to give leasing an advantage to firms seeking the maximum degree of financial leverage. First, it is frequently stated that firms can obtain more money for longer terms under a lease arrangement than under a secured loan agreement for the purchase of a specific piece of equipment. Second, leasing may not have as much of an impact on future borrowing capacity as borrowing and buying of equipment. This point is illustrated by examining the balance sheets of two hypothetical firms, A and B, in Table 13–4.

Initially, the balance sheets of both firms are identical, and they both have debt ratios of 50 percent. Next, they each decide to acquire assets costing $100. Firm A borrows $100 to make the purchase, so an asset and a liability go on its balance sheet and its debt ratio is increased to 75 percent. Firm B leases the equipment. The lease may call for as high or even higher fixed charges than the loan, and the obligations assumed under the lease can be equally or more dangerous to other creditors, yet the fact that the debt ratio of firm B is lower may enable it to obtain additional credit from other lenders. The amount of the annual rentals is shown as a note to the financial statements, but all available evidence suggests that credit analysts give less weight to firm B's lease than to firm A's loan.

Table 13–4 BALANCE SHEET EFFECTS OF LEASING

Before Asset Increase,			After Asset Increase					
Firms A and B			Firm A			Firm B		
Total	Debt	50	Total	Debt	150	Total	Debt	50
assets	100	Equity	50	assets	200	Equity	50	assets	100	Equity	50
Totals	100		100	Totals	200		200	Totals	100		100

This illustration indicates quite clearly a weakness of the debt ratio— if two companies are being compared and if one leases a substantial amount of equipment, then the debt ratio as we calculate it does not accurately show their relative leverage positions. It is, therefore, necessary to examine such cash flow figures as the "times fixed charges covered" ratio when making a comparative analysis of two or more firms.[4]

SUMMARY

Intermediate-term financing is defined as debt originally scheduled for repayment in more than one year but less than 5 years. Anything shorter is a current liability, while obligations due in 5 or more years are thought of as long-term debt. The major forms of intermediate-term financing include (1) *term loans,* (2) *conditional sales contracts,* and (3) *lease financing.*

Term Loans

A term loan is a business credit with a maturity of more than one year but less than 15 years. There are exceptions to the rule, but ordinarily term loans are retired by systematic repayments (amortization payments) over the life of the

---

[4] To help alleviate this problem, the accounting profession has given serious thought to capitalizing leases and showing them as both an asset and a liability on the balance sheet. The likelihood of this actually being done in the near future is remote, however. Cf. J. Myers, *Reporting of Leases in Financial Statements* (New York: American Institute of CPA's, 1961).

loan. Security, generally in the form of a chattel mortgage on equipment, is often employed, but the larger, stronger companies are able to borrow on an unsecured basis. Commercial banks and life insurance companies are the principal suppliers of term loan credit. Commercial banks typically make smaller, shorter term loans; life insurance companies make larger, longer term credit.

The interest cost of term loans, like rates on other credits, varies with the size of the loan and the strength of the borrower. For small loans to small companies, rates may go up as high as 10 percent; for large loans to large firms, the rate will be close to prime. Since term loans run for long periods, during which interest rates can change radically, many loans have variable interest rates, with the rate set at a certain level above the prime rate or above the Federal Reserve rediscount rate.

Another aspect of term loans is the series of *protective covenants* contained in most loan agreements. The lender's funds are tied up for a long period, and during this time the borrower's situation can change markedly. To protect himself, the lender will include in the loan agreement stipulations that the borrower will maintain his current ratio at a specified level, limit acquisitions of additional fixed assets, keep his debt ratio below a specified level, and so on. These provisions are necessary from the lender's point of view, but they necessarily restrict the borrower's actions.

Conditional Sales Contracts

Conditional sales contracts continue to be a major method by which firms obtain the use of equipment. Under the sales contract, the buyer agrees to buy a particular piece of equipment and to pay for it in installments over a one-to-five year period. Until payment is completed, the seller of the equipment continues to hold title to the equipment; thus the completion of the sale is *conditional* upon completion of the payments.

The cost of financing under sales contracts is relatively high—usually 6 percent discounted on the face amount of the contract, an effective rate of interest of 14 or 15 percent. On heavy machinery purchased by prime credit risks the rate may run as low as 8 to 9 percent.

Lease Financing

Leasing has long been used in connection with the acquisition of equipment by railroad companies. In recent years it has been extended to a wide variety of equipment. In the absence of major tax advantages, whether or not leasing is advantageous turns primarily on the firm's ability to acquire funds by other methods. Leasing has the advantage of a smaller down payment and increased opportunities for tax savings, and it probably increases the over-all availability of nonequity financing to the firm.

On the other hand, a leasing contract is very close to a straight-debt arrangement and uses some of the firm's debt-carrying ability. Also, the rental is a fixed obligation. Because of the importance of residual value, it will generally be advantageous to a firm to own its land and buildings. Because of the obsolescence factor, the residual value considerations may be less important in connection with the acquisition of equipment. Leasing of equipment may therefore continue to grow in importance.

QUESTIONS

13–1 "The type of equipment best suited for leasing has a long life in relation to the length of the lease; is a removable, standard product that could be used by many different firms; and is easily identifiable. In short, it is the kind of equipment that could be repossessed and sold readily. However, we would be quite happy to write a ten-year lease on paper towels for a firm such as General Motors." Discuss the statement.

13–2 On the basis of (a) the factors that make leasing a desirable means of financing and (b) your knowledge of the characteristics of different industries, name three industries that might be expected to use lease financing. Discuss.

13–3 Leasing is often called a hedge against obsolescence. Under what conditions is this actually true?

13–4 Is leasing in any sense a hedge against inflation for the lessee? for the lessor?

13–5 What qualities of railroad equipment certificates make them prime investment securities?

13–6 One of the alleged advantages of leasing is that it keeps liabilities off the balance sheet, thus making it possible for a firm to obtain more leverage than it otherwise could. This raises the question of whether or not both the lease obligation and the asset involved should be capitalized and shown on the balance sheet. Discuss the pros and cons of capitalizing leases and the related assets.

PROBLEMS

13–1 Suggest the form and source of financing for the following situations:

a) A manufacturer, after a long search for a particular type of equipment he needed, finally found it. The seller demanded cash in full or the deal was off, but the manufacturer had only enough cash for 20 percent of the total required.

b) A hardware dealer saw profits ahead if he could immediately stock up on certain items at favorable prices. He needed additional funds of $75,000 to take advantage of the opportunity.

c) An appliance dealer had recently moved to larger quarters. He needed $120,000 to finance additional inventory to handle increased business.

d) The growing business of a retail butcher on a busy thoroughfare warranted the cost of modernizing for customer convenience and more attractive display. The owner needed $3,000 to pay in full for items not eligible under FHA Title I financing.

e) An established partnership needed to purchase a heavy crane with special attachments which would increase earnings about $2,000 a month. The partnership was in the contracting business. It was able to make a one-third down payment, but did not have the balance of $60,000.

f) An automobile mechanic purchased a service station at a relatively low cost because of its previous poor earnings record. He had saved about $5,000, which he invested in the business and which mostly represented payment for equipment acquired. Increased volume necessitated employment of two men, and the owner required additional funds of $3,000 to carry inventory and meet payrolls.

g) A small manufacturer in the woodwork business with a record of stable earnings needed $500,000 to buy additional productive equipment to handle orders for houseware items that had become in short supply. The mortgage on his plant had been partially paid off.

13–2   The Johnson Department Store is considering a sale and leaseback of its major property, consisting of land and a building, because it is 35 days late on 80 percent of its accounts payable. The recent profit record and the balance sheet of Johnson are shown below. Profit before taxes in 1966 is $25,000; after taxes, $14,000.

JOHNSON DEPARTMENT STORE
BALANCE SHEET
December 31, 1966
(in thousands of dollars)

Cash		$ 200	Accounts payable	$1,000
Receivables		1,000	Bank loans, 6%	1,000
Inventories		1,300	Other current liabilities	500
Total current assets		2,500	Total current debt	2,500
Land	$800		Common stock	1,000
Building	500		Retained earnings	500
Fixtures and equipment	200			
Net fixed assets		1,500		
Total assets		$4,000	Total claims	$4,000

Annual depreciation charges are $40,000 a year on the building and $50,000 a year on the fixtures and equipment.

The land and building could be sold for a total of $2.3 million. The annual net rental will be $170,000.

a) How much capital gains tax will Johnson pay if the land and building are sold?

b) Compare the current ratio before and after the sale and leaseback if the net proceeds are used to "clean up" the bank loans and to reduce accounts payable and other current liabilities.

c) If the lease had been in effect during 1966, what would Johnson's profit for 1966 have been?

d) What are the basic financial problems facing Johnson? Will the sale and leaseback operation solve them?

13–3 The Altman Company is faced with the decision whether to purchase or to lease a new fork-lift truck. The truck can be leased on a 5-year contract for $1,000 a year, or it can be purchased for $4,000. The lease includes maintenance and service. The salvage value of the truck 5 years hence is $1,000. The company uses the sum-of-the-years'-digits method of depreciation. If the truck is owned, service and maintenance charges (a deductible cost) would be $250 a year. This cost should be added to the out-of-pocket expenses of owning (shown in the Total Payment column of your worksheet). The company has a 10 percent cost of capital.

Answer the questions shown below under each of the following alternative assumptions:

1) The firm borrows the $4,000 at an interest rate of 6 percent, and this same 6 percent is used as the discount factor in comparing the costs of leasing versus owning. (Assume the $4,000 loan is paid back in installments, not in a lump sum.) Taxes are 50 percent.

2) The firm borrows the $4,000 at an interest rate of 6 percent, which is used in computing the interest cost of owning, but the firm's 10 percent cost of capital is used in calculating the present values of the cash flows involved in leasing versus owning. Taxes are 50 percent.

a) Which method of acquiring the use of equipment should the company choose?

b) What factors could alter the results indicated by the quantitative analysis based on the above facts?

c) Discuss the use of 6 percent versus 10 percent as the discount factor.

Note:

Under the sum-of-years-digits' method of depreciation, one adds the years $1 + 2 + 3 + 4 + 5 = 15$ (in general, sum of $1 + \ldots + N$, where N = depreciable life of asset) to get a denominator. The numerator is N in the first year, $N - 1$ in the second, and so on. The fraction is multiplied by the cost of the asset minus the estimated salvage value to determine the depreciation for each year. In the present case, depreciation charges are calculated as follows:

Year	Fraction	(Cost-salvage)	Allowable Depreciation
1	5/15	$3,000	$1,000
2	4/15	3,000	800
3	3/15	3,000	600
4	2/15	3,000	400
5	1/15	3,000	200
			$3,000

PART VI

Long-Term Financing

Chapter 14

The Market for
Long-Term Securities

Short- and intermediate-term financial markets were discussed in Chapters 12 and 13. We now examine the markets in which long-term securities— stocks, bonds, warrants, and convertibles—are traded, and we consider efficient procedures for the financial manager to follow when raising funds by selling long-term securities. This background is necessary for an understanding of the characteristics and uses of the long-term financing instruments described in Chapters 15 through 20.

SECURITY MARKETS

There are two broad types of security markets—the *organized exchanges,* typified by the New York Stock Exchange, and the less formal *over-the-counter markets.*[1] Since the organized exchanges have actual physical market locations, hence are easier to describe and understand, we shall consider them first. With this background it will be easier to comprehend the nature of the over-the-counter market.

---

[1] There is also a "private" market in which the borrowing firm goes directly to the lending institutions; this is the market for *private placements* or *direct placements,* as it is frequently called. The primary instrument used in this market is the *term* loan, described in Chapter 13.

Organized Security Exchanges

The organized security exchanges are tangible, physical entities. Each of the larger ones occupies its own building, has specifically designated members, and has an elected governing body—its Board of Governors. Members are said to have seats on the exchange, although everybody stands up. These seats, which are bought and sold, represent the right to trade on the exchange. In 1967 seats on the New York Stock Exchange (NYSE) sold for about $250,000.

Most of the larger stock brokerage firms own seats on the exchanges and designate one of the officers of the firm as a member of the exchange. The designated officer occupies the seat. The exchanges are open daily, and the members meet in a large room equipped with telephones and telegraphs that enable each brokerage house member to communicate with the officers of his firm throughout the country.

Like other markets, a security exchange facilitates communication between buyers and sellers. For example, a Merrill Lynch, Pierce, Fenner, and Smith (the largest brokerage firm) office in Atlanta might receive an order from a customer to buy 100 shares of General Motors stock. Simultaneously, a brokerage house in Denver might receive an order from a customer to sell 100 shares of GM. Each broker would communicate by wire with his firm's representative on the NYSE. Other brokers throughout the country are also receiving customer orders to buy and sell GM, and they are also communicating with their own exchange members. The exchange members with *sell orders* offer the shares for sale, which are bid for by the members with *buy orders*. Thus, the exchanges operate as *auction markets.*[2]

Special procedures are available for handling large blocks of securities. For example, if a firm like General Motors, whose stock is already listed on the NYSE, plans to sell a new issue of stock, the exchange has facilities that make it easier for the market to absorb the new issue. Similarly, if a large mutual fund or pension fund wants to sell a large block of a listed stock, procedures are available that facilitate the sale without putting undue pressures on the stock price.

Two practices said to contribute to effectively functioning securities markets—*margin trading* and *short selling*—should be noted briefly.

Margin trading involves the buying of securities on credit. For example, when margin requirements are 70 percent, 100 shares of a stock selling for $100 a share can be bought by putting up in cash only $7,000, or 70 percent of the purchase price, and borrowing the remaining $3,000. The stock-

---

[2] This discussion is highly simplified. The exchanges have members known as "specialists," who facilitate the trading process by keeping an inventory of shares of the stocks in which they specialize. If a buy order comes in at a time when no sell order arrives, the specialist may sell off some of his inventory. Similarly, if a sell order comes in, the specialist will buy and add to his inventory.

broker lends the margin purchaser the funds, retaining custody of the stock as collateral. Margin requirements are determined by the Federal Reserve Board. When the Fed judges that stock market activity and prices are unduly stimulated by easy credit, it raises margin requirements and thus reduces the amount of credit available for the purchase of stocks. On the other hand, if the Fed desires to stimulate the market as a part of its overall monetary policy operations, it reduces margin requirements.

Short selling means selling a security that is not owned by the seller at the time of sale. Short selling is usually performed in anticipation of a decline in the market price. For example, a stock selling at $40 may be sold short. Suppose that in two months the market drops to $30. The short seller can buy at $30 and make delivery on stock which he sold at $40. The seller borrows the stock from his broker; often the broker has the stock because others of his customers either have purchased it on margin or have left the securities in the brokerage house's name—a so-called "street name." The advantage claimed for short selling is that it increases the number of participants operating in the market and thereby reduces fluctuations in stock prices. This is, however, a controversial subject.

Insofar as margin trading and short selling provide for a more continuous market, they encourage stock ownership and have two beneficial effects. (1) They broaden the ownership of securities by increasing the ability of people to buy securities. (2) They provide for a more active market; more active trading makes for narrower price fluctuations. However, when a strong speculative psychology grips the market, margin trading can be a fuel which feeds the speculative fervor. Short selling can also aggravate pessimism on the downside. However, there are restrictions on short selling which provide that a short sale may not be made at a price lower than on the last previously recorded sale. Current rules on short selling limit speculative and manipulative practices. Similarly, flexible margin requirements have had salutary effects on the use of credit in stock market transactions.

Benefits Provided by Security Exchanges

Organized security exchanges provide important benefits to businesses in at least four ways.

1. Security exchanges facilitate the investment process because they provide a marketplace in which to conduct transactions efficiently and relatively inexpensively. Investors are thus assured that they will have a place in which to sell their securities, if they decide to do so. The increased liquidity thus provided by the exchanges makes investors willing to accept a lower rate of return on securities than they would otherwise require. This means that exchanges lower the cost of capital to businesses.

2. By providing a market, exchanges create an institution in which continuous transactions test the values of securities. The purchases and

sales of securities record judgments on the values and prospects of companies and their securities. Companies whose prospects are judged favorable by the investment community will have higher values, facilitating new financing and growth.

3. Security prices are relatively more stable because of the operation of the security exchanges. Organized markets provide liquidity and continuous markets which make for more frequent, but smaller, price changes. In the absence of organized markets, price changes would be less frequent but more violent.

4. The securities markets aid in the digestion of new securities issues and facilitate their successful flotation.

OVER-THE-COUNTER SECURITY MARKETS

In contrast to the formal security exchanges, the over-the-counter market is a nebulous, intangible organization. Perhaps an explanation of the name "over the counter" will help clarify exactly what this market is. The exchanges operate as auction markets—buy and sell orders come in more or less simultaneously, and the exchanges are used to match these orders. But if a stock is traded less frequently, perhaps because it is the stock of a new or a small firm, few buy and sell orders come in and matching them within a reasonable length of time would be difficult. To avoid this problem, brokerage firms maintain an inventory of the stocks. They buy when individual investors wish to sell, and sell when investors want to buy. At one time the inventory of securities was kept in a safe and, when being bought and sold, the stocks were literally passed "over the counter."

Today, over-the-counter markets are defined as all facilities that provide for security transactions not conducted on the organized exchanges. These facilities consist primarily of the thousands of brokers who hold inventories of individual securities.

The majority of stocks in terms of the number of issues are traded over the counter. However, the stocks of larger companies are listed on the exchanges, and it is estimated that two thirds of the dollar volume of stock trading takes place on the exchanges. The situation is reversed in the bond market. Although the bonds of a number of the larger companies are listed on the NYSE bond list, in excess of 95 percent of bond transactions take place in the over-the-counter market. The reason for this is that bonds typically are traded among the large financial institutions—for example, life insurance companies, pension funds—and these institutions deal in very large blocks of securities. It is relatively easy for the over-the-counter bond dealers to arrange the transfer of large blocks of bonds among the relatively few holders of the bonds. It would be impossible to conduct similar operations in the stock market among the literally millions of large and small stockholders.

DECISION TO LIST STOCK

The exchanges require firms to meet certain requirements before their stock can be listed. These requirements relate to size of the company, number of years in business, earnings record, number of shares outstanding and their market value, and the like. In general, requirements become higher as we move from the regional exchanges toward the NYSE.

The firm itself makes the decision to seek to list or not list its securities on an exchange. Typically, the stocks of new and small companies are traded over the counter—there is simply not enough activity to justify the use of an auction market for such stocks. As the company grows, establishes an earnings record, expands the number of shares outstanding, and increases the list of stockholders, it may decide to apply for listing on one of the regional exchanges. For example, a Chicago company might list on the Midwest Stock Exchange, or a West Coast company might list its stock on the Pacific Coast Exchange. As the company grows still more, and as its stock becomes distributed throughout the country, it may seek a listing on the American Stock Exchange, the smaller of the two national exchanges. Finally, if it reaches a position as one of the nation's leading firms, it could switch to the Big Board, the New York Stock Exchange.

Assuming a company qualifies, it is generally felt that listing is beneficial both to it and to its stockholders. Listed companies receive a certain amount of free advertising and publicity, and their status as a listed company enhances their prestige and reputation. This probably has a beneficial effect on the sales of the products of the firm, and it certainly is beneficial in terms of lowering the required rate of return on the common stock. Investors respond favorably to increased information, increased liquidity, and increased prestige; by providing investors with these services in the form of listing their companies' stocks, financial managers lower their firms' cost of capital.[3]

---

[3] Two industries, banking and insurance, have a tradition against listing their stocks. The historic reason given by banks was that they were afraid that a falling market price of their stocks would lead depositors to think the bank itself was in danger and, thus, cause a run on the bank. Some basis for such fears may have existed before the creation of the Federal Deposit Insurance Corporation in 1935, but the fear is no longer justified. The other reason for banks not listing has to do with reporting financial information. The exchanges require that quarterly financial statements be sent to all stockholders; banks have been reluctant to provide financial information. Increasingly, bank regulatory agencies are requiring public disclosure of additional financial information. As this trend continues, it is expected that banks will increasingly seek listing on exchanges. A notable first is the Chase Manhattan Bank, which was listed on the New York Stock Exchange in 1965.

NATURE OF INVESTMENT BANKING

In the American economy, saving is performed by one group of persons while investing is performed by another. ("Investing" is used here in the sense of actually putting money into plant, equipment, and inventory, not "investing" in the sense of buying securities.) Thus, savings are placed with financial intermediaries who, in turn, make the funds available to firms wishing to acquire plant and equipment and to hold inventories.

One of the major institutions which perform this channeling role is known as *investment banking*. The term "investment banker" is somewhat misleading in that investment bankers are neither investors nor bankers. That is, they do not invest their own funds permanently, nor are they repositories for individuals' funds, as are commercial banks or savings banks. What, then, *is* the nature of investment banking? In defining any set of institutions a functional rather than a descriptive definition is required; for example, an elephant is best defined in terms of appearance, but a shovel is best defined in terms of what it does. Investment banking is best defined in terms of what investment bankers do.

The many activities of investment bankers may be described first in general terms and then with respect to specific functions. The historical and traditional function of the investment banker has been to act as the middleman in channeling driblets of savings and funds of individuals into the purchase of business securities, primarily bonds. The investment banker does this by purchasing and distributing the new securities of individual companies. Specifically, the investment banker has the following functions.

Underwriting

Underwriting is the insurance function of bearing the risks of adverse price fluctuations during the period in which a new issue of securities is being distributed. The nature of the underwriting function of the investment banker can best be conveyed through an example. A business firm needs $10 million. It selects an investment banker, conferences are held, and the decision is made to issue $10 million of bonds. An underwriting agreement is drawn up, and on a specific day the investment banker presents the company with a check for $10 million (less commission). In return, the investment banker receives bonds in denomination of $1,000 each, which he sells to the public.

The company receives the $10 million before the investment banker has sold the bonds. Between the time the investment banker pays the firm the $10 million and the time he has sold the bonds, the investment banker bears all the risk of market price fluctuations in the bonds. Conceivably, it can take the investment banker 10, 20, 30 days, 6 months, or longer to sell bonds. If in the interim the bond market collapses, the investment banker will be carrying the risk of loss in the sale of the bonds. There have been dramatic instances of bond market collapse within one week after an investment banker has bought $50 million or $100 million of bonds.

But the individual firm does not need to be concerned about the risk of market price fluctuations while the investment banker is selling the bonds. The firm has received its $10 million. *One fundamental economic function of the investment banker, then, is to underwrite the risk of a decline in the market price between the time the investment banker transmits the money to the firm and the time the bonds are placed in the hands of their ultimate buyers.* For this reason, the investment banker is often called an underwriter: he is an underwriter of risk during the distribution period.

Distribution

The second function of the investment banker is securities marketing. The investment banker is a specialist who has a staff and dealer organization to distribute securities. The investment banker can, therefore, perform the physical distribution function more efficiently and more economically than could an individual corporation. Sporadically, whenever it wished to sell an issue of securities, each corporation would find it necessary to establish a marketing or selling organization. This would be a very expensive and ineffective method of selling securities. The investment banker has a permanent, trained staff and dealer organization continuously available to distribute the securities. In addition, the investment banker's reputation for selecting good companies and pricing securities fairly builds up a broad clientele over a period, further increasing the ease with which he can sell securities.

Advice and Counsel

Since the investment banker is engaged in the origination and sale of securities, through experience he becomes an expert in advising about terms and characteristics of securities that will appeal to investors. The advice and guidance of the investment banker in determining the characteristics and provisions of securities so that they will be successfully marketed is valuable. Furthermore, the reputation of the investment banker, as a seller of the securities, depends upon the subsequent performance of the securities. Therefore, he will often sit on the boards of directors of firms whose securities he has sold. In this way he is able to provide continuing financial counsel and to increase the firm's probability of success.

Such, then, are the main economic functions provided by investment bankers. The investment houses engage in a wide variety of activities to provide many other services to business firms, but the other activities will best be understood after a more complete description of the investment banking operation.

INVESTMENT BANKING OPERATION

To understand clearly the investment banking function it is useful to trace the history of a new issue of securities.[4]

Pre-underwriting Conferences

First, the members of the issuing firm and the investment banker hold pre-underwriting conferences. At these conferences they discuss the amount of capital to be raised, the type of security to be issued, and the terms of the agreement.

Memorandums will be written by the treasurer of the issuing company, describing alternative proposals suggested at the conferences. Meetings of the board of directors of the issuing company will be held to discuss the alternatives and to attempt to reach a decision.

At some point the issuer enters an agreement with the investment banker that a flotation will take place. The investment banker will then begin to conduct what is called an underwriting investigation. If the company is proposing to purchase additional assets, the underwriter's engineering staff will make an engineering analysis of the proposed asset acquisition. A public accounting firm will be called upon to make an audit of the issuing firm's financial situation. In addition, the public accounting firm will aid in the preparation of the registration statements for the Securities and Exchange Commission (SEC) in connection with these issues.

A firm of lawyers will be called in to give interpretations and judgments about legal aspects of the flotation. In addition, the originating underwriter, who will be the manager of the subsequent underwriting syndicate, will make an exhaustive investigation of the prospects of the company.

---

[4] The process described here relates primarily to situations where the firm doing the financing picks an investment banker, then negotiates with him over the terms of the issue. An alternative procedure, used extensively only in the public utility industry, is for the selling firm to specify the terms of the new issue, then to have investment bankers bid for the entire new issue by use of *sealed bids*. The very high fixed costs that an investment banker must incur to thoroughly investigate the company and its new issue rule out sealed bids except for the very largest issues. The type of operation described in this section is called *negotiated underwriting;* competition is keen among underwriters, of course, to develop and maintain working relations with business firms.

When the investigations are completed, but before registration with the SEC, an underwriting agreement will be drawn up by the investment banker. Terms of the tentative underwriting agreement may be modified through discussions between the underwriter and the issuing company. Finally, agreement will be reached on all underwriting terms except the actual price of the securities.

Registration Statement

A registration statement will then be filed with the SEC. The commission requires a 20-day waiting period, during which time its staff analyzes the registration statement to determine whether there are any omissions or misrepresentations of fact. The SEC may file exceptions to the registration statement or may ask for additional information from the issuing company or the underwriters during the 20-day waiting period. During this period the investment bankers are not permitted to offer the securities for sale, although they may print preliminary prospectuses with all the information customarily contained in a prospectus except the offering price.

Setting the Price of the Securities

The actual price the underwriter pays the issuer is not generally determined until the close of the registration period. There is no universally followed practice, but one common arrangement for a new issue of stock calls for the investment banker to buy the securities at a prescribed number of points below the closing price on the last day of registration. For example, suppose the stock of XYZ Company has a current price of $38 and has sold in a range of $35 to $40 a share during the previous three months. The firm and the underwriter agree that the investment banker will buy 200,000 new shares at $2.50 below the closing price on the last day of registration. If the stock closes at $36 on the day the SEC releases the issue, then the firm will receive $33.50 a share. Typically, such agreements have an escape clause that provides for the contract to be voided if the price of the securities ends below some predetermined figure. In the illustrative case, this "upset" price might be set at $34 a share. Thus, if the closing price of the shares on the last day of registration is $33.50, the issuing firm will have an option of withdrawing from the agreement.

The Underwriting Syndicate

The investment banker with whom the issuing firm has conducted its discussions will not typically handle the purchase and distribution of the issue alone unless the issue is a very small one. If the sums of money involved are large and the risk of price fluctuation substantial, the investment banker forms a syndicate in an effort to minimize the amount of risk he carries. A syndicate is a temporary association for the purpose of carrying out a specific objective. The nature of the arrangements for a syndicate in the underwriting and sale of a security through an investment banker may best be understood with the aid of Figure 14-1.

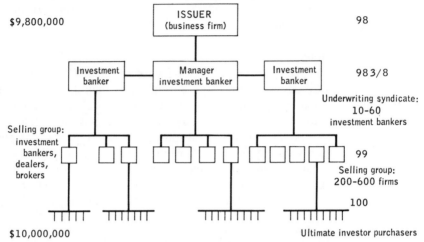

Figure 14-1   Diagram of Sales of $10 Million of Bonds through Investment Bankers

. The managing underwriter invites other investment bankers on the basis of their knowledge of the particular kind of offering to be made and on the basis of their strength and dealer contacts in selling securities of the type involved in the issue.

Each investment banker has business relations with other investment bankers and dealers; thus each investment banker has a selling group consisting of himself and other investment bankers and dealers. Some firms combine all these characteristics. For example, the firm of Merrill Lynch, Pierce, Fenner and Smith, Inc., underwrites some issues and manages the underwriting of others. On still other flotations it will be invited by the manager to join in the distribution of the issue. It also purchases securities as the dealer and carries an inventory of these securities. It publishes lists of securities it has for sale. In addition to being a dealer, Merrill Lynch, of course, carries on substantial activity as a broker. An individual investment firm may carry on all these functions, just as a department store sells many different types of merchandise.

But there are also firms with a narrower range of functions—specialty dealers, specialty brokers, and specialty investment counselors. Thus, in the financial field there is specialization of financial functions as well as department store types of operations. A *dealer* purchases securities outright, holds them in inventory as a grocery store would hold its inventory, and sells them at whatever price he can get. He may benefit from price appreciation or he may suffer a loss on declines, as any merchandiser does. A *broker,* on the other hand, takes orders for purchases and transmits them to the proper exchange; his gain is the commission he charges for the service.

Syndicates are used in the distribution of securities for three reasons. (1) A single investment banker may be financially unable to handle a large issue alone. (2) The originating house may desire to spread the risk even if it is financially able to handle the issue alone. (3) The utilization of several selling organizations, as well as other underwriters, permits an economy of selling effort and expense and encourages broader, nationwide distribution.

The participating underwriters and dealers are provided with full information on all phases of these financing transactions. They share in the underwriting commission. To show how the underwriting commission is shared, let us illustrate how a two-point spread would be divided. An investment banker buys $10 million worth of bonds to be sold at par, or $1,000 each. If the investment banker receives a two-point spread, he will buy the bonds from the issuer at 98; thus, he must pay the issuer $9.8 million for the issue of $10 million. Typically, on a two-point spread, the manager-underwriter will receive the first ¼ of 1 percent for originating and managing the syndicate. Next, the entire underwriting group will receive about ¾ of 1 percent. Members of the selling group receive about 1 percent as a sales commission.

If the manager of the underwriting group makes a sale to an ultimate purchaser of the securities, he will receive the ¼ percent as manager, ¾ percent as underwriter, and 1 percent as the seller—the full 2 percent. If he wholesales some of the securities to members of the selling group who make the ultimate sale, the latter will receive the 1 percent selling commission, and the manager will receive the other 1 percent for managing and underwriting the issue. If the issue is managed by one firm, underwritten by a second, and sold by a third, the 2 percent commission is divided, with 1 percent going to the selling firm, ¾ percent to the underwriter, and ¼ percent to the manager of the underwriting group.

Ordinarily, each underwriter's liability is limited to his agreed-upon commitment. For example, if an investment banker participates in a $20 million offering and agrees to see to it that $5 million of the securities are sold, his responsibility ends when he sells his $5 million.

The Selling Group

The selling group is formed primarily for the purpose of distributing securities; it consists of dealers, who take relatively small participations from the members of the buying group. The underwriters act as wholesalers; members of the selling group act as retailers. The number of houses in a selling group depends partly upon the size of the issue. A selling group may have as many as 300 to 400 dealers; for example, the one for Communications Satellite Corporation consisted of 385 members.

The operation of the selling group is controlled by the *selling group agreement,* which usually covers the following major points.

Description of the issue. The description is set forth in a report on the issue, the *prospectus,* which fully describes the issue and the issuer.

Concession. Members of the selling group subscribe to the new issue at a public offering price less the concession given to them as a commission for their selling service. In the preceding example, this was 1 percent.

Handling repurchased securities. The selling group agreement provides that no member of the selling group be permitted to sell the securities below the public offering price. The syndicate manager invariably pegs the quotation in the market by placing continuous orders to buy at the public offering price. A careful record is kept of bond or stock certificate numbers so that repurchased bonds may be identified with the member of the selling group who sold them. General practice is to cancel the commission on such securities and add brokerage costs incurred in the repurchase. Repurchased securities are then placed with other dealers for sale.[5]

Duration of selling group. The most common provision in selling group agreements is that the group have an existence of 30 days, subject to earlier termination by the manager. The agreement may be extended, however, for an additional 80 days by members representing 75 percent of the selling group.

Offering and Sale

After the selling group has been formed, the actual offering proceeds. Publicity in advance of the offering date is developed. Advertising material for release as soon as permissible is prepared. The actual day of the offering is chosen with a view to avoiding temporary congestion in the security market and other unfavorable events or circumstances.

The formal public offering is called "opening the books," an archaic term which reflects ancient customs of the investment banking trade. When the books are opened, the manager accepts subscriptions to the issue from both selling group participants and outsiders who may wish to buy.

If the demand for the issue is great, the books may be closed imme-

---

[5] Without these repurchase arrangements, a member of the selling group could sell his share of the securities on the open market instead of to new purchasers. Since the pegging operation is going on, there would be a ready market for the securities; consequently, a penalty is necessary to avoid thwarting of the syndicate operation.

diately. An announcement is then made that the issue is oversubscribed. On the other hand, when the reception is not strong, the books may remain open for an extended period.

Market Stabilization

During the period of the offering and distribution of securities, the manager of the underwriting group typically stabilizes the price of the issue. The duration of the price-pegging operation is usually 30 days. The price is pegged by placing orders to buy at a specified price in the market. The pegging operation is designed to prevent a cumulative downward movement in the price if it should soften. A downward price shift would result in losses for all members of the underwriting group. As the manager of the underwriting group has the major responsibility, he assumes the task of pegging the price.

This discussion raises the question of pricing the new issue. If the issue is simply more shares of an already outstanding stock, then the price of the existing stock is the main determinant of the price of the new shares. If the issue is a new one, the main guides to pricing it are the prevailing prices of similar outstanding issues. During the underwriting conferences, comparisons are made with other companies who have recently issued similar securities, and the prices and yields of these securities are analyzed. The new issue is priced to yield about the same as competitive securities.

The investment banker will have an easier job if the issue is priced low and has a high yield. The issuer of the securities naturally wants as high a price and as low a yield as possible. Some conflict of interest on price therefore arises between the investment banker and the issuer. If the issuer is financially sophisticated and looks to comparisons with similar issues of securities, the investment banker is forced to price close to the market.

If the market deteriorates during the offering period, the investment banker carries a rather substantial risk. For this reason, the pegging operation may not be sufficient to protect the underwriters. In the Pure Oil Company issue of $44 million convertible preferred stocks of September 3, 1937, at 100, only $1 million of shares were sold by the underwriters. At the conclusion of the underwriting agreement, initial trading took place at 74, giving the investment bankers a loss of over $11 million ($43 million × 26%). Not until 1941 did the stock again sell as high as 90. In the Textron issue of June 1967, the offering was reduced from $100 million to $50 million because of market congestion, and yet 5 percent of the bonds were unsold after the initial offering. Other similar cases can be cited.

It has been charged that pegging the price during the offering period constitutes a monopolistic price-fixing arrangement. On the other hand, investment bankers reply that not to peg the price would increase the risk and therefore the underwriting cost to the issuer. On balance, it appears that the pegging operation is a socially useful function. The danger of monopolistic pricing is avoided, or at least mitigated substantially, by competitive factors. If an underwriter attempts to set a monopolistic price on a particular issue of securities, the investor can turn to thousands of other securities not involved in price-pegging operations. The degree of control over the market by the underwriter in a price-pegging operation seems to be negligible.

Costs of Flotation

The cost of selling new issues of securities can be put into perspective by Table 14-1. The table summarizes the data on cost of flotation in the last available report on the subject by the Securities and Exchange Commission. Although these data are rather old, the figures are still appropriate, and important generalizations can be drawn from them.

1. The cost of flotation for common stock is greater than for preferred stocks, and the costs of both are greater than the cost of flotation for bonds.
2. The costs of flotation as a percentage of the gross proceeds are greater for small issues than for large ones.

What are the reasons for these relationships? The explanations are found in the amount of risk involved and the job of physical distribution. Bonds are generally bought in large blocks by a relatively few institutional investors, whereas stocks are bought by millions of individuals. For this reason the distribution job is greater for common stock, and the expenses of marketing it are greater.

The explanation for the variation in cost with the size of issue is also easily found. In the first place, certain fixed expenses are associated with any distribution of securities. Four items of expense account for 85 percent of the cost of flotation. Many of these expenses are fixed—the underwriting investigation, the preparation of the registration statement, legal fees, and so forth. Since they are relatively large and fixed, their percentage of the total cost of flotation runs high on small issues.

Second, small issues are typically those of relatively less well-known firms. The underwriting expenses may be larger than usual, because the danger of omitting vital information is greater for a small firm. Furthermore, the selling job is greater. More salesmen must exert greater effort to sell the securities of a less well-known firm. For these reasons the underwriting commission, as a percentage of the gross proceeds, is relatively high for small issues.

Table 14-1   COSTS OF FLOTATION, 1951–1955
(costs expressed as percentage of gross proceeds)

Size of Issue (in millions of dollars)	Debt			Preferred Stock			Common Stock		
	Underwriting Commission	Other Expenses	Total Costs	Underwriting Commission	Other Expenses	Total Costs	Underwriting Commission	Other Expenses	Total Costs
Under 0.5	—	—	—	—	—	—	21.0	6.2	27.2
0.5– 0.9	7.5	4.0	11.5	8.7	4.0	12.7	17.1	4.6	21.7
1.0– 1.9	5.8	2.4	8.2	6.0	2.0	8.0	11.2	2.3	13.5
2.0– 4.9	2.4	1.4	3.8	3.8	1.0	4.8	8.5	1.5	10.0
5.0– 9.9	1.0	0.8	1.8	2.9	0.8	3.7	5.3	0.9	6.2
10.0–19.9	0.9	0.6	1.5	2.4	0.5	2.9	4.2	0.5	4.7
20.0–49.9	0.9	0.5	1.4	2.8	0.4	3.2	5.0	0.4	5.4
50.0 and over	0.9	0.3	1.2	2.1	0.4	2.5	—	—	—

SOURCE: Securities and Exchange Commission, *Cost of Flotation of Corporate Securities, 1951–1955* (Washington, D. C.: U. S. Government Printing Office, June 1957).

It has been charged that the expenses of flotation have become high since the SEC, created in 1934, began requiring that relatively elaborate registration statements be filed prior to selling securities. An analysis of the costs of flotation has been made, breaking them down into costs associated with registration and those not affected by it. Underwriting commissions account for about 65 percent of the total cost of flotation. Registration expenses account for about 30 percent, and expenses not affected by registration account for the remainder, or about 5 percent. Registration expenses as a percentage of the gross proceeds are relatively minor and do not vary greatly with the size of flotation. Costs partly affected by registration—printing, engraving, legal, accounting, and engineering costs—do increase somewhat in percentage as the size of flotation decreases. The other costs are relatively minor.

These data demonstrate convincingly that the high percentage costs of flotation on small issues are not caused by discrimination against small issues. The fixed expenses of flotation are large when expressed as a percentage of the proceeds on small issues.

In addition to the factors discussed above, flotation costs are also influenced by whether or not the issue is a rights offering, and if it is, by the extent of the underpricing.[6] If rights are used and if the underpricing is sub-

---

[6] "Rights offerings" involve the sale of stock to existing stockholders. This topic is discussed extensively in Chapter 19.

stantial, then the investment banker bears little risk of inability to sell the shares. Further, very little selling effort will be required in such a situation. These two factors combine to enable a company to float new securities to its own stockholders at a relatively low cost.

REGULATION OF SECURITY TRADING

The operations of investment bankers, the exchanges, and the over-the-counter markets described in the previous sections of this chapter are significantly influenced by a series of federal statutes enacted during and after 1933. The financial manager is affected by these laws for several reasons. (1) Corporate officers are subjected to additional liabilities. (2) The laws affect the ease and costs of financing. (3) They also affect the behavior of the money and capital markets in which the corporations' securities are sold and traded. (4) Investors' willingness to buy securities is influenced by the existence of safeguards provided by these laws.

Securities Act of 1933

The first of the securities acts, the Securities Act of 1933, followed Congressional investigations after the stock market collapse of 1929–1932. The reasons motivating the act were (1) the large losses to investors, (2) the failures of many corporations on which little information had been provided, and (3) the misrepresentations that had been made to investors.

The basic objective of the Securities Act of 1933 is to provide for both *full disclosure* of relevant information and a *record of representations*. It seeks to achieve these objectives by the following means.

1. It applies to all interstate offerings to the public (some exemptions are government bonds and bank stocks) in amounts of $300,000 or more.

2. Securities must be registered at least 20 days before they are publicly offered. The registration statement provides financial, legal, and technical information about the company. A prospectus summarizes this information for use in selling the securities. If information is inadequate or misleading, the SEC will delay or stop the public offering.

3. After the registration has become effective, the securities may be offered if accompanied by the prospectus. Preliminary or "red herring" prospectuses may be distributed to potential buyers during the waiting period.

4. Any purchaser who suffers a loss may sue for damages if the registration statement or prospectus contains misrepresentations or omissions of material facts. Liabilities and severe penalties may be imposed on the issuer, its officers, directors, accountants, engineers, appraisers, underwrit-

ers, and others who participated in the preparation of the registration statement.

The act provides for full disclosure. It also has resulted in a procedure for obtaining a record of representations.

Securities Exchange Act of 1934

The Securities Exchange Act of 1934 extends the disclosure principle as applied to new issues by the act of 1933 to trading in already issued securities (the "secondhand" securities market). It seeks to accomplish this by the following measures.

1. It establishes a Securities and Exchange Commission (the Federal Trade Commission had been administering the act of 1933).

2. It provides for registration and regulation of national securities exchanges. Companies whose securities are listed on an exchange must file reports similar to registration statements with both the SEC and the stock exchange, and provide periodic reports as well.

3. It provides control over corporate "insiders." Officers, directors, and major stockholders of a corporation must file monthly reports of changes in holdings of the stock of the corporation. Any short-term profits from such transactions may have to be paid to the corporation, if stockholders take legal action.

4. The act gives the SEC the power to prohibit manipulation by such devices as pools (aggregations of funds used to affect prices artificially), wash sales (sales between members of the same group to record artificial transaction prices), and pegging the market. "Put-and-call" transactions were made subject to regulation.

5. The SEC is given control over the proxy machinery and practices.

6. Control over the flow of credit into security transactions is established by giving the Board of Governors of the Federal Reserve System the power to control margin requirements.

It will be noted that these powers extend only to listed securities. Many feel that the powers should be extended also to unlisted securities.

APPRAISAL OF REGULATION OF SECURITY TRADING

Why should security transactions be regulated? If a valid answer exists, it is found in the argument that a great body of relevant knowledge is necessary for an informed judgment of the value of a security. Moreover, security values are subject to great gyrations, which influence stability and business conditions generally. Hence, social well-being requires that orderly markets be promoted.

The objectives of the regulation may therefore be summarized into three points:

1. To protect the amateur investor from fraud and to provide him with a basis for more informed judgments.
2. To control the volume of bank credit to finance security speculation.
3. To provide orderly markets in securities.

Progress has been made on all three counts. There has been some cost in the increased time and expense involved in new flotations by companies. Though these burdens have not been so large as some persons have claimed, room for improvement exists. The regulations are powerless to prevent investors from investing in unsound ventures or to prevent stock prices from skyrocketing during booms and falling greatly during periods of pessimism. But requirements for increased information have been of great value.

From the standpoint of the financial manager, regulation has twofold significance. It affects the costs of issuing securities and also the effectiveness of the operation of the securities markets. With regard to the first, the data on costs of flotation reviewed above indicate that such costs have, in fact, been increased by regulation requirements. The increase, however, appears to have been only moderate except for smaller issues. The enactment of the regulatory acts of the 1930s restored public confidence in the securities markets and paved the way for renewed wide public participation in the securities markets with the post-World War II recovery in spending power. The net effect of regulation has therefore been to facilitate the raising of capital by business.

SUMMARY

Securities are traded both on *exchanges* and in the *over-the-counter market*. The stocks of larger industrial and utility companies are generally listed on an exchange, while stocks of financial institutions and bonds of practically all firms are traded over the counter. From the standpoint of the financial manager, listing on an exchange seems advantageous for seasoned issues. The over-the-counter market may aid in the seasoning process until the security can meet the requirements for listing.

The investment banker provides middleman services to both the seller and the buyer of new securities. He helps plan the issue, underwrites it, and handles the job of selling the issue to the ultimate investor. The cost of the service to the issuer is related to the magnitude of the total job the banker must perform to place the issue. The investment banker must also look to the interests of his brokerage customers; if these investors are not satisfied with the banker's products, they will deal elsewhere.

The financial manager should be familiar with the federal laws regulating the issuance and trading of securities, because they influence his liabilities and affect financing methods and costs. Regulation of securities trading seeks (1) to provide information that investors can utilize as a basis for judging the merits of securities, (2) to control the volume of credit used in securities trading, and (3) to provide orderly securities markets. The laws, however, do not prevent either purchase of unsound issues or wide price fluctuations. They raise somewhat the costs of flotation but have probably decreased the cost of capital by increasing public confidence in the securities markets.

Flotation costs are lowest for bonds, higher for preferred stocks, and highest for common stock. Larger companies have lower flotation costs than smaller ones for each type of security, and most companies can cut their stock flotation costs by issuing the new securities to stockholders through rights offerings.

QUESTIONS

14–1 State several advantages to a firm that lists its stock on a major stock exchange.

14–2 Would you expect the cost of capital of a firm to be affected if it changed its status from one traded over the counter to one traded on the New York Stock Exchange? Explain.

14–3 Evaluate the following statement: "Short selling is fundamentally a form of gambling; it is simply betting that a stock's worth will decline. Buying stocks, on the other hand, is more in the nature of true investment; stock is purchased in order to receive a dividend return on the invested capital. Consequently, if we do not wish to see Wall Street turned into an eastern Las Vegas, all short selling should be forbidden."

14–4 Evaluate the following statement: "The fundamental purpose of the federal security laws dealing with new issues is to prevent investors, principally small ones, from sustaining losses on the purchase of stocks."

14–5 Suppose two firms were each selling $10 million of common stock. The firms are identical—that is, they are of the same size, are in the same industry, have the same leverage, and have other similarities—except that one is publicly owned and the other is closely held. Would their costs of flotation be the same? If different, state the probable relationships. If the issue were $10 million of bonds, would your answer be the same?

14–6 Define these terms: brokerage firm, underwriting group, selling group, and investment banker.

14–7 Each month the Securities and Exchange Commission publishes a report of the transactions made by the officers and directors of listed firms in their own companies' equity securities. Why do you suppose the SEC makes this report?

14–8 The SEC forbids officers and directors to sell short the shares of their own company. Why do you suppose this rule is on the books?

14–9   Prior to 1933 investment banking and commercial banking were both carried on by the same firm. In that year, however, the Banking Act required that these functions be separated. Based on your knowledge of investment banking and commercial banking, discuss the pros and cons of this forced separation.

14–10   Before entering a formal agreement, investment bankers investigate quite carefully the companies whose securities they underwrite; this is especially true of the issues of firms going public for the first time. Since the bankers do not themselves plan to hold the securities, but plan to sell them to others as soon as possible, why are they so concerned about making careful investigations? Does your answer to the question have any bearing on the fact that investment banking is a very difficult field to "break into"?

14–11   If competitive bidding was required on all security offerings, would flotation costs be higher or lower? Would the size of the issuing firm be material in determining the effects of required competitive bidding?

14–12   Since investment bankers price new issues in relation to outstanding issues, should a spread eixst between the yields on the new and the outstanding issues? Discuss this matter separately for stock issues and bond issues.

14–13   What is there about the nature of insurance companies that causes them to make, on the average, (a) longer term loans, and (b) larger loans, than commercial banks?

14–14   What problems are raised by the increasing purchases of equities by institutional investors?

PROBLEMS

14–1   Listed below are salient facts on the terms of sale of several securities sold through investment bankers in recent years. All facts are taken from prospectuses issued in connection with the sales. Explain the differences in underwriting costs between the groups and among the firms within each group.

		Securities Issued		
Company Name, Business, Industry Characteristics	Date	Size (in millions of dollars)	Unit Price to Public (in dollars)	Total Underwriting Cost (in percentages)
I. Bonds				
A. Nonconvertible				
1. General Motors Acceptance Corporation. Organized 1919. Finances distribution of		(See next page.)		

Securities Issued

Company Name, Business, Industry Characteristics	Date	Size (in millions of dollars)	Unit Price to Public (in dollars)	Total Under- writing Cost (in percentages)
new cars and dealers' installment sales of General Motors products. Industry is competitive, discount rates fluctuate depending on competitive factor. 4½%, due 1985.	Nov. 1963	$150.00	$ 995.00	0.875
2. The Western Union Telegraph Company. Organized 1851. Furnishes communication services throughout the United States. Provides the only public telegraph message service. Competitive with telephone and mail. 5%, due 1992.	Mar. 1964	75.00	1,005.00	1.46
3. The Maston Company, Inc. Organized in 1923. Provides commercial and industrial loans up to three years. 5½%, due 1977.	Apr. 1962	5.00	1,000.00	2.29

B. Convertible with rights
   1. Litton Industry, Inc. Organized 1953. Manufacturing and sales business, commercial and military electrical systems. Industry is highly competitive and subject to changes in defense budget. 3½%, due 1987.

Company Name, Business, Industry Characteristics	Date	Securities Issued		
		Size (in millions of dollars)	Unit Price to Public (in dollars)	Total Underwriting Cost (in percentages)
Market price common: $138; conversion price: $160 until 1972, thereafter $170.	Apr. 1962	$50.70	$1,000.00	1.70*
2. Brunswick Corporation. Organized 1907. Principal product is bowling supplies. Company is one of the two leading manufacturers in its field. 4½%, due 1981. Market price common: $47; conversion price: $51.	Jan. 1961	25.60	1,000.00	2.06*
3. Chock Full O' Nuts. Organized 1932. Operates a chain of counter-service restaurants. Restaurants principally located in the Borough of Manhattan, New York City. 4½%, due 1981. Market price common: $26; conversion price: $28.50.	Aug. 1961	7.00	1,000.00	4.07*

C. Convertible: nonrights
1. Union Oil Company of California. Organized 1890. Engaged in substantially all branches of oil industry. The oil industry is characterized by intensive competition. 4¼%, due 1991. Market price com-

| | | Securities Issued | | |
| | | Size (in millions of dollars) | Unit Price to Public (in dollars) | Total Underwriting Cost (in percentages) |
Company Name, Business, Industry Characteristics	Date			
mon: $55; conversion price: $65.	June 1961	60.00	1,000.00	1.26
2. Baxter Laboratories, Inc. Organized 1931. One of the leading pharmaceutical companies in the manufacture and sale of parental solutions. Industry is extremely competitive. 4%, due 1982. Market price common: $31; conversion price: $38.	Apr. 1962	$10.00	$1,020.00	2.29
3. Standard Motor Products, Inc. Organized 1926. Engaged in the manufacture and sale of replacement parts for electrical and fuel systems, mainly for motor vehicles. Primary market is the automobile industry. 4¾%, due 1984. Market price common: $13; conversion price: $15.	Apr. 1964	3.00	1,000.00	4.27

II. Nonconvertible Preferred Stock

    1. Brockton Edison Company. Organized 1883. A Massachusetts electric utility serving an aggregate population of about 200,000. Is a member of the holding com-

		Securities Issued		
			Unit	Total
		Size	Price	Under-
		(in	to	writing
		millions	Public	Cost
Company Name, Business,		of	(in	(in
Industry Characteristics	Date	dollars)	dollars)	percentages)
pany system of Eastern Utilities Associates. No competition within its territory. 4.64%.	Oct. 1963	6.00	1,019.78	1.64

III. Common Stock
    A. With Rights
        1. Bank of America. Organized 1904. Provides banking services in California. Operates the largest system of branch banks in the nation. Market price: bid, $65.88, ask, $69.75; subscription price: $59.   Nov. 1961   94.4   59.00   1.19*
        2. The Western Casualty and Surety Company. Organized 1924. Engaged in the underwriting of all major types of insurance except life. In 1960, ranked forty-seventh among 115 leading insurance company groups of all types. Market price: bid, $60.50, ask, $62; subscription price: $57.   Mar. 1962 $ 10.7 $ 57.00 1.96*
        3. The Akron-Dime Banks. Organized in 1960 from the consolidation of the Dime Bank and the Bank of Akron. The Dime Bank was organized

| | | Securities Issued | | |
		Size *(in millions of dollars)*	Unit Price to Public *(in dollars)*	Total Under-writing Cost *(in percentages)*
Company Name, Business, Industry Characteristics	*Date*			
in 1900 and the Bank of Akron Company in 1918. Bank has 11 offices serving Summit County, Ohio. Is the second largest of 6 commercial banks in the county. Market price: bid, $34, ask, $35; subscription price: $26.	June 1965	1.7	26.00	1.92*
B. Nonrights				
1. Communications Satellite Corporation. Organized 1963. Plans to establish and operate a global commercial communication satellite system. Authorized by the Communication Satellite Act of 1962, but not an agency of the United States government. No previous market price.	June 1964	200.0	20.00	2.3
2. Delta Air Lines, Inc. Organized 1930. Engaged in air transportation of persons, property, and mail. Industry is regulated by the government. Market price: $38.	Apr. 1962	7.6	$37.25	6.38
3. Hudson Wholesale Groceries, Inc. Organized 1918. Engaged primarily in the				

		Securities Issued		
		Size (in millions of dollars)	*Unit Price to Public (in dollars)*	*Total Underwriting Cost (in percentages)*
Company Name, Business, Industry Characteristics	*Date*			
procurement, warehousing, and sale of groceries and nonfood items to supermarkets, discount stores, and neighborhood grocery stores. No previous market price.	May 1962	0.8	8.00	19.25

* The starred figures represent the minimum cost of financing, assuming that the subscription is fully subscribed. This cost will increase if the underwriter is required to buy any unsubscribed stock. In general, the subscription price is sufficiently below the market price to insure complete subscription.

14–2   Match each firm in list 1 with the most appropriate source of financing found in list 2, and set forth the key factors determining your choice. (There is no one right answer to this problem. Judgment is required, and where judgment is called into play, different people will reach different conclusions.)

List 1

a) Firm selling a large volume of small- and medium-sized orders to numerous medium-sized firms. Working capital position and ownership investment relatively small.

b) Medium-sized firm producing plastic toys. Profitability good, but dependent on independence of action by two owners. Growth good, requiring substantial investment in inventories of specialized packaging materials.

c) Medium-sized firm in growing industry. Needs a 15-to-20-year loan of $2 million; needs funds quickly; professional, financial, and business analysis indicates that the firm's outlook is promising.

d) Two scientists with strong technical competence have an idea for developing a product. Only technical experts could appraise the soundness of the idea. Need management guidance and encouragement as well as financing.

e) Large, highly reputable firm in the steel industry with expansion needs. Good credit rating with a 60 percent debt ratio. Fairly high price/earnings ratio.

f) Firm has large seasonal needs for funds in the autumn of each year.

g) Textile firm with declining profits because of competition of lower labor costs in other regions of the United States. Considering relocation in low-cost labor areas in cities interested in attracting new industry.

List 2
1. Commercial bank
2. Investment bankers
3. Life insurance company
4. Finance companies
5. Equity markets
6. Suppliers
7. Investment-development companies or **SBIC**.
8. Community-development companies
9. Friends and relatives

14–3 Excerpts from pospectuses, with particular focus on the underwriter agreements, are given below.

a) What differences do you find in the underwriting costs and agreements?
b) How do you explain the differences?

A summary of the financial information on the companies follows:

	Speedee Mart, Inc.	Spiegel, Inc.	Beckman Instru- ments, Inc.
Total assets, end of 1960	$2.3*	$291.3*	$39.0*
Net worth, end of 1960	0.7	64.2	19.5
Sales			
1958	0.097	152.7	39.8
1960	0.253	268.8	54.3
Net Income after taxes			
1958	0.018	5.0	(0.946)
1960	0.023	11.8	3.1

* Dollar amounts in millions

Speedee Mart, Inc. 90,000 shares, common stock, without par value.

	Price to Public	Underwriting Discounts and Commissions	Proceeds to Company
Per share	$ 6	$ 0.60	$ 5.40
Total	$540,000	$54,000.00	$486,000.00

Description of Business

Speedee Mart, Inc. (the "company"), whose principal offices are located at 7988 Normal Avenue, La Mesa, California, was incorporated in California on April 10, 1956. It is engaged in the business of enfranchising others (franchises) to manage and operate retail food stores under the name "Speedee Mart." From October 2, 1960, 51 stores have been doing business under franchises as herein described and the company was in varying stages of establishing 33 additional stores.

Speedee Mart markets are located primarily in areas where they provide convenient neighborhood food-shopping facilities away from metropolitan shopping centers. In a sense, these convenience markets, which are open from 7 A.M. to 11 P.M. 7 days a week, are in competition with several national supermarket chain store organizations, local chain stores, and large independent food stores, as well as other neighborhood markets. The Speedee Mart stores do not, however, purport to compete for the large weekly shopping trade, but rather to provide a convenient place for customers to make purchases for daily needs. The company believes that it meets supermarket prices on items comprising a majority of its sales volume.

Underwriting

The underwriter, J. A. Hogle & Company, 132 South Main Street, Salt Lake City, Utah, has made a firm commitment, subject to the terms and conditions of the underwriting agreement (a copy of which is filed as an exhibit to the registration statement), to purchase all the shares of the company offered hereby. The company has been advised by the underwriters that the common stock is proposed to be offered by the underwriter for sale initially at the public offering price set forth on the cover page of this prospectus. Concessions to selected dealers may be allowed in an amount not exceeding 35 cents a share, of which 15 cents a share may be reallowed to other dealers, provided such reallowance is retained. The public offering price and the concessions and reallowances to dealers may be changed by the underwriter after the initial public offering, by reason of changes in market conditions.

SOURCE: Prospectus, J. A. Hogle & Company, January 31, 1961.

Spiegel, Inc., $40,000,000, 5¼% debentures, dated April 1, 1961; due April 1, 1983.

	Price to Public	Underwriting Discounts and Commissions	Proceeds to Company
Per unit	100%	1.5%	98.5%
Total	$40,000,000	$600,000	$39,400,000

Description of Business

The company is engaged, and intends to continue to engage, in the sale of merchandise by mail. Customers are offered three ways to buy: cash with order, 30-day charge, and monthly payments. The company is believed to sell a substantially larger proportion of its total volume on the monthly payment plan than any other national retailer of general merchandise does.

The company expects to continue to concentrate its efforts in the specialized techniques of catalogue credit promotion, credit acceptance, collections, and credit finance. Experience has demonstrated that monthly payment selling is more profitable than selling for cash. Monthly payment customers tend to buy more frequently and in larger amounts than do cash customers. In addition, after being charged with the company's total interest expense, the servicing of the credit accommodation now contributes materially to consolidated profit.

Underwriting

Subject to the terms and conditions set forth in the underwriting agreement, the company has agreed to sell to each of the underwriters named below, and each of the underwriters for whom Wertheim & Company is acting as representative has severally agreed to purchase, at the price set forth on the cover page of this prospectus, the principal amount of debentures set opposite its name.

The nature of the underwriting commitments is such that the several underwriters are obligated, subject to certain conditions, to purchase all the debentures offered hereby. In the event of default by any underwriter, the underwriting agreement provides that in certain circumstances other underwriters may be substituted or the agreement terminated.

The company has been advised by Wertheim & Company that in connection with the sale of the debentures by the underwriters, concessions may be allowed to other dealers not in excess of 0.25 percent.

SOURCE: Prospectus, Wertheim & Company, April 12, 1961.

Beckman Instruments, Inc. 69,993 shares, common stock, par value $1 a share.

The company hereby offers to the holders of its common stock the right to subscribe for additional shares of its common stock at the rate of one additional share for each 20 shares held of record on the close of business on March 28, 1961, all as more fully set forth herein.

	Subscription Price	Underwriting Commissions	Proceeds to Company
Per share	$ 114	Min. $ 2.00	Max. $ 112.00
		Max. 5.40	Min. 108.60
Total	7,972,362	Min. 139,866.00	Max. 7,832,496.00
		Max. 377,638.20	Min. 7,594,723.80

Description of Business

The company and its subsidiaries are engaged in the business of designing, developing, manufacturing, and selling precision instruments for scientific, industrial, medical, and laboratory use.

Underwriting

In the underwriting agreement, the several underwriters, represented by Lehman Brothers, have agreed, subject to the terms and conditions therein set forth, to purchase from the company all the shares of common stock offered hereby not purchased on exercise of rights, at the subscription price set forth on the cover page of this prospectus. For their respective commitments the underwriters are to receive compensation as set forth below and on the cover page of this prospectus. Reference is made to the underwriting agreement filed as an exhibit to the registration statement.

The company has agreed to pay the underwriters $2 a share with respect to each share of common stock offered hereby, plus $3.40 a share on all shares (herein called the "unsubscribed stock") not purchased on the exercise of rights or which are purchased by the underwriters on the exercise of rights purchased by them. The minimum underwriting commissions and maximum proceeds to the company shown on the cover page of this prospectus are based on the assumption that all shares of common stock offered hereby will be subscribed for by other than the underwriters, and the maximum underwriting commissions and minimum proceeds to the company are based on the assumption that none of such shares will be so subscribed for.

If the aggregated sales price of all unsubscribed stock sold by the several underwriters during the period of the subscription offer and within 30 days thereafter is in excess of the aggregate subscription price of the unsubscribed stock, the underwriters will pay to the company 50 percent of such excess. Such excess is to be computed after deducting all costs and expenses (including selling concessions, brokerage commissions, and transfer taxes) and any losses paid or incurred, directly or indirectly, by the underwriters in connection with the distribution of the unsubscribed stock, the purchase of rights (whether or not exercised), stabilization operations, overallotments, short sales, and related transactions. For the purpose of this paragraph, unsubscribed stock not sold or contracted to be sold by the underwriters on the date on which such 30-day period terminates will be deemed to have been sold on such date of termination at the weighted average of the sales prices of the common stock of the company on the New York Stock Exchange on such date.

Name	
Lehman Brothers	20.00
A. C. Allyn and Company, Inc.	6.00
Ball, Burge & Kraus	2.00
J. Barth & Company	2.00
Bear, Stearns & Company	8.00
Blyth & Company, Inc.	8.00
Burnham and Company	2.00
Eastman Dillon, Union Securities & Company	8.00
Goodbody & Company	2.00
Hayden, Stone & Company	4.50
Hornblower & Weeks	4.50

Name

Paine, Webber, Jackson & Curtis	4.50
Paribas Corporation	8.00
Peltason, Tenebaum Company	2.00
Shearson, Hammill & Company	4.50
Stein Bros. & Boyce	2.00
Sutro & Company	2.00
Wagenseller & Durst, Inc.	2.00
Dean Witter & Company	8.00
Total	100.00

Lehman Brothers has advised the company that the underwriters may offer shares of common stock as set forth on the cover page of this prospectus, that initially they may allow concessions not in excess of $2.50 a share to certain dealers, and that the underwriters and such dealers initially may reallow concessions not in excess of 50 cents a share to other dealers. Such concessions to dealers may be changed by the representative.

SOURCE: Prospectus, Lehman Brothers, March 28, 1961.

Chapter 15

Common Stock

Common equity or, if unincorporated enterprises are considered, partner-ship or proprietorship interests constitute the first source of funds to a new business and the base of support for existing firms' borrowings. Accordingly, our discussion of specific forms of long-term financing will begin with an analysis of common stock.

APPORTIONMENT OF INCOME, CONTROL, AND RISK

The nature of equity ownership depends upon the form of the business organization. The central problem revolves around an apportionment of cer-tain rights and responsibilities among those who have provided the funds necessary for the operation of the business.

The rights and responsibilities attaching to equity consist of positive considerations—income potential and control of the firm—and negative con-siderations—loss potential, responsibility, and personal liability.

General Rights of Holders of Common Stock

The rights of holders of common stock in a business corporation are established by the laws of the state in which the corporation is chartered and by the terms of the charter granted by the state. The characteristics of charters are relatively uniform on many matters.

Collective Rights.   Certain collective rights are usually given to the holders of common stock. Some of the more important rights allow stockholders (1) to amend the charter with the approval of the appropriate officials in the state of incorporation; (2) to adopt and amend bylaws; (3) to elect the directors of the corporation; (4) to authorize the sale of fixed assets; (5) to enter into mergers; (6) to change the amount of authorized common stock; and (7) to issue preferred stock, debentures, bonds, and other securities.

Specific Rights.   Holders of common stock also have specific rights as individual owners. (1) They have the right to vote in the manner prescribed by the corporate charter. (2) They may sell their stock certificates, their evidence of ownership, and in this way transfer their ownership interest to other persons. (3) They have the right to inspect the corporate books.[1] (4) They have the right to share residual assets of the corporation on dissolution; however, the holders of common stock are last among the claimants to the assets of the corporation.

Apportionment of Income

There are two important positive considerations involved in equity ownership: income and control. The right to income carries risks of loss. Control also involves responsibility and liability. In an individual proprietorship, using only funds supplied by the owner, the owner has a 100 percent right to income and control and to loss and responsibility. As soon as the proprietor incurs debt, however, he has entered into contracts that place limitations on his complete freedom to control the firm and to apportion the firm's income.

In a partnership, these rights are apportioned among the partners in an agreed manner. In the absence of a formal agreement, a division is made by the laws of the locality. But the more significant issues arise concerning the rights of the owners of a business corporation.

Apportionment of Control

Through the right to vote, holders of common stock have legal control of the corporation. As a practical matter, however, in many corporations the principal officers constitute all, or a majority of, the members of the board of directors. In such circumstances the board of directors may be controlled by the management, rather than vice versa. Management con-

---

[1] Obviously, a corporation cannot have its business affairs disturbed by allowing every stockholder to go through any record that he would like to inspect. A corporation could not wisely permit a competitor who happened to buy shares of its common stock to look at all the corporation records. There must be, and there are, practical limitations to this right.

trol, or control of a business by others than its owners, results. However, numerous examples demonstrate that stockholders can reassert their control when dissatisfied. In recent years, proxy battles with the aim of altering corporation policies have occurred fairly often.

As receivers of residual income, holders of common stock are frequently referred to as the ultimate entrepreneurs in the firm. They are the ultimate owners and they have the ultimate control. Presumably the firm is managed on behalf of its owners, the holders of common stock, but there has been much dispute about the actual situation. The point of view has been expressed that the corporation is an institution with an existence separate from the owners, and that the corporation exists to fulfill certain functions for stockholders as only one among other important groups, such as workers, consumers, and the economy as a whole. This view doubtlessly has some validity, but it should also be noted that ordinarily the officers of a firm are also large stockholders. Furthermore, more and more firms are tying officers' compensation in with the firms' profit performance either by granting executives stock purchase options or by giving bonuses. These actions are, of course, designed to make management more stockholder-oriented.

Apportionment of Risk

The fact that, on liquidation, holders of common stock are last in the priority of claims signifies that the portion of capital they contribute provides a cushion for creditors if losses occur on dissolution. The equity-to-total-assets ratio indicates the percentage by which assets may shrink in value on liquidation before creditors will incur losses.

For example, compare two corporations, A and B, with these balance sheets.

BALANCE SHEETS

Corporation A			Corporation B		
	Debt	$ 20		Debt	$ 60
	Equity	80		Equity	40
Total assets $100	Total claims $100		Total assets $100	Total claims $100	

The ratio of equity to total assets in corporation A is 80 percent. Total assets would therefore have to shrink by 80 percent before creditors would lose money. By contrast, in corporation B the extent by which assets may shrink in value on liquidation before creditors lose money is only 40 percent.

Since the average equity-to-total-assets ratio for all manufacturing is approximately two thirds, a substantial equity cushion ordinarily exists. For some industries, such as airline transport and aircraft manufacturing, however, the equity cushion is only about one third of total assets.

COMMON STOCK FINANCING

Before undertaking an evaluation of common stock financing it is desirable to describe some of its additional important characteristics. These topics include (1) the nature of voting rights, (2) the nature of the pre-emptive right, (3) the significance of par value, and (4) variations in the forms of common stock.

Nature of Voting Rights

For each share of common stock owned, the holder has the right to cast a vote at the annual meetings of stockholders of the corporation or at such special meetings as may be called.

Proxy. Provision is made for the temporary transfer of this right to vote by an instrument known as a proxy. A proxy is defined as a transfer of the right to vote. The transfer is limited in its duration, typically for a specific occasion such as the annual meeting of stockholders.

The Securities and Exchange Commission supervises the use of the proxy machinery and issues frequent rules and regulations seeking to improve its administration. SEC supervision is justified for several reasons. First, if the proxy machinery is left wholly in the hands of management, there is a danger that the incumbent management will be self-perpetuated. Second, if it is made easy for minority groups of stockholders and opposition stockholders to oust management, there is danger that small groups of stockholders may gain control of the corporation for temporary advantages or place their friends in management positions. Sometimes, the minority may be seeking the prizes that go along with controlling the corporation, for example, income from real estate.

Eligibility to vote. In certain situations there may be some doubt about who has the right to vote. For example, in a *hypothecation of securities* (where securities are pledged as collateral for a loan), does the pledger or the lender have the right to vote? The law provides that in a simple hypothecation situation the pledger of the stock, rather than the lender, retains the right to vote. In a trust situation, where the donor has placed the stock in the hands of a trustee to be controlled for the benefit of the beneficiary, three possible parties might have the right to vote: the donor, the trustee, and the beneficiary. The law provides that the trustee shall have the right to vote.

Proxies may be mailed to stockholders of record of a specified date—for example, April 10. The voting may relate to an annual meeting to be held one month later, May 10. In the interim the stock may be sold. Who has the right to be proxy: the stockholder of record on April 10 or the new stockholder? Technically, the stockholder of record has the right to vote. He has the proxy and he may keep it. However, the new buyer may, and should, request the proxy from the seller.

Cumulative voting.   A method of voting which has come into increased prominence is cumulative voting.[2] Cumulative voting for directors is required in 22 states, including California, Illinois, Pennsylvania, Ohio, and Michigan. It is permissive in 18, including Delaware, New York, and New Jersey. Ten states make no provision for cumulative voting.

Cumulative voting permits multiple votes for a single director. For example, suppose six directors are to be elected. The owner of 100 shares can cast 100 votes for each of the six openings. Cumulatively, then, he has 600 votes. When cumulative voting is permitted, the stockholder may accumulate his votes and cast 600 votes for *one* director, instead of 100 each for *six* directors. Cumulative voting is designed to enable a minority group of stockholders to obtain some voice in the control of the company by electing at least one director to the board.

The nature of cumulative voting is illustrated by use of a well-known formula.

$$r = \frac{d \times S}{D + 1} + 1$$

$r =$ number of shares required to elect a desired number of directors
$d =$ number of directors stockholder desires to elect
$S =$ total number of shares of common stock outstanding and entitled to vote[3]
$D =$ total number of directors to be elected

The formula may be made more meaningful by an example. The ABC company will elect six directors. There are 15 candidates and

---

[2] For an excellent discussion of all aspects of cumulative voting, see C. M. Williams, *Cumulative Voting for Directors* (Boston: Graduate School of Business Administration, Harvard University, 1951).

[3] An alternative that may be agreed to by the contesting parties is to define S as the number of shares *voted,* not authorized to vote. This procedure, which in effect gives each group seeking to elect directors the same percentage of directors as their percentage of the voted stock, is generally followed. When it is followed, a group that seeks to gain control with a minimum investment must estimate the percentage of shares that will be voted, then obtain control of 51 percent of that number.

100,000 shares entitled to a vote. If a group desires to elect two directors, how many shares must it have?

$$\frac{2 \times 100,000}{6 + 1} + 1 = 28,572$$

Observe the significance of the formula. Here, a minority group wishes to elect one third of the board of directors. They can achieve their goal by owning less than one third the number of shares of stock.[4]

The question may be put in another way. Assuming that a group holds 40,000 shares of stock in this company, how many directors would it be possible for the group to elect, following the rigid assumptions of the formula? The formula can be used in its present form or can be solved for d and expressed as

$$d = \frac{(r - 1)(D + 1)}{S}$$

Inserting the figures, the calculation would be

$$d = \frac{39,999 \times 7}{100,000} = 2.8$$

The 40,000 shares could elect 2.8 directors. Since directors cannot exist as fractions, the group can elect only two directors.

As a practical matter, suppose that in the above situation the total number of shares is 100,000. Hence 60,000 shares remain in other hands. The voting of all the 60,000 shares may not be concentrated. Suppose the 60,000 shares (cumulatively, 360,000 votes) are distributed equally among 10 candidates, 36,000 shares per candidate. If the other 240,000 votes are distributed equally for each of six candidates, the minority group could elect all six directors.

In actuality, it is difficult to make assumptions about how the opposition votes will be distributed. What is shown here is a good example of game theory. One rule involved in the theory of games is to assume that your opponents will do the worst they can do to you and to counter with actions to minimize the maximum loss. This is the kind of assumption followed in the formula. If your opposition concentrates its votes in the optimum manner, what is the best you can do to work in the direction of your goal? Other plausible assumptions can be substituted if one has sufficient facts to support alternative hypotheses about the behavior of his opponents.

---

[4] Note also that at least 14,287 shares must be controlled to elect one director. So far as electing a director goes, any number less than 14,287 constitutes a useless minority.

Pre-emptive Right

The pre-emptive right gives holders of common stock the first option to purchase additional issues of common stock. In some states the pre-emptive right is made a part of every corporate charter. In other states it is necessary to insert the pre-emptive right specifically in the charter.

The purpose of the pre-emptive right is twofold. First, it protects the power of control of present stockholders. If it were not for this safeguard, the management of a corporation under criticism from stockholders could prevent stockholders from removing it from office by issuing a large number of additional shares at a very low price and purchasing these shares itself. Management would thereby secure control of the corporation to frustrate the will of the current stockholders.

The second, and by far the more important protection that the pre-emptive right affords stockholders, regards dilution of value. An example may clarify this. Assume that 1,000 shares of common stock with a market value of $100 are outstanding, making the total market value of the firm $100,000. An additional 1,000 shares are sold at $50 a share, or for $50,000, thus raising the total market value of the firm to $150,000. When the total market value is divided by the new total shares outstanding, a value of $75 a share is obtained. Thus, selling common stock at below market value will dilute the price of the stock and be detrimental to present stockholders and beneficial to those who purchased the new shares. The pre-emptive right prevents such occurrences.

Par Value versus No-Par Value

Some distinctions. Some distinctions need to be made among different concepts of value. *Par value* is the nominal value of common stock; it is the value arbitrarily stated on the shares. *Book value,* the concept that has been used here, is the historical value of the common stock. Book value per share is calculated by adding the balance sheet value of the common stock, plus earned surplus, plus capital surplus, and dividing this sum by the number of shares outstanding. If there is a goodwill account on the left-hand side of the balance sheet, the analyst may or may not deduct the goodwill item, depending upon whether it generates superior earning power.

Market value, as explained in Chapter 9, is the prevailing price paid for a share of common stock as registered in transactions between buyers and sellers of common stock.

Intrinsic value, or economic value, is not an objective amount. It represents a judgment of the long-run value of the common stock as determined by fundamental economic forces.

These distinctions facilitate analysis of the use of par value, the trend toward no-par value, and the reversal of that trend. Originally, the purpose of a par value was to protect creditors. It was to insure that the full amount of payment for common stock had actually been received by the company. By clearly stating a par value on the balance sheet, the creditors of the company had the assurance that, if the full amount had not been paid in, they had the right to levy deficiency judgments against the present holders of common stock.

For example, A buys a $100 par value stock *from the company* for $65. On insolvency he is liable up to $35 to a subsequent assessment by creditors. This deficiency assessment right holds even though A may have subsequently sold his stock. For example, B purchases the stock from A for $115, an amount that exceeds par value by $15. The deficiency assessment liability of $35 is acquired by B, because the company has never received the full par value of the stock. The deficiency provision follows stock ownership.

Having a high par value can cause other problems. For example, suppose a firm sells stock for $100 par at the time it is organized. Years later, the market price may be well below par—say $50. Now suppose the company has some good investment opportunities, but to take advantage of them it must raise funds by selling common stock. However, the market price of the stock is only $50, so this sets the practical maximum at which new shares can be sold. But if new shares are sold *by the company* at only $50, purchasers would be liable for a deficiency judgment. This, in turn, makes it impractical to sell new common stock.

No-par stock. Because of deficiency assessments and other reasons, no-par stock was developed. No-par stock was first permitted by a New York State statute in 1912. When no-par stock is issued, it is carried on the balance sheet at the price at which the stock is sold or at some other stated value. Sometimes when no-par stock is sold, a paid-in surplus is created. For example, assume 1,000 shares are sold at $10 a share, a total of $10,000. The stated value of the common stock sold may be stated, quite arbitrarily, as $8,000 with a paid-in surplus of $2,000.

No-par stock has several advantages. First, it avoids the problem of deficiency assessments. Second, it avoids misleading the investor who may feel that par value has some significance; the fact that par value is stated on the common stock certificate may lead some unwary and uninformed investors to feel that somehow the intrinsic worth of the stock is represented by its stated par value. Third, it may increase the marketability of the stock, since the company can sell additional shares of common stock at any time at whatever price the stock will bring.

Some possible disadvantages of no-par stock should also be examined. First, it is sometimes said that no-par stock may lead to possible manipulation of the accounts. Stock may be sold at $10 a share and carried on the books at $8, with a paid-in surplus for the difference. Unsophisticated investors might think this represents *earned* surplus and thus shows that the company is operating profitably. However, creation of surplus can also occur with par stock. For example, a company may sell stock at $8 a share, establishing a par value of $5 a share and showing the difference of $3 as paid-in surplus. Therefore, whether stock is par value or no-par value has little fundamental influence on possible manipulation.

Second, if stock is sold at a price below the present stated value, or book value of no-par stock, the value of the old stock may be diluted. But the book value of par stock can also be diluted if it is sold at less than book value. Typically, par value is less than book value; if a company has earned surplus, the book value of its stock will be greater than the par value.

For some years, no-par stock was taxed at $100 value for stock transfer tax purposes. This resulted in a trend toward the use of low-par stocks of $1 to $5. However, the stock transfer tax is now based on market prices. Hence, no general advantage for the use or nonuse of a nominal value for common stock exists.

Forms of Common Stock

Classified common stock. Classified common stock was used extensively in the late 1920s, sometimes in ways that misled investors. During that period Class A common stock was usually nonvoting, and Class B was typically voting. Thus promoters could control companies by selling large amounts of Class A stock while retaining Class B stock.

In more recent years there has been a revival of Class B common for sound purposes. It is used by a small, new company seeking to acquire funds from outside sources. Common stock A is sold to the public, and typically pays dividends of a consistent amount; it has full voting rights. Common stock B, however, is retained by the organizers of the company, but dividends are not paid on it until the company has established its earning power. By the use of the classified stock the public can take a position in a conservatively financed growth company without sacrificing income.

Founders' shares. Founders' shares are somewhat like Class B stock except that they carry *sole* voting rights. Class A stock does not carry voting rights; founders' shares do not have the right to dividends for a number of years. Thus the organizers of the firm are able to maintain complete control of the operations in the crucial initial development of the firm. At the same time, other investors are protected against excessive withdrawals of funds by owners.

EVALUATION OF COMMON STOCK AS A SOURCE OF FUNDS

The chapter has covered the main characteristics of common stock, frequently referred to as equity shares in the company. By way of a summary of the important aspects of common stock, common stock financing will be appraised from the standpoint of the issuer.

Advantages

First, common stock does not entail fixed charges. If the company generates the earnings, it can pay common stock dividends. In contrast to bond interest, however, there is no legal obligation to pay dividends.

Second, common stock carries no fixed maturity date.

Third, since common stock provides a cushion against losses for creditors, the sale of common stock increases the credit-worthiness of the firm.

Fourth, common stock may at times be sold more easily than debt. Common stock may appeal to certain investor groups for two reasons: (1) it typically carries a higher yield than does preferred stock or debt, and (2) it provides the investor with a better hedge against inflation than do straight preferred stock and bonds, because it represents the ownership in the firm. Ordinarily common stock increases in value when the value of real assets rises during an inflationary period.

Disadvantages

First, the sale of common stock extends voting rights or control to the additional stockowners who are brought into the company. For this reason, among others, additional equity financing is often avoided by small and new firms. The owner-managers may be unwilling to share control of their companies with outsiders.

Second, common stock gives more owners the right to share in income. The use of debt may enable the firm to utilize funds at a fixed low cost, whereas common stock gives equal rights to new stockholders to share in the net profits of the firm.

Third, the costs of underwriting and distributing common stock are usually higher than those for underwriting and distributing preferred stock or debt. Flotation costs for selling common stock are characteristically higher because, although certain investor groups may be interested in common stock, the broadest market for securities is for debt securities. Insurance companies, savings banks, and other investing institutions place a large proportion of their assets in debt; the potential market for debt securities is therefore greater than that for common stocks.

Fourth, common stock typically must be sold on a higher expected return basis than debt. When anticipated earnings or dividends are related to the price at which common stock is sold, the indicated yield is higher than the interest rate the firm would have to pay on debt.[5]

Fifth, common stock dividends are not deductible as an expense for calculating the corporations' income subject to the federal income tax, but bond interest is deductible.

Other Aspects of Equity Financing

Common stock also should be considered from a social standpoint. Common stock is a desirable form of financing because it renders business firms, hence a major segment of the economy, less vulnerable to the consequences of declines in sales and earnings. If sales and earnings decline, common stock financing involves no fixed charges, the payment of which might force the firm into reorganization or bankruptcy.

However, there is another aspect of common stock financing that may have less desirable social consequences. Common stock prices fall in recessions, and this causes a rise in the cost of equity capital.[6] The rising cost of equity raises the over-all cost of capital, which in turn reduces investment. This reduction further aggravates the recession. On the other hand, an expanding economy is accompanied by rising stock prices, and with rising stock prices comes a drop in the cost of capital. This, in turn, stimulates investment, which may add to a developing inflationary boom. In summary, a consideration of its effects on the cost of capital suggests that stock financing may tend to amplify cyclical fluctuations.

Just how these opposing forces combine to produce a net effect is unknown, but the authors believe that the first is the stronger; that is, stock financing tends to stabilize the economy.

DECISION MAKING IN COMMON STOCK FLOTATIONS

So far a number of characteristics of common stock financing have been presented. The advantages and disadvantages of external equity financing, compared with the use of preferred stock and debt, have been described. The purpose of the descriptive background material has been to provide a basis for making sound decisions when financing by common stock is being considered as a possible alternative.

Chapters 8, 9, and 10 have already provided a framework for analyz-

---

[5] In an economy experiencing inflation, bond yields may be higher than stock yields. The reasoning is that the prices of common stock may be bid up to high levels because such stock is regarded as an effective inflation hedge.

[6] See Table 9–1.

ing the advantages and limitations to the use of debt financing versus equity financing. The more specific aspects influencing financing decisions will now be considered. Among the numerous factors involved, eight have particular importance:

1. Patterns of sales and profits
2. Growth rate of sales and profits
3. Existing financial position
4. Age of firm
5. Control considerations
6. Cash flow requirements
7. Costs
8. Restrictions associated with the financing agreement

An important factor influencing financing decisions is the industry of the firm. In part, a firm's industry determines many of the above characteristics. The industry characteristics will strongly influence the asset structure, which in turn will influence the extent to which the firm will have collateral or meet other requirements of particular forms of financing.

With respect to the eight factors listed, some favor common stock financing, others favor other forms. The influence of each factor will now be discussed.

If sales and profit patterns are highly volatile, such as in the durable-goods industries, common stock financing is favored. Rarely will firms with serious profit instability employ significant amounts of long-term debt. The risks of having to meet fixed charges will be too large.

The existing financial position of the company in relation to its optimal or "target" capital structure is another crucial factor determining whether common stock will be employed. If the maximum debt ratio considered safe for the line of business is 50 percent and the firm already has a ratio of 60 percent, common stock financing will be indicated.

If the firm is new, it may have difficulty finding creditors willing to lend large sums on a long-term basis. The age of the firm may make equity financing the only available source. If the firm is established and its existing common stock is widely held, common stock financing will not raise problems of maintaining control of the company.

The absence of fixed interest or rental payments and the fact that there are no maturity and no sinking fund requirements will make future cash flows more stable with common stock financing. Although common stock is expected to pay dividends at some time, dividend payments are ordinarily not legally required, particularly if the earnings of the firm have been small.

The relative costs of common stock financing may be favorable at a particular point in time. If both stock prices and interest rates appear to be high, stock financing may be indicated. The converse is also true, of course, and Chapter 23 deals specifically with the timing of debt and equity issues.

Finally, debt financing may carry important disadvantages, such as loan agreements with restrictions on the management, including the requirement to maintain the current ratio at some prescribed level. Debt financing may call for collateral that is not available in the required amount or kind.

This discussion of eight factors important for decisions whether to use common stock financing when long-term funds are required may be regarded as a check list. Some factors will favor the use of common stock, but all need not be present to justify the selection of common stock. When some, but not all, of the conditions favoring common stock are present, the financial manager must exercise judgment in making the final decision. Differences in recommendations may arise because the decision, in part, depends upon such uncertain factors as the future level of the firm's sales and profits.

It is also important to note that one *cannot* go through the eight factors, decide that six or even seven favor common stock, and recommend common stock over debt. The one factor that favors debt may be dominant in the particular case—it may override all those favoring common stock. In other words, here, just as in all other aspects of financial management, analytical tools provide a basis for the exercise of judgment.

SUMMARY

Equity capital provides the foundation of a firm's operations, since it is the basis for obtaining other forms of financing. Equity funds carry the ultimate risk as well as the ultimate control and claim to the residual income of the business enterprise.

The main advantages of common stock from the point of view of the issuer are that it carries no maturity dates, does not require payment of fixed charges, and increases the firm's base for obtaining other kinds of funds. The disadvantages are that present owners must share voting rights and that dividends are not deductible as an expense for tax purposes, as is bond interest.

Another useful method of summarizing the role of common stock is to identify the conditions that favor its use. Circumstances favoring the use of common stock are:

1. The firm's sales and profits fluctuate widely.
2. Profit margins do not cover the cost of debt.
3. The firm already has a high debt equity ratio in relation to the prudent maximum for its line of business.
4. The firm is new, lacking access to debt financing.
5. Dilution of control of the firm is not a problem.

6. Cash flow considerations are important.
7. The relative costs of common stock financing are favorable.
8. Available debt financing would carry onerous loan-agreement restrictions.

It must be recognized, of course, that simply listing these factors is not enough to determine whether common stock should be used in a particular instance. Seven of the eight factors might favor the use of common stock, but the one favoring debt might be important enough in a particular case to swing the decision to the use of debt.

QUESTIONS

15–1 What percentage could total assets shrink in value on liquidation before creditors incurred losses in each of the following cases:

a) Equity to total asset ratio, 50 percent
b) Debt to equity ratio, 50 percent
c) Debt to total asset ratio, 40 percent

15–2 Distinguish between stated value and par value.
15–3 What factors, if any, are relevant to the decision to use par-value common stock versus no par stock?
15–4 What difficulties do small firms encounter in raising equity capital?
15–5 What characteristics of a new common stock issue would make its purchase more attractive to prospective investors?
15–6 How many shares must a minority group possess in order to assure election of two directors if nine new directors will be elected and 200,000 shares are outstanding? Assume cumulative voting exists.
15–7 Should the pre-emptive right entitle stockholders to purchase convertible bonds before they are offered to outsiders?

PROBLEMS

15–1 The Green Giant Company is principally engaged in the business of growing, processing, and marketing a variety of canned and frozen vegetables and is a major company in this field. High-quality products are produced and marketed at premium prices.

During each of the past several years the company's sales have increased and the needed inventories have been financed from short-term sources. The officers have discussed the idea of refinancing their bank loans with long-term debt or common stock. A common stock issue of 310,000 shares sold at this time (present market price is $24 a share) would yield $7 million after expenses. This same sum could be raised by selling 12-year bonds with an interest rate of 6½ percent and a sinking fund to retire the bonds over their 12-year life.

Canning Industry Financial Ratios

Current ratio (times)	2.2
Sales to total assets (times)	2.0
Sales to inventory (times)	5.6
Average collection period (days)	22.0
Current debt/total assets (percent)	25–30
Long-term debt/total assets (percent)	10–15
Preferred/total assets (percent)	0.5
Net worth/total assets (percent)	60–65
Profits to sales (percent)	2.3
Net profits to total assets (percent)	4.0
Profits to net worth (percent)	8.4
Expected growth rate of earnings and dividends (percent)	6.5

GREEN GIANT COMPANY
CONSOLIDATED BALANCE SHEET
March 31, 1968*
(in millions of dollars)

Current assets	$47	Accounts payable		$ 4
Fixed plant and equipment	19	Notes payable		12
Other assets	4	Accruals		5
		Total current liabilities		$21
		Long-term debt, 5%		21
		Preferred stock	3	
		Common stock	4	
		Retained earnings	21	
		Net worth		28
Total assets	$70	Total claims on assets		$70

* The majority of harvesting activities do not begin until late April or May.

GREEN GIANT COMPANY
CONSOLIDATED STATEMENT OF INCOME
Year Ended March 31
(in millions of dollars)

	1965	1966	1967	1968
Net sales	$75.0	$78.2	$97.6	$115.7
Cost of goods sold	48.7	52.2	65.1	76.8
Gross profit	26.3	26.0	32.5	38.9
Other expenses	20.6	22.0	27.0	29.5
Operating income	5.7	4.0	5.5	9.4
Other income (net)	(1.1)	(1.4)	(1.9)	(3.1)

	1965	1966	1967	1968
Earnings before tax	4.6	2.6	3.6	6.3
Taxes	2.4	1.1	1.8	3.2
Net profit	2.2	1.5	1.8	3.1
Preferred dividend	0.1	0.1	0.1	0.1
Earnings available to common stock	$ 2.1	$ 1.4	$ 1.7	$ 3.0
Earnings per share	$ 1.05	$ 0.70	$ 0.85	$ 1.50
Cash dividends per share	0.43	0.48	0.53	0.60
Price range for common stock				
High	22.00	23.00	22.00	27.00
Low	10.00	14.00	17.00	21.00

a) Should Green Giant refinance the short-term loans? Why?

b) If the bank loans should be refinanced, what factors should be considered in determining which form of financing to use?

This question should not be answered in terms of precise cost of capital calculations. Rather, a more qualitative and subjective analysis is appropriate. The only calculations necessary are a few simple ratios. Careful interpretation of these ratios is necessary, however, to understand and discuss the often complex, subjective judgment issues involved.

15–2 Pitney-Bowes has been practically the sole manufacturer of postage meters, which it leases or sells outright. Postage meters accounted for half of all the United States postage used by 1959. In addition, the company makes and sells a variety of mailing and business machines.

A few years ago the company incurred $6 million in short-term bank loans because of the expansion of its Stamford plant and offices. The officers of Pitney-Bowes discussed the desirability of refinancing the bank loans with long-term debt or common stock. Underwriters informed them that 20-year, 5½ percent sinking fund debentures or 200,000 shares of common stock could be sold to raise the desired funds. As the common stock was selling above $40 per share, the company could receive about $8,000,000 net from the sale of 200,000 shares. Financial data are shown on the following page.

PITNEY-BOWES, INC.
CONSOLIDATED BALANCE SHEET
December 31, 1959*
(in millions of dollars)

Current assets	$21	Accounts payable	$ 4
Fixed plant and equipment	29	Notes payable, 5%	6
		Income taxes payable	3
		Other accruals	2
		Total current liabilities	$15
		Prepaid rental income (net)	7
		Promissory notes, 3¾%, due in 1967	4
		Cumulative preferred stock, $50 par, 4¼%	1
		Common stock, $2 par value. 8	
		Capital surplus 4	
		Retained earnings 11	
		Net worth	23
Total assets	$50	Total claims on assets	$50

* The balance sheet and income statement figures have been altered to simplify the calculations.

PITNEY-BOWES, INC.
CONSOLIDATED STATEMENT OF INCOME
Year Ended December 31
(in millions of dollars)

	1956	1957	1958	1959
Sales (net)	17	17	20	22
Rental and service income	26	29	31	33
Operating income	43	46	51	55
Cost of products sold	7	7	9	9
Depreciation on rental equipment	2	3	3	3
Selling, administrative, and other expenses	26	27	30	33
	35	37	42	45
Net operating income	8	9	9	10
Income taxes	4	5	5	5
Net profit for the period	4	4	4	5
Earnings per share of common	1.00	1.00	1.00	1.25
Cash dividends per common share	0.50	0.52	0.53	0.60
Price range for common stock				
High	24	24	33	45
Low	15	15	18	35

Manufacturing Industry Financial Ratios

Current ratio (times)	2.0
Sales to total assets (times)	——
Sales to inventory (times)	9.0
Average collection period (days)	——
Current debt/total assets (percent)	20–25
Long-term debt/total assets (percent)	6–10
Preferred/total assets (percent)	——
Net worth/total assets (percent)	65–70
Profits to sales (percent)	4–6
Net profits to total assets (percent)	10–12
Profits to net worth (percent)	13–15
Expected growth in earnings and dividends (percent)	7.5

a) Should Pitney-Bowes have refunded the short-term bank loan? Why?
b) If you were to refinance the short-term loan, what factors would enter into your consideration of the two alternatives?
c) Indicate which means of refinancing you would suggest.

This question should not be answered in terms of precise cost of capital calculations. Rather, a more qualitative and subjective analysis is appropriate. The only calculations necessary are a few simple ratios. Careful interpretation of these ratios is necessary, however, to understand and discuss the often complex, subjective judgment issues involved.

Chapter 16

Preferred Stock

NATURE OF PREFERRED STOCK

Preferred stock has claims or rights ahead of common stock. The preference may be a prior claim on earnings; it may take the form of a prior claim on assets in the event of liquidation; or it may take a preferential position with regard to both earnings and assets.

Hybrid Form

The hybrid nature of preferred stock becomes apparent when one tries to classify it in relation to bonds and common stock. The priority feature and the (generally) fixed dividend indicate that preferred stock is similar to bonds. Payments to the preferred stockholders are limited in amount so that the common stockholders receive the advantages (or disadvantages) of leverage. On the other hand, if the preferred dividends are not earned, the company can forgo paying them without danger of bankruptcy. In this characteristic preferred stock is similar to common stock. Moreover failure to pay the stipulated dividend does not cause default of the obligation, as does failure to pay bond interest.

Debt and Equity

In some kinds of analysis preferred stock is treated as debt. For example, if the analysis is being made by a potential stockholder considering the earnings fluctuations induced by fixed-charge securities, preferred stock would be treated as debt. But suppose the analysis is by a bondholder studying the firm's vulnerability to *failure* brought on by declines in sales or in income. Since the dividends on preferred stock are not a fixed charge in the sense that failure to pay them would represent a default of an obligation, preferred stock represents a cushion; it provides an additional equity base. From the point of view of *stockholders,* it is a leverage inducing instrument much like debt. From the point of view of *creditors,* it constitutes additional net worth. Preferred stock may therefore be treated either as debt or as equity, depending on the nature of the problem under consideration.

MAJOR PROVISIONS OF PREFERRED STOCK ISSUES

The possible characteristics, rights, and obligations of any specific security vary widely, and a point of diminishing returns is quickly reached in a descriptive discussion of different kinds of securities. As economic circumstances change, new kinds of securities are manufactured. The possibilities are numerous. The kinds and varieties of securities are limited chiefly by the imagination and ingenuity of the managers formulating the terms of the security issues. It is not surprising, then, that preferred stock can be found in a variety of forms. One need only look at the main terms and characteristics in each case and examine the possible variations in relation to the kinds of situations or circumstances in which they could occur, as is done below.

Priority in Assets and Earnings
Many provisions in a preferred stock certificate are designed to reduce risk to the purchaser relative to the risk carried by the holder of common stock. Pieferred stock usually has priority with regard to earnings and assets. Two provisions designed to prevent undermining these preferred stock priorities are often found. The first states that, without the consent of the holders of the preferred stock, there can be no subsequent sale of securities having a prior or equal claim on earnings. The second provision seeks to hold earnings in the firm. It requires a minimum level of retained earnings before common stock dividends are permitted. In order to assure the availability of liquid assets that may be converted into cash for the payment of dividends, the maintenance of a minimum current ratio may also be required.

Par Value
Unlike common stock, preferred stock usually has a par value, and this par value is a meaningful quantity. First, it establishes the amount due

to the preferred stockholders in the event of a liquidation. Second, the preferred dividend is frequently stated as a percentage of the par value. For example, J. I. Case has preferred stock outstanding that has a par value of $100, and the dividend is stated to be 7 percent of par. It would, of course, be just as appropriate for the Case preferred stock to state simply that the annual dividend is $7, and on many preferred stocks the dividends are stated in this manner rather than as a percentage of par value.

Cumulative Dividends

A high percent of dividends on preferred stocks is cumulative—all past preferred dividends must be paid before common dividends may be paid. The cumulative feature is therefore a protective device. If the preferred stock was not cumulative, preferred and common stock dividends could be passed by for a number of years. The company could then vote a large common stock dividend, but only the stipulated payment to preferred stock. Suppose the preferred stock with a par value of $100 carried a 7 percent dividend. Suppose the company did not pay dividends for several years, so that it accumulated an amount which would enable it to pay in total about $50 in dividends. It could pay one $7 dividend to the preferred stock and a $43 dividend to the common stock. Obviously, this device could be used to evade the preferred position that the holders of preferred stock have tried to obtain. The cumulative feature prevents such evasion. Note, however, that compounding is absent in most cumulative plans. In other words, the arrearages themselves earn no return.

Arrearages on preferred stock would make it difficult to resume dividend payments on common stock for a long time. To avoid delays in resuming common stock dividend payments, a compromise arrangement with the holders of common stock is likely to be worked out.

A package offer is one possibility; for example, a recapitalization plan may provide for an exchange of shares. The arrearage will be wiped out by the donation of common stock with a value equal to the amount of the preferred stock arrearage; the holders of preferred stock are thus given an ownership share in the corporation. Whether this ownership share is worth anything depends on the future earnings prospects of the company. In addition, resumption of current dividends on the preferred may be promised.

The advantage to the company of substituting common stock for dividends in arrears is that it can start again with a clean balance sheet. If earnings recover, dividends can be paid to the holders of common stock without making up arrearages to the holders of preferred stock. The original common stockholders, of course, will have given up a portion of their ownership of the corporation.

Convertibility

A significant percentage of the preferred stock that has been issued in recent years is convertible into common stock. For example, one share of a particular preferred stock could be convertible into 2.5 shares of the firm's common stock at the option of the preferred shareholder. The nature of convertibility is discussed in Chapter 20.

Other Infrequent Provisions

Some of the other provisions occasionally encountered among preferred stocks include the following:

Voting rights. Sometimes a preferred stock is given the right to vote for directors. When this feature is present, it generally permits the preferred to elect a *minority* of the board, say three out of nine directors. The voting privilege becomes operative only if the company has not paid the preferred dividend for a specified period, for example, 6, 8, or 10 quarters.

Participating. A rare type of preferred stock is one that participates with the common stock in sharing the firm's earnings. The following factors generally relate to participating preferred stocks: (1) the stated preferred dividend is paid first—for example, $5 a share; (2) next, income is allocated to common stock dividends *up to* an amount equal to the preferred dividend—in this case, $5; (3) any remaining income is shared equally between the common and preferred stockholders.

Sinking fund. Some preferred issues have a sinking fund requirement. When they do, the sinking fund ordinarily calls for the purchase and retirement of a given percentage of the preferred stock each year.

Maturity. Preferred stocks almost never have maturity dates on which they must be retired. However, if the issue has a sinking fund, this effectively creates a maturity date.

Call provision. A call provision gives the issuing corporation the right to call in the preferred stock for redemption. If it is used, the call provision generally states that the company must pay an amount greater than the par value of the preferred stock, with this additional sum being defined as the *call premium.* For example, a $100 par value preferred stock might be callable at the option of the corporation at $105 a share.

EVALUATION OF PREFERRED STOCK AS A SOURCE OF FINANCING

Appraisal from Standpoint of Issuer

Advantages. An important advantage of preferred stock from the standpoint of the issuer is that, in contrast to bonds, the obligation to make fixed interest payments is avoided. Also, a firm wishing to expand because its earning power is high may obtain higher earnings for the original owners by selling preferred stock with a limited return rather than by selling common stock.

By selling preferred stock the financial manager avoids the provision of equal participation in earnings that the sale of additional common stock would require. Preferred stock also permits a company to avoid sharing control through participation in voting. In contrast to bonds, it enables the firm to conserve mortgageable assets. Preferred stock is often sold on a lower yield than is common stock. Since preferred stock typically has no maturity and no sinking fund, it is more flexible than bonds.

Disadvantages. There are several disadvantages associated with preferred stock. Characteristically, it must be sold on a higher yield basis than that for bonds. Preferred stock dividends are not deductible as a tax expense, a characteristic which makes their cost differential very great in comparison with that of bonds. As we have seen in Chapter 10, the after-tax cost of debt is approximately half the stated coupon rate for profitable firms. The cost of preferred, on the other hand, is the full percentage amount of the preferred dividend. This fact has greatly reduced the use of preferred stocks in recent years.

Appraisal from Standpoint of Investor

In fashioning securities, the financial manager needs to consider the investor's point of view. Frequently it is asserted that preferred stocks have so many disadvantages both to the issuer and to the investor that they should never be issued. Nevertheless, preferred stock is issued in substantial amounts. In fact, between 1930 and 1950, more preferred stock was issued and sold than common stock.

From the standpoint of the investor, preferred stock provides the following advantages. (1) Preferred stocks provide reasonably steady income. (2) Preferred stockholders have a preference over common stockholders in liquidation; numerous examples can be cited where the prior-preference position of holders of preferred stock saved them from losses incurred by holders of common stock. (3) Many corporations (for example, insurance companies) like to hold preferred stocks as investments because 85 percent of the dividends received on these shares is not taxable.

There are also some disadvantages to investors. (1) Although the holders of preferred stock bear a substantial portion of ownership risk, their returns are limited. (2) Price fluctuations in preferred stock are far greater than those in bonds, yet yields on bonds are only moderately lower than those on preferred stock. (3) There is no legally enforceable right to dividends. (4) Accrued dividend arrearages are seldom settled in cash comparable to the amount of the obligation that has been incurred.

Recent Trends

Because of the nondeductibility of preferred stock dividends as a tax expense, many companies have retired their preferred stock. Often debentures or subordinated debentures will be offered to preferred stockholders in exchange. The interest on the debentures is deductible as a tax expense, while preferred stock dividends are not deductible.

When the preferred stock is not callable, the company must offer terms of exchange that are sufficiently attractive to induce the preferred stockholders to agree to the exchange. Characteristically, bonds or other securities in an amount somewhat above the recent value of the preferred stock will be issued in exchange. Sometimes bonds equal in market value to the preferred stock will be issued, along with additional cash or common stock to provide an extra inducement to the preferred stockholders. Sometimes the offer will be bonds equal to only a portion of the current market value of the preferred with an additional amount, represented by cash or common stock, that will bring the total amount offered to the preferred stockholders to something over its market value as of a recent date.

U. S. Steel's replacement of its 7 percent preferred stock in 1965 illustrates one of the above exchange patterns. U. S. Steel proposed that its 7 percent preferred stock be changed into 4⅝ percent 30-year bonds at a rate of $175 principal amount of bonds for each preferred share. On August 17, 1965, when the plan was announced, the preferred stock was selling at $150. By September 29, 1965, the preferred stock was selling for $170. U. S. Steel announced also that the conversion would increase earnings available to common stock by $10 million yearly, or 18 cents a share at 1965 federal income tax rates; this was sufficient inducement to persuade the company to give the preferred stockholders the added $20 a share.

Tax considerations have reduced the use of preferred stock. But a countertrend has been the use of convertible preferred stock in mergers.[1] The reasoning here also involves taxes. The owners of the acquired firm frequently are willing to sell out because they are seeking to get away from the worries associated with ownership and management. Consequently, they can be more easily induced to sell out if they are offered a fixed income security. But if bonds (or cash) are offered for the shares of the acquired firm, the selling stockholders must pay a capital gains tax on any

---

[1] Convertibles are discussed in detail in Chapter 20 and financial aspects of mergers in Chapter 21.

proceeds received in excess of their cost basis. Frequently, this would involve a heavy capital gains tax liability. If the exchange is convertible preferred stock of the acquiring company for common stock of the acquired firm, the exchange can qualify for exemption on the capital gains liability. In this manner the stockholders of the acquired firm can receive a fixed income security, avoid an immediate capital gains liability, and receive additional benefits from the conversion feature if the price of the acquiring firm's common stock rises.

The use of convertible preferreds has been most noticeable among merger-minded conglomerate corporations. These conglomerates are frequently growth companies with low dividend payout policies, and they frequently buy out firms that have been paying substantial dividends. If the merger was accomplished by an exchange of stock, the stockholders of the acquired company would suffer a reduction in their dividend receipts. The use of a convertible preferred can avoid this dividend dilution and thus enhance the chances that the acquired firm's stockholders will approve the merger.

DECISION MAKING ON USE OF PREFERRED STOCK

The circumstances favoring the use of preferred stock can now be distilled from the foregoing analysis. As a hybrid security type, the use of preferred stock is favored by conditions that fall between those favoring the use of common stock and those favoring the use of debt.

When a firm's profit margin is high enough to more than cover preferred stock dividends, it will be advantageous to employ leverage. However, if the firm's sales and profits are subject to considerable fluctuations, the use of debt with fixed interest charges may be considered unduly risky. Preferred stock may offer a happy compromise. The use of preferred stock will be strongly favored if the firm already has a debt ratio that is heavy relative to the reference level maximum for the line of business.

Relative costs of alternative sources of financing are always important considerations. When the market prices of common stocks are relatively low, the costs of common stock financing are relatively high; this has been shown in Chapter 9. The costs of preferred stock financing follow interest rate levels more than common stock prices; in other words, when interest rates are low, the cost of preferred stock is also likely to be low. When the costs of income instruments such as preferred stock are low and the costs of variable value securities such as common stock are high, the use of preferred stock is favored.

Preferred stock may also be the desired form of financing when the use of debt would involve excessive risk or the issuance of common stock would result in problems of control for the dominant ownership group in the company.

SUMMARY

The characteristics of preferred stock vary with the requirements of the situation under which it is issued. However, certain patterns tend to remain. Preferred stocks usually have priority over common stocks with respect to earnings and claims on assets in liquidation. Preferred stocks are usually cumulative; they have no maturity but are sometimes callable. They are typically nonparticipating and have only contingent voting rights.

The advantages to the issuer are limited dividends and no maturity. These advantages may outweigh the disadvantages of higher cost and the nondeductibility of the dividends as an expense for tax purposes. But their acceptance by investors is the final test of whether they can be sold on favorable terms.

Companies sell preferred stock when they seek the advantages of trading on the equity but fear the dangers of the fixed charges on debt in the face of potential fluctuations in income. If debt ratios are already high or if the costs of common stock financing are relatively high, the advantages of preferred stock will be reinforced.

The use of preferred stock has declined significantly since the advent of the corporate income tax because preferred dividends are not deductible for income tax purposes while bond interest payments are deductible. However, in recent years there has been a strong shift back to a new kind of preferred stock—convertible preferred, used primarily in connection with mergers. If cash or bonds are given to the stockholders of the acquired company, they are required to pay capital gains taxes on any gains that might have been realized. However, if convertible preferred stock is given to the selling stockholders, this constitutes a tax-free exchange of securities. The selling stockholders can obtain a fixed income security and at the same time postpone the payment of capital gains taxes.

QUESTIONS

16–1 If preferred stock dividends are passed for several years, the preferred stockholders are frequently given the right to elect several members of the board of directors. In the case of bonds that are in default on interest payments, this procedure is not followed. Why does this difference exist?

16–2 Preferred stocks are found in almost all industries, but one industry is the really dominant issuer of preferred shares. What is this industry, and why are firms in it so disposed to use preferred stock?

16–3 From the point of view of the issuing firm, what are some of the advantages of preferred stock?

16–4 If the corporate income tax was abolished, would this raise or lower the amount of new preferred stock issued?

16–5   Investors buying securities have some expected or required rate of return in mind. Which would you expect to be higher, the required rate of return (before taxes) on preferred stocks or on common stocks (a) for individual investors and (b) for corporate investors (for example, insurance companies)?

16–6   Do you think the before-tax required rate of return is higher or lower on very high-grade preferred stocks or on bonds (a) for individual investors and (b) for corporate investors?

16–7   Discuss the pros and cons of a preferred stock sinking fund from the point of view (a) of the issuing corporation and (b) of a preferred stockholder.

16–8   For purposes of measuring a firm's leverage, should preferred stock be classified as debt or as equity? Does it matter if the classification is being made (a) by the firm itself, (b) by creditors, or (c) by equity investors?

PROBLEMS

16–1   In late 1968 the Brockton Edison Company of Massachusetts sought to raise $4 million to refinance present preferred stock issues at a lower rate. The company is a member of the Eastern Utilities Associates Holding Company system. The company could sell additional debt at 5 percent, preferred stock at 4.64 percent, or common stock at $80 a share. How should the company raise the money? Relevant financial information is provided below.

This question should not be answered in terms of precise cost of capital calculations. Rather, a more qualitative and subjective analysis is appropriate. The only calculations necessary are a few simple ratios. Careful interpretation of these ratios is necessary, however, to understand and discuss the often complex, subjective judgment issues involved.

Public Utilities Financial Ratios

Current ratio (times)	1.00
Interest earned (before taxes) (times)	4.0
Sales to total assets (times)	0.3
Average collection period (days)	28.0
Current debt/total assets (percent)	5–10
Long-term debt/total assets (percent)	45–50
Preferred/total assets (percent)	10–15
Common equity/total assets (percent)	30–35
Earnings before interest and taxes to total assets (percent)	5.9
Profits to common equity (percent)	10.1
Expected growth in earnings and dividends (percent)	4.625

BROCKTON EDISON COMPANY
BALANCE SHEET
July 31, 1968
(in millions of dollars)

Cash	$ 0.5	Current liabilities	$ 2.0
Receivables	1.0	Long-term debt, 3.5%	18.0
Material and supplies	0.8	Preferred stock, 5.60%	4.0
Total current	2.3	Common stock, $25 par value	7.5
		Paid-in surplus	4.4
Net property	37.7	Earned surplus	4.1
Total assets	$40.0	Total claims	$40.0

BROCKTON EDISON COMPANY
INCOME STATEMENT
For Year Ended July 31, 1968
(in millions of dollars)

Operating revenues	$12.6
Operating expenses (incl. taxes)	10.5
Net operating income	2.1
Interest deductions	0.6
Net income	1.5
Earnings per share	$ 5.00
Dividends per share	$ 3.50

16–2 Genesco, Inc., is a manufacturer of apparel and footwear. Although principally a manufacturer of shoes, it has in recent years acquired a number of companies that make men's and women's apparel.

The company seeks to retire its 4.5 percent unsecured notes due in 1969 and its outstanding 5 percent notes due in 1970. A substantial amount of funds ($10 million) from new financing is earmarked for additions to working capital and retirement of short-term bank notes as they mature. Genesco can issue new debt at 5½ percent, a preferred stock issue at 4.5 percent, or common stock at $30 a share. Total new financing is expected to be $20 million. How should the company raise the money? Relevant financial data are given below; some have been slightly changed.

This question should not be answered in terms of precise cost of capital calculations. Rather, a more qualitative and subjective analysis is appropriate. The only calculations necessary are a few simple ratios. Careful interpretation of these ratios is necessary, however, to understand and discuss the often complex, subjective judgment issues involved.

Footwear Industry Financial Ratios

Current ratio (times)	2.2
Sales to total assets (times)	2.3
Sales to inventory (times)	6.1
Average collection period (days)	46.0
Current debt/total assets (percent)	30.0
Long-term debt/total assets (percent)	10.0
Preferred/total assets (percent)	0–10
Common equity/total assets (percent)	50–60
Profits to sales (percent)	2.3
Net profits to total assets (percent)	5.0
Profits to common equity (percent)	9.0
Expected growth in earnings and dividends (percent)	3.33

GENESCO, INC.
CONSOLIDATED BALANCE SHEET
July 31, 1968
(in millions of dollars)

Current assets	$150	Current liabilities	$ 40
Plant and equipment (net)	28	Long-term debt	60
Other assets	22	Preferred stock $4.50	10
		Common stock $1 par value	3
		Paid-in capital	42
		Retained earnings	45
Total assets	$200	Total claims	$200

GENESCO, INC.
CONSOLIDATED INCOME STATEMENT
For Year Ended July 31, 1968
(in millions of dollars)

Net sales and other income	$400
Cost of sales and expenses	381
Earnings before interest and taxes	19
Taxes and interest ($3)	10
Net income	9
Earnings per share	3
Dividends	2

Chapter 17

Long-Term Debt

DEBT VERSUS EQUITY FINANCING

In Part IV the major factors underlying the decision to trade on the equity (utilize debt) were set out. It was noted that the use of debt magnifies gains and losses. Up to a point that varies with the characteristics of the firm's line of activity, additional debt is advantageous. Beyond that point, more debt is hazardous or excessively expensive, or both.

Since every firm has the option of using some debt, it is useful to examine the various forms and characteristics of debt so that the financial manager may employ it most effectively. Part V has already analyzed the use of some forms of debt financing. The present chapter deals with types and forms of long-term debt securities.

INSTRUMENTS OF LONG-TERM DEBT FINANCING

For an understanding of long-term forms of financing, some familiarity with technical terminology is necessary. However, the presentation will be limited to only that descriptive material necessary to analyze important problems and to formulate financial policies. The discussion of long-term debt therefore begins with an explanation of several important instruments.

Seven Key Concepts

Bond. Most people have had some experience with short-term promissory notes. A *bond* is a long-term promissory note.

Mortgage. A *mortgage* represents a pledge of designated property for a loan. Under a mortgage bond the corporation pledges certain real assets as security for the bond. A *mortgage bond* is therefore secured by real property.[1] The pledge is a condition of the loan.

Debenture. A *debenture* is long-term debt unsecured in the sense that it lacks a pledge of any specific property. However, like other general creditor claims, it is secured by any property not otherwise pledged.

Funded debt. *Funded debt* is simply long-term debt. When a firm is said to be planning to "fund" its floating debt, it will replace short-term securities by long-term securities. Funding does not imply placing money with a trustee or other repository; it is simply part of the jargon of finance and means long term.

Indenture. Since a bond is a long-term promissory note, a long-term relation between borrower and lender is established in a document called an *indenture.* When it is a matter of an ordinary 60- or 90-day promissory note, few new developments are likely to occur in the life or affairs of the borrower to endanger repayment. The lender looks closely at the borrower's current position because current assets are the main source of repayment. But a bond is a long-time contractual relation between the issuer of the bond and the bondholders, and over such an extended period the bondholder has cause to worry that the firm's position can change materially.

In the ordinary common stock or preferred stock certificate or agreement, the details of the contractual relation can be summarized in a few paragraphs. The bond indenture, however, may be a document of several hundred pages covering a large number of factors that will be important to the contractual parties. It discusses the form of the bond and the instrument. It provides a complete description of property pledged. It specifies the authorized amount of the bond issue. It contains protective clauses or *covenants,* which are detailed and which usually include limits on indebtedness, restrictions on dividends, and a sinking fund provision. Generally a minimum current ratio requirement during the bond indebtedness, as well as provisions for redemption or call privileges, are also added.

Trustee. Not only is a bond of long duration, but the issue is also likely to be of substantial size. Before the rise of the large aggregations of savings through insurance companies or pension funds, no single buyer was able to buy an issue of such size. Bonds were therefore issued in denominations of $1,000 each and were sold to a large number of purchasers. To

---

[1] There are also *chattel mortgages,* which are secured by personal property, but these are generally intermediate-term instruments.

facilitate communication between the issuer and the numerous bond-holders, another device was instituted—the *trustee,* who is the representative of the bondholders. He is presumed to act at all times for their protection and on their behalf.

Any legal person, including a corporation, is considered competent to act as a trustee. Typically, however, the duties of the trustee are handled by a department of a commercial bank.

The trustee has three main responsibilities. (1) The trustee certifies the issue of bonds. This duty involves making certain that all the legal requirements for drawing up the bond contract and the indenture have been carried out. (2) The trustee polices the behavior of the corporation in its performance of the responsibilities set forth in the indenture provision. (3) The trustee is responsible for taking appropriate action on behalf of the bondholders if the corporation defaults on payment of interest or principal.

It is said that in a large number of the corporate bond defaults in the early 1930s, trustees did not act in the best interests of the bondholders. The trustees did not conserve the assets of the corporation effectively. Often they did not take early action, so that corporation executives continued their salaries and disposed of assets under conditions favorable to themselves but detrimental to the bondholders. Assets pledged as security for the bonds were sold; specific security was, thus, no longer available. The result in many instances was that holders of mortgage bonds found themselves more in the position of general creditors than in that of secured bondholders.

As a consequence of such practices, the Trust Indenture Act of 1939 was passed in order to give more protection to bondholders. It provides that trustees must be given sufficient power to act on behalf of bondholders. The indenture must fully disclose rights and responsibilities and must not be deceptive. There is provision for changes in the indenture at the option of the bondholders. A specific requirement of prompt, protective action on the part of the trustees for bondholders on default is made. Provision is made for making certain that an arm's-length relation exists between the issuing corporation and the trustee. The obligor may not own more than 10 percent of the common stock of the trustee, nor the trustee more than 5 percent of the voting stock of the obligor. Finally, the corporation must make periodic reports to trustees to enable them to carry out their protective responsibilities.

Sinking Fund. A *sinking fund* is a provision that facilitates the orderly retirement of a bond issue (or, in some cases, an issue of preferred stock). Typically, the sinking fund provision requires the firm to buy and retire a portion of the bond issue each year. Sometimes the stipulated sinking fund payment is tied to sales or earnings of the current year, but usually it is a mandatory fixed amount. If it is mandatory, a failure to meet the sinking fund payment causes the bond issue to be thrown into default and possibly leads the company into bankruptcy. Obviously, then, a sinking fund can constitute a dangerous cash drain to the firm.

In most cases the firm is given the right to handle the sinking fund in either of two ways: (1) it may call a certain percentage of the bonds at a stipulated price each year—for example, 2 percent of the original amount at a price of $1,050—with the actual bonds, which are numbered serially, being determined by a lottery; or (2) it may spend the funds provided by the sinking fund payment to buy the bonds on the open market. The firm will do whichever results in the greatest reduction of outstanding bonds for a given expenditure. Therefore, if interest rates have risen (and the price of the bonds has fallen), the firm will choose the open market alternative. On the other hand, if interest rates have fallen and bond prices have risen, the company will elect to use the option of calling bonds.

It must be recognized that the call provision of the sinking fund may at times work to the detriment of bondholders. If, for example, the bond carries a 7 percent interest rate, and if yields on similar securities are 4 percent, the bond will sell for well above par. A sinking fund call at par would thus greatly disadvantage some bondholders. This would apply to bonds *subsequent* to their initial issue, however, and, on balance, securities that provide for a sinking fund and continuing redemption are likely to be offered initially on a lower yield basis than are securities without such a fund. Since sinking funds provide additional protection to investors, bonds with this feature are likely to sell initially at higher prices; hence, they have a lower cost of capital to the issuer.

SECURED LONG-TERM DEBT

Secured long-term debt may be classified according to (1) the priority of claims, (2) the right to issue additional securities, and (3) the scope of the lien.

Priority of Claims

1. A senior mortgage is a mortgage with prior claims on assets and earnings. Senior railroad mortgages have been called the mortgages next to the rail, implying that they have the first claim on the land and assets of the railroad corporations.

2. A junior mortgage is a subordinate lien, such as a second or a third mortgage. It is a lien or claim junior to others.

Right to Issue Additional Securities

Mortgage bonds may also be classified with respect to the right to issue additional obligations pledging already encumbered property.

In the case of a *closed-end mortgage* a company may not sell additional bonds, beyond those already issued, secured by the property specified in the mortgage. For example, assume that a corporation with plant and land worth $5 million has a $2 million mortgage on these properties. If the mortgage is closed end, no more bonds having first liens on this property may be issued. Thus a closed-end mortgage provides greater security to the bond buyer. The ratio of the amount of the senior bonds to the value of the property will not be increased by subsequent issues.

If the bond indenture is silent on this point, it is called an *open-end mortgage.* Its nature may be illustrated by the facts of the example cited. Against property worth $5 million, bonds of $2 million are sold. If an additional first mortgage bond of $1 million is subsequently sold, the property has been pledged for a total of $3 million bonds. If, on liquidation, the property sold for $2 million, the original bondholders would receive 67 cents on the dollar. If the mortgage had been closed end, they would have been fully paid.

Most characteristic is the *limited open-end mortgage.* Its nature may be indicated by continuing the example. A first mortgage bond issue of $2 million is sold secured by the property worth $5 million. The indenture provides that an additional $1 million worth of bonds—or an additional amount of bonds up to 60 percent of the original cost of the property—may be sold. Thus, the mortgage is open only up to a certain point.

These are some ways in which the limited feature of an open-end mortgage may be expressed. The limited open-end mortgage is flexible in that it provides for the issuance of additional securities. At the same time, it limits this right; thus the original bondholder is protected.

Scope of the Lien

Bonds may also be classified with respect to the scope of their lien. When it is a matter of a *specific lien,* the security for a first mortgage or a second mortgage is a specifically designated property. A lien is granted on certain described property. On the other hand, a *blanket mortgage* pledges all real property currently owned by the company. The definition of real property is land and those things affixed thereto. Hence a blanket mortgage would not be a mortgage on cash, accounts receivables, or inventories, but only on real property because these items are regarded as personal property. A blanket mortgage gives more protection to the bondholder than does a specific mortgage because it provides a claim on all real property owned by the company.

UNSECURED BONDS

Debentures

The debenture is an unsecured bond, and as such provides no lien on specific property as security for the obligation. Debenture holders are therefore general creditors whose claim is protected by property not otherwise pledged. The advantage of debentures from the standpoint of the issuer is that he leaves his property unencumbered for subsequent financing. However, in practice the use of debentures depends on the nature of the firm's assets and its general credit strength.

If the credit positions of the lending companies in an industry are exceptionally strong, these firms can issue debentures—they simply do not need specific security. On the other hand, the credit position of a company may be so weak that it has no alternative to the use of debentures—all its property may already be encumbered. American Telephone & Telegraph's vast financing program since the end of World War II has been mainly through debentures, both convertible and straight debentures. AT&T is such a strong institution that it does not have to provide security for its debt issues.

Debentures are also often issued by companies in industries where it would not be practical to provide a lien through a mortgage on fixed assets. An example of such an industry would be the large mail order houses, which characteristically do not have large fixed assets in relation to their total assets. The bulk of their assets is in the form of inventory, which is not satisfactory security for a mortgage lien.

Subordinated Debentures

The term *subordinate* means below, or inferior. Thus, subordinated debt has claims on assets after unsubordinated debt in the event of liquidation. Debentures may be subordinated to designated notes payable—usually bank loans—or to any or all other debt. In the event of liquidation or reorganization the debentures cannot be paid until senior debt *as named in the indenture* has been paid. Senior debt typically does not include trade accounts payable. How the subordination provision strengthens the position of senior-debt holders is shown in Table 17–1.

Where $200 is available for distribution, the subordinated debt has a claim of one half of $100, or $50. However, this claim is subordinated to the bank debt (senior debt) and is added to the $100 claim of the bank. As a consequence, 75 percent of the bank's original claim is satisfied.

Where $300 is available for distribution, the $75 allocated to the subordinated debt is divided into two parts: $50 goes to the bank and the other $25 remains for the subordinated-debt holders. In this situation, the senior bank debt holders are fully paid off, 75 percent of other debt is paid, and the subordinated debt receives only 25 percent of its claim.

Subordination is frequently required. Alert credit managers of firms supplying trade credit or commercial bank loan officers typically will insist upon subordination, particularly where debt is owed to the principal stockholders or officers of a company.

Table 17-1 ILLUSTRATION OF LIQUIDATING PAYMENTS TO SENIOR DEBT, OTHER DEBT, AND SUBORDINATED DEBT

Financial Structure	(1) Book Value	(2) Percent of Total Debt	(3) Initial Allocation	(4) Actual Payment	(5) Percent of Original Claim Satisfied
I. $200 available for claims on liquidation					
Bank debt	$200	50	$100	$150	75
Other debt	100	25	50	50	50
Subordinated debt	100	25	50	0	0
Total debt	400	100	$200	$200	
Net worth	300				0
Total	$700				
II. $300 available for claims on liquidation					
Bank debt	$200	50	$150	$200	100
Other debt	100	25	75	75	75
Subordinated debt	100	25	75	25	25
Total debt	400	100	$300	$300	
Net worth	300				0
Total	$700				

Steps: 1. Express each type of debt as a percentage of total debt (column 2).
2. Multiply the debt percentages (column 2) by the amount available, obtaining the initial allocations shown in column 3.
3. The subordinated debt is subordinate to bank debt. Therefore, the initial allocation to subordinate debt is added to the bank debt allocation until it has been exhausted or until the bank debt is finally paid off. This is given in column 4.

Preferred stock, in comparison to subordinated debt, suffers from the disadvantage that preferred stock dividends are not deductible as an expense for tax purposes. The interest on subordinated debentures is an expense for tax purposes. Some people have referred to subordinated debentures as being much like a special kind of preferred stock, the dividends of which are deductible as an expense for tax purposes. Subordinated debt has therefore become an increasingly important source of corporate capital.

The reasons for the use of subordinated debentures are clear. They offer a considerable tax advantage over preferred stock, and yet they do not restrict the ability of the borrower to obtain senior debt as would be the case if all debt sources were on an equal basis.

Subordinated debentures are further stimulated by periods of tight money when commercial banks may require a greater equity base for short-term financing. Subordinated debentures provide a greater equity cushion for loans from commercial banks or other forms of senior debt. The use of subordinated debentures also illustrates the development of hybrid securities which emerge to meet changing situations that develop in the capital market.

The amount of subordinated debt that may be employed is limited, as is the amount of any form of debt. The rule of thumb employed by investment bankers in connection with industrial issues of subordinated debentures appears to be about $2 of net worth for each $1 of subordinated debt.

Income Bonds

Income bonds typically arise from corporate reorganizations. These bonds pay interest only if income is actually earned by the company because the company, having gone through reorganization, has been in difficult financial circumstances. Interest is not a fixed charge; the principal, however, must be paid when due.

Income bonds are like preferred stock in that management is not required to pay interest if it is not earned. However, they differ from preferred stock in that if interest has been earned, management is usually required to pay it. In recent years, income bonds have been increasingly used as a source of ordinary financing.[2]

The main characteristic and distinct advantage of the income bond is that interest is payable only if the company achieves some earnings. Since earnings calculations are subject to differing interpretations, the indenture of the income bond carefully defines income and expenses. If it did not do so, long-drawn-out litigation might result.

---

[2] See S. M. Robbins, "A Bigger Role for Income Bonds," *Harvard Business Review,* 33 (November–December 1955), pp. 100–114.

Some income bonds are cumulative for a limited number of years; others are noncumulative for the first three to five years, after which time they become cumulative. Some issues are fully cumulative.

Income bonds usually contain sinking fund provisions to provide for their retirement. The payments to the sinking funds range between ½ and 1 percent of the face amount of the original issue. Because the sinking fund payments are typically dependent on earnings, a fixed-cash drain on the company is avoided.

Sometimes income bonds are convertible. There are sound reasons for their being convertible if they arise out of a reorganization. Creditors who receive income bonds in exchange for defaulted obligations have a less desirable position than they had before. Since they have received something based on an adverse and problematical forecast of the future of the company, it is appropriate that if the company should prosper, income bondholders should be entitled to participate. When income bonds are issued in situations other than reorganization, the convertibility feature is a "sweetener" likely to make the issue more attractive to prospective bond buyers.

Typically, income bonds do not have voting rights when they are issued. Sometimes bondholders are given the right to elect one, two, or some specified number of directors if interest is not paid for a certain number of years.

Income bonds have been used instead of preferred stock in situations other than reorganization. Armour & Company has made repeated use of such bonds.[3] In 1943, Armour used subordinated income bonds to substitute for a preferred stock issue. At the close of 1954, Armour replaced convertible preferred stock with dividend arrearages by 5 percent cumulative income bonds subordinated to other debt with a warrant to buy common stock. The replacement of preferred stock by income bonds resulted in a substantial tax saving for the company.

CHARACTERISTICS OF LONG-TERM DEBT

From Viewpoint of Holder

A critical framework for analyzing the position of any security holder in a corporation includes aspects of risk, control, and income.

Risk. Debt is favorable to the holder because it gives him priority both in earnings and in liquidation. Debt also has a definite maturity and is protected by the covenants of the indenture.

---

[3] Robbins, p. 106.

Income.   The bondholder has a fixed return; except in the case of income bonds, interest payments are not contingent on the level of earnings of the company. On the other hand, debt does not participate in any superior earnings of the company, and gains are limited in magnitude. Frequently, long-term debt is callable. If bonds are called, the investor receives funds which must be reinvested to be kept active.

Control.   The bondholder typically does not have the right to vote. Yet there are periods when a substantial portion of bonds sold are convertible bonds. If bonds are convertible into common stock, under certain conditions the bondholder may obtain the position of an equity holder rather than a debt holder.

An over-all appraisal of the characteristics of long-term debt would therefore show that it is strong from the standpoint of risk, it has limited advantages with regard to income, and it is weak with respect to control.

From Viewpoint of Issuer

Advantages.   (1) The cost of debt is definitely limited. Bondholders do not participate in superior profits if earned.

(2) Not only is the cost limited, but it is typically lower than the cost of common or preferred stock.

(3) The owners of the corporation do not share control of the corporation when debt financing is used.

(4) The interest payment on debt is deductible as a tax expense.

(5) Flexibility in the financial structure of the corporation may be achieved by inserting a call provision in the indenture of the debt.

Disadvantages.   (1) Debt is a fixed charge; there is greater risk if the earnings of the company fluctuate, because the corporation may be unable to meet these fixed charges.

(2) As was seen in Chapter 9, higher risk brings higher capitalization rates on equity earnings. Thus, even though leverage is favorable and raises earnings per share, the higher capitalization rates attributable to leverage may drive the common stock value down.

(3) Debt usually has a definite maturity date. Because of the fixed maturity date, the financial officers must make provision for repayment of the debt.

(4) Since long-term debt is typically a commitment for a long period, such debt involves risk; the expectations and plans on which the debt was issued may change. The debt may prove to be a burden, or it may prove to have been advantageous. For example, if income, employment, and the price level fall greatly, the assumption of a large amount of debt may prove to have been unwise financial policy. The railroads are always given as an

example in this regard. They were able to meet their ordinary operating expenses during the 1930s but were unable to meet the heavy financial charges they had undertaken earlier, when the prospects for the railroads looked more favorable than they turned out to be.

(5) In a long-term contractual relation, the indenture provisions are likely to be much more stringent than they are in a short-term credit agreement. Hence the firm may be subject to much more disturbing and crippling restrictions in the indenture of a long-term debt arrangement than would be the case if it had borrowed on a short-term basis or had issued common stock.

(6) There is a limit on the extent to which funds can be raised through long-term debt. Some of the generally accepted standards of financial policy dictate that the debt ratio shall not exceed certain limits. These standards of financial prudence set limits or controls on the extent to which funds may be raised through long-term debt.

DECISIONS ON USE OF LONG-TERM DEBT

The foregoing discussion of the various forms of debt illustrates an important principle in business finance: Any form of financing arrangement is likely to be developed as the economic environment and the needs of firms require. The only limitations are the imaginations of the issuers and investment bankers and the needs of investors—and these permit a wide degree of variation in securities forms.

The preceding review of the different kinds of equity and debt forms is purely *illustrative* of some of the readily explained types that have emerged. The future will doubtlessly see many new forms of hybrid securities as the economic environment changes, as the needs of issuers are altered, and as investors are educated to the benefits that may be derived from some of the new provisions of securities.

The conditions favoring the use of long-term debt when a number of alternative methods of long-term financing are under consideration include the following:

1. Sales and earnings are relatively stable or a substantial increase in sales and earnings is expected in the future, providing substantial benefit to the use of leverage.
2. A substantial rise in the price level is expected in the future, making it advantageous for the firm to incur debt which can be repaid with cheaper dollars.
3. The existing debt ratio is relatively low for the line of business.

4. Management thinks the price of the common stock in relation to that of bonds is temporarily depressed.
5. Sale of common stock would involve problems of maintaining the existing control pattern in the company.

REFUNDING A BOND ISSUE[4]

Suppose a company sells bonds at a time when interest rates are relatively high. Provided the issue is callable, as most bond issues are, the company can sell a new issue of low interest rate bonds and use the proceeds to retire the high interest rate issue. This is called a *refunding operation.*

The decision to refund a bond issue is analyzed in much the same manner as a capital budgeting expenditure. The costs of refunding—the "investment outlay"—are (1) the call premium paid for the privilege of calling the old issue and (2) the flotation costs involved in selling the new issue. The annual receipts, in the capital budgeting sense, are the interest payments that are saved each year; for example, if interest expense on the old issue is $1 million while that on the new issue is $700,000, the $300,000 saving constitutes the annual receipts.

In analyzing the advantages of refunding, the net present value method is the recommended procedure—discount the future interest savings back to the present and compare the discounted value with the cash outlays associated with the refunding. *In the discounting process, the interest rate on the new debt, not the average cost of capital, should be used as the discount factor.* The reason for this is that there is no risk to the savings—their value is known with complete certainty, which is quite unlike most capital budgeting decisions. Because no risk is involved in the refunding, a low discount rate should be used. The following example illustrates the calculations needed in a refunding operation decision.

The Culver City Company has outstanding a $60 million 20-year bond issue, carrying a 6½ percent interest rate. The bond indenture carries a call provision making it possible for the company to retire the bonds by calling them in at a 6 percent premium. Investment bankers have assured the company that it could sell an additional $60 to $70 million worth of 20-year bonds at an interest rate of 5 percent. Predictions are that interest rates are unlikely to fall below 5 percent. Flotation costs of the new issue will amount to $2,650,000. Should the company refund the $60 million worth of bonds?

---

[4] For an excellent discussion of refunding, see O. D. Bowlin, "The Refunding Decision," *Journal of Finance,* March 1966, pp. 55–68.

Step 1:   What is the investment outlay required to refund the issue?
    a) Call premium: 0.06 × $60,000,000 = $3,600,000
    b) Flotation costs of new issue: $2,650,000
    c) Total costs: $6,250,000
Step 2:   What are the annual savings?
    a) Old bonds: $60,000,000 × 0.065 = $3,900,000
    b) New bonds: $60,000,000 × 0.050 =   3,000,000
    c) Savings   = $ 900,000
Step 3:   What is the present value of the savings?
    a) 20-year annuity factor at 5 percent: 12.462
    b) P.V. of $900,000 a year for 20 years: 12.462 × $900,000 =
       $11,215,800

Conclusion: Since the present value of the receipts ($11,215,800) exceeds the required investment ($6,250,000), the issue should be refunded.

Two other points should be made. First, since the $900,000 savings is an absolutely riskless investment, its present value is found by discounting at the firm's most riskless rate—its cost of debt. Second, since the refunding operation is advantageous to the firm, it must be disadvantageous to bondholders—they must give up their 6½ percent bond and reinvest in one yielding 5 percent. This points out the danger of the call provisions to bondholders and explains why, at any given time, bonds without a call provision command higher prices than callable bonds.[5]

SUMMARY

A *bond* is a long-term promissory note. A *mortgage bond* is secured by real property. An *indenture* is an agreement between the firm issuing a bond and the numerous bondholders, represented by a *trustee*.

Secured long-term debt differs with respect to (1) the priority of claims, (2) the right to issue additional securities, and (3) the scope of the lien provided. These characteristics determine the amount of protection provided to the bondholder by the terms of the security. Giving the investor more security will induce him to accept a lower yield but will restrict the future freedom of action of the issuing firm.

The main forms of unsecured bonds are (1) *debentures,* (2) *subordinated debentures,* and (3) *income bonds.* Holders of debentures are unsecured general creditors. Subordinated debentures are junior in claim to bank loans. Income bonds are similar to preferred stock in that interest is paid only when earned.

The characteristics of long-term debt determine the circumstances under which it will be used when alternative forms of financing are under analysis. The

[5] Cf. F. C. Jen and J. E. Wert, "The Effects of Call Risk on Corporate Bond Yields," *Journal of Finance,* December 1967; and G. Pye, "The Value of Call Deferment on a Bond: Some Empirical Results," *Journal of Finance,* December 1967.

cost of debt is limited, but it is a fixed obligation. Bond interest is an expense deductible for tax purposes. Debt carries a maturity date and may require sinking fund payments to prepare for extinguishing the obligation. Indenture provisions are likely to include restrictions on the freedom of action of the management of the firm.

The nature of long-term debt encourages its use under the following circumstances:

1. Sales and earnings are relatively stable.
2. Profit margins are adequate to make trading on the equity advantageous.
3. A rise in profits or the general price level is expected.
4. The existing debt ratio is relatively low.
5. Common stock price/earnings ratios are low in relation to the levels of interest rates.
6. Control considerations are important.
7. Cash flow requirements under the bond agreement are not burdensome.
8. Restrictions of the bond indenture are not onerous.

Although seven of the eight factors may favor debt, the eighth can swing the decision to the use of equity capital. The list of factors is, thus, simply a check list of things to consider when deciding upon bonds versus stock; the actual decision is based on a judgment about the relative importance of the several factors.

QUESTIONS

17-1 There are many types of bonds, for example, mortgage, debentures, collateral trust, and varying maturities for each type. What are some factors that determine the particular type of bond a company should use?

17-2 A sinking fund is set up in one of two ways: (1) the corporation makes annual payments to the trustee, who invests the proceeds in securities (frequently government bonds) and uses the accumulated total to retire the bond issue on maturity; (2) the trustee uses the annual payments to retire a portion of the issue each year, either calling a given percentage of the issue by a lottery and paying a specified price per bond or buying bonds on the open market, whichever is cheaper. Discuss the advantages and disadvantages of each procedure from the standpoint of both the firm and the bondholders.

17-3 Why is a financial institution such as a bank, instead of an individual, a better choice for a bond trustee?

17-4 Since a corporation often has the right to call bonds at will, do you believe individuals should be able to demand repayment at any time they so desire?

17-5 What are the relative advantages and disadvantages of issuing a long-term bond during a recession versus during a period of prosperity?

17-6 On September 24, 1965, Missouri Pacific 4¾ percent income bonds due in

2020 were selling for $770, while the company's 4¼ percent first mortgage bonds due in 2005 were selling for $945. Why would the bonds with the lower coupon sell at a higher price? (Each has a $1,000 par value.)

17–7 When a firm sells bonds, it must offer a package acceptable to potential buyers. Included in this package of terms are such features as the issue price, the coupon interest rate, the term to maturity, any sinking fund provisions, and other features. The package itself is determined through a bargaining process between the firm and the investment bankers who will handle the issue. What particular features would you, as a corporate treasurer, be especially interested in, and which would you be most willing to give ground on, under each of the following conditions:

a) You believe that the economy is near the peak of a business cycle.

b) Long-run forecasts indicate that your firm will have heavy cash inflows in relation to cash needs during the next 5 to 10 years.

c) Your current liabilities are presently low, but you anticipate raising a considerable amount of funds through short-term borrowing in the near future.

17–8 Bonds are less attractive to investors during periods of inflation because a rise in the price level will reduce the purchasing power of the fixed-interest payments and also of the principal. Discuss the advantages and disadvantages to a corporation of using a bond whose interest payments and principal would increase in direct proportion to increases in the price level (an inflation-proof bond).

PROBLEMS

17–1 The Harris Company has a $100,000 long-term bond issue outstanding. This debt has an additional 10 years to maturity and bears a coupon interest rate of 8 percent. The firm now has the opportunity to refinance the debt with 10-year bonds at a rate of 6 percent. Further declines in the interest rate are not anticipated. The bond redemption premium (call premium) on the old bond would be $5,000; issue costs on the new would be $6,000. If tax effects are ignored, should the firm refund the bonds?

17–2 In early 1966, the Raymond Instrument Corporation planned to raise an additional $100 million for financing plant additions and for working capital. Raymond manufactures precision instruments and tools.

Investment bankers state that the company could sell common stock at a market price of $25.60 a share to net $25, or it could sell sinking fund debentures to yield 4 percent. Costs of flotation would be slightly higher for common stock but not enough to influence the decision.

The balance sheet and the income statement of Raymond Instrument prior to the financing are given below.

RAYMOND INSTRUMENT CORPORATION
BALANCE SHEET
March 31, 1966
(in millions of dollars)

Current assets	$250	Accounts payable	$ 20
Investments	25	Notes payable to banks	80
Net fixed assets	125	Taxes	40
		Other current liabilities	35
		Total current liabilities	$175
		Long-term debt	100
		Common stock, $1 par	25
		Earned surplus	100
Total assets	$400	Total claims	$400

RAYMOND INSTRUMENT CORPORATION
INCOME STATEMENT
March 31, 1966
(in millions of dollars)

Sales	$700
Net income before taxes, 10%	70
Interest on debt	6
Net income subject to tax	64
Tax, 50%	32
Net income after tax	32

a) Assuming that net income before interest and taxes remains at 10 percent of sales, calculate earnings per share under both the stock financing and debt financing alternatives at sales levels of $200, $400, $600, $800, and $1,000 million.

b) Make a break-even chart for the earnings under *a*.

c) Using a price/earnings ratio of 20 times, calculate the market value per share of common stock under both the stock financing and debt financing alternatives.

d) Make a break-even chart of the market value per share of the company for *c*.

e) *If the use of debt caused the price/earnings ratio to fall to 12.5*, what would the market value per share of common stock become under the debt financing alternatives in the range of sales being considered?

f) Make a break-even chart for *e*, keeping a price/earnings ratio of 20 for equity financing.

g) Using the data and assumptions set out, which form of financing should Raymond adopt? Why? (Answer in terms of both the quantitative factors listed above and the qualitative factors discussed in the chapter.)

17–3   The Frontier Steel Company is planning a capital improvement program to provide greater efficiency and versatility in its operations. It is estimated that by mid-1967 the company will need to raise $50 million. Frontier is a leading steel producer with an excellent credit rating.

You are asked to set up a program for obtaining the necessary funds. Using the following information, indicate the best form of financing. Some of the items you should include in your analysis are profit margins, relative costs, control, cash flows, ratio analysis, and *pro forma* analysis.

Frontier's common stock is selling at $80 a share. The company could sell debt (25 year) at 4.5 percent or preferred stock at 5 percent.

Steel Industry Financial Ratios

Current ratio (times)	2.1
Sales to total assets (times)	1.8
Coverage of fixed charges	7.0
Average collection period (days)	42.0
Current debt/total assets (percent)	20–25
Long-term debt/total assets (percent)	10.0
Preferred/total assets (percent)	0–5
Net worth/total assets	65–70
Profits to sales (percent)	3.3
Profits to total assets (percent)	6.0
Profits to net worth (percent)	9.5
Expected growth rate in earnings and dividends	5.3

FRONTIER STEEL COMPANY
CONSOLIDATED BALANCE SHEET
December 31, 1966
(in millions of dollars)

Assets		
Current	$190	
Other investments	35	
Properties (net)	285	
Deferred assets	10	
Total assets		$520
Liabilities		
Current	$ 80	
Long-term debt, 4.44%	45	
Total liabilities		$125
Common stock, $10 par	80	
Capital surplus	75	
Retained income	220	
Reserves	20	
Total net worth		395
Total liabilities and net worth		$520

FRONTIER STEEL COMPANY
CONSOLIDATED INCOME STATEMENT
For Years Ended December 31, 1964, 1965, and 1966
(in millions of dollars)

	1964	1965	1966
Sales	$610	$455	$540
Other income	5	5	5
Total	615	460	545
Costs and expenses	530	400	480
Income before taxes	85	60	65
Federal income tax	43	30	32
Net income	42	30	33
Cash dividends	23	23	23
Interest on long-term debt	1.0	1.3	2.0
Depreciation	20	16	17
Shares outstanding (widely held)	7,850,000		

Chapter 18

Dividend Policy and Internal Financing

Dividend policy determines the division of earnings between payments to stockholders and retained earnings. Retained earnings are one of the most significant sources of funds for the financing of corporate growth, but dividends constitute the cash flows that accrue to equity investors. Although both growth and dividends are desirable, these two goals are in conflict—a higher dividend rate means less retained earnings and, consequently, a slower rate of growth in earnings and stock prices. One of the financial manager's most important functions is to determine the allocation of profits after taxes between dividends and retained earnings, as this decision may have a critical influence on the value of the firm. The factors that influence the allocation of earnings to dividends or retained earnings are the subject of this chapter.

IMPORTANCE OF DIVIDEND POLICY

Table 18–1 sets forth the relation between corporate internal sources of funds and total uses of funds since 1954. For the 12-year period between 1955 and 1966, the total uses of funds by corporations was $705 billion. Internal sources financed over two thirds of the total uses—depreciation accounted for 45 percent, and retained earnings some 24 percent. If depreciation charges are deducted from gross total uses, net total uses of funds

359

Table 18–1   CORPORATE INTERNAL SOURCES AS PERCENT OF TOTAL FUNDS, 1955–1966
(in billions of dollars)

Year	Total Funds	Retained Earnings	Percentage of Retained Earnings to Total Funds	Depreciation	Percentage of Depreciation to Total Sources	Total Internal Sources	Percentage of Total Internal Sources to Total Sources
(1)	(2)	(3)	(4)	(5)	(6)	(7)	(8)
1955	$51.4	$ 13.9	27.0%	$ 17.0	33.1%	$ 30.9	60.1%
1956	43.1	13.2	30.6	18.4	42.7	31.6	73.3
1957	40.0	11.8	29.5	20.3	50.8	32.1	80.3
1958	42.1	8.3	19.7	21.4	50.8	29.7	70.5
1959	54.3	12.6	23.2	22.9	42.2	35.5	65.4
1960	45.3	10.0	22.0	24.2	53.4	34.2	75.5
1961	55.0	10.2	18.5	25.4	46.2	35.6	64.7
1962	61.6	12.4	20.1	29.2	47.4	41.6	67.5
1963	65.8	13.6	20.7	30.8	46.8	44.4	67.5
1964	67.1	18.5	27.6	32.8	48.9	51.3	76.5
1965	87.3	21.7	24.8	35.1	40.2	56.8	65.1
1966	92.0	23.0	25.0	37.6	40.9	60.6	65.9
1955–1960	276.2	69.8	25.3	124.2	44.9	194.0	70.2
1961–1966	428.8	99.4	23.2	190.9	44.5	290.3	67.7
1955–1966	$705.0	$169.2	24.3%	$315.1	44.7%	$484.3	68.9%

SOURCE: *Economic Report of the President* (Washington, D. C., U. S. Government Printing Office, 1967), p. 294.

in the amount of $390 billion is obtained. Retained earnings financed 43 percent of the net total uses of corporate funds—the firms' growth—during the 12-year period.

Significance of Internal Financing

Comprehensive studies in capital formation and their financing underscore the important role of internal financing. In commenting on the progress report of a National Bureau of Economic Research project on "Long-Term Trends in Capital Formation and Financing," [1] Professor Eli Shapiro has called attention to the significance of internal financing.

Indeed, it may be stated categorically that one of the most important features of all three papers is the stress placed on internal financing of capital formation over the first half of the twentieth century. The presence of the dominance of internal financing of capital formation is hard to rationalize in the light of the disproportionate space devoted to the role of financial institutions in the so-called business or corporate finance textbooks published as recently as the late forties or early fifties.

Because of the great importance of internal financing, dividend policy, which determines the division of corporate earnings between outflows and retained earnings, must be recognized as one of the central decision areas for financial managers.

Patterns in Dividend Payouts

Studies of dividend patterns over extended periods beginning in 1870 indicate that, over all, corporations have paid in dividends two thirds of their earnings after taxes. However, this percentage has varied considerably from year to year. Table 18–2 shows that immediately following World War II dividend payout dropped to about 36 percent. This decrease was due partly to the "overstatement" of earnings because of the use of historical methods of costing during a period of rising price levels. More importantly, it was due to the rapid growth of firms and their need for funds to finance inventories and fixed assets at higher price levels.

In the period 1950–1955, dividend payouts averaged about 41 percent of earnings. Writers in the mid-fifties observed that, of corporate earnings before taxes, one half was paid to the government. Of the remainder, 40 to 45 percent was distributed to the stockholders. Thus, if a corporation earned $20 million, the corporate income tax would take $10 million, corporate dividends would be about $4 million, and retained earnings would be about $6 million.

It is interesting to note the payout pattern during the 1960s (1960–

---

[1] *Journal of Finance,* 10 (May 1955), p. 281.

Table 18–2   CORPORATE PROFITS AND DIVIDENDS, 1929–1966
(dollar amounts in billions)

Year	Corporate Profits after Tax	Dividends	Payout Percentage
1929	$ 8.6	$ 5.8	6%
1930	2.9	5.5	190
1931	−0.9	4.1	0
1932	−2.7	2.5	0
1933	0.4	2.0	500
1934	1.6	2.6	163
1935	2.6	2.8	108
1936	4.9	4.5	92
1937	5.3	4.7	89
1938	2.9	3.2	110
1939	5.6	3.8	68
1940	7.2	4.0	56
1941	10.1	4.4	44
1942	10.1	4.3	43
1943	11.1	4.4	40
1944	11.2	4.6	41
1945	9.0	4.6	51
1946	15.5	5.6	36
1947	20.2	6.3	31
1948	22.7	7.0	31
1949	18.5	7.2	39
1950	24.9	8.8	35
1951	21.6	8.6	40
1952	19.6	8.6	44
1953	20.4	8.9	44
1954	20.6	9.3	45
1955	27.0	10.5	39
1956	27.2	11.3	42
1957	26.0	11.7	45
1958	22.3	11.6	52
1959	28.5	12.6	44
1960	26.7	13.4	50
1961	27.2	13.8	51
1962	31.2	15.2	49
1963	33.1	16.5	49
1964	38.7	17.3	45
1965	44.5	19.2	43
1966	48.1	20.9	43

Year	Corporate Profits after Tax	Dividends	Payout Percentage
1929–1939	31.2	41.5	133
1940–1945	58.7	26.3	45
1945–1950	110.8	39.5	36
1950–1955	134.1	54.7	41
1955–1960	157.7	71.1	45
1960–1966	249.5	116.3	47

SOURCE: *Economic Report of the President,* (Washington, D. C.: U. S. Government Printing Office, 1967), p. 290.

1966). In the early part of the period, payouts were high, averaging about 50 percent. This was a period of relatively slack economic activity—investment opportunities were not particularly strong, and debt funds were available at low rates of interest. Without an especially pressing need for funds, and with plenty of low-cost debt money available, dividend payouts were high. In 1964, 1965, and 1966, however, investment demand was booming and debt funds were scarce and expensive. This caused firms to reduce dividend payouts and to rely more heavily on retained earnings.

Cash Flows as Determinant of Payouts

Cash flows are earnings plus depreciation and depletion charges. When dividends are related to cash flows rather than to earnings, the payout patterns show two changes. First, the payout percentages drop to lower levels. For all manufacturing corporations, the payout appears to drop from the two-thirds ratio to a one-third ratio. The ratio would be expected to drop, but it is of interest that it dropped to almost precisely the complement of the payout ratio related to earnings.

The second change is that the payout ratio appears to be more stable when dividends are related to cash flows rather than to earnings. If dividends were tied more directly to cash flows than to earnings, this would suggest that cash flows rather than earnings may be the primary determinant of dividends. However, the apparent increased stability in the dividend-to-cash-flow ratio may be an arithmetical accident instead of a cause-and-effect relation. For example, consider the following data:

Year	Earnings	Dividends	Payout Percentage	Depreciation	Cash Flows	Payout Percentage
1	20	10	50	20	40	25
2	15	10	67	20	35	29
3	10	10	100	20	30	33
4	30	10	33	20	50	20

The payout percentage based on cash flows is clearly more stable than the payout based on earnings. But this result flows from adding a constant figure to the earnings. The greater stability may simply come about because a relatively fixed amount of depreciation is added to earnings.

FACTORS INFLUENCING DIVIDEND POLICY

The economic patterns described above indicate the great significance of retained earnings in financing the growth of firms. This poses the fundamental question: What determines the extent to which a firm will pay out dividends instead of retain earnings? This question may be answered by a consideration of the factors influencing dividend policy. First, the major influences on dividend policy will be described. Second, this check list will be used to attempt to explain differences in dividend patterns observed among different industries and among firms in the same industry.

Legal Rules

The state statutes and court decisions governing dividend policy are complicated, but their essential nature may be stated briefly. The legal rules provide that dividends be paid from earnings, either from the current year's earnings or from past years' earnings as reflected in earned surplus. State laws emphasize three rules: (1) the net profits rule, (2) the capital impairment rule, and (3) the insolvency rule.

The *net profits* rule provides that dividends may be paid from past and present earnings. The *capital impairment* rule protects shareholders and creditors by forbidding the payment of dividends from capital. Paying dividends from capital would be distributing the investment in the company rather than its earnings.[2] The *insolvency* rule provides that corporations may not pay dividends while insolvent. Insolvency is here defined in the bankruptcy sense that liabilities exceed assets.

Legal aspects are significant. They provide the framework within which dividend policies can be formulated. However, within these boundaries important financial and economic factors will have a major influence on policy.

Cash Position

Profits held as retained earnings (which show up in the right-hand side of the balance sheet in the surplus or retained earnings account) may be

---

[2] It is possible, of course, to return stockholders' capital, but when this is done it must be clearly stated as such.

invested in assets required for the conduct of the business. Thus, although a firm has had a record of earnings, it may not be able to pay cash dividends because of its liquidity position. Indeed, it was seen above that a growing firm, even a very profitable one, typically has a pressing need for funds. In such a situation the firm may elect not to pay cash dividends.

Need to Repay Debt

When a firm has sold debt to finance expansion or to substitute for other forms of financing, it is faced with two alternatives: it can refund the debt at maturity by replacing it with another form of security, or it can make provision for paying off the debt. Since the retained earnings of a growing firm are likely to be tied up in operating assets, it will not be able to liquidate assets. Therefore, a debt obligation implies that the firm is planning either retention of earnings to pay off the debt or new external financing in the future.

Rate of Asset Expansion

The more rapid the rate at which the firm is growing, the greater will be its needs for financing asset expansion. A fast-growing firm will anticipate a substantial need for funds in the future. The greater the future need for funds, the more likely the firm is to retain earnings rather than to pay them out.

Profit Rate

The profit rate of a firm is a highly important variable. The profitability with which the firm employs funds will determine the relative attractiveness of paying out earnings in the form of dividends to stockholders who will use them elsewhere, compared with the productivity of their use in the present enterprise. The internal profitability rate of the firm provides a basis for comparing the productivity of retained earnings to the alternative return which could be earned elsewhere.

Stability of Earnings

If earnings are relatively stable, a firm is better able to predict what its future earnings will be. It is therefore more likely to pay out a higher percentage of its earnings in dividends than is a firm with fluctuating earnings. The latter firm is not certain that in subsequent years the hoped-for earnings will be realized, and it is more likely to retain a high proportion of earnings in order to maintain dividends if earnings should fall off in the future.

Access to the Capital Markets

A large, well-established firm with a record of profitability and some stability of earnings will have easy access to capital markets and other forms of external financing. On the other hand, the small, new, or venturesome firm has a greater amount of risk for potential investors. Its ability to raise equity funds or debt from capital markets is restricted, and it must therefore retain more earnings to finance its operations. A well-established firm is likely to have a higher dividend payout rate than is a new or small firm.

Control

Another important variable is the effect of alternative sources of financing on the control situation in the firm. Some corporations, as a matter of policy, will expand only to the extent of their internal earnings. This policy is defended on the grounds that raising funds by selling additional common stock dilutes the control of the dominant group in the company. At the same time, selling debt increases the risks of fluctuating earnings to the present owners of the company. Reliance on internal financing in order to maintain control reduces the dividend payout.

Tax Position of Stockholders

The tax position of the owners of the corporation will greatly influence the desire for dividends. For example, a corporation closely held by a few taxpayers in high income tax brackets is likely to pay out a relatively low dividend. The owners of the corporation are interested in taking their income in the form of capital gains rather than in ordinary dividends, which are subject to higher personal income tax rates. On the other hand, the stockholders in a large, widely held corporation may be interested in a high dividend payout.

At times there is a conflict of interest in large corporations between stockholders in high income tax brackets and stockholders in low income tax brackets. The former will prefer to see a low dividend payout and a high rate of earnings retention in the hope of an appreciation of the capital stock of the company. The lower income stockholder will prefer a relatively high dividend payout rate.

Corporate Tax Liabilities

In order to prevent wealthy stockholders from using the corporation as an "incorporated pocketbook" by which to avoid the high rates of personal income tax, tax regulations applicable to corporations provide for a special surtax on improperly accumulated income. This was the subject of the famous Section 102 of the Internal Revenue Code, which is now Section 531 of the 1954 law. The Revenue Act of 1954 placed the burden of proof on the Internal Revenue Service to justify penalty rates for accumulation of earnings. That is, earnings retention is justified unless the Internal Revenue Service can prove otherwise.

The ten factors outlined above influence corporations to different degrees, depending upon the particular situation. The effects of these factors result in different dividend patterns from industry to industry and from company to company. How these forces influence dividend policy will be indicated in the following sections.

STABILITY OF DIVIDEND POLICY

A fundamental relation observed in dividend policy is the widespread tendency of corporations to pursue a relatively stable dividend policy. Profits of firms fluctuate considerably with changes in the level of business activity. Figure 18–1 shows that dividends are more stable.

As Professor John Lintner has observed, corporations seek to maintain

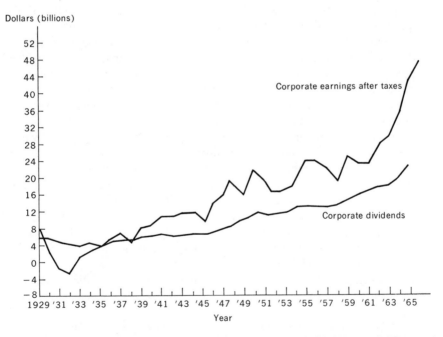

Figure 18-1   Corporate Earnings after Taxes and Dividends (billions of dollars)

a target dividend payout ratio.[3] However, dividends increase with a lag after earnings rise. Only after an increase in earnings appears clearly sustainable and relatively permanent are dividends increased. When dividends have been increased, strenuous efforts are made to maintain them at the new level. If earnings decline, until it is clear that an earnings recovery will not take place, dividends will be maintained.

The foregoing also explains the practice of firms of declaring dividend extras during the final quarter of their fiscal year. As earnings of the firm increase, at first the customary quarterly dividend will not be altered. Year-end "extras," however, will be declared. This explains why in Figure 18–1 the amount of dividends will rise moderately in years when earnings increase sharply. Only after it is clear that earnings have risen to a new plateau will the "customary" amount of dividends be increased.

We may now evaluate this practice of following a stable dividend payout policy. First, consider the stable dividend policy from the standpoint of the stockholders as owners of a company. Their acquiescence with the general practice must imply that stable dividend policies lead to higher stock prices on the average than do alternative dividend policies. Is this a fact? Does a stable dividend policy maximize security values for a corporation? As there has been no conclusive empirical study of this question, on a factual basis there is really no answer to the question.

On a priori grounds, however, it would be expected that a stable dividend policy would lead to higher stock prices. First, a stable dividend policy is likely to lead to higher stock prices because investors will value more highly dividends they are certain to receive. If dividends fluctuate, investors may discount, with some percentage probability factor, the likelihood of receiving any particular amount of dividends. That is, the same average amounts of dividends received under a fluctuating dividend policy are likely to have a higher discount factor applied to them than to dividends under a stable dividend policy. In the terms used in Chapter 10, this means that a firm with a stable dividend would have a lower required rate of return—or cost of capital—than one whose dividends fluctuated.

Second, many stockholders live on income received in the form of dividends. Such stockholders would be greatly inconvenienced by fluctuating dividends, and they would likely pay a premium for a stock with a relatively assured minimum dollar dividend.

A third advantage of a stable dividend from the standpoint of a corporation and its stockowners is the requirement of legal listing. Legal

---

[3] For an excellent discussion providing a foundation for understanding dividend policy, see J. Lintner, "Distribution of Incomes of Corporations among Dividends, Retained Earnings and Taxes," *American Economic Review,* 46 (May 1956), pp. 97–113.

lists are lists of securities in which state governments, mutual savings banks, pension funds, insurance companies, and other fiduciary institutions are permitted to invest. One of the criteria for placing a stock on the legal list is an uninterrupted payment of dividends. Thus, legal listing encourages pursuance of a stable dividend policy.

On the other hand, if a firm's investment opportunities fluctuate from year to year, should it not retain more earnings during some years in order to take advantage of these opportunities when they appear, then increase dividends when good internal investment opportunities are scarce? This line of reasoning would lead to the recommendation of a fluctuating payout for companies whose investment opportunities are unstable. However, the logic of the argument is diminished by recognizing that it is possible to maintain a reasonably stable dividend by using outside financing, especially debt, to smooth out the differences between the funds needed for investment and the amount of money provided by retained earnings.

A GRAPHIC THEORY OF DIVIDEND POLICY

In recent years a great deal of theoretical work has been done on dividend policy. Much of it is too technical and abstract for an introductory text, but it is possible to use part of the theoretical material to solidify some of the concepts discussed in the preceding sections. In this section we present what might be called *the residual theory of dividend policy*.[4] The theory draws on materials developed earlier in the book—capital budgeting and the cost of capital—and serves to provide a bridge between these key concepts.

The starting point in the theory is that investors prefer to have the firm retain and reinvest earnings rather than pay them out in dividends if the returns on reinvested earnings exceed the rate of return the investor could, himself, obtain on other investments. In other words, if the corporation can reinvest retained earnings and get a 20 percent rate of return, while the best rate the stockholder can obtain if the earnings are passed on to him in the form of dividends is 10 percent, then the stockholder would prefer to have the firm retain the profits.

We have seen in Chapter 10 that the cost of equity capital obtained from retained earnings is an *opportunity cost* which reflects rates of return open to equity investors. If a firm's stockholders could buy other stocks of equal risk and obtain a 10 percent dividends-plus-capital-gains yield, then 10 percent is the firm's cost of retained earnings. The cost of new

---

4 "Residual" implies "left over." The residual theory of dividend policy implies that dividends are paid after internal investment opportunities have been used up.

outside equity raised by selling common stock is higher because of the costs of floating the issue.

Most firms have an optimum debt ratio that calls for at least some debt, so new financing is done partly with debt and partly with equity. Debt has a different, and generally lower, cost than equity, so the two forms of capital must be combined to find the *weighted cost of capital.* So long as the firm finances at the optimum point, using an optimum amount of debt and equity, its marginal cost of capital is equal to the weighted average cost of capital.

Internally generated equity (retained earnings) is available for financing a certain amount of new investment; beyond this amount the firm must turn to more expensive new common stock. At the point where new stock must be sold, the cost of equity and, consequently, the weighted cost of capital, begins to rise. In other words, the minimum point on the weighted cost of capital curve—and this minimum point is the marginal cost of capital—rises when the firm uses up its retained earnings and must sell common stock.

These concepts, which were developed in Chapter 10, are illustrated in Figure 18-2. Panel A shows the construction of the weighted cost of capital for (1) internal equity (retained earnings) and (2) after the firm has exhausted its retained earnings and must sell new common stock. The optimum debt ratio is seen to be 50 percent in this hypothetical case, and the minimum points on the weighted cost of capital curves are designated points X and Y for retained earnings and for new common stock, respectively. Point X, which has a value of 10 percent, is the marginal cost of capital so long as equity comes only from retained earnings. Point Y, which has a value of 13 percent, is the marginal cost of all capital raised after the firm begins selling new common stock. We assume that the firm uses no preferred stock.

Our hypothetical firm has $50 million of retained earnings and a 50 percent optimum debt ratio. Therefore, it can make net investments (investments in addition to asset replacements financed from depreciation) up to $100 million—$50 million retained earnings plus $50 million new debt supported by the retained earnings. Therefore, its marginal cost of capital is constant at 10 percent for up to $100 million of capital. Beyond $100 million, the marginal cost of capital rises to 13 percent, as the firm begins to use more expensive new common stock. This is shown in panel B of Figure 18-2.

Next, suppose the firm's capital budgeting department draws up a list of investment opportunities, ranked in the order of their internal rates of return (IRR), and plots them on a graph. The investment opportunity curves of three different years—one for a "good" year (IRR_1), one for a

(a)

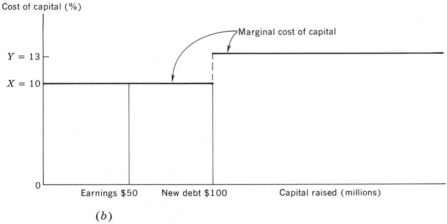

(b)

Figure 18-2   The Cost of Capital

"normal" year (IRR_2), and one for a "bad" year (IRR_3)—are shown in Figure 18–3. IRR_1 shows that the firm can invest more money at higher rates of return than it can when the investment opportunities are given in IRR_2 and IRR_3.

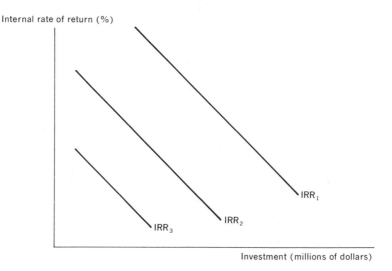

Figure 18-3   Investment Opportunities

Now we combine the investment opportunities schedules with the cost of capital; this is done in Figure 18–4. The point where the investment opportunity curve cuts the cost of capital curve defines the proper level of new investment. When investment opportunities are relatively poor, the optimum level of investment is $25 million; when opportunities are about normal, $75 million should be invested; and when opportunities are relatively good, the firm should make new investments in the amount of $125 million.

Consider the situation where IRR_1 is the appropriate schedule. The firm has $50 million in earnings and a 50 percent target debt ratio, so it can finance $100 million, $50 million earnings plus $50 million debt, from retained earnings plus new debt *if it retains all its earnings*. If it pays part of the earnings in dividends, then it will have to begin using expensive new common stock sooner, so the cost of capital curve will jump sooner. This suggests that under the conditions of IRR_1 the firm should retain all its earnings and actually sell some new common stock in order to take advantage of its investment opportunities. Its payout ratio is thus zero percent.

Under the conditions of IRR_2, however, the firm should invest only $75 million. How should this investment be financed? First, notice that if it retains the full amount of its earnings, $50 million, it will need to sell only $25 million of new debt. But retaining $50 million and selling only $25

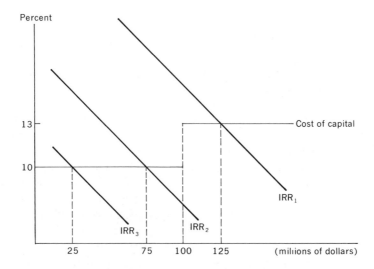

Figure 18-4   Interrelation among Cost of Capital, Investment Opportunities, and New Investment

million of new debt will cause the company to move away from its target capital structure. To stay on target, the required $75 million must be financed half by equity—retained earnings—and half by debt, or $37.5 million of retained earnings and $37.5 million of debt. Now if the firm has $50 million in total earnings and decides to retain and reinvest $37.5 million, it must pay $12.5 million in dividends.[5] In this case, the payout ratio is 25 percent ($12.5 divided by $50).

Finally, under the "bad" conditions of IRR₃ the firm should invest only $25 million. Because it has $50 million in earnings, it could finance the entire $25 million out of retained earnings and still have $25 million available for dividends. Should this be done? Under the assumptions, this would not be a good decision because it would move the firm away from its target debt ratio. To stay in the 50–50 debt/equity position, the firm must retain $12.5 million and sell $12.5 million of debt. When the $12.5 million of retained earnings is subtracted from the $50 million of earnings, we are left with a residual of $37.5, the amount that should be paid out in dividends. In this case the payout ratio is 75 percent.

---

[5] Actually it could buy back its common stock instead of paying dividends. Also, the firm might prefer to engage in merger activities rather than raise its payout ratio, using retained earnings to acquire other firms. This possibility is discussed in Chapter 21.

A LONG-RUN VIEWPOINT

There seems to be a conflict between the theory and the statement made in the preceding section that firms should and do maintain reasonably stable cash dividends. How can this conflict be reconciled?

Actually, this reconciliation is quite simple if we recognize that the theory is not meant to be applied *exactly*. In other words, we would not recommend that a firm adjust its dividend each and every year—indeed, this is not necessary. Firms do have target debt ratios, but they also have a certain amount of flexibility—they can be slightly above or below the target debt position in any one year with no adverse consequences. This means that if an unusually large number of good investments are available in a particular year, the firm does not necessarily have to cut its dividend to take advantage of them—it can borrow somewhat more heavily than usual in that particular year without getting its debt ratio too far out of line. Obviously, however, this excessive reliance on debt could not continue for too many years without getting the debt ratio seriously out of line, necessitating either a sale of new stock or a cut in dividends and an attendant increase in the level of retained earnings.

HIGH AND LOW DIVIDEND PAYOUT INDUSTRIES

Some industries are experiencing rapid growth in the demand for their products, providing the firms in these industries with many good investment opportunities. Electronics, office equipment, and color television are examples of such industries in recent years. Other industries, on the other hand, have experienced much slower growth, or perhaps even declines. Examples of such slow-growth industries are cigarette manufacturing, textiles, and coal mining. Still other industries are growing at about the same rate as the general economy—oil, steel, and banking are representative.

The theory suggests that firms in rapidly growing industries should generally have IRR curves that are relatively far out to the right on graphs such as Figure 18–4; for example, Xerox, Fairchild Camera, and Litton Industries might have investment opportunities similar to IRR_1. The tobacco companies, on the other hand, could be expected to have investment schedules similar to IRR_3, while IRR_2 might be appropriate for Standard Oil of New Jersey or U. S. Steel.

Each of these firms would, of course, experience shifts in investment opportunities from year to year, but the curves would *tend* to be in about the same part of the graph. In other words, firms like Xerox would *tend* to have more investment opportunities than money, so they would *tend* to have a zero (or very low) payout ratio. Reynolds Tobacco, on the other hand, would *tend* to have more money than good investments, so we would expect to find Reynolds paying out a relatively high percentage of earnings in dividends. These companies do, in fact, conform with our expectations.

DIVIDEND PAYMENTS

Dividends are normally paid quarterly. For example, Kern County Land Company paid dividends of $2.60 during 1966, 65 cents each quarter. In common financial language, we say that Kern County Land's *regular quarterly dividend* is 65 cents, or that its *regular annual dividend is* $2.60. Management, sometimes by an explicit statement in the annual report and sometimes by implication, conveys to stockholders an expectation that the regular dividend will be maintained if at all possible. Further, management conveys its belief that earnings will be sufficient to maintain the dividend.

Under other conditions, a firm's cash flows and investment needs may be too volatile for it to set a very high regular dividend, but, on the average, it needs a high dividend payout to dispose of funds not necessary for reinvestment. In such a case, the directors can set a relatively low regular dividend—low enough that it can be maintained even in low profit years or in years when a considerable amount of reinvestment is needed— and supplement it with an *extra dividend* in years when excess funds are available. General Motors, whose earnings fluctuate widely from year to year, has long followed the practice of supplementing its regular dividend with an *extra dividend* paid at the end of the year, when its profits and investment requirements are known.

The Payment Procedure

The actual payment procedure is of some importance; the following is the payment sequence.

1. The directors meet, say on November 15, and declare the regular dividend. The directors would, on this date, issue a statement similar to the following: "On November 15, 1967, the directors of the XYZ Company met and declared the regular quarterly dividend of $0.50 per share, plus an extra dividend of $0.75 per share, to holders of record on December 15, payment to be made on January 1, 1968."

2. On December 15, the *holder of record date,* the company closes its stock transfer books and makes up a list of the shareholders as of that date. If XYZ Company is notified of the sale and transfer of some stock before

December 15, the new owner receives the dividend. If notification is received on or after December 15, the old stockholder gets the dividend.

3. Suppose Edward Johns buys 100 shares of stock from Robert Noble on December 13; will the company be notified of the transfer in time to list Noble as the new owner and, thus, pay the dividend to him? To avoid conflict, the stock brokerage business has set up a convention of declaring that the right to the dividend remains with the stock until four days prior to the holder of record date; on the fourth day before the record date, the right to the dividend no longer goes with the shares. The date when the right to the dividend leaves the stock is called the *ex-dividend date.*

In this case, the ex-dividend date is four days prior to December 15, or December 11. Therefore, if Johns is to receive the dividend, he must buy the stock by December 10. If he buys it on December 11 or later, Noble will receive the dividend.

The total dividend, regular plus extra, amounts to $1.25, so the ex-dividend date is important. Barring fluctuations in the stock market, we would normally expect the price of a stock to drop by approximately the amount of the dividend on the ex-dividend date.

4. The company actually mails the checks to the holders of record on January 1, the payment date.

STOCK DIVIDENDS AND STOCK SPLITS

One of the significant issues of dividend policy in which the financial manager plays an important policy formulation role is that of stock dividends and stock splits. A *stock dividend* is paid in additional shares of stock instead of cash, and simply involves the transfer of surplus to the capital stock account.[6]

An interesting example of the use of stock dividends is the case of the Commonwealth Edison Company. In October 1958 it announced that almost all the annual earnings would be distributed each year in the form of cash and stock dividends. The company would continue to pay the regular 50 cents a share quarterly cash dividend, plus one annual dividend in stock, equivalent to the difference between the amount earned on common stock

---

[6] One point that should be made in connection with stock dividends is that the transfer from earned surplus to the capital stock account must be based on market value. In other words, if a firm's shares are selling for $100 and it has 1 million shares outstanding, a 10 percent stock dividend requires the transfer of $10 million (100,000 × $100) from earned surplus to capital stock. Quite obviously, stock dividends are thus limited by the size of earned surplus. The rule was put into effect to prevent the declaration of stock dividends unless the firm has had earnings. This is another in a long series of rulings designed to prevent investors from being fooled by the practices of unscrupulous firms.

in that year and the $2 cash dividend paid. This device gives investors a combination of both cash and stock dividends.

In a *stock split,* on the other hand, there is no change in the total capital account or surplus. A larger number of shares of common stock are issued. In a two-for-one split, each stockholder would have two shares for each one previously held. Book value per share would be cut in half. The par, or stated, value per share of common stock is similarly changed.

From a practical standpoint there is little difference between a stock dividend and a stock split. The New York Stock Exchange considers any distribution of stock totaling 24 percent or less of outstanding stock to be a stock dividend. Any distribution of stock of 25 percent or more is regarded as a stock split. Since the two are similar, the issues outlined below are discussed in connection with both stock dividends and stock splits.

Price Effects. The results of a careful empirical study of the effects of stock dividends are available and can be used as a basis for observations on the price effects of stock dividends.[7] The findings of the study are presented in Table 18-3. When stock dividends were associated with a cash dividend increase, the value of the company's stock six months after the ex-dividend date had risen by 8 percent. On the other hand, where stock dividends were not accompanied by cash dividend increases, stock values fell by 12 percent during the subsequent six-month period.

Table 18–3 PRICE EFFECTS OF STOCK DIVIDENDS

	Price at Selected Dates (in percentages)		
	Six Months Prior to Ex-dividend Date	At Ex-dividend Date	Six Months after Ex-dividend Date
Cash Dividend Variable			
1. Cash dividend increase	100	109	108
2. No cash dividend increase	100	99	88

These data seem to suggest that stock dividends are seen for what they are—simply additional pieces of paper—and that they do not represent true income. When they are accompanied by higher earnings and cash dividend increases, investors bid up the value of the stock. On the other hand, when stock dividends are not accompanied by increases in earnings and cash dividends, the dilution of earnings and dividends per share causes the

---

[7] C. A. Barker, "Evaluation of Stock Dividends," *Harvard Business Review,* 36 (July–August 1958), pp. 99–114.

price of the stock to drop. The fundamental determinant is underlying earnings and dividend trends.

Effects on Extent of Ownership. Table 18-4 shows the effect of stock dividends on common stock ownership. Large stock dividends resulted in the largest percent increases in stock ownership. The use of stock dividends increased ownership by 25 percent on the average. For companies and industries that did not offer stock splits or stock dividends, the percent increase in ownership was only 5 percent. Furthermore, the degree of increase in ownership increased with the size of the stock dividend.

Table 18–4   EFFECTS OF STOCK DIVIDENDS ON STOCK OWNERSHIP

	Percentage Increase in Stockholders, 1950–1953
Stock dividend, 25% and over	30
Stock dividend, 5–25%	17
All stock dividends	25
No stock dividends or splits	5

SOURCE: C. Austin Barker, "Evaluation of Stock Dividends," *Harvard Business Review,* 36 (July–August 1958).

This evidence suggests that stock dividends increase share ownership. Regardless of the effect on market price, the use of stock dividends effectively increases stock ownership by lowering the price at which shares are traded to a more popular range.

SUMMARY

Dividend policy determines the extent of internal financing by a firm. The financial manager decides whether to release corporate earnings from the control of the enterprise. Because dividend policy affects the financial structure, the flow of funds, corporate liquidity, stock prices, and investor satisfaction—to list a few ramifications—the manager exercises a high degree of judgment in establishing a dividend pattern.

In theory, once the firm's debt policy and cost of capital have been determined, dividend policy should automatically follow. Under our theoretical model, dividends are simply a residual after investment needs have been met, and if this policy is followed, stockholders are better off than under any other possible dividend policy. However, the financial manager simply does not have all the information assumed in the theory, and rule-of-thumb guidelines are needed.

As a guide to boards of directors responsible for dividend policy, the following check list summarizes the major economic and financial factors influencing dividend policy and the direction of the influence.

1. *Rate of growth and profit level.* Economic theory suggests that high growth rates are associated with higher profit opportunities and lower growth rates with smaller profit margins. The higher the growth rate and the larger the prospective margins, the lower the dividend payout is likely to be.

2. *Stability of earnings.* If earnings are relatively stable from the standpoint of both long-term growth and cyclical fluctuations, the dividend payout is likely to be higher.

3. *Age and size of firm.* A well-established, large firm has better access to the capital markets than has a new and small firm. Hence, the dividend payout, other things being equal, will be higher for the larger and older firm.

4. *Cash position.* The stronger a firm's cash or liquidity position in relation to its prospective future need for funds, the higher the probable dividend payout.

5. *Need to repay debt.* A firm that has incurred heavy indebtedness has implicitly committed itself to a relatively high rate of earnings retention unless it seeks to prepare the markets for a common stock or debt-refunding issue.

6. *Control.* If maintenance of existing control is an important consideration, the dividend payout may be lower to permit financing from retained earnings. The procedure avoids issuance of additional securities, which would involve dilution of ownership or the increased risks of debt. On the other hand, if a struggle for control of the firm with opposition groups is in progress or is threatened, the dividend payout may be higher to appeal to stockholder goodwill.

7. *Maintenance of a target dividend.* The objective of a stable dividend policy will make for low payouts when profits are temporarily high, and high payouts when profits are temporarily depressed; and it will cause dividends to lag behind profit growth until the establishment of new earnings levels is strongly assured.

8. *Tax position of stockholders.* Corporations closely held by a few taxpayers in high income brackets are likely to have a lower dividend payout. Corporations widely held by small investors will tend to have higher dividend payouts.

9. *Tax position of the corporation.* Potential penalties for excessive accumulation of retained earnings may cause dividend payouts to be higher than economic and financial considerations alone would indicate.

Of the factors listed, some make for higher dividend payouts, some for lower. It is not possible to provide a formula which can be used to establish the proper dividend payout for a given situation. This is a task requiring the exercise of judgment. The considerations summarized above provide a check list for guiding dividend decisions.

Empirical studies indicate a wide diversity of dividend payout ratios not only among industries but also among firms in the same industry. Studies also show that dividends are more stable than earnings. Firms are reluctant to raise dividends in years of good earnings, and they resist dividend cuts as earnings decline. In view of investors' observed preference for stable dividends and of the probability that a cut in dividends is likely to be interpreted as forecasting a cut in earnings, stable dividends make good sense.

Stock Dividends and Splits

Neither stock splits nor stock dividends alone exert a fundamental influence on prices. The fundamental determinant of the price of the company's stock is the company's earning power compared with the earning power of other companies. However, both stock splits and stock dividends can be used as an effective instrument of financial policy. They are useful devices for reducing the price at which stocks are traded, and studies indicate that stock dividends and stock splits tend to broaden the ownership of a firm's shares.

QUESTIONS

18–1   Discuss the advantages and disadvantages of each of the following dividend policies:

    a) Constant payout ratio.
    b) Constant dollar dividend per share.
    c) Constant regular quarterly dividend plus a year-end extra when earnings are sufficiently high or corporate investment needs are sufficiently low.

18–2   How would each of the following changes probably affect aggregate payout ratios? Explain your answer.

    a) An increase in the personal income tax rate.
    b) A liberalization in depreciation policies for federal income tax purposes.
    c) A rise in interest rates.
    d) An increase in corporate profits.
    e) A decline in investment opportunities.

18–3   Aggregate dividend payout ratios have been increasing since the end of World War II. Why?

18–4   Discuss the pros and cons of having the directors formally announce what a firm's dividend policy will be in the future.

18–5   What purpose do stock dividends and stock splits accomplish?

18–6   What is the difference between a stock dividend and a stock split? As a stockholder, would you prefer to see your company declare a 100 percent stock dividend or a two-for-one split?

18–7   "The cost of retained earnings is less than the cost of new outside equity capital. Consequently, it is totally irrational for a firm to sell a new issue of stock and, during the same year, pay dividends." Discuss this statement.

PROBLEMS

18–1   Listed below are pertinent financial data for the common stocks of Cerro Corp., Polaroid, and National Fuel Gas. Cerro is a leading producer of copper, zinc, and lead, whose product demand is quite cyclical. Polaroid manufactures cameras and film. National Fuel Gas is an integrated gas system serving Northeastern United States.

CERRO CORPORATION

Year	Earnings	Dividends	Price Range	Payout	Price/ Earnings* Ratio
1964	$4.59	$1.14	46–19	25%	10–4
1963	2.25	0.73	21–12	32	9–5
1962	0.99	0.69	21–11	70	18–10
1961	0.87	0.66	27–18	76	25–17
1960	2.01	0.58	24–15	29	11–7
1959	1.73	0.54	27–19	31	14–9
1958	0.95	0.46	25–13	48	20–10
1957	1.11	0.79	29–12	71	22–9
1956	2.19	0.75	37–26	34	12–8
1955	2.78	0.64	28–16	23	7–4

POLAROID

1964	$1.16	$0.06	46–32	5%	40–28
1963	0.71	0.05	53–30	7	88–32
1962	0.63	0.05	55–20	8	115–85
1961	0.52	0.05	60–44	10	116–72
1960	0.56	0.05	65–41	9	68–35
1959	0.69	0.05	47–24	7	59–23
1958	0.47	0.05	27–11	11	37–18
1957	0.36	0.04	13–6	11	30–13
1956	0.22	0.03	7–3	14	21–11
1955	0.13	0.02	3–2	15	23–15

NATIONAL FUEL GAS

1964	$2.17	$1.36	34–31	63%	16–14
1963	2.29	1.30	37–29	57	16–13
1962	2.15	1.23	31–23	57	14–11
1961	1.84	1.20	33–24	65	18–13
1960	1.86	1.20	24–22	64	13–12
1959	1.74	1.15	25–21	66	14–12
1958	1.78	1.10	24–17	62	13–10
1957	1.30	1.10	20–16	85	15–13
1956	1.58	1.03	22–19	65	14–12
1955	1.57	1.00	23–20	64	15–12

* Price/earnings ratios are the high and the low for the year according to *Standard & Poor's Reports*.

a) What differences are revealed by the data on the dividend policy of the three firms? What explanations can be given for these differences?

b) What is the relation of dividend policy to the market price of the stock?

18–2 In the following table, earnings and dividend data are shown for American Telephone and Telegraph and Sun Oil Company, a closely held, growing firm.

Explain the difference in the percentage of dividends paid out by each.

AMERICAN TELEPHONE AND TELEGRAPH

Year	Earnings	Dividend	Payout	Average Price
1964	$3.24	$1.95	60%	70
1963	3.03	1.80	59	64
1962	2.90	1.80	62	59
1961	2.76	1.73	63	60
1960	2.77	1.65	60	47
1959	2.61	1.58	60	40
1958	2.34	1.50	64	33
1957	2.17	1.50	69	28
1956	2.20	1.50	68	30
1955	2.19	1.50	68	30

SUN OIL COMPANY

Year	Earnings	Dividend	Payout	Average Price
1964	$4.30	$0.95	22%	59
1963	3.85	0.90	23	46
1962	3.29	0.85	26	41
1961	3.09	0.81	26	43
1960	3.05	0.75	25	37
1959	2.64	0.73	28	44
1958	1.98	0.70	35	46
1957	2.93	0.67	23	50
1956	3.48	0.63	18	49
1955	2.95	0.58	20	44

18–3 Union spokesmen have presented arguments similar to the following: "Corporations such as General Foods retain about one half their profits— that is, they do not pay them out in dividends. Therefore, their profits are too high, because if they financed by selling common stock instead of by retained earnings, their prices or profits would not need to be so high." Evaluate the statement.

18–4 Select a pair of companies in problems 1 and 2 and calculate dividend payout based on cash flows. Would your previous explanation of dividend policies be affected by the cash flow payout patterns? The following financial data are appropriately scaled.

CERRO CORPORATION

Year	Net Income*	Depreciation and Depletion*
1964	$26.00	$8.78
1963	12.69	8.83
1962	5.53	8.98
1961	4.94	8.18
1960	9.38	7.56
1959	8.00	6.95
1958	3.98	6.27

POLAROID CORPORATION

1964	$18.32	$5.24
1963	11.22	4.39
1962	9.96	3.41
1961	8.11	3.75
1960	8.81	2.87
1959	10.74	2.18
1958	7.21	1.58

NATIONAL FUEL GAS

1964	$11.05	$4.64
1963	11.66	4.65
1962	10.96	4.60
1961	9.35	4.20
1960	9.16	3.96
1959	8.56	3.95
1958	8.78	3.90

* After taxes, in millions of dollars.

AMERICAN TELEPHONE & TELEGRAPH

Year	Net Income*	Depreciation and Depletion*
1964	$1,658.6	$1,469.4
1963	1,479.5	1,332.1
1962	1,388.2	1,219.0
1961	1,284.6	1,099.9
1960	1,213.0	1,007.8
1959	1,113.2	930.0
1958	952.3	834.0

SUN OIL COMPANY

1964	$68.51	$57.71
1963	61.22	62.19
1962	53.19	57.12
1961	49.79	65.60
1960	49.27	63.33
1959	42.84	52.81
1958	32.06	56.42

Chapter 19

The Use of Rights
in Financing

When a corporation sells a new issue of common stock, it may make the sale to its existing stockholders or to an entirely new set of investors. If the sale is to the existing stockholders, the stock flotation is called a *rights offering*. Each stockholder is issued an option to buy a certain number of the new shares; the terms of the option are contained on a piece of paper called a *right*. Each stockholder receives one right for each share of stock he owns. The advantages and disadvantages of rights offerings are described in this chapter.

PRE-EMPTIVE RIGHT

The pre-emptive right gives a firm's stockholders the opportunity of purchasing additional issues of the company's securities; generally, the securities covered are limited to common stock and securities convertible into common stock. The pre-emptive right is a legal matter and is governed by state law. The situation in the 50 states and the District of Columbia is summarized in Table 19-1.

Only two states require that pre-emptive rights be carried by corporate charters. However, the dominant practice, found in almost three fourths of the states, provides that the pre-emptive right exists unless specifically denied in the corporate charter. A survey of the first 100 com-

384

panies listed in the 1958 *Fortune* directory of the 500 largest United States industrial corporations shows that 55 percent deny the pre-emptive right to their stockholders.[1]

Table 19-1   TREATMENT OF PRE-EMPTIVE RIGHTS IN STATE LAWS

Provisions of State Law	Number	Percentage
Pre-emptive right required	2	4
Pre-emptive right provided unless specifically denied in corporate charter	36	71
Pre-emptive right denied unless specifically granted in the corporate charter	5	10
No statutory provision	8	15
Total	51	100

SOURCE: J. R. Nelson, "Rights" (Unpublished Ph.D. dissertation, University of California, Los Angeles, 1961), p. 29. Computed from Commerce Clearing House, *Corporation Law Guide,* 1960.

Purpose

The purpose of the pre-emptive right is to enable stockholders to maintain their proportionate share of the ownership and control of the corporation. For example, if a stockholder owns 10 percent of the stock of a company and is permitted to subscribe to new shares, he will be able to maintain his 10 percent ownership of the company.

THEORETICAL RELATIONSHIPS

Several issues confront the financial manager who is deciding on the details of a rights offering. The various considerations can be made clear by the use of illustrative data on the Southeast Company, whose balance sheet and income statement are given in Table 19-2.

Southeast earns $4 million after taxes and 1 million shares are outstanding, so earnings per share are $4. The stock sells at 25 times earnings, or for $100 a share. The company plans to raise $10 million of new equity funds through a rights offering and decides to sell the new stock to shareholders for $50 a share. The questions now facing the financial manager are:

1. How many rights will be required to purchase a share of the newly issued stock?

---

[1] Unpublished study by the authors.

Table 19–2   *SOUTHEAST COMPANY*
                    BALANCE SHEET BEFORE RIGHTS OFFERING

		Total debt, 5%	$ 40,000,000
		Common stock ($10 par)	10,000,000
		Retained earnings	50,000,000
		Total liabilities and	
Total assets	$100,000,000	capital	$100,000,000

SOUTHEAST COMPANY
PARTIAL INCOME STATEMENT

Total earnings	$10,000,000
Interest on debt	2,000,000
Income before taxes	8,000,000
Taxes (50% assumed)	4,000,000
Earnings after taxes	4,000,000
Earnings per share (1,000,000 shares)	$ 4
Market price of stock (price-earnings ratio of 25 assumed)	$100

   2. What is the value of each right?
   3. What effect will the rights offering have on the price of the existing stock?

Each of these questions will now be analyzed.

Number of Rights to Purchase a New Share

Southeast plans to raise $10 million in new equity funds and to sell the new stock at a price of $50 a share. Dividing the subscription price into the total funds to be raised gives the number of shares to be issued.

$$\text{number of new shares} = \frac{\text{funds to be raised}}{\text{subscription price}} = \frac{\$10,000,000}{\$50} = 200,000 \text{ shares}$$

The next step is to divide the number of new shares into the number of previously outstanding shares to get the number of rights required to subscribe to one share of the new stock. Note that stockholders always get one right for each share of stock they own.

$$\text{number of rights needed to buy a share of the stock} = \frac{\text{old shares}}{\text{new shares}} = \frac{1,000,000}{200,000} = 5 \text{ rights}$$

Therefore, a stockholder will have to surrender five rights plus $50 dollars to get one of the newly issued shares. Had the subscription price been set at

$95 a share, 9.5 rights would have been required to subscribe to each new share, while only one right would have been needed if the price had been set at $10 a share.

Value of a Right

It is clearly worth something to be able to buy for less than $100 a share of stock selling for $100. The right provides this privilege, so the right must have a value. To see how the theoretical value of a right is established, we will continue with the example of the Southeast Company, assuming that it will raise $10 million by selling 200,000 new shares at $50 a share.

First, notice that the *market value* of the old stock was $100 million— $100 a share times 1 million shares. (The book value is irrelevant.) When the firm sells the new stock, it brings in an additional $10 million. As a first approximation, we assume that the market value of the common stock increases by exactly this $10 million. Actually, the market value of all the common stock would go up by more than $10 million if investors think the company will be able to invest these funds at a yield substantially in excess of the cost of equity capital, but by less than $10 million if investors are doubtful of the company's ability to put the new funds to work profitably in the near future.

Under the assumption, the total market value of the common stock after the new issue will be $110 million. Dividing this new value by the new total number of shares outstanding, 1.2 million, we obtain a new market value of $91.67 a share. Therefore, we see that after the financing has been completed, the price of the common stock will have fallen from $100 to $91.67.

Since the rights give the stockholders the privilege of buying for only $50 a share of stock that will end up being worth $91.67, thus saving $41.67, is $41.67 the value of each right? The answer is "no," because five rights are required to buy one new share; we must divide $41.67 by 5 to get the value of each right. In the example each one is worth $8.33.

Ex Rights

Rights are handled much like dividends in some regards. Recall that dividends go with the stock until the ex-dividend date, which is four days prior to the stock of record date. Rights are treated similarly when the old stock is traded prior to the issuance of the new stock but after the announcement of the financing. For example, on October 15 Southeast Company might announce the terms of the new financing, stating that rights will be mailed out on December 1 to stockholders of record as of the close of business on November 15. Anyone buying the old stock on or before November 11 will receive the rights; anyone buying the stock on or after

November 12 will *not* receive the rights. Thus, November 12 is the *ex-rights date;* before November 12 the stock sells *rights on.* In the case of Southeast Company, the *rights on price* is $100, the *ex-rights price* is $91.67.

Formula Value of the Rights

Rights On. Equations have been developed for determining the value of rights without going through all the procedures described above. While the stock is still selling rights on, the value at which the rights will sell when they are issued can be found by use of the following formula: [2]

$$\text{value of one right} = \frac{\text{market value of stock, rights on} - \text{subscription price}}{\text{number of rights required to purchase one share plus 1}}$$

$$R = \frac{M_o - S}{N + 1}$$

Here M_o is the rights-on price of the stock, S is the subscription price, N is the number of rights required to purchase a new share of stock, and R is the value of one right. Substituting in the appropriate values for the Southeast Company;

$$R = \frac{\$100 - \$50}{5 + 1} = \frac{\$50}{6} = \$8.33$$

This agrees with the value of the rights as found by the long procedure.

Ex Rights. Suppose you are a stockholder in the Southeast Company. When you return to the United States from a trip to Europe, you read about the rights offering in the newspaper. The stock is now selling ex rights for $91.67 a share. How can you calculate the theoretical value of a right? Simply using the following formula, which follows the logic described in preceding sections, you can determine the value of each right to be $8.33:

$$\text{value of one right} = \frac{\text{market value of stock ex rights} - \text{subscription price}}{\text{number of rights required to purchase one share}}$$

$$R = \frac{M_e - S}{N}$$

$$R = \frac{\$91.67 - \$50}{5} = \frac{\$41.67}{5} = \$8.33$$

Here M_e is the ex-rights price of the stock.

---

[2] The equation is derived in J. Fred Weston and Eugene F. Brigham, *Managerial Finance, Second Edition,* p. 492.

EFFECTS ON POSITION OF STOCKHOLDERS

A stockholder has the choice of exercising his rights or selling them. If he has sufficient funds and if he wants to buy more shares of the company's stock, the stockholder will exercise the rights. If he does not have the money or does not want to buy more stock, he will sell his rights. In either case, provided the formula values of the rights hold true, the stockholder will neither benefit nor lose by the rights offering. This statement can be made clear by considering the position of an individual stockholder in the Southeast Company.

The stockholder had 10 shares of stock before the rights offering. The 10 shares had a market value of $100 a share, so the stockholder had a total market value of $1,000 in the company's stock. If he exercises his rights, he will be able to purchase two additional shares at $50 a share, a new investment of $100; his total investment is now $1,100. He now owns 12 shares of his company's stock, which, after the rights offering, has a value of $91.67 a share. The value of his stock is $1,100, exactly what he has invested in it.

Alternatively, if he sold his 10 rights, which have a value of $8.33 a right, he would receive $83.30. He would now have his original 10 shares of stock plus $83.30 in cash. But his original 10 shares of stock now have a market price of $91.67 a share. The $916.70 market value of his stock plus the $83.30 in cash is the same as the original $1,000 market value of stock with which he began. From a purely mechanical or arithmetical standpoint, the stockholder neither benefits nor gains from the sale of additional shares of stock through rights.

Relation between Market Price and Subscription Price

We can now investigate the factors influencing the use of rights and, if they are used, the level at which the subscription price will be set. The articles of incorporation of the Southeast Company permit it to use rights or not, depending on whether it judges their use to be advantageous to the company and its stockholders. The financial vice-president of the company is considering three alternative methods of raising the additional sum of $10 million.

Alternative I. Southeast Company could sell additional shares through investment bankers to the public at approximately $100 a share, the company netting approximately $96 a share; thus, it would need to sell 105,000 shares in order to cover the underwriting commission.

Alternative II. The company could sell additional shares through rights, using investment bankers and paying a commission of 1 percent on the total dollar amount of the stock sold plus ¾ percent on all shares unsubscribed and taken over by the investment bankers. Allowing for the usual market pressure when common stock is sold, the new shares would be sold at a 15 percent discount, or at $85. Thus, 125,000 additional shares would be offered through rights. With eight rights, an additional share could be purchased at $85.

Alternative III. The company could sell additional shares through rights at $10 a share. Investment bankers would not be employed at all. The number of additional shares of common stock to be sold would be one million. For each right held, existing stockholders would be permitted to buy one share of the new common stock.

Under alternative I, investment bankers are used. Rights would not be utilized at all. In this circumstance the underwriting commission, or flotation cost, is approximately 4 percent. In alternative II, where rights are used with a small discount, the underwriting commission is reduced, because the discount removes much of the risk of not being able to sell the issue. The underwriting commission consists of two parts—1 percent on the original issue and an additional ¾ of 1 percent commission on all unsubscribed shares the investment bankers are required to take over and sell. Thus, the actual commission will range somewhere between 1 percent and 1¾ percent.

Under alternative III, the subscription price is $10 a share. With such a large concession the company does not need to use investment bankers at all, because the rights are certain to have value and to be either exercised or sold.

Which of the three alternatives is superior?

Alternative I will provide a wider distribution of the securities sold, thus lessening any possible control problems. Also, it provides the assurance from the investment bankers that the company will receive the $10 million involved in the new issue. The company pays for these services in the form of underwriting charges. The stock price, after the issue, should be $100.

Under alternative II, by utilizing rights, underwriting expenses are reduced. There is also a small reduction in the unit price per share, from $100 to $98 a share. Also, since the rights do have a low value, some stockholders may neither exercise them nor sell them, thus suffering a loss.[3]

---

[3] The value of each right is computed as

$$R = \frac{\$100 - \$85}{8 + 1} = \frac{\$15}{9} = \$1.67$$

The value of the stock, after financing, is $100 — $1.67 = $98.33 a share.

Because existing stockholders will buy some of the new shares, the distribution is likely to be less wide.

Alternative III involves no underwriting expense, and it results in a substantial decrease in the unit price of shares. Initially, however, the shares will be less widely distributed. Notice that alternative III has a large stock-split effect which results in a much lower final stock price per share. Many people feel that there is an optimal stock price—one that will produce a maximum total market value of the shares—and that this price is generally in the range of $30 to $60 a share. If this is the feeling of Southeast's directors, they may believe that alternative III permits them to reach this more desirable price range, while at the same time reducing flotation costs on the new issue. Also, since the rights have a substantial value, few stockholders will fail either to exercise or to sell them, so there should be a minimum of stockholder loss from inaction.

The three alternatives are summarized below.

	Advantages	*Disadvantages*
Alternative I	1. Wider distribution 2. Certainty of receiving funds	1. High underwriting costs
Alternative II	1. Smaller underwriting costs 2. Lower unit price of shares	1. More narrow distribution
Alternative III	1. No underwriting costs 2. Substantial decrease in unit price of shares	1. More narrow distribution

The alternative that is most advantageous depends upon the company's needs. If the company is strongly interested in a wider distribution of its securities, alternative I is preferable. If it is most interested in reducing the unit price of its shares and is confident that the lower unit price will induce wider distribution of its shares, alternative III will be chosen. If the company's needs are moderate in both directions, alternative II may offer a satisfactory compromise. Whether rights will be used and the level of the subscription price both depend upon the needs of the company at a particular time.

Exercise of Rights

Interestingly enough, it is expected that a small percentage of stockholders may neglect to exercise their rights or to sell them. In an offering in 1955, the holders of 1½ percent of the shares of General Motors common stock did not exercise their rights.[4] The loss involved to these stockholders

---

[4] E. A. Grimm, "The Money You Save May Be Your Own," *Exchange,* 16 (December 1955), pp. 17–20.

was $1.5 million. Those who failed to exercise their rights in a number of offerings during 1955 held from 1.5 to 2.75 percent of the shares of stock outstanding. In an AT&T issue in that year, the loss to shareholders who neglected to exercise their rights was $960,000.[5]

As a consequence of the failure of a small percentage of shareholders to exercise their rights, the financial manager must increase slightly the size of the new security issue to compensate for the nonexercise of rights.

Market Price and Subscription Price

Measured from the registration date for the new issue of the security, the average percentage by which the subscription prices of new issues were below their market prices was 22.8 percent during the years 1946–1947 and 15.3 percent during the years 1956–1957. Examples of price concessions of 40 percent or more were observed in a small percentage of issues. The most frequently encountered discounts are from 10 to 20 percent.

Effect on Subsequent Behavior of Market Price of Stock

It is often stated that new issues of stock through rights will depress the price of the existing common stock of the company. To the extent that a subscription price in connection with the rights offering is lower than the market price, there will be a "stock split effect" on the market price of the common stock. With the prevailing market price of Southeast Company's stock at $100 and a $10 subscription price, the new market price will probably drop to $55.

But the second question is whether, because of the rights offering, the actual new market price will be $55 or lower or higher. Again, empirical analysis of the movement in stock prices during rights offerings indicates that generalization is not practical. What happens to the market prices of the stock ex rights and after the rights trading period depends upon the prospects of the issuing company.

SIGNIFICANCE OF RIGHTS BEHAVIOR

To this point the material on rights has sought to develop an understanding of the nature and behavior of rights and their values. Much of this may have appeared to be from the standpoint of the investor. But such an approach is necessary to uncover the basic properties of rights. With this understanding as a background, it is now possible to focus directly on the significance of the use of rights in formulating financing policies. This ma-

---

[5] Grimm, *op. cit.*

terial may be conveniently organized in terms of advantages to the use of rights.

Advantages of Use of Rights in New Financing

It has been seen that the pre-emptive right gives the shareholders the protection of preserving their pro rata share in the earnings and surplus of the company. The firm also benefits. By offering new issues of securities to the existing stockholders, it increases the likelihood of a favorable reception for the stock. By their ownership of common stock in the company, these investors have already indicated a favorable evaluation of the company. They may be receptive to the purchase of additional shares, particularly when the additional reasons indicated below are taken into account.

The shares purchased with rights are subject to lower margin requirements. For example, margin requirements since November 1963 have been 70 percent; in other words, a person buying listed stocks must have at least $70 of his own funds for every $100 of securities purchased. However, if shares of new issues of stocks are purchased with rights, only $25 per $100 of common stock purchased must be furnished by the investor himself; he is permitted by law to borrow (if feasible) up to 75 percent of the purchase price. Furthermore, the absence of a clear pattern in the price behavior of the adjusted market price of the stocks and rights before, during, and after the trading period may enhance interest in the investment possibilities of the instruments.

These factors may offset the tendency toward a downward pressure on the price of the common stock occurring at the time of a new issue.[6] With the increased interest and advantages afforded by the rights offering, the "true" or "adjusted" downward price pressure may actually be avoided.

A related advantage is that the flotation costs to an issuer associated with a rights offering will be lower than the costs of a public flotation. Costs referred to here are cash costs. For example, the flotation costs of industrial issues of common stock in 1955 were 9 percent on public issues compared with 3.8 percent of the proceeds to the company on rights offerings.[7] Underpricing on rights offerings increases their "costs" to 20.6 percent. However, the underpricing is not a cash outlay and, as we have seen, the underpricing accrues to stockholders by making their rights more valuable.

---

[6] The downward pressure develops because of an increase in the supply of securities without a necessarily equivalent increase in the demand. Generally, it is a temporary phenomenon and the stock tends to return to the theoretical price after a few months. Obviously, if the acquired funds are invested at a very high rate of return, the stock price benefits; if the investment does not turn out well, the stock price suffers.

[7] H. W. Stevenson, *Common Stock Financing* (Ann Arbor: University of Michigan, 1957), p. 61.

The financial manager may obtain positive benefits from underpricing. Since a rights offering is a stock split to a certain degree, it will cause the market price of the stock to fall to a level lower than it otherwise would have been. But stock splits will increase the number of shareholders in a company by bringing the price of a stock into a more attractive trading level. Furthermore, because a rights offering is an indirect stock split, it may result in additional dividends for the stockowners.

Finally, the total effect of the rights offering may be to stimulate an enthusiastic response from stockholders and the investment market as a whole, with the result that opportunities for financing become more attractive to the firm. Thus, the financial manager may be able to engage in common stock financing at lower costs and under more favorable terms.

SUMMARY

This chapter focuses on the key decisions confronting the financial manager when he considers a rights offering and indicates the major features bearing on such decisions. Rights offerings may be used effectively by financial managers to increase the goodwill of shareholders. If the new financing associated with the rights represents a sound decision—one likely to result in improved earnings for the firm—a rise in stock values will probably result. The use of rights will permit shareholders to preserve their positions or to improve them. On the other hand, if investors feel that the new financing is not well advised, the rights offering may well cause the price of the stock to decline by more than the value of the rights.

Because the rights offering is directed to existing shareholders, it may be possible to reduce the costs of floating the new issue. However, these savings are possible only if the benefits provided by nonrights offerings—broadened distribution of the securities and protection against adverse price development during the flotation period—are not needed.

A major decision for financial managers in a rights offering is to set the subscription price, or the amount of the concession from the existing market price of the stock. Formulas reflecting the static effects of a rights offering indicate that neither the stockholders nor the company benefits or loses from the price changes. The rights offering has the effect of a stock split. The level set for the subscription price will to a great degree reflect the objectives and effects of a stock split.

The subsequent price behavior of the rights and the common securities in the associated new offering will reflect the earnings and dividends prospects of the company, as well as the underlying developments in the securities markets. The new financing associated with the rights offering may be an indicator of prospective growth in the sales and earnings of the company. The stock-split effects of the rights offering may be used to alter the company's dividend payments. The effects of these developments on the market behavior of the rights and the securities before, during, and after the rights trading period will reflect the expectations of investors toward the outlook for earnings and dividends per share.

QUESTIONS

19–1 It is frequently stated that the primary purpose of the pre-emptive right is to allow individuals to maintain their proportionate share of the ownership and control of a corporation. Just how important do you suppose this consideration is for the average stockholder of a firm whose shares are traded on the New York or American stock exchanges? Is the pre-emptive right likely to be of more importance to stockholders of closely held firms?

19–2 How would the success of a rights offering be affected by a declining stock market?

19–3 What are some of the advantages and disadvantages of setting the subscription price on a rights offering substantially below the current market price of the stock?

19–4 Is a firm likely to get a wider distribution of shares if it sells new stock through a rights offering or directly to underwriters? Why would a company be interested in getting a wider distribution of shares?

PROBLEMS

19–1 The common stock of the Industrial Research Company is selling for $99 on the market. The stockholders are offered one new share at a subscription price of $75 for every three shares held. What is the value of each right? Prove your answer.

19–2 Lewis has 20 shares of Northwood Industries. The market price per share is $70. The company now offers stockholders one new share to be purchased at $40 for every five shares held.

a) Determine the value of each right.
b) Assume that Lewis (1) uses 15 rights and sells the other 5, or (2) sells 20 rights at the market price you have calculated. Prepare a statement showing the changes in his position under the above assumptions.

19–3 National Appliance Company common stock is priced at $43 a share on the market. Notice is given that stockholders may purchase one new share at a price of $25 for every five shares held. You hold 80 shares at the time of notice.

a) At approximately what price will each right sell on the market?
b) Why will this be the approximate price?
c) What effect will the issuance of rights have on the original market price? Why?

19–4 The Wilson Company has the following balance sheet and income statement.

THE WILSON COMPANY
BALANCE SHEET BEFORE RIGHTS OFFERING

		Total debt, (5%)	$ 5,000,000
		Common stock ($20 par value)	2,000,000
		Retained earnings	3,000,000
Total assets	$10,000,000	Total liabilities and capital	$10,000,000

Earnings rate: 10% on total assets

Total earnings	$1,000,000
Interest on debts	250,000
Income before taxes	750,000
Taxes (40% rate assumed)	300,000
Earnings after taxes	$ 450,000

Earnings per share	$ 4.50
Dividends per share (56%)	$ 2.50
Price/earnings ratio	20 times
Market price per share	$90.00

The Wilson Company plans to raise an additional $4 million through a rights offering. The additional funds will continue to earn 10 percent. The price/earnings ratio is assumed to remain at 20 times, dividend payout will continue to be 56 percent, and the 40 percent tax rate will remain in effect.

a) Assuming subscription prices of $20, $40, and $60 a share:
   (1) How many additional shares of stock will have to be sold?
   (2) How many rights will be required to purchase one new share?
   (3) What will be the new earnings per share?
   (4) What will be the new market price per share?
   (5) Selling stock through a rights offering with the subscription price set below the current market price has an effect that is somewhat similar to a stock split or stock dividend. A stock split of approximately what degree would have the same effect on earnings per share as does the rights offering under each of the three subscription prices?
   (6) What will be the new dividend per share if the dividend payout ratio is maintained?
b) What is the significance of your results?

Chapter 20

Warrants and Convertibles

Thus far in the discussion of long-term financing, we have examined the nature of common stock, preferred stock, and long-term debt. Further, we saw how offering common stock through the use of rights can facilitate low-cost stock flotations. In this chapter we see how the financial manager can make his company's securities attractive to a broader range of investors, thereby lowering his cost of capital, through the use of warrants and convertibles.

WARRANTS

A *warrant* is an option to buy a stated number of shares of stock at a specified price. For example, Trans World Airlines has warrants outstanding that give the warrant holders the right to buy one share of TWA stock at a price of $22 for each warrant held. The warrants generally expire on a certain date—TWA's warrants expire on December 1, 1973—although some have perpetual lives. An illustrative list of warrants is shown in Table 20-1

Theoretical Value of a Warrant

Warrants have a calculated, or theoretical, value and an actual value, or price, that is determined in the marketplace. The theoretical value is found by use of the equation shown on page 399.

Table 20–1 ILLUSTRATIVE LIST OF WARRANTS LISTED ON AMERICAN STOCK EXCHANGE

Name of Company	Price on 7/24/67		Option to Purchase Common Shares		Date Option Expires	Theoretical Value	Premium
	Common	Warrants	No.	Price			
Allegheny Airlines	20	15	1.0	$10.50	5/1/69	$ 9.50	$ 5.50
Allegheny Corp.	11⅜	8⅝	1.0	3.75	Perpetual	7.63	0.99
Atlas Corp.	5⅝	3	1.0	6.25	Perpetual	0.00	3.00
Braniff Airways	65¾	30	1.0	73.00	12/1/86	0.00	30.00
General Acceptance Corporation	29¼	11¼	1.0	20.00	10/31/69	9.25	2.00
Hilton Hotels Corp.	38	19¾	1.0	46.00	10/15/70	0.00	19.75
Indian Head Corp.	29½	14½	1.0	20.00	5/15/70	9.50	5.00
Jefferson Lake Petrochemicals	39½	30½	1.04	10.00	6/1/71	30.68	(0.18)
Martin Marietta	24½	29⅛	2.73	16.50	11/1/68	21.84	7.28
McCrory	21	6⅝	1.0	20.00	3/15/76	1.00	5.62
National General	16½	7	1.0	15.00	5/15/74	1.50	5.50
Pacific Petroleum	16¼	5	1.1	19.00	3/13/68	0.00	5.00
Sperry Rand	34¼	10½	1.08	28.00	9/15/67	6.75	3.75
Textron, Inc. *	73	57⅜	1.0	15.00	5/1/84	58.00	(0.62)
Trans World Airlines	64½	46⅞	1.0	22.00	12/1/73	42.50	4.38
Tri-Continental Corporation	27⅞	48	2.54	8.88	Perpetual	48.31	(0.31)
United Industrial Corp.	15¼	3⅜	.05	17.00	11/15/69	0.00	3.38
Uris Buildings	24¾	15⅝	1.06	12.50	5/1/75	12.98	2.64

* Price at which common may be purchased increases by $2.50 in 1969, 1974, and 1979.

$$\text{theoretical value} = \left(\begin{matrix}\text{market price} \\ \text{of} \\ \text{common stock}\end{matrix} \cdot less \begin{matrix}\text{option} \\ \text{price}\end{matrix}\right) \times \begin{matrix}\text{number of shares each} \\ \text{warrant entitles owner} \\ \text{to purchase}\end{matrix}$$

For example, a TWA warrant entitles the holder to purchase one share of common stock at $22 a share. If the market price of the common stock is $64.50, the formula price of the warrant may be obtained as follows:

$$(\$64.50 - \$22) \times 1.0 = \$42.50$$

Actual Price of a Warrant

Generally, warrants sell above their theoretical values. For example, when TWA stock was selling for $64.50, the warrants had a theoretical value of $42.50 but was selling at a price of $46.87. This represented a premium of $4.33 above the theoretical value.

A set of TWA stock prices, together with actual and theoretical warrant values, is given in Table 20-2 and plotted in Figure 20-1. At any stock price below $22, the theoretical value of the warrant is zero; beyond $22, each $1 increase in the price of the stock brings with it a $1 increase in the theoretical value of the warrant.[1] The actual market price of the warrants lies above the theoretical value at each price of the common stock. Notice, however, that the premium of market price over theoretical value declines as the price of the common stock increases. For example, when the common sold for $22 and the warrants had a zero theoretical value, their actual price, and the premium, was $9.

Table 20–2 THEORETICAL AND ACTUAL VALUES OF TWA
WARRANTS AT DIFFERENT MARKET PRICES

	Value of Warrant		
Price of Stock	*Theoretical*	*Actual Price*	*Premium*
$ 0.00	$ 0.00	Not Available	—
22.00	0.00	$ 9.00	$9.00
23.00	1.00	9.75	8.75
24.00	2.00	10.50	8.50
33.67	11.67	17.37	5.70
52.00	30.00	32.00	2.00
75.00	53.00	54.00	1.00
100.00	78.00	79.00	1.00
150.00	128.00	Not Available	—

[1] The formula gives a *negative* theoretical value when the stock is selling for less than the option price. This makes no sense, so we define the theoretical value to be zero when the stock is selling for less than the option price.

**Figure 20-1   Theoretical and Actual Values of TWA Warrants at
Different Common Stock Prices**

As the price of the stock rises, the theoretical value of the warrants matches the increase dollar for dollar, but for a while the market price of the warrant climbs less rapidly and the premium declines. The premium is $9 when the stock sells for $22 a share, but declines to $1 by the time the stock price has risen to $75 a share. Beyond this point the premium seems to be constant.

Why do you suppose this pattern exists? Why should the warrant ever sell for more than its theoretical value, and why does the premium decline as the price of the stock increases? The answer lies in the speculative appeal of warrants—they enable a person to gain a high degree of personal leverage when buying securities. To illustrate, suppose TWA warrants always sold for exactly their theoretical value. Now suppose you are thinking of investing in the company's common stock at a time when it is selling for $25 a share. If you buy a share and the price rises to $50 in a year, you have made a 100 percent capital gain. However, had you bought the warrants at their theoretical value ($3 when the stock sells for $25), your capital gain would have been $25 on a $3 investment, or 833 percent. At the same time, your total loss potential with the warrant is only $3, while the potential loss from the purchase of the stock is $25. However, a $3 decline in the stock price produces only a 12 percent loss if the stock is purchased, but a 100 percent loss if you buy the warrant. The huge capital gains potential, combined with the loss limitation, is clearly worth something—the exact amount that it is worth to investors is the amount of the premium.

But why does the premium decline as the price of the stock rises? The answer here is that both the capital gains leverage effect and the loss protection feature decline at high stock prices. For example, if you are thinking of buying the stock at $75 a share, the theoretical value of the warrants is $53. If the stock price doubles to $150, the theoretical value of the warrant goes from $53 to $128. The percentage capital gain on the stock is still 100 percent, but the percentage gain on the warrant declines from 833 percent to 142 percent. Also, notice that the loss potential on the warrant is much greater when the warrant is selling at high prices. These two factors, the declining leverage impact and the increasing danger of losses, explain why the premium diminishes as the price of the common stock rises.

Use of Warrants in Financing

Warrants are generally used by small, rapidly growing firms as "sweeteners" when selling either debt or preferred stocks. Such firms frequently are regarded by investors as being highly risky, so their bonds could be sold only if the firms are willing to accept extremely high rates of interest and very restrictive indenture provisions. However, giving warrants along with the bonds enables investors to share in the company's growth if it does, in fact, grow and prosper; therefore, investors are willing to accept a lower bond interest rate and less restrictive indenture provisions. A bond with warrants has some of the characteristics of debt and some of the characteristics of equity. It is a hybrid security that provides the financial manager with an opportunity to expand his mix of securities, appeal to a broader group of investors, and thus possibly lower his firm's cost of capital.

Also, notice that warrants can bring in additional funds. The option price is set 15 to 20 percent above the market price of the stock at the time of the bond issue. If the firm does grow and prosper and if its stock price rises above the option price at which shares may be purchased, warrant holders will surrender their warrants and buy stock at the stated price. This happens for several reasons. First, it will surely happen if the warrants are about to expire with the market price of the stock above the option price.

Second, it will happen voluntarily as the company raises the dividend on the common stock. No dividend is earned on the warrant, so it provides no current income. However, if the common stock pays an attractive dividend, it provides an attractive dividend yield. This induces warrant holders to exercise their option to buy the stock. Third, warrants sometimes have *stepped-up option prices*. For example, the Williamson Scientific Company warrants have an option price of $25 until December 31, 1975, at which time the option price rises to $30. If the price of the common stock is above $25 just before December 1975, many warrant holders will exercise their option before the stepped-up price takes effect.

One desirable feature of warrants is that they tend to bring in additional funds only if these funds are needed. If the company grows and prospers, causing the price of the stock to rise, the warrants are exercised and bring in needed funds. On the other hand, if the company is not successful and cannot profitably employ additional money, the price of its stock will probably not rise sufficiently to induce exercise of the options.

CONVERTIBLES

Convertible securities are bonds or preferred stocks that are exchangeable, at the option of the holder, under specified terms and conditions. The *conversion ratio* gives the number of shares of common stock the holder of the convertible receives when he surrenders his security on conversion, and the *conversion price* is the effective price paid for the common stock when conversion occurs.

The relation between the conversion ratio and the conversion price is illustrated by the Adams Electric Company $1,000 par value convertible debentures. At any time prior to July 1, 1989, a debenture holder can turn in his bond and receive in its place 20 shares of common stock; therefore, the conversion ratio is 20 shares for one bond. The bond has a par value of $1,000, so the holder is giving up this amount when he converts. Dividing the $1,000 by the 20 shares received gives a conversion price of $50 a share.

$$\text{conversion price} = \frac{\text{par value of bond}}{\text{shares received}} = \frac{\$1,000}{20} = \$50$$

The conversion price and the conversion ratio are established at the time the convertible bond is sold. Generally, these values are fixed for the life of the bond, although sometimes a stepped-up conversion price is

used.[2] Litton Industries' convertible debentures, for example, are convertible into 12.5 shares until 1972, into 11.76 shares from 1972 until 1982,
and into 11.11 shares from 1982 until they mature in 1987. The conversion
price thus starts at $80, rises to $85, then to $90. Litton's convertibles, like
most, are callable at the option of the company.

Like warrant option prices, the conversion price is characteristically
set from 10 to 20 percent above the prevailing market price of the common
stock at the time the convertible issue is sold. Exactly how the conversion
price is established can best be understood after examining some of the
reasons why firms use convertibles.

Relative Use of Convertibles

A study by Professor C. James Pilcher on the use of convertibles during the period 1933 through 1952 showed that 182 convertible debentures
were issued during the 20-year period. Another study, made by the late
Professor Robert R. McKenzie of New York University, estimated that 419
issues were placed in the 10-year period 1956–1965. Thus, there has been
a pronounced increase in the use of convertibles in more recent years.

There were clear and definite advantages to investors who bought convertibles in the post-World War II period. This was a time of great uncertainty. Many economists were forecasting a major postwar recession; others
were forecasting an unprecedented boom. The use of convertibles permitted the investor to hedge against both. In the event of a postwar collapse,
he had the protection of his senior position. But if a boom and inflation
caused common stock prices to soar, the convertible would rise with the
price of the common stock. Thus, convertibles offered the investor both
lower risk and speculative potentialities—a hedge against both deflation and
inflation. Note, however, that the coupon interest rate on a convertible is
always lower than the interest rate of an equivalent nonconvertible bond.
Accordingly, an investor who buys a convertible gives up interest income
in the hope of a capital gain.

A sampling of the price behavior of convertibles issued in 1962 shows

---

[2] Another factor that may cause a change in the conversion price and ratio is
a standard feature of practically all convertibles—the clause protecting the convertible against dilution from stock spilts, stock dividends, and the sale of common
stock at low prices (as in a rights offering). The typical provision states that no
common stock can be sold at a price below the conversion price, and that the conversion price must be lowered (and the conversion ratio raised) by the percentage
amount of any stock dividend or split. For example, if Adams Electric had a two-
for-one split, the conversion ratio would automatically be adjusted to 40 and the
conversion price lowered to $25. If this protection was not contained in the con-
tract, a company could completely thwart conversion by the use of stock splits and
dividends. Warrants are similarly protected against dilution.

that by 1965 the market price of the common stock was approximately 150 percent of the conversion price. In other words, the market price of the stock rose approximately 50 percent above its market price at the time the convertibles were issued. Correspondingly, through 1965 there were marked profits for people who bought convertibles at the time they were originally issued. Note also, however, that profits would have been even greater had the holders of these convertibles purchased the common stock for which they were exchangeable. The reason is that the conversion price is set higher than the initial market price of the common stock.

Reasons for Use of Convertibles

Convertibles offer advantages to corporations as well as to individual investors. The most important of these advantages are discussed below.

As a sweetener when selling debt. Sometimes a company can sell debt with reasonable interest rates and protective covenants only by giving investors a chance to share in the capital gains; convertibles, like bonds with warrants, offer this possibility.

To sell common stock at prices higher than those now prevailing. Many companies actually want to sell common stock, not debt, but feel that the price of the stock is temporarily depressed. Management may know, for example, that earnings are depressed because of a strike but that they will snap back during the next year and pull the price of the stock up with them. To sell stock now would require giving up more shares to raise a given amount of money than management thinks is necessary. However, setting the conversion price 15 to 20 percent above the present market price of the stock will require giving up 15 to 20 percent fewer shares when the bonds are converted than would be required if stock was sold directly.

Notice, however, that management is counting on the stock price rising above the conversion price to make the bonds actually attractive in conversion. If the stock price does not rise and conversion does not occur, then management is saddled with debt.

How can the company be sure that conversion will occur when the price of the stock rises above the conversion price? Characteristically, convertibles have a provision that gives the issuing firm the opportunity of calling the convertible at a specified price. Suppose the conversion price is $50, the conversion ratio is 20, the market price of the common stock has risen to $60, and the call price on the convertible bond is $1,050. If the company called the bond (by giving the usual notification of 20 days), bondholders could either convert into common stock with a market value of $1,200 or allow the company to redeem the bond for $1,050. Naturally, bondholders prefer $1,200 to $1,050, so conversion occurs. The call provision therefore gives the company a means of forcing conversion, provided that the market price of the stock is greater than the conversion price.

To have low-cost capital during a construction period.   Another advantage from the standpoint of the issuer is that a convertible issue may be used as a temporary financing device. During the years 1946 through 1957, American Telephone & Telegraph Company sold $10 billion of convertible debentures. By 1959 about 80 percent of these convertible debentures had been converted into common stock. AT&T could not have sold straight debt in this amount because its financial structure would have been unbalanced. On the other hand, if AT&T had simply issued large amounts of common stock periodically, there would have been price pressure on its stock because the market is slow to digest large blocks of stock.

By using convertible debentures, however, which provided for a lag of some six to nine months before they were converted into common stock, AT&T received relatively cheap money to finance growth. Transmission lines and telephone exchange buildings must first be built to provide the basis for ultimately installing phones. While AT&T is installing transmission lines and telephone exchange buildings, these investments are not earning any money. Therefore it was important to AT&T to minimize the cost of money while these installations were being made. After six to nine months had elapsed and these installations were translated into telephones that were bringing in revenues, AT&T was better able to pay the regular common stock dividend. Thus, convertibles provide for stages in financing by a firm.

Disadvantages of Convertibles

From the standpoint of the issuer, convertibles have a possible disadvantage. Although the convertible stock gives the issuer the opportunity to sell the common stock at a price 15 to 20 percent higher than it could otherwise be sold, if the common stock greatly increases in price the issuer may find that he would have been better off if he had waited and simply sold the common stock. Further, if the company truly wants to raise equity capital and if the price of the stock declines after the bond is issued, then it is stuck with debt.

But the plain fact of the matter may well be that the company has no alternative, especially if it is a small and growing company. A sufficient investment demand in the company's debt securities or preferred stock may not be present. For this reason the company may be virtually forced to use convertibles. In this kind of situation the convertibles perform a very useful function in that they enable management to raise additional debt and equity money and maintain control in the company.

DECISIONS ON THE USE OF WARRANTS AND CONVERTIBLES

The Winchester Company, an electronic circuit and component manufacturer with assets of $12 million, illustrates a typical case where convertibles are useful.

Winchester's profits have been depressed as a result of its heavy expenditures on research and development for a new product. This situation has held down the growth rate of earnings and dividends, and the price/ earnings ratio is only 18 times, as compared with an industry average of 22. At the current $2 earnings per share and P/E of 18, the stock is selling for $36 a share. The Winchester family owns 70 percent of the 300,000 shares outstanding, or 210,000 shares. It would like to retain majority control, but cannot buy more stock.

The heavy R&D expenditures have resulted in the development of a new type of printed circuit that management believes will be highly profitable. Five million dollars is needed to build and equip new production facilities, and profits will not start to flow in to the company for some 18 months after construction on the new plant is started. Winchester's debt amounts to $5.4 million, or 45 percent of assets, well above the 25 percent industry average. Present debt indenture provisions restrict the company from selling additional debt unless the new debt is subordinate to that now outstanding.

Investment bankers inform J. H. Winchester, Jr., the financial vice-president, that subordinated debentures cannot be sold unless they are convertible or have warrants attached. Convertibles or bonds with warrants can be sold with a 5 percent coupon interest rate if the conversion price or warrant option price is set at 15 percent above the present market price of $36, or at $41 a share. Alternatively, the investment bankers are willing to buy convertibles or bonds with warrants at a 5½ percent interest rate and a 20 percent conversion premium, or a conversion (or exercise) price of $43.50. If the company wants to sell common stock directly, it can net $33 a share.

Which of the alternatives should Winchester choose? First, note that if common stock is used, the company must sell 151,000 shares ($5 million divided by $33). Combined with the 90,000 shares held outside the family, this amounts to 241,000 shares versus the Winchester holdings of 210,000, so the family will lose majority control if common stock is sold.

If the 5 percent convertibles or bonds with warrants are used and the bonds are converted or the warrant is exercised, 122,000 new shares will be added. Combined with the old 90,000, the outside interest will then be 212,000, so again the Winchester family will lose majority control. However, if the 5½ percent convertibles or bonds with warrants are used, then after conversion or exercise only 115,000 new shares will be created. In this case the family will have 210,000 shares versus 205,000 for outsiders; absolute control will be maintained.

In addition to control, using the convertibles or warrants also benefits earnings per share in the long run—the total number of shares is less because fewer new shares must be issued to get the $5 million, so earnings per share will be higher. Before conversion or exercise, however, the firm has a considerable amount of debt outstanding. Adding $5 million raises the total debt to $10.4 million against a new total assets of $17 million, so the debt ratio will be over 61 percent versus the 25 percent industry average. This could be dangerous. If delays are encountered in bringing the new plant into production, if demand does not meet expectations, if the company should experience a strike, if the economy should go into a recession —if any of these things occurs, the company will be extremely vulnerable because of the high debt ratio.

In the present case the decision was made to sell the 5½ percent convertible debentures. Two years later earnings climbed to $3 a share, the P/E ratio to 20, and the price of the stock to $60. The bonds were called, but, of course, conversion occurred. After conversion, debt amounted to approximately $5.5 million against total assets of $17.5 million (some earnings had been retained), so the debt ratio was down to a more reasonable 31 percent.

Convertibles were chosen rather than bonds with warrants for the following reason. If a firm has a high debt ratio and its near-term prospects are favorable, it can anticipate a rise in the price of its stock and thus be able to call the bonds and force conversion. Warrants, on the other hand, have a stated life, and even though the price of the firm's stock rises, the warrants may not be exercised until near their expiration date. If, subsequent to the favorable period (during which convertibles could have been called), the firm encounters less favorable developments and the price of its stock falls, the warrants may lose their value and never be exercised. The heavy debt burden will then become aggravated. Therefore, the use of convertibles gives the firm greater control over the timing of future capital structure changes. This factor is of particular importance to the firm if its debt ratio is already high in relation to the risks of its line of business.

USE OF OPTIONS IN SMALL BUSINESS FINANCING

Most of the principles of financing are equally applicable to large and small firms. However, one aspect of small business financing has received considerable attention—the fact that organizers and owners of small businesses are often reluctant to share control of the firm as it grows. This presents problems, for growth brings with it the need to obtain additional funds. Small firms characteristically do not present a record of earnings or stability that justifies long-term debt financing, and the sale of equity shares would result in dilution of ownership and control.

This basic dilemma of small business financing can be eased considerably by the use of convertibles and warrants, the subject of the present chapter. Until the necessary background on convertibles and warrants had been set forth, we could not present a rounded discussion of small business financing. We can now do so. The use of convertibles and warrants enables a small firm to raise long-term debt money from the capital markets and at the same time provide investors in such securities with a degree of participation in the potential increase in equity values. Since the convertibles and warrants provide for future purchase of the common stock at a price usually at a premium over the current common stock price, the extent of dilution of control by the present owners is diminished to some degree.

Investment Banker Sponsorship of Small Firms

With the background of the use of options such as convertibles and warrants, it is now possible to discuss another important aspect of investment banker operations since the mid-1950s. One of the barriers to small firms' security issues has been the high cost of flotation, which until the mid-1950s according to SEC data, averaged around 20 percent of gross proceeds. Since the mid-1950s, warrants have been used to reduce direct flotation costs on both equity and debt issues for small firms. A common practice among investment bankers has been to reduce their commission from 20 percent to about 5 to 10 percent and to receive warrants to purchase up to 10 percent of the common stock of the small firm. With these kinds of inducements, investment bankers have vigorously sponsored small equity issues and have maintained a continued program of financing for small firms, especially those with good growth potential.

Small Business Investment Corporations

The original intention of the Small Business Investment Company (SBIC) Act of 1958 was to create, with federal government financing help, institutions that would provide funds to small business firms on a debt basis with the added inducement of equity participation through the use of convertibles and warrants. Since the adoption of the act in 1958, the SBICs have gone through alternate periods of optimistic and pessimistic evaluations of their prospects. Both government regulations providing for the nature and extent of government assistance and the investment powers of the SBICs have undergone a series of changes. Throughout all these changes, two broad policies have characterized the operations of the small business investment corporations. First, they emphasize convertible securities and obligations with warrants, giving the SBIC a residual equity position in the companies to which funds are provided. Second, they emphasize the provision for SBIC management counsel, for which a fee is charged.

In order to promote small business financing, the SBICs were granted advantageous tax provisions. Dividends received by the SBICs from their small business investments are 100 percent deductible from the SBIC's income, compared with 85 percent for ordinary corporations. Losses from convertible debentures of the stocks into which these are converted can be treated as losses chargeable against ordinary income, not against capital gains. SBICs are exempt from penalties for improper accumulation of income if they meet certain requirements. Also, investors in SBICs may treat their own stock losses as ordinary losses chargeable against ordinary income.

OTHER ACTIVITIES OF THE SMALL BUSINESS ADMINISTRATION

Since one of the activities of the Small Business Administration was discussed in connection with the SBIC program, it may be useful to round out the discussion by describing some of the other important activities of the Small Business Administration (SBA).

Scope of Operations of the SBA

The Small Business Administration (SBA) helps small business firms in a number of ways. It aids small business in obtaining a fair share of government contracts and it also emphasizes assistance in management and production problems. These two objectives recognize that a substantial number of small business firms need management counseling and assistance. In addition, the SBA actively aids small firms with their financial problems; this aspect of SBA operations will be emphasized here.

For business loans, the SBA defines a small business as one that is independently owned and operated and is nondominant in its field. Specific standards depend upon the industry of the firm. Any manufacturing concern is defined as small if it employes 250 or fewer persons; it is defined as large if it employs more than 1,000 persons. On the other hand, if a manufacturing concern operates in an industry that has few competitors, and if it has less than 5 percent of sales, it may be called a small business; American Motors is classed as a small business under this definition. A wholesale concern is classified as small if its yearly sales are $5 million or less. Most retail businesses and service trades are defined as small if their total annual receipts do not exceed $1 million. A business operating under a franchise may obtain a loan if the SBA can be assured that the firm is not a large business through its affiliation with the franchiser. The Department of Commerce estimates that, as of the end of 1966, 95 percent of all firms were classified as small businesses. There is, therefore a wide scope for SBA operations.

Loan Policies and Types

By law, the SBA makes loans to small business concerns only when financing is not available to them on reasonable terms from other sources. The SBA loans are of two types: direct and participating. In a direct loan, there is no participation by a private lender—the loan is made directly by the SBA to the borrower. In participating loans, the SBA joins with a bank or other private lending institution in making a loan to a small business firm.

A participating loan may be made under a loan guarantee or on an immediate basis. A participating loan on a *guarantee basis* provides that the SBA will purchase its guaranteed portion of the outstanding balance of the loan if the borrower defaults. When the SBA participates in a loan on an *immediate basis,* it purchases immediately a fixed percentage of the original principal amount of the loan. By law, the SBA may not enter into an immediate participation if it can arrange a guaranteed loan.

SUMMARY

Both warrants and convertibles are forms of options used in financing business firms. The use of long-term options such as warrants and convertibles is encouraged by an economic environment combining prospects of both boom or inflation and depression or deflation. The senior position of the securities protects against recessions. The option feature offers the opportunity for participation in rising stock prices.

Both the convertibility privilege and warrants are used as sweeteners. The option privileges they grant may make it possible for small companies to sell debt or preferred stock which otherwise could not be sold. For large companies, the sweeteners result in lower costs of the securities sold. In addition, the options provide for the future sale of the common stock at prices higher than could be obtained at the time. The options thereby permit the delayed sale of common stock at more favorable prices.

The exercise of convertibles by their holders does not ordinarily bring additional funds to the company. The exercise of warrants will provide these funds.[3]

---

[3] An outstanding exception is the convertible debenture issued by AT&T since the end of World War II. For each $100 principal amount of debentures, an additional $35 to $45 (varying with the issue) was required to obtain one share of common stock.

The conversion of securities will result in reduced debt ratios. The exercise of warrants will strengthen the equity position but will still leave the debt or preferred stock on the balance sheet. In comparing the use of convertibles with senior securities carrying warrants, a firm with a high debt ratio should choose convertibles. A firm with a moderate or low debt ratio may employ warrants.

Options such as warrants and convertibles have been increasingly used to facilitate small business financing. One of the ways in which options have stimulated investment banker sponsorship of small firms has been in reducing the cash expenses of floating new issues of securities. SEC data showed that for a number of years flotation costs on small issues averaged as high as 20 percent of gross proceeds. The use of options has caused cash flotation costs to be reduced. The characteristic pattern has been for the investment banker to charge a commission of 5 to 10 percent of gross proceeds plus taking warrants exercisable at the issue price on up to 10 percent of the number of new shares issued.

Another institutional arrangement that encouraged the use of options in the financing of small business resulted from the establishment of Small Business Investment Corporations in 1958. The SBICs were empowered to make debt investments in small business and to take warrants and conversion features as an inducement for making the loans.

In addition to their operations through SBICs, the Small Business Administration has provided financing to small business firms in a number of ways. First, the SBA helps small businesses obtain government contracts. Second, the SBA has emphasized management counseling to small business. Finally, the SBA itself makes two types of loans to small business—direct loans to borrowers and participating loans through other financial institutions. Participating loans are either *immediate* loans in which a fixed percentage of the loan is made by the SBA to the small business, the remainder of the funds being supplied by a bank, or a loan guarantee under which the SBA will purchase its guaranteed portion if the borrower defaults.

QUESTIONS

20–1 Why do warrants typically sell at prices greater than their theoretical values?

20–2 Why do convertibles typically sell at prices greater than their theoretical values (the higher of the conversion value or straight debt value)? Would you expect the percentage premium on a convertible bond to be greater or less than that on a warrant? (The percentage premium is defined as the market price minus the theoretical value, divided by the market price.)

20–3 What effect does the trend in stock prices (subsequent to issue) have on a firm's ability to raise funds (a) through convertibles and (b) through warrants?

20–4 If a firm expects to have additional financial requirements in the future, would you recommend that it use convertibles or bonds with warrants? Why?

20–5 How does a firm's dividend policy affect each of the following:

  a) The value of long-term warrants.
  b) The likelihood that convertible bonds will be converted.
  c) The likelihood that warrants will be exercised.

20–6 Evaluate the following statement: "Issuing convertible securities represents a means by which a firm can sell common stock at a price above the existing market."

20–7 Why do corporations often sell convertibles on a rights basis?

PROBLEMS

20–1 The Marfield Manufacturing Company's capital consists of 8,000 shares of common stock and 4,000 warrants, each good to buy two shares of common at $80 a share. The warrants are protected against dilution (that is, the subscription price is adjusted downward in the event of a stock dividend or, if the firm sells common stock at less than the $80 exercise price). The company issues rights to buy one new share of common at $60 for every two shares held. With the stock selling rights on at $90, compute:

  a) The theoretical value of the rights before the stock sells ex rights.
  b) The new subscription price of the warrant after the rights issue.

20–2 The Baker Electronics Corporation was planning to finance an expansion in the summer of 1967. The principal executives of the company were agreed that an industrial company of this type should finance growth by means of common stock rather than of debt. However, they felt that the price of the company's common stock did not reflect its true worth, so they were desirous of selling a convertible security. They considered a convertible debenture but feared the burden of fixed interest charges if the common stock did not rise in price to make conversion attractive. They decided on an issue of convertible preferred stock.

  The common stock was currently selling at $60 a share. Management projected earnings for 1967 at $4 a share and expected a future growth rate of 8 percent a year. It was agreed by the investment bankers and the management that the common stock would sell at 20 times earnings.

  a) What conversion price should be set by the issuer?
  b) Should the preferred stock include a call-price provision? Why?

20–3 Baker Electronics, Inc., has the following balance sheet:

BALANCE SHEET 1

Current assets	$ 50,000	Current debt	$ 20,000
Net fixed assets	50,000	Common stock, par value $2	20,000
		Earned surplus	60,000
Total assets	$100,000	Total claims	$100,000

a) The firm earns 20 percent on total assets before taxes (assume a 50 percent tax rate). What are earnings per share?

b) If the price/earnings ratio for the company's stock is 20 times, what is
the market price of the company's stock?

c) What is the book value of the company's stock?

In the following few years, sales are expected to double and the financing
needs of the firm will double. The firm decides to sell debentures to meet
these needs. It is undecided, however, whether to sell convertible debentures or debentures with warrants. The new balance sheet would appear as
follows:

BALANCE SHEET 2

Current assets	$100,000	Current debt	$ 40,000
Net fixed assets	100,000	Debentures	60,000
		Common stock, par value $2	20,000
		Earned surplus	80,000
Total assets	$200,000	Total claims	$200,000

The convertible debentures would pay 5 percent interest and would be
convertible into 25 shares of common stock for each $1,000 debenture. The
debentures with warrants would carry a 6 percent coupon and entitle each
holder of a $1,000 debenture to buy 20 shares of common stock at $40.
Richard Baker owns 80 percent of Electronics before the financing.

d) Assume that convertible debentures are sold and all are later converted.
Show the new balance sheet, disregarding any changes in retained
earnings.

BALANCE SHEET 3

	Current debt	_____
	Debentures	_____
	Common stock, par value $2	_____
	Paid-in surplus	_____
	Earned surplus	_____
Total assets _____	Total claims	_____

e) Complete the firm's income statement after the debentures have all been
converted:

INCOME STATEMENT

Net income after all charges except debenture interest and before taxes (20% of total assets)	_____
Debenture interest	_____
Federal income tax, 50%	_____
Net income after taxes	_____
Earnings per share after taxes	_____

f) Now, instead of convertibles, assume that debentures with warrants were issued. Assume further that the warrants were all exercised. Show the new balance sheet figures.

BALANCE SHEET 4

Total assets	Current debt _____
	Debentures _____
	Common stock, par value $2 _____
	Paid-in surplus _____
	Earned surplus _____
	Total claims _____

g) Complete the firm's income statement after the debenture warrants have all been exercised.

INCOME STATEMENT

Net income after all charges except debenture interest and before taxes	_____
Debenture interest	_____
Taxable income	_____
Federal income tax	_____
Net income after taxes	_____
Earnings per share after taxes	_____

20-4 The Dixon Company has grown rapidly during the past five years. Recently its commercial bank has urged the company to consider increasing permanent financing. Its bank loan had risen to $200,000, carrying 6 percent interest. Dixon has been 30 to 60 days late in paying trade creditors.

Discussions with an investment banker have resulted in the suggestion to raise $400,000 at this time. Investment bankers have assured Dixon that the following alternatives will be feasible (flotation costs will be ignored):

Alternative 1: Sell common stock at $8.
Alternative 2: Sell convertible bonds at a 6 percent coupon, convertible into common stock at $10.
Alternative 3: Sell debentures at a 6 percent coupon, each $1,000 bond carrying 100 warrants to buy common stock at $10.

Additional information is given below.

DIXON COMPANY
BALANCE SHEET
December 31, 1968

		Current liabilities	$350,000
		Common stock, par $1.00	100,000
		Retained earnings	50,000
		Total liabilities and	
Total assets	$500,000	capital	$500,000

DIXON COMPANY
INCOME STATEMENT
December 31, 1968

Sales	$1,000,000
All costs except interest	900,000
Gross profit	$ 100,000
Interest	12,000
Profit before taxes	$ 88,000
Taxes at 50%	44,000
Profits after taxes	$ 44,000
Shares	100,000
Earnings per share	$0.44
Price/earnings ratio	20×
Market price of stock	$8.80

E. E. Bradley, the president, owns 68 percent of the common stock of Dixon Company and wishes to maintain control of the company.

a) Show the new balance sheet under each of the alternatives. For 1 and 2 show the balance sheet after conversion of the debentures or exercise of warrants. Assume that one half the funds raised will be used to pay off the bank loan and one half to increase total assets.
b) Show Bradley's control position under each alternative, assuming he does not purchase additional shares.
c) What is the effect on earnings per share of each of the alternatives, if it is assumed that profits before interest and taxes will be 20 percent of total assets?
d) What will be the debt ratio under each alternative?
e) Which of the three alternatives would you recommend to Bradley, and why?

PART VII

Valuation in Mergers and Corporate Readjustment

Chapter 21

External Growth: Mergers and Holding Companies

Growth is vital to the well-being of a firm; without it a business cannot attract able management because it cannot give them recognition in promotions and challenging creative activity. Without able executives, the firm is likely to decline and die. Much of the material in the previous chapters dealing with analysis, planning, and financing has a direct bearing on the financial manager's potential contribution to the growth of a firm. However, because of the central importance of the growth requirement, the present chapter is focused on strategies for promoting it.

Merger activity has played an important part in the growth of firms in the United States, and financial managers are required both to appraise the desirability of a prospective purchase and to participate directly in evaluating the respective companies involved in a merger.[1] Consequently, it is essential that the study of financial management provide the background necessary for effective participation in merger negotiations and decisions.

Financial managers—and intelligent laymen—also need to be aware of the broader significance of mergers. Despite the heightened merger activities in the 1920s, again after World War II, and during the mid-1960s, recent merger movements have neither approached the magnitude nor

---

[1] As we use the term, "merger" means any combination that forms one economic unit from two or more previous ones. For legal purposes there are distinctions between the various ways these combinations can occur, but our emphasis is on fundamental business and financial aspects of mergers or acquisitions.

had the social consequences of the mergers that took place from 1890 to 1905. During this period more than 200 major combinations were effected, thus resulting in the concentration that has characterized the steel, tobacco, and other important industries. Regardless of the business objectives and motives of merger activity, the social and economic consequences of mergers must also be taken into account.

REASONS FOR SEEKING GROWTH

One of the objectives of growth, whether by external acquisitions or by internal development, is large size for the purpose of achieving economies of large-scale operations. Economies of scale result from the following factors.

Research. Research activities are especially crucial in today's dynamic economy. The large firm can finance large-scale research which may benefit a great number of its diverse operations. But suppose a large firm is broken into ten units. Could not the ten units each contract to hire research from a research organization? It is true that research in the large firm is often conducted by executives hired on a salary basis, and independent research firms do sell their services on a fee basis. There are some kinds of research, however, that are the unique contribution of the large firm.

For example, suppose that a large firm which spends $50 million a year on research is divided into ten firms, each of which could allocate $5 million a year for research. If each of these ten firms hires the services of a research organization, each would attempt to buy $5 million worth of research designed to give it a competitive advantage over its nine rivals and any other firms in the industry. It seems reasonable to suppose that certain kinds of research could not be purchased by the $5 million a year but could be achieved by the $50 million budget.

Modern large-scale business organizations represent the combination of centralized and decentralized decisions. Research is an activity performed most efficiently when centralized. Although the amounts of money spent on research are relatively small, its significance is critical for the progress of the firm.

Top-management skills. Related to indivisibility of research expenditures is the value of the highly able executive. The very competent individual is another one of the indivisible factors that make for an advantage of large-scale operations. It cannot be denied that many decisions are decentralized and that for many matters delegation of authority to committees and subordinates takes place. On the other hand, some of the centralized decisions and the catalytic process of a great mind on policy matters are of pervasive and powerful influence on the growth pattern and performance of an organization.

Operating economies. Often there are other economies of multiprod-uct operations. Lower salary ratios may be achieved by consolidating certain departments (accounting, marketing, advertising, switchboard, cler-ical); marketing costs may be lowered by consolidating salesmen covering the same territory for several companies, thus reducing the total number of salesmen required; production savings may come from the ability to utilize large, high-output machinery or to obtain quantity discounts on purchases.

Risk reduction. Still another important factor is the risk reduction of multiplant operations, which is heightened by the tax structure. If a new firm attempts an innovation or a new product line and fails, the loss may force it out of business completely. On the other hand, if an established firm attempts a change or an innovation, any loss can be offset against as-sured income from other sources. The higher the tax rate, the higher the proportion of the innovation costs borne by taxes. This is another reason why multiproduct and multiplant firms confer economic advantages, not only on the firm itself but also on the economy as a whole, in terms of the potential rate of economic progress.

Market capitalization rates. While it is not strictly an operating econ-omy, the fact that the earnings of larger economic units are capitalized at lower rates and, hence, produce higher market values has stimulated many mergers. The securities of larger firms have better marketability, these firms are more able to diversify and thus reduce risks, and they are generally better known. All these factors lead to higher price/earnings ratios. As a result, it may be possible to consolidate firms and have the resulting market value greater than the sum of their individual values, even if there is no increase in aggregate earnings. To illustrate, three companies may each be earning $100 and selling at 10 times earnings, for a total market value of ($100)(10)(3) equals $3,000. When these companies combine, the new company may obtain a Stock Exchange listing or take other actions to im-prove the price of its stock. If so, the price/earnings ratio may rise to 15, in which case the market value of the consolidated firm would be $4,500.[2]

The five factors just discussed provide a plausible rationale for the existence and operation of larger multiproduct and multiplant enterprises.

MERGERS VERSUS INTERNAL GROWTH

Many of the objectives of size and diversification may be achieved either through internal growth or by external growth through acquisitions and mergers. In the post-World War II period considerable diversification was

---

[2] The market capitalization rate is related to the cost of equity, as was ex-plained in Chapter 10. A lower capitalization rate results in a lower cost of capital. Therefore, the same actions that raise the market value of the equity also lower the firm's cost of new capital.

achieved by many firms through external acquisition. The reasons for utilizing external acquisition instead of internal growth to achieve diversification may be briefly indicated.

Speed. New facilities may be acquired more quickly through mergers. New products, new processes, new plants, and new productive organizations can be acquired in a fully operative condition by a merger.

Cost. The desired facilities may be obtained more cheaply by purchasing the ownership stock of each existing company. For many reasons the securities of a company may be selling below the replacement costs of the firm's assets. For example, stock market prices were relatively depressed from 1946 to 1953, and the market values of common stocks were low in relation to earnings levels. A basis was provided for developing favorable merger terms.

Mergers in the steel industry in the period immediately following 1946 are good examples of this influence. A steel company could add new capacity much more cheaply by buying another company than by building new plants to achieve the same increase in capacity. Furthermore, the speed factor mentioned above was important here. The duration of the seller's market in steel was unknown. The sooner a steel company could acquire additional facilities and get them into operation for making sales, the more likely it would be to benefit from the favorable market conditions.

Related to the above is the objective of obtaining the services of desired personnel. Sometimes the inducement of higher compensation to attract an outstanding individual or management group might be either unduly expensive or useless. Simply buying the company that employs these people may prove to be the most effective means of obtaining their services. In such circumstances a merger may be the only practicable method of obtaining the kind of superior management talent or technical skill that the acquiring firm is seeking to obtain.

Financing. Sometimes it is possible to finance an acquisition when it is not possible to finance internal growth. A large steel plant, for example, involves a large investment. Steel capacity may be acquired in a merger through an exchange of stock more cheaply than it can be obtained by buying the facilities themselves. Sellers may be more willing to accept the stock of the purchaser in payment for the facilities sold than would investors in a public distribution. The use of stock reduces cash requirements for the acquisition of assets.

Risk. The desired new product, new process, or new organization may be developed with less uncertainty of investment loss. The purchased facility may already have demonstrated its revenue-yielding capacity.

Stabilizing effects. A merger may represent the most effective method of achieving stability and progress at a given stage of industrial development. It may represent the most efficient method of combining facilities and disposing of obsolete and inefficient properties, as was probably true at some stages in the development of industries such as railroad transport, air transport, banking, agricultural implements, and steel.

Taxes. Without question, the high level of taxation was a factor in the postwar period. A study by a Harvard group indicates that taxes appear to have been a major reason for the sale of about one third of the firms acquired by merger.[3] Inheritance taxes precipitated these sales in some cases; in others the advantage of buying a company with a tax loss, which was discussed in Chapter 2, provided the motivation.

Competitive advantages. The development of new products and market areas may be accomplished through mergers. Firms in the early stages of development can in this way avoid combating difficult competition. Market control may be obtained more rapidly and with less risk through mergers than by internal expansion. The merger of two large firms may result in market dominance by the combined firms. Coordinated price and output policies that might be illegal in separate firms may be achieved legally by a single, consolidated enterprise.

Regardless of the motives or objectives of mergers from a business standpoint, the consequences of the market-control position of the acquiring company may lead to intervention by governmental regulatory agencies. Hence, it is not enough for the financial manager to consider only the business aspects of the merger. He must also consider the effects on market control. If the merger will have potentially adverse effects on competition, there is a strong likelihood that government action will be interposed against the merger.

TERMS OF MERGERS

For every merger actually consummated, a number of other potentially attractive combinations fail during the negotiating stage. In some of these cases, negotiations are broken off when it is revealed that the companies' operations are not compatible. In others, tangible benefits would result, but the parties are unable to agree on the merger terms. Of these terms, the most important is the price paid by the acquiring firm for the firm acquired. Factors that influence this important aspect of a merger are now considered.

---

[3] J. K. Butters, J. Lintner, and W. L. Cary, *Effects of Taxation: Corporate Mergers* (Boston, Mass.: Division of Research, Graduate School of Business Administration, Harvard University, 1951).

Effects on Price and Earnings

A merger carries potentialities for either favorable or adverse effects on earnings, market prices of shares, or both. Previous chapters have shown that investment decisions should be guided by the effects on market values and that these effects should in turn be determined by the effects on future earnings and dividends. These future events are difficult to forecast, however, so stockholders as well as management give considerable weight to the immediate effects of a contemplated merger on earnings per share. Directors of companies will often state, "I do not know how the merger will affect the market price of the shares of my company because so many forces influencing market prices are at work. But the effect on earnings per share can be seen directly."

An example will illustrate the effects of a proposed merger on earnings per share and thus suggest the kinds of problems that are likely to arise. Assume the following facts for two companies:

	Company A	Company B
Total earnings	$20,000	$50,000
Number of shares of common stock	5,000	10,000
Earnings per share of stock	$ 4.00	$ 5.00
Price/earnings ratio per share	15×	12×
Market price per share	$ 60.00	$ 60.00

Suppose the firms agree to merge, with B, the surviving firm, acquiring the shares of A by a one-for-one exchange of stock. The exchange ratio is determined by the respective market prices of the two companies. Assuming no increase in earnings, the effects on earnings per share are shown in the following tabulation:

	Shares of Company B Owned after Merger	Earnings per share	
		Before Merger	After Merger
A's stockholders	5,000	$4	$4.67
B's stockholders	10,000	5	$4.67
Total	15,000		

Since total earnings are $70,000 and a total of 15,000 shares will be outstanding after the merger has been completed, the new earnings per share will be $4.67. Earnings will increase by 67 cents for A's stockholders, but they will decline by 33 cents for B's.

The effects on market values are less certain. If the combined companies sell at the 15 times price/earnings ratio of company A, the new market value per share of the new company will be $70. In this case shareholders of both companies will have benefited. This result comes about because the combined earnings are now valued at a multiplier of 15, whereas prior to the merger a portion of the earnings was valued at a multiplier of 15 and a portion valued at a multiplier of 12.

If, on the other hand, the earnings of the new company are valued at B's multiplier of 12, the indicated market value of the shares will be $56. The shareholders of each company will have suffered a $4 dilution in market value.

Because the effects on market value per share are less certain than those on earnings per share, the impact on earnings per share tends to be given greater weight in merger negotiations. Because of this, the following analysis also emphasizes effects on earnings per share, while recognizing that maximizing market value is the valid rule for investment decisions.

If the merger takes place on the basis of earnings, neither earnings dilution nor earnings appreciation will take place. This follows from the results shown below:

	Shares of Company B Owned after Merger	Earnings per Old Share	
		Before Merger	After Merger
A shareholders [4]	4,000	$4	$4
B shareholders	10,000	$5	$5
Total	14,000		

It is clear that the equivalent earnings per share after the merger are the same as before the merger. The effects on market values will depend upon whether the 15-times multiplier of A or the 12-times multiplier of B obtains.

Of the numerous factors affecting the valuation of the constituent companies in a merger, all must ultimately be reflected in the earnings per share or market price of the companies. Hence, all the effects on the earn-

---

[4] Based on earnings, the exchange ratio is 4:5; that is, company A's shareholders receive four shares of B stock for each five shares of A stock they own. Earnings per share of the merged company is $5, but since A's shareholders now own only 80 percent of the number of their old shares, their equivalent earnings per *old* share is the same $4. For example, suppose one of A's stockholders formerly held 100 shares. He will own only 80 shares of B after the merger, and his total earnings will be 80 × $5 = $400. Dividing their $400 total earnings by the number of shares they formerly owned, 100, gives the $4 per *old* share.

ings position or wealth position of stockholders are encompassed by the foregoing example. The discussion may, therefore, turn to a consideration of the factors that will influence the terms on which an acquisition or a merger is likely to take place. Both quantitative and qualitative factors receive consideration.

Quantitative Factors Affecting Terms of Mergers

Five factors have received the greatest emphasis in arriving at merger terms:

Earnings and growth rates	Market values
Dividends	Book values
Net current assets	

Analysis is typically based on the per share values of the foregoing factors. The relative importance of each factor and the circumstances under which each is likely to be the most influential determinant in arriving at terms will vary. The nature of these influences is now described.

Earnings and growth rates. Both expected earnings and capitalization rates (P/E ratios) are important in determining the values that will be established in a merger. The analysis necessarily begins with historical data on the firms' earnings, whose past growth rates, future trends, and variability are important determinants of the earnings multiplier, or P/E ratio, that will prevail after the merger.

How future earnings growth rates affect the multiplier can be illustrated by extending the preceding example. First, we know that high P/E ratios are commonly associated with rapidly growing companies. Since company A has the higher P/E ratio, it is reasonable to assume that its earnings are expected to grow more rapidly than those of company B. Suppose A's expected growth rate is 10 percent and B's 5 percent. Looking at the proposed merger from the point of view of company B and its stockholders and assuming that the exchange ratio is based on present market prices, it can be seen that B will suffer a dilution in earnings when the merger occurs. However, B will be acquiring a firm with more favorable growth prospects; hence its earnings after the merger should increase more rapidly than before. In fact, the new growth rate may turn out to be a weighted average of the growth rates of the individual firms, weighted by their respective total earnings before the merger. In the example, the new expected growth rate is 6.43 percent.

With the new growth rate it is possible to determine just how long it will take company B's stockholders to regain the earnings dilution. That is, how long will it take earnings per share to be back to where they would have been without the merger? This can be determined graphically from Figure 21–1.[5] Without the merger, B would have initial earnings of $5 a share, and these earnings would have grown at a rate of 5 percent a year.

With the merger, earnings drop to $4.67 a share, but the rate of growth increases to 6.43 percent. Under these conditions the earnings dilution is overcome after five years; from the fifth year on, B's earnings will be higher, assuming the merger is consummated.

This same type of relationship could be developed from the point of view of the faster growing firm. Here there would be an immediate earnings increase but a reduced rate of growth. Working through the analysis would show the number of years before the earnings accretion would be eroded.

It is apparent that the critical variables are (1) the respective rates of growth of the two firms, (2) their relative sizes, which determine the actual amount of the initial earnings per share dilution or accretion, as well as the new weighted average growth rate, (3) the firms' P/E ratios, and (4) the exchange ratio. These factors interact to produce the resulting pattern of earnings per share for the surviving company. It is possible to generalize the relationships somewhat,[6] but for our purposes here it is necessary simply to note that in the bargaining process the exchange ratio is the variable that must be manipulated in an effort to reach a mutually satisfactory earnings pattern.

Dividends. Dividends, because they represent the actual income received by stockholders, may influence the terms of merger. However, as the material in Chapter 17 indicates, dividends are likely to have little influence on the market price of companies with a record of high growth and high profitability. For example, some companies, such as Litton Industries, have not yet paid cash dividends but command market prices representing a high multiplier of current earnings. At the end of 1964, Litton was selling at a multiplier of approximately 40 times. On the other hand, for utility companies and for companies in industries where growth rates and profitability have declined, the dollar amount of dividends paid may have a relatively important influence on the market price of the stock. Dividends may therefore influence the terms on which these companies would be likely to trade in a merger.

Market values. The price of a firm's stock reflects expectations about its future earnings and dividends, so one might expect current market values to have a strong influence on the terms of a merger. However, one could predict that the value placed on a firm in an acquisition is likely to exceed its current market price for a number of reasons. (1) If the company is in a depressed industry, its stockholders are likely to overdiscount the dismal

---

[5] The calculation could also be made algebraically by solving for N in the following equation: $E_1(1 + g_1)^N = E_2(1 + g_2)^N$, where $E_1 =$ earnings before the merger, $E_2 =$ earnings after the merger, g_1 and g_2 are the growth rates before and after the merger, and N is the break-even number of years.

[6] For a generalization, as well as for a more detailed examination of the interrelations, see D. F. Folz and J. Fred Weston, "Looking Ahead in Evaluating Proposed Mergers," *N.A.A. Bulletin* (April 1962).

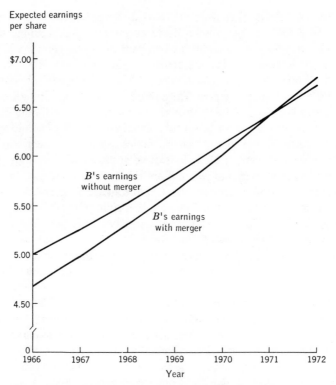

Expected earnings
per share

$7.00

6.50

6.00

B's earnings
without merger

5.50

B's earnings
with merger

5.00

4.50

0
1966   1967   1968   1969   1970   1971   1972

Year

Figure 21-1   Effect of Merger on Future Earnings

outlook for the company and this will result in a very low current market price. (2) The prospective purchaser may be interested in acquiring the company for the contribution that it may make to the acquiring company. Thus, the acquired company is worth more to an informed purchaser than it is in the general market. (3) Unless stockholders are offered more than current market prices for their stock, they may have no inducement to sell.

Book value per share. Book values are now generally considered to be relatively unimportant in determining the value of a company; they merely represent the historical investments that have been made in the company. These historical investments may have little relation to current values or prices. At times, however, especially when book values substantially exceed market values, they may well have an impact on merger terms. The book value is an index of the amount of physical facilities made available in the merger. Despite a past record of low earning power, it is always possible that, under effective management, a firm's assets may once again achieve normal earning power. If this is the case, the market value of the company will rise. Because of the potential contribution of physical properties to improved future earnings, book values may have an important influence on actual merger or acquisition terms.

Net current assets per share. Net current assets (current assets minus current liabilities) per share are likely to have an influence on merger terms because they represent the amount of liquidity that may be obtained from a company in a merger. In the postwar textile mergers, net current assets were very high, and this was one of the characteristics making them attractive to the acquiring firms. By buying a textile company, often with securities, an acquiring company was in a position to look for still other merger candidates, paying for the new acquisition with the just-acquired liquidity. In this same connection, if the acquired company is debt-free, the acquiring firm may be able to borrow the funds required for the purchase, using the acquired firm's assets and earning power as security for the loan.

Relative Importance of Quantitative Factors

Attempts have been made to determine statistically the relative weights assigned to each of these factors in actual merger cases. However, these attempts have been singularly unsuccessful—in one case one factor seems to dominate, in another some other determinant appears to be most important. This absence of consistent patterns among the quantitative factors suggests that qualitative forces are also at work, and we now turn our attention to these more nebulous variables.

Qualitative Influences

Sometimes the most important influence on the terms of a merger is a business consideration not reflected at all in historical quantitative data. A soundly conceived merger is one in which the combination produces what may be called a *synergistic,* or "two plus two equals five" effect. By the combination, more profits result than could be achieved by the individual firms operating separately.

For example, in the 1953 merger between Merck and Company and Sharp and Dohme, it was said that each company complemented the other in an important way. Merck had a strong reputation for its research organization. Sharp and Dohme had a most effective sales organization. The combination of these two pharmaceutical companies added strength to both. Another example is the merger in late 1954 between Carrier Corporation and Affiliated Gas Equipment, Inc. The merger enabled the combined company to provide a complete line of air-conditioning and heating equipment. The merger between Hilton Hotels and Statler Hotels led to economies in the purchase of supplies and materials. One Hilton executive estimated that the savings accruing simply from the combined management of the Statler Hotel in New York and Hilton's New York Hotel amounted to $700,000 a year. The bulk of the savings were in laundry, food, advertising, and administrative costs.

The qualitative factors may also reflect such influences as the following. The merger or acquisition may enable one company to obtain general-management ability that it lacks but which the other company possesses. Another factor may be the acquisition of a technically competent scientific or engineering staff; one of the companies may have fallen behind in the technological race and may need to combine with another company if it expects to catch up at all. In such a situation the company lacking the technical competence possessed by the other firm may be willing to pay a substantial premium over previous levels of earnings, dividends, or market or book values.

Or the purpose of the merger may be to develop a production capability a firm does not possess. Some firms are strong in producing custom-made items with high-performance characteristics, yet these firms, on entering new markets, must make use of mass-production techniques. If the firm has had no experience in mass-production techniques, this skill may have to be obtained by means of a merger. Or the firm may need to develop an effective sales organization. For example, some of the companies previously oriented to the defense market, such as the aircraft companies, found that they had only a limited industrial sales organization; merger was the solution to the problem.

The foregoing are the kinds of qualitative considerations that may have an overriding influence on the actual terms of merger; the values of these contributions are never easy to qualify. The all-encompassing question, of course, is how these factors will affect the contribution of each company to future earnings per share in the combined operation. The historical data and the qualitative considerations described above, in addition to judgment and bargaining, combine to determine merger terms.

ACCOUNTING POLICIES IN MERGERS[7]

After merger terms have been agreed upon, the financial manager must be familiar with the principles for recording the financial results of the merger and for reflecting the initial effect on the earnings of the surviving firm. This section deals with these matters.

The financial statements of the survivor in a merger must follow the regulations and supervision of the Securities and Exchange Commission. The SEC's requirements follow the recommendations of professional accounting societies on combinations, but interpretations of actual situations require considerable financial and economic analysis.

Both the Securities and Exchange Commission and the *Accounting*

---

[7] The material in this section is rather technical and is generally covered in accounting courses. The section may be omitted without loss of continuity.

Research Bulletin No. 48 make a distinction between "purchase" and "pooling of interests." Three main tests must be met to establish that a "pooling of interests" has occurred:

1. The net worth of the two firms must be roughly the same size at the time of combination.
2. The relative asset sizes of the two firms must be approximately equal.
3. Both managements must continue to carry on important functions in the resulting firm.

In a purchase, an important part of one or more of the ownership interests is absorbed, and the other tests of pooling of interests are not met.

In practice it is difficult to distinguish between purchase and merger, especially when combinations show characteristics of each. However, the Securities and Exchange Commission spends long hours in conferences with representatives of registrants discussing the financial treatment of combinations.

Another aspect of the distinction between purchase and pooling of interests relates to the creation of goodwill. In a purchase, the excess (or deficit) over the book value of net worth purchased is set up as goodwill, and capital surplus is increased (or decreased) accordingly. In a pooling of interests, any premium over book value is charged against capital surplus. As a consequence, the combined total assets after the merger represent a simple sum of the asset contributions of the constituent companies. Further, the writing-off of goodwill can have a marked impact on the surviving firm's reported profits for years to come.

If the merger is handled as a purchase, the acquired firm is treated as an investment, just as would the acquisition of any other capital asset. The goodwill, or difference between the purchase price and the acquired net worth, is considered to be "depreciable." Goodwill must therefore be written off against earnings over some "reasonable" period, just as any other depreciable asset must be written off. (However, goodwill written off is not deductible for tax purposes.) Therefore, if a merger is treated as a purchase, reported profits will be lower than if it is handled as a pooling of interests. This is the reason that most firms prefer the pooling-of-interest to the purchase treatment, and also the reason for the SEC's interest in the accounting method followed.

These general statements may be made more meaningful by concrete illustrations of first a purchase and then a pooling of interests.

Financial Treatment of a Purchase

The financial treatment of a purchase may best be explained by the use of a hypothetical example. The Mammoth Company has just purchased the Petty Company under an arrangement known as a *purchase*. The facts are as given in Table 21-1, which also shows the financial treatment. The illustration conforms to the general nature of a purchase. Measured by total assets, the Mammoth Company is twenty times as large as Petty, while its total earnings are fifteen times as large. Assume that the terms of the purchase will be one share of Mammoth for two shares of Petty, based on the

Table 21–1   FINANCIAL TREATMENT OF A PURCHASE

	Mammoth Company	Petty Company	Adjustments Debit	Adjustments Credit	Pro Forma Balance Sheet
Assets					
Current	$80,000	$4,000			$84,000
Other assets	20,000	2,000			22,000
Net fixed assets	100,000	4,000			104,000
Intangible assets			$54,000		54,000
Total assets	$200,000	$10,000			$264,000
Liabilities and net worth					
Current liabilities	$40,000	$4,000			$44,000
Long-term debt	20,000				20,000
Common stock	40,000	1,000	1,000	$ 4,000	44,000
Capital surplus	20,000			56,000	76,000
Retained earnings	80,000	5,000	5,000		80,000
Total	$200,000	$10,000			$264,000

Explanation	Mammoth	Petty
Par value per share common stock	$4	$0.50
Number of shares outstanding	10,000	2,000
Book value per share	$14	$3
Total earnings	$ 30,000	$ 2,000
Earnings per share	$3	$1
Price/earnings ratio	20×	30×
Market value per share	$60	$30

prevailing market value of their shares of common stocks. Thus, Mammoth is giving $30 of market value and $7 of book value for each share of Petty stock. Petty's market value is $30 a share and its book value is $3 a share. The total market value of Mammoth paid for Petty is $60,000. The goodwill involved may be calculated as follows:

Value given by Mammoth	$60,000
Net worth of Petty purchased	6,000
Goodwill	$54,000

The $54,000 goodwill represents a debit in the Adjustments column and is carried to the *pro forma* balance sheet. The *pro forma* balance sheet is obtained by simply adding the balance sheets of the constituent companies.

The other adjustments to complete the entry are described below.

Common stock, Petty	$ 1,000	
Retained earnings, Petty	5,000	
Goodwill	54,000	
Common stock, Mammoth		$ 4,000
Capital surplus, Mammoth		56,000

Thus, a total value of $60,000 has been given by Mammoth. This amount represents a payment of $1,000 for the common stock of Petty, $5,000 for the retained earnings, and $54,000 goodwill. The corresponding credit is the 1,000 shares of Mammoth given in the transaction at their par value of $4 a share, resulting in a credit of $4,000. Capital surplus of Mammoth is increased by $56,000. When these adjustments are carried through to the *pro forma* balance sheet, total assets are increased from the combined total of $210,000 by the $54,000 increase in goodwill; the result is new total assets of $264,000. Total tangible assets, however, still remain $210,000.

The effects on earnings per share for stockholders in each company are now shown.

Total earnings	$32,000.00
Total shares	11,000
Earnings per share	$2.91
For Petty Shareholders	
New earnings per share [8]	$1.46
Before-purchase earnings per share	$1.00
Accretion per share	$0.46
For Mammoth Shareholders	
Before-purchase earnings per share	$3.00
New earnings per share	2.91
Dilution per share	$0.09

[8] Petty shareholders, after the 1 for 2 exchange, have only one half as many shares as before the merger. Therefore their earnings per *old* share are $2.91 ÷ 2 = $1.46. The example does not reflect the write-off of goodwill.

Total earnings represent the combined earnings of Mammoth and of Petty. The total shares are 11,000, because Mammoth has given one share of stock for every two shares of Petty previously outstanding. The new earnings per share are therefore $2.91. The calculation of earnings accretion or dilution proceeds on the same principles as the calculations set forth earlier in the chapter. The results require two important comments, however.

It will be noted that although the earnings accretion per share for Petty is $0.46, the earnings dilution per share for Mammoth is relatively small, only 9 cents per share. The explanation is that the size of Mammoth is large in relation to that of Petty. This example also illustrates a general principle—when a large company acquires a small one, it can afford to pay a high multiple of earnings per share of the smaller company. In the present example, the price/earnings ratio of Petty is 30, whereas the price/earnings ratio of Mammoth is 20. If the acquiring company is large relative to the acquired firm, it can pay a substantial premium and yet suffer only small dilution in its earnings per share.

But it is unrealistic to assume that the same earnings on total assets will obtain after the merger. After all, the purpose of the merger is to achieve something that the two companies could not have achieved alone. When in late 1953 Philip Morris & Company purchased Benson & Hedges, maker of Parliament, a leading filter-tip brand, it was buying the ability and experience of Benson & Hedges. By means of this merger Philip Morris & Company was able to make an entry into the rapidly growing filter-cigarette business more quickly than it could otherwise have done. The combined earnings per share are likely to be higher.

In the previous illustration it will be noted that the earnings rate on the tangible assets of Mammoth are 15 percent and on the total assets of Petty are 20 percent. Let us now assume that the return on total tangible assets of the combined companies rises to 20 percent. With the same total shares of 11,000 outstanding, the new earnings per share will be $3.82. Thus there will be accretion of $0.91 for the Petty shareholders, a rise of almost a dollar per share. Here, however, there will be an accretion of 82 cents for the Mammoth shareholders as well.

Another general principle is illustrated. If the purchase of a small company adds to the earnings of the consolidated enterprise, earnings per share may increase for both participants in the merger. Even if the merger results in an initial dilution in earnings per share of the larger company, the merger may still be advantageous. The initial dilution in the earnings per share may be regarded as an investment. The investment will have a payoff at some future date in terms of increased earnings per share of the consolidated company.

Treatment of Goodwill

In a purchase, goodwill is likely to arise, and since goodwill represents an intangible asset, its treatment is subject to the exercise of judgment. It will therefore be useful to set out a few generalizations on good practice with respect to the treatment of goodwill.

1. When goodwill is purchased, it should not be charged to surplus immediately on acquisition. Preferably, goodwill should be written off against income and should go through the income statement. Since goodwill is to be written off against income, it would not be appropriate to write it off entirely on acquisition, because an immediate write-off would be of such magnitude that distortion of earnings for that year would result.

2. The general view is not to write off purchased goodwill by charges to capital surplus. Purchased goodwill is supposed to represent, and to be reflected in, a future rise of income. It should be written off against income rather than against capital surplus. If goodwill is set up and capital surplus is created where no actual goodwill exists, it would be appropriate to write off such goodwill, but such writing off is more in the nature of correcting an error.[9]

3. When goodwill is purchased, an estimate should be made of its period of life. Annual charges, based on the estimated life of the goodwill, should then be made against income, to amortize the goodwill over the estimated period of the usefulness of the goodwill purchased.

4. If the life of intangibles does not appear to be limited, no systematic write-off is required. However, a conservative policy may justify a systematic write-off in amounts that will not distort income.

When goodwill is purchased, it should be treated as the purchase of any other valid asset. It should be written off to the extent that the value represented by any part of goodwill has a limited life, as is likely to be the situation. In a free enterprise economy, the existence of high profits represented by superior earning power attracts additional resources into that line of business. The growth of capacity and the increase in competition are likely to erode the superior earning power over time.

Financial Treatment of Pooling of Interests

When a business combination is a pooling of interests rather than a purchase, the accounting treatment is simply to combine the balance sheets of the two companies. Goodwill will not ordinarily arise in the consolidation.

The financial treatment may be indicated by another example, which

---

[9] W. W. Werntz, "Intangibles in Business Combinations," *Journal of Accountancy,* 103 (May 1957), pp. 47–48.

reflects the facts as they are set forth in Table 21–2. In order to focus on the critical issues, the balance sheets are identical in every respect. A difference in the amount and rate of profit (after interest) of the two companies is indicated.

Book value per share is $24. The amount of profit after interest and taxes is $40,000 for Company A and $20,000 for Company B. Earnings per share are therefore $8 and $4, respectively. The price/earning ratio is 15 for A and 10 for B, so that the market price of stock for A is $120 and for B $40. The working capital per share is $10 in each instance. The dividends per share are $4 for A and $2 for B.

For the example, assume that the terms of the merger would reflect either earnings or market price per share. If the terms of merger are based on earnings, 15,000 shares of stock will be outstanding. Total earnings are $60,000. The number of shares of stock in the new company AB is 15,000; hence, earnings per share in the company will be $4. As the owners of company A receive two shares, they are receiving the equivalent of $8 per share of stock which they originally held. Stockholders of both A and B have experienced neither earnings dilution nor earnings accretion.

When the terms of exchange are based on market price per share, the terms of exchange are 3 to 1. The number of shares of stock outstanding increases to 20,000, so that earnings per share become $3. The stockholders in company A now each receive three shares of stock with earnings per share of $3. Nine dollars of earnings per original share represents an accretion of $1 for the stockholders of company A. The earnings per share of $3 for the stockholders of company B represents dilution of $1 a share.

The general principle is that when terms of merger are based on the market price per share and the price/earnings ratios of the two companies are different, earnings accretion and dilution will occur. The company with a higher price/earnings ratio will attain earnings accretion; the company with the lower price/earnings ratio will suffer earnings dilution. If the sizes of the companies are greatly different, the effect on the larger company will be relatively small, whether in earnings dilution or in earnings accretion. The effect on the smaller company will be large.

HOLDING COMPANIES

In 1889 New Jersey became the first state to pass a general incorporation law permitting corporations to be formed for the sole purpose of owning the stocks of other companies. This law was the origin of the holding company. The Sherman Act of 1890, which prohibits combinations or collusion in restraint of trade, gave an impetus to holding company operations as well

Table 21-2 FINANCIAL TREATMENT OF POOLING OF INTEREST

	A	B	Adjustments or Ratios	New Firm AB If Exchange Basis Is 2/1	New Firm AB If Exchange Basis Is 3/1
Current assets	$100,000	$100,000		$200,000	$200,000
Fixed assets	100,000	100,000		200,000	200,000
Total assets	$200,000	$200,000		$400,000	$400,000
Current liabilities	$ 50,000	$ 50,000		$100,000	$100,000
Long-term debt	30,000	30,000		60,000	60,000
Total debt	80,000	80,000		160,000	160,000
Common stock, par value $10	50,000	50,000	$ 50,000* 100,000†	150,000	200,000
Capital surplus	60,000	60,000	$ 50,000* 100,000†	70,000	20,000
Earned surplus	10,000	10,000		20,000	20,000
Total claims on assets	$200,000	$200,000		$400,000	$400,000
Number of shares of stock	5,000	5,000		15,000	20,000
Book value	$ 24.00	$ 24.00	1.0		
Amount of profit after interest and taxes	$ 40,000	$ 20,000	2.0	$ 60,000	$ 60,000
Earnings per share	$8	$4		4.0	3.0
Price/earnings ratio	15	10			
Market price of stock	$120	$40	3.0		
Working capital per share	$10	$10	1.0		
Dividends per share	$4	$2	2.0		
Exchange ratio No. 1—earnings basis	2/1	1/1	2/1		
Equivalent earnings per share	$8	$4			
Exchange ratio No. 2—price basis	3/1	1/1			
Equivalent earnings per share	$9	$3			

* = 2/1 ratio basis.
† = 3/1 ratio basis.

437

as to outright mergers and complete amalgamations, because companies could do as one company what they were forbidden to do, by the terms of the act, as separate companies.

Many of the advantages and disadvantages of holding companies are no more than the advantages and disadvantages of large-scale operations already discussed in connection with mergers and consolidations. Whether a company is organized on a divisional basis or with the divisions kept as separate companies does not affect the basic reasons for conducting a large-scale multiproduct, multiplant operation. However, the holding company form of large-scale operations has different advantages and disadvantages from those of completely integrated divisionalized operations.

Advantages

Control with Fractional Ownership. Through a holding company operation a firm may buy 5, 10, or 50 percent of the stock of another corporation. Such fractional ownership may be sufficient to give the acquiring company effective working control or substantial influence over the operations of the company in which stock ownership has taken place. An article in the *New York Times* of November 16, 1958, makes this point clearly.

Working control is often considered to entail more than 25 percent of the common stock, but it can be as low as 10 percent if the stock is widely distributed. One financier says that the attitude of management is more important than the number of shares owned, adding that "if they think you can control the company, then you do." In addition, control on a very slim margin can be held through friendship with large stockholders outside the holding company group.

Sometimes holding company operations represent the initial stages of the transformation of an operating company into an investment company, particularly when the operating company is in a declining industry. When the sales of an industry begin to fall off permanently and the firm begins to liquidate its operating assets, it may use these liquid funds to place the investments of its stockholders in industries having a more favorable growth potential. An illustration of this is provided by the same *New York Times* article.

Former investment banker Gordon W. Wattles, who holds many corporate directorships, is the architect of the pyramid built on Century Investors and Webster Investors. The former was once an aviation investment concern, while the latter began as a cigar maker.

Isolation of Risks. Because the various operating companies in a holding company system are separate legal entities, the obligations of any one unit are separate from the obligations of the other units. Catastrophic losses incurred by one unit of the holding company system are therefore not transmitted as claims on the assets of the other units.

Though this is the customary generalization of the nature of a holding company system, it is not completely valid. In extending credit to one of the units of a holding company system, an astute financial manager or loan officer will look through the holding company veil and require a guarantee or a claim on the assets of all the elements in a complete holding company system. Therefore, to some degree, the assets in the various elements of a holding company are joined. The advantage remains to the extent that unanticipated catastrophies which may occur to one unit in a holding company system will not be transmitted to the other units.

Approval Not Required.   If a holding company group is seeking to obtain effective working control of a number of companies, it may quietly purchase a portion of the stock of the companies in which it is interested. This is a completely informal operation; the permission or approval of the stockholders of the acquired company or companies is not required. Thus the guiding personalities in a holding company operation are not dependent upon negotiations and approval of the other interest groups in order to obtain their objectives.

Tender Offers.   In a tender offer, one party, generally a corporation seeking a controlling interest in another corporation, asks the stockholders of the firm it is seeking to control to submit, or "tender," their shares in exchange for a specified price. The price is generally stated as so many dollars per share of acquired stock, although it can be stated in terms of shares of stock in the acquiring firm. The tender offer is a direct appeal to stockholders, so the tender need not be cleared with the management of the acquired firm. Tender offers have been used for a number of years, but the pace greatly accelerated after 1965.

If one firm wishes to gain control over another, the acquiring firm typically approaches the to-be-acquired firm's management and seeks its approval of the merger. If approval cannot be obtained, the company wishing to gain control can appeal directly to stockholders by means of the tender offer, unless the management of the to-be-acquired firm holds enough stock to retain control. If the potential acquiring firm has reason to believe that the to-be-acquired firm's management will not approve the merger, it may use a tender offer without ever informing the to-be-acquired firm's management of its intentions. In this situation, the potential acquirer will frequently buy the stock of the acquired firm in the name of a stockbroker ("street name") to conceal its intentions. Because of the frequency of tender offers and because of the views of some that (1) the recent merger trend is leading to "too much concentration" in the economy and (2) the feeling that tender offers are somehow "unfair" to the managements of firms acquired through this vehicle, Congressional investigations were conducted during 1967 with the idea of obtaining information that could be used to legislate controls over the use of tender offers. The controls most likely to be imposed are the following: (1) The acquiring firm must give thirty days' notice of its intentions to make the acquisition to both the management of the acquired firm and to the Securities and Exchange Commission. (2) When substantial blocks are purchased through tender offers (or through open market purchases—that is, on the stock exchange), the beneficial owner of the stock must be disclosed together with the name of the party putting up the money for the transaction.

The example of Tenneco's acquisition of Kern County Land Company illustrates many of these points. First, Kern was a relatively old, conservatively managed company whose assets consisted largely of oil properties and agricultural land together with some manufacturing subsidiaries. Many informed investors believed that Kern's assets had a potential long-run value in excess of its current market price. Occidental Petroleum, a relatively aggressive company, made an investigation of Kern's assets and decided to make a tender offer for the company. At that time, Kern's market price was about $60 a share, while the price Occidental decided to offer Kern's stockholders was $83.50 a share. According to Kern's management, Occidental's management got in touch with the former over a weekend and informed Kern that the tender offer would be made the following Monday.

Kern's management resisted the offer. Because the published statements of Occidental indicated that it felt Kern's undervalued position was partly the result of an unaggressive management, Kern's management could anticipate being replaced in the event that Occidental effected the takeover. One could anticipate that Kern's management would resist the takeover, and it did indeed. Kern's president wrote a letter to stockholders condemning the merger and published the letter as an advertisement in the *Wall Street Journal*. His position was that Kern's stock was indeed valuable, but it was worth more than had been offered by Occidental Petroleum.

How would Kern County's stockholders react to this exchange? In the first place, the stock had been selling at about $60 a share, and now they were offered $83.50 a share. One might anticipate that stockholders would accept the tender unless Kern's management could do something to keep the price above $83.50. What Kern did was to obtain "marriage proposals" from a number of other companies. Kern's management reported to the newspapers—while Occidental's tender offer was still outstanding—that it had received a substantial number of proposals calling for the purchase of Kern's stock at a price substantially in excess of $83.50.

The offer Kern's management finally accepted—and presumably the one giving Kern's stockholders the highest price—was from Tenneco Corporation. Tenneco offered one share of a new $5.50 convertible preferred stock for each share of Kern's stock. The market value of this convertible preferred was estimated at the time of Tenneco's offer to be worth about $105 a share. Further, Kern's stockholders would not have to pay capital gains tax on this stock at the time of the exchange. (Had they accepted Occidental's offer, the difference between $83.50 and the cost of their stock would be taxable income to Kern's stockholders.) According to newspaper reports, Tenneco planned to keep Kern's existing management after the merger was completed.

The Kern-Tenneco merger was completed in the fall of 1967. Tenneco owns the Kern stock and is thus a holding company, with Kern being one of its operating subsidiaries.

Disadvantages

Partial Multiple Taxation. Provided the holding company owns at least 80 percent of a subsidiary's voting stock, it is allowed to deduct the entire amount of dividends received from the affiliate. However, if less than 80 percent of the stock is owned, only 85 percent of the dividends may be deducted. With a tax rate of 48 percent, this means that the effective tax on intercorporate dividends is 7.2 percent. This partial double taxation somewhat offsets the benefits of holding company control with limited ownership, but whether the penalty of 7.2 percent of dividends received is sufficient to offset other possible advantages is a matter that must be decided in individual situations.

Risks of Excessive Pyramiding. While pyramiding magnifies profits if the operations are successful, as was seen in the trading-on-the-equity analysis, it also magnifies losses. The greater the degree of pyramiding, the greater the degree of risk involved for any degree of fluctuations in sales or earnings of the company. This is one of the potential disadvantages of pyramiding operations through holding companies.

Ease of Enforced Dissolution. In the case of a holding company operation that falls into disfavor with the United States Department of Justice, it is relatively easy to require dissolution of the relation by disposition of stock ownership. A clear case in point is the recent requirement that du Pont dispose of its 23 percent stock interest in General Motors Corporation. The acquisition took place in the early 1920s. Because there was no fusion between the corporations, there were no difficulties, from an operating standpoint, in requiring the separation of the two companies. On the other hand, if complete amalgamation had taken place, it would have been much more difficult to break up the company after a lapse of so many years.

Leverage in Holding Companies

The problem of excessive leverage is worthy of further note, for the degree of leveraging in certain past instances has been truly staggering. For example, in the 1920s Samuel Insull and his group controlled electric utility operating companies at the bottom of a holding company pyramid by a 1/20 of 1 percent investment. As a ratio, this represents 1/2000. In other words, $1 of capital at the top holding company level controlled $2,000 of assets at the operating level. A similar situation existed in the railroad field. It has been stated that Robert R. Young, with an investment of $254,000, obtained control of the Allegheny system consisting of total operating assets of $3 billion.

The nature of leverage in a holding company system and its advantages and disadvantages are illustrated by the hypothetical example developed in Table 21–3. As in the previous examples, although this is a

Table 21–3   LEVERAGE IN A HOLDING COMPANY SYSTEM

Holding Company 2			
Common stock B of Holding		Debt	2,000
Company 1	5,000	Preferred stock	1,000
		Common stock: class A*	1,000
		Common stock: class B	1,000
Holding Company 1			
Common stock B of operating		Debt	50,000
company	100,000	Preferred stock	10,000
		Common stock: class A*	30,000
		Common stock: class B	10,000
Operating Company			
Total assets	2,000,000	Debt	1,000,000
		Preferred stock	150,000
		Common stock: class A*	650,000
		Common stock: class B	200,000

* Common stock A is nonvoting.

hypothetical case, it illustrates actual situations. One thousand dollars of class B common stock of holding company 2 controls $2 million of assets at the operating company level. Further leverage could, of course, have been postulated in this situation by setting up a third company to own the common stock B of Holding Company 2.

Table 21–4 shows the results of holding company leverage on gains

Table 21–4   RESULTS OF HOLDING COMPANY LEVERAGE
ON GAINS AND LOSSES

	Assume that each company pays:	4% on debt
		5% on preferred stock
		8% on common stock A

	Earnings before Taxes	
Operating Company	*12%*	*8%*
Amount earned	$240,000	$160,000
Less: Tax*	100,000	60,000
Available to meet fixed charges	140,000	100,000
Debt interest	40,000	40,000
Preferred stock	7,500	7,500
Common stock A	52,000	52,000
Total charges	99,500	99,500
Available to common B	40,500	500
Dividends to common B	40,000	500
Holding Company 1		
Amount earned	20,000	250
Less: Tax (0.5 × 0.15 × $18,000)*	1,350	0
Available to meet fixed charges	18,650	250
Debt interest	2,000	2,000
Preferred stock	500	500
Common stock A	2,400	2,400
Total charges	4,900	4,900
Available to common B	13,750	loss
Dividends to common B	10,000	
Holding Company 2		
Amount earned	5,000	
Less: Taxes (0.5 × 0.15 × $4,920)*	369	
Available to meet fixed charges	4,631	
Debt interest	80	
Preferred stock	50	
Common stock A	80	
Total	210	
Available to common B	4,421	
Percent return on common B	442%	

* Tax computed on earnings less interest charges at a 50% tax rate.

and losses at the top level. In the first column it is assumed that the operating company earns 12 percent before taxes on its $2 million of assets, while in the second column it is assumed that the return on assets is 8 percent. The operating and holding companies are the same ones described in Table 21–3.

A return of 12 percent on the operating assets of $2 million represents a total profit of $240,000. The debt interest of $40,000 is deducted from this amount, and the 50 percent tax rate applies to the remainder. The amount available to common stock after payment of debt interest, preferred stock dividends, and an 8 percent return to the nonvoting common stock A is $40,500. Assuming a $40,000 dividend payout, the amount earned on the assets of holding company 1 is $20,000. If the same kind of analysis was followed through, the amount available to the common stock B in holding company 2 would be $4,421. This return is on an investment of $1,000, representing a return on the investment in common stock B of holding company 2 of about 440 percent. The power of leverage in a holding company system can indeed be great.

On the other hand, if a decline in revenues caused the pretax earnings to drop to 8 percent of the total assets of the operating company, the results would be disastrous. The amount earned under these circumstances is $160,000. After deducting the bond interest, the amount subject to tax is $120,000, resulting in a tax of $60,000. The after-tax-but-before-interest earnings are $100,000. The total prior charges are $99,500, leaving $500 available to common stock B. If all earnings are paid out in dividends to common stock B, the earnings of holding company 1 are $250. This is not enough to meet the debt interest. The holding company system would be forced to default on the debt interest of holding company 1 and, of course, holding company 2.

This example illustrates the potentiality for tremendous gains in a holding company system. It also illustrates that a small decline in earnings on the assets of the operating companies would be disastrous.

Although holding companies offer the potential opportunity of controlling other companies with only partial ownership, in a high percentage of industrial companies the parent company owns virtually all the stock of the subsidiary. One of the reasons for the high percentage of ownership is the legal requirement that the parent own at least 80 percent of the stock of the subsidiary to receive dividends without paying full taxes on them. As the discussion in Chapter 2 indicated, unless the subsidiary is at least 80 percent owned, the parent must pay a 7.2 percent tax on dividends received.

SUMMARY

Growth is vital to the well-being of a firm, for without it a business cannot attract able management because it cannot give men recognition in promotions and challenging creative activity. Mergers have played an important part in the growth of firms, and since financial managers are required both to appraise the desirability of a prospective merger and to participate in evaluating the respective companies involved in the merger, the present chapter has been devoted to background materials on merger decisions.

One of the objectives of growth, whether by external acquisitions or by internal development, is large size for the purpose of achieving economies of scale. Economies of scale result from the following factors.

Research. Certain types of research can be performed best by large firms.

Top-management skills. Skilled executives are an extremely scarce commodity, and it is often economical to spread their talents over a relatively large enterprise.

Operating economies. For some types of production, the average cost per unit of output is lower when large-scale plants and distribution systems are used.

Risk reduction. Risk is reduced by diversification in large enterprises. Tax considerations add to the importance of this factor.

Market capitalization rates. Market capitalization rates are lower for larger firms.

While the size necessary to take advantage of these aspects of economies of scale may be attained by internal expansion, there are certain advantages to growth by merger.

Speed. Growth may be attained much more rapidly by merger than by internal expansion.

Cost. Frequently, the cost of expansion is lower if new facilities and talents are obtained by merger.

Financing. Sometimes it is possible to finance an acquisition when it is not possible to finance internal growth.

Risk. Risks may be reduced by acquiring a going concern rather than starting a new division.

Stabilizing effects. Certain economies may arise that result in stabilizing a particular industry. The railroad mergers in the late 1960s may be cited as an example.

Taxes. Taxes appear to have been a factor in about one third of all mergers.

Competitive advantages. Two firms may merge and coordinate their price and output decisions. Antitrust considerations make this motive of doubtful importance today, however.

Terms of Mergers

The most important term that must be negotiated in a merger arrangement is the price the acquiring firm will pay for the acquired business. Some of the factors that influence this decision are given below.

Earnings. Present earnings and expected future earnings after the merger, which are reflected in expectations about the effects of the merger on the surviving firm's *growth rate,* are perhaps the most important determinant of the price that will be paid for a firm that is being acquired.

Market prices. Current market prices are the second most important determinant of prices in mergers.

Book value. Depending on whether or not asset values are indicative of the approximate value of the merged firm, book values may exert an important influence on the terms of the merger.

Net current assets. Net current assets are an indication of the amount of liquidity being purchased in a merger; this can be an important factor.

The factors listed above are all *quantitative;* qualitative, or nonmeasurable, factors are sometimes the overriding determinant of merger terms. Qualitative considerations may suggest that *synergistic,* or "two plus two equals five," effects may be present to a sufficient extent to warrant paying more for the acquired firm than the quantitative factors would suggest.

If the terms of merger reflect the respective earnings per share of the two companies, neither earnings dilution nor earnings accretion will result. If the exchange terms are based on the market price of the shares of the company and if the prevailing price/earnings ratios of the two companies differ, earnings accretion and dilution are likely to result. Any initial earnings dilution may be offset by the improved earnings of the combined operation. After a period, appreciation of earnings per share for all the constituent companies in the merger may be achieved.

Accounting Policies and Mergers

A merger may be treated as either a *purchase* or a *pooling of interests.* Generally, in a purchase a larger firm takes over a smaller one and assumes all management control. The amount actually paid for the smaller firm is reflected in the acquiring firm's balance sheet; if more was paid for the acquired firm than the book value of its assets, goodwill is reflected on the acquiring firm's financial statements. In a pooling of interests, on the other hand, the merged firms are generally of about the same size, and both managements carry on important functions after the merger. The total assets of the surviving firm are equal to the sum of the assets of the two independent companies, so no goodwill is created.

Holding Companies

In mergers, one firm disappears. However, an alternative is for one firm to buy all or a majority of the common stock of another and to run the acquired firm as an operating subsidiary. When this occurs, the acquiring firm is said to be a *holding company.* A number of *advantages* arise when a holding company is used.

Control with fractional ownership. It may be possible to control the acquired firm with a smaller investment than would be necessary if a merger were to occur.

Isolation of risks. Each firm in a holding company is a separate legal entity; the obligations of any one unit are separate from the obligations of the other units.

Approval not required. Stockholder approval is required before a merger can take place. This is not necessary in a holding company situation.

There are also some *disadvantages* to holding companies; some of these are given below.

Partial multiple taxation. If the holding company does not own 80 percent of the subsidiary's stock and does not file consolidated tax returns, it is subject to taxes on dividends received from the subsidiary.

Risks from excessive pyramiding. The leverage effects possible in holding companies can subject the holding company to a great deal of risk.

Ease of dissolution. The Antitrust Division of the United States Department of Justice can much more easily force the breakup of a holding company situation than it can the dissolution of two completely merged firms.

QUESTIONS

21–1   The number of mergers tends to fluctuate with business activity, rising when GNP rises and falling when GNP falls. Why does this relation exist?

21–2   A large firm has certain advantages over a smaller one. What are some of the *financial* advantages of large size?

21–3   What are some of the potential benefits that can be expected by a firm which merges with a company in a different industry?

21–4   Mergers can often be important to rapidly growing firms. How?

21–5   Distinguish between a holding company and an operating company. Give an example of each.

21–6   Which appears to be more risky, the use of debt in the holding company's capital structure or the use of debt in the operating company? Why?

21–7   Is the public interest served by an increase in merger activity? Give arguments both pro and con.

21–8   Would the book value of a company's assets be considered the absolute minimum price to be paid for a firm? Why? Is there any value that would qualify as an absolute minimum?

21–9   Discuss the situation where one firm, California Motors, for example, calls off merger negotiations with another, American Space Labs, because the latter's stock price is overvalued. What assumption concerning dilution is implicit in the above situation?

21–10   Thus far, many methods by which a company can raise additional capital

have been discussed. Can a merger or a purchase be considered a means
of raising additional equity capital? Explain.

21–11 A particularly difficult problem regarding business combinations has been
whether to treat the new company as a purchase or as a pooling of
interests.

    a) What criteria can be set down to differentiate between the above forms
of business combinations?

    b) Would you as a stockholder in one of the firms prefer a purchase or a
pooling arrangement? Why?

    c) Which combination would you prefer if you were a high-ranking
manager in one of the firms?

21–12 The previous question discusses purchases and pooling arrangements. Why
is it important to make a distinction between these two combination forms?

21–13 Are the negotiations for merger or purchase agreements more difficult if
the firms are in different industries or in the same industry? if they are
about the same size or quite different in size? Why?

21–14 How would the existence of long-term debt in a company's financial structure affect its valuation for merger purposes? Could the same be said for
any debt account regardless of its maturity?

21–15 During 1964–1965, the Pure Oil Company was involved in merger negotiations with at least three other firms. The terms of these arrangements
varied from a transfer of stock to a direct cash purchase of Pure Oil. Discuss the relative advantages to a corporation of paying for an acquisition
in cash or in stock.

PROBLEMS

21–1 Given the following balance sheets:

H COMPANY
CONSOLIDATED BALANCE SHEET

Cash	$ 800	Borrowings	$ 600
Other current assets	600	Common stock	1,000
Net property	1,000	Surplus	800
Total assets	$2,400	Total claims on assets	$2,400

A COMPANY
BALANCE SHEET

Current assets	$200	Net worth	$400
Net property	200		
Total assets	$400	Total net worth	$400

a) The holding company, H, buys the operating company, A, with "free" cash of $400. Show the new consolidated balance sheet for H after the acquisition.

b) Instead of buying A, H buys operating company B with free cash of $600. The balance sheet of B follows:

B COMPANY
BALANCE SHEET

Current assets	$ 400	Borrowings	$ 400
Net property	600	Net worth	600
Total assets	$1,000	Total claims on assets	$1,000

Show the new consolidated balance sheet for H after acquisition.

c) What are the implications of your consolidated balance sheets for measuring the growth of firms resulting from acquisitions?

21-2   H Company is a holding company owning the entire common stock of Minor Company and Operating Company. The balance sheet as of December 31, 1966, for each subsidiary is identical with the following one.

BALANCE SHEET
December 31, 1966

Current assets	$3,000,000	Current liabilities	$ 500,000
Fixed assets, net	2,000,000	First mortgage bonds (4%)	1,000,000
		Preferred stock (5%)	1,000,000
		Common stock (par $10)	2,000,000
		Surplus	500,000
Total assets	$5,000,000		$5,000,000

Each operating company earns $550,000 annually before taxes and before interest and preferred dividends. A 50 percent tax rate is assumed.

a) What is the annual rate of return on each company's net worth (common stock plus surplus)?

b) Construct a balance sheet for H Company based on the following assumptions: (1) The only asset of the holding company is the common stock of the two subsidiaries; this stock is carried at par (not book) value. (2) The holding company has $700,000 of 4 percent coupon debt and $1,300,000 of 6 percent preferred stock.

c) What is the rate of return on the book value of the holding company's common stock?

d) How could the rate of return in c be increased?

e) What investment is necessary to control the three companies under the assumptions of the initial conditions?

f) If ownership of 25 percent of the holding company's common stock

($2 million of common) could control all three firms, what percentage would this be of the total assets?

21–3   You are given the following data on two companies:

TERMS OF MERGER ANALYSIS

	A	B	Adjust-ments or Ratio	Consoli-dated Statement
Current assets	$120,000	$120,000		1. _____
Fixed assets	80,000	80,000		2. _____
Total assets	$200,000	$200,000		3. _____
Current liabilities	$ 60,000	$ 60,000		4. _____
Long-term debt	40,000	40,000		5. _____
Total debt,* 5%	$100,000	$100,000		6, _____
Common stock, par value $5	$ 50,000	$ 50,000	1. _____	7. _____
Capital surplus	40,000	40,000	2. _____	8. _____
Earned surplus	10,000	10,000	3. _____	9. _____
Total claims on assets	$200,000	$200,000		10. _____

			Ratios	
(1) Number of shares of stock	10,000	10,000		1. _____
(2) Book value per share	_____	_____	1. _____	2. _____
(3) Amount of profit before interest and taxes†	$ 65,000	$ 25,000		3. _____
(4) Earnings per share	_____	_____	2. _____	4. _____
(5) Price/earnings ratio	20	15		
(6) Market price of stock	_____	_____	3. _____	
(7) Working capital per share	_____	_____	4. _____	
(8) Dividends per share, 50% payout	_____	_____	5. _____	
(9) Exchange ratio	_____	_____	6. _____ (A/B)	
(10) Equivalent earnings per share	_____	_____		

* Average rate on interest-bearing and noninterest-bearing debt combined.
† Assume a 50 percent tax rate.

     a) What in your judgment would be a reasonable basis for determining the terms at which shares in A and in B would be exchanged for shares in the new AB company? What exchange ratio would you recommend and why?

b) Use the market price of stock relation as the basis for the terms of exchange of stock in the old company for stock in the new company (2 shares of AB for 1 share of A, or 1/2 share of AB for 1 share of B). Then complete all calculations for filling in all the blank spaces, including the adjustments for making the consolidated statement. Treat this problem as a situation which the SEC and accountants would refer to as a pooling of interests.

21–4 The Titan Company has just purchased the Miniature Company under an arrangement known as a purchase. The purchase was made by stock in a settlement based exactly on the indicated market prices of the two firms. The data on the two companies are given below.

a) Fill in the blank spaces and complete the Adjustments and *Pro Forma* Balance Sheet columns, and show the journal entries for the stock purchase. Give an explanation for your entries.

b) Calculate earnings dilution or accretion for both companies on the assumption that total earnings are unchanged.

c) Calculate the earnings dilution or accretion on the assumption that the return on combined tangible assets rises to 20 percent after interest and taxes.

d) Comment on your findings.

	Titan	Miniature	Adjust-ments	Pro Forma Balance Sheet
Current assets	$ 900,000	$14,000		
Other assets	300,000	10,000		
Fixed assets	800,000	16,000		
Intangibles				
Total assets	$2,000,000	$40,000		
Current liabilities	$ 400,000	$16,000		
Long-term debt	300,000			
Common stock	400,000	4,000		
Capital surplus	300,000			
Retained earnings	600,000	20,000		
Total claims	$2,000,000	$40,000		
Par value	$ 8.00	$ 1.00		
Number of shares	_____	_____		
Total earnings available to common	$ 250,000	$16,000		
Book value	_____	_____		
Earnings per share	_____	_____		
Price/earnings ratio	10 times	25 times		
Market value per share	_____	_____		

21-5   Every merger agreement is subject to negotiation between the companies
involved. One significant indicator of the compensation received by the
acquired company is the respective market prices of the companies' stocks
relating to the merger items. Some actual merger data are given below.

Calculate the percent premium or discount received by the acquired
company, using market prices as the criteria. Compare the results of your
calculations based on the stock prices of the two previous quarters with that
of your results based on the prices immediately preceding the merger.
Which is the proper measure of the actual discount or premium received:
the one indicated by the earlier stock prices or the one indicated by the
stock prices immediately preceding the merger? Explain.

	Company	Date	Terms	Market Price Two Quarters before Merger		Market Price Preceding Merger	
				(A)	(B)	(A)	(B)
1	(A) Celanese Corp.	9/21/64	2 shares of Celanese				
	(B) Champlain Oil		for every 3 shares				
			of Champlain	62	34	67	42
2	(A) Cities Service Co.	6/14/63	0.9 shares (2.25 pref.)				
	(B) Tennessee Corp.		for each Tenn. Corp.				
			share (common)	65	48	61	55
3	(A) Ford Motor Co.	12/11/61	1 share of Ford for				
	(B) Philco Corp.		every 4½ shares of				
			Philco	81	22	113	25
4	(A) General Telephone	3/5/59	Share for share basis				
	(B) Sylvania Elec.			52	46	69	69

Chapter 22

Failure, Reorganization, and Liquidation

Thus far the text has dealt with issues associated mainly with the growing, successful enterprise. Not all businesses are so fortunate, however, so we must examine financial difficulties, their causes, and their possible remedies. This material is significant for the financial manager of successful, as well as potentially unsuccessful, firms. The successful firm's financial manager must know his firm's rights and remedies as a creditor and must participate effectively in efforts to collect from financially distressed debtors. Conversely, the financial manager must know how to handle his own firm's affairs if financial difficulties arise. Often such understanding may mean the difference between loss of ownership of the firm and rehabilitation of the operation as a going enterprise.

THE FIRM'S LIFE CYCLE

The life cycle of an industry or firm is often depicted as an S-shaped curve, as shown in Figure 22–1. The figure represents a hypothetical life cycle of a representative firm. Although it is an oversimplification, it provides a useful framework for analysis. The hypothesis represented by the four-stage life-cycle concept is based on a number of assumptions. It assumes competent management in the growth periods and insufficient management foresight prior to the decline phase. Obviously, one of management's

453

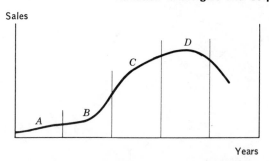

Figure 22-1   Hypothetical Life Cycle of a Firm

primary goals is to prolong phase *B* and completely forestall phase *D,* and a great many firms are apparently successful in these endeavors.

If an industry experiences the period of decline, financial readjustment problems will arise, affecting most firms in the industry. In addition, specific events may result in business failure—for example, a prolonged strike, a fire not adequately covered by insurance, or a bad decision on a new product.

FAILURE

Although failure can be defined in several ways, according to various applications of the term, it does not necessarily result in the collapse and dissolution of a firm.

Economic Failure

Failure in an economic sense usually signifies that a firm's revenues do not cover costs. Another formulation states that a firm has failed if the rate of earnings on the historical cost of investment is less than the going rate of interest. According to still another possible definition, a firm can be considered a failure if its actual returns have fallen below expected returns. There is no consensus on the definition of failure in an economic sense.[1]

Financial Failure

Failure from a financial standpoint is a less ambiguous term than the concept of economic failure. Financial failure signifies insolvency; even here, however, two aspects are generally recognized.

---

[1] In still another economic sense, a firm that goes bankrupt may not be a failure at all. To illustrate, suppose someone starts a business to *attempt* to develop a product which, if successful, will produce very large returns, and if unsuccessful, will result in a total loss of invested funds. The entrepreneur *knows* that he is taking a risk, but thinks the potential gains are worth the chance of loss. If the loss in fact results, then it was expected (in a probability sense).

1. A firm can be considered a failure if it is insolvent in the sense that it cannot meet its current obligations as they come due, even though its total assets may exceed its total liabilities.

2. A firm is a failure or is bankrupt if its total liabilities exceed a fair valuation of its total assets. The "real" net worth of the firm is negative.

When we use the word "failure" hereafter, we include both of these aspects.

CAUSES OF FAILURE

According to data compiled regularly by Dun & Bradstreet, Inc., the yearly rate of failure per 10,000 firms was about 50 immediately prior to World War II.[2] In the years immediately following World War II the failure rate was low, about 20 to 30 per 10,000 firms, because of the vigorous rate of business activity in making up the war postponements of production. In recent years the failure rate has risen to 60 per 10,000 firms, reflecting the resumption of stronger competition between firms.

The liability per failure averaged about $20,000 prewar, but has risen to nearly $100,000 in recent years. The Dun & Bradstreet compilations indicate also that about 60 percent of these firms fail during the first five years of their lives; another 25 percent fail during the second five years.[3]

Different studies assign the causes of failure to different factors. The Dun & Bradstreet compilations assign these causes as follows:

Cause of Failure	Percentage of Total
Neglect	4
Fraud	2
Disaster	1
Management incompetence	91
Unknown	2

A number of other studies of failures may be generalized into the following groupings: [4]

---

[2] *The Failure Record through 1965* (New York: Dun & Bradstreet, Inc. 1966), p. 3.

[3] *The Failure Record*, p. 12.

[4] See studies referred to in A. S. Dewing, *The Financial Policy of Corporations* (New York: Ronald, 1953), Vol. II, Chap. 28.

Cause of Failure	Percentage of Total
Unfavorable industry trends	20
Management incompetence	60
Catastrophes	10

Both classifications presumably include the effects of recessions and place the resulting failures in the category of managerial incompetence. This method is logical—managements should be prepared to operate in environments in which recessions take place, and should frame their policies to cope with downturns as well as to benefit from business upswings.

A number of financial remedies are available to management when it becomes aware of the imminence or occurrence of insolvency.

1. Extension
2. Composition
3. Reorganization
4. Liquidation
   a) Assignment
   b) Bankruptcy

These remedies are described in the remainder of this chapter in the order listed.

EXTENSION AND COMPOSITION

Extension and composition are discussed together because they both represent voluntary concessions by creditors. Extension *postpones* the date of required payment of past-due obligations. Composition voluntarily *reduces* the creditor's claim on the debtor. Both have the purpose of keeping the debtor in business and of avoiding court costs. Although creditors absorb a temporary loss, the recovery is often greater than if one of the formal procedures had been followed, and the hope is that a stable customer will emerge.

Procedure

A meeting of the debtor and his creditors is held. The creditors appoint a committee consisting of four or five of the largest creditors and one or two of the smaller ones. These meetings are typically arranged and conducted by adjustment bureaus associated with local credit managers' associations or by trade associations. The factors are presented in a general statement to the adjustment bureaus.

After a meeting is held at the adjustment bureau and it is judged that the case can be worked out, the bureau assigns investigators to make an exhaustive report. The bureau and the creditors' committee use the facts of the report to formulate a plan for adjustment of claims. Another meeting between the debtor and the creditors is then held in an attempt to work out an extension or a composition or a combination of the two. Subsequent meetings may be required to reach final agreements.

Necessary Conditions

At least three conditions are typically necessary to make an extension or composition feasible.

1. Debtor is a good moral risk.
2. Debtor shows ability to effect recovery.
3. General business conditions are favorable to recovery.

Extension

An extension is preferred by creditors in that it provides for payment in full. The debtor buys current purchases on a cash basis and pays off his past balance over an extended time. In some cases, creditors may agree not only to extend time of payment but also to subordinate existing claims to new debts incurred in favor of vendors extending credit during the period of the extension. The creditors must have faith that the debtor will solve his problems. Because of the uncertainties involved, however, creditors will want to exercise controls over the debtor while waiting for their claims to be paid.

As examples of controls, the committee may insist that an assignment (turnover of assets to the creditors' committee) be executed, to be held in escrow in case of default. Or if the debtor is a corporation, the committee may require that stockholders transfer their stock certificates into an escrow until performance under the extension. The committee may also designate a representative to countersign all checks. Furthermore, the committee may obtain security in the form of notes, mortgage, or assignment of accounts receivable.

Composition

In a composition a pro rata cash settlement is made. Creditors receive from the debtor in cash a uniform percentage of the obligations. The cash received is taken as full settlement of the debt. The ratio may be 10 percent or higher. Bargaining will take place between the debtor and the creditors over the savings that result in avoiding certain costs associated with the bankruptcy: costs of administration, legal fees, investigators, and so on. In addition to financial considerations, the debtor gains in that the stigma of bankruptcy is avoided, and thus he may be induced to part with most of the savings that result from avoiding bankruptcy.

Combination Settlement

Often the bargaining process will result in a compromise involving both an extension and a composition. For example, the settlement may provide for a cash payment of 25 percent of the debt and six future installments of 10 percent each. Total payment would thereby aggregate 85 percent. Installment payments are usually evidenced by notes. Creditors will also seek protective controls.

Appraisal of Voluntary Settlements

The advantages of voluntary settlements are informality and simplicity. Investigating, legal, and administrative expenses are held to a minimum. The procedure is the most economical and results in the largest return to creditors.

One possible disadvantage is that the debtor is left in control of his business. This situation may involve legal complications or erosion of assets still operated by the debtor. However, numerous controls are available to give the creditors protection.

A second disadvantage is that small creditors may take a nuisance role in that they may insist on payment in full. As a consequence, settlements typically provide for payment in full for claims under $50 or $100. If a composition is involved and all claims under $50 are paid, all creditors will receive a base of $50 plus the agreed-on percentage of the balance of their claims.

Significance to the Financial Manager

Substantial opportunities for asset conservation are provided by voluntary settlements. Since the formal methods are expensive, prompt action by the financial manager and a clear understanding of the potentials of working through the local credit association groups may achieve substantial savings for his firm.

REORGANIZATION

Reorganization is a form of extension or composition of the firm's obligations. However, the legal formalities are much more involved than the procedures thus far described. Regardless of the legal procedure followed, the reorganization processes have several features in common.

1. The firm is insolvent either because it is unable to meet cash obligations as they come due or because claims on the firm exceed its assets. Hence, some modifications in the nature or amount of the firm's obligations must be made. A scaling down of terms or amounts must be formulated. This procedure may represent scaling down fixed charges or converting short-term debt into long-term debt.

2. New funds must be raised for working capital and for property rehabilitation.

3. The operating and managerial causes of difficulty must be discovered and eliminated.

The procedures involved in effecting a reorganization are highly legalistic and are, in fact, thoroughly understood only by attorneys who specialize in bankruptcy and reorganization. We shall therefore confine our remarks to the general principles involved.

A reorganization is, in essence, a composition, a scaling down of claims. In any composition, two conditions must be met: (1) the scaling down must be fair to all parties and (2) in return for the sacrifices, the likelihood of successful rehabilitation and profitable future operation of the firm must be feasible. These are the standards of *fairness* and *feasibility,* which are analyzed further in the next section.

FINANCIAL DECISIONS IN REORGANIZATIONS

When a business becomes insolvent, a decision must be made whether to dissolve the firm through liquidation or to keep it alive through reorganization.[5] Fundamentally, this decision depends upon a determination of what the value of the firm will be if it is rehabilitated versus the value of each part if the firm is dismembered.

Liquidation values depend upon the degree of specialization of the capital assets used in the firm and, hence, their resale value. In addition, liquidation itself involves costs of dismantling, including legal costs. Successful reorganization also involves costs. Typically, better equipment must be installed, obsolete inventories must be disposed of, and improvements in management must be made.

Net liquidation values are compared with the value of the firm after reorganization, net of the costs of rehabilitation. The procedure that prom-

---

[5] This discussion is based on the excellent treatment by N. S. Buchanan, *The Economics of Corporate Enterprise* (New York: Holt, Rinehart and Winston, 1940), pp. 363–388.

ises the higher returns to the creditors and owners will be the course of action favored. Often the greater indicated value of the firm in reorganization, compared with its value in liquidation, is used to force a compromise agreement among the claimants in a reorganization, even when they feel that their relative position has not been treated fairly in the reorganization plan.

In reorganizations both the SEC and the courts are called upon to determine the *fairness* and the *feasibility* of proposed plans of reorganization.[6] In developing standards of fairness in connection with such reorganizations, both the courts and the SEC have adhered to two court decisions which established precedent on these matters.[7]

Standards of Fairness

The basic doctrine of fairness states that claims must be recognized in the order of their legal and contractual priority. Junior claimants may participate only to the extent that they have made an additional cash contribution to the reorganization of the firm.

The carrying out of this concept of fairness involves the following steps:

1. An estimate of future sales must be made.
2. An analysis of operating conditions must be made so that the future earnings on sales can be estimated.
3. A determination of the capitalization rate to be applied to these future earnings must be made.
4. The capitalization rate must be applied to the estimated future earnings to obtain an indicated value of the properties of the company.
5. Provision for distribution to the claimants must then be made.

Illustrative case. The meaning and content of these procedures may best be set out by the use of an actual example of reorganization involving the Northeastern Steel Corporation.

Table 22–1 gives the balance sheet of the Northeastern Steel Corporation as of March 31, 1957. The company had been suffering losses running to $2.5 million a year, and on February 1, 1957, it filed a petition for reorganization with a federal court. The court, in accordance with the law, appointed a disinterested trustee. On June 13, 1957, the trustee filed with

---

[6] The federal bankruptcy laws specify that reorganization plans be worked out by court-appointed officials and be reviewed by the Securities and Exchange Commission.

[7] *Case* vs. *Los Angeles Lumber Products Co.*, 308 U.S. 106 (1939) and *Consolidated Rock Products Co.* vs. *duBoise*, 213 U.S. 510 (1940). Securities and Exchange Commission, Seventeenth Annual Report, 1951 (Washington, D. C.: U. S. Government Printing Office), p. 130.

Table 22–1   *NORTHEASTERN STEEL CORPORATION*
BALANCE SHEET
March 31, 1957
(amounts in millions)

Current assets	$ 3.50
Net property	12.50
Miscellaneous assets	0.70
Total assets	$16.70
Accounts payable	$ 1.00
Taxes	0.25
Notes payable	0.25
Other current liabilities	1.75
4½% First-mortgage bonds, due 1970	6.00
6% Subordinated debentures, due 1975	7.00
Common stock ($1)	1.00
Paid-in capital	3.45
Earned surplus	(4.00)
Total liabilities and capital	$16.70

the court a plan of reorganization, which was subsequently analyzed by the SEC.

The trustee found that the company could not be internally reorganized; he concluded that the only feasible program would be to combine Northeastern with an established producer of stainless and alloyed steel. Accordingly, the trustee solicited the interest of a number of steel companies. Late in March 1957, Carpenter Steel Company showed an interest in Northeastern. On June 3, 1957, Carpenter made a formal proposal to take over the $6 million of 4½ percent first-mortgage bonds of Northeastern, to pay $250,000 taxes owed by Northeastern, and to pay 40,000 shares of Carpenter Steel common stock to the company. Since the stock had a market price of $75 a share, the value of the stock was equivalent to $3 million. Thus, Carpenter was offering this sum, plus the $6 million takeover and the $250,000 taxes, a total of $9.2 million on assets that had a net book value of $16.7 million.

Trustee's Plan.   The trustee's plan, based on 40,000 shares at $75 equaling $3 million, is shown in Table 22–2. The total claims of the unsecured creditors equal $10 million. However, the amounts available total only $3 million. Thus, each claimant would be entitled to receive 30 percent before the adjustment for subordination. Before this adjustment, holders of notes payable would receive 30 percent of their claim of

Table 22–2   *NORTHEASTERN STEEL CORPORATION*
                         TRUSTEE'S PLAN

Prior Claims	Amount	Receives
Taxes	$ 250,000	Cash paid by Carpenter
First mortgage, 4½%, 1970	6,000,000	Same assumed by Carpenter

Trustees' plan for remainder of claims
    Valuation based on 40,000 shares at $75 equals $3 million, or 30% of $10 million liabilities.

Claims	Amount	30 Percent × Amt of Claim	Claim after Sub-ordination	No. of Shares of Common Stock
Notes payable	$ 250,000	$ 75,000	$ 250,000	3,333
General unsecured creditors	2,750,000	825,000	825,000	11,000
Subordinated debentures	7,000,000	2,100,000	1,925,000	25,667
	$10,000,000	$3,000,000	$3,000,000	40,000

$250,000, or $75,000. However, the debentures are subordinated *to the notes payable,* so an additional $175,000 would be transferred to notes payable from the subordinated debentures.

    SEC Evaluation.   The Securities and Exchange Commission, in evaluating the proposal from the standpoint of fairness, made the following analysis. The SEC began with an evaluation of the prospective value of Northeastern Steel (Table 22–3). After a survey and discussion with various experts, they arrived at estimated sales of Northeastern Steel Corporation of $25 million a year. It was further estimated that the profit margin on sales would equal 6 percent, thus giving an indicated future earnings of $1.5 million a year.

    The SEC analyzed price/earnings ratios for comparable steel companies and arrived at 8 times future earnings for a capitalization factor. Multiplying 8 by $1.5 million gave an indicated total value of the company of $12 million. Since the mortgage assumed by Carpenter Steel was $6 million, a net value of $6 million is left for the other claims. This value is exactly double that of the 40,000 shares of Carpenter Steel stock paid for the remainder of the company. Because the SEC felt that the value of these claims was $6 million rather than $3 million, the SEC concluded that the trustee's plan for reorganization did not meet the test of fairness. It will be noted that under both the trustee's plan and the SEC plan, the holders of

Table 22–3   *NORTHEASTERN STEEL CORPORATION*
                SEC EVALUATION OF FAIRNESS

Valuation

Estimated sales of Northeastern Steel Corp.	$25,000,000 per year
Earnings at 6% of sales	1,500,000
Price/earnings ratio of 8 (total value)	12,000,000
Mortgage assumed, $6,000,000	6,000,000
Net value	$ 6,000,000

Claims	*Amount*	*Claim*	*Claim after Subordination*
Notes payable	$ 250,000	$ 150,000	$ 250,000*
General unsecured creditors	2,750,000	1,650,000	1,650,000
Subordinated debentures (subordinate to notes payable)	7,000,000	4,200,000	4,100,000*
Totals	$10,000,000	$6,000,000	$6,000,000
Total available	6,000,000		
Percentage of claims	60%		

* Notes payable must be satisfied before subordinated debentures receive anything.

common stock would receive nothing, while the holders of the first-mortgage bond were paid in full.

Because no better alternative offer could be obtained, the proposal of Carpenter Steel was accepted despite the SEC disagreement with the valuation. This example illustrates how the implementation of the standard of fairness is actually applied in a reorganization plan.

Standards of Feasibility

The primary test of feasibility is that the fixed charges on the income of the corporation after reorganization are amply covered by earnings. Adequate coverage of fixed charges for a company in need of reorganization generally requires an improvement in earnings or a reduction of fixed charges, or both.

Policies Required.   Among the actions that will have to be taken to improve the earning power of the company are the following:

1. Where the quality of management has been inefficient and inadequate for the task, new talents and abilities must be brought into the company if it is to operate successfully subsequent to the reorganization.
2. If inventories have become obsolete to a considerable degree, the useless inventory should be disposed of and the operations of the company streamlined.

3. Sometimes the plant and the equipment of the firm need to be modernized before it can operate and compete successfully on a cost basis.
4. Reorganization may also require an improvement in production, marketing, advertising, and other functions, to enable the firm to compete successfully and earn satisfactory profits.
5. Sometimes it is necessary to develop new product activity of the firm so that it can move from areas where economic trends have become undesirable into areas where the growth and stability potential is greater.

Application of Feasibility Tests. Referring again to the Northeastern Steel Corporation example, the SEC observed that the reorganization involved taking over the properties of the Northeastern Steel Corporation by the Carpenter Steel Company. It judged that the direction and aid of the Carpenter Steel Company would remedy the production and operating deficiencies that had troubled Northeastern Steel. Whereas the debt-to-assets ratio of Northeastern Steel had become unbalanced, the Carpenter Steel Company went into the purchase with only a moderate amount of debt. After the consolidation had taken place, the total debt of Carpenter Steel was approximately $17.5 million compared with total assets of more than $63 million. Thus the debt ratio of 27 percent after the reorganization was not unreasonable.

The net income after taxes of Carpenter Steel had been running at a level of approximately $6 million. The interest on the debt of Carpenter steel would run $270,000 on the long-term debt and, taking other borrowings into account, would total a maximum of $600,000 a year. The $6 million profit after taxes would therefore provide a 10-times coverage of fixed charges; this exceeds the standard of 8 times set forth in Chapter 8.

LIQUIDATION PROCEDURES

Liquidation of a business takes place when the estimated value of the firm is greater "dead than alive."

Assignment is a liquidation procedure that does not go through the courts, although it can be used to achieve full settlement of claims on the debtor. *Bankruptcy* is a legal procedure carried out under the jurisdiction of special courts in which a business firm is formally liquidated and claims of creditors are completely discharged.

Assignment

Assignment (as well as bankruptcy) takes place when the debtor is insolvent and the possibilities of restoring profitability so remote that the enterprise should be dissolved—that is, when the firm is "worth more dead than alive." Assignment is a technique for liquidating a debtor and yielding a larger amount to the creditors than is likely to be achieved in bankruptcy.

Technically, there are three types of assignments:

1. Common law assignment
2. Statutory assignment
3. Assignment plus settlement

Common Law Assignment.   The common law provides for an assignment whereby a debtor transfers his title to assets to a third person, known as an assignee or a trustee. The trustee is instructed to liquidate the assets and to distribute the proceeds among the creditors on a pro rata basis.

Typically, an assignment is conducted through the adjustment bureau of the local credit managers' association. The assignee may liquidate the assets through what is known as a bulk sale, which is a public sale through an auctioneer. The auction is preceded by sufficient advertising so that there will be a number of bids at the auction. Liquidation may also be by a piecemeal auction sale conducted on the premises of the assignor by a competent licensed auctioneer, rather than by a bulk sale. On-premises sales are particularly advantageous in the liquidation of large machine shops or manufacturing plants.

The common law assignment, as such, does not discharge the debtor from his obligations. If a corporation goes out of business and does not satisfy all its claims, there will still be claims against the corporation, but in effect the corporation has ceased to exist. The people who have been associated with the corporation can then proceed to organize another corporation free of the debts and obligations of the previous corporation. There is always the danger, however, that the court may look through the corporate veil and hold the individuals responsible. It is therefore usually important to obtain a statement from creditors that claims have been completely settled.

Although a common law assignment has taken place, the assignee, in drawing up checks paying the creditors, may write on the check the requisite legal language to make the payment a complete discharge of the obligation. There are technical legal requirements for this process, which are best carried out with the aid of a lawyer, but essential is a statement that endorsement of this check represents acknowledgment of full payment for the obligation.

A common law assignment is often used by an individual debtor (a sole proprietorship) or a partnership. Following the execution of such an assignment, the assignor requests voluntarily signed releases from the creditors. Such releases are usually forthcoming in situations of "honest failures," thus avoiding the necessity of bankruptcy.

Statutory Assignment. Statutory assignment is similar in concept to common law assignment. Legally, it is carried out under state statutes regulating assignment; technically, it requires more formality. The debtor executes an instrument of assignment, which is recorded. This recordation provides notice to all third parties. A court is utilized: the court appoints an assignee and supervises the proceedings, including the sale of the assets and distribution of the proceeds. As in the common law assignment, the debtor is not automatically discharged from the balance of his obligations. He can discharge himself, however, by printing the requisite statement on the settlement checks.

Assignment Plus Settlement. Both the common law assignment and the statutory assignment may take place with recognition and agreement beforehand with the creditors that the assignment will represent a complete discharge of obligation. Normally, the debtor will communicate with the local credit managers' association. The adjustment bureau of the association will arrange a meeting of all the creditors. A trust instrument of assignment is drawn up. The adjustment bureau is designated to dispose of the assets, which are sold through regular trade channels, by bulk sales, by auction, or by private sales. The creditors will, typically, leave all responsibility for the liquidation procedure with the assignee, the adjustment bureau of the local credit managers' association.

Having disposed of the assets and obtained funds, the adjustment bureau will then distribute the dividends pro rata among the creditors, with the designation on the check that this is in full settlement of the claims on the debtor. Ordinarily, a release is not agreed upon prior to the execution of the assignment. After full examination of the facts, the creditors' committee will usually make a recommendation for the granting of a release following the execution of the assignment. If releases are not forthcoming, the assignor may, within four months of the date of the assignment, file a voluntary petition in bankruptcy. In this event, the assignment is terminated and the assignee must account and report to the trustee and the referee in bankruptcy, and deliver to the trustee all assets in the estate (usually by that time assets have been reduced to cash).

Assignment has substantial advantages over bankruptcy. Bankruptcy through the courts involves much time, legal formalities, and accounting and legal expenses. An assignment saves the substantial costs of bankruptcy proceedings, and it may save time as well.

Furthermore, an assignee usually has much more flexibility in disposing of property than does a bankruptcy trustee. He may be more familiar with the normal channels of trade. Since he takes action much sooner, before the inventories become more obsolete, he may achieve better results.

BANKRUPTCY

Though the bankruptcy procedures leave room for improvement, the Federal Bankruptcy Acts themselves represent two main achievements. (1) They provide safeguards against fraud by the debtor during liquidation and at the same time provide for an equitable distribution of the debtor's assets among his creditors. (2) Insolvent debtors may discharge all their obligations and start new businesses unhampered by a burden of prior debt.

Prerequisites for Bankruptcy

A voluntary petition of bankruptcy may be filed by the debtor. But if an involuntary petition of bankruptcy is to be filed, three conditions must be met.

1. The total debts of the insolvent must be $1,000 or more.
2. If the debtor has less than 12 creditors, any one of the creditors may file the petition if the amount owed him is $500 or more. If there are 12 or more creditors, the petition must be signed by three or more creditors with provable total claims of $500 or more.
3. Within the four months preceding, the debtor must have committed one or more of the six acts of bankruptcy.

Acts of Bankruptcy

The six acts of bankruptcy can be summarized briefly.

1. *Concealment or fraudulent conveyance.* Concealment constitutes hiding assets with intent to defraud creditors. Fraudulent conveyance is transfer of property to a third party without adequate consideration and with intent to defraud creditors.

2. *Preferential transfer.* A preferential transfer is the transfer of money or assets by an insolvent debtor to a creditor, giving the creditor a greater portion of his claim than other creditors would receive on liquidation.

3. *Legal lien or distraint.* If an insolvent debtor permits any creditor to obtain a lien on his property and fails to discharge the lien within 30 days, or if the debtor permits a landlord to distrain (to seize property that has been pledged as security for a loan) for nonpayment of rent, he has committed an act of bankruptcy. In this way creditors, by obtaining a lien, may force an insolvent but obdurate debtor into bankruptcy.

4. *Assignment.* If a debtor makes a general assignment for the benefit of his creditors, an act of bankruptcy likewise exists. Again, this enables creditors who have become distrustful of the debtor in the process of as-

signment to transfer the proceedings to a bankruptcy court. As a matter of practice, typically in common law assignments, creditors will require that a debtor execute a formal assignment document to be held in escrow, to become effective if informal and voluntary settlement negotiations fail. If they do fail, the assignment becomes effective and the creditors have their choice of throwing the case into the bankruptcy court.

5. *Appointment of receiver or trustee.* If an insolvent debtor permits the appointment of a receiver or a trustee to take charge of his property, he has committed an act of bankruptcy. In this event, the creditors may remove a receivership or an adjustment proceeding to a bankruptcy court.

6. *Admission in writing.* If the debtor admits in writing his inability to pay his debts and his willingness to be judged bankrupt, he has committed an act of bankruptcy. The reason for this sixth act of bankruptcy is that debtors are often unwilling to engage in voluntary bankruptcy because it carries some stigma of avoidance of obligations. Sometimes therefore, negotiations with a debtor reach an impasse. Admission in writing is one of the methods of forcing the debtor to commit an act of bankruptcy and of moving the proceedings into a bankruptcy court, where the debtor will no longer be able to reject all plans for settlement.

Adjudication and the Referee

On the filing of the petition of involuntary bankruptcy, a subpoena is served on the debtor. There is usually no contest by the debtor, and the court adjudges him bankrupt. On adjudication, the case is transferred by the court to a referee in bankruptcy. A referee in bankruptcy is generally a lawyer appointed for a specified term by the judge of the bankruptcy court to act in his place after adjudication.

In addition, on petition of the creditors, the referee in voluntary proceedings, or the judge in involuntary proceedings, may appoint a receiver, who serves as the custodian of the property of the debtor until the appointment of a trustee. This arrangement was developed because a long period elapses between the date of the filing of a petition in bankruptcy and the election of a trustee at the first creditors' meeting. To safeguard the creditors' interest during this period, the court, through either the referee or the judge, may appoint a receiver in bankruptcy. The receiver in bankruptcy has full control until the trustee is appointed.

First Creditors' Meeting

At the first meeting of the creditors, a trustee is elected. If different blocks of creditors have a different candidate for trustee, the election may become drawn out. Frequently, the trustee will be the adjustment bureau of the local credit managers' association. At this first meeting the debtor may also be examined for the purpose of obtaining necessary information.

Subsequent Procedure

The trustee and the creditors' committee act to convert all assets into cash. The trustee sends a letter to people owing the debtor money, warning that all past-due accounts will result in instant suit if immediate payment is not made, and if necessary he will institute such suit. Appraisers are appointed by the courts to set a value on the property. With the advice of the creditors' committee and by authorization of the referee, the merchandise is sold by approved methods. As in an assignment, auctions may be held.

Property may not be sold without consent of the court at less than 75 percent of the appraised value that has been set by the appraisers appointed by the court. Cash received from the disposition of the property is used first to pay all expenses associated with the proceedings of the bankruptcy. The trustee will then pay any remaining funds to the claimants.

Final Meeting and Discharge

When the trustee has completed his liquidation and has sent out all the claimants' checks, he makes an accounting, which is reviewed by the creditors and the referee. After all the payments have been made by the trustee, the bankruptcy is discharged and the debtor is released from all debts.

If the hearings before the referee indicate the probability of fraud, the FBI is required to undertake an investigation. If fraud was not committed and the bankruptcy is discharged, the debtor is again free to engage in business. Since business is highly competitive in many fields, he will probably not have great difficulty in obtaining credit again. Under the National Bankruptcy Act, however, a debtor may not be granted a discharge more often than at six-year intervals.

Priority of Claims on Distribution of Proceeds of a Bankruptcy

The order of priority of claims in bankruptcy generally takes the following pattern:

1. Costs of administrating and operating the bankrupt estate.
2. Wages due workers if earned within three months prior to the filing of the petition in bankruptcy. The amount of wages is not to exceed $600 a person.
3. Taxes due the United States, state, county, or any other governmental agency.
4. Secured creditors with the proceeds of the sale of specific property pledged for a mortgage.

5. General or unsecured creditors. This claim consists of the remaining balances after payment to secured creditors from the sale of specific property, and includes trade credit, bank loans, and debenture bonds.
6. Preferred stock.
7. Common stock.

To illustrate how this priority of claims works out, let us take a specific example. The balance sheet of the Bankrupt Firm is shown in Table 22–4. Assets total $90 million. The claims are those indicated on the right-hand side of the balance sheet. It will be noted that the subordinated debentures are subordinated to the notes payable to commercial banks.

Table 22–4   *BANKRUPT FIRM*
          BALANCE SHEET

Current assets	$80,000,000	Accounts payable	$20,000,000
Net property	$10,000,000	Notes payable (due bank)	10,000,000
		Accrued wages,	
		1,400 @ $500	700,000
		U. S. taxes	1,000,000
		State and local taxes	300,000
		Current debt	$32,000,000
		First mortgage	$ 6,000,000
		Second mortgage	1,000,000
		Subordinated debentures*	8,000,000
		Long-term debt	$15,000,000
		Preferred stock	2,000,000
		Common stock	26,000,000
		Capital surplus	4,000,000
		Earned surplus	11,000,000
		Net worth	$43,000,000
	$90,000,000	Total	$90,000,000

* Subordinated to $10 million notes payable to the First National Bank.

Now assume that the assets of the firm are sold. The following amounts are realized on liquidation:

Current assets	$28,000,000
Net property	5,000,000
Total	$33,000,000

The order of priority of payment of claims is shown by Table 22–5. Fees and expenses of administration typically are about 20 percent of gross proceeds. In this example they are assumed to be $6 million. Next in priority are wages due workers, which total $700,000. The total amount of taxes to be paid is $1.3 million. Thus far the total paid from the $33 million is $8 million. The first mortgage is then paid from the net proceeds of $5 million from the sale of fixed property, leaving $20 million available to the general creditors.

Table 22–5   *BANKRUPT FIRM*
                        ORDER OF PRIORITY OF CLAIMS

Distribution of Proceeds on Liquidation

1. Proceeds of sale of assets	$33,000,000
2. Fees and expenses of administration of bankruptcy	$ 6,000,000
3. Wages due workers earned 3 months prior to filing of bankruptcy petition	700,000
4. Taxes	1,300,000
	$25,000,000
5. First mortgage, paid from net property	5,000,000
6. Available to general creditors	$20,000,000

Claims as *General Creditors*	*Claim*	*Application of 50 Percent*	*After Subordination Adjustment*	*Percentage of Original Claims Received*
Unsatisfied portion of first mortgage	$ 1,000,000	$ 500,000	$ 500,000	92
Unsatisfied portion of second mortgage	1,000,000	500,000	500,000	50
Notes payable	10,000,000	5,000,000	9,000,000	90
Accounts payable	20,000,000	10,000,000	10,000,000	50
Subordinated debentures	8,000,000	4,000,000	0	0
	$40,000,000	$20,000,000	$20,000,000	56

Percentage of payment $\dfrac{\$20,000,000}{\$40,000,000} = 50$

The amount therefore available to the general creditors is $20 million. The claims of the general creditors total $40 million. Since $20 million is available, each claimant would receive 50 percent of his claim before the subordination adjustment. The subordination adjustment requires that the subordinated debentures turn over to the notes to which they are subordinated all amounts received until the notes are satisfied. In this situation, the claim of the notes payable is $10 million, but only $5 million is available. The deficiency is $5 million. After transfer by the subordinated debentures of $4 million, there remains a deficiency of $1 million, which will be unsatisfied. It will be noted that 92 percent of the bank claim is satisfied, whereas only 50 percent of other unsecured claims will be satisfied. These figures illustrate the usefulness of the subordination provision to the security to which the subordination is made. Since no other funds remain, the claims of the holders of preferred and common stock are completely wiped out.

Studies of the proceeds in bankruptcy liquidations reveal that unsecured creditors receive, on the average, about 15 cents on the dollar. Consequently, where assignment to creditors is likely to yield more, assignment is to be preferred to bankruptcy.

SUMMARY

Problems associated with the decline and failure of a firm, as well as methods of rehabilitating or liquidating one that has failed, were the subjects treated in this chapter. The major cause of failure is incompetent management. Bad managers should, of course, be removed as promptly as possible, but if failure has occurred, a number of remedies are open to the interested parties.

The first question to be answered is whether the firm is better off dead or alive—whether it should be liquidated and sold off piecemeal or rehabilitated. Assuming the decision is made that the firm should survive, it must be put through what is called a *reorganization*. Legal procedures are always costly, especially in the case of a business failure. Therefore, if it is at all possible, both the debtor and the creditors are better off if matters can be handled on an informal basis rather than through the courts. The informal procedures used in reorganization are (1) *extension*, which postpones the date of settlement, and (2) *composition*, which reduces the amount owed.

If voluntary settlement through extension or composition is not possible, the matter is thrown into the courts. If the court decides on reorganization rather than liquidation, it will appoint a trustee (1) to control the firm doing the reorganization and (2) to prepare a formal plan of reorganization. The plan, which must be reviewed by the SEC, must meet the standards of *fairness* to all parties and *feasibility* in the sense that the reorganized enterprise will stand a good chance of surviving rather than being thrown back into the bankruptcy courts.

The application of standards of fairness and feasibility developed in this chapter are tools to determine the probable success of a particular plan of reorganization. The concept of fairness involves the estimation of sales and earnings and the application of a capitalization rate to the latter to determine the appropriate distribution to each claimant.

The *feasibility test* examines the ability of the new enterprise to carry the fixed charges resulting from the reorganization plan. The quality of management and the company's assets must be assured. Production and marketing may also require improvement.

Finally, where liquidation is treated as the only solution to the debtor's insolvency, the creditors should attempt procedures that will net them the largest recovery. *Assignment* of the debtor's property is the cheaper and the faster procedure. In addition, there is more flexibility in disposing of the debtor's property and thus providing larger returns. *Bankruptcy* provides formal procedures in liquidation to safeguard the debtor's property from fraud and provides equitable distribution to the creditors. The procedure is long and cumbersome. In addition, the debtor's property is generally poorly managed during bankruptcy proceedings unless the trustee is closely supervised by the creditors.

QUESTIONS

22–1 "A certain number of business failures is a healthy sign. If there are no failures, this is an indication (1) that entrepreneurs are overly cautious, hence not as inventive and as willing to take risks as a healthy, growing economy requires, (2) that competition is not functioning to weed out inefficient producers, or (3) that both situations exist." Discuss, giving pros and cons.

22–2 How can financial analysis be used to forecast the probability of a given firm's failure? Assuming that such analysis is properly applied, can it always predict failure?

22–3 Why do creditors usually accept a plan for financial rehabilitation rather than demand liquidation of the business?

22–4 Would it be possible to form a profitable company by merging two companies both of which are business failures? Explain.

22–5 Distinguish between a reorganization and a bankruptcy.

22–6 Would it be a sound rule to liquidate whenever the liquidation value is above the value of the corporation as a going concern? Discuss.

22–7 Why do liquidations of all types usually result in losses for the creditors or the owners, or both? Would partial liquidation or liquidation over a period limit their losses? Explain.

22–8 Are liquidations likely to be more common for public utility, railroad, or industrial corporations? Why?

PROBLEMS

22–1 The financial statements of the Blough Publishing Company for 1966 were as follows:

BLOUGH PUBLISHING COMPANY
BALANCE SHEET
December 31, 1966
(in millions of dollars)

Current assets	$40	Current liabilities	$ 14
Investments	16	Advance payments for sub-	
Net fixed assets	51	scriptions	26
Goodwill	5	Reserves	2
		$4 preferred stock, $75 par	
		(600,000 shares)	45
		$7 preferred stock, no par	
		(300,000 shares, callable	
		at $100)	3
		Common stock, par value	
		of $1 (3,000,000 shares	
		outstanding)	3
		Retained earnings	19
Total assets	$112	Total claims	$112

BLOUGH PUBLISHING COMPANY
CONSOLIDATED STATEMENT OF INCOME AND EXPENSE
For Year Ended December 31, 1966
(in millions of dollars)

Operating income		$180.0
Operating expense		172.0
Net operating income		$ 8.0
Other income		1.0
Other expense		0.0
Earnings before income tax		$ 9.0
Income tax at 50 percent		4.5
Income after taxes		$ 4.5
Dividends on $4 prior preferred stock	$2.4	
Dividends on $7 preferred stock	0.2	2.6
Income available for common stock		$ 1.9

A recapitalization plan is proposed in which each share of the $4 preferred will be exchanged for one share of $1.60 preferred (stated value, $25) plus one 6 percent subordinated income debenture (stated principal, $50). The $7 preferred would be retired from cash.

a) Show the *pro forma* balance sheet (in millions of dollars) giving effect to the recapitalization and showing the new preferred at its stated value and the common stock at its par value.

b) Present the *pro forma* income statement (in millions of dollars carried to two decimal places).

    c) How much does the firm increase income available to common stock by the recapitalization?

    d) How much less is the required pretax earnings after the recapitalization compared to those before the change? Required earnings is that amount which is just enough to meet fixed charges, debenture interest, and/or preferred dividends in this case.

    e) How is the debt-to-net-worth position of the company affected by the recapitalization?

    f) Would you vote for the recapitalization if you were a holder of the $4 prior preferred stock?

22–2   The Perfecto Instrument Company produces precision instruments. The company's products are designed and manufactured according to specifications set out by its customers and are highly specialized.

    Declines in sales and increases in development expenses in recent years resulted in a large deficit by the end of 1966.

PERFECTO INSTRUMENT COMPANY
BALANCE SHEET
December 31, 1966
(in thousands of dollars)

Current assets	$ 500	Current liabilities	$ 600
Fixed assets	500	Long-term debt	
		(unsecured)	300
		Capital stock	200
		Earned surplus or	
		(deficit)	(100)
Total assets	$1,000	Total claims	$1,000

Independent assessment led to the conclusion that the company would have a liquidation value of about $600,000. As an alternative to liquidation, the management concluded that a reorganization was possible with additional investment of $300,000. The management was confident of eventual success of the company and stated that the additional investment would restore earnings to $150,000 a year after taxes and before fixed charges. The appropriate multiplier to apply is 8 times. The management is negotiating

PERFECTO INSTRUMENT COMPANY
SALES AND PROFITS
1963–1966
(in thousands of dollars)

Year	Sales	Net Profit After Tax Before Fixed Charges
1963	$3,500	$350
1964	$3,200	300
1965	$1,900	(100)
1966	$1,800	(150)

with a local investment group to obtain the additional investment of $300,-000. If the funds are obtained, the holders of the long-term debt would be given one half the common stock in the reorganized firm in place of their present claims.

Should the creditors agree to the reorganization or should they force liquidation of the firm?

22–3[8] On September 13, 1956, a voluntary petition for reorganization under Chapter X of the Bankruptcy Act was filed by Green River Steel Corporation in the U.S. District Court for the Western District of Kentucky, Owensboro Division. The petition was approved and a trustee was named. On November 12, 1956, the trustee filed a plan for reorganization with the court.

GREEN RIVER STEEL COMPANY
BALANCE SHEET
July 31, 1956
(in thousands of dollars)

Assets		Current liabilities	
Current assets	$ 4,000	4½ % mortgage due RFC	
Net property account	9,000	($2,100 past due)	$ 4,000
		Notes payable to banks	1,000
		Accounts payable	1,500
		Interest due to RFC	1,000
		Accruals	200
		Total current liab.	$ 7,700
		Long-term debt	
		4½ % mortgage due RFC	$ 4,500
		Deferred interest	300
		3½ % debentures, due 1961	4,000
		Interest accrued on 3½ % debentures	18
		Total long-term debt	$ 8,818
		Capital stock	
		Common (10 cents par)	7
		Paid-in surplus	80
		Earned surplus (deficit)	(3,605)
Total assets	$13,000	Total claims	$13,000

[8] Based on SEC Reorganization Release No. 1940. *In the matter of Green River Steel Corporation, Debtor, in proceedings for the reorganization of a corporation pursuant to Chapter X of the Bankruptcy Act* (Washington, D. C.: January 24, 1957), pp. 1–25. Facts altered and rounded to facilitate calculations.

On November 22, 1950, Green River Steel was incorporated under the laws of Kentucky for the purpose of engaging in the production and sale of semifinished steel products. In July 1953, Green River started operations. In early 1954, when the plant was ready to produce at its rated capacity, the entire industry was hit by a recession. In addition, the company lacked working capital as shown by the balance sheet below.

All attempts to secure additional funds failed. In spite of the difficulties, there has been a steadily improving trend in both sales and net profits.

However, with the entire $4 million principal amount of one of the mortgage notes held by RFC falling due on January 1, 1957, it was obvious to the management that the company could not meet its obligations.

GREEN RIVER STEEL COMPANY
SALES AND PROFITS, 1954–1956
(in thousands of dollars)

Year Ended	Net Sales	Net Operating Profit Before Interest Charges	Net Profits
July 31, 1954	$ 5,413	(1,603)	(2,185)
July 31, 1955	10,790	47	575
July 31, 1956	17,270	826	204

The trustee's plan of reorganization was based on an offer by Jessop Steel Company. The trustee's plan follows:

1) The United States, as the holder of RFC notes, will receive a new first-mortgage note in the principal amount of $9.8 million at the date of consummation, maturing 18 years thereafter and bearing interest at 3 percent a year for the first 3 years and 4½ percent a year thereafter.

2) The holders of outstanding debentures will receive, in exchange for each $1,000 principal amount and the interest accumulated thereon to the date of consummation, a new $1,000 income subordinated debenture note, maturing 25 years thereafter and bearing interest if earned, but noncumulative, of 2 percent for the third through the sixth years, 2½ for the seventh and eighth years, and 3½ percent thereafter. The new debentures will be subordinate (a) to a $9.8 million first-mortgage note, (b) to new 10-year notes payable to Jessop in the principal amount of not less than $1.5 million, and (c) to bank loans of $3 million.

3) The holders of the common stock of the debtor will receive in exchange for each 10 shares of such stock one share of common stock of Jessop. New common stock will be issued by Green River to Jessop, which will become the sole stockholder of the reorganized enterprise.

4) The trustee's plan provides for the issuance of 10-year notes to Jessop in exchange for cash advanced to the debtor in the principal amount of $1.5 million at the consummation date, maturing in 10 years and bearing interest of 4 percent a year.

5) The plan also provides for sinking funds for the retirement of the first-mortgage note, the 10-year note, and the new debentures.

The *pro forma* liabilities and net worth, giving effect to the trustee's plan, are:

Notes payable to banks	$3,000	
Accounts payable	1,500	
Accruals	200	
Current liabilities		$ 4,700
First mortgage due RFC	$9,800	
10-year note to Jessop	1,500	
Subordinated income debentures	4,000	
Long-term debt		15,300
Common stock, par value $10	$3,000	
Capital surplus	1,000	
Net worth		4,000
Total claims		$24,000

The *pro forma* statement is based on continuing the accounts payable at $1.5 million, on increasing the bank loans to $3 million, and on additional investment of $1.5 million by Jessop Steel.

a) What is the value of the assets of Green River less the new capital invested in the business?

b) Using the capitalization of income method, if the sales of Green River rise to $30 million, the profit rate on sales (before interest) is 7 percent and the price/earnings ratio is 8, what is the amount of the total assets of Green River after reorganization?

c) What is the amount of total assets of Green River if sales are $25 million but all other conditions are as in (b)?

d) Assume that sales of Green River are $25 million but that the profit rate rises to 8 percent. What is the amount of total assets of Green River now?

e) Because Jessop Steel would become the sole owner of Green River, does it make any difference whether Jessop's $1.5 million is treated as debt or as ownership investment?

f) What is your appraisal of the fairness of the proposed reorganization plan?

g) What is your opinion of the feasibility of the reorganization plan?

22-4 On May 10, 1965, the Simpson Company filed an involuntary petition in bankruptcy, having defaulted interest on its outstanding debt. At this date, it issued the following balance sheet.

SIMPSON COMPANY
BALANCE SHEET
May 10, 1965

Cash	$ 10,000	Accounts payable	$ 500,000
Receivables	190,000	Notes payable, 8%	500,000
Inventory	800,000	First mortgage, 5%	1,000,000
Machinery	2,000,000	Second mortgage, 6%	1,000,000
Plant	5,000,000	Debentures, 6%	2,000,000
Surplus	1,000,000	Preferred stock, 7%	1,000,000
		Common stock	3,000,000
Total	$9,000,000	Total	$9,000,000

The Simpson Company, after the necessary reorganization, can earn $320,-000. You have determined that 8 percent is an appropriate capitalization rate.

a) State your plan of reorganization, using (1) absolute priority doctrine and (2) relative priority doctrine.
b) Defend both your plans for (1) "fairness" in legal connotation and (2) "feasibility" in legal connotation.

22–5   The Pomona Pipe Company has suffered several years of operating losses. Because of the unfavorable outlook for the firm, it goes into bankruptcy and is dissolved. How much would each class of claimant on assets receive in liquidation?

POMONA PIPE COMPANY
BALANCE SHEET
September 30, 1965
(last balance sheet before dissolution)

Cash	$ 20,000	Accounts payable	$ 1,000,000
Accounts receivable	100,000	Loans from banks	2,000,000
Inventories	2,000,000	Property taxes	5,000
Building	10,000,000	Accrued wages*	60,000
Equipment	5,000,000	Federal income taxes	5,000
		First mortgage on building	4,000,000
		Second mortgage on building	2,000,000
		Subordinated convertible debentures†	1,000,000
		Preferred stock	3,000,000
		Common stock	3,000,000
		Retained earnings	1,050,000
Total	$17,120,000	Total	$17,120,000

* Incurred during the last two months, no claim exceeds $600.
† Subordinated to bank loan only.

On liquidation, the following amounts are received from respective items:

Cash	$ 20,000
Receivables	50,000
Inventories	1,000,000
Building	5,000,000
Equipment	2,000,000

What would be the priority of payment, and how much would each class of creditor receive?

PART VIII

An Integrated View of Financial Management

Chapter 23

The Timing of
Financial Policy

This chapter deals with the timing of financial policy. Variations in the relative cost and availability of funds require comparison of the changes in the cost and availability of equity money, long-term money, and short-term money over time. Fluctuations in the level of business activity produce a number of impacts on the firm. For good timing of financial policy, the financial manager must take into account prospective changes in asset requirements that will have to be financed over time. He must also consider prospective prices and return from capital assets. Finally, he must plan his needs to meet future maturing obligations.

SIGNIFICANCE TO FINANCIAL MANAGEMENT

The significance of financial timing of firms is suggested by the following comments in *Business Week:*

Since 1951, when the Federal Reserve won the right to pursue an independent monetary policy, the cost and availability of money have been a constant problem for corporate management. At times, as in the tight money squeeze of 1957, it has been a major worry.

Company treasurers resented the high rates that banks charged on loans; they resented even more banks' insistence that they hold compensating balances, depriving them of the full use of their borrowed money. And because they feared

483

that rates would go even higher and that credit might not be available at all, they stepped up their demands—which had the effect of further tightening an already tight situation.[1]

The concern of financial managers over the cost of money in 1960 was mild compared with their reactions to the "credit crunch" that developed in August 1966 and again in the summer and fall of 1967. This is evidenced by another quotation from *Business Week* seven years later.

Even a modest increase in monetary restraint will be hard for most companies to handle. Ever since the end of last year's credit drought, companies have worked hard to rebuild liquidity.

However, there's a "difference between actual and desired liquidity," says an economist for a major New York City bank, "and companies haven't succeeded in loosening up balance sheets".

In contrasting money market conditions that lie ahead with 1966, economists stress the expected impact of inflation itself. During late 1966, the wholesale price index remained relatively stable. But if price increases get larger in coming months, interest rates are almost sure to climb.

"People who borrow under conditions of sharp inflation are willing to pay any amount for money," says Milton Friedman of the University of Chicago, "and people who lend ask high rates to protect themselves from loss of purchasing power." If the Fed doesn't tighten, Friedman expects prices to rise by at least 5% and possibly 7% during 1968 and predicts that interest rates will be in the "9% to 10% range." [2]

Financial managers are concerned with variations in money and capital market conditions—sharp changes in the cost and availability of funds have been experienced in the past, and similar fluctuations will undoubtedly be experienced in the future.

Table 23–1 gives an indication of the pattern of interest changes in the U. S. economy during the period of 1929–1966. One outstanding characteristic of interest rate behavior is made most clear by the table—the wide magnitude of the changes in the price of money over the years. For example, the borrowing rate on 4 to 6 months commercial paper, which is the best indication of the cost of short-term money to large corporations, reached a low of 0.53% in 1941. By 1953, this rate stood at 2.52%, but it declined to 1.58% during the business recession of the following year. In the early 1960's prime commercial paper rates rose to over 3%, and during the credit stringency of 1966 the rate reached 6%. However, it had declined to 4.75% by September 1967.

Yields on high grade long-term corporate bonds have fluctuated simi-

---

[1] "Where the Credit Pinch Hurts," *Business Week*, February 27, 1960, p. 65.
[2] "Is a Money Crunch on Its Way?" *Business Week*, September 29, 1967, p. 36.

larly, but not to the same degree. For example, the corporate Aaa bond rate reached a low of 2.53% in 1946. It rose to over 3% in 1953 and, after declining to 2.90% during the business downturn of 1954, climbed to 4.41% by 1960. During August 1966, yields on Aaa corporates rose above 5½ percent, and the rise continued in 1967. By the fall of 1967, new Aaa issues were yielding over 6%.

This brief review of fluctuations in short-term and long-term interest rates is sufficient to demonstrate that fluctuations in the cost of capital to business represents one of the most volatile of the inputs purchased by firms. Within relatively short time periods, money costs have fluctuated by over 100 percent.

The significance of fluctuations in interest rates is seen to be especially important when one considers the large amounts of financing that may be involved. On July 11, 1967, Texaco came to the market with a $200 million offering of bonds due in 1997, carrying a rating of Aaa and a coupon of 5¾ percent. On August 30, 1967, Alcoa issued $125 million of similarly rated bonds sold to yield 6.07 percent. Had Texaco waited another month to issue its bonds and incurred a ¼ percent higher cost, this would have represented a difference in interest charges of $500,000 a year.

While the cost variations associated with interest rate fluctuations are substantial, the greatest significance of interest rates is their role as an index of the availability of funds. A period of high interest rates reflects a period of tight money, which is in turn associated with tight reserve positions at commercial banks. At such times interest rates will rise, of course, but there are conventional limits on interest rates. As a consequence, a larger quantity of funds is demanded by borrowers than banks are able to make available. Banks therefore begin to ration funds among prospective borrowers by continuing lines of credit to traditional customers but restricting loans to borrowers whose credit standards are not as strong.

Small firms will characteristically have greater difficulty obtaining financing during periods of tight money. Even among large borrowers, the bargaining position of the financial institutions is stronger in a period of tight money. It is a lender's market rather than a borrower's market. As a consequence, the availability of loans is likely to be restricted. Furthermore, the restrictive conditions in term loan agreements are likely to be more onerous when the demand for funds is high.

Interest rates are therefore of very great significance to financial managers as an index to the availability of funds. For small- and medium-sized firms, a period of rising interest rates may indicate increasing difficulty in obtaining any financing at all. Or, if financing is obtained, it will be obtained at a higher cost and under less favorable conditions.

A period of tight money will have a particularly heavy impact on the

Table 23–1 BOND YIELDS AND INTEREST RATES, 1929–1966

[percent per year]

Year or Month	U.S. Government Securities				Corporate Bonds (Moody's)		High-grade Municipal Bonds (Standard & Poor's)	Average Rate on Short-term Bank Loans to Business—Selected Cities	Prime Commercial Paper, 4–6 Months	Federal Reserve Bank Discount Rate
	3-Month Treasury Bills	9–12 Month Issues	3–5 Year Issues	Taxable Bonds	Aaa	Baa				
1929	—	—	—	—	4.73	5.90	4.27	—	5.85	5.16
1930	—	—	—	—	4.55	5.90	4.07	—	3.59	3.04
1931	1.402	—	—	—	4.58	7.62	4.01	—	2.64	2.11
1932	0.879	—	—	—	5.01	9.30	4.65	—	2.73	2.82
1933	0.515	—	2.66	—	4.49	7.76	4.71	—	1.73	2.56
1934	0.256	—	2.12	—	4.00	6.32	4.03	—	1.02	1.54
1935	0.137	—	1.29	—	3.60	5.75	3.40	—	0.75	1.50
1936	0.143	—	1.11	—	3.24	4.77	3.07	—	0.75	1.50
1937	0.447	—	1.40	—	3.26	5.03	3.10	—	0.94	1.33
1938	0.053	—	0.83	—	3.19	5.80	2.91	—	0.81	1.00
1939	0.023	—	0.59	—	3.01	4.96	2.76	2.1	0.59	1.00
1940	0.014	—	0.50	—	2.84	4.75	2.50	2.1	0.56	1.00
1941	0.103	—	0.73	—	2.77	4.33	2.10	2.0	0.53	1.00
1942	0.326	—	1.46	2.46	2.83	4.28	2.36	2.2	0.66	1.00
1943	0.373	0.75	1.34	2.47	2.73	3.91	2.06	2.6	0.69	1.00
1944	0.375	0.79	1.33	2.48	2.72	3.61	1.86	2.4	0.73	1.00

Year										
1945	0.375	0.81	1.18	2.37	2.62	3.29	1.67	2.2	0.75	1.00
1946	0.375	0.82	1.16	2.19	2.53	3.05	1.64	2.1	0.81	1.00
1947	0.594	0.88	1.32	2.25	2.61	3.24	2.01	2.1	1.03	1.00
1948	1.040	1.14	1.62	2.44	2.82	3.47	2.40	2.5	1.44	1.34
1949	1.102	1.14	1.43	2.31	2.66	3.42	2.21	2.68	1.49	1.50
1950	1.218	1.26	1.50	2.32	2.62	3.24	1.98	2.69	1.45	1.59
1951	1.552	1.73	1.93	2.57	2.86	3.41	2.00	3.11	2.16	1.75
1952	1.766	1.81	2.13	2.68	2.96	3.52	2.19	3.49	2.33	1.75
1953	1.931	2.07	2.56	2.94	3.20	3.74	2.72	3.69	2.52	1.99
1954	0.953	0.92	1.82	2.55	2.90	3.51	2.37	3.61	1.58	1.60
1955	1.753	1.89	2.50	2.84	3.06	3.53	2.53	3.70	2.18	1.89
1956	2.658	2.83	3.12	3.08	3.36	3.88	2.93	4.20	3.31	2.77
1957	3.267	3.53	3.62	3.47	3.89	4.71	3.60	4.62	3.81	3.12
1958	1.839	2.09	2.90	3.43	3.79	4.73	3.56	4.34	2.46	2.16
1959	3.405	4.11	4.33	4.08	4.38	5.05	3.95	5.00	3.97	3.36
1960	2.928	3.55	3.99	4.02	4.41	5.19	3.73	5.16	3.85	3.53
1961	2.378	2.91	3.60	3.90	4.35	5.08	3.46	4.97	2.97	3.00
1962	2.778	3.02	3.57	3.95	4.33	5.02	3.18	5.00	3.26	3.00
1963	3.157	3.28	3.72	4.00	4.26	4.86	3.23	5.01	3.55	3.23
1964	3.549	3.76	4.06	4.15	4.40	4.83	3.22	4.99	3.97	3.55
1965	3.954	4.09	4.22	4.21	4.49	4.87	3.27	5.06	4.38	4.04
1966	4.881	5.17	5.16	4.65	5.13	5.67	3.82	6.00	5.55	4.50

SOURCE: *The Annual Report of the Council of Economic Advisers* (Washington, D. C.: U.S. Government Printing Office, 1967), p. 272.
Note: Rates are annual averages; variations within a given year can be pronounced.

487

ANNUALLY

Percent per year

Common stocks
Earnings/price ratio

Dividend/price ratio

High-grade preferred stocks
Dividend/price ratio

Figure 23-1 Stock Yields

SOURCE: Historical Supplement to *Federal Reserve Chart Book on Financial and Business Statistics*, p. 37

utilities and other heavy industries, state and local governments, and the housing and construction sectors. For the heavy, long-term investments made in these areas, the impact of interest rates on profitability is likely to be very great.

The preceding paragraphs have described the conditions that exist when money is tight and interest rates are high. The situation is just the reverse when money is easy. Then funds are readily available at low costs and under relatively unrestrictive loan agreements.

DATA ON RELATIVE COSTS OF FINANCING OVER TIME

It has been seen that the cost of money can vary widely over the business cycle. In addition, costs of different forms of financing differ, and the timing of swings in the cost of money and in the relative cost of financing by different sources changes over time. Detailed data are presented to provide a factual foundation for decision making in choosing between the alternatives available to financial managers. The data in Figure 23–1 present stock yields since 1912.

Cost of Equity Funds

Both earnings/price ratios and dividend yields on common stocks have exhibited wide fluctuations. Earnings/price ratios have been as high as 16 percent and as low as 5 to 6 percent, excluding years when earnings were negative. Dividend/yield ratios have also fluctuated widely, not so much because dividends have fluctuated greatly but because the price factor in the denominator has gyrated widely.

The pattern in recent years is shown more clearly in Figure 23–2, which is an enlargement of the segment of Figure 23–1 from 1960 through the first half of 1967. Common stock earnings/price ratios during the 1960s have averaged about 6 percent, ranging from 4.5 to 7.1 percent. Common stock dividend yields fluctuated between 3 and 3.75 percent during this same period. Preferred stocks yields have shown more moderate fluctuations than either earnings/price ratios or dividend yields. Since the late 1950s, preferred stock dividend yields have been about 2 percentage points higher than common stock dividend yields, reflecting the market's expectation that common stock earnings, dividends, and stock prices will grow and provide capital gains to supplement the dividend yield.

Relation between Long-Term and Short-Term Interest Rates

One of the important elements in the financial manager's timing decisions is an understanding of the relation between long-term and short-term interest rates. Long-term interest rates are rates on securities with

STOCKS

EARNINGS RATIO, END OF QUARTER; DIVIDEND RATIO, MONTHLY

Percent

Standard and Poor's Corporation

COMMON STOCKS
Earnings/price ratio

PREFERRED STOCKS
Dividend/price ratio

COMMON STOCKS
Dividend/price ratio

YEAR

Figure 23-2   Security Yields

SOURCE: *Federal Reserve Chart Book, Financial and Business Statistics,* September, 1967, p. 27

maturities in excess of 15 years. Short-term interest rates are those on securities with maturities of under one year.

Figure 23–3 graphs the relationship between long-term and short-term interest rates. In some periods, short-term interest rates were higher than long-term interest rates; this was true in late 1959 and late 1966, when the money market was extremely tight. These data refute the theory set out by some distinguished economists who argued on the basis of the evidence of the 1930s that short-term rates of interest are always lower than long-term rates. Their case was based on the reasoning that long-term securities represent a greater degree of risk than do short-term securities. These economists argued that because of the greater risk involved in holding long-term bonds, long-term rates would always be higher than short-term rates. Their reasoning was partially sound, as there is greater risk to holding long-term securities than short-term securities. For one thing, the longer the maturity of the security in an uncertain economic environment, the greater the danger that the firm that issued it may not make an effective adaptation to its environment and, therefore, may not be able to meet its obligations in 10 ,15, or 20 years. In addition, the *prices* of long-term bonds are much more volatile than short-term bond prices when interest rates change; the reason for this is largely arithmetic and was described in Chapter 9.

However, many other kinds of uncertainties are faced by the firm and the investor, and these other considerations may dominate at some point in time.

One of these uncertainties is changes in the supply and demand of loanable funds over time. When the supply of funds is tight relative to the demand for them at prevailing prices, there will be strong pressure for short-term interest rates to rise. Short-term interest rates reflect current supply-and-demand situations. Long-term interest rates reflect an average of supply-and-demand conditions over the life of the security. This characteristic accounts for the fact that short-term interest rates are much more volatile than long-term interest rates (Figure 23–3).

A theory (economists call it the *expectations theory*) has been put forth that long-term interest rates may appropriately be regarded as an average of short-term interest rates. Thus the relation between long rates and short rates will depend upon what is happening to the future of short-term interest rates, as illustrated by Table 23–2. In section A it is assumed that short-term interest rates rise 1 percent each year, beginning at 2 percent in year 1. The corresponding long-term interest rate in year 1 for a five-year period can be approximated by taking a simple arithmetic average of the five short-term rates, 4 percent. Thus, in year 1, the long-term rate would be double the short-term rate.

Figure 23-3   Long and Short-Term Interest Rates
SOURCE: *Federal Reserve Chart Book, Financial and Business Statistics, September, 1967,* p. 23

Table 23-2   RELATION BETWEEN SHORT-TERM AND
             LONG-TERM INTEREST RATES

	A		B	
Year	5-Year Note	Short-Term Rates	5-Year Note	Short-Term Rates
1	4	2	4	6
2		3		5
3		4		4
4		5		3
5		6		2

Consider, however, the situation under section B. Here, in a tight-money situation in year 1, short-term rates are 6 percent, but they are expected to decline by 1 percent each year. The average of these rates would be the same as in section A, because the numbers are identical—their order is simply reversed. Now, however, the long-term rate of 4 percent lies below the short-term rate of 6 percent.

These examples do not prove the relation between short-term rates and long-term rates. They do, however, illustrate the pattern that would exist if the only factor operating was expected changes in interest rate movements, themselves reflecting a broad group of supply-and-demand factors. However, many other uncertainty factors do operate on the market. Some of these include differences in the risks of loss and failure among individual business firms, in the economic outlook for different industries, in the degree to which price-level changes affect different products in industries, and in the impact that changes in government legislation will have on different firms in an industry.

Interest Rate Structure

The discussion now turns to an analysis of the wide range of relations between money costs in the postwar period. The basic data on bond yields and interest rates since 1929 for ten categories of instruments were presented in Table 23–1. The table indicates that when a person speaks of "the interest rate," he is in fact referring to an interest rate structure, or cost-of-money structure.

The data in Table 23–1 indicate the range of variations *between* rates on different securities at any moment of time, variations in rates on a particular security over time, and changes in the structure of rates through time. It provides the basic factual background for money cost patterns that will be discussed later. Furthermore, it provides a factual foundation

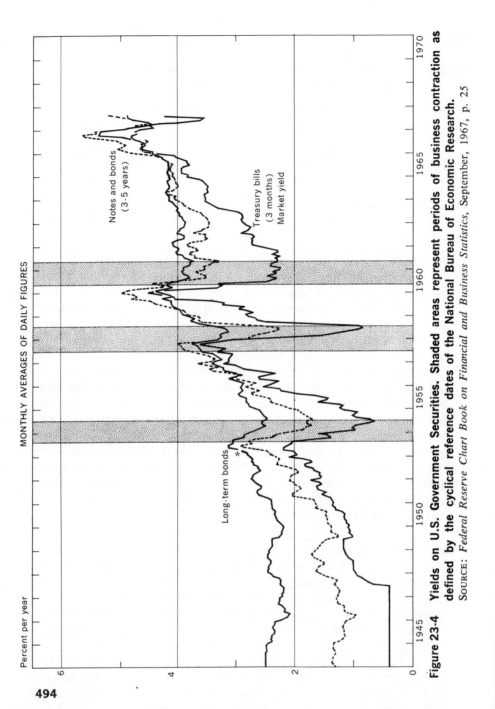

Figure 23-4   Yields on U.S. Government Securities. Shaded areas represent periods of business contraction as defined by the cyclical reference dates of the National Bureau of Economic Research.

SOURCE: *Federal Reserve Chart Book on Financial and Business Statistics,* September, 1967, p. 25

for evaluating the timing of financial policy of firms during the post-World War II period. Reference to the table may be made when solving the problems at the end of this chapter.

As a starting point toward understanding the patterns exhibited in Table 23–1, the data are graphed in Figures 23–4 and 23–5. Figure 23–4 illustrates the relation between interest rates on 20-year Treasury bonds and three-month Treasury bills over the post-World War II cycles. The relative costs typically spread widely apart during a business downturn and tend to narrow during a business upswing. Not only does the spread vary over time, but the absolute level also varies over time. It will be observed also that the movements in short-term rates are much more volatile than movements in long-term interest levels.

Further aspects are presented in Figure 23–5, which presents movements over time in prime commercial paper rates and rates on corporate Triple A bonds. With this abundant factual material on the movements of the cost of money, some generalizations may now be made and systematic patterns observed.

CHARACTERISTIC PATTERNS IN COST OF MONEY

The general nature of the relations between long- and short-term interest rates and between rates and GNP are shown in Figure 23–6. Short-term interest rates show the widest amplitude of swings. Long-term interest rates are not as sensitive as short-term rates. Short-term rates move more quickly than long-term rates. The costs of debt money tend generally to lag movements in general business conditions, both at the peak and at the trough. But the movements of long-term rates lag more than short-term rates.

The cost of equity funds may best be approximated by equity yields, dividends plus capital gains. To understand the behavior of equity yields, the behavior of earnings, dividends, and prices must be analyzed. Corporate earnings are highly volatile. They lead the business cycle both on the upturn and on the downturn, and dividends follow earnings. Prices of common stocks anticipate changes in corporate earnings. Prices of equities are also influenced by money market conditions. Owing to the gradual tightening in money market conditions as expansion continues, bond yields rise and attract money out of stocks and into bonds, causing the prices of equities to turn down before corporate profits reach their peak. Hence, the cost of equity financing turns up because firms receive lower prices for the stocks they sell. In other words, the cost of equity capital begins to rise in the later stages of the business cycle.

ANNUALLY

Percent per year

Bonds High-grade railroad

High-grade corporate AAA

Corporate
(30 years)
Basic yields

Prime commercial paper
(4-6 months)

Figure 23-5   Long-Term and Short-Term Interest Rates
SOURCE: *Federal Reserve Chart Book on Financial and Business Statistics*, September, 1967, p. 23

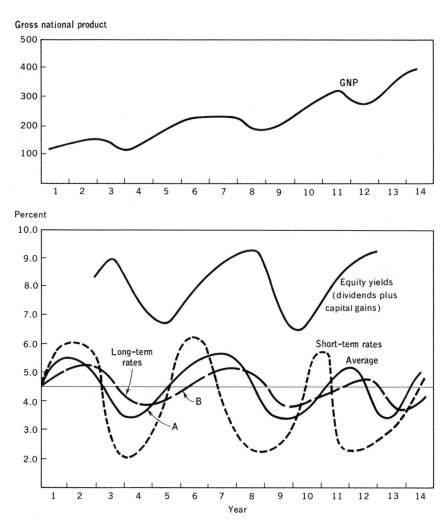

Figure 23-6   Illustrative Relation between Movements of Gross National Product and Interest Rates

If the financial manager is to apply these guidelines effectively, he must know the current stage of the financial cycle whenever he contemplates the acquisition of funds. A forecast of interest rate movements is therefore required. As an approach to laying a framework and foundation for forecasting interest rates, two kinds of material are covered: first, broad trends to provide a basic foundation; second, data for short-term forecasting.

PATTERNS IN FUND FLOWS

Within the broad framework described above, the forecaster of short-term movements in interest rates must look at immediate prospects for changes in the short-run supply and demand for funds. In the analysis of the supply and demand for funds, attention will be focused first on the supply of savings. National savings have averaged about 13½ percent of the net national product.[3] Personal savings account for 70 to 75 percent of total savings, with corporate savings making up the remaining 20 to 25 percent of total national savings. The share of savings by nonfarm households and by agricultural and unincorporated business enterprises related to the total personal disposable income has averaged about 12 percent. National income statistics presented on a current basis show personal savings as a percentage of disposable personal income running at about a 6-to-7 percent rate.

There has been an increase in the amount of indirect savings. Indirect savings are transmitted through a financial intermediary (banks, insurance companies, investment funds, pension funds) by the saver to the ultimate user. This percentage has risen from about 25 percent between 1900 and 1929 to about 40 percent in the 1950s and 1960s. Thus a considerable portion of saving does not bring the user and the saver into direct contact.

Another aspect of saving of some significance is that contractual saving, in which the saver makes a long-term commitment to save (for example, life insurance, pensions, mortgage repayments) has risen from 10 percent of the total amount of individual savings around 1900 to 20 percent in the 1920s and well over 50 percent in the 1950s and 1960s. Savings are therefore less subject to discretionary decisions by individuals on a current basis than they were in the past.

The principal uses of funds have been nonfinancial corporate bonds and stocks, real estate mortgages, state and local government net debt, and federal government and agency debt. These are mainly long-term funds. The principal uses of short-term funds have been consumer credit and various types of bank loans, principally short-term bank loans to business. Thus the principal competitors to business borrowers are residential real estate mortgages and federal, state, and local government borrowings.

External long-term corporate financing can be divided into three major categories—common stock, preferred stock, and bonds and notes. Until the bull market in stocks began to surge in 1953, bonds and notes ac-

---

[3] These data and related material are taken from the *Conference on Savings and Residential Financing, 1958 Proceedings* (United States Savings and Loan League, September 1958). The present data are taken from the paper by Raymond W. Goldsmith, "The Supply of Savings."

counted for about 80 percent of external financing (Table 23–3). In recent years, common stock financing has fluctuated markedly, rising in bull market years such as 1961 and declining in weak markets such as 1966.

Table 23–3 CORPORATE SECURITIES OFFERED FOR CASH SALE IN THE UNITED STATES,* 1934–1967

Year	Common Stock (millions of dollars)	(percentages)	Preferred Stock (millions of dollars)	(percentages)	Bonds and Notes (millions of dollars)	(percentages)	Totals (millions of dollars)
1934	19	4.8	6	1.5	372	93.7	397
1935	22	0.9	86	3.7	2,224	95.4	2,332
1936	272	6.0	271	5.9	4,028	88.1	4,572
1937	285	12.4	406	17.6	1,618	70.0	2,310
1938	25	1.2	86	4.0	2,044	94.8	2,155
1939	87	4.0	98	4.5	1,980	91.5	2,164
1940	108	4.1	183	6.8	2,386	89.1	2,677
1941	110	4.1	167	6.3	2,390	89.6	2,667
1942	34	3.2	112	10.4	917	86.4	1,062
1943	56	4.8	124	10.6	990	84.6	1,170
1944	163	5.1	369	11.5	2,670	83.4	3,202
1945	397	6.6	758	12.6	4,855	80.8	6,011
1946	891	12.9	1,127	16.3	4,882	70.8	6,900
1947	779	11.8	762	11.6	5,036	76.6	6,577
1948	614	8.7	492	7.0	5,973	84.3	7,078
1949	736	12.2	425	7.0	4,890	80.8	6,052
1950	811	12.8	631	9.9	4,920	77.3	6,361
1951	1,212	15.7	838	10.8	5,691	73.5	7,741
1952	1,369	14.4	564	5.9	7,601	79.7	9,534
1953	1,326	14.9	489	5.5	7,083	79.6	8,898
1954	1,213	12.7	816	8.6	7,488	78.7	9,516
1955	2,185	21.3	635	6.2	7,420	72.5	10,240
1956	2,301	21.0	636	5.8	8,002	73.2	10,939
1957	2,516	19.5	411	3.2	9,957	77.3	12,884
1958	1,334	11.6	571	4.9	9,653	83.5	11,558
1959	2,027	20.8	531	5.4	7,190	73.8	9,748
1960	1,664	16.4	409	4.0	8,081	79.6	10,154
1961	3,294	25.0	450	3.4	9,420	71.6	13,165
1962	1,314	12.3	422	3.9	8,969	83.8	10,705
1963	1,022	8.4	342	2.8	10,872	88.8	12,237
1964	2,679	19.2	412	3.0	10,865	77.8	13,957
1965	1,547	9.7	725	4.5	13,720	85.8	15,992
1966	1,940	10.5	570	3.1	15,908	86.4	18,418
Jan.–July 1967	946	6.6	384	2.7	12,941	90.7	14,270

* Gross proceeds.
SOURCE: SEC Statistical Bulletins.

In 1965 and 1966, bond financing again rose to over 85 percent of financing. Since convertibles, when initially offered, are counted in the bond and preferred stock categories, the great increase in convertible financing causes the role of fixed-charge financing to be greater than it actually is on a longer term basis. Most convertibles will be converted into common stock, so it is somewhat misleading to classify convertible financing with regular preferred stock or debt issues.

FORECASTING THE LEVEL OF INTEREST RATES

Although profound and impressive studies of the theory of interest rates have been made, from the practical standpoint it is necessary merely to assess the future behavior of the major supply-and-demand factors. The major categories of the sources and uses of funds for the economy are set out in Table 23–4. By projecting the sources and uses of funds in different categories, the direction of the pressure on interest rates can be estimated.[4]

The table can be used in the following way. Historical patterns can be established to show uses and sources of funds in relation to the growth of the economy as a whole as measured by gross national product. When in any particular year the demand for funds grows faster than the supply in relation to historical patterns, interest rates are likely to rise. These extra funds are supplied by drawing on the commercial banking system, which is the pivot in the financial mechanism. Whenever the demand for funds must be met by drawing on the commercial banking system to a greater-than-normal degree, interest rates rise.

The data for 1966 present an interesting pattern. Statistics for 1966 reflect the impact of the tight money policy followed by the Federal Reserve System during most of the year. As a consequence of this policy, the total supply of funds in 1966 *decreased* by over $10 billion from the $61.6 billion total of 1965. The realized use (demand) for funds necessarily declined by a like amount, but it is estimated that at least $20 billion of unsatisfied demands for funds existed during 1966.

Another significant statistic in the table is the rise in the supply of funds from Individuals and Miscellaneous; funds from this source rose by almost $6 billion during 1966, and a further increase of $13 billion was estimated for 1968. With tight money, the ability of the commercial banks and other financial institutions to supply funds is restricted relative to demand. This produces high interest rates, and these high rates induce individuals, businesses, and others to make their surplus funds available to

---

[4] Compilations of studies of these kinds are facilitated by the flow of funds data developed by the Federal Reserve System, published in the monthly Federal Reserve Bulletins.

Table 23-4 DEMAND AND SUPPLY FOR CREDIT (billions $)

Demand	1961	1962	1963	1964	1965	1966	1967E	1968E
Mortgages (after Agency purchases)	18.9	21.9	26.7	25.6	25.1	17.5	19.5	20.5
Corporate Bonds	5.2	4.9	5.6	6.6	8.1	11.1	15.2	13.1
Term Loans (SB&H) est.)	1.0	1.4	2.0	2.8	5.3	4.8	3.5	4.2
State and Local Securities	5.0	5.3	6.3	5.6	7.1	5.6	9.0	9.2
Foreign Bonds	0.5	0.9	1.1	0.9	1.2	0.9	0.9	0.8
Investment Demand, Long Term	30.6	34.4	41.7	41.5	46.8	39.9	48.1	47.8
Other Bank Loans (ex Term and Mortgages)	4.6	8.6	9.1	10.8	14.3	8.2	7.5	8.5
U.S. Government Debt (Publicly Held)*	5.8	6.1	2.5	3.2	0.5	2.9	3.2	12.2
Total Demand	41.0	49.1	53.3	55.5	61.6	51.0	58.8	68.5
Supply †								
Savings Banks	2.2	3.0	3.6	4.1	3.6	2.5	4.7	3.5
Savings and Loan Associations	9.4	10.4	13.0	10.9	9.3	4.3	7.3	6.0
Life Insurance Companies	4.9	5.3	5.9	6.4	6.6	7.1	7.0	7.0
Fire and Casualty Insurance Companies	0.9	0.9	0.9	0.8	1.0	1.1	1.0	1.1
Private Pension Funds	1.5	1.7	1.9	2.1	2.1	1.9	2.1	2.3
Public Retirement Funds	2.1	2.2	2.5	2.7	2.9	3.2	3.7	4.0
Mutual Funds	0.2	0.7	-0.1	0.4	0.4	0.9	0.1	0.3
Nonbank Institutions	21.2	24.2	27.7	27.4	25.9	21.0	25.9	24.2
Commercial Banks	15.9	19.2	18.8	21.5	27.9	17.2	35.0	30.0
Corporations, State and Local Governments, Foreigners	-0.6	2.1	2.5	-0.5	0.6	-0.2	-3.0	0.5
Individuals and Miscellaneous	4.5	3.6	4.3	7.1	7.2	13.0	0.9	13.8
Total Supply	41.0	49.1	53.3	55.5	61.6	51.0	58.8	68.5

* Includes direct debt, Federal agencies and P.C. sales.
† Excludes funds for equities, cash, and miscellaneous demands not tabulated above.
SOURCE: Henry Kaufman, "Pressure on Capital and Money Markets," *Commercial and Financial Chronicle*, vol. 206 (October 5, 1967), p. 24.

borrowers. Thus the supply of funds is augmented from nonbanking sources, but only at substantially higher interest rates.

The importance of monetary and fiscal policy when making forecasts of interest rate movements has been suggested. The nature of these governmental influences is now briefly treated.

FEDERAL RESERVE POLICY

No discussion of interest rate behavior would be complete without an analysis of the role of the central bank, which in the United States is the Federal Reserve System. The central bank is equipped with a set of powers having a significant influence on the operations of commercial banks, whose loan and investment activities in turn have an important influence on the supply of money. Of these powers the most powerful, and hence the one used sparingly, is *changing reserve requirements*. The one most often used, which can be applied in a more direct and pinpointed fashion, is changing the pattern of *open-market operations*. Changes in the *discount rates* are likely to have more of a psychological influence than direct quantitative effects.

Changes in discount rate levels are shown in the last column of Table 23–1. These changes represent the announcement by Federal Reserve authorities that a change in economic conditions has taken place calling for a future tightening or easing of monetary conditions, signaled by the direction of change in the discount rate. The data in Table 23–1 demonstrate that increases in the Federal Reserve bank discount rate have been associated with rising interest rate levels, and conversely.

Selective controls over real estate and consumer credit have been enforced periodically, but experience with them is not sufficient to determine whether the Federal Reserve authorities can effectively utilize these instruments of selective credit control. Changes in stock margin requirements have been used to counter strong movements in stock prices and probably perform some useful role. However, the underlying influences which determine stock prices are so strong and pervasive that changes in margin requirements typically are not of sufficient power to determine the future course of stock market prices.

FISCAL POLICY

The fiscal policy of the federal government has considerable impact on the movements in interest rates. A cash budget deficit represents a stimulating influence by the federal government, and a cash surplus exerts a restraining influence from the government-spending sector of the economy. However, this generalization must be modified to reflect the way a deficit is financed and by the way a surplus is used. To have the most stimulating effect, the deficit should be financed by sale of securities through the banking system, particularly the central bank. To have the most restrictive effect, the surplus should be used to retire bonds held by the banking system, particularly the central bank.

The impact of Treasury financing programs will be different at different times. Ordinarily, when the Treasury needs to draw on funds from the money market, it competes with other potential users of funds; the result may be a rise in interest rate levels. On the other hand, the desire to hold down interest rates also influences Treasury and Federal Reserve policy. To ensure the success of a large new offering, Federal Reserve authorities may temporarily ease money conditions, a procedure that will tend to soften interest rates. If the Treasury encounters resistance in selling securities in the nonbanking sector, securities may be sold in large volume to the commercial banking system, which expands its reserves and thereby increases the monetary base. This change in turn tends to lower the level of interest rates.

The interaction of monetary and fiscal policies is illustrated by the events since the early 1960s. Figure 23–7 presents the pattern of growth rates in gross national product in both current dollars and in constant dollars since 1959. Gross national product in current dollars increased at a 6.8 percent compound annual rate from the first quarter of 1961 through the fourth quarter of 1964. Real national product during the same period increased at a 5.4 percent annual rate, indicating that price inflation was about 1.4 percent a year. When growth in GNP rose to a 9.9 percent rate during 1965, the economy was able to achieve a growth in real product of 7.7 percent, indicating a 2.2 percent price inflation.

The role of monetary and fiscal policies during these periods is suggested by Figure 23–8. In the earlier period with moderate growth in GNP, both the monetary stock and federal government expenditures grew at moderate rates. During 1965, however, the rate of increase in the monetary stock jumped from about 3 percent to about 6 percent a year. Defense spending increased 18.7 percent in this one year, causing total federal government spending to rise by almost the same percentage. Fearing that the rate of inflation would increase, in 1966 the Federal Reserve System caused the money stock to shrink at a 2 percent annual rate. This produced a reduction in the annual growth rate of GNP from about 9 percent during the fourth quarter of 1966 to a rate of about 3.4 percent in the second quarter of 1967. Since defense spending increased at a 24.1 percent annual rate between the second quarter of 1966 and the second quarter of

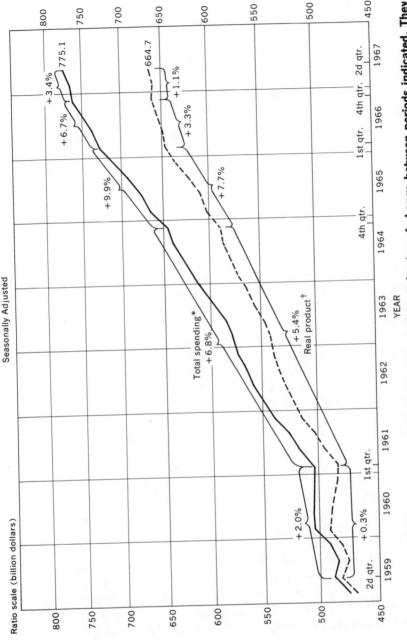

Quarterly Totals at Annual Rates
Seasonally Adjusted

Ratio scale (billion dollars)

Figure 23-7 Demand and Production. Percentages are annual rates of change between periods indicated. They are presented to aid in comparing most recent developments with past "trends." (Latest data plotted: second quarter.)

* GNP in current dollars.
† GNP in 1958 dollars.
SOURCE: U.S. Department of Commerce. Prepared by Federal Reserve Bank of St. Louis.

(a)

(b)

Figure 23-8 **(upper) Money Stock; (lower) Federal Government Expenditures—National Income Accounts Budget. Percentages are annual rates of change between periods indicated. They are presented as an aid in comparing most recent developments with past trends.**

SOURCE: Federal Reserve Bank of St. Louis, *Monthly Review*, September, 1967, pp. 5, 6.

1967, the slowdown in GNP growth must have occurred in the nondefense sector of the economy.

To combat the decline in the GNP growth rate, the Fed allowed the money stock to grow at a 9 percent annual rate during early 1967. This action by the monetary authorities exerted an expansionary influence on the economy, but it brought with it fears of another tight-money period, which resulted in a considerable amount of anticipatory long-term financing by corporate financial managers.

These events of 1966 and 1967 are described to illustrate different types of economic conditions and to show that fluctuations in money costs and availability, which have confronted financial managers in past decades, are still present and will continue to challenge the knowledge and judgment of these men in the years ahead. The financial manager will find it necessary and desirable to keep in close touch with federal budgetary developments and the nature of governmental policy, particularly interactions between fiscal and monetary policies, in order to judge trends in costs of money.[5] This subject deserves much more detailed and analytical treatment than can be given here, for it is of great significance for sound decision making by financial managers.

IMPLICATION OF COST OF MONEY PATTERNS FOR TIMING OF FINANCIAL POLICY

Variations in the cost of money and its availability are likely to be of great significance for decisions by financial managers. The importance of the sound timing of financial policy is further underscored by the mistakes observed in practice.[6]

Financial managers have tended to shift from short-term funds to long-term funds too late during the business upswing. Characteristically, firms have relied on short-term financing during the early stages of a business upswing. The reason for this can clearly be seen from Figure 23–5. The cost of short-term money remains below the cost of long-term money until well into the boom. Furthermore, as recovery takes place the major need for funds is for working capital purposes. Although these needs are

---

[5] Useful sources of current information in addition to the monthly issues of the *Federal Reserve Bulletin* are *Economic Indicators,* prepared for the Joint Economic Committee of the U. S. Congress by the President's Council of Economic Advisers, and *Business Cycle Developments,* prepared by the Bureau of the Census of the U. S. Department of Commerce. Both of the latter publications are available on a subscription basis from the Superintendent of Documents, Government Printing Office, Washington, D. C., 20402.

[6] For illustrations, see J. Weston, "Financial Implications of Growth," *Controller,* March 1958, pp. 118–120.

permanent, as has been demonstrated previously, many financial managers in the past have tended to regard the financing of working capital as only a temporary use of funds.

As a consequence, the acquisition of long-term funds has been delayed until relatively late in the business upswing. Specifically, long-term funds have been acquired at point B in Figure 23–6 rather than at point A. At point B there is an apparent logic in obtaining long-term funds rather than short-term funds. Compared with acquiring long-term funds at point A, the timing of the acquisition of long-term funds is unsound. It leads to obtaining long-term funds at a 4¼ percent rate, when they could have been obtained at something like a 3¾ percent rate earlier in the upswing. Another advantage of obtaining the funds at point A is that credit conditions are relatively much easier at this stage, and the terms under which funds may be acquired are likely to be much less onerous than they will be near the peak of the boom.

It is likely, therefore, that by making proper financial requirement projections, as described earlier, and by keeping historical perspective on the growth of the economy and the pattern of interest rate behavior, financial managers can improve the timing of their acquisition of debt funds. They can lower the cost and improve the terms of financing by obtaining long-term funds early in the upswing. As the upturn in business conditions improves, the firm will have the benefit of trading on the equity with the use of long-term debt money.

Before the peak of the business upswing, the firm may properly sell equity securities, replacing some of its debt. By selling equities near the highs of common stock prices, the firm is enabled to increase its equity base to the degree necessary to facilitate the sale of additional long-term debt money at the low point of the next business cycle.

Although all the strategies of the timing of financial policy are not encompassed by this brief overview, it does serve to focus attention on the need for awareness of changes in the cost of different forms of money during different stages of fluctuations in the level of business activity.

SUMMARY

In general, the financial manager should seek to time the acquisition of funds for his business enterprise in relation to trends and cycles in general business and in interest rates. At the beginning of a business upswing it is likely to be advantageous to raise funds through long-term debt sources. Although short-term rates are lower than long-term rates at this stage of the cycle, the magnitude of swings in short-term rates is large. In the later stages of a business upswing, short-term rates exceed long-term rates, and both are much higher.

Qualitative aspects of financing reflected in credit terms will also be considerably more favorable if long-term borrowing is arranged during the beginning of the upswing. The firm will also obtain larger benefits from trading on the equity.

Later in the upswing, the equity markets are likely to be strong. Equity financing should be used for expansion and for replacing long-term debt financing arranged early in the upswing. At this time interest rates will be relatively high, and equity yields relatively low. This situation allows refunding of debt issues and builds the equity base for protection during the downswing and for trading on the equity during the next upswing.

QUESTIONS

23-1   "It makes good sense for a firm to fund its floating debt, because this relieves the possibility that it will be called upon to pay off debt at an awkward time. However, from the standpoint of cost, it is always cheaper to use short-term debt than long-term debt." Discuss the statement.

23-2   Historical data indicate that more than twice as much capital is raised yearly by selling bonds than by selling common stocks. Does this indicate that corporate capital structures are becoming overburdened with debt?

23-3   Distinguish between the money market and the capital market. How are they related?

23-4   Is the Federal Reserve's tight money policy restraining the country's economic growth? Discuss the pros and cons from the corporation's viewpoint.

23-5   Why do interest rates on different types of securities vary widely?

23-6   What does GNP represent? Why are its level and growth significant to the financial manager?

23-7   Figure 23-5 indicates that short-term interest rates were higher than long-term interest rates for most of the period 1900–1930. Is there any reason to believe that this relation may again prevail during the period 1970–1980?

23-8   Are short-term rates of any value in forecasting the rates for the long-term market?

PROBLEMS

23-1   In mid-1958 the Central Company made a reappraisal of its sales forecasts for the next one, two, and five years. It was clear that the product development program which had been under way for the previous five years was now coming to fruition. The officers of Central were confident that a sales growth of 12 to 15 percent a year (on a compound basis) for the next five years was strongly indicated unless general business declined.

The Central Company has total assets of $10 million. It has a debt-to-total assets ratio of 29 percent. Since it has been spending heavily on research and development during the past five years, its profits have been depressed and the stock has not been favorably regarded by investors.

The Central Company learned that it could borrow on a short-term basis at 2.5 percent (the rate for prime commercial paper at mid-1958 was 1.6 percent) and sell some common stock or float some nonconvertible long-term bonds at 4 percent. Central financed by selling $2 million of common stock (the maximum to avoid control problems) and by short-term loans at the lower rates until early 1960, when it found that its growing financial requirements could not be met by short-term borrowing. Its need for financing was so great that Central sold $10 million convertible debentures at 5.5 percent (the rate on prime commercial paper at this time was almost 5 percent) and with terms requiring a strong current ratio and limitations on fixed assets purchases. The price of its common stock had quadrupled by mid-1959 but had dropped by 10 percent in early 1960.

Evaluate the timing of the selection of forms of financing by the Central Company.

23-2 In July 1958, as the economy in general was emerging from the 1957–1958 downturn and the Flexible Container Corporation's business was resuming its strong growth in sales, Fred Bolden, the treasurer, concluded that the firm would require more working capital financing during the year ending June 30, 1959. Below are the historical and *pro forma* income statements and balance sheets of the Flexible Container Corporation.

How should the financing needs be met? Why?

FLEXIBLE CONTAINER CORPORATION
BALANCE SHEETS
1958 and 1959, *Pro Forma*
(in thousand dollars)

Assets	1958	1959
Cash	$ 200	$ 600
Receivables	800	1,200
Inventories	1,000	1,600
Total current assets	$2,000	$3,400
Fixed assets, net	1,000	2,000
Total assets	$3,000	$5,400
Liabilities and Capital		
Accounts payable	300	500
Accruals	100	200
Reserves for taxes	600	800
Total current liabilities	$1,000	$1,500
Additional financing	0	800
Common stock, $10 par	1,000	1,000
Surplus	1,000	2,100
Total liabilities and capital	$3,000	$5,400

FLEXIBLE CONTAINER CORPORATION
INCOME STATEMENTS
For Years Ended June 30, 1958 and 1959

	1958	1959
Sales, net	$10,000	$14,000
Cost of sales	8,000	10,000
Gross profit	2,000	4,000
Operating expenses	1,000	1,500
Operating profit	1,000	2,500
Other income, net	200	100
Profits before taxes	1,200	2,600
Taxes	600	1,300
Net profit after taxes	600	1,300
Dividends	100	200
Retained earnings	$ 500	$ 1,100

Chapter 24

The Financial Life
Cycle of the Firm

The preceding chapter showed the importance of relating financial plans and policies to the underlying economic and financial environment. In addition, financing patterns should change as the characteristics of the firm itself evolve. Analogies are always dangerous, but the analogy to the life cycle of the individual is useful if it is not taken too literally and is not carried too far. The individual finds, as the old saying has it, that certain things are appropriate to the behavior of a child, to the behavior of a young man, to the behavior of the head of a mature and established family, and to an aged person for his elder statesmanship and wisdom.

Just as the outside world changes, so the individual, regardless of his age or stage in life, must make adjustments. But further, even if the external environment does not change, the individual must adjust as the aging process goes on. In a similar fashion, the financial policies of a firm must be related to the stages of its development.

STAGES OF GROWTH AND FINANCING

The inspiration to view the financing of a firm over its life cycle comes from comments dealing with historical series on sources and uses of funds made by Professor George Evans at a National Bureau of Economic Research conference.[1]

Evans's Hypothesis

Professor Evans states his hypothesis succinctly: "Asset financing during the early, rapid stages of growth is carried on largely through stock and bond issues; thereafter, retained earnings are likely to become very important and, finally, annual depreciation charges bulk large as a source of funds for gross additions to plant." [2] The hypothesis suggests that there are three stages of growth in a business firm, which might be referred to as (1) the early stage, (2) the maturity stage, and (3) the leveling-off stage. In stage one, the firm is said to rely on stock and bond issues; in stage two, on retained earnings; and in stage three, on depreciation charges.

A preliminary empirical basis for the generalizations is provided by Figure 24–1, which reproduces findings for the relative importance of different forms of financing over time for six steel companies and five chemical companies. The data are clearly consistent with the hypothesis set out.

A further corroboration of the Evans approach is suggested in the book by the Oxford financial economists analyzing the business financing of the firm. Their conclusion likewise was that for an understanding of the financial policies of business enterprise in the United Kingdom, it was much more important to group the firms by size and growth rate of sales rather than by industry.

It is also highly significant that the contributors of the general studies (Chapters 2–8) usually found it more illuminating to compare and contrast the companies in different size and growth groups than those in different industrial groups. This is not to say that any of the size groups or growth groups were homogenous—far from it—but at least such groups were often found to be significantly different (and frequently in some systematic and explicable fashion) than were the twenty-one industrial groups.[3]

Rate of Growth

The influence of the rate of sales growth, referred to in the Oxford study, can be shown by the example in Table 24–1, which compares two manufacturing firms. One grows from $800,000 sales to $1.2 million in

---

[1] George Herbeston Evans, Jr., "Discussion: The Development of Historical Series on Sources and Uses of Corporate Funds," *Conference on Research in Business Finance* (New York: National Bureau of Economic Research, Inc., 1952), pp. 28–34.

[2] Evans, p. 23.

[3] Brian Tew and R. F. Henderson (eds.), *Studies in Company Finance* (Cambridge, England: Cambridge University Press, 1959), p. 255.

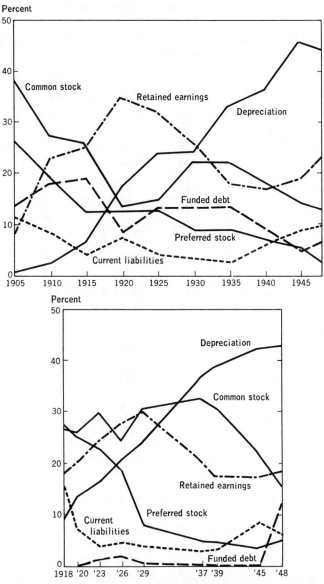

Figure 24-1 **(upper) Chief Sources of Funds for Asset Financing: Six Steel Companies; (lower) Five Chemical Companies. Medians of percentage of total are computed for each company on data cumulated to indicated dates.**

Source: Loc. cit., p. 33. Reprinted by permission of the National Bureau of Economic Research

Table 24–1   FINANCIAL EFFECTS OF DIFFERENT RATES OF GROWTH
(in thousands of dollars)

	Firm 1		Firm 2				
	1	2	1	2	3	4	5
Sales	$800	$1,200	$800	$900	$1,000	$1,100	$1,200
Current assets (30%)	240	360	240	270	300	330	360
Fixed assets (20%)	160	240	160	180	200	220	240
Total assets	$400	$ 600	$400	$450	$ 500	$ 550	$ 600
Accounts payable (10%)	80	120	80	90	100	110	120
Notes payable	96	172	96	79	56	27	(8)
Other accruals (3%)	24	36	24	27	30	33	36
Current liabilities	$200	$ 328	$200	$196	$ 186	$ 170	$ 148
Common stock	100	100	100	100	100	100	100
Retained earnings*	100	172	100	154	214	280	352
Net worth	$200	$ 272	$200	$254	$ 314	$ 380	$ 452
Total claims	$400	$ 600	$400	$450	$ 500	$ 550	$ 600
Key ratios							
Current ratio (times)	1.2	1.1	1.2	1.4	1.6	1.9	2.4
Debt to assets (percentage)	50	55	50	44	37	31	25
Sales to total assets (times)	2	2	2	2	2	2	2
Profit to net worth (percentage)	24	26.5	24.0	21.3	19.1	17.3	15.9

* Profit is 6% of sales, retained earnings are equal to profit plus retained earnings from the previous year.

one year; the other grows by the same amount, but over a four-year period.[4]

It will be observed that when firm 1 achieves a 50 percent sales growth in one year, the current ratio, which was weak in the beginning, deteriorates further. The debt ratio, which was 50 percent initially, moves beyond generally accepted prudent levels. The financial community always likes to feel that the owner has as much money in the business as the creditors have, but in the second year, the creditors have supplied over half the total funds. The profit rate has improved because the firm is using

---

[4] Parenthetically, it may be observed that a 50 percent sales growth rate is not at all unusual for a new firm starting out in the electronics industry or the plastics industry, or for almost any small firm in other than retail or wholesale trade. Even in the latter industries, in the early stages of the life cycle of the firm, if a firm is going to succeed it must have a very rapid growth rate.

debt more heavily; that is, it is receiving the benefit of financial leverage.

The consequences may be contrasted when the firm uses four periods to achieve the same amount of growth. The financial ratios give a profile of what has happened. The current ratio has improved; it has risen above the 2-to-1 bankers' rule of thumb to 2.4 to 1. The debt ratio has dropped to 25 percent, very low compared with the average of 40 percent for all manufacturing. (See Chapter 3.) However, the profit-to-net-worth ratio has declined to the norm for all manufacturing.

A paradox is encountered. Rapid sales growth means high profitability but a precariousness in the firm's financial position unless equity financing is obtained in relatively large amounts. On the other hand, slow growth can be encompassed by the plowback from retained earnings and depreciation charges. The example suggests that a firm growing by only 10 percent a year should not have serious financial problems if it obtains normal profits and retains a high percentage in the business. But owners of rapidly growing firms may find that when their sales are growing at a high rate, they may have difficulty financing the required asset growth necessary to support the rising sales level. Or, alternatively, a firm that increasingly holds net earnings in the business as a substitute for the use of debt may find that with declining leverage its rate of return on net worth also declines. Both paradoxes are readily unraveled if one looks at the simple dynamics of this growth situation.

FINANCING IN RELATION TO A CROSS SECTION OF STAGES

The situation described in Table 24–1 purports to be a general statement of a particular kind of phenomenon comparing rapid growth with less rapid growth, and high retention of earnings with other alternatives. We may generalize further by considering a summary of firms and their financial characteristics in terms of their different sizes and ages.

The relation between the growth of a firm and its requirements is exhibited by Figure 24–2, which presents the sales and the total assets of the Bethlehem Steel Corporation during the last half century. With the exception of the disruptions brought about by World War I and World War II and their aftermaths, the growth of sales of the Bethlehem Steel Corporation has roughly followed the S-shaped growth curve.

Financing requirements of the firm have paralleled the growth pattern in sales. After 1940 the firm has been able to achieve a sales-total-asset ratio exceeding 1 during most years. Yet the sales-total-asset ratio is substantially below the characteristic 2-to-1 ratio observed for manufacturing firms in less capital-intensive industries.

Table 24-2 GENERAL SUMMARY OF FINANCIAL PATTERNS IN RELATION TO SIZE AND AGE OF FIRM*

	Growth Rate (in percentages)	Profit to Sales	Financial Position		Main Forms	Main Sources	Dividend Payout (in percentages)	Mergers
Small Rapid growth	20–30	8	Current ratio Asset turnover Debt ratio	1 3 67%	Current liabilities	Trade credit	0–10	Need for full range of management capabilities
Moderate growth	5–8	5	Current ratio Asset turnover Debt ratio	2 2 33–50%	Long-term debt Common stock Retained earnings	Privately placed term loans	20–25	Cost reduction incentives
Medium Rapid growth	16–20	6–7	Current ratio Asset turnover Debt ratio	1.4 2.5 50%	Long-term debt Current liabilities Common stock	Privately placed term loans	5–15	Cost reduction, rounding out of sales lines
Moderate growth	4–7	5	Current ratio Asset turnover Debt ratio	2 2 33%	Long-term debt Common stock Retained earnings	Bonds, equity capital market	40–50	Diversification into new product lines
Large Moderate growth	4–6	5	Current ratio Asset turnover Debt ratio	2 2 33%	Retained earnings Depreciation	Retained earnings	50–60	Diversification into new product lines

* Based on the institutional framework of the United States.

516

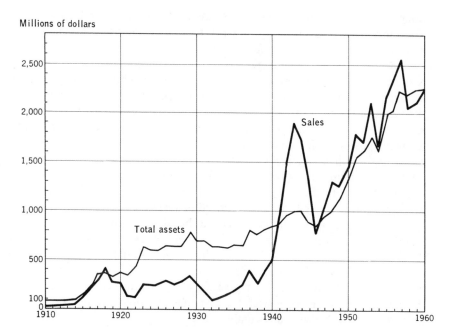

Figure 24-2   Bethlehem Steel Corporation, 1910-1960

A relation exists between a firm's growth in sales and the nature of its financing requirements. A general framework for obtaining perspective on the financial life cycle of the firm can be developed. Table 24–2 sets forth a summary of leading financial characteristics of manufacturing firms, classified by size and age. This panorama is based on a review of studies of the growth of individual firms and on the Financial Research Program of the National Bureau of Economic Research on capital formation and its financing in a number of industries.

The summary is idealized in that many exceptions can be found in actuality. It is not an ideal picture in the sense that each set of characteristics represents the optimal situation. It indicates how the age and the growth rate of a firm and the nature of its financial environment are reflected in its financial patterns over time. In the following sections, the table is discussed to convey the idea of how a firm is likely to move from one stage to another.

Small, Rapidly Growing Firm

The small, successful firm will typically have a high sales growth rate —20 to 30 percent a year. Its profit rate on sales will be somewhat higher than the average for large manufacturing companies. Compared with tradi-

517

tional and customary standards, its financial position is relatively weak. The current ratio is probably under 1 to 1. The sales-to-total-assets ratio will be high. The debt ratio is 67 percent.

Because Table 24–2 provides the profit on sales, the asset turnover, and the debt ratio, the return on net worth can be calculated. In the present instance the return on total assets would be 24 percent, more than double the norm of about 10 to 12 percent for all manufacturing.[5] The return on net worth would be 72 percent (after taxes).[6] Because of its precarious financial position, the underfinanced small firm shows a high return on net worth. With a relatively normal profit on sales, the high turnover of total assets results in a favorable profit rate on total assets. The relatively high debt ratio further magnifies the return on net worth. The result is a profit rate on net worth of 72 percent after taxes.

Studies of new, small firms indicate that 80 to 90 percent of the initial financing comes from the funds of the owners of the business and their relatives and friends. As the sales grow, the major initial source of external financing is likely to be trade credit. Suppliers provide credit of both an informal and a formal kind. This practice is fortunate, because trade credit thereby performs the very useful social function of providing small firms with financing otherwise unavailable.

With regard to dividend policy (the term is here used to include withdrawals), the small firm should pay out very little, if anything, in dividends. Here is a case where the pattern is idealized in the sense that many small firms may fail to observe this rule or guide to action.

Small firms will sometimes sell out to large firms as they grow to a certain point. A small firm is created and receives its initial propulsion because of a specific ability of the owner-manager-entrepreneur. He may be a good salesman, a good engineer, or a good production man. He strikes out on his own because of his one strong competence. While the firm is small, a specific ability may be sufficient for the firm's success.

But very soon a firm reaches "that awkward age" in which more than the dynamic force of one or two individuals is needed to enable it to continue to prosper. At this stage the owner-managers of the firm realize that it takes a full range of managerial abilities to succeed. It is not enough to have only sales, technical, or financial skills. A firm begins to find that it is making numerous mistakes because it does not have a full range of balanced managerial skills. As a consequence, it may join with other firms with which it can complement strengths and weaknesses. Or, more typically, a

---

[5] Sales margin $\times$ turnover $= 8 \times 3 = 24\%$ return on assets

[6] $\dfrac{\text{return on assets}}{1.0 - \text{debt ratio}} = \dfrac{24\%}{1.0 - 0.67} = \dfrac{24}{0.33} = 72\%$ return on net worth (after taxes)

large firm sees that it can use the particular managerial talents of the small firm and can supply everything else lacking in the small firm. For these reasons, many small firms are likely to sell out to larger firms.

Small, Long-Established Firm

If a firm is small and old, it is probably not in a growing industry. Since manufacturing firms are being discussed, the long-established firm is probably producing a particular product to which large firms do not give much attention. Its growth rate in sales is probably no better than the over-all average of the industry. The profit rate is not likely to be more than normal.

Its financial position is likely to meet conventional standards. It meets the traditional standard for the current ratio, the bankers' rule of thumb of 2 to 1. Its sales-to-total-assets ratio approximates the 1.9 for all manufacturing. The debt ratio probably is from 33 to 50 percent, reflecting the fact that because it is small it may have difficulty raising equity funds.

Because the firm has been in existence for a time, its past performance record may have enabled it to obtain moderate amounts of long-term debt. Also, it probably has had time to build up fairly large retained earnings. As it meets the bankers' traditional financial standards, it qualifies for some bank financing.

Dividend payouts are probably still on the low side, because the small firm by nature has only limited access to the external financial markets. Hence, it relies on internal financing to a great degree.

The firm is likely to engage in mergers. It may be acquired by a large firm for its special product contribution. Large firms seek vertical integration as they reach the stage of maturity. In older firms, in the later stages of the life cycle of an industry, profit margins may decline. For this reason, such firms may engage in mergers to encompass an additional product stage or product splinter to broaden its product line. If larger volume per dollar of investment can thereby be generated, improved profit margins may be achieved.

Medium-Sized, Rapidly Growing Firms

The remainder of the firms in the summary table have some relation to the two categories already discussed. For the medium-sized firm, growth rates and net profit rates will not be so high as those for the new, small firm. The medium firm will be in a somewhat better financial position. Because it is medium-sized, although new, it probably has been in operation long enough to have established a performance record which gives it at least a degree of access to the external capital markets.

Such a firm's dividend payout is still relatively low because of its high profit rate and the need to finance further growth. It is likely to seek mergers to round out production or sales lines and thus to spread the relatively fixed costs of the sales organization or production organization over a larger number of product lines, making it more able to compete effectively with the larger firms in its line of business.

Medium-Sized, Moderately Growing Firm

The firm of medium size with a moderate growth rate will have characteristics similar to those of small firms with moderate growth rates. The profit rate will approximate the profit rate of industry generally. The firm will satisfy the financial standards generally regarded as sound. It will doubtlessly achieve a current ratio of at least 2 to 1. It will have a normal sales-to-total-assets ratio of about 2. It will have reduced its debt ratio to about 33 percent of assets.

The medium-sized firm will have greater access to the capital markets than will the small firm of moderate growth rate. The fixed costs of capital flotations will bear less heavily on the larger firm than on the small firm. For this reason, the medium-sized firm of moderate growth and profitability will have a somewhat higher dividend payout than will the smaller firm.

The lower growth rate of the medium-sized firm may lead it to seek product diversification in an effort to enter new product-market areas with more favorable growth opportunities. It will seek to acquire smaller, rapidly growing firms which have products with favorable growth potentialities.

Large Firm with Moderate Growth Rate

The large firm with a moderate growth rate is likely to be an established firm in an industry that has reached its maturity. The firm will generally exhibit the characteristics of a medium-sized firm. However, its larger size implies a higher fixed-assets-to-total-assets ratio. Thus the fixed assets will provide a throw-off of funds from depreciation charges. The large firm will therefore draw on the capital markets for financing to a smaller degree. Instead, it will rely to a greater extent on internal financing.

Illustrative Patterns

The influence of industry, age, size, and rate of growth on financing of firms can also be indicated by Table 24–3. Firms in the textiles and shoe-manufacturing industries generally have a large peak seasonal investment in receivables. This seasonal investment does not justify a proportionate amount of permanent capital. Consequently, such firms are likely to make use of receivables to provide a secured basis for financing large temporary investment requirements during each year.

Table 24–3 ILLUSTRATIVE FINANCING STRATEGIES

Characteristic of Firm	Critical Financing Need	Strategic Financing Requirement
Small		
Textiles and Shoes	Peak seasonal in receivables	Receivables financing
Scientific	Equipment and research outlays	Leasing, venture capital
Canning	Peak seasonal in inventories	Field warehousing, other commodity loans
Manufacturing	Equipment	Conditional sales contract, leasing, venture capital
Moderate Size		
Manufacturing	Plant and equipment	Long-term debt and equity financing
Rapid growth	Working capital and fixed assets	Convertible debt or debt with warrants
Large		
Moderate growth	Fixed asset replacement	Internal funds

Similarly, a canning manufacturer is likely to experience a peak seasonal growth in inventories. Again, such large investments do not justify permanent capital sufficient to finance the seasonal peak inventories. Therefore, field warehousing or other types of commodity loans are the strategic financing requirements.

The many new scientifically oriented firms with rapid growth have a different financing requirement. Their investment in equipment is likely to be heavy, and their large outlays on research may require a number of years before a profitable series of products results. The initial outlays for research must require venture capital—capital willing to assume substantial risks. Permanent investment requirements are reduced by the opportunities for leasing their heavy equipment needs.

The small, basic manufacturing company is likely to have its heaviest investment in equipment. Conditional sales contracts or leasing may take care of this strategic financing requirement. In addition, the initial period of operations is likely to require an investment of venture capital. On the other hand, a manufacturing firm that has been in business for a number of years and has achieved moderate size is likely to have heavy investment in both plant and equipment. With a record of sales, profitability, and some stability of management, a moderate-sized manufacturing firm is likely to have access to the open capital market. It will have access to long-term debt and equity financing from the financial markets.

The rapidly growing, moderate-sized firm will probably have a record of reasonably stable and rising sales and profits, and it will experience a need to finance both fixed assets and working capital. Such a firm is likely to use a certain amount of straight debt, supplemented by subordinated convertibles or debt with warrants that will, in time, provide additional equity capital.

The large firm in a mature industry is likely to be experiencing only moderate growth. With reasonably stable profits and a heavy investment in fixed assets (which contributes to cash flow due to depreciation charge-off), its main financing requirement is for replacement of fixed assets. Most of these needs will be met from internal sources.

The purpose of this review of some illustrative financing strategies has been to place characteristic financing needs in proper perspective and to relate them to financing forms and sources. It has not been possible to generalize on the financing patterns and requirements of every type of firm and every type of industry. However, these illustrations have served to indicate that some basic patterns emerge when firms are viewed analytically in terms of their industry characteristics, age, size, and growth rate. With a foundation based on an understanding of the basic patterns and relationships, in addition to a sound analytical framework, practical experience will develop the maturity and good judgment essential to making good financial decisions.

INFLUENCE OF ECONOMIC CLIMATE

These broad patterns and the financing of the firm over its life cycle are likely to be substantially modified by variations in money market conditions over time. During a strong bull market in equities, such as occurred in the late 1920s, the advantages to equity financing become substantial. During depressed periods like that of the 1930s the characteristic life-cycle pattern of growth and sales is likely to be seriously disturbed. The occurrence of wars will cause erratic disturbances in the growth cycle of the firm.

In addition, characteristics of the general economic environment are likely to influence the forms of financing employed. For example, during the post-World War II period, the fear of inflation, coupled with the danger of a postwar depression, made convertible securities popular. The convertible securities, of course, provided a hedge against deflation and at the same time offered some participation in the growth potentialities of firms and industries during a period characterized by attractive growth records among many firms.

FINANCIAL GUIDELINES

On the basis of the perspectives provided by a review of the financial life cycle of firms, some generalizations may be drawn. These generalizations summarize many of the topics discussed previously and provide a statement of guidelines for the financial manager.

1. Permanent needs should not be financed from short-term sources.

2. A substantial portion of current assets represents permanent investment and should be financed from long-term sources.

3. Financing should be arranged before needs become immediately pressing. "The best time to get money is the time it is not needed."

4. It is better to obtain financing in larger "chunks" than in a series of small amounts, because each financing transaction carries a large element of fixed costs.

5. Anticipate needs so that future needs will also be met.

6. Financing is a personal business. The financial manager should cultivate personal and professional contacts with credit men, bank loan officers, investment bankers, and financial executives of insurance companies and finance companies.

7. The financial manager should have some element of flexibility in his financing programs so that the unexpected does not find him in a vulnerable position.

8. The financial manager should be prepared to bargain strenuously on the terms of financial agreements. He should not permit his firm to be tied up in loan terms that will hamper its freedom of action in the future.

9. Especially in a new firm, the commitment of funds should be held to a minimum. Buildings and equipment should be rented initially, or used equipment should be employed to the extent permitted by fund-raising capacity.

10. Irrational aversion to debt reduces profits. Judicious use of debt provides valuable leverage.

11. On the other hand, small and new firms, especially, must recognize that growth requires a large plowback of earnings if excessive debt is to be avoided or equity ownership is not to be shared. Growth of sales may lead to a feeling of prosperity and large withdrawals, which may hamper the healthy growth of a firm.

SUMMARY

The framework provided by the concept of the financial life cycle of the firm gives the perspective on the financing alternatives available to the firm. Acquisition of funds at one stage of a firm's development should be made with a view to establishing the best foundation for the forms of financing most likely to be required at subsequent stages.

The overview of the financial life cycle of firms also highlights the inter-relations between growth rates, financial position, forms and sources of financing, and dividend and merger policies. Understanding these relations will prevent mutually inconsistent policies.

A widespread fault of small firms in their early stages is excessive withdrawals of funds by owner-managers. Failure to recognize the financing requirements of rapid growth and the necessity for obtaining the major portion of such financing from internal sources during the early stages of a firm's development will lead to financial difficulties. As a firm establishes a performance record, the opportunities for financing are broadened. The possibilities for obtaining external sources of funds on favorable terms improve during the later stages of a firm's development. At the same time, the reduced rate of growth makes it probable that a larger proportion of needs will be provided from internal sources.

Application of the life cycle framework can yield useful guidelines for financial decisions. The financial policies of the firm constitute an important area of managerial decisions required for successful operations.

QUESTIONS

24–1   Discuss the relation between size of firm and the life-cycle concept.

24–2   Discuss the relation between diversification and the life-cycle concept.

24–3   Should a firm always attempt to forestall the declining phase of the life cycle? What about a firm created for the purpose of exploiting a given mineral deposit, say an iron ore mine?

24–4   Explain how each of the following factors could be expected to influence the extent to which actual firms conform to the life-cycle hypothesis:

   a) Development of the corporate form of organization
   b) Corporate diversification
   c) Research and development expenditures
   d) Trend toward larger firms

24–5   If the average cost of capital is actually minimized when the firm has a certain amount of debt in its capital structure, is it logical for older, slower growing firms to retire all their debt by retaining earnings? If such a tendency is observed, what is the implication for the economists' notion that firms seek to maximize profits?

24–6   A fast-growing firm usually has a higher profit rate than a firm growing more slowly. Yet the former will be less able to finance its growth from retained earnings. Explain.

24–7   A large, well-established firm typically retains a lower percentage of its earnings than does a smaller, faster growing firm. Yet the larger firm finances a higher percentage of its financing needs from retained earnings than does the smaller firm. Explain.

24–8   Two firms each earn 6 percent on sales and have an asset turnover of 2 times. Firm A has a debt-to-total-assets ratio of one third. Firm B has a ratio of two thirds. What is the respective profit rate on net worth for each firm?

24–9   A firm has a 5 percent return on sales. It has a debt-to-net-worth ratio of 100 percent. What turnover of total assets is required for a 20 percent return on net worth?

24–10   Which firms are likely to have the higher asset turnover—new, small, rapidly growing firms or the largest firms in American industry?

24–11   What are the major sources of initial financing of new, small firms? Why?

24–12   Are large firms likely to have a higher or a lower ratio of trade receivables to trade payables than have smaller firms in the same line of business?

24–13   At what stage in its development is an industrial firm likely to make the greatest use of long-term debt? Explain.

24–14   Explain the characteristics of the economy and the stage of development of a firm and of its financial structure that will favor the use of convertible debt to raise funds equal to 20 percent of its present total assets.

PROBLEMS

24–1   Match each firm in list 1 with the most appropriate form of financing found in list 2. Present the key factors that determine your choice.

List 1

a) A medium-sized specialty steel company in Texas expects to double its sales in 12 years. Stock prices are expected to more than double over that period. Existing short-term debt is somewhat high; it has no long-term debt.

b) A laundromat plans expansion by the installation of ten additional washing machines and three new driers.

c) A plastics manufacturing company of $8 million sales volume, 70 percent owned by the founder and chief engineer, sells 60 percent of its output to a small number of large aircraft firms and finds itself continually short of working capital.

d) An electronics company doing $25 million of sales needs $5 million to finance its expansion. It has a debt-to-total-assets ratio of 60 percent, and its common stock, which is widely held, has tripled in price during the past year.

e) A manufacturing company with steadily growing sales (currently at $20 million) needs $2 million to finance new equipment which will substantially increase sales 10 to 14 months after the investment is made. Profits are expected to increase more than proportionally to the sales increase. Its debt-to-total-assets ratio runs about 30 percent.

f) A finance company with good prospective sales growth, relatively low debt ratio, stock prices temporarily depressed, and very good banking relations seeks to finance a prospective 10 percent increase in assets during the forthcoming year.

g) A medium-sized electrical utility ($100 million total assets) with a debt ratio of 40 percent needs an additional $20 million to finance the growth taking place in the early stages of a business upswing.

h) A small chemical company producing many competitive lines has been growing on the average at about 10 percent a year—at a higher rate in good years and at a lower one in poor years. To finance growth the firm is attempting to decide between a convertible debenture issue or debt with warrants to buy common stock. Its existing total debt ratio is 10 percent of total assets.

List 2

1) Common stock
2) Convertible preferred stock
3) Subordinated debentures
4) Conditional sales contract
5) Accounts receivables financing or factoring
6) Mortgage bonds
7) Debt with warrants
8) Convertible debentures

24-2 United Engineers, Inc., has experienced the following sales, profit, and balance sheet patterns. Identify the financial problem that has developed, and recommend a solution for it.

UNITED ENGINEERS, INC.
FINANCIAL DATA
1959–1968
(in millions of dollars)

Income Statements	*1959*	*1960*	*1961*	*1962*	*1963*	*1964*	*1965*	*1966*	*1967*	*1968*
Sales	$50	$70	$90	$100	$120	$200	$180	$220	$240	$340
Profits after tax	5	7	9	10	12	20	18	22	24	34
Dividends	4	5	6	6	7	10	10	14	18	24
Retained earnings	1	2	3	4	5	10	8	8	6	10
Cumulative retained earnings	1	3	6	10	15	25	33	41	47	57
Balance Sheets										
Current assets	10	15	20	25	30	50	40	55	60	80
Net fixed assets	15	20	25	25	30	50	50	55	60	90
Total assets	$25	$35	$45	$ 50	$ 60	$100	$ 90	$110	$120	$170

Income Statements	1959	1960	1961	1962	1963	1964	1965	1966	1967	1968
Trade credit	4	6	8	9	10	18	15	20	40	60
Bank credit	4	6	10	10	13	29	14	20	—	20
Other	1	5	6	6	7	8	8	9	8	8
Total current liab.	9	17	24	25	30	55	37	49	48	88
Long-term debt	0	0	0	0	0	5	5	5	10	10
Total debt	9	17	24	25	30	60	42	54	58	98
Common stock	15	15	15	15	15	15	15	15	15	15
Retained earnings	1	3	6	10	15	25	33	41	47	57
Net worth	16	18	21	25	30	40	48	56	62	72
Total claims on assets	$25	$35	$45	$ 50	$ 60	$100	$ 90	$110	$120	$170

24–3 a) A firm with $20 million of assets judges that it is at the beginning of a three-year growth cycle. It is a manufacturing firm with a total-debt-to-assets ratio of 16 percent. It expects sales and net earnings to grow at a rate of 10 percent a year.

Stock prices are expected to rise 30 percent a year over the 3-year period. The firm will need $2 million at the beginning of the 3-year period and another $1 million by the middle of the third year. It is at the beginning of a general business upswing, when money and capital costs are what they generally are after about a year of recession and at the beginning of an upswing. By the middle of the third year, money and capital costs will have their characteristic pattern near the peak of an upswing.

How should the firm raise the $2 million and the $1 million?

b) An aerospace company with sales of $50 million a year needs $10 million to finance expansion. It has a debt-to-total-assets ratio of 65 percent. Its common stock, which is widely held, is selling at a price/earnings ratio of 25 times. It is comparing the sale of common stock and convertible debentures.

Which do you recommend? Why?

c) A chemical company has been growing steadily. To finance a growth of sales from $80 million a year to $100 million over a 2-year period, it needs $4 million in additional equipment. When additional working capital needs are taken into account, the total additional financing required during the first year is $10 million. Profits will rise by 50 percent after the first 10 months. The stock is currently selling at 20 times earnings. It can borrow on straight debt at 5½ percent. It could borrow with a convertibility or warrant "sweetener" for ¾ percent less. The present debt-to-total-asset ratio is 25 percent.

Which form of financing should it employ?

Compound Interest Tables

Appendix A

Table A–1 COMPOUND SUM OF $1

Year	1%	2%	3%	4%	5%	6%	7%
1	1.010	1.020	1.030	1.040	1.050	1.060	1.070
2	1.020	1.040	1.061	1.082	1.102	1.124	1.145
3	1.030	1.061	1.093	1.125	1.158	1.191	1.225
4	1.041	1.082	1.126	1.170	1.216	1.262	1.311
5	1.051	1.104	1.159	1.217	1.276	1.338	1.403
6	1.062	1.126	1.194	1.265	1.340	1.419	1.501
7	1.072	1.149	1.230	1.316	1.407	1.504	1.606
8	1.083	1.172	1.267	1.369	1.477	1.594	1.718
9	1.094	1.195	1.305	1.423	1.551	1.689	1.838
10	1.105	1.219	1.344	1.480	1.629	1.791	1.967
11	1.116	1.243	1.384	1.539	1.710	1.898	2.105
12	1.127	1.268	1.426	1.601	1.796	2.012	2.252
13	1.138	1.294	1.469	1.665	1.886	2.133	2.410
14	1.149	1.319	1.513	1.732	1.980	2.261	2.579
15	1.161	1.346	1.558	1.801	2.079	2.397	2.759
16	1.173	1.373	1.605	1.873	2.183	2.540	2.952
17	1.184	1.400	1.653	1.948	2.292	2.693	3.159
18	1.196	1.428	1.702	2.026	2.407	2.854	3.380
19	1.208	1.457	1.754	2.107	2.527	3.026	3.617
20	1.220	1.486	1.806	2.191	2.653	3.207	3.870
25	1.282	1.641	2.094	2.666	3.386	4.292	5.427
30	1.348	1.811	2.427	3.243	4.322	5.743	7.612

Year	8%	9%	10%	12%	14%	15%	16%
1	1.080	1.090	1.100	1.120	1.140	1.150	1.160
2	1.166	1.188	1.210	1.254	1.300	1.322	1.346
3	1.260	1.295	1.331	1.405	1.482	1.521	1.561
4	1.360	1.412	1.464	1.574	1.689	1.749	1.811
5	1.469	1.539	1.611	1.762	1.925	2.011	2.100
6	1.587	1.677	1.772	1.974	2.195	2.313	2.436
7	1.714	1.828	1.949	2.211	2.502	2.660	2.826
8	1.851	1.993	2.144	2.476	2.853	3.059	3.278
9	1.999	2.172	2.358	2.773	3.252	3.518	3.803
10	2.159	2.367	2.594	3.106	3.707	4.046	4.411
11	2.332	2.580	2.853	3.479	4.226	4.652	5.117
12	2.518	2.813	3.138	3.896	4.818	5.350	5.936
13	2.720	3.066	3.452	4.363	5.492	6.153	6.886
14	2.937	3.342	3.797	4.887	6.261	7.076	7.988
15	3.172	3.642	4.177	5.474	7.138	8.137	9.266
16	3.426	3.970	4.595	6.130	8.137	9.358	10.748
17	3.700	4.328	5.054	6.866	9.276	10.761	12.468
18	3.996	4.717	5.560	7.690	10.575	12.375	14.463
19	4.316	5.142	6.116	8.613	12.056	14.232	16.777
20	4.661	5.604	6.728	9.646	13.743	16.367	19.461
25	6.848	8.623	10.835	17.000	26.462	32.919	40.874
30	10.063	13.268	17.449	29.960	50.950	66.212	85.850

Table A-1 (continued)

Year	18%	20%	24%	28%	32%	36%
1	1.180	1.200	1.240	1.280	1.320	1.360
2	1.392	1.440	1.538	1.638	1.742	1.850
3	1.643	1.728	1.907	2.067	2.300	2.515
4	1.939	2.074	2.364	2.684	3.036	3.421
5	2.288	2.488	2.932	3.436	4.007	4.653
6	2.700	2.986	3.635	4.398	5.290	6.328
7	3.185	3,583	4.508	5.629	6.983	8.605
8	3.759	4.300	5.590	7.206	9.217	11.703
9	4.435	5.160	6.931	9.223	12.166	15.917
10	5.234	6.192	8.594	11.806	16.060	21.647
11	6.176	7.430	10.657	15.112	21.199	29.439
12	7.288	8.916	13.215	19.343	27.983	40.037
13	8.599	10.699	16.386	24.759	36.937	54.451
14	10.147	12.839	20.319	31.691	48.757	74.053
15	11.974	15.407	25.196	40.565	64.359	100.712
16	14.129	18.488	31.243	51.923	84.954	136.97
17	16.672	22.186	38.741	66.461	112.14	186.28
18	19.673	26.623	48.039	85.071	148.02	253.34
19	23.214	31.948	59.568	108.89	195.39	344.54
20	27.393	38.338	73.864	139.38	257.92	468.57
25	62.669	95.396	216.542	478.90	1033.6	2180.1
30	143.371	237.376	634.820	1645.5	4142.1	10143.

Year	40%	50%	60%	70%	80%	90%
1	1.400	1.500	1.600	1.700	1.800	1.900
2	1.960	2.250	2.560	2.890	3.240	3.610
3	2.744	3.375	4.096	4.913	5.832	6.859
4	3.842	5.062	6.544	8.352	10.498	13.032
5	5.378	7.594	10.486	14.199	18.896	24.761
6	7.530	11.391	16.777	24.138	34.012	47.046
7	10.541	17.086	26.844	41.034	61.222	89.387
8	14.758	25.629	42.950	69.758	110.200	169.836
9	20.661	38.443	68.720	118.588	198.359	322.688
10	28.925	57.665	109.951	201.599	357.047	613.107
11	40.496	86.498	175.922	342.719	642.684	1164.902
12	56.694	129.746	281.475	582.622	1156.831	2213.314
13	79.372	194.619	450.360	990.457	2082.295	4205.297
14	111.120	291.929	720.576	1683.777	3748.131	7990.065
15	155.568	437.894	1152.921	2862.421	6746.636	15181.122
16	217.795	656.84	1844.7	4866.1	12144.	28844.0
17	304.914	985.26	2951.5	8272.4	21859.	54804.0
18	426.879	1477.9	4722.4	14063.0	39346.	104130.0
19	597.630	2216.8	7555.8	23907.0	70824.	197840.0
20	836.683	3325.3	12089.0	40642.0	127480.	**375900.0**
25	4499.880	25251.	126760.0	577060.0	2408900.	9307600.0
30	24201.432	191750.	1329200.	8193500.0	45517000.	230470000.0

TABLE A-2

PRESENT VALUE OF $1

Year	1%	2%	3%	4%	5%	6%	7%	8%	9%	10%	12%	14%	15%
1	.990	.980	.971	.962	.952	.943	.935	.926	.917	.909	.893	.877	.870
2	.980	.961	.943	.925	.907	.890	.873	.857	.842	.826	.797	.769	.756
3	.971	.942	.915	.889	.864	.840	.816	.794	.772	.751	.712	.675	.658
4	.961	.924	.889	.855	.823	.792	.763	.735	.708	.683	.636	.592	.572
5	.951	.906	.863	.822	.784	.747	.713	.681	.650	.621	.567	.519	.497
6	.942	.888	.838	.790	.746	.705	.666	.630	.596	.564	.507	.456	.432
7	.933	.871	.813	.760	.711	.665	.623	.583	.547	.513	.452	.400	.376
8	.923	.853	.789	.731	.677	.627	.582	.540	.502	.467	.404	.351	.327
9	.914	.837	.766	.703	.645	.592	.544	.500	.460	.424	.361	.308	.284
10	.905	.820	.744	.676	.614	.558	.508	.463	.422	.386	.322	.270	.247
11	.896	.804	.722	.650	.585	.527	.475	.429	.388	.350	.287	.237	.215
12	.887	.788	.701	.625	.557	.497	.444	.397	.356	.319	.257	.208	.187
13	.879	.773	.681	.601	.530	.469	.415	.368	.326	.290	.229	.182	.163
14	.870	.758	.661	.577	.505	.442	.388	.340	.299	.263	.205	.160	.141
15	.861	.743	.642	.555	.481	.417	.362	.315	.275	.239	.183	.140	.123
16	.853	.728	.623	.534	.458	.394	.339	.292	.252	.218	.163	.123	.107
17	.844	.714	.605	.513	.436	.371	.317	.270	.231	.198	.146	.108	.093
18	.836	.700	.587	.494	.416	.350	.296	.250	.212	.180	.130	.095	.081
19	.828	.686	.570	.475	.396	.331	.276	.232	.194	.164	.116	.083	.070
20	.820	.673	.554	.456	.377	.319	.258	.215	.178	.149	.104	.073	.061
25	.780	.610	.478	.375	.295	.233	.184	.146	.116	.092	.059	.038	.030
30	.742	.552	.412	.308	.231	.174	.131	.099	.075	.057	.033	.020	.015

Year	16%	18%	20%	24%	28%	32%	36%	40%	50%	60%	70%	80%	90%
1	.862	.847	.833	.806	.781	.758	.735	.714	.667	.625	.588	.556	.526
2	.743	.718	.694	.650	.610	.574	.541	.510	.444	.391	.346	.309	.277
3	.641	.609	.579	.524	.477	.435	.398	.364	.296	.244	.204	.171	.146
4	.552	.516	.482	.423	.373	.329	.292	.260	.198	.153	.120	.095	.077
5	.476	.437	.402	.341	.291	.250	.215	.186	.132	.095	.070	.053	.040
6	.410	.370	.335	.275	.227	.189	.158	.133	.088	.060	.041	.029	.021
7	.354	.314	.279	.222	.178	.143	.116	.095	.059	.037	.024	.016	.011
8	.305	.266	.233	.179	.139	.108	.085	.068	.039	.023	.014	.009	.006
9	.263	.226	.194	.144	.108	.082	.063	.048	.026	.015	.008	.005	.003
10	.227	.191	.162	.116	.085	.062	.046	.035	.017	.009	.005	.003	.002
11	.195	.162	.135	.094	.066	.047	.034	.025	.012	.006	.003	.002	.001
12	.168	.137	.112	.076	.052	.036	.025	.018	.008	.004	.002	.001	.001
13	.145	.116	.093	.061	.040	.027	.018	.013	.005	.002	.001	.001	.000
14	.125	.099	.078	.049	.032	.021	.014	.009	.003	.001	.001	.000	.000
15	.108	.084	.065	.040	.025	.016	.010	.006	.002	.001	.000	.000	.000
16	.093	.071	.054	.032	.019	.012	.007	.005	.002	.001	.000	.000	
17	.080	.060	.045	.026	.015	.009	.005	.003	.001	.000	.000		
18	.069	.051	.038	.021	.012	.007	.004	.002	.001	.000	.000		
19	.060	.043	.031	.017	.009	.005	.003	.002	.000	.000			
20	.051	.037	.026	.014	.007	.004	.002	.001	.000	.000			
25	.024	.016	.010	.005	.002	.001	.000	.000					
30	.012	.007	.004	.002	.001	.000	.000						

Table A-3 SUM OF AN ANNUITY OF $1 FOR N YEARS

Year	1%	2%	3%	4%	5%	6%
1	1.000	1.000	1.000	1.000	1.000	1.000
2	2.010	2.020	2.030	2.040	2.050	2.060
3	2.030	3.060	3.091	3.122	3.152	3.184
4	4.060	4.122	4.184	4.246	4.310	4.375
5	5.101	5.204	5.309	5.416	5.526	5.637
6	6.152	6.308	6.468	6.633	6.802	6.975
7	7.214	7.434	7.662	7.898	8.142	8.394
8	8.286	8.583	8.892	9.214	9.549	9.897
9	9.369	9.755	10.159	10.583	11.027	11.491
10	10.462	10.950	11.464	12.006	12.578	13.181
11	11.567	12.169	12.808	13.486	14.207	14.972
12	12.683	13.412	14.192	15.026	15.917	16.870
13	13.809	14.680	15.618	16.627	17.713	18.882
14	14.947	15.974	17.086	18.292	19.599	21.051
15	16.097	17.293	18.599	20.024	21.579	23.276
16	17.258	18.639	20.157	21.825	23.657	25.673
17	18.430	20.012	21.762	23.698	25.840	28.213
18	19.615	21.412	23.414	25.645	28.132	30.906
19	20.811	22.841	25.117	27.671	30.539	33.760
20	22.019	24.297	26.870	29.778	33.066	36.786
25	28.243	32.030	36.459	41.646	47.727	54.865
30	34.785	40.568	47.575	56.085	66.439	79.058

Year	7%	8%	9%	10%	12%	14%
1	1.000	1.000	1.000	1.000	1.000	1.000
2	2.070	2.080	2.090	2.100	2.120	2.140
3	3.215	3.246	3.278	3.310	3.374	3.440
4	4.440	4.506	4.573	4.641	4.770	4.921
5	5.751	5.867	5.985	6.105	6.353	6.610
6	7.153	7.336	7.523	7.716	8.115	8.536
7	8.654	8.923	9.200	9.487	10.089	10.730
8	10.260	10.637	11.028	11.436	12.300	13.233
9	11.978	12.488	13.021	13.579	14.776	16.085
10	13.816	14.487	15.193	15.937	17.549	19.337
11	15.784	16.645	17.560	18.531	20.655	23.044
12	17.888	18.977	20.141	21.384	24.133	27.271
13	20.141	21.495	22.953	24.523	28.029	32.089
14	22.550	24.215	26.019	27.975	32.393	37.581
15	25.129	27.152	29.361	31.772	37.280	43.842
16	27.888	30.324	33.003	35.950	42.753	50.980
17	30.840	33.750	36.974	40.545	48.884	59.118
18	33.999	37.450	41.301	45.599	55.750	68.394
19	37.379	41.446	46.018	51.159	63.440	78.969
20	40.995	45.762	51.160	57.275	72.052	91.025
25	63.249	73.106	84.701	98.347	133.334	181.871
30	94.461	113.283	136.308	164.494	241.333	356.787

Table A–3 (continued)

Year	16%	18%	20%	24%	28%	32%
1	1.000	1.000	1.000	1.000	1.000	1.000
2	2.160	2.180	2.200	2.240	2.280	2.320
3	3.506	3.572	3.640	3.778	3.918	4.062
4	5.066	5.215	5.368	5.684	6.016	6.362
5	6.877	7.154	7.442	8.048	8.700	9.398
6	8.977	9.442	9.930	10.980	12.136	13.406
7	11.414	12.142	12.916	14.615	16.534	18.696
8	14.240	15.327	16.499	19.123	22.163	25.678
9	17.518	19.086	20.799	24.712	29.369	34.895
10	21.321	23.521	25.959	31.643	38.592	47.062
11	25.733	28.755	32.150	40.238	50.399	63.122
12	30.850	34.931	39.580	50.985	65.510	84.320
13	36.786	42.219	48.497	64.110	84.853	112.303
14	43.672	50.818	59.196	80.496	109.612	149.240
15	51.660	60.965	72.035	100.815	141.303	197.997
16	60.925	72.939	87.442	126.011	181.87	262.36
17	71.673	87.068	105.931	157.253	233.79	347.31
18	84.141	103.740	128.117	195.994	300.25	459.45
19	98.603	123.414	154.740	244.033	385.32	607.47
20	115.380	146.628	186.688	303.601	494.21	802.86
25	249.214	342.603	471.981	898.092	1706.8	3226.8
30	530.312	790.948	1181.882	2640.916	5873.2	12941.0

Year	36%	40%	50%	60%	70%	80%
1	1.000	1.000	1.000	1.000	1.000	1.000
2	2.360	2.400	2.500	2.600	2.700	2.800
3	4.210	4.360	4.750	5.160	5.590	6.040
4	6.725	7.104	8.125	9.256	10.503	11.872
5	10.146	10.846	13.188	15.810	18.855	22.370
6	14.799	16.324	20.781	26.295	33.054	41.265
7	21.126	23.853	32.172	43.073	57.191	75.278
8	29.732	34.395	49.258	69.916	98.225	136.500
9	41.435	49.153	74.887	112.866	167.983	246.699
10	57.352	69.814	113.330	181.585	286.570	445.058
11	78.998	98.739	170.995	291.536	488.170	802.105
12	108.437	139.235	257.493	467.458	830.888	1444.788
13	148.475	195.929	387.239	748.933	1413.510	2601.619
14	202.926	275.300	581.859	1199.293	2403.968	4683.914
15	276.979	386.420	873.788	1919.869	4087.745	8432.045
16	377.69	541.99	1311.7	3072.8	6950.2	15179.0
17	514.66	759.78	1968.5	4917.5	11816.0	27323.0
18	700.94	1064.7	2953.8	7868.9	20089.0	49182.0
19	954.28	1491.6	4431.7	12591.0	34152.0	88528.0
20	1298.8	2089.2	6648.5	20147.0	58059.0	159350.0
25	6053.0	11247.0	50500.0	211270.0	824370.0	3011100.0
30	28172.0	60501.0	383500.0	2215400.0	11705000.0	56896000.0

535

Present Worth of an Annuity of $1

Year	1%	2%	3%	4%	5%	6%	7%	8%	9%	10%
1	0.990	0.980	0.971	0.962	0.952	0.943	0.935	0.926	0.917	0.909
2	1.970	1.942	1.913	1.886	1.859	1.833	1.808	1.783	1.759	1.736
3	2.941	2.884	2.829	2.775	2.723	2.673	2.624	2.577	2.531	2.487
4	3.902	3.808	3.717	3.630	3.546	3.465	3.387	3.312	3.240	3.170
5	4.853	4.713	4.580	4.452	4.329	4.212	4.100	3.993	3.890	3.791
6	5.795	5.601	5.417	5.242	5.076	4.917	4.766	4.623	4.486	4.355
7	6.728	6.472	6.230	6.002	5.786	5.582	5.389	5.206	5.033	4.868
8	7.652	7.325	7.020	6.733	6.463	6.210	6.971	5.747	5.535	5.335
9	8.566	8.162	7.786	7.435	7.108	6.802	6.515	6.247	5.985	5.759
10	9.471	8.983	8.530	8.111	7.722	7.360	7.024	6.710	6.418	6.145
11	10.368	9.787	9.253	8.760	8.306	7.887	7.499	7.139	6.805	6.495
12	11.255	10.575	9.954	9.385	8.863	8.384	7.943	7.536	7.161	6.814
13	12.134	11.348	10.635	9.986	9.394	8.853	8.358	7.904	7.487	7.103
14	13.004	12.106	11.296	10.563	9.899	9.295	8.745	8.244	7.786	7.367
15	13.865	12.849	11.938	11.118	10.380	9.712	9.108	8.559	8.060	7.606
16	14.718	13.578	12.561	11.652	10.838	10.106	9.447	8.851	8.312	7.824
17	15.562	14.292	13.166	12.166	11.274	10.477	9.763	9.122	8.544	8.022
18	16.398	14.992	13.754	12.659	11.690	10.828	10.059	9.372	8.756	8.201
19	17.226	15.678	14.324	13.134	12.085	11.158	10.336	9.604	8.950	8.365
20	18.046	16.351	14.877	13.590	12.462	11.470	10.594	9.818	9.128	8.514
25	22.023	19.523	17.413	15.622	14.094	12.783	11.654	10.675	9.823	9.077
30	25.808	22.397	19.600	17.292	15.373	13.765	12.409	11.258	10.274	9.427

Year	12%	14%	16%	18%	20%	24%	28%	32%	36%
1	0.893	0.877	0.862	0.847	0.833	0.806	0.781	0.758	0.735
2	1.690	1.647	1.605	1.566	1.528	1.457	1.392	1.332	1.276
3	2.402	2.322	2.246	2.174	2.106	1.981	1.868	1.766	1.674
4	3.037	2.914	2.798	2.690	2.589	2.404	2.241	2.096	1.966
5	3.605	3.433	3.274	3.127	2.991	2.745	2.532	2.345	2.181
6	4.111	3.889	3.685	3.498	3.326	3.020	2.759	2.534	2.339
7	4.564	4.288	4.039	3.812	3.605	3.242	2.937	2.678	2.455
8	4.968	4.639	4.344	4.078	3.837	3.421	3.076	2.786	2.540
9	5.328	4.946	4.607	4.303	4.031	3.566	3.184	2.868	2.603
10	5.650	5.216	4.833	4.494	4.193	3.682	3.269	2.930	2.650
11	5.988	5.453	5.029	4.656	4.327	3.776	3.335	2.978	2.683
12	6.194	5.660	5.197	4.793	4.439	3.851	3.387	3.013	2.708
13	6.424	5.842	5.342	4.910	4.533	3.912	3.427	3.040	2.727
14	6.628	6.002	5.468	5.008	4.611	3.962	3.459	3.061	2.740
15	6.811	6.142	5.575	5.092	4.675	4.001	3.483	3.076	2.750
16	6.974	6.265	5.669	5.162	4.730	4.033	3.503	3.088	2.758
17	7.120	5.373	5.749	4.222	4.775	4.059	3.518	3.097	2.763
18	7.250	6.467	5.818	5.273	4.812	4.080	3.529	3.104	2.767
19	7.366	6.550	5.877	5.316	4.844	4.097	3.539	3.109	2.770
20	7.469	6.623	5.929	5.353	4.870	4.110	3.546	3.113	2.772
25	7.843	6.873	6.097	5.467	4.948	4.147	3.564	3.122	2.776
30	8.055	7.003	6.177	5.517	4.979	4.160	3.569	3.124	2.778

Appendix B

Glossary

Glossary

ACCRUALS   Continually recurring short-term liabilities. Examples are accrued wages, accrued taxes, and accrued interest.

AGING SCHEDULE   A report showing how long accounts receivable have been outstanding. It gives the percent of receivables not past due and the percent past due by, for example, one month, two months, or other periods.

AMORTIZE   To liquidate on an installment basis; an amortized loan is one in which the principal amount of the loan is repaid in installments during the life of the loan.

ANNUITY   A series of payments of a fixed amount for a specified number of years.

ARREARAGE   Overdue payment; frequently, omitted dividends on preferred stocks.

ASSIGNMENT   A relatively inexpensive way of liquidating a failing firm that does not involve going through the courts.

BALLOON PAYMENT   When a debt is not fully amortized, the final payment is larger than the preceding payments and is called a "balloon" payment.

BANKRUPTCY   A legal procedure for formally liquidating a business carried out under the jurisdiction of courts of law.

BOND   A long-term debt instrument.

BOOK VALUE   The accounting value of an asset. The book value of a share of common stock is equal to the net worth (common stock plus surplus) of the corporation divided by the number of shares of stock outstanding.

BREAK-EVEN ANALYSIS   An analytical technique for studying the relation between fixed cost, variable cost, and profits. A break-even *chart* graphically depicts the nature of break-even analysis. The break-even *point* represents that volume of sales at which total costs equal total revenues (that is, profits equal zero).

539

CALL   (1) An option to buy (or "call") a share of stock at a specified price within a specific period. (2) The process of redeeming a bond or preferred stock issue before its normal maturity.

CALL PREMIUM   The amount in excess of par value that a company must pay when it calls a security.

CALL PRICE   The price that must be paid when a security is called. The call price is equal to the par value plus the call premium.

CALL PRIVILEGE   A provision incorporated into a bond or a share of preferred stock that gives the issuer the right to redeem (call) the security at a specified price.

CALLING   The action of exercising the call privilege and redeeming securities prior to their maturity date.

CAPITAL ASSET   An asset with a life of more than one year that is not bought and sold in the ordinary course of business.

CAPITAL BUDGETING   The process of planning expenditures on assets whose returns are expected to extend beyond one year.

CAPITAL GAINS   Profits on the sale of capital assets held for six months or more.

CAPITAL LOSSES   Losses on the sale of capital assets.

CAPITAL STRUCTURE   The permanent long-term financing of the firm represented by long-term debt, preferred stock, and net worth (net worth consists of capital, capital surplus, and earned surplus). Capital structure is distinguished from *financial structure,* which includes short-term debt plus all reserve accounts.

CAPITALIZATION RATE   A discount rate used to find the present value of a series of future cash receipts; sometimes called *discount rate.*

CARRY-BACK; CARRY-FORWARD   For income tax purposes, losses that can be carried backward or forward to reduce federal income taxes.

CASH BUDGET   A schedule showing cash flows (receipts, disbursements, and net cash) for a firm over a specified period.

CASH CYCLE   The length of time between the purchase of raw materials and the collection of accounts receivable generated in the sale of the final product.

CHATTEL MORTGAGE   A mortgage on personal property (not real estate). A mortgage on equipment would be a chattel mortgage.

COLLATERAL   Assets that are used to secure a loan.

COMMERCIAL PAPER   Unsecured, short-term promissory notes of large firms, usually issued in denominations of $1 million or more. The rate of interest on commercial paper is typically somewhat below the prime rate of interest.

COMMITMENT FEE   The fee paid to a lender for a formal line of credit.

COMPENSATING BALANCE   A required minimum checking account balance that a firm must maintain with a commercial bank. The required balance is generally equal to 15 to 20 percent of the amount of loans outstanding. Compensating balances can raise the effective rate of interest on bank loans.

COMPOSITION   An informal method of reorganization that voluntarily reduces creditors' claims on the debtor firm.

COMPOUND INTEREST   An interest rate that is applicable when interest in succeeding periods is earned not only on the initial principal but also on the accumulated interest of prior periods. Compound interest is contrasted to *simple interest,* in which returns are not earned on interest received.

COMPOUNDING The arithmetic process of determining the final value of a payment or series of payments when compound interest is applied.

CONDITIONAL SALES CONTRACT A method of financing new equipment by paying it off in installments over a one- to five-year period. The seller retains title to the equipment until payment has been completed.

CONSOLIDATED TAX RETURN An income tax return that combines the income statement of several affiliated firms.

CONVERSION PRICE The effective price paid for common stock when the stock is obtained by converting either convertible preferred stocks or convertible bonds. For example, if a $1,000 bond is convertible into 20 shares of stock, the conversion price is $50 ($1,000/20).

CONVERSION RATIO OR CONVERSION RATE The number of shares of common stock that may be obtained by converting a convertible bond or share of convertible preferred stock.

CONVERTIBLES Securities (generally bonds or preferred stocks) that are exchangeable at the option of the holder for common stock of the issuing firm.

COST OF CAPITAL The discount rate that should be used in the capital budgeting process.

COUPON RATE The stated rate of interest on a bond.

COVENANT Detailed clauses contained in loan agreements. Covenants are designed to protect the lender and include such items as limits on total indebtedness, restrictions on dividends, minimum current ratio, and similar provisions.

CUT-OFF POINT In the capital budgeting process, the minimum rate of return on acceptable investment opportunities.

DEBT RATIO Total debt divided by total assets.

DEBENTURE A long-term debt instrument that is not secured by a mortgage on specific property.

DEFAULT The failure to fulfill a contract. Generally, default refers to the failure to pay interest or principal on debt obligations.

DISCOUNT RATE The interest rate used in the discounting process; sometimes called *capitalization rate.*

DISCOUNTING The process of finding the present value of a series of future cash flows. Discounting is the reverse of compounding.

DISCOUNTING OF ACCOUNTS RECEIVABLE Short-term financing where accounts receivable are used to secure the loan. The lender *does not* buy the accounts receivable but simply uses them as collateral for the loan. Also called "pledging of accounts receivable."

DIVIDEND YIELD The ratio of the current dividend to the current price of a share of stock.

EARNINGS MULTIPLIER The price/earnings ratio (the P/E ratio).

E.B.I.T. Abbreviation for "earnings before interest and taxes."

E.P.S.   Abbreviation for "earnings per share."

ECONOMICAL ORDERING QUANTITY(EOQ)   The optimum (least cost) quantity of merchandise which should be purchased.

EQUITY   The net worth of a business, consisting of capital stocks, capital (or paid-in) surplus, earned surplus (or retained earnings), and, occasionally, certain net worth reserves. *Common equity* is that part of the total net worth belonging to the common stockholders. *Total equity* would include preferred stockholders. The terms "common stock," "net worth," and "equity" are frequently used interchangeably.

EXCISE TAX   A tax on the manufacture, sale, or consumption of specified commodities.

EX-DIVIDEND DATE   The date on which the right to the current dividend no longer accompanies a stock. (For listed stock, the ex-dividend date is four working days prior to the date of record.)

EXERCISE PRICE   The price that must be paid for a share of common stock when it is bought with a warrant.

EXTENSION   An informal method of reorganization in which the creditors voluntarily postpone the date of required payment on past-due obligations.

FACTORING   A method of financing accounts receivable under which a firm sells its accounts receivable (generally without recourse) to a financial institution (the "factor").

FIELD WAREHOUSING   A method of financing inventories in which a "warehouse" is established at the place of business of the borrowing firm.

FINANCIAL LEVERAGE   The ratio of total debt to total assets. There are other measures of financial leverage, especially ones that relate cash inflows to required cash outflows: in this book the debt/total asset ratio is generally used to measure leverage.

FINANCIAL STRUCTURE   The entire right-hand side of the balance sheet—the way in which a firm is financed.

FIXED CHARGES   Costs that do not vary with the level of output.

FLOAT   The amount of funds tied up in checks which have been written but are still in process and have not yet been collected.

FLOTATION COST   The cost of issuing new stocks or bonds.

FUNDED DEBT   Long-term debt.

FUNDING   The process of replacing short-term debt with long-term securities (stocks or bonds).

GOODWILL   Intangible assets of a firm established by the excess of the price paid for the going concern over its book value.

HOLDING COMPANY   A corporation operated for the purpose of owning the common stocks of other corporations.

IMPROPER ACCUMULATION   Earnings retained by a business for the purpose of enabling stockholders to avoid personal income taxes.

INCOME BOND   A bond that pays interest only if the current interest is earned.

INDENTURE   A formal agreement between the issuer of a bond and the bond-holders.

INSOLVENCY   The inability to meet maturing obligations.

INTEREST FACTOR (IF)   Numbers found in compound interest and annuity tables.

INTERNAL RATE OF RETURN   The rate of return on an asset investment. The internal rate of return is calculated by finding the discount rate that equates the present value of future cash flows to the cost of the investment.

INTRINSIC VALUE   That value which, in the mind of the analyst, is justified by the facts. It is often used to distinguish between the "true value" of an asset (the intrinsic value) and the asset's current market price.

INVESTMENT BANKER   One who underwrites and distributes new investment securities; more broadly, one who helps business firms to obtain financing.

INVESTMENT TAX CREDIT   A credit (reduction) from federal income taxes that is computed as a percentage of the initial cost of certain capital assets.

LEVERAGE FACTOR   The ratio of debt to total assets.

LINE OF CREDIT   An arrangement whereby a financial institution (bank or insurance company) commits itself to lend up to a specified maximum amount of funds during a specified period. Sometimes the interest rate on the loan is specified; at other times it is not. Sometimes a commitment fee is imposed for obtaining the line of credit.

LIQUIDITY   Refers to a firm's cash position and to its ability to meet maturing obligations.

LISTED SECURITIES   Securities traded on an organized security exchange—for example, the New York Stock Exchange.

LOCK-BOX PLAN   A procedure used to speed up collections and to reduce float.

MARGIN—PROFIT ON SALES   The *profit margin* is the percentage of profit after tax to sales.

MARGIN—SECURITIES BUSINESS   The buying of stocks or bonds on credit; known as *buying on margin.*

MARGIN TRADING   Buying securities on credit (margin).

MARGINAL COST   The cost of an additional unit. The *marginal cost of capital* is the cost of an additional dollar of new funds.

MARGINAL EFFICIENCY OF CAPITAL   A schedule showing the internal rate of return on investment opportunities.

MARGINAL REVENUE   The additional gross revenue produced by selling one additional unit of output.

MERGER   Any combination that forms one company from two or more previously existing companies.

MONEY MARKET   Financial markets in which funds are borrowed or loaned for short periods. (The money market is distinguished from the capital market, which is the market for long-term funds.)

MORTGAGE   A pledge of designated property as security for a loan.

NET WORTH   The capital and surplus of a firm—capital stock, capital surplus (paid-in capital), earned surplus (retained earnings), and, occasionally, certain reserves. For some purposes, preferred stock is included, but generally net worth refers only to the common stockholder's position.

OPERATING LEVERAGE   The extent to which fixed costs are used in a firm's operation. Break-even analysis is used to measure the extent to which operating leverage is employed.

OPPORTUNITY COST   The rate of return on the best *alternative* investment that is available. It is the highest return which will *not* be earned if the funds are invested in a particular project. For example, the opportunity cost of *not* investing in common stocks yielding 8 percent might be 6 percent, which could be earned on bonds.

ORDINARY INCOME   Income from the normal operations of a firm. Operating income specifically excludes income from the sale of capital assets.

ORGANIZED SECURITY EXCHANGES   Formal organizations having tangible, physical locations. Organized exchanges conduct an auction market in designated ("listed") investment securities. For example, the New York Stock Exchange is an organized exchange.

OVER-THE-COUNTER MARKET   All facilities that provide for security transactions not conducted on organized exchanges. The over-the-counter market is typically a "telephone market," as most business is conducted over the telephone.

OVER-THE-COUNTER SECURITIES   Securities that are not traded on an organized security exchange.

PAR VALUE   The nominal or face value of a stock or bond.

PAYBACK PERIOD   The length of time required for the net revenues of an investment to return the cost of the investment.

PAYOUT RATIO   The percentage of earnings paid out in the form of dividends.

PERPETUITY   A stream of equal future payments expected to continue forever.

PLEDGING OF ACCOUNTS RECEIVABLE   Short-term borrowing from financial institutions where the loan is secured by accounts receivable. The lender may physically take the accounts receivable but typically has recourse to the borrower; also called *discounting of accounts receivable.*

POOLING OF INTEREST   An accounting method for combining the financial statements of two firms that merge. Under the pooling of interest procedure, the assets of the merged firms are simply added together to form the balance sheet of the surviving corporation. This method is different from the "purchase" method, where goodwill is put on the balance sheet to reflect a premium (or discount) paid in excess of book value.

PRE-EMPTIVE RIGHT   A provision contained in the corporate charter and bylaws that gives holders of common stock the right to purchase on a pro rata basis new issues of common stock (or securities convertible into common stock).

PRESENT VALUE   The value today of a future payment, or stream of payments, discounted at the appropriate discount rate.

PRICE/EARNINGS RATIO (P/E)   The ratio of price to earnings. Faster growing firms typically have higher P/E ratios than slower growing firms.

PRIME RATE   The rate of interest commercial banks charge very large, strong corporations.

PRO FORMA   A projection. A *pro forma* financial statement is one that shows how the actual statement will look if certain specified assumptions are realized. *Pro forma* statements may be either future or past projections. An example of a backward *pro forma* statement is when two firms are planning to merge and show what their consolidated financial statements would have looked like had they been merged in preceding years.

PROFIT MARGIN   The ratio of profits after taxes to sales.

PROGRESSIVE TAX   A tax that requires a higher percentage payment on higher incomes. The personal income tax in the United States, which is at a rate of 14 percent on the lowest increments of income to 70 percent on the highest increments, is progressive.

PROSPECTUS   A document issued for the purpose of describing a new security issue. The Securities and Exchange Commission (SEC) examines prospectuses to insure that statements contained therein are not "false and misleading."

PROXY   A document giving one the authority or power to act for another. Typically, the authority in question is the power to vote shares of common stock.

PUT   An option to sell a specific security at a specific price within a designated period.

RATE OF RETURN   The internal rate of return on an investment.

RECOURSE ARRANGEMENT   A term used in connection with accounts receivable financing. If a firm sells its accounts receivable to a financial institution under a recourse agreement, then, if the account receivable cannot be collected, the selling firm must repurchase the account from the financial institution.

REFUNDING   The process of retiring an old bond issue and replacing it with a new issue.

REGRESSION ANALYSIS   A statistical procedure for predicting the value of one variable (dependent variable) on the basis of knowledge about one or more other variables (independent variables).

REORGANIZATION   When a financially troubled firm goes through reorganization, its assets are restated to reflect their current market value, and its financial structure is restated to reflect any changes on the asset side of the statement. Under a reorganization the firm continues in existence; this is contrasted to bankruptcy, where the firm is liquidated and ceases to exist.

REQUIRED RATE OF RETURN   The rate of return that stockholders expect to receive on common stock investments.

RESIDUAL VALUE   The value of leased property at the end of the leased term.

RETAINED EARNINGS   Profits after taxes that are retained in the business rather than being paid out in dividends.

RIGHT   A short-term option to buy a specified number of shares of a new issue of securities at a designated "subscription" price.

RIGHTS OFFERING   A securities flotation offered to existing stockholders.

RISK PREMIUM   Investors dislike risk; therefore, higher risk securities require a higher rate of return. Disregarding liquidity differences and certain other factors, the difference between the rate of return on a safe investment (sometimes called *the pure rate of interest*) and that on a more risky investment is defined as the "risk premium" attached to the risky investment.

SALVAGE VALUE   The value of a capital asset at the end of a specified period. It is the current market price of an asset being considered for replacement in a capital budgeting problem.

SELLING GROUP   A group of stock brokerage firms formed for the purpose of distributing a new issue of securities; part of the investment banking process.

SHORT-SELLING   Selling a security that is not owned by the seller at the time of the sale. The seller borrows the security from a brokerage firm and must at some point repay the brokerage firm by buying the security on the open market.

SECURITIES, JUNIOR   Securities that have lower priority in claims on assets and income than other securities (*senior securities*). For example, preferred stock is junior to debentures, but debentures are junior to mortgage bonds. Common stock is the most junior of all corporate securities.

SECURITIES, SENIOR   Securities having claims on income and assets that rank higher than certain other securities (*junior securities*). For example, mortgage bonds are senior to debentures, but debentures are senior to common stock.

SINKING FUND   A required annual payment designed to amortize a bond or a preferred stock issue. The sinking fund may be held in the form of cash or marketable securities, but more generally the money put into the sinking fund is used to retire each year some of the securities in question.

STOCK DIVIDEND   A dividend paid in additional shares of stock rather than in cash. It involves a transfer from earned surplus to the capital stock account; therefore, stock dividends are limited by the amount of earned surplus.

STOCK SPLIT   An accounting action to increase the number of shares outstanding; for example, in a 3-for-1 split, shares outstanding would be tripled and each stockholder would receive three new shares for each one formerly held. Stock splits involve no transfer from surplus to the capital account.

SUBORDINATED DEBENTURE   A bond having a claim on assets only after the senior debt has been paid off in the event of liquidation.

SUBSCRIPTION PRICE   The price at which a security may be purchased in a rights offering.

SURTAX   A tax levied in addition to the normal tax. For example, the normal corporate tax rate is 22 percent, but a surtax of 26 percent is added to the normal tax on all corporate income exceeding $25,000.

TANGIBLE ASSETS Physical assets as opposed to such intangible assets as goodwill and the stated value of patents.

TERM LOAN A loan generally obtained from a bank or insurance company with a maturity greater than one year. Term loans are generally amortized.

TRADE CREDIT Interfirm debt arising through credit sales and recorded as an account receivable by the seller and as an account payable by the buyer.

TRUST RECEIPT An instrument acknowledging that the borrower holds certain goods in trust for the lender. Trust receipt financing is used in connection with the financing of inventories for automobile dealers, construction equipment dealers, appliance dealers, and other dealers in expensive durable goods.

UNDERWRITING (1) The entire process of issuing new corporate securities. (2) The insurance function of bearing the risk of adverse price fluctuations during the period in which a new issue of stock or bonds is being distributed.

UNDERWRITING SYNDICATE A syndicate of investment firms formed to spread the risk associated with the purchase and distribution of a new issue of securities. The larger the issue, the more firms will typically be involved in the syndicate.

WARRANT A long-term option to buy a stated number of shares of common stock at a specified price. The specified price is generally called the "exercise price."

WORKING CAPITAL Refers to a firm's investment in short-term assets—cash, short-term securities, accounts receivable, and inventories. *Gross working capital* is defined as a firm's total current assets. *Net working capital* is defined as current assets minus current liabilities. If the term "working capital" is used without further qualification, it generally refers to gross working capital.

YIELD The rate of return on an investment—the internal rate of return.

Index

549